THE

ACTS OF THE APOSTLES

EXPLAINED

BY

JOSEPH ADDISON ALEXANDER

IN TWO VOLUMES

VOLUME II

THIRD EDITION.

NEW YORK:
CHARLES SCRIBNER, 124·GRAND STREET,
CORNER OF BROADWAY.
1862.

ENTERED, according to Act of Congress. in the year 1857 by
JOSEPH ADDISON ALEXANDER,
In the Clerk's Office of the United States District Court for the District of New Jersey.

JOHN F. TROW,
PRINTER, STEREOTYPER, AND ELECTROTYPER,
46, 48 & 50 Greene Street,
New York.

THE

ACTS OF THE APOSTLES.

CHAPTER XIII.

The first great movement, from Jerusalem to Antioch, having been recorded in the previous twelve chapters, the historian now enters on the second, beginning at Antioch and ending at Rome, in which the field of operations is the Gentile world, and the principal agent the Apostle Paul (xiii–xxviii.) The first and largest portion of this narrative is occupied with the Apostle's active ministry, or his official labours while at liberty (xiii–xxi.) The historical account of these commences with his first foreign mission, that to Cyprus and certain parts of Asia Minor (xiii, xiv.) The division of the text now immediately before us contains the first part of this mission, from its inception in the church at Antioch to the arrival of the missionaries at Iconium (xiii.)

We are first told how Barnabas and Saul were designated to the missionary work (1–3). They then sail from Syria to Cyprus (4.) They visit Salamis and Paphos in that island (5, 6.) A sorcerer resists them and is struck with blindness (6–11.) The Roman Proconsul is converted (12.) Saul, henceforth called Paul, as Apostle of the Gentiles, conducts the mission into Asia Minor, landing at Perga in Pamphylia, where their attendant, John Mark, leaves them (13.) They proceed to Antioch in Pisidia, and attend the synagogue (14, 15.) Paul preaches his first sermon upon record (16–41.) It produces a powerful effect upon the people (42–44.) The unbelieving Jews make violent opposition (45.) Paul avows his mission to the Gentiles (46, 47.) Many Gentiles are converted (48, 49.) The Jews excite a persecution (50.) Paul departs to Iconium, leaving the new converts in a happy state (51, 52.)

1. Now there were in the church that was at Antioch certain prophets and teachers; as Barnabas, and Simeon that was called Niger, and Lucius of Cyrene, and Manaen, which had been brought up with Herod the tetrarch, and Saul.

At Antioch in the being (or *existing*) *church.* The participle (*being*) is emphatic, and has been variously explained, as meaning the real or true church, in opposition to the false Judaic one; or the church as it then was, in its actual condition, still requiring inspired teachers, until uninspired ones could be provided; or the church now really existing, and so well established that it could spare labourers to go abroad. All these interpretations supply something not expressed or necessarily suggested by the text or context. The only natural construction is the one adopted in our version, which supposes *being* to denote nothing more than the existence of a church there, or the fact that Antioch had not only heard the Gospel and invented the name *Christian* (see above, on 11, 26), but was now the seat of a regularly organized church, with a full and efficient corps of ministers. 'There were at Antioch in the church which now existed there.' The powers of this church were exercised, according to the apostolical principle and practice, through divinely constituted officers, here described as *Prophets and Teachers* (see above, on 2, 18), i. e. either inspired teachers, as a single class, or inspired and uninspired teachers, as distinct classes. Or, still more probably than either, the two words are generic and specific terms, applied to the same persons, one denoting their divine authority, the other the precise way in which it was exercised. Other distinctions which have been assumed, such as that between itinerant and settled ministers, or occasional and stated preachers, or exhorters and instructors, are possible enough, but not susceptible of proof. *As* may seem to imply that there were others not here mentioned; but the Greek word (τε) simply means *both*, i. e. not only Barnabas, but those who follow. (See the very same form in 1, 13 above.) *Barnabas* is probably named first, as the oldest man and oldest minister, or as the one who had been sent down from Jerusalem (see above, on 11, 22), or perhaps as being really the pastor or presiding elder of the church at Antioch. *Simeon* (or *Simon*), a very common Hebrew name (see above, on 1, 13. 8, 9. 9, 43. 10, 6), here distinguished by the Roman surname *Niger* (*Black*), which has led some to identify the person here meant with Simon the Cyrenian, who bore our Saviour's cross (Matt. 27, 32. Mark 15, 21. Luke 23, 26.) *Lucius* is expressly described as a Cyrenian, and may be the same whom Paul salutes (Rom. 16, 21) among his kinsmen, either in the wide or narrow sense. (See above, on 10, 24.) That this was Luke himself, is an ancient but improbable conjecture. *Manaen* is a Hellenistic form of the Hebrew *Menahem* (2 Kings 15, 14.) *Which had been brought up with Herod* is more concisely and exactly rendered in the margin, *Herod's foster-brother*. *The tetrarch*, i. e. Herod Antipas, the one so often mentioned in the Life of Christ. Josephus and the Talmud speak of a Menahem, an Essene, who predicted the elevation and long reign of Herod the Great, and was therefore an object of his special favour. It is very possible that this man's son was nursed or educated with the king's sons, and afterwards converted to the Christian faith. (For another follower of Christ connected with the court of Herod, see Luke 8, 3.) As the same Greek particle (τε) is repeated with this name, although here translated simply *and*, some suppose a distinction to be thereby made between the first three as prophets and the last two as mere teachers. But who can suppose Saul to have been less a prophet than Barnabas? (Compare 1 Cor. 14, 1–5.) The place assigned to Saul in this list has been variously explained; but the most satisfactory solution is, that his apostolical commission had not yet been made known, and that until its disclosure, he was to remain undistinguished from his fellow-labourers, or even to take the lowest place among them, as on this occasion. (See below, on vs. 9. 13.) The word *certain* (τινες) in the first clause is omitted by the oldest manuscripts and latest critics.

2. As they ministered to the Lord and fasted, the Holy Ghost said, Separate me Barnabas and Saul for the work whereunto I have called them.

They ministering, the Greek word from which *liturgy* is derived, but which is never elsewhere used in the New Testament with any special or exclusive reference to prayer. According to its derivation, it means any public service or official function. The cognate verb and noun are applied to the ministry of angels (Heb. 1, 7. 14), to Christian charity and kindness (Rom. 15, 27. 2 Cor. 9, 12. Phil. 2, 30), to magistrates as ministers of God (Rom. 13, 6), to the Christian ministry and missions (Rom. 15, 16), to public worship, and especially the Jewish ritual (Luke 1, 23. Heb. 10, 11.) Later ecclesiastical usage restricted it to the Sacraments, and Chrysostom explains it here to mean preaching. But its true sense is the general one expressed in the translation, *ministering*, engaged in the discharge of their official functions, with particular reference to public worship, and with the special addition, in this case, of fasting, not as a stated periodical observance, which is rather discountenanced than recommended in the New Testament, but as a special aid to prayer, no doubt for the spread of Christianity, and perhaps for guidance as to their own duty at this interesting crisis. *The Holy Ghost said*, while they were thus engaged, perhaps to all at once by audible communication, or by special revelation to some one among them. *Separate*, a verb used elsewhere in a bad sense, (see Matt. 13, 49. 25, 32. Luke 6, 22), but here (as in Rom. 1, 1. Gal. 1, 15) meaning, *set apart*, designate, implying separation from the rest, and from the ordinary work in which they had been all engaged, to another special and extraordinary business. *Called them*, i. e. Barnabas and Saul, but not the rest of you. This work was not to supersede or take the place of the stated ministry, but to be superadded to it. The very form of the command shows that this was no reception of Barnabas and Saul by the others to their own body, but a solemn and extraordinary separation from it.

3. And when they had fasted and prayed, and laid (their) hands on them, they sent (them) away.

This verse records the execution of the previous command. *Then having fasted and prayed* may be a mere continuation of the fast already mentioned, or a subsequent observance of the same kind, implying a continued need of this auxiliary to their prayers for the divine blessing on this new and most important measure. *Laid hands on them*, as a sign of transfer from the ordinary service of the church to an extraordinary mission. (See above, on 6, 6. 8, 17. 9, 12.) *Sent them away*, dismissed, discharged them, let them go (see above, on 3, 13. 4, 21. 23. 5, 40), again implying separation from their own body, as prophets and teachers of the church at Antioch. The nature and design of this proceeding have been variously understood, in accordance with various conclusions or hypotheses as to church-organization. It could not be an ordination to the ministry; for the very two now set apart were already eminent and successful ministers, far more illustrious in the church than those who are supposed to have ordained them. It could not be a consecration (so called) to the diocesan episcopate; for, even admitting its existence, why should all these prelates be attached to one church (v. 1)? Or if not prelates, how could they bestow a higher office than they held themselves? Least of all could it be (as some allege) an elevation of these two men to the Apostleship, to fill the places of the two Jameses; for how could ordinary ministers, or even bishops, create Apostles? Or how could such an act be reconciled with Paul's asseveration (Gal. 1, 1) that his Apostleship was not from men, nor even through men? Or with the fact that Barnabas is nowhere subsequently called an Apostle, except on one occasion in conjunction with Paul, and even then in a dubious sense? (See below, on 14, 4. 14.) The only remaining supposition is, that this was a designation, not to a new rank or office, but to a new work, namely, that of foreign missions, or rather to this single mission, which they are subsequently said to have "fulfilled." (See below, on 14, 26.) It is not necessarily implied that this was the first intimation made to Barnabas and Saul of their vocation to the work of missions. The divine communication mentioned in 22, 21, below, may have been previously made; and they may have come to Antioch for the very purpose of obtaining a dismission from the church there; and it may have been in reference to this request, that the Prophets and Teachers were engaged in special prayer and fasting for divine direction.

4. So they, being sent forth by the Holy Ghost,

departed unto Seleucia; and from thence they sailed to Cyprus.

As it had just been said that they were dismissed or let go by the church, their divine legation is again asserted, to prevent mistake. *Being sent forth by the Holy Ghost*, not merely by their associates at Antioch. *Departed*, literally, *came down*, which might seem to mean down the Orontes, on which Antioch is situated; but it more probably means, from the interior to the seacoast. (See above, on 12, 19.) *Seleucia*, a Syrian port, near the mouth of the Orontes, west of Antioch, built by Seleucus Nicator, and called by his own name, as Antioch was by that of his father. (See below, on v. 14.) *Sailed*, or more emphatically, *sailed away*, i. e. from Syria, where they had so long been labouring. *Cyprus*, a large island off the coast of Palestine, renowned in the remotest times for wealth, fertility and luxury. It was now a Roman province, ruled by a Proconsul. (See below, on v. 7.) This island may have been selected as their first field of missionary labour, not merely on account of its proximity to Syria, but because it was the native land of Barnabas (see above, on 4, 36), and perhaps of John Mark also (see the next verse, and compare Col. 4, 10.) It could hardly be fortuitous that this first mission was directed to the native countries of the missionaries, and to Cyprus first, as Barnabas still took the lead.

5. And when they were at Salamis, they preached the word of God in the synagogues of the Jews: and they had also John to (their) minister.

Being in Salamis, or having got there. This was an ancient city in the south-eastern corner of the island, afterwards called Constantia, and now Famagusta. *Preached* (announced, declared) *the word of God* (the new or Christian revelation.) *Synagogues*, assemblies, meetings, whether large or small. It is not probable that Salamis contained more than one such building, nor certain that it had even one; but the Greek word, as we have already seen (on 6, 9), admitted of a wider application than the one assigned to it in later usage. The first preachers of the Gospel, being Jews by birth and education, obtained access, through the synagogues, not only to their countrymen, but also to the serious and devoutly disposed Gentiles, who were in the habit of attending Jewish worship. (See above, on 9, 20. 10, 1.) *To* (or *for*) *their minister*, attendant, servant. (For the origin and usage of the Greek word, see above, on 5, 22.) As the same word is elsewhere used by Luke to designate an officer or servant of the synagogue in Nazareth (see Luke 4, 20), it might seem here to have specific reference to what immediately precedes. 'They preached in the synagogues of Salamis, and in so doing were assisted or attended on by John.' It is generally understood, however, in a wider sense, to wit, that he attended them upon this journey; but in what capacity, has been disputed. Some make him a mere personal attendant, like the young men who accompanied the ancient prophets; others an ordained minister of lower rank, to aid in preaching and administering baptism; others still, avoiding these extremes, regard him as a personal attendant, but preparing for more sacred duties. (See below, on 16, 1–3.)

6. And when they had gone through the isle unto Paphos, they found a certain sorcerer, a false prophet, a Jew, whose name (was) Bar-jesus:

Having gone through the whole island, is the reading of the five oldest manuscripts, i. e. through its whole length, from east to west. Though not expressly mentioned, it is highly probable that in this, as in other previous cases of the same kind, they preached in smaller towns upon the road. (See above, on 8, 25. 40. 9, 32.) *Unto*, even to, as far as, the particle again suggesting that they had traversed the whole island. *Paphos*, a city on the western coast of Cyprus, famous for the worship of Venus in a temple near it, whence she is called *Paphian* by Homer and Horace. It was now the seat of Roman government, i. e. the residence of the Proconsul. *Found*, met with, learned that he was there before them. (For the passive of the Greek verb, see above, on 8, 40, and compare v. 9 of the same chapter.) Several of the oldest manuscripts and latest editors read, *a certain man, a sorcerer.* For the true meaning of this last word (*magus* or *magician*), see above, on 8, 9. *A false prophet* (*and*) *a Jew*, or a *Jewish false prophet*, as the last word in Greek may be either an adjective or a substantive. This man was, therefore, not a heathen sorcerer, like Simon Magus, but a Jewish renegade, or still more probably, a professed Jew, but falsely claiming inspiration. There were probably many such among the *Goetes* or impostors who abounded in the Apostolic age, not as mere jugglers, but as teachers of a higher kind of science, in which trade Jews would have a great advantage from their real superiority in religious knowledge. *Whose name* (Gr. *to whom the name*) was *Bar-jesus*, an Aramaic form, meaning the *Son of Joshua.* See above, on 7, 45, and compare the kindred forms, Barabbas (Matt. 27, 16), Bartholomew (see above, on 1, 13), Barjonas (Matt. 16, 17), Barnabas (vs. 1. 2), Barsabas (1, 23), Bartimeus (Mark 10, 46.)

7. Which was with the deputy of the country, Sergius Paulus, a prudent man; who called for Barnabas and Saul, and desired to hear the word of God.

Was with, not merely at some one time, such as that of their arrival, but habitually, in his service or his company. We know, from contemporary writers, that such associations were not uncommon at the courts or residences of distinguished public men, arising no doubt, at least partially, from the prevailing discontent of the most serious heathen with their own religion, and perhaps, in some degree, from their prevailing expectation of a great deliverer from among the Jews, which would account still further for the presence of Bar-Jesus in the case before us. (See above, on 2, 5, vol. 1, p. 47.) *Deputy of the country* is in Greek a single word, used by the later writers, such as Polybius and Plutarch, to represent the Latin *Proconsul.* We have here a striking instance of a supposed error becoming a conclusive proof of accuracy even in minute points. The Roman provinces were divided by Augustus into two great classes, senatorial and imperial, the former governed by Proconsuls, and the latter by Proprætors or Consular Legates. Now as Cyprus was originally an Imperial province, the use of the word Proconsul, or its Greek equivalent, was once regarded as an error, though of no importance; but it was afterwards discovered, by a more minute examination of original authorities, that before the date of these events, the island had been transferred from the one class to the other, and was now actually under a Proconsul, a fact confirmed by the existence of a Cyprian coin, belonging to the same reign, on which Proclus, the successor of Sergius Paulus, bears the very title given to the latter in the verse before us. *Prudent*, though always used to represent this Greek word in the English version (see Matt. 11, 25. Luke 10, 21. 1 Cor. 1, 19), is not so expressive of its meaning as *intelligent* or *sensible.* Perhaps, however, it was not here used to denote capacity or knowledge so much as disposition or habit of mind, and might therefore be still better rendered *thoughtful* or *reflecting*, with particular allusion to religious subjects. This state of mind, so far from being inconsistent with his patronage of Elymas, explains it, by suggesting that he had precisely that kind of uneasiness or curiosity, which one acquainted with the Hebrew Scriptures would be best prepared, however partially, to satisfy. *Who*, literally, *this*, the latter, i. e. Sergius Paulus, the name last mentioned. *Called for*, literally, *calling to*, i. e. to himself, or to his presence, summoning, requiring to attend. (See above, on 5, 40. 6, 2, and compare the application of the same verb to the call of God, in 2, 39.) *Desired*, in Greek an emphatic or intensive compound, much stronger than the simple verb employed in the next verse, and meaning *sought for*, *inquired after*, but here construed with another verb (*to hear.*) It is clear from the tense and collocation of this verb, that it was not meant to express (although it certainly implies) his previous state of mind, but rather that occasioned by the news of their arrival, or their actual appearance in obedience to his summons. (Whereupon) *he sought* (or earnestly requested) *to hear the word of God*, i. e. the gospel, claiming to be a new revelation or divine communication. (See above, on v. 5, and on 4, 31. 6, 2. 7. 8, 14. 11, 1. 12, 24.)

8. But Elymas the sorcerer (for so is his name by interpretation) withstood them, seeking to turn away the deputy from the faith.

Then withstood them Elymas, the same Greek verb with that in 6, 10, where it is translated *resist.* The kind of opposition, which the word most readily suggests in this connection, is open argument or disputation; but it does not necessarily exclude more indirect and private methods, which would be facilitated by his previous relations to the governor. *Elymas* is commonly explained as the Greek form of an Arabic word meaning *wise* or *learned*, the plural of which (*Ulema*) is applied to the collective body of Mahometan doctors in the Turkish empire. While the verbal root in Arabic means to *know*, the corresponding root in Hebrew means to *hide*, both which ideas (*occult science*) are included in the term by which

Luke here explains it (*Magus.*) The last clause gives the motive of this opposition. *Seeking*, the uncompounded form of the verb used in the preceding verse; not only *wishing* but *attempting*, using active means to gain his end. *To turn away*, a very strong Greek word, used in the classics to denote the act of twisting or distorting, but commonly employed in the New Testament to signify moral perversion or perverseness. (See below, on 20, 30, and compare Matt. 17, 17. Luke 9, 41. 23, 2. Phil. 2, 15.) It here means to divert attention or withdraw the mind, but with an implication of violence or great exertion. The same verb is applied, in the Septuagint version of Ex. 5, 4, to the diversion of the Hebrews from their work by the visits and discourses of Moses and Aaron. *The Deputy*, or rather the *Proconsul*, as in v. 7. *From the faith* may either mean from the Christian faith, the new religion, which these strangers preached; or from the act of faith, i. e. believing the new doctrine thus made known to him.

9. Then Saul, who also (is called) Paul, filled with the Holy Ghost, set his eyes on him—

There is here a sudden change in Saul's relative position, not only with respect to Barnabas, but also to the whole conduct of the mission, and the whole course of the history. From holding an inferior place, as indicated even by the order of the names (see above, on vs. 1. 2, and compare 11, 30. 12, 25), he now comes forward in this singular emergency, addresses Elymas in tones of high authority, and acts as the organ of the divine justice, in predicting or inflicting a retributive calamity. This change in his position is accompanied, as in the case of Abraham, Jacob and Peter (Gen. 17, 5. 32, 28. John 1, 42), by a change of name. *Then* (δὲ) *Saul, the* (*one*) *also* (*called*) *Paul.* It is not improbable that Saul, according to the custom of the Jews in that age (see above, on v. 1, and on 1, 23. 9, 36. 12, 12), had already borne the Roman name of *Paulus;* and Luke might seem to introduce it here merely because of the coincidence with the name of the Proconsul. But this does not account for its invariable use, from this point onwards, to the absolute exclusion of the Hebrew name by which he had been always before called. (See above, 7, 58. 8, 1. 3. 9, 1. 4. 8. 11. 17. 19. 22. 24. 26. 11, 25. 30. 12, 25. 13, 1. 2. 7.) Jerome's idea, that he now assumed the name, in commemoration of the victory achieved by the conversion of the Roman governor, exaggerates the value and importance of that incident, and assumes an adulation of great men entirely at variance with apostolic principles and practice, as well as a violation of the early Christian usage, according to which, teachers gave their names to their disciples, and not vice versa. Augustin, on the contrary, supposes that the name is an expression of humility (originally meaning *little.*) But such humility is too much like that of the Pope, who calls himself a servant of servants; and the Latin name would not so readily suggest this idea as that of a noble Roman family who bore it. Besides, why should it be assumed just here, either in point of fact or in the narrative? The only supposition which is free from all these difficulties, and affords a satisfactory solution of the facts in question, is, that this was the time fixed by divine authority for Paul's manifestation as Apostle of the Gentiles, and that this manifestation was made more conspicuous by its coincidence with his triumph over a representative of unbelieving and apostate Judaism, and the conversion of an official representative of Rome, whose name was identical with his own apostolical title. The critical juncture was still further marked by Paul's first miracle or sign of his apostleship (see 2 Cor. 12, 12), preceded by a few words, but conceived and uttered in the highest tone of apostolical authority. *Filled with the Holy Ghost*, not for the first time (see above, on 9, 17), but renewedly and specially inspired to utter this denunciation, which is therefore not the natural expression of any merely human sentiment or feeling, but an authoritative declaration of God's purposes and judgments. *Set his eyes on him*, a phrase very variously rendered in our Bible, but the strict sense of which is *gazing* (or *intently looking*) *into him* (see above, on 1, 10. 3, 4. 12. 6, 15. 7, 55. 10, 4. 11, 6.) This was no doubt intended to arrest the attention of the sorcerer as well as the spectators, and to awe them under an impression of God's presence and authority. With the following address of Paul to Elymas, compare that of Peter to the Magus of Samaria. (See above, on 8, 20–23.)

10. And said, O full of all subtilty and all mischief, (thou) child of the devil, (thou) enemy of all righteousness, wilt thou not cease to pervert the right ways of the Lord?

Full, not merely tinged or tainted with these qualities, but full of them, composed of them. (See above, on 8, 23.) *Subtilty*, so translated also in Matt. 26, 4, but twice *deceit* (Mark 7, 22. Rom. 1, 29), once *craft* (Mark 14, 1), and often *guile* (e. g. John 1, 47. 2 Cor. 12, 16. 1 Pet. 2, 22. Rev. 14, 5.) The Greek word primarily means a bait for fish; then any deception; then a desire or disposition to deceive. *Mischief*, unscrupulousness, recklessness, facility in doing evil, which is the original and etymological import of the word. It occurs only here in the New Testament, but a kindred form (translated *lewdness*) in 18, 14, below. *All*, before these nouns, denotes both quality and quantity, variety and high degree. (See above, on 4, 29. 5, 23. 12, 11.) *Child* (literally, *Son*) *of the devil*, i. e. like him, a partaker of his nature, belonging to his party, "the seed of the serpent." (See above, on 5, 16, and compare Gen. 3, 15. John 8, 44.) *The devil* (i. e. slanderer, false accuser) is always so translated, except in 2 Tim. 3, 3. Titus 2, 3. (See above, on 10, 38.) *Enemy of all righteousness*, i. e. of all that is right and good. The pronoun (*thou*) twice supplied by the translators rather weakens the expression than enforces it. *Wilt thou not cease?* may be also read affirmatively, *thou wilt not cease*. But the interrogative form has more force, as conveying a severe expostulation, like the famous exordium of Cicero's first oration against Catiline (*Quousque tandem abutere patientia nostra?*) *To pervert*, literally, *perverting*, the participle of the verb translated *turn away* in v. 8. The essential meaning is the same in either case, but the construction different, the object of the action being there a person, here a thing. The truth, from which Barjesus sought to turn the governor away, is here described as turned away itself, i. e. distorted or perverted, by misrepresentation or misapplication. *The ways of the Lord*, i. e. here, most probably, his methods of salvation or his purposes of mercy. *Right*, in the physical sense, *straight*, as applied in mathematics (a right line or a right angle.) The term here has reference to the figure of a path, the *ways of the Lord* which, although straight in themselves, Elymas was trying to make crooked. (Compare Isai. 5, 20.) The essential idea is not the specific one of doctrinal error or of practical misconduct, but the general one of interference with God's purposes, and the impious attempt to hinder their accomplishment. As he tried to turn away Sergius Paulus from the faith, so he tried to turn away the grace of God from Sergius Paulus.

11. And now, behold, the hand of the Lord (is) upon thee, and thou shalt be blind, not seeing the sun for a season. And immediately there fell on him a mist and a darkness; and he went about seeking some to lead him by the hand.

And now is a phrase often used to mark the close of a preamble and to introduce the main proposition (see above, on 3, 17. 7, 34. 10, 5); but here it seems to have its strict sense as a particle of time, 'and now (at length) your hour is come, your career is at an end, your course is finally arrested.' *Behold*, as usual, introduces something unexpected. (See above, on 1, 10. 12, 7.) *The hand of the Lord*, i. e. his power, especially in active exercise, whether in mercy or in judgment. (See above, on 4, 28. 30. 11, 21. 12, 11, and compare Ex. 9, 3. 1 Sam. 5, 11. Ezr. 7, 9. Neh. 2, 8. Job 19, 21.) At the same time, it suggests that this was no fortuitous or human stroke, 'the hand of the Lord and not of man.' (*Is* or *shall be*) *upon thee;* as the verb is not expressed, it may be either descriptive of the present or prophetic of the future. If the first, it is equivalent to saying, 'already (or even now) upon thee.' *Blind and not seeing* may be an idiomatic combination of the positive and negative expression of the same idea. (Compare Luke 1, 20, where a similar form is used in reference to speech and dumbness.) Or *not seeing* (even) *the sun* may be a strong expression for total blindness. *For a season*, literally, *to* (or *till*) *a time*, i. e. a set time, which is the proper meaning of the Greek word, as explained above (on 1, 7. 3, 19. 7, 20. 12, 1.) This may mean, as long as it shall please God, and does not therefore necessarily imply that Elymas should be restored to sight. That is certainly, however, the most natural construction, and the one which has been commonly adopted. Chrysostom says that this was not a word of punishment but of conversion; and the Venerable Bede, that Paul knew by experience how the darkness of the eyes might be followed by illumination of the mind. There is certainly a singular resemblance between this first recorded miracle of Paul and the miraculous accompaniments of his own conversion. (See above, on 9, 8. 9.) Some have inferred from Gal. 4, 15, and other passages, that Paul's own sight was never perfectly restored. The same phrase (*till a time* or *for a season*) is used by Luke in reference to the intermission of our

Lord's temptation (Luke 4, 13.) *Immediately*, or on the spot, the same word that is used above in 3, 7. 5, 10. 9, 18. 12, 23, and there explained. *Fell on him*, the same verb with that used in 8, 16. 10, 10. 44. 11, 15, in reference to spiritual influences. Common to both cases is the idea of suddenness and also of descent from above, or the agency of a superior power. *Mist*, a poetical Greek word, applied by Homer to the failure of the sight at death or in a swoon. *Darkness* may be either the more usual prosaic word expressive of the same thing, or denote the effect as distinguished from the cause, or mark a gradation in the blindness, first a mist, then total darkness, the reverse of that in one of our Lord's miracles. (See Mark 8, 24.) As the word translated *mist* is also used by Galen, the Greek medical writer, some regard it as a trace of Luke's profession. *Went about*, literally, *leading about* or *around* (as in 1 Cor. 9, 5), a verb often used in the intransitive sense first given, perhaps by an ellipsis of the reflexive pronoun (*leading himself about.*) See Matt 4, 23. 9, 35. 23, 15. Mark 6, 6, and compare the like use of the simple verb in Matt. 26, 46. Mark 1, 38. 14, 42. John 11, 7. 15. 16. 14, 31. *Went about seeking* just reverses the original construction, which is *going about sought.* The last seven words in English correspond to one in Greek, meaning *hand-guides* or *hand-leaders.* (See the active and passive participles of the corresponding verb in 9, 8 above, and 22, 11, below.) The scene so vividly described in this clause has been realized, or rendered visible, in one of Raphael's cartoons.

12. Then the deputy, when he saw what was done, believed, being astonished at the doctrine of the Lord.

Then, in its strict sense, as a particle of time, equivalent to saying, when (or after) this had happened. *The deputy*, used by our translators here and in vs. 7, 8 above, though more specific, is less accurate than Tyndale's *ruler*, as the Greek word (ἀνθύπατος) does not mean a deputy in general, but the deputy of a supreme magistrate (ὕπατος), i. e. of a Roman Consul, to whom the uncompounded form is constantly applied by the later Greek historians. The Vulgate and its copyists in English (Wiclif and the Rhemish Version) give the corresponding Latin form (*Proconsul.*) *When he saw* (literally, *having seen* or *seeing*) *what was done*, or more exactly, *the* (*thing*) *done*, come to pass, or happened, i. e. the sudden blindness of Barjesus, in immediate execution of Paul's sentence or prediction. *Believed* can only mean that he believed in Christ, or in the truth of the religion thus attested. *Astonished*, literally, *struck* or *smitten*, not with wonder merely, but with admiration, as appears from Mark 11, 18, where mere amazement would be insufficient to account for the effect described. The same verb is often used (see Matt. 13, 54. Mark 6, 2. 7, 37. Luke 2, 48), and sometimes with the very same construction (Matt. 7, 28. 22, 33. Mark 1, 22. 11, 18. Luke 4, 32), to express the effect produced upon the people by our Saviour's miracles and teachings. In all those cases, as in that before us, *doctrine* does not mean the truth taught, but the mode of teaching. *The doctrine of the Lord*, i. e. Paul's doctrine with respect to Christ, is a grammatical construction, but at variance with the first clause and its obvious relation to the last, as well as with the numerous analogies just cited from the Gospels. What *struck* the mind of the Proconsul and commanded his belief was the *Lord's* (*mode of*) *teaching* (his own religion), both by word and miracle. Here, as in the case of Simon Magus (see above, on 8, 24), we are not told what became either of Elymas or Sergius Paulus. The tradition which describes the latter as accompanying Paul to Spain, and afterwards as Bishop of Narbonne in France, is probably entitled to no credence.

13. Now when Paul and his company loosed from Paphos, they came to Perga in Pamphylia; and John departing from them returned to Jerusalem.

Now, and, or but. *Paul and his company* (in the older English versions, *Paul and they that were with him*) is in Greek, *those about Paul*. This peculiar idiom is common in the classics, sometimes literally meaning the attendants or companions (as in Mark 4, 10), sometimes only the persons named (as in John 11, 19), sometimes both together, as in this place. The expression seems to have been chosen here, to render prominent the change in Paul's position, and to show that he was now the leader. (See above, on v. 9.) This change may possibly have been deferred till they were leaving Cyprus and about to enter Asia Minor; whereas Barnabas had been allowed to take the lead as long as they were in his native country. (See above, on v. 4, and compare 4, 36.) *Loosed* is so translated in two other places (16, 11. 27, 21), but elsewhere *launched* (21, 1. 27, 2. 4), *launched forth* (Luke 8, 22), *sailed* (20, 3. 13), *set forth* (21, 2), *departed* (27, 12. 28, 10. 11.) The Greek verb, thus variously rendered, strictly means *to lead* (or *to be led*) *up* (as in 9, 39. 12, 4 above), but as a nautical expression to go out to sea, being so used by Herodotus and Homer. Its form is here that of a passive participle but may be translated, *having sailed* or *put to sea.* They enter Asia Minor, not through Cilicia, which was Paul's native province, where he had already laboured (see above, on 9, 30. 11, 25), but through Pamphylia, the adjacent province on the west. *Perga,* its capital, a few miles from the coast, was famous for the worship of Diana, as Paphos was for that of Venus (see above, on v. 6, and below, on 19, 24.)* Its ruins are supposed to be still visible. *John,* who was mentioned in v. 5 above, as their attendant. That *John Mark* is the person meant, appears from a comparison of 12, 25 above with 15, 37 below. *Departing* denotes not mere local separation, but secession or desertion, being elsewhere used in an unfavourable sense (see Matt. 7, 23, and compare Luke 9, 39.) A term still stronger is employed in 15, 39 below. John's motive for abandoning the mission has been variously conjectured to be weariness, home-sickness, feeble health, important business at Jerusalem, &c. &c. That it was not understood from the beginning that he should take leave of them at this point, appears, not only from the terms here used and just explained, but still more clearly from Paul's censure of his conduct as a species of apostasy (see below, on 15, 39.) The most satisfactory solution seems to be, that he was discontented with the unexpected transfer of precedence and authority from Barnabas his kinsman (see Col. 4, 10) to one who had hitherto occupied a lower place. This feeling, though a wrong one, will not seem unnatural, when we consider, that Barnabas was not only older as a Christian and a minister (see above, on 4, 36), but had been the means of introducing Paul to active labour, both in Jerusalem (9, 27) and Antioch (11, 26.) That he did not share in Mark's resentment, may be ascribed to his superior piety and wisdom, or to a less ardent temper, which required time for its excitement. (See below, on 15, 37.)

14. But when they departed from Perga, they came to Antioch in Pisidia, and went into the synagogue on the sabbath day, and sat down.

* Pergae fanum antiquissimum et sanctissimum scimus esse.—CICERO (in Verrem.)

They is expressed in Greek and therefore emphatic, meaning Paul and Barnabas, as the remaining members of the mission after Mark's desertion. *Departed*, literally, *passing through*, or *having passed through*, i. e., through the country between Perga and Antioch. (See above, on 8, 40. 9, 32. 11, 19. 22.) Some of the older English versions have the strange translation, *wandered through the countries*, as if the words were intended to describe an itinerant ministry, and not a direct passage from one point to another. They seem to have visited Pamphylia at this time, only as the key or entrance to Pisidia, the next province on the north, reserving missionary labour in the former until their return. (See below, on 14, 25.) Antioch is referred by different ancient writers to the adjacent provinces of Phrygia, Pamphylia, and Pisidia, a variation owing either to actual change in the political arrangements of the country, or more probably to vagueness and uncertainty in the boundaries themselves. The ruins of this Antioch have been discovered in our own day. The frequent occurrence of this name in ancient history arises from its application by the Greek King of Syria, Seleucus Nicator, to a number of towns founded or restored by himself, in honor of his father, Antiochus the Great. *The synagogue*, meeting, or assembly, of the Jews for worship, whether in a private house or public building. (See above, on v. 5, and on 6, 9.) *The sabbath-day*, literally, *day of the sabbath*, the Aramaic form of the Hebrew name (שׁבתא) resembling a Greek plural, and being often so declined, and construed by all the evangelists excepting John, who always treats it as a singular. *Sat down*, i. e., as some suppose, in a place usually occupied by public teachers; but see the next verse.

15. And after the reading of the law and the prophets, the rulers of the synagogue sent unto them, saying, (Ye) men (and) brethren, if ye have any word of exhortation for the people, say on.

The reading of the Law (i. e. the books of Moses) seems to have formed a part of public worship, from the earliest times to which its history can be traced. That of the Prophets is said, in a tradition of the later Jews, to have been introduced as an evasion of an edict of Antiochus Epiphanes prohibiting the reading of the law, and afterwards continued as a permanent usage. *The rulers of the synagogue* (in Greek one compound word) were probably the elders of the Jews in Antioch, i. e. the heads of families, or other hereditary chiefs and representatives, as such conducting or controlling public worship. It is not impossible, however, that in foreign countries, the synagogue had more of a distinct organization than in Palestine itself. (See above, on 6, 9. 9, 2. 20.) But most of the minute details now found in Jewish books are probably posterior in date to the destruction of Jerusalem and the dissolution of the Jewish nation with its hereditary eldership, a change which would naturally lead to the separate organization of the synagogue or Jewish church. *Sent to them*, not said to them, implying that they were not in the chief seats of the synagogue (Matt. 23, 6), but had probably sat down near the entrance. They were no doubt recognized as strangers, and perhaps as teachers, by some circumstance of dress or aspect. The message was probably conveyed by the "minister" or servant of the synagogue. (See above, on v. 5, and compare Luke 4, 20.) *Men and brethren*, the same courteous and kindly form of speech which we have already had occasion to explain. (See above, on 1, 16. 2, 29. 37. 7, 2.) It implies a recognition of the strangers by the rulers of the synagogue, as fellow Jews, the Christian schism being probably as yet unknown to them. *If ye have*, literally, *if there is in you*, i. e. in your minds or your possession, (any) *word of exhortation*, i. e. any exhortation to be spoken or delivered. (See above, on 4, 36. 9, 31.) *Say on* is in Greek simply *say* or speak.

16. Then Paul stood up, and beckoning with (his) hand said, Men of Israel, and ye that fear God, give audience.

As Barnabas derived his very name from his experience and gifts as an exhorter (see above, on 4, 36), it is the more remarkable that Paul should now appear as the chief speaker, not only in this one case but before and afterwards. (See above, on v. 9, and below, on 14, 12.) The uniformity of this proceeding, and the seeming acquiescence of Barnabas himself, confirm the previous conclusion, that Paul's commission as Apostle of the Gentiles (Rom. 11, 13), although given long before (see above, on 9, 15, and below, on 22, 21. 26, 17. 18), was now first publicly made known and acted on. *Arising*, standing up, see above, on 2, 15. 5, 34. 11, 28. *Beckoning*, see above, on 12, 17. *Men of Israel*, i. e. Jews by birth, descendants of Jacob, hereditary members of the chosen people. (See above, on 2, 22. 3, 12. 5, 35.) *Ye that fear* (literally, *those fearing*) *God*, a phrase applicable in itself to all devout men, but specially applied in the New Testament to Gentiles, whether Proselytes, i. e. professed converts to the Jewish faith (see above, on 2, 10. 6, 5), or merely well disposed to it and more or less influenced by it (see above, on 10, 2. 22, 35.) Of this class many seem to have been found, wherever there was access to the Jewish worship, and from this class the Apostles gathered some of their earliest and most important converts. *Give audience*, literally, *hear*, implying, as in all like cases, that they might hear something to which they were not accustomed, or for which they were not prepared. (See above, on 2, 14. 22. 29.) The discourse which follows has peculiar interest and value, as the first of Paul's on record, and most probably the first that he delivered after the avowal of his Apostolical commission. When compared with those of Peter and his own epistles, the degree of difference and sameness is precisely such as might have been expected from the circumstances under which they were composed or uttered. (See above, on 3, 26. vol. 1, p. 122.)

17. The God of this people of Israel chose our fathers, and exalted the people when they dwelt as strangers in the land of Egypt, and with a high arm brought he them out of it.

Beginning with a brief sketch of the early history of Israel, as the ancient church or chosen people, from their first vocation to the reign of David (17–22), the Apostle suddenly exhibits Jesus, as the heir of that king and the promised Saviour (23), citing John the Baptist as his witness and forerunner (24–25) ; then makes the offer of salvation through Christ to both classes of his hearers (26), describing his rejection by the Jews at Jerusalem (27), his death, burial, and resurrection (28–31) ; all which he represents as the fulfilment of God's promise to the fathers (32), and of specific prophecies, three of which he quotes, interprets, and applies to Christ (33–37) ; winding up with another earnest offer of salvation (38–39), and a solemn warning against unbelief (40–41.) The mixture of law and gospel, threatening and promise, doctrine and exhortation, in this sermon, are highly characteristic of its author, and yet too peculiar, both in form and substance, to have been compiled, as some allege, from his epistles. In the verse before us, he describes the vocation of the Hebrews, and their organization as the chosen people. *This people* (*of Israel* is omitted by the latest critics) seems addressed rather to the Gentiles than the Jews. *Chose*, or more emphatically, chose out for himself, or for his own use and service. (See above, on 1, 2. 24. 6, 5.) *Our fathers*, thus acknowledging his own hereditary kindred to them. (See above, on 3, 13. 25. 5, 30. 7, 2. 11. 12. 15. 19. 38. 39. 44. 45.) This first clause may relate to the original vocation of the Patriarchs, and the second to the national organization, for which the people were prepared in Egypt; or the whole may be referred to the Egyptian period, the choice mentioned in the first clause being then the choice of Israel, not as a family, but as a nation. The last of these constructions is the one most readily suggested by the words, although the first gives more completeness to Paul's retrospect, by including the Patriarchal period. (See above, on 7, 2–16.) *The people*, thus chosen and separated from all others. *Exalted*, literally, *heightened*, made high, applied elsewhere to the raising of the brazen serpent and to Christ's elevation on the cross (John 3, 14. 8, 28. 12, 32. 34); to his ascension and exalted state in heaven (see above, on 2, 33. 5, 31); in a moral sense, to self-exaltation or elation (Matt. 23, 12. Luke 14, 11. 18, 14); and in an outward sense, to extraordinary privileges and prosperity (Matt. 11, 23. Luke 10, 15. 2 Cor. 11, 7. Jas. 4, 10. 1 Pet. 5, 6.) This last appears to be the meaning here, in reference either to the honour put upon the chosen people, even under persecution, or to their miraculous increase and national development. *When they dwelt as strangers*, literally, *in the sojourn*. (For a cognate form, applied to the same subject, see above, on 7, 6. 29.) *A high arm*, an idiomatic expression for the manifest exertion of extraordinary power, corresponding to the *stretched out arm* of the Old Testament, and like it specially applied to the exertion of Jehovah's power in the exodus from Egypt. (Compare Ex. 6, 6 Deut. 5, 15. Jer. 32, 21. Ps. 136, 12.)

18. And about the time of forty years suffered he their manners in the wilderness.

Next to the Exodus he puts the Error, or forty years'

wandering in the wilderness. *About*, literally, *as*, see above, on 1, 15. 2, 41. 4, 4. 5, 7. 36. This expression is the more appropriate, because the actual error lasted only thirty-eight years. (See above, on 7, 42.) *Suffered their manners*, i. e. bore with them, endured them. Another reading, differing in a single letter, and preferred by most modern critics, yields the meaning, *bore them as a nurse does*, i. e. nursed or nourished. The same figure is applied by Moses to this period in the history of Israel (see Num. 11, 12. Deut. 1, 31, in which last place the Septuagint version exhibits the same textual variation) and by Paul to his own treatment of the Thessalonians (1 Thess. 2, 7.)

19. And when he had destroyed seven nations in the land of Canaan, he divided their land to them by lot.

Next to the Error comes the Conquest of Canaan. *When he had* (literally, *having*) *destroyed.* (For a very different meaning of the same verb, see below, on v. 29.) *Seven nations*, i. e. tribes of the Canaanites, to wit, those enumerated in Deut. 7, 1. Josh. 3, 10. Neh. 9, 8. *Gave by lot*, or, according to the oldest manuscripts and latest editors, *gave as an inheritance*, or caused them to inherit. Neither of the two Greek verbs occurs elsewhere in the New Testament, but both are used in the Septuagint, and sometimes to translate the same Hebrew word (e. g. Num. 33, 54. Josh. 14, 1, compared with Deut. 21, 16. Josh. 19, 51.) It is a curious inference of Bengel, that because three rare words used in these two verses occur also in the Septuagint version of the first chapters of Deuteronomy and Isaiah, these are the portions of the law and Prophets read, in the synagogue of Antioch for that day, as he says they still are in the Jewish service.

20. And after that he gave (unto them) judges about the space of four hundred and fifty years, until Samuel the prophet.

After that, literally, *after these* (*things*), i. e. the conquest and settlement of Canaan. *About*, literally, *as*; see above, on v. 18. By adding together all the periods mentioned in the book of Judges, i. e. the periods of foreign domination and the intervals of rest under the Judges, we obtain almost the very number here affirmed. This agreement between Paul and the inspired record of the time to which he here refers cannot be shaken by the seeming discrepancy in 1 Kings 6, 1, the solution of which belongs to the interpretation of that book. *Gave them Judges*, who were therefore not self-constituted rulers, but divinely commissioned. *Until Samuel the Prophet*, the next one of eminence after Moses (see above, on 3, 24.) He was also the last in the series of Judges, under whom the regal form of government was introduced.

21. And afterward they desired a king, and God gave unto them Saul the son of Cis, a man of the tribe of Benjamin, by the space of forty years.

Afterward, literally, *thence*, from there, a local particle applied, in this one case, to time, as we say in English, thenceforth, henceforth. The expression may involve an allusion to the regular succession of the history which Paul was tracing, like a line or path presented to the eye. *They asked* (for themselves), to gratify their own desires, and not to answer any higher end. (For the exact force of the verbal form here used, see above, on 3, 14. 7, 46. 9, 2.) *God gave*, in displeasure and in judgment, but so that Saul was nevertheless a legitimate though not a theocratical sovereign. *Cis* should have been written *Kis*, the nearest approach that could be made in Greek letters to the Hebrew *Kish*. The coincidence, in name and tribe, between this king and the Apostle speaking, is undoubtedly remarkable. (Compare 1 Sam. 9, 1. 16. 21, with Rom. 11, 1. Phil. 3, 5.) One of the early Fathers (Tertullian) makes one Saul a type of the other, and even explains Gen. 49, 27 as a prophecy of Paul's persecutions and conversion. *By the space of* is needlessly supplied by Tyndale, and transcribed by his successors. Wiclif has simply *by*, which seems to be equivalent to *for* in modern English, when prefixed to chronological specifications. The most simple and exact translation is the Rhemish (*forty years.*) This is understood by some as the age of Saul at his accession, but by most as the length of his reign. We have no account of its duration in Scripture; but Josephus states with great precision, perhaps relying upon public records or tradition not preserved in Scripture, that Saul reigned eighteen years in Samuel's lifetime, and twenty-two years after his decease.

22. And when he had removed him, he raised up unto them David to be their king; to whom also he gave testimony and said, I have found David the (son) of Jesse, a man after mine own heart, which shall fulfil all my will.

Having removed (or *deposed*) *him*, i. e. from his kingly office, as recorded in 1 Sam. 15, 11. 23. 35. 16, 1. Some suppose it to refer to his death, as a removal out of life; but this would be otherwise expressed, and the Greek verb here used is repeatedly applied to removal from office, both in the Septuagint (2 Kings 17, 23. Dan. 2, 21) and the New Testament (Luke 16, 4.) *Raised up* then relates, not merely to David's coronation (2 Sam. 2, 4), but to his original designation and anointing (1 Sam. 16, 1. 13.) *To be their king*, literally, *as* (or *for*) *a king*. *To whom also*, i. e. besides making him a king, he testified expressly of his character. *Gave testimony and said*, in Greek, *said testifying*. The words that follow are not found in the Old Testament, precisely as they stand here, but are made up of two passages, "The Lord hath sought him a man after his own heart" (1 Sam. 13, 14), and "I have found David my servant" (Ps. 89, 20.) They are not combined through inadvertence or a lapse of memory, as some pretend, but as real expressions of what God did say, through Samuel and otherwise, on different occasions, or as the spirit and the meaning of his whole mode of dealing with this favoured servant, like the prophetic summary in Matt. 2, 23 (see above, on 2, 22.) The same explanation will apply to the last clause, which describes him not as personally free from fault or even crime, but as merely blameless in his character and conduct as a theocratic sovereign. *Fulfil all my will*, or more exactly, *do all my wills*, i. e. all the things that I shall will or order.

23. Of this man's seed hath God, according to (his) promise, raised unto Israel a Saviour, Jesus:

The particular promise here referred to must be that recorded in 2 Sam. 7, 12, and frequently repeated elsewhere. *Raised*, or according to the text now commonly adopted, *brought*. (This expression occurs in the Septuagint version of Zech. 2, 9, as the other does in that of 3, 9. 15.) *Unto Israel*, as the chosen people, to whom the offer must be first made. *A Saviour* (even) *Jesus*, such being the import of the Hebrew name. (See Matt. 1, 21.)

24. When John had first preached, before his coming, the baptism of repentance to all the people of Israel.

John having heralded (proclaimed) *beforehand*, the same Greek verb that appears in the common text of 3, 20. *Before*, literally, *before the face*, an expression commonly applied to persons (Matt. 11, 10. Mark 1, 2. Luke 1, 76. 7, 27), but here used in imitation of the corresponding Hebrew phrase (לפני.) *His coming*, not his birth or incarnation, which was before John's public appearance, but *his entrance* on his office, in which sense the Greek word is used by Isocrates. Etymologically it is the correlative or converse of *exodus*, which is twice applied to death in the New Testament, being rendered in both instances *decease* (Luke 9, 31. 2 Pet. 1, 15), as it is *departure*, when the reference is to the exodus from Egypt (Heb. 11, 22.) *Baptism of repentance*, of which repentance was not only the condition but the meaning or thing signified. (See above, on 2, 38, and below, on 19, 4; and compare Mark 1, 4. Luke 3, 3.) *To all the people of Israel*, not necessarily to every individual, but to the body of the nation as such. (See above, on 5, 31.)

25. And as John fulfilled his course, he said, Whom think ye that I am? I am not (he). But, behold, there cometh one after me, whose shoes of (his) feet I am not worthy to loose.

Fulfilled, or was fulfilling, i. e. as some explain it, was engaged in executing his commission (see above, on 12, 25, below, on 14, 26), without reference to any particular period of his ministry; while others understand it as referring to its close, *while he was finishing his course* (see above, on 2, 1. 7, 23. 30. 9, 23, and below, on 24, 27.) *Course*, in its proper sense of *race* or *running*, a figure borrowed from the ancient games and used in the New Testament by Paul alone, who twice applies it to his own official life or ministry. (See below, on 20, 24, and compare 2 Tim. 4, 7.) The qualities which it suggests are those of energy and swiftness. *He said*, in the imperfect tense, not once for all, or on a single occasion, but habitually, he was wont to say. The next clause is construed in the Vulgate and by Luther without interrogation, and in this sense, *I am not he whom ye suppose me to be.* But this is now admitted to be ungrammatical, although it gives the true sense of the language. *Whom do ye suppose* (or *suspect*) *me to be?* (The Messiah, but) *I am not.* (See the same form of negation in Mark 13, 6. Luke 21, 8. John 13, 19.) The historical fact here referred to is recorded in John 1, 19–28. See John 1, 20. 27. Luke 3, 15. With the remainder of the verse compare Matt. 3, 11. Mark 1, 7. Luke 3, 16. *Shoes of his feet* is pleonastic in English, but not in Greek, where the first noun strictly denotes *underbinding*, and the feet are mentioned to determine or define it. (See above, on 7, 33, and compare John 1, 27.) *To unloose*, untie, or take off, the lowest kind of menial service, used by John to signify the vast disparity between himself and Christ.

26. Men (and) brethren, children of the stock of Abraham, and whosoever among you feareth God, to you is the word of this salvation sent.

This was not a matter of local or temporary interest, but an offer of salvation to the very persons whom he now addressed, both Jews and Gentiles. The former he describes as his *brethren* (see above, on 1, 16. 2, 29), *sons* (or *children*) *of the stock* (race or lineage) *of Abraham;* the latter as those *fearing God* (i. e. the true God), although not belonging to the chosen people (see above, on v. 16.) The form of the original is, *those among you fearing God. To you*, i. e. as some understand it, you as distinguished from the Jews of Palestine, referred to in the next verse. But as we know that these were not excluded from forgiveness and salvation, the meaning rather seems to be, that the rejection of the Gospel by the people at Jerusalem ought not to occasion its rejection elsewhere. *The word of this salvation* is a similar expression to the *words of this life* in 5, 20. There is no need of resolving it into *this word of salvation*, i. e. this saving word or doctrine. It simply means *the word* (or tidings) *of this* (method of) *salvation* (through Christ.) *Is sent*, literally, *was sent*, i. e. was intended to be sent from the beginning, although necessarily presented to the Jew first (Rom. 2, 9. 10.) This agrees better with the form of expression, as well as with the known facts of the case, than the explanation, *has been sent*, i. e. now, since the Jews at home have rejected it. This would rather have deterred the Jews of Antioch from hearing than incited them to do so.

27. For they that dwell at Jerusalem, and their rulers, because they knew him not, nor yet the voices of the prophets which are read every sabbath day, they have fulfilled (them) in condemning (him).

The conduct of the Jews at home, far from discrediting the claims of Jesus, had confirmed them, by contributing to verify the prophecies respecting him. Not the rabble merely, but their rulers, their chief men and most enlightened spiritual guides, had failed to recognize him as the Messiah foretold in the Scriptures, which were weekly read in their assemblies; but in the act of judging him as an impostor, they fulfilled those very Scriptures, which predicted his rejection. *Voices*, i. e. audible predictions, in allusion to the circumstance just mentioned, of their being read aloud every sabbath. *Judging*, i. e. acting as judges, sitting in judgment; the idea of *condemning* is suggested by the context. (See above, on 7, 7.) The construction of the sentence is ambiguous, as the verb *not knowing* (or *ignoring*) seems to govern an accusative both before and after it. Some avoid this syntax by construing *voices* with *fulfilled* directly (*and the voices of the prophets, every sabbath read, judging they fulfilled.*) But the construction adopted in our version is more natural, and yields a stronger sense, by expressly stating that the Jews mistook the meaning of their Scriptures, as well as the person of their Messiah *Nor yet* is simply *and* in the original.

28. And though they found no cause of death (in him), yet desired they Pilate that he should be slain.

So completely blinded were they to their own Messiah, and so bent on his destruction, that being unable to convict him of any capital offence, they asked it as a favour to themselves, and that too of a heathen governor, that he might be put to death. *Cause of death*, or ground of capital punishment. (See above, on 9, 15, and below, on 26, 25. 28, 18.) *Finding* (or *having found*), implying search and effort, on the part of accusers, witnesses, and judges. *Desired*, requested for themselves; see above, on v. 21, and compare 3, 14. 7, 46. 9, 2. 12, 20. *Slain*, despatched, made away with; see above, on 12, 2. Here again, *though* is simply *and* in the original. With the whole verse compare Matt. 27, 24. Lu. 23, 22. John 18, 31.

29. 30. And when they had fulfilled all that was written of him, they took (him) down from the tree, and laid (him) in a sepulchre. But God raised him from the dead.

The very acts which seemed to put an end to Christ and his pretensions, were fulfilments of prophecy, and preparations for his reappearance. In venting their own spite, *they* (unwittingly) *accomplished all the* (*things*) *written* (in the prophecies) *concerning him.* They might have thought their work complete when, *taking* (*him*) *down from the wood* (or *tree*, i. e. the cross, see above, on 5, 30. 10, 39), *they placed him in a tomb* (or monument, a word akin to that used in 2, 29, and there explained.) *But God raised* (or *roused*) *him from* (among) *the dead.* So that even his burial was only a preliminary to his resurrection. The ascription of his death and burial to the same agents has been variously explained. Some suppose that, as Nicodemus and Joseph of Arimathea were themselves rulers of the Jews, as well as those by whom Christ was condemned, that whole class is here described as performing both acts. Others suppose the reference to be not to the immediate agents, either in the crucifixion or the burial, but to the prime movers in this whole judicial murder, of which the burial was the natural conclusion. A third opinion is, that even this part of the process, by itself considered, although at first accomplished by the hands of friends, was transferred, as it were, to those of enemies, by the sealing and guarding of the sepulchre (Matt. 28, 66.) Paul here presents the contrast of which Peter is so fond, between the acts of men and the acts of God, in reference to Jesus. (See above, on 10, 39. 40.) This resemblance is no argument against the authenticity of the discourse, but rather for it, since this was no peculiarity of Peter's, but a view which every Christian must have taken, and which every preacher to the Jews was bound to set before his hearers.

31. And he was seen many days of them which

came up with him from Galilee to Jerusalem, who are his witnesses unto the people.

The resurrection of Christ was not assumed or asserted without evidence. He not only rose, but he was seen after he had risen; not for a moment, but for many days; not by strangers, but by those who knew him well, and had accompanied him on his last journey from the chief scene of his labours to the Holy City. Nor had these witnesses all passed away; they were still bearing testimony to the great event. This last point is particularly prominent in the text of the oldest manuscripts and latest editors (*who* NOW *are*) witnesses. Lastly, this testimony to the resurrection of the Saviour was not private or informal, but public and official, addressed directly to the chosen people.

32. And we declare unto you glad tidings, how that the promise which was made unto the fathers—

The same testimony which was thus addressed by the companions of the risen Saviour to the body of the Jewish church in Palestine, was now borne by Paul and Barnabas, to Jews and Gentiles, in the synagogue at Antioch; not as a mere historical fact, but as joyful intelligence, good news; yet not as something altogether strange and unconnected with their previous religious faith and hope, but as the fulfilment of a promise made to former generations of God's people, the natural progenitors of the Jews then present, and the spiritual fathers of believing Gentiles. *We* and *you*, at the beginning of the sentence, stand together in Greek, which gives great force and point to the antithesis; 'What they are telling the people yonder, we tell you.' *Declare glad tidings* is in Greek one word, often translated *preach* in this book (see above, on 5, 42. 8, 4. 12. 35. 40. 10, 36. 11, 20), sometimes more fully, *preach the gospel* (see above, on 8, 25, and below, on 14, 7. 21. 16, 10), but nowhere so exactly rendered as in this place (and in Luke 1, 19. 2, 10. 8, 1.) *The promise* meant is that of the Messiah's Advent, which pervades the Hebrew Scriptures.

33. God hath fulfilled the same unto us their children, in that he hath raised up Jesus again; as it

is also written in the second psalm, Thou art my Son, this day have I begotten thee.

This oft-repeated, long-continued promise to the fathers God has now performed to us, their natural and spiritual children, by raising up or bringing forward, in our day and to our view, the long expected Saviour of his people, and as such called Jesus; and this he does not only in fulfilment of the promises in general, but of that one in particular, which is contained in the second Psalm, where God is represented as proclaiming the organic law or constitution of Messiah's kingdom, and uttering as its fundamental principle, the intimate relation of Messiah to himself, not merely mutual affection, but community of nature. The idea is derived from the great Messianic promise made to David (2 Sam. 7, 14), "I will be his father, and he shall be my son." The expression in the Psalm, *I have begotten thee*, means, I am he who has begotten thee, i. e. I am thy father. *To-day* refers to the date of the decree itself, (*Jehovah said, To-day*, &c.); but this, as a divine act, was eternal, and so must be the sonship it affirms. *Raising up* is here applied by some, not to Christ's incarnation, but his resurrection, on the ground that it is certainly so used in the next verse. But this rather proves the contrary; for there the meaning is defined or specified by adding, *from the dead*, which cannot retroact upon its absolute use here, especially when it has been repeatedly employed before, in this same book, to signify the act of giving him existence as a man. (See above, on 2, 30. 3, 22. 26. 7, 37.) In the only other place where it seems to be used absolutely of the resurrection (see above, on 2, 32), it is really determined by the previous reference to death and dissolution. (For a fuller view of the passage quoted, in its original connection, see the writer's exposition of Ps. 2, 7.) Instead of *second psalm*, the latest editors read *first psalm*, but on very doubtful manuscript authority. Even admitting it to be the true text, it is not a lapse of memory, but a relic of the old opinion that the first Psalm is a preface to the whole collection.

34. And as concerning that he raised him up from the dead, (now) no more to return to corruption, he said on this wise, I will give you the sure mercies of David.

But this was not the only sense in which Christ had been *raised up*, or the only scripture which his raising up had verified. As his incarnation was the advent of that Son of God predicted in the second Psalm, so his resurrection from the dead was the redemption of the promise, *I will give you the sure mercies of David.* That this is a quotation, is clear from the formula which introduces it, *he said on this wise*, or, *he thus hath spoken.* The passage quoted is Isai. 55, 3, but with some variation, both from the Hebrew and the Septuagint version. Thus the promise, *I will make with you an everlasting covenant*, Paul contracts into the brief phrase, *I will give you*, which is only a conciser and less definite expression of the same idea. On the other hand, he follows the Greek version in translating (חסדי) *favours*, *mercies*, by a word (ὅσια) which properly means *sacred*, *holy* (*things*), particularly such as have respect to God, and not to human usages or institutions (δίκαια.) Besides this passage, and 2, 27 above, the word occurs in reference to God (Rev. 15, 4), to Christ (Heb. 7, 26), and to men (1 Tim. 2, 8. Tit. 1, 8), in all which places it is rendered *holy*. In the verse before us, and the Septuagint version of Isai. 55, 3, it appears to have the sense of solemn, sacred, or inviolable, as applied to the divine engagements. 'I will give you (or fulfil to you) the sacred promises once made to David.' This explanation is given in the margin of the English Bible, while the text retains the original expression (*mercies.*) *Sure*, i. e. sure to be accomplished, literally, *faithful*, credible, or worthy of belief and trust. The reference is to 2 Sam. 7, 8–16 (compare 1 Chr. 17, 11–14. Ps. 89, 3. 2.) As the burden of this promise was perpetual succession on the throne of David, it was fulfilled in Christ (compare Isai. 9, 6. 7. Luke 1, 32. 33), but only on the supposition, that his resurrection was not a mere temporary restoration, but the pledge of an endless immortality. Hence the Apostle speaks of this prophetic promise as fulfilled in the momentous fact, that God raised him from the dead, *no more to return to corruption*, i. e. into the condition, of which dissolution is a natural and in every other case a necessary incident. This perpetuity of Christ's restored life, as a necessary element in the doctrine of his resurrection, is insisted on by the Apostle elsewhere. (See Rom. 6, 9, and compare Rev. 1, 18.) The English version inserts one word (*now*) and omits another (μέλλοντα), which can be translated only by the use of an enfeebling paraphrase, *no more about* (or *being about*) *to return.*

(See above, on 3, 3. 5, 35. 11, 28. 12, 6; and for the origin and usage of the word *corruption*, on 2, 27. 31.) In the foregoing exposition of this verse, the original order of the clauses is inverted, for the sake of the logical connection. The actual connection of both verses is as follows. 'That God raised up Jesus (i. e. brought him into being as a man), is a verification of that passage in the second Psalm, Thou art my Son, this day have I begotten thee: that he raised him from the dead, no more to be subjected to the power of corruption, is a verification of that promise in Isaiah, I will give you the sure mercies of (or things inviolably pledged to) David.'

35. Wherefore he saith also in another (psalm), Thou shalt not suffer thine Holy One to see corruption.

The necessity and certainty of Christ's perpetual exemption from corruption, i. e. from dissolution of the body, was not a matter of mere inference or implication, but a subject of explicit prophecy and promise. To evince this, Paul adduces the same passage which Peter had expounded and applied in his Pentecostal sermon (see above, on 2, 25–31.) He also argues with respect to it precisely in the same way, namely, by denying that the words quoted (Ps. 16, 10) could apply to David, and affirming that they did apply to Christ. Here again the sameness of the two discourses has been made a ground of argument against their independent authenticity; as if each of the Apostles must use different methods of proving the Messiahship of Jesus; or as if the one here used belonged exclusively to Peter. We may even suppose that Paul heard Peter's exposition of this passage, or heard of it afterwards, without detracting from his independent apostolical authority (see above, on v. 3.) That one discourse is not compiled or copied from the other, is sufficiently apparent from the difference of form, Paul quoting only one verse, and that only in part, of the four which Peter had made use of, and connecting that one with a passage of Isaiah, not alluded to by Peter, while he passes by the latter's kindred argument derived from Ps. 110. (See above, on 2, 34. 35.) All this goes to show the independence of the two Apostles and their two discourses, but at the same time their exact agreement in the exposition of a Messianic prophecy. The logical connection of Paul's arguments is indicated in the text itself. *Wherefore*, for which reason, i. e. because *the sure mercies of David* comprehended the Messiah's perpetual exemption from mortality when once arisen from the dead. *In another* (psalm), or less specifically, *in another* (place or part of scripture.) For the meaning of the last clause, see above, on 2, 27.

36. 37. For David, after he had served his own generation by the will of God, fell on sleep, and was laid unto his fathers, and saw corruption. But he, whom God raised again, saw no corruption.

The perfect independence of the two Apostles, even in expounding the same passage and employing the same argument, is furthermore apparent from the curious fact, that while the end they aim at is identical, namely, to show that David's words were inapplicable to himself, and the proof coincident, to wit, that he did die and see corruption, this last phrase is the only one common to both speakers, their other expressions being wholly different. While Peter (see above, on 2, 29) begs leave to remind his hearers that the Patriarch, or founder of their royal family, was dead and buried, and his sepulchre among them at the time of speaking, Paul, with exact agreement as to substance but a beautiful variety of form, describes him as an eminent servant both of God and man while he lived, but as sleeping with his fathers for a course of ages, and subjected long since to that process of corruption, from which this prophecy (Ps. 16, 10) declared its subject to be free. He could not therefore be that subject; whereas Jesus, being raised up from the dead by God himself, before the process of corruption had begun, did really enjoy that very exemption which is here foretold. The consequence is plain, that he must be the Messiah. (See above, on 2, 32.) The marginal translation, *having* (*in*) *his own age* (or *generation*) *served the will of God*, is not so natural in its construction of the dative (γενεᾷ) as denoting time, and in giving the verb (*served*) an impersonal or abstract object (*will*); nor does it yield so rich a sense, as it obliterates the fine idea of his serving man as well as God. *His own generation*, or contemporary race, is here emphatic and exclusive, as distinguished from all later times and generations. (See above, on 2, 40.) *Served* or *ministered*, by doing good, officially and privately. (Compare Paul's description of his own voluntary service, 1 Cor. 9, 19.) *By* (i. e. according to, or in obedience to) *the will of God* (see above, on 2, 23. 4, 28. 5, 38.) *Fell on sleep*, an unusual expression even in old English, but entirely synonymous with the common phrase, *fell asleep* (or still more simply and exactly, *slept*), which here means *died*, perhaps with an implication of serenity and peace, as in the case of Stephen. (See above, on 7, 60, where the same Greek word is rendered *fell asleep.*) *Laid* (literally, *added*, as in 2, 41. 47. 5, 14. 11, 24. 12, 3. Gal. 3, 19) *unto his fathers*, i. e. with them, but implying close proximity and union (as in John 1, 1. 2.) This is usually understood of burial in the same grave or family vault; but in the earliest instances of the expression, it seems to be distinguished both from death and burial, and has therefore been supposed to imply the separate existence of disembodied spirits. (See Gen. 25, 8. 35, 20. 2 Kings 22, 20, and compare Matt. 22, 32.) Even here, it may have reference to the soul, and the words following to the body, thus corresponding more exactly to the language of Ps. 16, 10, as fully quoted and applied to Christ by Peter. (See above, on 2, 27.) *He whom God raised* (*again*), i. e. Jesus, as stated in v. 34. *Raised*, however, is not the verb there used, but that employed in v. 30, and in 3, 15. 4, 10. 5, 30. 10, 40, in the same sense; while in vs. 22, 23 above, it has the general sense of calling into being; so that this double usage really belongs to both verbs, one of which originally means to stand or cause to stand, the other (the one here used) to arouse or awaken out of sleep. *Saw no corruption*, literally, *did not see* (perceive, experience) *corruption* (i. e. dissolution of the body.) We have thus the authority of two Apostles, and those the two most eminent, for denying that David is the subject of his own prophecy in Ps. 16, 10.

38. Be it known unto you, therefore, men (and) brethren, that through this man is preached unto you the forgiveness of sins.

It was not mere historical, nor even doctrinal or exegetical instruction that the Apostle here intended to communicate, but practical and experimental knowledge of the utmost moment, as relating to the only method of salvation. Having shown therefore that the Jesus, whom the people at Jerusalem had crucified, must be the Christ predicted both by David and Isaiah, he now brings the matter home to the bosoms of his hearers, by announcing that this Jesus is not only the Messiah, but the vehicle or medium through whom alone forgiveness is now offered to the guilty. *Be it known* is the same solemn formula, employed by Peter in the beginning of his Pentecostal sermon (2, 14), and again when he ascribed the healing of the lame man to the name of Jesus Christ of Nazareth (4, 10.) It implies that the truth declared was one of which the hearers had been ignorant, but which it was important they should know. *Therefore*, as the logical no less than the practical conclusion of the whole preceding argument. *Men and brethren*, the respectful and affectionate address, with which he had already introduced the offer of salvation (see above, on v. 26), and with which he now impressively repeats it. *Through this* (*one*), this same Jesus, whom our brethren in Judea crucified, but whom I have just proved to be the promised Christ. *Remission of sins*, see above, on 2, 38. 5, 31. 10, 43. There is something impressive in the very order of the words in this clause—*that through this* (*man*) *unto you remission of sins is preached*—i. e. declared, announced, proclaimed. See above, on v. 5, and compare 4, 2. The idea of an offer or an invitation is implied, as when a government proclaims peace or pardon.

39. And by him all that believe are justified from all things, from which ye could not be justified by the law of Moses.

The gift thus offered was not only pardon, or deliverance from punishment, but justification, or deliverance from guilt, reaching to all the sins of all believers, and effecting what the law, in which they trusted, had completely failed to bring about, through their fault, not its own. *By him* and *by the law* are correlative expressions, strictly meaning *in him* and *in the law*, i. e. in union with, and in reliance on, him and the law, as grounds of hope and means of justification. By some this verse is understood as drawing a distinction between sins which could and sins which could not be atoned for by the law of Moses, and asserting the necessity of justification only in relation to the latter. These suppose the contrast to be that between mere ceremonial offences, for which ceremonial expiation was sufficient, and sins or offences against God, for which legal observances could make no satisfaction, though they might prefigure it. But most interpreters and readers take the words in an exclusive sense, 'from all which sins ye were not able to be justified in the law of Moses.' The English version has departed here materially from the form of the original, by substituting the plural, *all that believe*, for the singular, *every one believing*, and by changing the whole order of the sentence, not without some diminution of its force and beauty. The original arrangement is as follows: *and from all (the things from) which ye were not able to be justified in the law of Moses, in this man every one believing is justified.*" This collocation is entitled to the preference, not only as that chosen by the writer, but because it puts the two antagonistic phrases, *in the law of Moses* and *in this man*, side by side, and ends the sentence with the sum of the whole matter, *every one believing is justified.* The antithesis just mentioned shows that *in this man* depends upon the verb *is justified*, and not, as some suppose, upon *believing.* It is needless to show how much more this part of Paul's discourse resembles his epistles than any part of Peter's. (Compare Rom. 1, 16. 3, 22. 4, 25. 5, 10. 11. 6, 7. 8, 3. 10, 4. Gal. 3, 11. 22.) *From* after *justified* implies deliverance from guilt and righteous condemnation.

40. Beware, therefore, lest that come upon you, which is spoken of in the prophets:

The offer of salvation is accompanied, as usual in Scripture, by a warning against the danger of rejecting it, here clothed in a peculiar form, derived from the Old Testament, and threatening the despisers of this offered mercy with as sudden and terrific judgments as Jehovah brought of old upon his faithless people, by allowing fierce and cruel foreign nations to invade and conquer them. *Take heed*, literally, *see, look*, i. e. see to it, or look out, be upon your guard; an expression nowhere else employed in this book, but of frequent occurrence in the writings of the Apostle who is here speaking. (See 1 Cor. 3, 10. 8, 9. 10, 12. Gal. 5, 15. Eph. 5, 15. Phil. 3, 2. Col. 2, 8. 4, 17. Heb. 3, 12. 12, 25.) The coincidence is here so slight and yet so striking, that a later writer could not have invented it, or would not have left it to be brought to light by microscopic criticism, ages after it was written. *Therefore*, since the true Messiah has appeared and been rejected at Jerusalem, and you are now in danger of committing the same sin. *Come upon you*, suddenly, and from above, or as a divine judgment. (See above, on 8, 24, and compare Luke 11, 22. 21, 26. 35.) As it sometimes has a good sense (see above, on 1, 8, and compare Luke 1, 35), the unfavourable sense here is determined by the context. *Spoken of*, or rather *spoken*, not merely mentioned or referred to, but recorded as directly uttered by Jehovah. *In the prophets*, the division of the Hebrew Canon so called. (See above, on v. 15. 7, 42, and compare John 6, 45.)

41. Behold, ye despisers, and wonder, and perish: for I work a work in your days, a work which ye shall in no wise believe, though a man declare it unto you.

These words are from the Septuagint version of Habakkuk 1, 5, which varies considerably from the Hebrew. *Behold ye despisers* is, in the original, *behold* (or *see*) *among the nations*. *Wonder and perish* (or be wasted, consumed) is there, *wonder* (*and*) *wonder* (or as the English version of Habakkuk has it, *wonder marvellously*.) The remainder of the verse agrees almost exactly with the Hebrew, the chief difference of form consisting in the substitution of the impersonal construction (*if one tell you*) for the passive (*when it is told*.) The necessity of trying to account for these departures from the Hebrew text is precluded by the obvious consideration, that this passage is not quoted, expounded, and declared to be fulfilled, like those from David and Isaiah in vs. 33–37 above, but merely made the vehicle of a warning similar to that contained in the original prediction. As if he had said, 'Be upon your guard lest, by rejecting the salvation which I have now offered in the name of your Messiah, you should call down judgments on yourselves as fearful and incredible as those predicted by Habakkuk, and inflicted by the hands of the Chaldeans, on our unbelieving fathers.' The Septuagint version is retained without correction, because no interpretation or application of the passage is intended, but a simple use of its expressions to convey the Apostle's own ideas to the minds of his hearers in a striking manner. This is the less surprising or improbable, because that part of the quotation which he had especially in view, is that which agrees best with the original. For although the word *despisers*, in the first clause, may seem specially appropriate to the Jews who rejected Christ, Paul seems to have intended to dwell chiefly on the greatness of the threatened judgment or prediction, as incredible in either case. This quotation, therefore, does not of itself prove that Paul spoke in Greek, though this is highly probable for other reasons; but it does prove that he thought himself at liberty to use the words of the Old Testament in application to new cases, and even in a version not entirely accurate. But let it be observed, that in neither of these things is he an example to us, because in both he acted under the control of inspiration and by virtue of his apostolical authority, without which we are utterly incompetent to say what new application may be made of words prophetically uttered, or how far an imperfect version may be used with safety. Let it also be observed that no such use is made by the Apostle Paul of Scripture, where his doctrine or his argument depends upon it, as in a previous portion of this very chapter. (See above, on vs. 33–37.)

42. And when the Jews were gone out of the synagogue, the Gentiles besought that these words might be preached to them the next sabbath.

The text of the first clause varies very much in the editions. According to the latest critics, the words *Jews*, *Synagogue*, and *Gentiles*, have all been interpolated by the copyists, either to supply some supposed deficiency, or to make the verse intelligible, as the abrupt beginning of an ancient pericope or lesson, to be read in public worship. The reading now adopted, on the authority of the five oldest manuscripts and two oldest versions, is, *and they having gone out, they besought*, &c. The subjects of the verbs are not expressed, which makes the clause obscure; and to remove this ambiguity was probably the motive of the textual changes in the later copies. The first verb most probably refers to the preachers, and the second to their hearers, whether Jews or Gentiles. *These words*, this doctrine, or this new religion. (See above, on 5, 20. 32. 10, 22. 44. 11, 14.) *Might be preached*, literally, *to be spoken*. *The next sabbath*, or, as the margin of the English Bible has it, *in the week between*, or *in the sabbath between*. The last appears to be unmeaning, as no points can be assigned, between which this sabbath is described as intermediate; whereas *the week between* would naturally mean the week between the sabbath when these things happened and the next. That the Greek word sometimes has the sense of *week*, is plain from Mark 16, 9. Luke 18, 12; but this usage is so rare, that it is not to be preferred without necessity. *Between* is certainly the strict sense, and in classic Greek the common one, of the particle (μεταξύ), and it always has that meaning elsewhere in the New Testament (see above, on 12, 6, and below, on 15, 9, and compare John 4, 31, where the sense is, in the time between, or in the meanwhile.) But the later writers, such as Plutarch and Josephus, give it the sense of next or afterward; and this is preferred here by almost all interpreters. It seems, then, that they were invited to repeat their instructions, no doubt in the synagogue, to which both Jews and Gentiles were accustomed to resort. (See above, on v. 5.)

43. Now when the congregation was broken up, many of the Jews and religious proselytes followed Paul and Barnabas; who, speaking to them, persuaded them to continue in the grace of God.

The congregation is in Greek *the synagogue*, a clear instance of its primary or strict sense. (See above, on vs. 5. 14, and on 6, 9. 9, 2. 20.) *Being broken up*, dissolved, or dismissed. *Religious proselytes*, (Tyndale, *virtuous converts*,) i. e. serious and devout Gentiles, who had become Jews, either wholly or in part. (See above, on 2, 10. 6, 5.) As Paul and Barnabas were said in the preceding verse to have gone out of the synagogue, this mention of the meeting's being broken up occasions some confusion. One solution of the difficulty is that they withdrew when they had spoken, but before the service was concluded; another, that it was the Jews who went out, and the Gentiles who requested them to preach again; a third, that these two verses relate to two successive sabbaths, and that between them something is to be supplied, e. g. they did so, or they did repeat their teachings the next sabbath, and then, when the assembly was dissolved on that day, some of the hearers followed Paul and Barnabas. In the last clause of this verse, as in the first of that before it, the subjects of the verbs are not expressed, so that it may either mean, that these Jews and proselytes persuaded Paul and Barnabas to persevere in the good work which they had begun, or that Paul and Barnabas persuaded them to persevere in their inquiries after saving truth, here called the grace of the Lord, i. e. the new revelation of the divine favour made in and by the Lord Jesus Christ. Although Calvin thought the first of these constructions probable, the second has been almost universally regarded as the true one. Besides other reasons in its favour, it agrees better with the verb *persuaded*, which is so often used to denote the effect produced by public teaching and official exhortation. (See below, on 18, 4. 19, 8. 26. 26, 28. 28, 23.)

44. And the next Sabbath day came almost the whole city together to hear the word of God.

The next Sabbath (*day* is not expressed here, any more than in v. 42), i. e. the second or the third, according to the meaning put upon the two preceding verses. If they relate to the same sabbath, this is a second; if to two sabbaths, this is a third. *Next*, in the received text, is literally *coming*, i. e. following, ensuing; but several of the oldest manuscripts have a word which differs only in a single letter (see above, on v. 18), but which means holding fast to, adjacent, next, as applied both to place (as in Mark 1, 38) and to time (see below, on 20, 15. 21, 26, and compare Luke 13, 33.) *Almost* is a slight but significant proof how little the historian is given or inclined to exaggeration. *The whole city*, all the city, i. e. all the people. *Came together*, or, adhering to the passive form of the original, *was gathered* (or assembled), the same verb that is applied to the assembly of the Sanhedrim and of the disciples (see above, on 4, 6. 26. 27. 31. 11, 26.) *To hear the word of God*, the Gospel, the new revelation. It is worthy of remark that nothing is here said of miracles, so that the desire of instruction and salvation would appear to be the only cause of this great concourse, which resembles that occasioned by our Lord's appearance as a public teacher. (See Mark 2, 2. Luke 8, 19.) The place of meeting was no doubt the synagogue, or customary place for the assembling of the Jews. The crowd itself was probably increased by the instructions and appeals of Paul and Barnabas, during the interval between these sabbaths.

45. But when the Jews saw the multitudes, they were filled with envy, and spake against those things which were spoken by Paul, contradicting and blaspheming.

However patiently the Jews of Antioch might have borne with the new doctrine preached by Paul and Barnabas, so long as it was limited to their own body, the extraordinary popular effect which it produced would naturally rouse their jealousy or party spirit. *Seeing the multitudes* (or *crowds*), not merely the great numbers but the various characters and classes (see above, on 1, 15), which assembled, no doubt at the place of worship, where the strangers were expected to appear again. *Envy*, or rather emulation, jealousy, and party-spirit. Both *zeal* and *indignation* were of course included, but neither of these terms expresses the full force of the original (see above, on 5, 17.) Among the feelings thus excited was no doubt the fear of forfeiting that influence upon the Gentiles which the Jews appear to have derived from their possession of the true religion, even when they were the objects of oppression or contempt, and which they actually exercised on this occasion (see below, on v. 50.) This moral power of the true religion in overcoming even the most serious social disadvantages, is among the clearest evidences of its being what it claims to be. *Spake against* and *contradicting* are in Greek but two forms of the same verb which includes the meaning of both English ones, to wit, the idea of denial and that of vituperation or abuse. *Blaspheming* Paul and Barnabas, i. e. reviling them as heretics and false teachers; or *blaspheming* Christ himself, as an impostor and a false Messiah. (For the twofold usage of this verb and its cognate forms, see above, on 6, 11. 13.) The second participle (*contradicting*) is not found in several of the oldest manuscripts and versions but the very critics who have commonly most deference for such authority, regard this as an unauthorized omission, intended to remove what was considered an inelegant repetition. It really adds strength to the expression, whether taken as an idiomatic combination of two cognate forms for emphasis (see above, on 4, 17. 5, 28), or as a natural resumption and reiteration for the same effect, resulting in a kind of climax; *contradicting and* (not only contradicting but) *blaspheming*. Here again Paul appears as the chief speaker, or perhaps the only one, and therefore as the object against whom this opposition was directed. (See above, on v. 9, and below, on 14, 12.)

46. Then Paul and Barnabas waxed bold, and said, It was necessary that the word of God should first have been spoken to you; but seeing ye put it from you, and

judge yourselves unworthy of everlasting life, lo, we turn to the Gentiles.

This opposition, far from intimidating the Apostles, only served to hasten an explicit declaration of their purpose and commission, with respect to Jews and Gentiles. *Then* (δέ), and, but, or so. *Waxed bold*, or more exactly, *speaking freely*, talking plainly, the idea of boldness being rather implied than expressed. (See above, on 9, 27. 29, and compare 2, 29. 4, 13. 29. 31.) What might have been disclosed in a more gradual and gentle manner, was, in consequence of this malignant opposition, plainly and abruptly stated. As this declaration is ascribed expressly both to Paul and Barnabas, some argue that the previous speaking must have been by both alike; while others from the same fact draw the opposite conclusion, that where only one is mentioned, as in the preceding verse, the other is thereby excluded. Here again, the emphasis, though not the meaning, of the sentence is affected by a change of the original arrangement, which, however, may have been necessary to accommodate our idiom. *To you*, the Jews, who had been just described as contradicting and blaspheming. *Necessary*, i. e. to the execution of the divine plan and purpose, with respect to the first proclamation of the Gospel. (See above, on 1, 16. 21.) *Put it from you*, thrust it away, scornfully reject it; a kindred form to that employed by Stephen in relating the rejection of Moses by his countrymen in Egypt. (See above, on 7, 27. 39.) *Judge yourselves unworthy*, literally, *not worthy judge yourselves*. The thought suggested, although not immediately expressed, is that they *condemned* themselves as thus unworthy (see above, on v. 27), not in word, nor even in thought, but by their conduct. They proved themselves unworthy of salvation by refusing to accept of it, when freely offered through their own Messiah. To the striking but unusual expression here employed a fine parallel is found in Cicero, who says that Catiline had judged himself worthy of confinement or imprisonment: *Qui se ipsum dignum custodia judicaverit.* The interjection, *lo*, behold, as usual, introduces something unexpected and surprising. (See above, on vs. 11. 25.) As if he had said, however strange it may appear to you, however unprepared you may be to receive it. *We turn* (or *are turning* at this moment) to the *Gentiles* (or *the nations*), not considered as far distant (see above, on 2, 39), but as represented here, in this assembly (see above, on 11, 1. 18.) This cannot mean that Paul was now commissioned for the first time as the Apostle of the Gentiles (see above, on vs. 3, 9, and compare 9,15. 22, 21. 26, 17. 18); nor can it mean that he was henceforth to abandon all attempts at the conversion of the Jews (see below, on 18, 5. 19, 8, and compare Rom. 1, 16. 2, 9. 10.) The primary idea is the obvious one, that they were thus to turn from Jews to Gentiles where they were, i. e. in Antioch of Pisidia, but with an implication that the same course was to be repeated, whenever and wherever the occasion should present itself. And this agrees exactly with Paul's later practice, as for instance in Corinth (18, 6), Ephesus (19, 9), and Rome (28, 28.)

47. For so hath the Lord commanded us, (saying), I have set thee to be a light of the Gentiles, that thou shouldest be for salvation unto the ends of the earth.

This was not a voluntary self-imposed commission, but a necessary part of their divine vocation. *The Lord*, according to New Testament usage, might be understood to mean the Lord Jesus Christ (see above, on 1, 24.) But as the words which follow are addressed to the Messiah, *the Lord* may be regarded as the usual translation of *Jehovah*. The passage quoted is Isai. 49, 6 (compare 42, 6), where the Messiah is described as a source of light, not merely to the Jews, but to the nations, not merely in the Holy Land, but to the ends of the earth. The same description had already been applied to Christ by Simeon (Luke 2, 31. 32.) *Commanded us* is not an arbitrary transfer or accommodation of the passage, but a faithful reproduction of its original and proper import, as relating both to the Head and the Body, the Messiah and the Church in their joint capacity, as heralds of salvation to the world. (See Isaiah Translated and Explained, vol. II. p. 216.)

48. And when the Gentiles heard this, they were glad, and glorified the word of the Lord: and as many as were ordained to eternal life believed.

Hearing this announcement, that the apostolical ministry was now to be directed to themselves, *the Gentiles*, literally, *nations* (as in v. 46) *rejoiced*, that they were no longer to be shut out from the privileges hitherto monopolized by Jews and proselytes, *and glorified*, or praised and honoured, *the word of the Lord*, the doctrine of Christ, the new revelation which had now been preached to them, not merely as a theme of speculation, nor even as a system of divine truth, but also as a method of salvation, so that *they believed*, not merely in the truth of what they heard, but in the Lord Jesus Christ as the only Saviour. *As many as were ordained*, ordered or appointed, *to eternal life*, a favourite expression of John and Paul to signify salvation. It occurs in this book only here, but is several times employed by Luke in his Gospel (10, 25. 18, 18. 30.) The violent attempts which have been made to eliminate the doctrine of election or predestination from this verse, by rendering the last verb *disposed*, *arrayed*, &c., or by violent constructions, such as that adopted by Socinus (*as many as believed were ordained to everlasting life!*) can never change the simple fact, that wherever this verb occurs elsewhere, it invariably expresses the exertion of power or authority, divine or human, and being in the passive voice, cannot denote mere disposition, much less self-determination, any more than the form used in 2, 40 above, which some have cited as a parallel example.

49. 50. And the word of the Lord was published throughout all the region. But the Jews stirred up the devout and honourable women, and the chief men of the city, and raised persecution against Paul and Barnabas, and expelled them out of their coasts.

The purpose which had been announced in v. 46, was carried into execution. *The word of the Lord*, the doctrine of Christ, the new religion, *was published* (literally *carried*, i. e. circulated or diffused) *throughout all the region*, meaning that part of Asia Minor, without reference to any political division into provinces. *Stirred up*, excited, instigated, no doubt by misrepresentation, as well as by appealing to the prepossessions of these female proselytes in favour of their new religion, and against all further change. The number of female converts from Heathenism to Judaism in that age, we know from Josephus to have been very great. *Devout*, literally, *worshipping*, a term commonly applied to Gentiles who acknowledged the true God, and were more or less under Jewish influence, whether open professors of that faith or not. (See above, on

v. 43, and below, on 16, 14. 17, 4. 17. 18, 7.) Neither *devout* nor *honourable* is here descriptive of personal character, so much as of social relations and position. The word translated *honourable* means originally handsome, comely (as in 1 Cor. 12, 24); then respectable in point of rank and station (as in Mark 15, 43.) *The chief* (or *first*) *men* (see below, on 25, 2. 28, 7. 17) may have been the husbands, or other near connections, of these honourable women. *Raised*, aroused, or awakened, a compound form of the verb used above in vs. 22. 23. 30. 37. *Persecution*, see above, on 8, 1. *Expelled*, literally, *cast out*, but not always used to express violent exclusion (see above, on 9, 40), although sometimes so used (see above, on 7, 58), and most probably in this case. *Coasts*, in the old English sense of borders, bounds, or frontiers, often put for the whole country thus defined or bounded. The word is used repeatedly by Mark and Matthew, but in no other part of the New Testament, with the exception of the verse before us.

51. But they shook off the dust of their feet against them, and came unto Iconium.

The act described in the first clause was symbolical, expressive of unwillingness to have the least communication or connection with the place or country, even by suffering its flying dust (κονιορτόν) to settle or remain upon the person. It is said to have been practised by the ancient Jews whenever they re-entered Palestine from other countries. Paul and Barnabas performed this ceremony in obedience to our Lord's express command. (See Matt. 10, 14. Mark 6, 11. Luke 9, 5. 10, 11.) A similar act of the same signification was the shaking of the raiment. (See below, on 18, 6.) *Against them*, either in the local sense of towards, on, at them, or in the figurative sense of testifying against them; probably the latter, as it is expressed in Luke 9, 5. *Iconium*, an important town of Asia Minor, referred by Xenophon to Phrygia, by Strabo to Lycaonia, by Ammian to Pisidia, while Pliny seems to represent it as the seat of a distinct provincial government. It is still a place of some importance under the corrupted name of *Conieh* or *Koniyeh*.

52. And the disciples were filled with joy, and with the Holy Ghost.

We have here another instance of a fact already noticed, that the primitive disciples are repeatedly described as rejoicing in the very circumstances which might seem peculiarly adapted to produce an opposite effect. (See above, on 5, 41, and compare Luke 24, 52.) That the cause of this effect was supernatural, we learn from the concluding words. Although not the grammatical construction, it is really the import of this verse, that they were filled with what Paul elsewhere calls "joy in the Holy Ghost" (Rom. 14, 17), "all joy and peace in believing" (Rom. 15, 13.) *The disciples* who were thus affected were no doubt the converted Jews and Gentiles, whom the missionaries left behind at Antioch in Pisidia, and against whom the persecution was perhaps continued for a time. (See below, on 14, 22.) The prosperous condition of the early churches, even in the midst of outward trials, is a characteristic feature of this history. (See above, on 4, 32–35. 9, 31. 12, 24.)

CHAPTER XIV.

This division of the text records the ministry of Paul and Barnabas at Iconium, Lystra, and Derbe; their return through these places to Pisidia and Pamphylia; their voyage from Attalia to Antioch; their report to the church and resumption of their work there. They preach at Iconium with great success (1.) But here again the unbelieving Jews oppose them (2.) They remain there long, however, and are greatly blessed (3.) The city is divided into two parties (4.) At length all their enemies combine against them (5.) They flee to Lycaonia and there introduce the Gospel (6.) At Lystra Paul performs a signal miracle (8–10.) The heathen population offer to worship him and Barnabas (11–13.) They indignantly refuse it (14.) They avow the object of their mission (15.) They contrast the idols of the heathen with the true God (16, 17.) With difficulty they prevent their own deification (18.) Even here they are pursued by their old enemies (19.) Paul narrowly escapes destruction (20.) They preach at Derbe without opposition, and return as they had come, organizing churches by the way (21–24.) They preach now for the first time at Perga (25.) They sail from Attalia to Antioch in Syria (26.) They make a report of their mission to the church there (27.) After this they resume their old position and employment (28.)

1. And it came to pass in Iconium, that they went both together into the synagogue of the Jews, and so spake that a great multitude, both of the Jews and also of the Greeks, believed.

It came to pass, i. e. (something) *happened* (or took place, while they were) *in Iconium* (see above, on 13, 52.) *Together*, not *as usual*, or *according to custom*, but *at the same* (time), either with one another (as in 3, 1), or with the congregation or the multitude. The synagogue was still the medium of access, not only to the Jews, but to the serious Gentiles. (See above, on 13. 14. 15.) *So spake* is commonly explained to mean, in so remarkable a manner, with such force, warmth, unction, or assistance of the Spirit. The original order of the words is, *spake so that*, which some explain as making the effect described dependent simply on their speaking, not on any thing peculiar in their mode of speaking upon this occasion. But as this would have been sufficiently expressed by one of the Greek particles here used (ὥστε), the other (οὕτως) must have a distinctive sense (*in such a manner*), and the common explanation is the true one. (See above, on 1, 11. 3, 18. 7, 1. 6. 8. 8, 32. 12, 8. 15. 13, 47.) The original order of the last clause is, *believed, both of the Jews and Greeks, a great multitude. Believed*, i. e. in Christ, or were converted to the new religion. *Greeks*, not foreign Jews, but Gentiles. (See above, on 6, 1. 9, 29. 11, 20.) Some deny that heathen Greeks would frequent the synagogue; but such a practice is not only natural and probable, but actually mentioned in the classics, which bear witness to the interest felt in Judaism and the practice of attending on its worship, even in Rome. It is said, indeed, that these were proselytes; but how could they become such, if entirely unacquainted with the Jewish worship?

2. But the unbelieving Jews stirred up the Gentiles, and made their minds evil affected against the brethren.

Unbelieving, and also *disobedient*, both which ideas are suggested by the Greek verb (compare 1 Pet. 2, 7. 3, 20. Rom. 10, 21, and the Septuagint version of Isai. 65, 2.) Belief in the Gospel was not a matter of indifference or option, but of duty and obedience to divine authority, a favourite idea both with Paul and Peter. (See above, on 6, 7, and compare Rom. 1, 5, 15, 18. 16, 19. 26. 2 Cor. 7, 15. 10, 5. 6. 1 Pet. 1, 2. 14. 22.) *Excited and embittered*, literally, *made bad*, i. e. disaffected, hostile, or malignant. (See above on 7, 6. 19. 12, 1.) *The Gentiles*, literally, *the nations*, (see above, on 4, 27. 9, 15. 10, 45. 11, 1. 18. 13, 42. 46. 47. 48.) *The brethren*, the new converts, whether Jews or Gentiles, sometimes called *disciples* (see above, on 13, 52.) What is here recorded shows, not only the determined ill-will of the unbelieving Jews, but also their extraordinary influence upon the Gentiles. (See above, on 13, 50.)

3. Long time therefore abode they speaking boldly in the Lord, which gave testimony unto the word of his grace, and granted signs and wonders to be done by their hands.

Long time, literally, *sufficient time*, or time enough. (See above, on 5, 37. 8, 11. 9, 23. 43. 11, 24. 26. 12, 12, and compare Luke 8, 32 with Matt. 8, 30.) The precise time is purposely left undetermined, but, as the very form of expression may suggest, it should suffice us to know that it was long enough to carry out the divine purpose. *Therefore*, or rather, *so then*, a resumptive or continuative particle, connecting this verse more directly with the first than with the second, which may be regarded as a sort of parenthesis or interruption, the author's main design being rather to record the success of the Gospel than the opposition to it, which is therefore only mentioned by the bye. But although the opposition of the Jews and Gentiles is not given as the reason of their stay (*long time therefore*), it is plain that it had no effect in hindering it. *Abode*, literally, *wore out*, *wore away*, but commonly applied to time, even when not expressly mentioned. (See above, on 12, 19.) *Boldly*, or *freely* (Geneva Bible, *frankly*), as opposed not merely to timidity or cowardice, but to all reserve, obscurity, or partiality. (See above, on 2, 29. 4, 13. 29. 31. 9, 27. 28. 13, 46.) *In the Lord*, or rather *on him*, i. e. in reliance on him, and by his authority, both which ideas are suggested by the next clause. (See above, on 2, 38. 3, 16. 4, 18. 9, 42. 11, 17.) *The Lord*, i. e. God, as manifested in the Lord Jesus Christ. (See above, on 13, 49.) *The Lord, the (one) testifying*, bearing witness, *to the word of his grace*, his gracious word, or the doctrine of his grace, the proclamation of his mercy in the Gospel. *Signs and wonders*, i. e. miracles, as proofs of the divine approbation, and as prodigies or wonders. (See above, on 2, 19. 22. 43. 4, 30. 5, 12. 6, 8. 7, 36.) *Giving*, granting or permitting, miracles to be performed by their hands, through their agency as simple instruments, in order to attest their divine legation. (See above, on 2, 4. 27. 4, 29. 13, 35.)

4. But the multitude of the city was divided; and part held with the Jews, and part with the Apostles.

Divided (rent, split, the Greek verb from which *schism* is derived) *was the multitude*, the mass or body of the people (see above, on v. 1. and compare 2, 6 4, 32. 5, 16. 6, 2. 5.) *Part held with*, literally, *some were with*, i. e. on the side of, joined with, in the schism or separation now in question (see above, on 4, 13. 5, 17. 21.) *The Jews*, i. e. the unbelieving Jews, so called in v. 2. *The Apostles*, i. e. the body of Apostles, represented by the missionaries; or more probably, *the (two) Apostles*, i. e. Paul, the Apostle of the Gentiles, and Barnabas, either as holding the same office and equal in authority, or simply so called as Paul's colleague and companion, which explains the fact that he is never so called separately or in the singular number, nor indeed at all, except in this one passage, though he is so often mentioned. Some find an analogy in the case of Silas (see below, on 16, 37. 38.) But a still more natural and satisfactory solution is, that Paul and Barnabas are both here called Apostles, not in the technical distinctive sense, but in the primary and wider one of *missionaries*, ministers sent forth upon a special service. (Compare John 13, 16. Rom. 16, 7. 2 Cor. 8, 23. Phil. 2, 25.)

5. And when there was an assault made both of the Gentiles, and also of the Jews, with their rulers, to use (them) despitefully, and to stone them,

When, literally, *as*, suggesting both the time and cause of the departure mentioned in the next verse. (See above, on

1, 10. 5, 24. 7, 23. 8, 36. 9, 23. 10, 7. 17. 25. 11, 25. 29.) *An assault*, properly a rush, a violent onward movement, but sometimes applied to an internal impulse, resolution, plan, or purpose (compare James 3, 4), which some prefer here, as agreeing better with the first words of the sixth verse. *Their rulers* may refer to the Jews alone, as the nearest antecedent, or to both Jews and Gentiles, which seems more natural. By the rulers of the Jews we are probably to understand, not elective or self-constituted officers, but their natural, hereditary chiefs and representatives, the heads of families or elders, according to the patriarchal system, which the Jews carried with them in their wide dispersion, as an organization reconcileable with any social or political condition, because really a mere extension of the family relation. (See above, on 4, 5. 5, 21. 6, 12. 11, 30.) *To insult*, outrage, treat with insolence, wantonly abuse. The idea of physical violence is not necessarily included in the meaning of this word, but suggested by what follows. The Greek verb is once rendered by *reproach* in English (Luke 11, 45), but always elsewhere by *entreat* (i. e. *treat*) or *use despitefully* (Matt. 22, 26. Luke 18, 32. 1 Th. 2, 2, and here), while the cognate noun is represented by *reproach* in one place (2 Cor. 12, 10), and by *hurt* and *harm* in another, within the compass of a dozen verses (see below, on 27, 10. 21.) The essential idea is not so much that of spite or malignity as that of insolence and outrage. *To stone them*, either as an act of brutal rage and violence, or as a sort of judicial testimony against the impiety of Paul and Barnabas. (See above, on 5, 26. 7, 58. 59.) If the latter, it must have been confined to the Jews; or rather, they alone can be supposed to have attached this symbolical meaning to the act, while the Gentiles regarded it, and perhaps took part in it, merely as a public ignominious insult.

6. 7. They were aware of (it), and fled unto Lystra and Derbe, cities of Lycaonia, and unto the region that lieth round about; and there they preached the Gospel.

Being aware (of it), literally, *knowing with* (one's self, i. e. being conscious), or *knowing with* (others, i. e. being privy, cognizant, or in the secret.) See above, on 5, 2. 12, 12. Some infer from this expression, that the movement mentioned in

v. 5 must have been a secret plot, and not an open assault; but even the latter might have been discovered or perceived in its inception or first movements. Observe the exact agreement here between Luke's speaking of a plan or plot to stone them, which was not carried into execution, and Paul's saying (2 Cor. 11, 25), "Once was I stoned," i. e. at Lystra (see below, on v. 19.)* *Fled*, not in terror, or in undue care for their own safety, but in the exercise of that discretion, which sometimes prompted them to stand and sometimes to retreat before danger. (See above, on 4, 13. 20. 5, 29, 42. 8, 1. 9, 20. 25. 29. 30. 12, 17. 13, 51.) The original order of the next clause is, *to the cities of Lycaonia, Lystra and Derbe.* The definite expression (*the cities*) does not necessarily exclude Iconium, which Strabo and Pliny reckon also to that province, but may be equivalent to *the* (other) *cities.* This construction is not necessary, however, as the limits of these provinces were always vague and often shifting. (See above, on 13, 51.) The sense may therefore be, *the* (principal or well known) *cities of* (the neighboring province) *Lycaonia.* Thus Xenophon calls Iconium, "the last town of Phrygia." *Lycaonia* was an inland tract of Asia Minor, lying between Phrygia, Galatia, Cappadocia, and Cilicia. *Lystra* was in the southern part of it, thirty miles south of Iconium. Ptolemy includes it in Isauria, which was probably not a political division, but a district on the frontier of several provinces, infested by a race of robbers called *Isauri.* The site of Lystra is supposed to have been recently discovered. *Derbe* was east of Lystra and south-east of Iconium, mentioned by Cicero as the residence of his friend Antipater. Some travellers suppose both the site and name to be preserved in the modern *Divle. The region that lieth round about* (one word in Greek) i. e. about Lystra and Derbe, not about Lycaonia, but within it. *Preached,* or more exactly, *were preaching,* i. e. for a time not specified, but necessarily implying more than a mere transient visit. *Preaching,* evangelizing, telling the good news of Christ and his salvation. (See above, on 5, 42. 8, 4. 12. 25. 35. 40. 10, 36. 11, 20. 13, 32.)

8. And there sat a certain man at Lystra, impotent

* "Truth is necessarily consistent; but it is scarcely possible that independent accounts, not having truth to guide them, should thus advance to the very brink of contradiction without falling into it."—PALEY.

in his feet, being a cripple from his mother's womb, who never had walked.

Having given, in the two preceding verses, a summary description of their missionary work in the region of Lystra and Derbe, the historian now gives a more particular account of what occurred at Lystra, including a miracle (8–10), an apotheosis (11–13), an apostolical discourse (14–18), and a persecution (19–20.) They may have performed many miracles in Lystra, as they did during their long stay in Iconium (v. 3), and this one may have been recorded merely on account of the events to which it led. Or it may have been the only one performed, because Paul and Barnabas were soon after driven from the place (vs. 19, 20.) The strong resemblance between these occurrences and those recorded in the third and fourth chapters, where a miracle is likewise the occasion both of a discourse and a persecution, so far from tending to discredit either narrative, serves rather to confirm both as authentic, on the principle that like causes produce like effects, so that these two narratives, instead of being copied one from the other, are only specimens of what was frequently experienced in that age, on a larger or a smaller scale. That one of these remarkable examples is recorded in each great division of the history, is no proof of a disposition to assimilate the life of Paul to that of Peter, but a natural result of the plan on which the whole book is constructed, and agreeably to which one Apostle is especially conspicuous in one part, and the other in the other. The resemblance in the miracles themselves can be a difficulty only on the supposition that they were fortuitous and under no particular divine direction. *A certain man*, as in 3, 2. 5, 1. 34. 6, 9. 8, 9. 9, 10. 33. 36. 10, 1. 23. 11, 20. 12, 1. 13. 1, 6, in all which cases, by a sort of antiphrasis, *certain* seems really to mean *uncertain*, the Greek word being merely an indefinite pronoun, corresponding both to *some* and *any*. *Impotent*, literally, *unable* (to make use of them.) *Sat*, not *dwelt*, as some dilute the meaning, by a false comparison of Matt. 4, 16, where *sat* is also the true version. (Compare Gen. 23, 10, where the meaning is not that Ephron dwelt among the children of Heth, which there was no need of affirming, as he was their chief, but that Ephron was then sitting in the midst of them or surrounded by them.) *Sat*, which in Mark 5, 15 was a proof of cure, in this case only proved the need of it. He sat because he could not stand or walk. *Being* is not found in the oldest manuscripts, and is rejected by the latest critics, as an unauthorized assimilation to the narrative in 3, 2. *Cripple* is a more exact translation than the *lame man* of that passage. Both men had been so from their birth, and of this one it is added negatively, *he had never walked.* Congenital infirmities of this kind being commonly regarded as incurable, the man's condition seemed to be a hopeless one.

9. 10. The same heard Paul speak, who steadfastly beholding him, and perceiving that he had faith to be healed, said with a loud voice, Stand upright on thy feet. And he leaped and walked.

This (*man*) *heard*, or according to the common text, *was hearing*, listening, when the cure was wrought; but the oldest manuscripts and latest editors have the aorist instead of the imperfect. *Paul speaking*, i. e. publicly, not merely talking but preaching. *Gazing at him*, as in 3, 4. 13, 9 (compare 1, 10. 3, 12. 6, 15. 7, 55. 10, 4. 11, 6.) This act, when connected with miraculous performances, was probably intended, first, to fix attention on the person, then to arrest his own, also to ascertain his actual condition, and lastly by divine assistance to discern his spirit or read his heart, as Paul did in the case before us. *Faith to be healed* (literally, *to be saved*) is variously understood to mean what theologians call saving faith, and which was often, if not commonly, connected with miraculous healing, as a previous condition or a subsequent effect (see above, on 3, 16); or confident assurance that he could or would be healed of (saved from) his disease (see above, on 4, 9); or, intermediate between these two extremes, such a confiding state of mind as made him a fit object of compassion, and in a good sense qualified him to be saved both from bodily and spiritual maladies. *With a great* (or *loud*) *voice*, like our Saviour in the case of Lazarus (see John 11, 43.) There was no need of Peter's doing likewise, as the cripple whom he healed was lying at the gate through which he was about to pass (3, 2. 3); whereas the one whom Paul healed may have been at a considerable distance, in the midst of the assembly which he was addressing. In some of the old manuscripts, and one modern critical edition, Paul begins by saying, *I say unto thee in the name of the Lord Jesus Christ*, which is commonly rejected by the critics as an evident assimilation to the words of

Peter in 3, 6. But the words, though not recorded here, may have been uttered in both cases, or if not pronounced by Paul, were certainly implied in his avowed relation to the Saviour, and perhaps anticipated in his previous discourse, which may have included or wound up with an account of Christ's own miracles of healing (compare that of Peter to Cornelius and his company, 10, 38), and by this "hearing" (Rom. 10, 17) may have come the cripple's "faith to be healed" (v. 9.) *Arise*, stand up, *upon thy feet*, which he had never used (v. 8), *erect*, straight, upright, a word occurring elsewhere only in Heb. 12, 13, where it is translated *straight*. This implies that he was previously bent or otherwise deformed (compare Luke 13, 16.) *He leaped and walked*, the same gradation or succession as in 3, 8, but more concisely stated. The leaping here most probably denotes the first exertion of his newly acquired power in an effort to obey the Apostle's mandate. Leaping for joy is not distinctly mentioned here as in the other narrative (3, 9.)

11. And when the people saw what Paul had done, they lifted up their voices, saying in the speech of Lycaonia, The gods are come down to us in the likeness of men.

The crowds, i. e. the assembled masses who had witnessed the miracle, perhaps called *crowds*, not merely in reference to their numbers, but to their promiscuous composition (see above, on 1, 15. 6, 7. 8, 6. 11, 24. 26. 13, 45.) *Seeing what Paul did*, to wit, that he had healed the cripple. *Raised their voices*, shouted, cried aloud, with one voice (see above, on 2, 6, and compare 4, 24. 7, 57. 8, 7. 13, 27.) *In Lycaonian*, *Lycaonically* (lat. *Lycaonice*), an adverb similar in form to those translated, *in Hebrew*, *Greek*, *and Latin* (John 19, 20.) This was the vernacular language of the country, supposed by some to be a dialect of Greek, by others a Semitic tongue, but evidently meant to be distinguished from the Greek which the Apostles spoke, and which was no doubt understood by the people, as the English is in Wales, Ireland, and the Highlands of Scotland, even where the native language of the people is Welsh, Erse, or Gaelic. This sudden falling back upon their mother-tongue, when strongly excited, is exquisitely true to nature and experience. But why is it recorded? Most interpreters (since Chrysostom) agree that it is mentioned to account for the delay of the Apostles in refusing divine honours, which they seem not to have done until they saw the priest approaching with the victims and the garlands (v. 13), so that the acclamations of the people were either not heard, although apparently uttered on the spot as soon as they had seen the miracle, or not understood, because uttered in an unknown tongue. From this fact various conclusions have been drawn, e. g. that the gift of tongues was not constant but occasional or temporary; that it was not universal but restricted in the case of individual apostles; and therefore that it was not a mere practical convenience in the preaching of the Gospel, but a token of God's presence and a symbol of the calling of the Gentiles. (See above, on 2, 4. 10, 46.) *Likened* (assimilated, made like) *to men* (or having been so) for the nonce, on this particular occasion, *Have* (or *are*) *come down to us*, descended from above, from heaven or Olympus, where the gods resided. This language agrees perfectly, not only with the general belief in such epiphanies or theophanies, divine appearances in human form, as found in Homer and the later classics, but also with the local superstitions and traditions of the very country where the words were spoken, *Lycaonia*, so called from *Lycaon*, whose fatal entertainment of Jupiter is one of Ovid's fables in the first book of his Metamorphoses, while in the eighth he tells the fabulous but interesting story of the visit paid to Philemon and Baucis, in the adjacent province of Phrygia, by Jupiter and Mercury, the very gods named in the next verse.

12. And they called Barnabas Jupiter; and Paul Mercurius, because he was the chief speaker.

Jupiter, the Roman name of the divinity whom the Greeks called *Zeus*, and in the early ages *Dis*, the accusative of which word (*Dia*) is the one here used. *Mercurius* (more usually written with an English termination, *Mercury*, like *Timotheus* and *Timothy*, 2 Cor. 1, 1. 19), the Roman name corresponding to the Greek *Hermes*, the interpreter or spokesman of the gods, and represented in the popular mythology, as commonly attending Zeus or Jupiter in his visits to the earth (see above, on v. 11.) This accounts for the application of the name to Paul, as being *the chief speaker*, literally, *the* (*one*) *leading in the word* (or *in discourse*), not merely (if at all) the one that said most, but the one that spoke for both, or acted as the spokesman of the party. (See above, on 1, 13. 15.) Having thus named Paul for a specific reason, they inferred of course that Barnabas was Jupiter, for which no reason is assigned at all. Not content with this simple, unembellished explanation of the text, interpreters have chosen to imagine other reasons, some of which may possibly be true, but none of which are either expressed or necessarily implied. Such are the usual hypotheses, that Barnabas was older and of more majestic presence, Paul younger and more active; while others have gone further and described him as diminutive in stature and contemptible in aspect, on the ground of certain dubious expressions in his own epistles (2 Cor. 10, 1. 10.) But even granting this to be the true interpretation of his language, how would such a picture correspond to the ideal forms of Mercury, with which they were familiar, and some of which are still preserved, as an athletic, graceful, active youth? This discrepancy is enough to prove, either that Paul was not such a looking person as these writers represent him, or, which is probably at all events a true and safe conclusion, that the people of Lystra, in calling him Mercurius, had no regard at all to his appearance, but exclusively to what is here expressly stated, that he was *the leading speaker* in behalf of both. To this absurd depreciation of Paul's person or physique, the opposite extreme is that of making them describe him as Mercurius, because of his extraordinary eloquence, an art or gift of which that god was the reputed patron. This hypothesis, though in itself far better founded than the other, is excluded, in the case before us, partly by the fact that Barnabas himself received his name from the Apostles on account of his excelling in this very gift (see above, on 4, 36. 11, 23); but chiefly by the silence of the narrative, which does not say that Paul was eloquent, or more eloquent than Barnabas, who cannot be supposed to have been speechless (see below, on v. 15), but simply that he was *the leading speaker*, took the lead in speaking, really because he was superior in rank as an Apostle, but as they very naturally thought, because he held the same position of interpreter, ambassador, or spokesman, which the Mercury or Hermes of their own mythology sustained to Zeus or Jupiter.

13. Then the priest of Jupiter, which was before their city, brought oxen and garlands unto the gates, and would have done sacrifice with the people.

The excited heathen followed up their words with corresponding acts. Having recognized two gods as present, they consistently proceed to offer sacrifice. *The priest* does not specifically mean *the chief priest* (see above, on 5, 24), as some contend because there must have been a number. Even granting this, which is by no means certain, it may mean the priest who happened to be present, or the one then officiating at the temple. *Which was before the city* might seem to describe the priest as standing or residing there; but there is no such ambiguity in the original, *the priest of the Jupiter* (to wit) *the* (Jupiter) *being* (or *that was*) *before the city.* This may be figuratively understood as meaning its protector or champion, which is really implied; but the words should rather have their literal or local sense, as describing the position of the image, or more probably the temple, of the tutelary god, which is often mentioned in the classics as without the city (*extra urbem.*) The very phrase here used is applied by Æschylus to Pallas as the Queen before the city (ἄνασσα πρὸ πόλεως), and the tutelary Jupiter derived one of his titles from it (*Zeus Propylus*, or Jupiter before the gates.) *Bulls* or *bullocks* were regarded, both by Jews and Gentiles, as the most costly victims, and as such were offered to the chief or father of the gods, a fact abundantly attested by Homer, Virgil, and Ovid, who moreover says that cows were offered to Minerva and calves to Mercury; but another poet (Persius) expressly speaks of bulls as also sacrificed to Mercury. The offering in this case therefore may have been designed for both; or that to Jupiter may be considered as superseding or including any other. *Bulls and crowns* is by some explained as an example of the figure called *hendiadys*, equivalent, in ordinary language, to the phrase, *crowned bulls;* but the occurrence of this forced construction in a famous line of Virgil, though relating also to a sacrificial service (that of pouring libations from *cups and gold*, i. e. *golden cups*) cannot warrant its assumption in the plain prose of a narrative like that before us. *Crowns* or *garlands*, wreaths of flowers, were profusely and continually used in ancient sacrifice, and are so still, at least in India. It has been disputed whether those here mentioned were designed to decorate the victims or the god; but the authorities appealed to upon both both sides of the question have most clearly shown that they were used, not only for both purposes, but also to adorn the priests, the altars, and the temples, and indeed whatever else, connected with the sacrifice, admitted of such decoration. Here again the ancient heathen ceremonial agrees with that still practised by the idolatrous Hindoos. *Bulls and crowns to the gates having brought*, i. e. as some suppose to the entrance of the temple ; but why there, when the supposed gods themselves were elsewhere ? Others understand the door of the house where Paul and Barnabas were lodging; but this requires another supposition, namely, that they had returned home in the mean time. A third hy- pothesis, more probable than either, is that the *gates* (literally, vestibules, porticoes, or porches, see above, on 10, 17. 12, 13) were those of the city itself, near which there was probably an image or a temple of the tutelary deity, and to which Paul and Barnabas were now conducted, either from within or from without, according as the scene of the miraculous performance which occasioned this idolatrous proceeding lay in the suburbs or the city proper. *With the crowds* (which comes next in the Greek), i. e. accompanied or followed by them, when he brought the victims and the garlands. There is no need of connecting these words with the following verbs, as in the English version, and in some editions of the Greek text. *Would have done sacrifice*, in modern English, means that he would have done so but for what is afterwards recorded as preventing him. But *would have*, even in this version, is not an auxiliary tense but a distinct and independent verb, meaning that *he wished* (intended, or was just about) *to sacrifice*. It is not said to whom; but this is sufficiently apparent from the context.

14. (Which) when the Apostles, Barnabas and Paul, heard (of), they rent their clothes, and ran in among the people, crying out—

Hearing (or *having heard*) stands first in the original, and either means that they were told by others, possibly by Christian friends, what was passing; or that they now heard and understood the words of the idolaters themselves, as they proceeded to effect their purpose, either because they had come nearer, or were speaking more loudly and distinctly, or because some or all of them were speaking Greek instead of Lycaonian (see above, on v. 11.) *The Apostles Barnabas and Paul*, as in v. 4, where they were intended, although not expressly named, as here. It is a fine stroke in this simple but most graphic narrative, that Barnabas is here again restored to his old place, because he occupied it in the scene described, as being the Jupiter, for whom the sacrifice was chiefly or exclusively intended. *Rending* (tearing open or apart) *their* (upper or outer) *garments* (see above, on 7, 57. 9, 39. 12, 8), a customary oriental method of expressing grief, and also indignation and abhorrence of impiety or blasphemy committed in one's presence. (Compare the conduct of the High Priest when our Lord avowed himself the Son of God, Matt. 26, 65, Mark 14, 63.) In this case it was no doubt a spontaneous or involuntary burst of feeling, prompted by the sudden and astonishing discovery just made by the Apostles, and not intended as a demonstration to the multitude, although these were probably no less familiar with this ancient exhibition of strong feeling. But Paul and Barnabas were not contented with this typical expression of repugnance. *They ran in*, literally, *leaped* (or *sprang*) *in*, or according to the text now commonly preferred, *leaped* (or sprang) *out*, i. e. from the house, or from the city-gate, or more indefinitely, from the place where they were standing. *Into the crowd*, not merely ran about among the people, but plunged into the heart of the excited mass, now bent upon their own deification. This movement of the two was not a silent one. *Calling*, shouting, crying out, may denote the inarticulate but noisy sounds, by which they tried to interrupt the service and divert the attention of the people, before uttering the words that follow. Or the two participles, although strangely placed in different verses, may be construed together, as qualifying one another, *calling and saying*, that is saying with a loud voice, shouting or vociferating, what is given in the following verses. There are few passages, in history or poetry, at once so simple and so vivid as this narrative, of which no higher proof can be demanded than its being chosen by the greatest of modern painters, as the subject of one of his most masterly though not most finished works. (See above, on 13, 11.)

15. And saying, Sirs, why do ye these (things?) We also are men of like passions with you, and preach unto you that ye should turn from these vanities unto the living God, which made heaven, and earth, and the sea, and all things that are therein:

Sirs, literally, *men*, nearly equivalent to our *gentlemen* (see above on 1, 11. 16.) The question in the first clause implies censure or expostulation, for which the other clause assigns the reason. *We are men*, a different word from that at the beginning of the verse, and meaning mere men, mortals, human beings. *Of like passions* corresponds to one Greek adjective (the root of our familiar word *homœopathic*) meaning similarly constituted or affected. *Passions*, in the English versions, has not its moral sense of violent affections or desires, but its physical sense of suffering (as applied to the death of Christ in 1, 3) or liability to suffering. The whole phrase means, therefore, subject to the same infirmities, partakers of the same mortal nature, with yourselves, and consequently not entitled to divine honours. *Preach unto you*, bringing you glad tidings of deliverance from your present superstitious bondage, by calling you to turn from the worship of these very gods with which you have confounded us. *Vanities*, or rather *vain* (*things*), not only useless but unreal, without personal existence, in which sense Paul says that "an idol is nothing in the world" (1 Cor. 8, 4, compare 10, 19.) Similar epithets are applied to false gods in the Old Testament (e. g. Jer. 2, 5. Zech. 11, 17, compare 1 Kings 16, 2.) *The living God*, i. e. really existing, as distinguished from these lifeless or imaginary deities; and also *life-giving*, or the source of all existence. (See Matt. 16, 16. 26, 63. John 6, 69. 2 Cor. 3, 3. 6, 16. 1 Th. 1, 9. 1 Tim. 3, 15. 4, 10. 6, 17. Heb. 3, 12. 9, 14. 10, 31. 12, 22. Rev. 7, 2.) This naturally leads to the description of him as Creator of the Universe, the principal parts of which are here enumerated, not in scientific but in popular form, with the contents of each.

16. Who in times past suffered all nations to walk in their own ways.

Of this supreme God they were ignorant, because he had not fully revealed himself to them. *Past*, departed, gone by. *Times*, literally, *generations*, or contemporary races (see above, on 2, 40. 13, 36.) *Suffered*, permitted, or allowed; not approved, much less required, but did not hinder or prevent. The word used in the version is the nearest equivalent that could be chosen. *All nations*, i. e. all but one, to whom he granted an exclusive revelation. It is therefore equivalent to *all the Gentiles* (see above, on vs. 2, 5, and on 4, 27. 7, 45. 9, 15. 10, 45. 11, 1. 18. 13, 42. 46–48.) *To walk*, advance, move onward, implying not merely active but progressive motion.

(See above, on 1, 10. 25. 9, 31.) *Ways*, paths, a common figure for the course of life. (See above, on 2, 28. 9, 2. *Their own ways*, as opposed to God's, which sometimes means the ways in which he walks himself (as in 13, 10 above), and sometimes those which he prescribes to man, as here.

17. Nevertheless he left not himself without witness, in that he did good, and gave us rain from heaven, and fruitful seasons, filling our hearts with food and gladness.

And yet, notwithstanding this rejection of the Gentiles, by withholding from them an explicit and a written revelation, they were still without excuse. (Compare Paul's statement of the same truth in Rom. 1, 18–21.) *Not unattested* (or untestified), as really existing and as infinite in power and goodness. *Doing good*, bestowing benefits or favours (compare the similar but not identical expression in 10, 38 above.) *Us* and *our hearts* are in the oldest manuscripts and latest texts, *you* and *your hearts*. The original order is, *from heaven to you rains giving*. *Rains* may be understood as a generic plural, simply equivalent to *rain;* or as referring to the stated periodical rains of certain climates, especially the early and the latter rains of Scripture (James 5, 7); or more naturally still, as signifying mere abundance, frequency or constancy. It is said to have been usual with the heathen to ascribe rain not to the gods, but to God, the Supreme Being. It has also been observed that *rain* was peculiarly appropriate here, as the phenomenon or element which keeps up the connection between heaven, earth, and sea, the great divisions of the universe enumerated in the context (see above, on v. 15.) It is chiefly spoken of, however, as a source of good to man, by its fertilizing and productive power. *Fruitful*, fruit-bearing, or productive. *Filling*, sufficing, satisfying, abundantly supplying, not only what is necessary to subsistence, but the means of bodily enjoyment. *Food*, nourishment, support of life. *Joy*, pleasure, happiness, as something more than mere existence. *Hearts*, not stomachs, as some writers would explain the word from the analogy of *heartburn* and other like expressions; but *minds* or *souls*, as the only real seat of all enjoyment, even when afforded by the body. It is a strong though incidental proof of authenticity, that when the Apostles address heathen hearers, unacquainted even with the Hebrew Scriptures, they begin with the great truths of natural theology, and not by appealing to the prophecies or proving the Messiahship of Jesus, as they did in their addresses to the Jews (see above, on 2, 16-36. 3, 22-26. 4, 11-12. 13, 17-41, and below, on 17, 22-31.) As these words are ascribed both to Barnabas and Paul (v. 14), they may be regarded as the sum and substance of what both said, more at large and perhaps in a variety of forms.

18. And with these sayings scarce restrained they the people, that they had not done sacrifice unto them.

With these sayings, literally, *these* (*things*) *saying*. *Scarce*, scarcely, i. e. almost not at all; but the original expression, from its very etymology, answers more exactly to our *hardly*, i. e. with difficulty, (see below, on 27, 7. 8.) It implies however that they did succeed. *Restrained*, or more exactly, *quieted*, arrested, caused to cease. (The Greek word occurs elsewhere only in Heb. 4, 4. 8. 10.) *The people*, crowds, or masses, as in vs. 11. 13. 14. *That they had not done sacrifice*, a singular and awkward use of the pluperfect to translate an infinitive present, *not to sacrifice*. This, with the negation implied in the preceding verb, amounts to a double or emphatic negative, a point in which the Greek idiom differs most remarkably, not only from the English but the Latin. (See above, on 8, 16.) We express the same idea without a negative by saying, 'they restrained them *from* sacrificing.' It may however be resolved into our idiom thus, 'restrained them *so as not* to sacrifice.' (See above, on 10, 47.) *To them*, i. e. to Paul and Barnabas, as representatives or incarnations of Mercurius and Jupiter (v. 12.)

19. And there came thither (certain) Jews from Antioch and Iconium, who persuaded the people, and, having stoned Paul, drew (him) out of the city, supposing he had been dead.

By a violent reaction, persecution follows the apotheosis, but a persecution prompted from without and by inveterate enemies. *Came thither*, literally, *came upon* (them), i. e. suddenly assailed them (see above, on 8, 24. 13, 40.) *Antioch and Iconium*, from both which places Paul and Barnabas had been expelled by the same influence. (See above, on v. 5, and on 13, 50.) *Having persuaded the crowds* (or *masses*) *and stoned Paul* may possibly mean, having persuaded them to stone Paul, but more probably, having persuaded them to let the Jews themselves stone him. ('Having gained the consent of the people and then stoned him.') This agrees better with the form of expression, as well as with the fact that stoning was a Jewish punishment (see above, on v. 5.) The persuasion was effected no doubt by the same arts of misrepresentation and appeal to evil passions, as at Antioch and Iconium (see above, on v. 2, and on 13, 45.) *Drew*, violently pulled, or dragged (see above, on 8, 3, and below, on 17, 6.) This was not for burial, but for exposure, and to free the city from the impurity incurred by the presence of a corpse so odious, according to the notions both of Jews and Gentiles. Stephen was first brought out and then stoned (see above, on 7, 58), a minute but not unimportant difference, so far from involving inconsistency between the two accounts, that it illustrates the exactness of the writer in distinguishing between Jerusalem and Lystra, the Holy City of the Jews, in which it was unlawful to put any one to death, and a provincial city of the Gentiles; where no such scruple could be entertained by either class. *Supposing*, thinking, being of opinion. *That he had been dead*, another antique use of the pluperfect (see above, on v. 18), meaning simply *that he was dead*, or adhering still more closely to the form of the original, *supposing him to be dead.* This expression does not necessarily imply that he was not so really; but that is certainly the natural and obvious suggestion (see below, on 21, 29), as the word *suppose* is otherwise superfluous, the fact asserted being then simply that *he was dead*, whether they supposed him to be so or not. (But see below, upon the next verse.)

20. Howbeit, as the disciples stood round about him, he rose up, and came into the city; and the next day he departed with Barnabas to Derbe.

There is nothing corresponding to *howbeit* but the usual continuative particle (δέ), so often rendered *and*, *but*, *now*, or *then*. *The disciples*, converts, Christians, called *the brethren* in v. 2, but *disciples* also in 13, 52. *Stood round about him*, literally, *having encircled* (or *surrounded*) *him*, some think to bury him; others, to lament (over) him; others, to see whether he was still alive; others, to conceal that fact from his oppressors. *Rising* (or *standing up*) *he came into the city*, out of which he had been dragged (v. 19.) Some maintain that Paul was only stunned or in a swoon, from which he naturally soon recovered. Others, on the contrary, regard it as a case of real death and miraculous resuscitation. Intermediate between these two extremes is the opinion, that he was not actually dead (see above, on v. 19), but that the miracle consisted in the preservation of his life and his immediate restoration to his usual activity and vigour after being stoned by an infuriated mob, or by still more vindictive and malignant enemies. The restoration was so perfect that he *went out* (or departed) *to Derbe* (see above on v. 6) *on the morrow* (or *the next day*) after these events occurred. An ingenious living writer thinks it probable, that this deliquium or swoon at Lystra was the trance or ecstasy described by Paul in one of his epistles (2 Cor. 12, 1–4), whether in the body or out of the body he did not know. *With Barnabas*, who seems to have escaped the persecution, which would naturally fall with most severity on Paul as the "chief speaker" (v. 12), not only in behalf of Christianity, but in opposition both to Heathenism and anti-Christian Judaism, not in Lystra only but in Antioch and Iconium. The first of these three places seems to have differed from the others as a seat of unmixed heathenism, without a Synagogue or Jewish settlers, which accounts for their excessive superstition and credulity, and is itself explained by their secluded residence beyond Mount Taurus, in the heart of Asia Minor.

21. And when they had preached the Gospel to that city, and had taught many, they returned again to Lystra, and (to) Iconium, and Antioch,

Having both evangelized that city and discipled many. They not only preached the Gospel, but received converts, which implies a church-organization. (See Matt. 28, 19, and compare Matt. 13, 52. 27, 57.) *Both* (τε), not both Paul and Barnabas, but both evangelized and discipled, a distinction obliterated in the English version (*preached* and *taught.*) Their ministry at Derbe was none the less successful on account of its affording so little historical material, according to the adage that the best times to live in are the worst to write about. They here encountered probably neither heathen flattery nor Jewish persecution; and although they may have performed miracles, these probably produced no ulterior effects and are therefore not recorded. Instead of returning to Syria by the nearest way, i. e. through Cilicia, Paul's native country, they retraced their steps from Derbe, and revisited Lystra, Iconium, and Antioch in Pisidia, in an order opposite to that of their first journey, and for reasons given in the next verse.

22. Confirming the souls of the disciples, (and) exhorting them to continue in the faith, and that we must through much tribulation enter into the kingdom of God.

Confirming (strengthening, establishing) *the souls* (or *minds*) *of the disciples* (Christian converts in those places), by additional instruction in the doctrines of their new faith, and by exhortation to perform its duties. *Exhorting* (and entreating) *them to continue in* (adhere to or abide by) *the* (Christian) *faith* (which they had recently embraced.) Before the last clause some supply *saying*, or *assuring them*, because what follows is not exhortation but instruction. Two instances, however, of the very same construction (*to exhort that*) have been cited from Polybius and Xenophon. What follows is the statement of a general or universal fact common to the experience of all believers, and presented as a reason why they should not be deterred from holding fast their profession by distress or opposition. *Much tribulation*, literally, *many tribulations*, which expresses not mere quantity or number but variety. *Tribulations*, literally, *pressures*, straits, through which the Christian is described as struggling. (See above, on 7, 10. 11. 11, 19, and compare Matt. 7, 14. 2 Cor. 2, 4.) *It is necessary* (δεῖ) *for us to go in*, a necessity resulting from the will of God, and from the nature of the evils which attend our fallen state. *The kingdom of God*, the new economy or dispensation of his grace, sometimes viewed in its inception (see above, on 1, 3. 6), and sometimes in its consummation, as a state of future blessedness, which seems to be the meaning here. Compare Paul's favourite idea of inheriting this kingdom, 1 Cor. 6, 9. 10. 15, 50. Gal. 5, 21. Eph. 5, 5, also found in James 2, 5.

23. And when they had ordained them elders in every church, and had prayed with fasting, they commended them to the Lord on whom they believed.

Besides these exhortations and instructions, they gave their converts a distinct organization as societies or churches. The meaning of the word *ordained* has been the subject of protracted and vehement dispute between Presbyterian and Episcopal interpreters. The latter grant that the original etymological import of the Greek word is to vote by stretching out the hand, but they contend that usage had so modified its meaning as to generate the secondary sense of choosing or appointing, without any reference to votes or popular election; and this they insist upon as the unquestionable use of the word here, where the act is predicated, not of the people but of Paul and Barnabas, who cannot be supposed to have voted for these elders with the outstretched hand. Some go further and adopt the patristical usage of the word to denote imposition of hands, as the ordaining act; but this is commonly agreed to be an ecclesiastical usage of the word long posterior in date to the times of the Apostles. The opposite extreme is that of making the word here denote, directly and exclusively, the act of suffrage or election by the people. To meet the objection, which has been already stated, that the act described is not that of the people, but of Paul and Barnabas, some modify this explanation of the term, so as to make it mean that Paul and Barnabas appointed or ordained the elders chosen by the people. The philological objection to this modification, that the same verb cannot denote both these processes at once, can only be removed by taking one step further and thus reaching the true mean between the opposite extremes. This middle ground is, that the verb itself, expressing as it clearly does the act of Paul and Barnabas, can only mean that they appointed or ordained these elders, without determining the mode of election or the form of ordination; but that the use of this particular expression, which originally signified the vote of an assembly, does suffice to justify us in supposing that the method of selection was the same as that recorded (not in 1, 26, where the election was by lot and by direct divine authority, but) in 6, 5. 6, where it is explicitly recorded that the people chose the seven and the twelve ordained them. Another question, as to this verse, is the question whether *Elders* means diocesan bishops, presbyters (i. e. teaching elders), ruling elders, deacons, or church-officers in general, including perhaps all these special officers, except the first, which was of later date. In favour of this comprehensive meaning is the fact that Deacons are not mentioned, and the corresponding usage of the word in the organization of the old theocracy or Jewish church, from which the term was silently transferred to that of Christ, and not from the human and most probably much later institution of the synagogue, considered as a separate society. (See above, on 6, 9. 9, 2. 20. 13, 5. 15. 43.) As the Jewish elders were the heads of families, and other men of like position in society, these Christian elders were most probably selected from the same class. *In every church*, or rather, as a distributive phrase, *church by church* (see above, on 2, 46. 47. 3, 2. 5, 42. 8, 3. 13, 27), which does not necessarily imply that there were several ordained in each, though this is the most natural construction of the language, and the one most agreeable to Jewish usage, as well as to the fact of a plurality of bishops, no less than of deacons, in the church at Philippi (Phil. 1, 1.) *Prayed with fasting*, literally, *fastings*, *fasts*, the plural form referring to successive ordinations in the several churches. The practice of combining these attendant services with ordination has extensively prevailed throughout the church in later times. This organization of the churches may have been deferred till the return of the apostles, to allow time for some progress in the Christian life and some development of character before the choice of elders; or it may have been a matter of necessity arising from the persecution and expulsion of the Apostles out of all these places. On their journey back, the persecution may have ceased (but see above, on v. 22); or they may have escaped it by not preaching as before in public, but conversing only with the Christian converts. *Commended*, deposited, entrusted for safe keeping, as a precious charge. (See below, on 20, 32, and compare Luke 12, 48. 23, 46. 1 Tim. 1, 18. 2 Tim. 2, 2. 1 Pet. 4,19.) *To the Lord* (Jesus Christ) *in whom they had believed* (as their Redeemer) and thereby become members of his church, before they were thus organized externally. The pluperfect form, inappropriately used in the translation of vs. 18, 20, is here peculiarly expressive, as denoting that their faith or their conversion did not now begin, but dated back from the first visit of Paul and Barnabas to these three cities.

24. 25. And after they had passed throughout Pisidia, they came to Pamphylia. And when they had preached the word in Perga, they went down into Attalia:

Having come (or *gone*) *through Pisidia*, on their way to Antioch its capital (see above, on v. 21 and on 13, 14), and also after leaving it, so that they passed through the whole length of the province. *When they had preached*, literally, *having spoken*, for the first time in Perga, where they merely landed on their first arrival (see above, on 13, 13), and where they now seem to have met with no opposition or maltreatment. *Attalia*, a city of Pamphylia, at the mouth of the river Catarrhactes, built by Attalus Philadelphus, king of Pergamus, and still a seaport of considerable size and commerce, under a slightly altered name.

26. And thence sailed to Antioch, from whence they had been recommended to the grace of God for the work which they fulfilled.

Sailed, or more exactly, *sailed away*, implying distance. *Antioch*, in Syria, see above, on 11, 19–27. 13, 1. From the same port to the same port sailed a fleet of French Crusaders, in the year 1147, after passing through a part of the same region which had twice been traversed more than a thousand years before by Paul and Barnabas, on a very different errand and with very different success. *Recommended* is not, as it might seem from the version, a compounded form of the synonymous verb used in v. 23, but a similar derivative of the verb to *give*, meaning here *delivered*, *given up*, in a good sense, although often employed elsewhere in a bad one (see above, on 3, 13. 7, 42. 8, 3. 12, 4.) *Whence*, i. e. from Antioch, they had thus been committed or entrusted *to the grace of God*, i. e. to the divine care and protection, not in general merely, but with special reference to *the work* of missions in their native countries (see above, on 13, 4. 13), *which* (work) *they* (now) *fulfilled*, completed, brought to a conclusion, by returning to the point from which they had set out. The last words of this verse show that *the work* to which they had been solemnly *separated* by the church at Antioch, and in obedience to an express direction of the Holy Ghost, was not an office in the church or an order in the ministry, nor even the whole missionary work, but this one mission, *which they* (*now*) *fulfilled.* (See above, on 13, 2. 3.)

27. And when they were come, and had gathered the church together, they rehearsed all that God had done with them, and how he had opened the door of faith unto the Gentiles.

Being there (or having got there, see above, on 5, 21. 22. 25. 9, 26. 39. 10, 32. 33. 11, 23. 13, 14) *and having assembled* (or *convened*) *the church* (still spoken of as one) by which they had been "separated to the work," and from which they had been "sent forth by the Holy Ghost" (13, 41), *they rehearsed* (reported, brought back word) *how many* (or *how great*) *things* (see above, on 2, 39. 3, 24. 4, 34. 13, 48.) *God did* (or *had done*) *with them*, in conjunction with them, as his instruments, his agents, his co-workers. The objection, that this interpretation shares the honour between God and man, applies with equal force to Paul's express declaration (1 Cor. 3, 9), "We are labourers together with God," and to others like it (e. g. Mark 16, 20. 2 Cor. 6, 1.) The same double use of the preposition *with* prevails in English, as when one is said to travel with a sword, and to fight with a sword, the first *with* denotes merely that the sword is in his company, the second that he uses it. There is no need, therefore, of resorting to the Hebrew use of the corresponding particle, after words denoting treatment, just as we speak of dealing *with* one (well or ill); especially as this would seem to limit their report to what God had done for them, instead of making it include what he had done through them for the Gentiles. (See below, on 15, 4. 12.) The beautiful figure in the last clause is a favourite with Paul (1 Cor. 16, 9. 2 Cor. 2, 12. Col. 4, 3), but here employed in a peculiar sense or rather application, to denote the opportunity afforded to the Gentiles of believing upon Christ and being saved, whereas elsewhere it denotes the opportunity afforded to himself of preaching that salvation. (See 1 Cor. 16, 9. 2 Cor. 2, 12. Col. 4, 3, and compare Rev. 3, 8.) *Gentiles*, literally, *nations*, see above, on vs. 2. 5. 16. This report was not made to the local church of Antioch, as such, but as a sort of missionary board or council for the Gentiles (see below, upon the next verse.)

28. And there they abode long time with the disciples.

There is omitted by the oldest manuscripts and latest critics. *Abode long time*, literally, *spent* (the same verb as in v. 3, and in 12, 19) *time not a little* (literally *few*, see above, on 12, 18), *with the disciples*, converts, brethren, Christians (see above, on 11, 26), still considered as learners, and as such requiring teachers, which suggests a reason for their long stay above and beyond that of repose or relaxation; not however as mere visitors or temporary labourers, but as having now resumed their place among the prophets and teachers of the church at Antioch (13, 1), not as a single, much less as an independent congregation, but as the Jerusalem or radiating centre of the Gentile world, from which they were in due time to go forth again, not only to the old Jerusalem (15, 2), but also to the heathen (15, 36. 40.)

CHAPTER XV.

This chapter contains an account of the controversy with respect to the observance of the ceremonial law, as a condition of reception to the Christian church (1–35); and also the beginning of Paul's second foreign mission (36–41.) The church at Antioch is disturbed by Judaizing teachers (1.) Paul and Barnabas oppose them, and are sent to consult the Apostles and Elders at Jerusalem (2.) They report the conversion of the Gentiles, on their way and after their arrival (3. 4.) The converted Pharisees insist upon the circumcision of the Gentiles (5.) The Apostles and Elders are assembled (6.) Peter shows that the question has already been decided by divine authority (7–11.) Paul and Barnabas confirm this by a statement of their own experience (12.) James shows from prophecy that it had always been a part of the divine plan, (13–18.) He proposes a conciliatory and temporary compromise (19–21.) It is adopted and deputies to Antioch are chosen (22.) The decision of the council is reduced to writing (23–29.) It is received at Antioch with great joy (30, 31.)

The deputies continue there for some time and are then dismissed (32, 33.) (Silas,) Paul and Barnabas continue preaching there (34–35.) Paul proposes to revisit the churches planted in their former mission (36.) He and Barnabas differ as to John Mark, and separate in consequence (37–39.) Paul goes with Silas through Syria and Cilicia (40, 41.)

1. And certain men which came down from Judea taught the brethren, (and said), Except ye be circumcised after the manner of Moses, ye cannot be saved.

As the division of the chapters is conventional and arbitrary, this verse is to be read in the closest connection with the one before it. *And* (while Paul and Barnabas were thus employed at Antioch) *certain men* (*some* persons, see above, on 14, 8). The suppression of the names may be contemptuous, or at least intended to suggest that they were personally men of no note or authority, although they may have been lawfully commissioned teachers (see below, on v. 24.) *Coming down* (see above, on 11, 27) *from Judea* may mean from Jerusalem (see above, on 11, 1), or from Palestine, as opposed to Syria, from the mother-country and the mother-church, between which and the church at Antioch the communication seems to have been frequent. *Taught*, in the imperfect tense, implies something more than a mere transient visit or occasional address, and also makes it probable, as nothing is suggested to the contrary, that these men had a regular commission or authority as public teachers. *The brethren*, the disciples, the converted Gentiles. The last clause gives their own words, not on any one occasion, but the sum of what they used to say upon the subject. (See above, on 14, 17.) *Except*, in Greek, *if not*, unless. *Circumcision* is here put for the whole law, as the cross is sometimes put for the whole Gospel (1 Cor. 1, 18. Gal. 6, 12. 14. Phil. 3, 18), and the baptism of John for his whole ministry (see above, on 1, 22.) *After the manner* is too weak a version of the Greek, which means (*according to*) *the institute* (or *institution*) *of Moses*, including the idea both of law and custom (see above, on 6, 14.) The clause does not mean that being circumcised would save them, or that faith in Christ was not required, but that it would not avail them without circumcision or observance of the law. This was afterwards the doctrine of the Jewish-Christian sect called Ebionites, whose origin indeed may be traced back to the very controversy here recorded.

2. When therefore Paul and Barnabas had no small dissension and disputation with them, they determined that Paul and Barnabas, and certain other of them, should go up to Jerusalem unto the Apostles and Elders about this question.

There being (or *arising*) *therefore*, i. e. in consequence of this erroneous teaching. *No small*, precisely the same phrase that is translated *long* in 14, 28. *Dissension*, a Greek word which in Greek means *standing* (as in Heb. 9, 8), then the act of *standing up* or *rising* in rebellion, *insurrection* (Matt. 15, 7, from the Latin verb *insurgo*, to rise up against), once translated *uproar* (19, 40), thrice *sedition* (24, 5. Luke 23, 19. 25), here denoting violent contention and commotion. This does not necessarily imply that they succeeded in forming a party, or gained any followers, but only that the preaching of this doctrine produced great excitement, as it naturally would among the Gentiles, who had been received into the church without conforming to the ceremonial law. *Disputation*, literally, *seeking*, search, investigation, but always applied in the New Testament to that of a polemic kind, whether the form be compounded (as in v. 7. 28, 29, and in the common text of this verse) or uncompounded (as in John, 3, 25. 1 Tim. 1, 4. 6, 4. 2 Tim. 2, 23. Tit. 3, 9, and here, according to the latest critics.) *Paul and Barnabas had*, literally, *being* (or *arising*) *to Paul and Barnabas*, not merely as distinguished "prophets and teachers in the church at Antioch" (13, 1), but as the first two missionaries to the Gentiles, who had organized their converts into Christian churches (14, 23), without any reference whatever to the principle which these men laid down as essential to salvation, and who therefore, being specially attacked, were under the necessity of specially opposing this false doctrine, in their own defence as well as for the truth's sake. *With them*, literally, *to*, at, or against them (see above, on 11, 2), i. e. the Judaizing teachers, who appear as the only champions of their cause at Antioch. *They determined*, ordered, or appointed (see above, on 13, 48, and below, on 22, 10. 28, 23), must be construed with neither of the nearest antecedents, but indefinitely (so as to mean, *it was ordered*), or referred to the church-officers or members, although not expressly mentioned. *Should go up*, literally, (*appointed Paul and Barnabas*) *to go up* (see above, on 11, 2, and below, on 18, 22. 21, 4. 12. 15. 24, 11. 25, 1. 9.) *Certain other* (or in modern phrase, *some others*) *of them* (out of them, or from among them), i. e. other ministers or members of the church at Antioch, one of whom is commonly supposed to have been Titus (see below, on v. 4.) *The Apostles*, who were probably always returning to Jerusalem, as Paul and Barnabas to Antioch, from their missions and official journeys, so that some were always present in the Holy City, thus preserving to the mother-church its representative and normal character, and giving it authority to act for the whole body. *Elders*, presbyters, or local officers of that church. (See above, on 11, 30. 14, 23.) *Question*, or *dispute*, a kindred form to that translated *disputation*, the Greek words differing only in the final syllable, one denoting the act, the other the subject, of contention.

3. And being brought on their way by the church, they passed through Phenice and Samaria, declaring the conversion of the Gentiles: and they caused great joy unto all the brethren.

And, or more exactly, *so then* (see above, on 1, 6. 18. 2, 41. 5, 41. 8, 4. 25. 9, 31. 11, 19. 12, 5. 13, 4. 14, 3.) *They being brought on their way*, or more exactly, *forwarded*, *sent forward*, i. e. publicly escorted to a certain distance and then formally dismissed or taken leave of. This ancient mark of kindness and respect was often practised by the early Christians. (See below, on 20, 38. 21, 5, and compare Rom. 15, 24. 1 Cor. 16, 6. 11. 2 Cor. 1, 16. Tit. 3, 13. 3 John 6.) It was not an act of private friendship merely, but performed *by the church* as a collective body, represented either by its elders, or by delegates appointed for the purpose, or more probably than either, by as many of its members as could be assembled. This method of dismissing them or parting from them, was a kind of additional commission, over and above the written one, with which they were of course provided. *Passed* (*went* or *came*) *through Phenice*, i. e. Phenicia (see above, on 11, 19. 12, 20) *and Samaria*, not the city but the province (see above, on 8, 5. 9. 14.) *Galilee*, which lay between these provinces, is here omitted (as it is above, in 1, 8); perhaps because it was not customary to distinguish it in such enumerations (but see above, on 9, 31); or perhaps because they went by sea from Tyre to Ptolemais or Cesarea, as in Paul's last visit to Jerusalem (see below, on 21, 2–8); or because they did not publish the conversion of the Gentiles there, the Galilean Christians being Jewish converts, which was not so in Phenicia, nor (strictly speaking) even in Samaria (see above, on 1, 8. 8, 1. 14, and compare John 4, 9.) *Declaring*, not in general terms merely, but relating fully, giving a particular account (compare the use of the same emphatic compound in 13, 41 above.) *Conversion*, turning, i. e. in this case, from the worship of idols, as well as from the service of Satan, to the true God (see above, on 14, 15, and below, on 26, 18.) *Caused*, literally, *made*, created, or occasioned. *All the brethren*, or disciples, i. e. Christian converts, in Phenicia and Samaria, who would naturally feel peculiar interest in the tidings thus announced to them, which no doubt reminded the Samaritan disciples of their own conversion and the joy which followed it. (See above, on 8, 8, and compare John 4, 39–42.)

4. And when they were come to Jerusalem, they were received of the church, and (of) the apostles and elders, and they declared all things that God had done with them.

Being come (or *having arrived.*) *They were received*, or more emphatically, *welcomed*, received gladly, as the same verb is translated in Luke 8, 40. *Of* (i. e. *by*) *the church*, the body of believers, not as individuals merely, but as a collective body (see above, on v. 3.) *The Apostles*, still residing there, at least as their headquarters (see above, on v. 2); or as some with less probability suppose, assembled to attend this meeting; while others gather from Gal. 2, 9, that the Apostles here meant are the three there named. It is commonly agreed now that the visit to Jerusalem referred to in that chapter of Galatians is the one recorded in the narrative before us, although some identify it with the one in 11, 30. 12, 25, some with that in 18, 22, and some with an additional journey not recorded in the history. It is objected to the first hypothesis that Paul speaks of having gone up "by revelation" (Gal. 2, 2), i. e. by express divine command, whereas Luke represents him as a delegate from Antioch. But the two things are perfectly compatible, as appears from a comparison of 13, 3. 4, where Barnabas and Saul are expressly said, in two successive verses, to have been sent both by the Church and by the Holy Ghost. In the present case, we may suppose the "revelation" to have been made, as in that case, to the "Prophets and Teachers in the Church at Antioch" (13, 1), directing them to act as they are said to have done in v. 2 above; or secretly to Paul himself, directing him to undertake the task imposed upon him by his brethren. It is on the supposition of the identity of these two journeys, that one of the "some others" who went up with Paul and Barnabas (v. 2) is commonly supposed to have been Titus (see Gal. 2, 1), who is nowhere named in Acts, if we except a spurious or doubtful reading in a single passage. (See below, on 18, 7.) The date of these transactions has been variously fixed from A. D. 47 to 52, but the best modern writers are in favour of the year 50, or at the latest the beginning of the next year. *The elders* may be here described as giving Paul and Barnabas a separate welcome or reception, as well as the Apostles; or both may be mentioned as the organs through which they were welcomed by the church. It would not be ungrammatical indeed, though not perhaps so natural, to construe the clause thus, 'they were welcomed by the church, *both* the apostles and the elders,' i. e. both these classes acting as the organs or channels of communication, between the church at Jerusalem and the deputies from Antioch. *Declarèd*, reported, brought back word, a different verb from that in v. 3, and expressing more distinctly the idea of official statement, as distinguished from popular narration. *All things*, literally, *how great* (or *how many*) *things;* see above, on 3, 24. 4, 34. 13, 48. *With them*, see above, on 14, 27.

5. But there rose up certain of the sect of the Pharisees which believed, saying, That it was needful to circumcise them, and to command (them) to keep the law of Moses.

This is not a part of their report, relating the same fact that is recorded in v. 1 above, which would require "saying" or "said they" to be prefixed (as in the Geneva Bible), but Luke's own statement of what happened at Jerusalem, after Paul and Barnabas had made their report. The only argument in favour of the first construction mentioned is that otherwise the reason of their coming is not given at all. The answer to this is, not that they probably did state it, though it is not here recorded, which supposes the main theme of their discourse to be omitted, but that it was really involved in their report of "what God had done with them" (v. 4), which of course included the immediate reception of the Gentiles without circumcision. This would at once raise the same question that had been discussed at Antioch, with or without a formal narrative of that discussion. *Rose up*, in Greek a double compound, meaning that they *rose up out of* something, probably their place in the assembly, or *rose up from among* the persons who composed it. This would not be a natural expression in the mouth of Paul or Barnabas, but is perfectly appropriate in Luke's own narrative, where the fact of a meeting is implied, if not expressed, in the preceding context. *Some of those from* (i. e. belonging to, or who had come out from) *the sect* (school or party), *of the Pharisees* (see above, on 5, 17. 34.) The form of expression implies that there were other converts from that sect, besides those who acted upon this occasion, and also accounts for the rise of such a doctrine, which might naturally spring from Pharisaic habits and associations, even in the case of such as *had believed*, i. e. in Jesus as the true Messiah. *It is necessary*, in the present tense (see above, on 1, 16. 21) *to circumcise them*, i. e. the Gentile converts, showing that their reception without circumcision had formed part of the preceding statement. The last clause is explanatory of the one before it; to circumcise them was in fact to require them to observe the whole law, of which circumcision was the distinctive badge and sacramental seal.

6. And the apostles and elders came together for to consider of this matter.

Came together is in Greek a passive form meaning *were collected* or *assembled.* (Then were convened the Apostles, &c.) That the Apostles did not undertake to settle the dispute alone, is a strong proof that the permanent organization of the church had already taken place, and that the system was in active operation. *The elders*, not the diocesan bishops of Judea, for as yet there were none; nor the pastors of Judea, or of a still wider region, for of this we have no intimation in the text or context; but the local rulers of the mother-church, acting in conjunction with the Apostles as representatives of the church at large. (*For to*, see above, on 5, 31.) *Consider of*, literally, *see about*, an expression common to both idioms. *This matter*, literally, *this word*, which may either mean *this doctrine*, as to the necessity of circumcision, or *this statement*, this report, of Paul and Barnabas. That it cannot simply mean *this thing*, without regard to word or speech at all, see above, on 5, 24. 8, 21. 10, 29.

7. And when there had been much disputing, Peter rose up, and said unto them, Men (and) brethren, ye know how that a good while ago God made choice among us, that the Gentiles by my mouth should hear the word of the gospel and believe.

And much discussion (see above, on v. 2) *having taken place, Peter standing up* (or *rising*, see above, on 1, 15) *said to them* (i. e. to the Apostles and the Elders, mentioned in the verse preceding), *Men* (and) *brethren* (see above, on 1, 16.) *Ye know* is very strong in the original, *Ye* (*yourselves*) *are* (*well*) *aware* (see above, on 10, 28.) *A good while ago*, literally, *from old* (or *ancient*) *days*, a strong but indefinite and relative expression, the precise extent of which must be determined by the context, and which here evidently means at the beginning of this work among the Gentiles, referring no doubt to his own vision at Joppa and his subsequent reception of Cornelius and his household into the Christian Church, without requiring circumcision or subjection to the law of Moses. *Among us*, literally, *in us*, which some regard as a Hebraism for *chose us*, the verb *choose* being followed in Hebrew by a preposition often rendered *in*. But although this idiom is sometimes copied in the Septuagint version, there is no other instance of it in the Greek of the New Testament, and the common version is no doubt correct. *Among us*, or according to some manuscripts, *among you*, i. e. the Apostles, whom, in either case, he may be considered as addressing. *Made choice*, or more exactly, *chose out*, selected for himself or for his own use (see above, on 1. 2. 24. 6, 5. 13, 17.) The verb may either govern *me* understood, or be understood to mean *chose this* (to wit, that) *by my mouth*, i. e. through my preaching and oral instruction. *The Gentiles*, literally, tho *nations*, see above, on 10, 45. 11, 1. 18. *Should hear*, in the original, *chose the Gentiles to hear. The word of the Gospel*, i. e. its utterance or proclamation, as a joyful message to mankind. *And believe*, in Jesus, admitting him to be the true Messiah, and trusting in him as the only Saviour. The fact which Peter here refers to, as familiar to his hearers, is not the general fact that Gentiles had already been converted and received into the church, but that it was through his agency, though known as the Apostle of the circumcision.

8. 9. And God, which knoweth the hearts, bare them witness, giving them the Holy Ghost, even as (he did) unto us; and put no difference between us and them, purifying their hearts by faith.

The heart-knowing God, or *God the heart-knower*, the same expression that is used above, in 1, 24. *Bare witness*, testified, *to them*, the Gentiles thus received into the Church. Peter's argument is here the same as in 10, 47. 11, 17, to wit, that all doubt was precluded by the act of God himself, who had decided the whole question by dealing with those Gentiles precisely as he did with the converted Jews, bestowing the same spiritual influence on both, and with the same moral effect. *Put* (or *made*) *no difference*, did not distinguish or discriminate, *between us* (as Jews) *and them* (as Gentiles.) *By faith*, not merely by the truth objectively considered, but by the belief of it, including personal acceptance of the Saviour, without which even the truth can have no sanctifying influence (see John 17, 17). Both these, i. e. sanctification and the faith from which it springs, are the fruits of that Spirit who was given equally to Jews and Gentiles.

10. Now therefore why tempt ye God, to put a yoke upon the neck of the disciples, which neither our fathers nor we were able to bear?

And now seems to be used both as a temporal and logical phrase. 'Such was the divine decision in the former case, *and now*, in the case before us, why &c.' (See above, on 3. 17. 7, 34. 10, 5. 13, 11.) *Tempt ye God*, i. e. put him to the proof, try his patience and forbearance, by requiring further evidence of what he has already made so plain. (See above, on 5. 9, and compare Ex. 17, 2. Deut. 6, 16. Isai. 7, 12. Mal. 3, 15. Matt. 4, 7. Luke 4, 12. 1 Cor. 10, 9.) When God had so explicitly declared that faith, with its effects, entitled men to be received into the church, it would be tempting him to look for other evidence or prescribe other terms of admission. Especially would this be so if the conditions thus insisted on were not only gratuitous but intrinsically onerous, and proved so by the experience of those who now wished to impose them, and of their predecessors. The intolerable yoke of which he speaks is not merely the complex requisitions of the ceremonial law; for these they and their fathers could and did bear, and were only too prone to increase the burden in the hope of being thereby saved. The yoke meant is the whole law, as distinguished from the Gospel, and of which the ceremonial system was a mere form or expression; the covenant of works as distinguished from the covenant of grace in the economy of man's salvation; the hope of deliverance by merit or obedience, as distinguished from deliverance by grace or favour. This had always been a yoke or burden, even to believers, who were now delivered from it by the change of dispensations, being taught to come at once to Christ without obstruction or delay, a privilege of which these Christian Pharisees were anxious to deprive the Gentiles.

11. But we believe that through the grace of the Lord Jesus Christ we shall be saved, even as they.

But, on the contrary, so far from hoping to be saved ourselves by that which we are asked to impose upon the Gentile converts. *Through the grace of the Lord Jesus Christ*, i. e. the divine mercy exercised through him alone, and here contrasted with the heavy yoke of legal, ceremonial bondage. *We* (the converted Jews) *believe* (i. e. confidently expect) *to be saved. Even as*, literally, *after* (or *according to*) *what manner* (see above, on 1, 11. 7, 28, where the same noun and pronoun are used, but without the preposition.) This phrase denotes exact resemblance, even in minute particulars. *They* is explained by some to mean the gentile converts, by others the fathers, both which classes are referred to in the verse preceding. Both constructions are grammatical, and each affords a good sense in itself and in relation to the context. According to the first, the meaning is, we ought to lay no unnecessary yoke upon them, for our own hope of salvation is the same with theirs. According to the other, it is, we ought not to lay upon the Gentiles the same yoke which our fathers found so useless, since they as well as we were obliged after all to be saved by grace. On the whole, the former explanation is more natural, and now commonly preferred. The reference of *we* and *they* to Peter and Paul or to Peter and James, Paul and Barnabas, respectively, is a forced construction needing no refutation.

12. Then all the multitude kept silence, and gave audience to Barnabas and Paul, declaring what miracles and wonders God had wrought among the Gentiles by them.

Then, and, or but. *All the multitude*, the whole mass, of those present, implying a much larger number than the Apostles and the Elders (v. 6), unless these were very numerous. (See below, on vs. 22. 23.) *Kept silence* is a single word in Greek, to which there is no exact equivalent in English. There was no continuation or renewal of the previous dispute, but silent attention to the statement made by Barnabas and Paul in confirmation of Peter's argument. *Gave audience*, literally, *heard* or *listened*. As Paul was not one of the twelve, but the Apostle of the Gentiles, his name stands naturally after that of Barnabas, by whom he was originally introduced and recommended to the brethren at Jerusalem. (See above, on 9, 27.) *Declaring*, see above, on 10, 8, and below, on 21, 19. *Miracles* (or rather *signs*) *and wonders* (see above, on 2, 43. 4, 30. 5, 12. 6, 8. 7, 36. 8, 13. 14, 31) is not a figure for extraordinary moral changes, such as conviction and conversion, which might be described as "miracles of grace;" but literal miracles, attesting their divine legation and the authority by which they received Gentile converts and organized Gentile churches.

13. And after they had held their peace, James answered, saying, Men (and) brethren, hearken unto me:

Held their peace, were silent, ceased; the same verb that is used in the preceding verse. *Answered*, not merely *spoke* (see above, on 3, 12. 5, 8. 10, 46), but *responded* to what Peter,

Paul and Barnabas had just said; or replied to the question which had brought them together. *James* is supposed by many to be "James the brother of the Lord" (Gal. 1, 19), not one of the twelve, but an unbeliever (John 7, 5), till convinced by Christ's appearing to him after his resurrection (1 Cor. 15, 7), surnamed the Just, and put to death by the Jews soon after the close of the New Testament history. There is however a strong presumption that the person holding so distinguished a position in the church at Jerusalem, while the Apostles still survived, was himself one of their number; and as James the son of Alpheus was probably a cousin of our Saviour (see above, on 1, 13), he might be called his brother (Gal. 1, 19) in strict accordance with biblical and oriental usage. (See Gen. 14, 16. 29, 12. 15. Rom. 1, 13. 9, 3. 1 Cor. 1, 1.) It is very possible that James resided in Jerusalem more constantly than any other of the twelve, and had special charge of the church there, not however as an ordinary pastor, much less as a diocesan bishop, but as a resident Apostle. (See above, on 12, 17, and below, on 21, 18.) *Hearken unto me*, or simply *hear me*, i. e. me too, or me also; hear what I, as well as they who have already spoken, have to say upon the subject. This request is very far from favouring the notion that James spoke with superior authority, or even as the president of the assembly.

14. 15. Simeon hath declared how God at the first did visit the Gentiles, to take out of them a people for his name. And to this agree the words of the prophets; as it is written:

Simeon, the Septuagint form of the Hebrew name, found also in 13, 1 above, and in Luke 2, 25. 34. 3, 30. Rev. 7, 7, and used by Peter himself in one of his epistles (2 Peter 1, 1.) The more usual form (*Simon*) is rather Greek than Hebrew; but both occur in Jewish books. Some have strangely supposed that James has reference here to the words of Simeon in Luke 2, 30–32. *At the first*, or simply *first*, i. e. before Paul and Barnabas had preached to the Gentiles, thus deciding the whole question in advance (see above, on vs. 7–9.) *Visited*, or viewed, surveyed, with a view to choosing (see above, on 6, 3. 7, 23.) *Gentiles*, nations (see above, on vs. 3. 7. 12. *A people*, chosen people, church (see above, on 13, 17. 24, 31.)

For his name, i. e. to be called his people, or perhaps, to be founded on his name, or in reliance on it (see above, on 2, 38. 4, 17. 18. 5, 28. 40.) *For his honour or glory* is not expressed though necessarily implied. The whole verse refers to the important fact, alleged by Peter, that this direct reception of the Gentiles was no new thing introduced by Paul and Barnabas, but practised long before by Peter, with express divine approval. The fact thus historically proved James now shows to have been no afterthought or departure from the purpose previously revealed, but a part of the divine plan from the beginning, as attested by the Prophets, the inspired writers of the Old Testament, and more particularly those who were commissioned to predict the advent of Messiah (see above, on 3, 21. 24. 7, 52. 10, 43. 13, 27.)

16. After this I will return, and will build again the tabernacle of David, which is fallen down; and I will build again the ruins thereof, and I will set it up.

These are not given as the words of more than one prophet, but as a specimen or single instance of the way in which the prophets, as a class, contemplate the vocation of the Gentiles. The quotation is made from the Septuagint version, even where it varies most from the original; not because the latter would not answer the Apostle's purpose, but because he no doubt spoke in Greek, and therefore used the current version, without regard to its inaccuracies, as they did not interfere with the design of his quotation. The original passage is Amos 9, 11. 12. *After these things*, although not a literal translation of the Hebrew, conveys the same essential meaning, that of mere posteriority or subsequence. *I will return* is neither in the Hebrew nor the Septuagint, but supplied by the Apostle, in perfect keeping with the sense of both, as an introductory suggestion that the prophecy is one of restoration and returning favour. Some, with less probability, regard it as a Hebrew idiom for *again* (I will again rebuild), which would be singularly out of place in a translation when it is not found in the original. (As to the idiom in question, see above, on 7, 42.) *Build again*, or *rebuild*, answering to one Greek word. *Tabernacle*, tent, not put for house or dwelling in general, but for the meanest and least durable of human habitations, contrasted with a royal palace, to denote the low condition to which David's family must be reduced before the prophecy could be fulfilled. The same change is elsewhere represented by a shoot springing from the root or stump of a prostrate tree (Isai. 11, 1.) The image here presented is not merely that of a tent, but of a fallen tent. *Ruins*, breaches, fragments, or remains. *Set it up* (or rather *upright*) is again a single word in Greek and might be rendered, *re-erect.*

17. That the residue of men might seek after the Lord, and all the Gentiles, upon whom my name is called, saith the Lord, who doeth all these things.

The original is, *that they may inherit* (or *possess*) *the remnant of Edom and all the nations.* Edom is particularly named as a hereditary enemy of Israel, who had been subdued by David, but revolted under his successors. That it is merely used to represent the Gentiles, appears from the generic terms that follow. That the conquest here foretold is a spiritual one, is clear from the last clause, *upon whom my name is called*, which is often applied to Israel, as Jehovah's consecrated or peculiar people. (See Deut. 28, 9. 10. Isai. 63, 19. Jer. 7, 10. 11. 14, 9, and compare Deut. 12, 5. Jer. 15, 16. 33, 2.) The essential meaning of the passage, therefore, is that the restoration of the kingdom of David was to be connected with the spiritual conquest of the Gentiles; and as such a subjugation is not merely passive, but involves the act of seeking after God, it is expressed sufficiently though not exactly in the Septuagint version here adopted. *All these things* is merely an amplification of the original expression (*this.*) *All*, however, is omitted in the oldest manuscripts and versions.

18. Known unto God are all his works from the beginning of the world.

According to the received text, here translated, this verse expresses still more strongly and directly than v. 15, the important fact that the reception of the Gentiles into the church was no afterthought or innovation, but a part of the divine plan from the beginning. But as the greater part of this verse is very variously given in the manuscripts, and wholly wanting in several of the oldest, the modern critics have expunged it, leaving only the words, *known from the beginning*, which must then be read as the concluding words of the preceding sentence, *saith the Lord, the* (*one*) *doing these things* (which are or have been) *known from the beginning.* This is then a supplementary or exegetical clause added by the Apostle to the passage quoted, and perhaps on that account converted by transcribers into an independent proposition. *Beginning of the world* is a single word in Greek, the same that is used in 3, 25, and there explained as an indefinite or relative expression, sometimes denoting absolute eternity, sometimes endless existence, sometimes a particular period, age, or dispensation. Hence some would make it here equivalent to Peter's phrase (*from ancient days*) in v. 7 above, i. e. from the first promulgation of the Gospel to the Gentiles. But there seems to be no sufficient reason, even if the shorter reading is adopted, for diluting or extenuating this expression, as its strongest sense is equally appropriate and far more striking. *Thus saith the Lord who doeth these things, known* (to himself as part of his own plan or purpose) *from eternity.* Or the verb and adjective may be connected, as in 7, 19, *making these things known from the beginning* of the world, or of the old dispensation, or of the prophetic ministry (see above, on 3, 21, and compare Luke 1, 70.)

19. Wherefore my sentence is, that we trouble not them, which from among the Gentiles are turned to God:

Wherefore, because this mode of dealing with the Gentiles has been fully sanctioned by divine authority, and long ago predicted by the prophets. *My sentence is*, literally, *I judge* (as in the Rhemish version ; Wiclif has, *I deem*), a common formula, by which the members of the Greek assemblies introduced the expression of their individual opinion, as appears from its repeated occurrence in Thucydides, with which may be compared the corresponding Latin phrase (*sic censeo*) of frequent use in Cicero's orations. That James here settles the whole question by a decision *ex cathedra*, is as groundless an opinion as that Peter had already done so by his *dictum*. There is no trace in the narrative of any such superiority on either side. The whole proceeding is analogous to that which continually takes place in our own church-courts, when the roll is called to give the members present an opportunity of stating their judgment upon some important question. Even in Tyndale's version, copied by King James's Bible, *sentence* no doubt means opinion (*sententia*) not a final decision. *That we trouble not*, literally, *not to trouble*, or more emphatically, not to trouble in addition, i. e. besides (or over and above) the indispensable conditions of salvation, by imposing a gratuitous and supererogatory burden of mere ritual observance. (The same emphatic compound is used in the Septuagint version of Job 16, 3 Micah 6, 3.) *Those from the Gentiles* (literally, *nations*) *turning unto God*, i. e. from false gods to the true God (see above, on 14, 15.)

20. But that we write unto them, that they abstain from pollutions of idols, and (from) fornication, and (from) things strangled, and (from) blood.

But to charge them, in writing or by letters, as the verb (from which *epistle* comes) specifically means in later Greek. *To abstain*, or as the middle voice emphatically means, *withhold themselves*, implying self-control and some restriction of their Christian liberty. *Pollutions* is in Greek an abstract form, found nowhere else either in classical or hellenistic usage, and derived from a verb found only in the Septuagint version of Dan. 1, 8. Mal. 1, 7. 12, and in a single text of the Apocrypha. Some construe it with all the nouns that follow, *pollutions of idols, and of fornication*, &c. But this makes the first particular denote idolatry in general, from which it can hardly be supposed that Gentile converts needed any special exhortation to abstain, inasmuch as it was from this that they had just *turned to God*. It is therefore commonly agreed that by *pollutions of idols* the Apostle means participation in something that had been connected with idolatrous worship, especially the flesh remaining after sacrifice, on which the heathen used to feast, and the residue of which was often sold in the market. Now since the eating of such food, as Paul expressly teaches (1 Cor. 10, 19–33), was not sinful in itself, and yet to be avoided out of tenderness to those who thought it so, the abstinence here recommended must be understood in the same manner; not as an essential Christian duty, but as a concession to the consciences of others, i. e. of the Jewish converts, who still regarded such food as unlawful and abominable in the sight of God. It would seem to follow that the next particular must be explained in the same way, as relating not to an intrinsic evil (*malum per se*), but merely to what seemed to be so in the eyes of Jewish converts. This has led to various explanations of the Greek word, as a metaphorical description of idolatry itself as spiritual whoredom; or as meaning the licentiousness inseparably joined with certain forms of heathen worship; or concubinage, as substituted by them for marriage or connected with it; or marriage itself within the degrees forbidden by the law of Moses; besides many other still less obvious interpretations. But to all these it has been objected that the word occurs, not only in the speech of the Apostle James, but in the written formula to which it gave occasion (see below, on v. 29), and which was to be generally circulated in the Gentile churches (see below, on 16, 4.) The term must therefore be explained as they would naturally understand it, even without oral explanation, i. e. in the proper sense of fornication. This is indeed intrinsically evil, but it was not so regarded by the heathen, and the Gentile converts were in danger of at least appearing to retain this false view, and thereby offending the more scrupulous believers of the circumcision. James proposes, therefore, to enjoin upon them the most careful abstinence from every semblance of this sin, as well as from the more indifferent and in itself innoxious practice of eating flesh which had been sacrificed to idols. This combination of an essential with a ceremonial sin has led to much dispute respecting the two last particulars, or rather to the one which is expressed in two forms. *Strangled* i. e. killed without shedding the blood; so that this clause denotes flesh with the blood still in it, as the next does blood itself, either separate from the meat, or in a generic sense, including both. That *blood* here means *bloodshed*, i. e. homicide, is a notion which appears to be confined to one or two of the Fathers (such as Cyril and Cyprian); as the application of the ancient prohibitions to the use of flesh from the living animal appears to be peculiar to the Jewish Rabbins. The use of blood for food had been forbidden, not only in the law of Moses, but in the covenant with Noah, as being the vehicle or seat of life, which some regard as a physiological fact attested by divine authority, while others understand it as an arbitrary designation of the blood as the appointed representative of life *for sacrificial purposes*, without affirming or denying their physical relation in the animal economy. Connected with the first of these hypotheses is the belief, that the use of blood is here forbidden on the same ground with the practice of licentiousness, to wit, that both are necessary and intrinsic evils. In accordance with this view, the prohibition is enforced as a perpetual one by some of the ancient Fathers and Councils, and in the practice of the Greek Church to the present day. The Western Churches, both reformed and unreformed, adhere, with individual exceptions, to the doctrine of Augustin, that the prohibition was prudential and temporary, founded on no natural necessity or principle, the Old Testament restriction having ceased with the sacrificial services to which it had relation, and the one before us being merely an expedient for maintaining peace between converted Jews and Gentiles, during the anomalous and doubtful interval between the organization of the Christian Church and the outward as well as inward abrogation of the Jewish one. (See above, on 2, 46.) This is now commonly regarded as the import and design of all these prohibitions, which as being purely negative could not be regarded even as a temporary "yoke" imposed upon the Gentiles.

21. For Moses of old time hath in every city them that preach him, being read in the synagogues every sabbath day.

The sense of this verse by itself seems clear, but its connection with what goes before has been very variously understood. Some suppose it to assign a reason why it was not necessary to enjoin such abstinence upon the Jewish converts, namely, because they had the law of Moses to enforce it. But such a statement is entirely superfluous, as the point at issue had no reference at all to the converted Jews, except as being those for whose sake these restrictions were to be imposed upon the Gentiles. Another explanation is, that it contains a reason why the Jewish Christians need not fear that Moses would grow obsolete in consequence of this indulgence to the Gentiles, being still read every sabbath in the Christian synagogues or congregations. A third regards it as a reason why the Gentile Christians should not allow themselves, by any heathen usages, to fall behind their Jewish brethren, who were constantly preserved from such corruptions by the reading of the law in public worship. It cannot be denied that there is some obscurity in the connection, from the obvious suppression of an intermediate or connecting thought, which may be variously supplied; but on the whole, the simplest supposition seems to be, that the Apostle here assigns a reason why the Gentile converts ought to spare the feelings of their Jewish brethren, in this respect and for a time, to wit; that the continued reading of the Law, in services accessible to both, afforded some excuse for the remaining prepossessions of the one class, and at the same time left without excuse the disregard or violation of them by the other. As if he had said, 'these Gentile Christians know, by continually hearing the law read, to what the Jews have been accustomed, and have no right therefore to abuse their own exemption from its ceremonial precepts, by wounding the consciences of those who reckon some of these to be still binding.' *From ancient generations* is a much stronger expression than *from ancient days* in v. 7, and can hardly denote any thing, in this connection, but the immemorial use of the Hebrew scriptures in the Jewish worship; which again seems to determine that by *synagogue*, though in itself denoting any meeting or assembly (see above, on 6, 9. 13, 43), we are here to understand, as usual, the meetings of the Jews for public worship, not the separate assemblies of the Christians (compare James 2, 2), in which it could be scarcely said that Moses was *proclaimed* or *preached*, implying his continued recognition as a legislator and supreme authority. The reference to the synagogues at all is sufficiently explained by the fact so often mentioned or referred to, that they were frequented both by Gentiles and by Christians, who had therefore every opportunity of knowing what the Jews had been accustomed to believe and practise. So too the word *sabbath* does not mean the Lord's Day, or the first day of the week, which is not so called in the New Testament, nor by the oldest Christian writers, but the seventh day or Jewish sabbath, which is known to have been long observed by Christians in addition to the Lord's Day, a practice not entirely unconnected with the one just mentioned of attending at the Synagogue or Jewish worship, which was open constantly, if not exclusively, upon the last day of the week.

22. Then pleased it the apostles and elders, with the whole church, to send chosen men of their own company to Antioch with Paul and Barnabas, (namely), Judas surnamed Barsabas, and Silas, chief men among the brethren.

It pleased, or seemed good, and according to Greek usage still more strongly, was decided, or determined. Hence the derivative noun *dogma*, meaning that which is determined or decreed by competent authority (see below, on 16, 4. 17, 7.) This word, and not that *judge* used in v. 19, denotes the final decision of the question. James no more determined it than the mover of a judgment or a resolution in any deliberative or judicial body. *The Apostles and Elders*, not as independent bodies, nor as one body separate from the church itself, but acting in harmonious conjunction *with the whole church*, as there represented, not by human delegation but by divine appointment. *Having chosen men out of* (or *from among*) *themselves*, i. e. members of the mother-church and probably belonging to the number of its elders. *To Antioch*, as the secondary centre of the Gentile church (see above, on 14, 28.) *With Paul and Barnabas*, thereby confirming their authority and at the same time saving them from the suspicion of a partial or interested statement. *Chief* (literally *leading*) *men among the brethren* (Christians or believers in Jerusalem.) The restricted application of the term to ministers or elders may be true in point of fact, but is without foundation in the text or context. *Barsabas* was also the surname of the person mentioned in 1, 23, hence supposed by some to be his brother, and by some himself. *Silas*, the contracted form of *Silvanus*, (compare Lucas from Lucanus, Demas from Demetrius, Antipas from Antipater, &c.) the latter being always used in the epistles (1 Thess. 1, 1. 2 Th. 1, 1. 2 Cor. 1, 19. 1 Pet. 5, 12) and the former in the book before us (see below, on vs. 27. 32. 34. 40. 16, 19. 25. 29. 17, 4. 10. 14. 15. 18, 5.)

23. And they wrote (letters) by them after this manner: The apostles and elders and brethren (send) greeting unto the brethren which are of the Gentiles in Antioch and Syria and Cilicia—

Writing by the hand of them (or *by their hand*) does not mean employing them to write the letter, but sending it, when written, through their agency to Antioch (see above, on 2, 23. 5, 12. 7. 25. 35 11, 30. 14, 3.) *Writing* is there a compendious expression for sending a written message or a letter, as when we speak of one man's *writing to* another. *After this manner*, in Greek simply, *these* (*things.*) Some manuscripts omit *and the* in the superscription of the letter, so as to make it read, *the Apostles and Elders*, *brethren* (i. e. being brethren, or your brethren); but this is commonly regarded as an emendation of the text, perhaps intended to remove the appearance of co-operation on the part of the whole body of believers. *To the brethren* (fellow Christians, believers, or disciples) *those from* (out of, from among) *the Gentiles, those at Antioch, and* (in or throughout) *Syria and Cilicia.* Hence it appears that there were Gentile converts, and perhaps Christian churches, throughout both these regions, probably gathered by Paul on his return home after his conversion (see above, on 9, 30.) *Send greeting*, literally, *to rejoice*, i. e. tell them to rejoice, wish them joy, salute them. This was the usual salutatory formula in Greek epistles, and as such is used by Claudius Lysias in his letter to Felix (see below, on 23, 26.) The only other instance of its use in the New Testament is in the title or inscription of the Epistle of James, which has been regarded as an incidental proof that he wrote both epistles. That he wrote the one before us is highly probable, apart from this consideration, as it really embodies his proposal, which had been adopted by the whole assembly.

24. Forasmuch as we have heard, that certain which went out from us have troubled you with words, subverting your souls, saying, (Ye must) be circumcised, and keep the law; to whom we gave no (such) commandment—

Forasmuch as, whereas, since, referring to what follows, as *because* most generally does to something said before. Here, as in Luke 1, 1, it introduces a preamble or preliminary reason for their writing. *Certain*, i. e. some, indefinitely. *From us going out*, is usually taken in the literal or local sense, as meaning simply that they went from Judea or Jerusalem to Antioch (see above, on v. 1); or more emphatically, that they were members of the church there. A still stronger sense might be put upon the words, to wit, that they were clothed with a regular commission as religious teachers. But the strongest sense of all, and one directly opposite to this, is that suggested by the use of the same phrase elsewhere (see 1 John 2, 19) to signify desertion or apostasy. But the other seems more natural in this connection, and agrees better with the negative expression in the last clause. *Troubled*, disturbed, destroyed your peace, by insinuating doubts of your safety and acceptance in the sight of God. *With words*, i. e.

discourses, speeches, or perhaps with forms or modes of expression, which were new to them. *Subverting*, turning upside down, confounding, may be taken as a stronger synonyme of *troubling*, or in the more emphatic sense of *ruining*, destroying, by teaching a false method of salvation. The original meaning of the Greek verb is to pack up, then to carry off, used in a military sense by Xenophon to signify the spoliation of an enemy. *Saying ye must* (or *telling you to*) *be circumcised and keep* (observe, obey) *the law*, not the moral law, which is perpetually binding as a rule of duty, but the ceremonial system, or the whole law as a means of justification and salvation. (See above, on v. 10.) *Such*, in the last clause, is supplied by the translators, introducing a restriction which, although it may be true, is not expressed. The meaning may be a much wider one, 'we gave them no commission or authority to teach at all.'

25. 26. It seemed good unto us, being assembled with one accord, to send chosen men unto you with our beloved Barnabas and Paul, men that have hazarded their lives for the name of our Lord Jesus Christ.

It seemed good is the same verb that is rendered *pleased* in v. 22. *Being assembled with one accord*, or rather, *having become of one mind* (or unanimous), implying previous disagreement, not among the Apostles (see above, on vs. 14. 15), but among the brethren, and perhaps among the elders (see above, on 9, 26. 27.) Their being *assembled* is implied but not expressed either by the verb (which simply means *being* or *becoming*) or the adverb, which cannot mean *together* in the local sense, but by its very etymology denotes unity of mind or coincidence of judgment and of feeling. (See above, on 1, 14, 2, 1. 46. 4, 24. 5, 12. 7, 57. 8, 6. 12, 20.) *To send chosen men*, or more exactly, *having chosen men to send* (*them.*) *Chosen out*, selected for ourselves, as in v. 7 (see above, on 1, 2. 24. 6, 5. 13, 17), and therefore independently of Paul and Barnabas, who might have been accused of selecting the messengers themselves. *Our beloved*, not an empty compliment or ceremonious form of speech, but an important attestation of the light in which these two men were regarded by the Apostles and the brethren at Jerusalem, with whom their Judaizing adversaries may have represented them as being utterly at variance. But besides this general expression of regard and confidence, the letter indirectly sanctions their missionary labours by describing them as having *hazarded* (literally *given up*, exposed, or risked) *their lives*, not merely as a proof of courage, or without a moral and religious motive, but expressly and specifically, *for the name of our Lord Jesus Christ*, i. e. for all denoted by his names, in his service, in his cause, for his honour, as the Sovereign and the Saviour, the anointed Priest and Prophet of his people. (See above, on vs. 14. 17.) To have hazarded their lives in this cause was indeed an honour, which the church here recognizes as belonging to her two first foreign missionaries.

27. We have sent therefore Judas and Silas, who shall also tell (you) the same things by mouth.

Sent is not the same verb that is used in v. 25, but the one from which *Apostle* is derived, and a favourite of Luke's, though convertible and often interchanged with the other. (Compare 10, 5. 8. 21. 33. 11, 29. 30.) *Who shall also tell you*, or retaining more exactly the peculiar form of the original, *also themselves telling*, or reporting, carrying back word, in answer to the message sent from Antioch (v. 2.) The present participle represents the future scene at Antioch as actually passing (see above, on 7, 25), as the perfect tense at the beginning of the sentence represents the sending as already past. *Also*, and *the same* (*things*), are referred by some to Paul and Barnabas, by others to the letter, both which ideas are compatible and probably included. Judas and Silas were not only to confirm what Paul and Barnabas had said and done, but also to state orally, and no doubt with the necessary explanations, what was briefly recorded in the letter. *By mouth*, literally *by word*, through speech, or as the Latins phrased it *ore tenus*, *viva voce*.

28. For it seemed good to the Holy Ghost, and to us, to lay upon you no greater burden than these necessary things—

The preceding reference to the oral statements of the deputies accounts for the brief summary here given of the resolution which had been adopted. *It seemed good*, as in vs. 22. 25, denotes not mere opinion but authoritative judgment. *To the Holy Ghost and us*, as his accredited organs of communication. (See above, on 6, 11, and compare Ex. 14, 31. Judg. 7, 18. 20. 1 Sam. 12, 18.) Some refer the first words to a miraculous ratification of their judgment; others to the witness of the Spirit in the case of Cornelius (10, 44–46), and no doubt in others like it; but the natural and obvious construction is, that the Apostles, and those joining with them in this act, claim for their own decision a divine authority, as having been suggested or inspired by the Holy Ghost. Nothing can therefore be inferred from this phrase, with respect to the authority of Councils and their canons, except so far as they are known to be under the same guidance and control. *To lay* (put, place, or impose) *upon you no greater burden* (literally, *more weight*) *than* (save or except) *these necessary* (*things*), or retaining the original adverbial construction, *these* (*things*) *necessarily* (enjoined, exacted.) The necessity alleged is not, as some suppose, perpetual or absolute, but on the contrary, as indicated by the whole connection, and by all the circumstances of the case, provisional and temporary, so that the expression might be fairly paraphrased or amplified by saying, 'except these things, necessarily required by present exigencies, although in themselves, and at a future day, of no importance.' This must of course be qualified in reference to *fornication*, if that word be taken in its proper sense, in which case the necessity was temporary only with respect to the immediate reasons for peculiar circumspection in relation to that class of sins, to wit, the morbid and excessive jealousy of Jewish converts, as to Gentile liberty or license in such matters.

29. That ye abstain from meats offered to idols, and from blood, and from things strangled, and from fornication; from which if ye keep yourselves, ye shall do well. Fare ye well.

That ye abstain, literally, *to abstain* (see above, on v. 20.) *Meats offered to idols* corresponds to one Greek compound meaning *idol-sacrifices*, or as an adjective, *sacrificed to idols. Meats* is supplied by the translators, and no doubt correctly, both in the specific modern sense of *flesh*, and in the wider ancient sense of *food*, which was probably intended, but which really includes the other. This unambiguous expression must determine the more obscure one in v. 20 (*pollutions of idols.*) The only other difference between the verses is, that here the prohibitions which relate to food are put together, and that of fornication at the end, an improvement in the order which agrees exactly with the natural relation of an oral proposition as originally uttered, to the same idea afterwards reduced to writing; thus affording an unstudied but most interesting proof of authenticity and genuineness in the record. *From which* is by one distinguished writer understood to mean, *from which statements*, or *according to which rules*, *keeping yourselves*, i. e. acting circumspectly, *ye shall do well.* He objects to the usual and obvious construction (*keeping yourselves from which*, i. e. from these prohibited indulgences) as contrary to usage; but at least one clear example of the same verb (in its uncompounded form) followed by the same preposition in the same sense has been found in the New Testament.* *Ye shall* (or *will*) *do well*, in accordance with Greek usage, suggests three distinct ideas, all compatible and all appropriate in this connection. The first is, 'you will do right,' do your duty, act acceptably to God. The next is, 'you will do good,' do a favour to your brethren, by your tender care of their weak consciences. The third is, 'you will do well' for yourselves, promote your own best interest, or prosper. This last idea is repeated in the form of a concluding valediction. *Fare ye well*, literally, *be ye strong* (or healthy), corresponding to the Latin word (*valete*) used in the same way at the conclusion of a letter, a common expression in the classics, but confined in the New Testament to this place and the one before referred to. (See above, on v. 23, and below, on 23, 30.)

30. 31. So when they were dismissed, they came to Antioch; and when they had gathered the multitude together, they delivered the epistle, (which) when they had read, they rejoiced for the consolation.

So when, or rather *so then*, the resumptive or continuative phrase, of which Luke makes such frequent use. (See above, on v. 3, and compare 1, 6. 18. 2, 41. 5, 41. 8, 4. 25. 9, 31. 11,

* I pray not that thou shouldest take them out of the world, but that thou shouldest keep them from the evil (τηρήσῃς αὐτοὺς ἐκ τοῦ πονηροῦ). John 17, 15.

19. 12, 5. 13, 4.) *They having been dismissed*, allowed to go, or sent away (see above, on 3, 13. 4, 21. 23. 5, 40. 13, 3.) *Gathered together* answers to one compound Greek word meaning *collected*, assembled, or convened. *The multitude*, the whole mass or body of believers (see above, on 6, 12, and compare 2, 6. 4, 32. 5, 16. 6, 2. 5. 14, 41), called *the church* in 14, 27. The decision of the council being one in which all Christians were concerned, as well as one in which the whole mass of believers at Jerusalem had taken part, this public and promiscuous announcement was not only admissible but indispensable. *Delivered* and *read* belong to different subjects, the former to the messengers of the church in Jerusalem, the latter to the members of the church in Antioch. The meaning therefore is not, that they delivered the epistle by reading it, but that they delivered the epistle to the church (i. e. to the church-officers) who read it. *Which when they had read*, literally, *and having read* (*it*). The plural participle refers to *the multitude* as a collective, or to the church-officers who represented it; more probably the former, as it must have been the whole church that *rejoiced*, and not the elders merely. *Reading* has no doubt here its primary and proper sense of reading aloud. (See above, on v. 21, and compare 8, 28. 30. 32. 13, 27.) *For the consolation*, or as some prefer to render it, *the exhortation*. Both senses may be justified by usage (see above, on 4, 36. 9, 31. 13, 15); but the stronger sense of consolation seems to agree better with the effect described, as it was not the requisitions of the apostolical epistle that excited joy at Antioch, but the comforting assurance that their faith was not vain or their souls in jeopardy.

32. And Judas and Silas, being prophets also themselves, exhorted the brethren with many words, and confirmed (them.)

Prophets, inspired teachers (see above, on 11, 27. 13, 1.) *Also*, as well as leading men and delegates. *Themselves*, as well as Paul and Barnabas. *With many words*, literally, *through* (or by means of) *much speech* (word or discourse; see above, on v. 27.) *Exhorted*, the verb corresponding to the noun in v. 31, and including the ideas of exhortation and consolation (see above, on 11, 23.) *The brethren*, the disciples or believers, there called Christians (see above, on 11, 26.) *Confirmed*, strengthened, or established in the faith, by further instruction and animating exhortation. (See above, on 13, 43. 14, 22.)

33. And after they had tarried (there) a space, they were let go in peace from the brethren unto the apostles.

After they had tarried there a space, literally, *having made time*, i. e. passed or spent some time there. This use of the verb is rare, but found at least once in Demosthenes. *Let go*, dismissed, discharged, the same verb that occurs above in v. 30. *In peace*, or more exactly, *with peace*, i. e. with the usual benediction or good wishes, the most ancient form of which is probably the invocation of peace or prosperity upon the person thus saluted. (Compare the Latin *Pax vobiscum* with the Arabic *Salaam alaikum*, still the customary oriental salutation.) *The brethren* of the church at Antioch, as in v. 32. *To the apostles*, or as several of the oldest manuscripts and latest critics read, *to those who sent them.*

34. Notwithstanding it pleased Silas to abide there still.

Notwithstanding is in Greek the usual continuative particle (δέ) rendered *and* in the preceding verse. *It pleased*, or seemed best, as in vs. 22. 25. 28. *Abide there still*, stay on, remain over, as in 10, 48. This verse seems inconsistent with the one before it, where Silas and Judas are both said to have been sent back to Jerusalem. This seeming inconsistency may account for the omission of the whole verse in several of the oldest copies; but the latest critics rather suppose it to have been inserted in the others, to explain how Silas could be there to take the place of Barnabas, as Paul's companion in his second mission. (See below, on v. 40.) The communication seems, however, to have been so frequent (see above, on 11, 26. 30. 12, 25. 15, 2), that there is no improbability in supposing, either that Paul sent for Silas before setting out upon his second mission, or that Silas had returned to Antioch in the mean time.

35. Paul also and Barnabas continued in Antioch, teaching and preaching the word of the Lord, with many others also.

Continued, literally, *wore* or *spent* (time), see above, on 12, 19. 14, 3. 28. *Teaching and preaching*, either distinct official acts, the one more public than the other, or a twofold description of their ministry, both public and private, as didactic or instructive and yet cheering or encouraging. *Evangelizing the word of the Lord*, proclaiming it as good news or glad tidings (see above, on 5, 42. 8, 4. 12. 35 11, 20. 13, 32. 14, 7. 21.) *With many others also* (Gr. *also many others*), so that Antioch appears to have abounded more and more in "prophets and teachers" (see above, on 13, 1), probably because it had become a centre both of radiation and attraction, from which preachers were now sent forth in various directions, and to which there was a concourse of inquiring Gentiles, from the surrounding provinces, if not from distant countries. (See above, on 14, 28.)

36. And some days after, Paul said unto Barnabas, Let us go again and visit our brethren in every city where we have preached the word of the Lord, (and see) how they do.

Some days after, literally, *after some days*, an indefinite expression, which however seems more naturally to suggest a short time than a long one (see above, on 8, 36.) *Let us go again and visit*, literally, *returning let us visit* (or *look after;* see above, on 6, 3. 7, 23.) Between the participle and the verb in Greek there is a particle (δή), which might be rendered *now*, as it is a contraction of (ἤδη) *already*, but commonly employed to emphasize the word to which it is attached. (See above, on 13, 2, and compare Luke 2, 15. 1 Cor. 6, 20.) This proposition shows the same concern in Paul for the churches founded by himself that is displayed in his epistles and indeed occasioned them. *In every city* is in Greek still more expressive, as the preposition (κατά) corresponds not only to our *in*, but also to our *through*, *throughout*, *along*, and is also used distributively (see above, on vs. 21, 23. 2, 10, 46. 5, 15. 42. 8, 1. 3. 36. 9, 31. 42. 10, 37. 11, 1. 13, 1. 27. 14, 23.) *Where*, literally, *in which*, a plural form referring to the collective, *every city*. *We have preached*, or more exactly, *we preached*, i. e. upon our former mission. *Preached*, announced, proclaimed, declared, the same verb that is used in 4, 2. 13, 5. 38. *The word of the Lord*, the doctrine of Christ, i. e. the

Gospel. *How they do*, literally, *how they have* (themselves), i. e. how (or in what state) they are (see above, on 7, 1. 12, 15.) The words supplied in the translation (*and see*) give the sense, but not the syntax, as this last clause (*how they do*) must be grammatically construed with the verb *let us visit*, which includes, both in Greek and English, the idea of seeing, inquiring, or examining.

37. 38. And Barnabas determined to take with them John, whose surname was Mark. But Paul thought not good to take him with them, who departed from them from Pamphylia, and went not with them to the work.

Determined is too strong a version, even of the common text, which simply means that *he intended*, purposed, or that such was his design and plan; and still more of the reading given by the modern critics, *he desired* or *wished*. Some light is thrown upon this wish or purpose by Col. 4, 10, where we learn that Mark and Barnabas were cousins, either in the strict sense or the wide one common to both idioms. Tyndale's version (*sister's son*), retained in our Bible, is entirely too specific. The Rhemish (*cousin-german*) is better, and Wiclif's (*cousin*) better still. *Thought not good to take him*, or retaining the original construction, *thought good not to take him*. *Thought good* is a single word in Greek which strictly means *thought worthy* (as in Luke 7, 7. 2 Th. 1, 11. 1 Tim. 5, 17. Heb. 3, 3. 10, 29), but when absolutely used, *thought right* or *proper*. It sometimes means in classic Greek to *ask*, *demand*, but only as a matter of right, in which sense it is so translated by the Vulgate here (*rogabat*) and in 28, 22 below (*rogamus*), where it is copied by the English version (*we desire*.) If this sense be adopted in the case before us, the idea is, that Paul *demanded* or *insisted*, upon principle, or as a right, that John should not go with them. This differs only by suggesting the idea of oral expression, from the common version, *thought not good* or *right*. But it seems best to adhere to the common usage of the verb in the New Testament, and understand it as at least implying, that he did not think Mark *fit* or *worthy* to be taken with them. The ground of his objection is distinctly stated by referring to a fact recorded in its proper place (see above, on 13, 13.) *The work*, i. e. the missionary work in which they were engaged. Here, as in several other cases, the point of the sentence is impaired by a needless change of collocation. In the original the sentence closes, *not to take along with* (*them*) *this* (*man*), i. e. such a person, one who had thus acted. Paul's objection to so doing gathers strength if we suppose, as was before suggested (in the comment upon 13, 13), that Mark was guilty of resisting or refusing to acknowledge Paul's apostolical authority. There was thus a motive upon each side for the difference here recorded, the one being private or personal, the other public and official.

39. 40. And the contention was so sharp between them, that they departed asunder one from the other, and so Barnabas took Mark, and sailed unto Cyprus; and Paul chose Silas, and departed, being recommended by the brethren unto the grace of God.

And should be *therefore*, i. e. because they were divided in opinion upon this point. This English clause is not a version but a paraphrase of the original, which may be strictly rendered, *there was therefore* (or *arose*, began to be) *a paroxysm*, i. e. an excitement, elsewhere used in the good sense of incitement, provocation, to good works (Heb. 10, 24.) The idea of anger is suggested by the context, and confirmed by the usage of the verbal root (see below, on 17, 18, and compare 1 Cor. 13, 5.) It is not to be magnified, however, into any thing beyond a sudden and a temporary irritation (*sharpening*, as the Greek words primarily signify,) sufficient to account for the effect here mentioned, and, we may add, to carry out the divine purpose of multiplying labourers and even missions by a painful but momentary alienation between Paul and Barnabas. *Departed asunder* is in Greek a passive verb properly denoting violent division or forcible separation. (See above, on 1, 4, where an uncompounded form of the same verb is used.) It might here be rendered, *they were parted*, severed, sundered. *And so*, or rather *both* (τε), or on the one hand, placing this clause in antithesis to that which follows. *Took Mark*, taking Mark along, as he at first proposed and Paul refused to do. *Sailed out* (or *away*) *to Cyprus*, his own country, and perhaps that of his kinsman also. (See above, on 4, 36. 13, 4.) *Chose Silas* is a feeble although not an incorrect translation of a very expressive Greek verb, which denotes the act of choosing for himself in addition to (or in the place of) some one else, thus conveying the whole process of exchange and substitution by a single word. *Departed*, literally, *went forth* (compare 13, 4 above), it is not said how soon after the dispute, and therefore, if v. 34 be excluded from the text, it is not at all improbable that Silas was summoned from Jerusalem, no doubt with the consent of the church there as well as at Antioch, expressly to supply the place of Barnabas. *Being recommended*, literally, *given up* (as in 14, 26 above), which may include the idea of release from service there, as well as that of consignment to divine protection. *By the brethren*, as in v. 32 above. The inference usually drawn from the omission of any similar expression as to Barnabas and Mark, to wit, that their mission was without authority, divine or human, seems a little forced, since Luke is writing the history of Paul as the Apostle of the Gentiles, and had mentioned the dispute with Barnabas at all, only to account for the subsequent appearance of Silas as his substitute. It is equally admissible, and much more pleasant, to suppose that the "paroxysm," although directly caused by human frailty, was a providential means of sending out four men instead of two, on the same errand but in different directions, so as at the same time to avoid collision and enlarge the field of missionary labour. This hypothesis is favoured by the fact that it supposes the leader of each mission to have gone again to his own country (see above, on 13, 4. 13), and the two to have revisited, apart but simultaneously, the whole field of their first joint mission; whereas if Barnabas went forth without authority, Paul's proposal of a second visitation (see above, on v. 36) was not realized at all in relation to the island where he may be said to have achieved his first conquest, and indeed to have been first acknowledged as Apostle of the Gentiles (see above, on 13, 9.) This view of the matter also supersedes the disagreeable necessity of inquiring whether Paul was chargeable with undue rigour or Barnabas with nepotism, or both, or neither, all which alternatives have been maintained. The simplest and most satisfactory conclusion is, that the "paroxysm" here recorded was permitted to take place for the important reasons which have been suggested, and had no ulterior effects whatever on the mutual relations of the three men, whom we find in several of Paul's epistles reunited in the closest bonds of Christian friendship. (See 2 Cor. 9, 6. Col. 4, 10. 2 Tim. 4, 11. Philem. 24.) The same state of feeling is implied in

Gal. 2, 13, where Paul seems to express surprise that "even Barnabas," his old friend and associate, shared in that unhappy inconsistency of Peter, which by some is referred to the "certain days" of v. 36, though some put it later, and others think it could not possibly have happened after the decision of the council at Jerusalem.

41. And he went through Syria and Cilicia, confirming the churches.

He went through, i. e. Paul, as leader of the mission and Apostle of the Gentiles, Silas holding a subordinate position, because although a prophet (see above, on v. 32) not of Apostolic rank, and moreover just enlisted in the foreign service. *Syria and Cilicia*, the regions of which Antioch and Tarsus were the capitals, and to the Gentile converts of which the epistle from Jerusalem was formally addressed (see above, on v. 23.) This was the natural and necessary course to be pursued by one who went by land from Antioch into Asia Minor. The Gospel had most probably been first preached in Cilicia, and perhaps in the adjacent parts of Syria, by Paul himself, a few years after his conversion (see above, on v. 23, and on 9, 30); but churches may not have been organized till now, when the great Judaic controversy had been settled, and this organization may be here included under the term *confirming*, *establishing*, or at least connected with it, as it seems to be in 14. 22. 23.

CHAPTER XVI.

Continuing his second foreign mission, Paul revisits Derbe and Lystra, where he enlists Timothy in the service, after circumcising him (1-3.) They deliver the decrees of the council at Jerusalem in the towns through which they pass, and find the churches in a prosperous condition (4-5.) After visiting Phrygia and Galatia, and being excluded from other parts of Asia Minor, they arrive at Troas (6-8.) There a vision calls them into Macedonia (9-10.) Leaving Asia, they begin their European labours at Philippi, and a church is gathered in the house of Lydia (11–15.) A miracle performed by Paul occasions his arrest and imprisonment with Silas (16–24.) They prevent a suicide and baptize a household (25–34.) They assert their right as Roman citizens, and are honourably discharged and suffered to proceed upon their journey (35–40.)

1. Then came he to Derbe and Lystra; and, behold, a certain disciple was there, named Timotheus, the son of a certain woman which was a Jewess and believed; but his father (was) a Greek:

Then is the usual continuative particle, connecting this verse in the closest manner with what goes before, the division of the chapters being here mechanical. *Came down*, or down upon, a favourite verb of Luke's (see below, on 18, 19. 24.) The additional idea of return or coming back, which the word sometimes has in later Greek, would be appropriate here, but does not seem to belong to the New Testament dialect. *Derbe and Lystra* are named together as in 14, 6, but in the reverse order, as they were now approached from the opposite direction. Paul and Silas had probably come through the famous Cilician Gates, a pass in the Taurus range, leading from north to south, and eighty miles in length. *Behold* (or *lo*) usually introduces something unexpected, and may here imply that Timothy was not at home, though in a place where he was well known, as appears from the next verse. This may seem to favour the opinion that he was a native of Derbe (see below, on 20, 4), or of Antioch in Pisidia (see 2 Tim. 3, 11); but nothing can be certainly deduced from any of these texts as to that point. *There* no doubt refers to *Lystra*, as the nearest antecedent, and as named again in the next verse; or to *Derbe and Lystra* together, as being not far apart, or for some other reason spoken of as one place. *Disciple*, Christian, probably one of Paul's converts on his former visit (14, 7), and hence called his son or child (1 Cor. 4, 17. 1 Tim. 1, 2. 18. 2 Tim. 1, 2. 2. 1.) *Named* (literally, *by name*) *Timotheus*, sometimes written in our Bible with an English termination, *Timothy*. *Certain* before *woman* is omitted in the oldest manuscripts. *Son of a believing Jewish woman*, i. e. a Christian or converted Jewess. From 2 Tim. 1, 5, we learn that his mother's name was Eunice, and his grandmother's Lois, both eminent for faith, by whom he had been early made acquainted with the scriptures (2 Tim. 3, 14. 15.) This exclusive mention of his female relatives agrees exactly with the fact here stated that his father was a Greek, and as "*believing*" is not added, no doubt a heathen; as well as with the fact that he had not been circumcised. Intermarriage with the heathen was forbidden by the law (see Deut. 7, 4. Ezra 10, 2. 44. Neh. 13, 23); but some suppose a distinction between strange wives and strange husbands, founded on the cases of Esther and Drusilla (see below, on 24. 24.)

2. Which was well reported of by the brethren that were at Lystra and Iconium.

Well reported of, literally, *testified*, attested, testified to be (what is not expressed, but suggested by the context.) He had probably been labouring in these cities since Paul's former visit, either in a private way, or by express divine appointment (1 Tim. 1, 18), and ordination by the presbytery or elders of these churches (see above, on 14, 23, and compare 1 Tim. 4, 14. 2 Tim. 1, 6.) All this however may have happened after what is here recorded. *Iconium*, see above, on 14, 21. Besides this testimony from the church itself, Paul instructs Timothy himself to require that of those without (1 Tim. 3, 7.)

3. Him would Paul have to go forth with him, and took and circumcised him because of the Jews which were in those quarters; for they knew all that his father was a Greek.

Him (literally, *this one*) *Paul would have* (literally, *wished*, desired) *with him to go forth* (or *out*), i. e. upon this foreign mission, in the place of Mark, or as some say, of Titus, which supposes Paul's visit to Crete (Tit. 1, 1) to have been made just before; but this is mere conjecture on a point not here revealed or ascertainable. *And took* (literally, *taking*) seems to imply decision and authority, and also that he performed the rite himself, as it was not a sacerdotal act, but rather belonged to the father or his representative. It was not done as a necessary act, on Paul's part or on Timothy's, but *because of the Jews that were* (literally, *the ones being*) *in those quarters* (literally, *places*), i. e. Derbe, Lystra, and perhaps Iconium. *For they all knew his father*, *that he was a*

Greek (or Gentile), and therefore concluded that the son had not been circumcised. As one reason for selecting Timothy was no doubt his connection with both races, fitting him to be an instrument of good to both, Paul acted on the principle avowed in 1 Cor. 9, 22, and availed himself of the liberty enjoyed, as to ceremonial usages, during the interval between the advent and the downfall of Jerusalem. (See above, on 2, 46, and below, on 21, 23.) As this concession, though intended to conciliate the Jews, could scarcely have been misunderstood either by them or the Christian converts, it involves no sacrifice of principle, as the very same act would have done in the case of Titus, who seems to have had no connection with the Jews at all, and whose subjection to the rite would therefore have acknowledged the necessity of the legal ceremonies to salvation. (See above, on 15, 1, and compare Gal. 2, 3–5.) *Was a Greek* may mean *was* (*still*) *a Greek*, the original expression being not the mere verb of existence, but one sometimes denoting change of state and sometimes its continuance. (See above, on 2, 30. 3, 2. 6. 4, 34. 37. 5, 4. 7, 55. 8, 16. 10, 12. 14, 8.)

4. And as they went through the cities, they delivered them the decrees for to keep, that were ordained of the apostles and elders which were at Jerusalem.

Went (journeyed, travelled) *through the cities*, where Paul had preached before, Derbe and Lystra, Iconium and Antioch. *Decrees*, literally, *dogmas*, see above, on 15, 22. 25. 28. *Ordained*, decreed, decided. *The apostles and elders* of the church at Jerusalem, representing the whole body. (See above, on 15, 2.) These decrees, though temporary or provisional, were highly important to the present peace and unity of the church, and therefore perfectly consistent with the doctrine taught by Paul in his epistles (Rom. 14, 2. 17. 1 Cor. 8, 8. 10, 25. Tit. 1, 5.)

5. And so were the churches established in the faith, and increased in number daily.

So then, in consequence of this visitation (see above, on 15, 36, and compare, 14, 22), not merely by means of the decrees, the Greek connective (μὲν οὖν) commonly referring to a remoter antecedent. *Established*, settled, or confirmed, as opposed to doubt and vacillation. (Compare Eph. 4, 14.) *The faith*, not merely the doctrine of Christ, but their belief of it, and trust in him. *Increased*, abounded, were abundant. *Daily*, literally, *by day*, that is, *day by day*, the same expression that is used above in 2, 46. 47. 3, 2.

6. Now when they had gone throughout Phrygia and the region of Galatia, and were forbidden of the Holy Ghost to preach the word in Asia—

And having gone through Phrygia, a district of dubious or variable extent, in the interior of Asia Minor, divided at one time into two, and at another into three parts. It included not only Colosse, Hierapolis, and Laodicea, but according to the classical writers, Antioch in Pisidia. *The Galatian region*, elsewhere called *Galatia*, another inland district of the same peninsula, occupied by Gauls and Celts in the third century before Christ, and still retaining the language of those settlers six centuries later. The mixed population were called *Gallo-grecians*. To the churches of this province, probably founded by himself, Paul addressed one of his epistles. The phrase *Galatian region* may include more than Galatia proper. *Forbidden*, hindered, or prevented, either by express command or by insurmountable hinderances, most probably the former, as it is referred specifically to the Spirit. The omission of details in this account of Paul's visit to Galatia might lead to the conclusion that it was marked by no occurrences of interest; and yet to this date may be probably referred various facts mentioned in the epistle, showing a strong mutual attachment, and implying intimate acquaintance. The details are probably omitted here because no radiating centre was established, and the churches may have been in rural districts rather than in large towns, none of which are mentioned, either in Acts or in Galatians.

7. 8. After they were come to Mysia, they assayed to go into Bithynia, but the Spirit suffered them not; and they passing by Mysia came down to Troas.

Having come down to Mysia, the north-west province of Asia Minor. *Assayed*, endeavored, tried. As the Greek word is usually applied to moral trial or temptation, it may possibly imply that there was something presumptuous in this attempt.

(See above, on 15, 10.) *Bithynia*, a province on the northern coast of Asia Minor, to the east of Mysia. Here again they were forbidden by the *Spirit of Jesus*, a phrase occurring only here, but probably denoting the mission of the Spirit by the Son (see above, on 2, 33.) These prohibitions were no doubt intended gradually to disclose to them their mission or vocation to introduce the Gospel into Europe. *Passing by* may mean passing through without stopping, or at least without preaching, as they must have traversed Mysia to reach *Troas*, a seaport near the site of ancient Troy (see below, on 20, 5. 6, and compare 2 Cor. 2, 12. 2 Tim. 4, 13.) Here they were opposite to Greece and near it, so as to be ready to enter on their new field of missionary labour when commanded.

9. And a vision appeared to Paul in the night. There stood a man of Macedonia, and prayed him, saying, Come over into Macedonia, and help us.

The divine will is now more fully made known by a *vision* or preternatural appearance (see above, on 7, 31. 9, 10. 12. 10, 3. 17. 19. 11, 5. 12, 9.) *In* (through, during, in the course of) *the night*, perhaps the night of their arrival. *Appeared to Paul*, or *was seen by him*, as in 2, 3. 7, 2. 26. 30. 35. 9, 17. 13, 31. It is not said *in a dream*, which expression occurs only in the case of Joseph (Matt. 2, 13. 19. 22) and of Pilate's wife (Matt. 27, 19.) Some believe the supposition of a dream to be excluded here, as the lowest form or stage of divine communication, never used with the Apostles. *There was a certain man, a Macedonian, standing and beseeching;* but the latest editors omit *there was a certain*, and read simply, *a Macedonian man standing and beseeching*, or *exhorting*, as the same word often means (see above, on 2, 40. 11, 23. 15, 32), but the stronger sense is also fully justified by usage (see above, on 8, 31. 9, 38. 13, 42. 15, 32.) The essential idea, of which these are only modifications, is that of calling on (or to) a person, whether in the way of exhortation or entreaty. *Come over*, literally, *passing through* or *crossing over*, which some explain as implying difficulties or obstructions to be broken through, but which rather implies nearness and at the same time separation, both which ideas are appropriate to Paul's position at the moment, on the confines of Europe and Asia. There is no need of inquiring whether he was known to be a Macedonian by his dress, voice, or words; as the whole communication being preternatural might immediately suggest this fact without any reasoning at all. (See above, on 9, 12.) *Help us*, to be saved, or to obtain salvation. *Us*, the Macedonians, Greeks, or Europeans, as well as thy own countrymen of Asia Minor. Macedonia is thus specified, because it was the part of Europe nearest to the scene of this vision, and the part where his European work was to begin.

10. And after he had seen the vision, immediately we endeavoured to go into Macedonia, assuredly gathering that the Lord had called us for to preach the gospel unto them.

After he had seen, literally, *as* (or *when*) *he saw* (see above, on 1, 10.) *Immediately*, without any mention of his rising from sleep, as in the case of Joseph (Matt. 2, 14. 21.) *Endeavoured*, literally, *sought*, i. e. means or a conveyance. *To go*, or more exactly, *to go out* (or *forth*), implying a departure from their previous field of labour, and a migration into foreign parts. *Assuredly gathering* is in Greek one word, which we have already met with in the sense of *proving* (see above, on 9, 25), but which here seems to retain more of its primary or strict sense, that of combining, putting things together, in the way of argument, and as the ground of a conclusion. (Compare the similar expression in 4, 15 above, and Luke 2, 19.) In the present case, they may have reasoned by comparing this vision with the previous obstructions to their work in Asia (vs. 6. 7.) *Called us*, literally, *called to us*, or *called us to* (himself), as in 5, 40. 6, 2. 13, 7, but also used to signify a choice or designation of individuals, either to salvation (see above, on 2, 39), or to special service (see above, on 13, 2.) *To preach the gospel to them*, literally, *to evangelize them*, as in 8, 25. 40. 13, 32. Here, for the first time, the writer uses the first person (*we sought*), implying his own presence and participation in the facts recorded. Some explain this by supposing it to have been transferred from the narrative or journal of one who accompanied Paul from Troas to Philippi, where this form of expression is discontinued, but resumed again in 20, 5. To this ingenious combination it may be objected that so abrupt an introduction of another's language, without any intimation or change of form, is far less probable than an abrupt change in the author's own mode of expression, even if he had been present from the first. Still more natural is the supposition that the writer of the book joined Paul at Troas, perhaps as his physician (see Col. 4, 10), which agrees well with the supposition, that the infirmities of which Paul speaks in his epistles (see Gal. 4, 13. 14, and compare 2 Cor. 12, 7) arose from bodily disease, though some refer them to the cares and doubts occasioned by the interruption of his labours (see above, on vs. 6. 7), and others deny any direct reference to this part of his history. That Timothy is not the person here appearing for the first time, see below, on 20, 5. Had it been either Timothy or Silas, it would be wholly unaccountable that this form of expression should begin just here and not before, and also that the ancient and uniform tradition of the church, attested by such names as those of Clemens Alexandrinus, Irenæus, and Tertullian, should have dropped so eminent a name and substituted that of Luke, as the author both of this book and of the third gospel. That the use of the first person ceases at Philippi (see below, on v. 17), and is resumed there on a subsequent voyage (see below, on 20, 6), is a plausible reason for supposing that Luke remained there during that whole interval, or even that it was his place of residence. It is very possible, however, that he may have been in constant attendance upon Paul, but only wrote in the first person when he took part himself in that which he relates as a historian. Compare the similar interval between 21, 17 and 27, 1, during which we have no means of determining whether Luke was in Paul's company or separated from him. That he does not name himself, or explain how he happened to be present, is ascribed by some to modesty, by others to the fact that Theophilus, for whom he wrote in the first instance (see above, on 1, 1), was already acquainted with these circumstances. The suppression was altogether natural if Luke attended Paul as his physician, and not as an assistant in the missionary work, for which, however, then as now, his profession offered great advantages.

11. Therefore loosing from Troas, we came with a straight course to Samothracia, and the next (day) to Neapolis—

Therefore, in several of the oldest manuscripts, is simply *and* or *but*. *Loosing*, sailing, putting out to sea, the same term that is used in 13, 13, and there explained. According to some classical authorities, it originally means to loose the ropes. *Came with a straight course*, or more briefly and exactly, *ran straight*, i. e. sailed before the wind, without tacking, another nautical expression, implying that the wind was fair. This must have been from the south, to overcome the current which sets constantly in that direction from the Dardanelles. *Samothrace*, an island midway between Troas and Neapolis, called *Thracian Samos* to distinguish it from Samos on the coast of Lydia (see below, on 20, 15), and still known by the slightly altered name of Samotraki or Samandriki. It is the highest land in the northern Archipelago except Mount Athos, and was anciently renowned for the worship of Cybele and the mysteries of the Cabiri, forming a sort of link between Greek and Oriental heathenism. This historical association, with its local position between Europe and Asia, connects it, in an interesting manner, with Paul's transit from one to the other, though he seems not even to have landed there. *The next* (literally, *coming*, coming on, ensuing), an abbreviation of the phrase employed in 7, 26 above, and there explained. (See below, on 20, 15. 21, 18. 23, 11.) *Neapolis*, a maritime city, properly belonging to Thrace, but afterwards annexed by Vespasian to the Roman province of Macedonia. Its site, though doubtful, is supposed to be still marked by remains of Roman pavements, aqueducts and cisterns, at the Turkish village of Kavalla (or Cavallo.)

12. And from thence to Philippi, which is the chief city of that part of Macedonia, (and) a colony; and we were in that city abiding certain days.

The direct continuation of the sentence seems to show that they merely landed at Neapolis, without unnecessary stay, perhaps because there were no Jews there, but more probably because Paul was impatient to arrive at towns of primary importance, in which radiating centres of Christian influence might be established. Such a place was *Philippi*, anciently called Datos and Crenides (from its many springs), but afterwards named in honour of Philip of Macedon, by whom it was rebuilt and fortified. In the year 42 before the Christian era, it was the scene of the great battle, which decided the fate of the Roman republic, and in which Brutus and Cassius were defeated by Octavian and Anthony. In commemoration of this victory, and also as a safeguard of the empire, Augustus afterwards established there a colony, i. e. a military settlement chiefly composed of soldiers who had been partisans of Anthony. These Roman colonies were organized precisely on the model of the great metropolis, as to government, laws, language, and external forms, so that each exhibited a Rome in miniature. To some were granted in addition the *jus italicum*, or the same exemption from all taxes on the land, which Julius Cæsar had extended to the whole of the Italian peninsula. Troas and Antioch in Pisidia were also colonies; but the fact is particularly mentioned here, because connected with occurrences which took place at Philippi. (See below, on vs. 37. 38.) Luke describes Philippi, not only by the Latin term *colonia* (as distinguished from the Greek ἀποικία, which coincides more nearly with our modern use of *colony*, as meaning any foreign settlement or emigration), but also as *the first* (or rather, *a first*) *city of that part* (literally, *the part*) *of Macedonia.* This description has been variously explained, some understanding *first* of rank or dignity, and others of local situation, i. e. the first to which Paul came, Neapolis being then regarded either as a Thracian (not a Macedonian) city, or as the landing-place or harbour of Philippi, to which it is nearer than Seleucia to Antioch (see above, on 13, 4) or Ostia to Rome, and not much further than Cenchrea from Corinth (see below, on 18, 18), or even than the Piraeus from Athens. The present tense (*which is* not *which was*) is urged in favour of the other explanation of *first*, as meaning first in rank or importance. It cannot, however, mean the capital of Macedonia, which was Thessalonica, and the word *part* or *portion* cannot naturally signify a province or division of the Roman Empire. It is true that the old kingdom of Philip and Alexander, when subdued by Paulus Æmilius, was divided into four provinces or districts; but the capitals of these have been preserved by Livy, and that of the most easterly was not Philippi but Amphipolis. (See below, on 17, 1.) Some connect *first* with *colony*, 'the first colony in that part of Macedonia,' either in point of time, or dignity, or local situation, i. e. the first colony to which they came. But this construction is forbidden by the collocation of the sentence, although not by the conjunction *and*, which is supplied in the translation. All these interpretations introduce the article before *first*, though found in no Greek manuscript, the only reading extant being simply (πρώτη πόλις) *a first city*, i. e. a city of the highest rank, as we might say *a first-class* (or *a first-rate*) *city*, not in reference to political arrangements, but to population, wealth, &c. The same epithet (*first*) is applied, on coins still extant, to Pergamus and Smyrna, as well as to Ephesus, which was the political capital of Asia Proper. (See below, on 18, 19. 19, 1.) The fact that there are no such coins belonging to Philippi, or to any city out of Asia Minor, only renders improbable the technical and formal, not the popular descriptive use of the expression in the case before us. We were in *that* (literally, *this*) *city*, *abiding* (literally, *spending;* see above, on 12, 19. 14, 3. 28. 15, 35) *certain* (i. e. *some*) *days*, an indefinite expression, but most readily suggesting the idea of a short time. (See above, on 9, 19. 10, 48. 15, 36, and compare 8, 36.)

13. And on the sabbath we went out of the city by a river side, where prayer was wont to be made; and we sat down, and spake unto the women which resorted (thither.)

On the sabbath, literally, *the day of the sabbaths*, the Aramaic form of the Hebrew word resembling a Greek plural, and being often so inflected, even when a single day is meant. (See above, on 13, 14.) *Out of the city*, or according to the oldest manuscripts, *out of the gate*. The Syriac version combines both readings (*out of the gate of the city*.) *By a river side*, literally, *along a river*, i. e. the small stream flowing near Philippi into the Strymon, which is several miles distant. *Where prayer was wont to be made*, i. e. by the Jews of Philippi, whose worship may have been excluded from the city by the strict laws or the prejudices of a Roman colony; or they may have been too few to have a synagogue, in which case it was usual to have a place of prayer, with or without a building, often without the walls, and where it could be so arranged, near water, probably on account of the ablutions which accompanied the Jewish worship. Thus Tertullian speaks in one place of the Jews as praying on every shore (*per omne litus*), and in another of their sea-shore prayers (*orationes litorales*.) From this usage the Hellenistic word for *prayer* (προσευχή) acquired a local sense, being sometimes synonymous with *synagogue*, and sometimes used to distinguish the minor places of worship which have just been mentioned. The Latin form (*proseucha*) is thus used by Juvenal. The Greek word is most commonly explained so here, *where there was wont to be a prayer-place* (or *house of prayer.*) But the very same phrase is employed by Philo in explaining what a *proseucha* was (viz. a place where prayer was wont to be made), which seems to determine the sense here, or rather to confirm the invariable usage of the word in the New Testament, where it occurs nearly forty times, and always in the sense of *prayer*. The verb occurs fifteen times, and always elsewhere in the sense of thinking or supposing. (See above, on 7, 25. 8, 20. 14, 19.) Adhering to this constant usage of both words in the New Testament, the simplest version is, *where prayer was supposed to be*, i. e. where the missionaries were informed that the Jews were accustomed to assemble, or still more probably, where they saw a company of women gathered, and themselves supposed that they were met for prayer. That this explanation is an ancient one, appears from the various reading found in several of the oldest manuscripts, *they supposed prayer to be*. But although this is the most natural interpretation, and the one most in accordance with New Testament usage, the modern interpreters are almost unanimous in preferring the secondary sense of the noun (*a place of prayer*) and the primary or classical usage of the verb (*was wont* or *was accustomed.*) The mention of women only has been variously explained, by supposing that the men were inattentive, or came later; or that there were no male Jews at Philippi; or that the men and women prayed apart, as they are separated in the synagogue. But here again, the simplest supposition, and the one most readily suggested by the text itself, is that Paul and his associates, seeing a company of women there upon the sabbath, supposed them to be met for prayer, although they may have been mistaken, which agrees well with the usage of the verb in this book (see above, on 7, 25. 8, 20. 14, 19, in all which cases it suggests the idea of a false impression or erroneous judgment.) On any supposition, it is worthy of remark with what fidelity Paul carried out his plan of addressing the Jews first, and through them gaining access to the Gentiles. (See above, on 13, 5. 14. 46. 14, 1.)

14. And a certain woman named Lydia, a seller

of purple, of the city of Thyatira, which worshipped God, heard (us); whose heart the Lord opened, that she attended unto the things which were spoken of Paul.

Lydia, or a *Lydian*, as the name originally means, and as some explain it here, because Thyatira was situated on the confines of Lydia and Mysia in Asia Minor; but *named a Lydian*, or *a Lydian by name*, would be a very unusual expression, and we know that *Lydia* was in common use among the Greeks and Romans as a proper name. It may indeed have been a surname, given to her as a Lydian by the strangers among whom she dwelt. Thyatira, between Pergamus and Sardis, was famous in the ancient world for its purple dye, and old inscriptions have been found there which originated with the Dyers (*Bapheis*) as a craft or a society. The purple colour, so extravagantly valued by the ancients, included many shades or tints, from rose-red to sea-green or blue. Lydia's occupation may have been the sale of the dye itself, procured from a shell-fish (*purpura murex*), but more probably was that of cloth or clothes dyed with it, an art expressly mentioned in the classics as practised by the Lydian women. She seems to have been temporarily residing at Philippi for this purpose, as Luke would scarcely have named Thyatira, merely as her birth-place, if it was not still her home. *Worshipping God*, i. e. the true God, a phrase constantly applied to Gentiles who had obtained some knowledge of the Scriptures by attendance on the Jewish worship (see above, on 13, 43. 50, and compare 10, 2. 7), whether proselytes, i. e. professed converts to Judaism, or not. The technical distinction between different kinds of proselytes is probably of later date. (See above, on 2, 10. 6, 5. 13, 43.) *Opened her heart* (i. e. disposed the understanding and affections) *to attend* (apply the mind, but often in the classics with the accessory notion of believing, giving credence) *to the* (things) *spoken of Paul* (not concerning or about him, as the phrase would mean in modern English, but by him), or the things which Paul spake.

15. And when she was baptized, and her household, she besought (us), saying, If ye have judged me to be faithful to the Lord, come into my house, and abide (there). And she constrained us.

When she was baptized, not necessarily at this first meeting, but rather, as this phrase would seem to intimate, after an interval. In the former case, the natural expression would have been, *she was baptized*, whereas the idea now suggested is, that the Lord opened her heart at once, and then when she was afterwards baptized, &c. *Her household*, lit. *house*, supposed by some to mean her family, by others her assistants in her business. Both being mere conjectures, and entirely compatible with one another, there is nothing in the text to decide the controverted question, whether children were baptized on this occasion. Both parties reason in a circle from foregone conclusions; one contending that as infants are incapable of faith, there either were none, or they were excluded from the ordinance; the other, that as households include children, we have no right to except them from the general statement. The real strength of the latter argument lies not in any one case, but in the repeated mention of whole houses as baptized. (See above, on 10, 2. 48. 11, 14, and below, on v. 33.) The whole dispute, however, rests on grounds entirely independent of these cases, and every reader will interpret these according to his views of those. He who believes in the perpetuity of he patriarchal covenant, with a change in the accompanying eal, will need no proof that children were baptized with their arents upon such occasions; whereas, he whose very definiion of the ordinance excludes children, will of course deny heir actual reception of it in all given cases. *She besought*, ntreated, or invited (see above, on 8, 31. 9, 38. 13, 42); *us* s supplied by the translators. *If ye have judged* is commonly xplained to mean, *since ye have done so*, i. e. by baptizing me see above, on 4, 9.) *Faithful to the Lord* (Jesus Christ), or ather a believer in him (see above, on v. 1, and on 10, 45.) *Entering into my house*, *stay* (or *lodge*) *there*, i. e. during heir visit to Philippi. *Abide*, at least in modern English, s too strong, as it suggests the idea of permanent residence. *onstrained*, or forced, i. e. by urgent importunity, as in uke 24, 29, and often in the classics. *Us*, i. e. Paul's whole ompany, including the historian.

16. And it came to pass, as we went to prayer, a ertain damsel possessed with a spirit of divination met s, which brought her masters much gain by soothayying.

It happened, at a time still later, as the words seem naturally to suggest, though some have strangely understood them to mean, on the same day, after baptizing Lydia and her household, but before they had gone into the proseucha. Still more improbable is it that he here goes back to relate what had happened on their way to the river-side. The natural impression made by the whole context is, that Paul and his company took up their residence at the house of Lydia, as requested by her, and there formed a church or congregation of disciples, and that on their way to worship upon some occasion not particularly specified, *it came to pass*, &c. *As we went*, literally, *we going*, a Greek verb not denoting simple entrance, but a walk or journey of some length (see above, on v. 7, and on 1, 10. 11. 25. 8, 26. 36. 39. 9, 3. 10, 20. 12, 17.) *A certain damsel*, girl, young woman, commonly applied to servants (see above, on 12, 13), and perhaps denoting here a slave. *Possessed with*, literally, having, or possessing. *A spirit of divination*, or as the margin reads, *of Python*. In the Greek mythology this was the name of a serpent which guarded an oracle on mount Parnassus and was slain by Apollo, thence called *Pythius*, as being himself the god of divination. That she was not, as some suppose, a mere ventriloquist or sheer impostor, nor a mere somnambulist or lunatic, but a demoniac (see above, on 5, 16), is clear from Paul's address to her (see below, on v. 18.) *Brought*, literally, yielded or afforded. *Masters*, joint-owners or employers, such partnerships in valuable slaves being not unusual in ancient times. *Soothsaying*, divining, telling fortunes, by the aid of the spirit which possessed her.

17. The same followed Paul and us, and cried, saying, These men are the servants of the most high God, which shew unto us the way of salvation.

The same, literally, *this* (woman), i. e. the one just described *Followed*, literally, *following down*, dogging or pursuing *Paul and us*, i. e. Silas, Timothy, and Luke, who therefore uses the first person. *Cried*, not once but often, as suggested by the form of the Greek verb and expressly stated in the next verse. *Shew*, literally, *tell*, declare, announce, proclaim (See above, on 4, 2. 13, 5. 38. 15, 36.) These expressions she had probably heard used by Paul and Silas in their preaching and now repeated, either without knowing what they meant or in a sort of scornful irony, or as an involuntary testimony to the truth, like that borne to the Sonship and Messiahship of Jesus by the demons whom he dispossessed. (See Mark 1, 8. 5, 7. Luke 4, 34. 8, 28.) There is no need, therefore, of supposing any particular motive on the woman's part, such as a desire to conciliate the strangers, or to increase her masters' profits, or her own fame as a prophetess. Some have even imagined that she was impelled by a desire of salvation, and that this was gratified. But see below, upon the next verse.

18. And this did she many days ; but Paul, being grieved, turned and said to the spirit, I command thee in the name of Jesus Christ to come out of her. And he came out the same hour.

Many days, literally, *for many days*, the omission of the preposition being allowed both by Greek and English usage. (See above, on 1, 3.) *Grieved*, or more exactly, *wearied*, worn out, out of patience, from the frequent repetition of the same annoyance (see above, on 4, 9.) The common version, borrowed from the Vulgate (*dolens*), seems to favour the idea, entertained by some, that Paul was not offended at her constant cries, but only *grieved* (Rhemish version, *sorry*) that she was under demoniacal possession, and therefore, instead of reproving her, expelled the demon. But this is equally intelligible on the supposition that, although he was displeased or vexed with her repeated outcries, he considered her responsibility as merged in that of the demon who controlled her actions, and whose testimony, even to the truth, especially when thus obtruded, Paul rejected, as more likely to impede than to advance his work, and no doubt with intentional conformity to Christ's example (Mark 1, 34.) *Turning*, i. e. towards the woman, who was following them through the street as usual. *To the spirit*, present in her and acting through her, a sufficient proof that, in the view of the Apostle, it was not a case of mere disease, somnambulism, or derangement, but of actual possession by a personal spirit (see above, on 5, 16.) *Command*, or order peremptorily, as an officer his soldiers (but see above, on 1. 4.) *In the name of Jesus Christ*, by his authority, and as his representative. *Come out of her*, withdraw the preternatural control now exercised, and cease to influence her as at present. *The same hour*, or as the same phrase is rendered elsewhere (Luke 2, 38), *that instant.* The word translated *hour* is more comprehensive than its English derivative, meaning properly a *season* (of the year) in classical usage, and in that of the New Testament sometimes a whole day (as in Matt. 14, 15. Mark 6, 35), sometimes any short time (as in John 5, 35. 2 Cor. 7, 8), sometimes any definite or set time, whether long or short (as in John 4, 21. Matt. 24, 42), but most frequently a definite division of the day, corresponding to our use of *hour*, though varying in length according to the season. All that is here intended is, that the miraculous effect, as usual, was instantaneous. (See above, on 3, 7. 5, 10. 9, 18. 34. 13, 11.)

19. And when her masters saw that the hope of their gains was gone, they caught Paul and Silas, and drew (them) into the market-place unto the rulers—

Her masters, owners, or employers (see above, on v. 16.) *Seeing*, by her silence, or the change in her demeanour at the moment; or perceiving afterwards, that her extraordinary gift was lost. *Gains*, in the plural, is derived from Tyndale and Cranmer, whereas the other old English versions give it more exactly in the singular. *The hope of their gain*, or *their hope of gain*, not only their actual immediate profit, but their prospect of it for the future, upon which they may have been depending for subsistence. *Was gone*, literally, *gone out*, with obvious allusion to the use of the same word in the preceding verse. The spirit went out, and their hope of gain went out with it. *Caught*, literally, *catching*, seizing, or arresting, as in 18, 17. 21, 30. 33, though the Greek verb does not always imply violence (see above, on 9, 27, and below, on 17, 19. 23, 19.) *Paul and Silas* are not put for the whole company, but specifically mentioned as the only two arrested, Timothy and Luke having probably attracted no attention, from their silence or their obvious subordination to the others. *Drew* is not so strong a word as that employed in 8, 3. 14, 19, being sometimes applied to the drawing of a sword (John 18, 10), or of a net (John 21, 6. 11), or of men by moral, spiritual influence (John 6, 44. 12, 32.) The *market-place*, *agora*, or *forum*, the chief place of concourse in an ancient city (compare Matt. 11, 16. 20, 3. 23, 7. Mark 6, 56. 7, 4), sometimes in the centre, sometimes just within the gate, where business was transacted, both commercial and judicial. *Rulers*, a generic term, denoting those who take the lead, especially in government, and rendered more specific in the next verse. (See above, on 3, 17. 4, 5. 8. 26. 7, 27. 35. 13, 27. 14, 5.)

20. And brought them to the magistrates, saying, These men, being Jews, do exceedingly trouble our city—

Brought (literally, *bringing*), i. e. formally presenting or arraigning, as distinguished from the violent, tumultuous drawing, which had just been mentioned. (For a very different use of the same verb as a nautical term, see below, on 27, 27.) *Magistrates*, literally, *generals*, or leaders of an army, but transferred in military governments or those of a military origin, to civil rulers of a certain rank. By the Greek historians of Rome, it is used as an equivalent to *Prætores*, a title which (as Cicero informs us) was affected by colonial and provincial rulers. Philippi, as a Roman colony (see above, on v. 12), was no doubt organized in imitation of the great metropolis, with its *Duumviri* or miniature Consuls, who are probably the persons here intended, not as a distinct class from the *rulers* of v. 19, but as a more exact specification of that vague description. They drew them to the forum, as the place where the magistrates or rulers usually sat, and actually brought them up before the Duumviri or Prætors whom they found there. The real ground of the original disturbance is entirely suppressed, and one of a more public nature substituted; just as Christ himself was condemned by the Sanhedrim as a blasphemer, and then accused by them to Pilate as a traitor and a rebel. (See Luke 22, 66–71. 23, 1. John 18, 19. 19, 12.) *Exceedingly trouble* is in Greek an emphatic compound, strictly meaning to *out-trouble*, or to *trouble out*, i. e. to drive out of the regular and normal state by stirring up disturbance. "*Being Jews* to begin with," as an English writer somewhat quaintly phrases it; but this agrees better with the English than the Greek collocation of the sentence, in which the phrase (*being Jews*) comes after the chief accusation. It is, however, no doubt introduced as an additional or aggravating circumstance, intended to excite the national antipathy of the Roman colonists. As if he had said, 'who, by the bye, are Jews, and therefore less excusable for this intrusion.'

21. And teach customs, which are not lawful for us to receive, neither to observe, being Romans.

This is not a new charge, but a mere specification of the one in the preceding verse, explaining how these Jews disturbed the city, namely, by attempting to introduce a new religion. *Teach* is precisely the same word that is translated *show* in v. 17, though really meaning in both cases to *announce, declare*, but not without an implication of requirement and authority, like that suggested by the word *proclaim*, from its habitual association with the acts of governments or rulers. *Customs*, or rather *institutions*, whether established by law or usage. See above, on 6, 14. 15, 1, where the term is applied, both in the singular and plural, to the Law of Moses. This is also the sense here, as the Philippian colonists had probably no notion of the difference between Jews and Christians. *Are not lawful* gives the sense but not the form of the original, in which the construction is impersonal, *it is not lawful*, or still more strictly, *possible*, but in a moral, not a physical sense, i. e. admissible, right, proper. The same form occurs above in 8, 37, and the participle in 2, 29. *To receive*, admit, or adopt in theory. *To observe* (literally, *do*) in practice. (For a similar combination of *work* and *counsel*, see above, on 5, 38.) *Being Romans*, an obvious antithesis to *being Jews* in the preceding verse, and intended as a double aggravation of the charge, that Jews should dare to force their own religion upon Romans. The appeal is rather to the pride of race or national connection than to the Roman laws, which allowed the exercise of different religions, but forbade conversions and innovations without public sanction and authority. Mæcenas is said to have advised Augustus to abide by the hereditary worship, and make others do the same, prohibiting all novelties, as tending necessarily to insubordination and confusion. It was this worldly policy, rather than any bigoted hostility, with which Christianity at first had to struggle in the Roman Empire.

22. And the multitude rose up together against them; and the magistrates rent off their clothes, and commanded to beat (them).

The appeal to the prejudices of the Roman population was successful. *The multitude*, crowd, mob, or rabble, as distinguished from the magistrates or rulers, before whom Paul and Silas were arraigned. *Rose up together*, not with one another merely, by a general and simultaneous movement, but with the accusers, in conjunction or in concert with them. The charges, prompted by the selfish wishes or resentments of the owners of the slave, were now effectually seconded by the excited passions of the populace. The first clause of this verse explains the second. It is plain that the rulers were unable or unwilling to resist the multitude, and therefore, it would seem, without even the form of a judicial process, hastened to inflict a painful and disgraceful punishment upon the strangers. *Rent off their clothes*, literally, *tore around* (or *from around*) *them the clothes*, not their own, as some imagine, which would be wholly out of character in Romans, but those of Paul and Silas. *Clothes*, not their outer garments merely, as the Greek word means when used distinctively (see above, on 7, 58. 9, 39. 12, 8. 14, 14), but their garments generally, as it was the custom to inflict this punishment upon the naked back and shoulders. *To beat them with rods*, as the original word, from its very etymology, specifically signifies. (The nearest equivalent in English is *to cane them.*) This is one of the three cases, to which Paul refers in 2 Cor. 11, 25; the other two are not on record. He also alludes to this disgraceful punishment in 1 Thess. 2, 2. As the magistrates commanded them to be beaten by others, some suppose them to have also torn off their clothes by proxy; but as this is not expressed, they may have performed that act themselves, in order to convince the mob of their zeal in executing its commands, and possibly by this unlawful violence to save the prisoners from something worse.

23. And when they had laid many stripes upon them, they cast (them) into prison, charging the jailer to keep them safely—

Having laid, imposed, inflicted, by the hands of their officers or others, whom they are said to have commanded in 22. *Many stripes*, strokes or blows, there being no such merciful restriction in the Roman practice, as in that of the Jews (2 Cor. 11, 24), or rather in the law of Moses (Deut. 25, 3.) *Cast* (or *threw*) *them* does not necessarily imply literal violence, but may simply mean *committed* them to prison. (See below, on 22, 4. 26, 10.) But considering the violent, tumultuary character of the whole proceeding, and the way in which the magistrates were evidently urged on by the people, the word may be strictly understood as denoting, not only the imprisonment of Paul and Silas, but the harshness with which it was effected, by the agents of the magistrates, if not by their own hands. This last, though not a necessary suppo sition, agrees well, not only with the view already taken of their motives, but with the words of the remaining clause, which seem more naturally to suggest the idea of personal or oral charge than that of a mere message or a written order The scene thus presented is a vivid one, but not without its parallels in real life; the magistrates, unable to resist the mob apparently complying with its wishes, but really providing for the safety of the victims, first by an unjust punishment, and then by false imprisonment, officiously demanding of the jailer more than usual fidelity and strictness in the execution of his trust; for these words cannot mean mere ordinary diligence or care, as appears from the whole connection, and especially from what is added in the following verse. *Safely*, surely, or infallibly. (See above, on 2, 36, and compare Mark 14, 44.)

24. Who, having received such a charge, thrust them into the inner prison, and made their feet fast ir the stocks.

The jailer (literally, prison-guard or keeper) is not her represented as exceeding his commission, and cruelly aggra vating the condition of his prisoners, as some suppose, by wanton and gratuitous severities, but simply as obeying th command of his superiors, which is therefore here repeat ed, or again referred to, as a sort of explanation or apo ogy for his proceedings. *Having received such a charge* (c peremptory order), what was there left but to obey it? C the sense may be otherwise expressed in this way: it was no from any cruelty or malice upon his part, but because he ha received such a special order that he did what follows. Tl slight but obvious suggestion of this extenuating circumstana may possibly be owing to the fact that when the history wa written this Philippian jailer was an eminent disciple. (S below, on vs. 33. 40.) *Thrust* is precisely the same verb the is translated *cast* in the preceding verse, and admits of th same wide or strict interpretation. *The inner prison* is b some understood to mean a subterranean dungeon; but th phrase necessarily expresses nothing more than greater di tance from the entrance, and as a consequence of this, mo security, not only from the chances of escape, but also fro the fury of the mob. *Made their feet fast*, literally, *safe*, secure, *in the stocks*, literally, *into* (i. e. by putting them into) *the wood*, log, or block, an instrument employed in ancient times, not only for safe-keeping, but for punishment, the limbs being stretched as well as fastened. This implement of torture (called in Latin *nervus*) was sometimes more and sometimes less complex in structure, which accounts for the various descriptions given by the ancient writers.

25. And at midnight Paul and Silas prayed, and sang praises unto God, and the prisoners heard them.

At, about, or towards. (See above, on 12, 1, and below, on 19, 23. 27, 27.) *Praying*, *hymned* (or *sang to*) *God*, seems to express, not two distinct acts, as in the English version, but the single act of lyrical worship, or praying (i. e. worshipping or calling upon God) by singing or chanting, perhaps one or more of the many passages in the Book of Psalms peculiarly adapted and intended for the use of prisoners and others under persecution. Or the reference may be to similar expressions of religious feeling, spontaneously suggested by their circumstances, or by a special divine influence, but not to metrical, much less to rhymed hymns, and to artificial melodies, with which we now associate the term, but which are usages of later date. This psalmody of Paul and Silas showed their confidence in God and their superiority to human spite and violence. The difference in this respect between their case and that of Peter, as described in 12, 6, shows that the one account has not, as some pretend, been copied from the other, but that each is independently authentic and original. That two such imprisonments and two such liberations should have taken place, is less improbable and strange, than that God should have thus interposed in one case only. *Heard them* should rather be *were listening to them*, the imperfect tense suggesting the idea of continued action. That Luke may have received an account of what took place in the prison from one of these ear-witnesses, is not impossible, though quite unnecessary to account for his minute description.

26. And suddenly there was a great earthquake, so that the foundations of the prison were shaken: and immediately all the doors were opened, and every one's bands were loosed.

There was (began to be, took place, or happened) *a great earthquake*, strictly a commotion, shaking, once translated *tempest* (Matt. 8, 24), but always elsewhere used in the specific sense of earthquake. *Immediately*, at once, simultaneously, and not successively, as when they were opened by the hands of men. *All the doors*, not only the external entrance, but the intermediate ones conducting to the "inner prison." (See above, on v. 24.) *Every one's*, in Greek a plural form, *of all*. *Bands*, i. e. fetters, chains, or other means used to confine the limbs. *Loosed*, relaxed, let go, also used as a nautical term (see below, on 27, 40), and in a metaphorical or moral sense (Eph. 6, 9. Heb. 13, 3.) Some understand it here as denoting mere relaxation or diminished pressure; but the context seems to indicate the stronger sense of total liberation from constraint (but see below, upon the next verse.)

27. And the keeper of the prison awaking out of his sleep, and seeing the prison doors open, he drew out his sword, and would have killed himself, supposing that the prisoners had been fled.

Becoming sleepless or *awake* (ἔξυπνος.) *Seeing*, either from the place where he was lying, or more probably, on rising and passing through the several wards or subdivisions of the prison, which he found all *open*, or more exactly *opened*, i. e. just opened, implying that they had been shut and locked as usual. (See above, on 7, 56.) *Having drawn a sword*, perhaps one that happened to be near him, but more probably the one which he habitually wore, it may be even in his sleep, or which he seized as soon as he awoke. There can be little doubt that the keeper of this prison in a military colony of Rome (see above, on v. 1) was himself a Roman soldier, or at least subjected to the Roman discipline. His very title (see above, on v. 23) seems indicative of military service. *Would have killed*, or more exactly, *was* (*just*) *about to kill*, or on the point of despatching (making away with) *himself*. (For the usage of the two verbs, see above, on 3, 3. 5, 35. 11, 28. 12, 6. 13, 34, and on 2, 23. 5, 33. 36. 7, 28. 9, 23. 24. 29. 10, 39. 12, 2. 13, 28.) Self-destruction was considered by the Romans as not only lawful, but a duty or a virtue under certain circumstances. Cato's suicide was celebrated as a heroic act, and by a singular historical coincidence, this very city of Philippi, or its neighbourhood, had been signalized, within a hundred years, not only by the great defeat of Brutus and Cassius (see above, on v. 1), but by the suicide of both, and by a sort of wholesale self-destruction on the part of their adherents who had been proscribed by Octavian and Anthony. There is something rather providential than fortuitous in this rescue of a virtual self-murderer on a spot which had been consecrated, as it were, to suicide by such examples. *Supposing the prisoners to have escaped*, and considering himself liable, according to the rigorous requirements of the Roman law or discipline, to suffer in their stead. This penalty, including the disgrace of having forfeited his trust, and literally slept upon his post, which could not have been justified to his superiors, or even to himself, by any allegation of a miracle, seemed worse, at least to the excited feelings of this heathen jailer, than any thing to be expected in a future state; a delusion which might seem incredible, but for the daily proofs of its existence in our own times, and amidst the clearest light of Christianity.

28. But Paul cried with a loud voice, saying, Do thyself no harm, for we are all here.

Cried, called, or as the verb itself originally means, raised his voice, which is then separately expressed, *with a loud* (literally, *a great*) *voice.* (See above, on 7, 57. 60. 8, 7. 14, 10.) *Harm*, literally *evil*, which may perhaps suggest the ideas both of bodily violence and moral wrong. As if he had said, 'Neither hurt thy body nor sin against thy soul.' *We are all here*, i. e. all the prisoners, not only Paul and Silas, but those who were confined before them, and who were described in v. 25 as listening to the prayers and praises of the two new comers. This seems to imply, that if not in the same apartment, i. e. the inner prison (see above, on v. 23), they were near at hand, and that Paul could therefore see them to be still there when he spoke; although he may, with equal probability, be understood as making this assertion on direct divine authority. The fact itself, that all the prisoners remained, without embracing the occasion of escape, is supposed by some to prove that their chains were only loosened, not entirely removed (see above, on v. 27), while others more correctly refer it to a special divine influence, or to the natural effect of certain physical phenomena, such as storms, eclipses, earthquakes and the like, in generating a religious awe, even where there is nothing properly miraculous. If prisoners, even in such cases, might forego the opportunity of liberation, how much more credible is such forbearance or neglect in this case, where the circumstances were so evidently preternatural, and where the supposition of a special divine influence upon their minds, although not requisite, is so admissible.

29. Then he called for a light, and sprang in, and came trembling, and fell down before Paul and Silas,

Having asked for (or *demanded*) is the active form of the verb used in 3, 2. 14. 7, 46. 9, 2. 12, 20. 13, 21. 28. *A light*, literally, *lights*, which may either be a generic plural simply equivalent in meaning to the singular, or really denote a plurality of lamps or torches, brought by different attendants and from different apartments of the prison. *Sprang in* is by some understood to mean that he *leaped down* into the subterranean dungeon, with which they identify the "inner prison" of v. 23. But it probably denotes nothing more than his abrupt and hurried entrance into the ward or cell where Paul and Silas were confined. *Came trembling* introduces an idea not expressed in the original, which strictly means, *becoming tremulous*, i. e. beginning to tremble, as a natural external sign of fear. The very same phrase is translated elsewhere by the one word *trembled*, and almost the same by *quake*. (See above, on 7, 32, and compare Heb. 12, 21.) *Fell down before*, in Greek a very strong expression, meaning *fell to* or *against*, conveying the idea of a passive or powerless rather than an active and deliberate prostration. It is usually rendered as it is here (see Luke 8, 28. 47. Mark, 3, 11. 5, 33), but once *fell at* (Mark 7, 25), once *fell down at* (Luke 3, 8), and once, in reference to a tempest, *beat upon* (Matt. 7, 25, the only place where it is not applied to persons.) It here expresses, in the strongest and most vivid form, the terror and despair of the awakened jailer, and the awe with which he looked upon the two men whom he had so recently committed to the closest and most rigorous confinement.

30. And brought them out, and said, Sirs, what must I do to be saved?

Brought out, literally, *leading forth* (or *forward*), not from the house into the street or open air, but from the "inner" to the "outer prison," which was no doubt a more spacious, light, and airy place. This was, therefore, of itself an act of deference, if not of kindness, which prepares the way for what subsequently passed between them. *Sirs* is not the word so rendered in 7, 26. 14, 15, and in many other places *Men*, which is its proper meaning (see above, on 1, 11. 16. 2, 14. 22. 29. 37. 3, 12. 5, 35. 7, 2. 13, 15. 26. 15, 7. 13), but the word translated *Masters* in vs. 16. 19, and used in Greek, as that word is in English, to express respect and courtesy, especially to strangers. *What must I do*, or retaining the original impersonal construction, *what is it necessary for me to do*, a stronger and more definite expression, though substantially equivalent to that used in 2, 37 (*what shall we do?*) and there explained. It is rendered still more pointed and explicit by the additional words, *that I may be saved?* This does not mean delivered from the wrath of his superiors, which he had not incurred, as the prisoners were all safe, and from which Paul and Silas could not be expected to protect him, or even to advise him how to save himself. Nor does it mean delivered from the anger of the gods, by whom these strangers seemed to be protected, and who might therefore be expected to avenge their wrongs. If this had been his meaning, it would have been otherwise expressed, and not in terms appropriated in this history and throughout the New Testament to the expression of a wholly different idea. Nor would the Apostles have replied to such a question as they did, unless we adopt the forced hypothesis, that he inquired in one sense and they answered in another. The only natural and satisfactory interpretation is the obvious and common one, that *saved* is here used in its highest and most comprehensive sense, that of deliverance from sin and ruin, guilt and punishment, the wrath of God and everlasting exclusion from his presence. The assertion that a heathen could not seek salvation in this sense, is an absurdity, refuted by the case of every Gentile convert; and that this person in particular had heard of the new doctrine, and had even heard it preached by Paul and Silas, is decidedly more probable than that he had not.

31–33. And they said, Believe on the Lord Jesus Christ, and thou shalt be saved, and thy house. And they spake unto him the word of the Lord, and to all that were in his house. And he took them the same hour of the night, and washed (their) stripes; and was baptized, he and all his, straightway.

This answer, though entirely different in form from that of Peter to the same inquiry on the day of Pentecost (see above, on 2, 38), is perfectly harmonious in substance, saving faith and evangelical repentance being inseparable in experience, and mutually implying one another. Baptism, although not included in Paul's answer, as it is in Peter's, was actually administered in either case. *Thou and thy house* (or *household*, see above, on v. 15), does not mean that they were to be saved by his faith, but by faith in the same Saviour. Before receiving them as converts or disciples, Paul and Silas now instructed them more fully in the doctrine of Christ, or *the word of the Lord* (see above, on 8, 25. 13, 48. 49. 15, 35. 36.) *Spake* (or *talked*) may here denote a more colloquial instruction than in other cases (see above, on vs. 6. 13. 14, and on 4, 1. 17. 31. 5, 20. 40. 6, 10. 8, 25. 9, 29. 10, 44. 11, 19. 20. 13, 42. 46. 14, 1. 9. 25); but the difference, if real, is suggested by the context. *All those*, or *all the* (*persons*) *being in his house* or dwelling, which may include his family and all dependent on him. *Taking them*, the same word that is used above in 15, 39, where it evidently means taking away as well as taking along or with one. As Barnabas there leaves the company of Paul and takes Mark with him, so here the jailer takes Paul and Silas from the society of their fellow-prisoners into that of his own household. *The same hour*, literally, *in that* (*very*) *hour*, late and unseasonable as it was (see above, on v. 18.) *Washed their stripes*, literally, *from the stripes*, i. e. from the blood or wounds occasioned by them. The Greek verb (λούω) usually means to bathe or wash the body, as another (νίπτω) does to wash the face, hands, or feet (see Matt. 6, 17. Mark 7, 3. John 13, 5); but the former does not necessarily imply a greater quantity of water, or require the supposition of a cistern or a swimming bath. Even granting Chrysostom's suggestion, therefore, that the washing was reciprocal, he cleansing them and they baptizing him, perhaps in the same water, nothing follows as to his immersion, since both ablutions may have been performed at the mouth of a deep well, or even with a bowl of water brought in for the purpose. Here again, the narrative proves nothing by itself, but will always be interpreted according to the previous conclusions of the reader.

He who regards immersion as the essence of the rite, will of course assume the one wherever the other is mentioned; he who does not will find it hard to believe that the jailer of Philippi and his household were immersed at midnight (*straightway*, on the spot, or at the moment, see above, on v. 26. 3, 7. 5, 10. 9, 18. 12, 33. 13, 11), either inside or outside of the prison. The same thing may be said, *mutandis mutatis*, of the phrase *all his.* He who considers infants as excluded from this ordinance by its very nature, will of course exclude them from the *all* here mentioned; he who regards them as entitled to it by the stipulations of a divine covenant will just as naturally give the word its widest application. What is most important is to settle this disputed question upon other grounds and higher principles, and then explain these historical details accordingly.

34. And when he had brought them into his house, he set meat before them, and rejoiced, believing in God with all his house.

Leading (or *having led*) *them up into his house*, which was probably above the prison, or perhaps the upper part of the same building. *He set meat before them* is in Greek *he set a table*, placed a table near (or by them), a natural expression in all languages for giving food, and more especially for furnishing a regular repast or meal. There is no need, therefore, of supposing an allusion to the moveable tables of the East, or of the Greeks and Romans in the age of the apostles. That this was a communion or a love-feast, although not a necessary supposition, agrees well with the customary combination, in the early church, of social intercourse and sacramental services. (See above, on 2, 42. 46.) *Rejoiced*, exulted, a peculiar Hellenistic verb, not found in classic Greek (see above, on 2, 26.) *With all his house*, in Greek an adverb, used to signify what men do with their whole families or households, not excepting children, whom none perhaps would here exclude, as they are capable of joy, if not of baptism. But their comprehension in the phrase here used requires still stronger proof that they are not so comprehended in the equally wide terms of vs. 31 and 32 above. That there were no children, may be easily assumed in one case, but is highly improbable in many. *Believing* (or more exactly, *having believed* or *trusted*) *in God*, i. e. in his mercy for salvation.

This may denote mere sequence or succession, that after his conversion he was joyful, but more probably assigns the cause or reason of his joy, to wit, that he had now believed. (See above, on 2, 41. 46. 8, 8. 13, 52. 15, 3.)

35. 36. And when it was day, the magistrates sent the serjeants, saying, Let those men go. And the keeper of the prison told this saying to Paul, The magistrates have sent to let you go; now therefore depart, and go in peace.

Day having come, begun, or dawned. *The magistrates*, commanders, duumviri, or prætors (see above, on vs. 20. 22.) *Serjeants*, literally, *rod-bearers*, the ministerial officers of the colonial rulers, corresponding to the lictors of the Roman consuls. (Wiclif translates it by the homely English *catch-poles.*) *Those men* is hardly a contemptuous expression, being the only one that could well have been used, if the magistrates, as seems most likely, did not know their names. *Let go*, release, dismiss, the proper term for a judicial discharge (see above, on 3, 13. 4, 21. 23. 5, 40), or any formal and official dismission (see above, on 13, 3. 15, 30. 33.) Whether this proceeding was intended by the rulers from the first, or occasioned by a change of mind on better information, or extorted by the earthquake and their superstitious fears, can only be determined by conjecture. *Told*, announced, reported, as in 4, 23. 5, 22. 25. 11, 13. 12, 14. 17. 15, 27. He would naturally look upon this order as a happy deliverance for his prisoners as well as for himself, and expected them no doubt to accept it thankfully, as an unexpected condescension on the part of his superiors. *Now therefore*, so then, or accordingly, since such an opportunity of quietly withdrawing is afforded you. *Depart*, literally, *going out*, not only from the jail but from the city. *Go*, go away, depart, or journey. *In peace* may mean the same as *with peace* in 15, 33, that is, with the blessing or good wishes of those left behind. But in this connection, it suggests the somewhat different though not incompatible idea of withdrawing quietly, without disturbance.

37. But Paul said unto them, They have beaten us openly uncondemned, being Romans, and have cast

(us) into prison; and now do they thrust us out privily? Nay verily, but let them come themselves and fetch us out.

Unto them, the messengers, who therefore seem to have been present when the jailer told their errand, unless we suppose that Paul's answer was communicated through him, which appears less probable. *They have beaten*, literally, *having flayed or skinned us*, a strong expression often used in the New Testament for the severest kind of scourging. (See above, on 5, 40, and below, on 22, 19.) This is the first aggravating circumstance of which Paul here complains. *Openly*, publicly, before the people (see above, on 5, 18, and below, on 18, 28. 20, 20.) This, as adding to the ignominy of their treatment, was a second aggravation. *Uncondemned* is a third, which does not mean that they were tried and found not guilty, but that they were not tried at all and could not therefore be condemned, a statement very similar to one of Cicero's, in charging Verres with a like violation of the rights of others. *Being Romans* (literally, *Roman men*) is the fourth and highest aggravation which he mentions of their false imprisonment, itself a gross injustice, if committed against any one, without authority of law, but fearfully enhanced in Roman eyes by its commission against Roman citizens. This does not mean natives or inhabitants of Rome, nor even of Italy, for Paul was neither. Nor does it mean merely subjects of the empire, for this was no distinction. But it means the honorary *civitas* or citizenship, granted as a special favour or reward to certain individuals or families, entitling them to many of the same immunities and positive advantages enjoyed by native Romans, and among the rest to absolute exemption from imprisonment and corporal punishment, except as the result of a judicial process. This sanctity of the person had become a part of their religion, and any violation of it was esteemed a sacrilege. The almost fanatical extreme to which this feeling had been carried is exemplified in Cicero's orations against Verres, one of whose offences was a violation of this privilege, which the orator describes as being known and reverenced not only throughout the empire but among barbarians, so that the simple words, "I am a Roman citizen," had hitherto sufficed as a protection anywhere. All this illustrates the effect produced by Paul's disclosure of his civic rights, as described in the next verse. But why was this disclosure not made sooner, so as to prevent both scourging and imprisonment? Some say, because he was not questioned and had no opportunity of putting in his claim; but we find him, on a subsequent occasion, urging it without challenge or interrogation (see below, on 22, 25.) Another explanation is that he was not heard in the tumult, or knew that he would not be heard and therefore remained silent. But it was in such critical emergencies that Cicero describes the three talismanic words (*Romanus civis sum*) as instantly disarming the most lawless violence; and these words, or their Greek equivalents, might certainly have reached some ears amidst the riot at Philippi. The only remaining supposition seems to be, that Paul intentionally suffered his own rights and person to be outraged, in order to secure a greater good than mere exemption from disgrace and suffering, not only by admonishing the magistrates to shun a repetition of their error, but by so departing from Philippi as to leave the infant church there under the protection of the laws and in possession of the popular respect. As to the origin of Paul's civic rights, we only know that he possessed them by hereditary right (see below, on 22, 29), not as a citizen of Tarsus, for although that city was a free one, i. e. allowed to govern itself, as a reward for public services, this did not protect Paul from the punishment of scourging on a subsequent occasion (compare 21, 39 with 22, 24), till he had besides declared himself a Roman by hereditary right (22, 29), i. e. most probably in recompense of services rendered by his father, or some other ancestor, to one or more of the contending parties in the civil wars. The same thing may have been true in the case of Silas, who had a Roman name (Silvanus) as well as Paul; but some suppose that he is here included in the general description, just as Barnabas and Paul are called Apostles (see above, on 14, 4. 14.) *And now*, after all this public injury and insult. *Do they thrust us* (literally, *cast us*) *out*, the converse of the term used in vs. 23. 24, and like it necessarily suggesting the idea of some force or violence, to wit, that of freeing them or sending them away against their will, at least in point of time and manner. The clause may also be affirmatively rendered, *they are thrusting us out* (or driving us away); but the interrogative construction has a stronger tone of indignation and expostulation. It also agrees better with the next clause, in which Paul seems to answer his own question. *Nay verily*, if closely rendered, would be *no, for*, an elliptical expression wholly foreign from our idiom, but which may thus be amplified, *no* (they shall not do so), for (we will not submit to it), *but let them come*, &c. The original construction of the last clause is, *coming let them fetch us out*, or lead us forth, another compound form of the verb used above in v. 30. Two things have always been admired in this verse; Paul's condensed and pointed statement of the case, in which it has been said that every word is full of meaning; and the moral courage, calm decision, and sound judgment, which he showed in the assertion of his legal rights, precisely when it was most likely to be useful to himself and others. This is enough to show how far he was from putting a fanatical or rigorous interpretation on our Saviour's principle of non-resistance (Matt. 5, 39. Luke 6, 29), which, like many other precepts in the same discourse, teaches what we should be willing to endure in an extreme case, but without abolishing our right and duty to determine when that case occurs. Thus Paul obeyed it, both in letter and in spirit, by submitting to maltreatment and by afterwards resenting it, as either of these courses seemed most likely to do good to men and honour to God.

38. 39. And the serjeants told these words unto the magistrates, and they feared, when they heard that they were Romans. And they came and besought them, and brought (them) out, and desired (them) to depart out of the city.

Told, the same verb that is elsewhere rendered *rehearsed* (14, 27), and *declared* (15, 4), but in all these cases has the more specific sense, *reported*, carried back, implying previous departure or communication. *Feared*, or adhering to the passive form of the original, *were frightened*, or *afraid*, which is itself a passive participle, although now used only as an adjective. *When they heard*, having heard, or hearing. *That they were*, literally, *that they are*, the present tense, in this as in many other cases, calling up the scene before the reader's mind as actually passing. (See above, on 7, 25.) *Came and* (literally, *coming*) *besought*, invited, or exhorted (see above, on vs. 9. 15); but the strongest sense is here the most appropriate. What they besought them to do is stated in the last clause. *And brought* (literally, bringing, or having brought) *them out*, i. e. out of the prison or the jailer's house, which were probably the same (see above, on v. 37.) *Desired*, literally, *asked*, inquired, but in Hellenistic Greek also meaning to ask a favour, or inquire whether one will do it, which agrees exactly with the usage of the corresponding word in English. (See above, on 3, 3. 10, 48.) *Depart out* is in Greek simply *go out*, as in v. 36 above. This was not intended as an insult, but as a precautionary measure to ensure their safety and the public peace.

40. And they went out of the prison, and entered into (the house of) Lydia: and when they had seen the brethren, they comforted them, and departed.

Even in complying with this natural request, Paul and Silas seem to have avoided all appearance of timidity or haste, for which indeed they had a double motive; first, to make such an impression of their own respectability and innocence, as might serve to neutralize their previous maltreatment, and prevent its repetition in the case of the disciples whom they left behind; and secondly, to part from these disciples in a suitable and edifying manner. This they did by deliberately going from the prison to the house of Lydia, where the church had been originally formed, and where it was accustomed to assemble (see above, on v. 16.) *And having seen the brethren*, no doubt gathered for the purpose, *they exhorted them*, the more specific sense of consolation being really included, *and departed*, went out, from Philippi. Such was the first organization of a Christian church in Europe, of which we have any authentic record, that of Rome resting merely on a vague tradition, though its date may certainly have been much earlier, as well as that of many others, founded by the foreign converts on the day of Pentecost, who afterwards returned to their respective homes. It is remarkable, however, that of such organizations there is no memorial in Scripture, while the narrative before us leaves the natural impression, that the one which it records, if not really the first in time, was designed to hold the first place in the memory of men, as the earliest fruits of Apostolical labour in the territory settled by the sons of Japhet. Another claim to this preeminence is founded on the singular affection which the great Apostle cherished towards this people, and which still appears as fresh as ever in his short epistle to the church of the Philippians, between which and the narrative before us there are many cross lights of reciprocal elucidation. A peculiar mark of his attachment was his breaking or suspending his own rule of self-support among the Gentiles, by accepting contributions from this church when he refused them from all others. (See Phil. 4, 10–16. 2 Cor. 11, 7–12.) As the subjects of the verbs in this verse, and the whole preceding context, must be Paul and Silas, they alone are here expressly said to have departed. This does not forbid the supposition that both Timothy and Luke went with them, and in 17, 14, we find the former with them at Berea; but the use of the first person, which is commonly regarded as the token of Luke's presence, does not reappear until the close of Paul's next European mission (see above, on v. 10, and below, on 20, 5.) This, although not conclusive evidence, creates a strong presumption that Paul left him at Philippi, either to attend to his own business, or more probably to nurse and train the infant church, which may have owed to him, as a chosen instrument in God's hand, that early advancement in the spiritual life which Paul so thankfully acknowledges long after. (See Phil. 1, 3–5.)

CHAPTER XVII.

THE account is still continued of Paul's apostolical and missionary labours in the two great provinces of Greece, Macedonia and Achaia. He passes through Amphipolis and Apollonia to Thessalonica (1.) He preaches there with great success (2–4.) The Jews raise a persecution (5–9.) The same things happen at Berea (10–13.) Paul, leaving Silas and Timothy behind, removes to Athens (14–15.) He preaches in the synagogue and in the market (16–18.) He is brought to the Areopagus and requested to gratify the curiosity of the Athenians (19–21.) Taking occasion from an altar to an unknown God, he teaches them that the Creator cannot be confined to temples or in need of human care (22–25.) He is himself the source of all existence, and the common father of all nations, whose history is ordered by his providence, with a view to his own glory (26–27.) As the father of the human race, he is dishonoured by the use of images to represent him (28–29.) This practice he has hitherto endured, but now forbids and will inexorably judge, through Christ whom he has raised from the dead (30–31.) At this point his audience refuse to hear him further, and he leaves them, but not without having gained some converts, two of whom are named (32–34.)

1. Now when they had passed through Amphipolis and Apollonia, they came to Thessalonica, where was a synagogue of the Jews.

The history of the Macedonian mission is continued without interruption. *Having made their way* (or *journeyed*) *through Amphipolis and Apollonia*, it would seem without stopping, probably because there were no Jews, or at least no synagogues, in those two cities. *Amphipolis*, an Athenian colony, famous in the history of Greece, almost surrounded by the river Strymon, a circumstance indicated by its name. It was above thirty miles west of Philippi; Apollonia as many miles still further west; Thessalonica about as far, still in the same direction. When Paulus Æmilius, the Roman conqueror of Macedonia, divided it into four provinces or districts, Amphipolis was the chief town of the first, and Thessalonica of the second. When all Greece was afterwards divided into two great provinces, Macedonia and Achaia, Thessalonica was the capital of the former. It was anciently called Thermae, but Cassander, who rebuilt and fortified it, named it in honour of his wife, the sister of Alexander the Great, who had herself been so named by her father Philip in commemoration of a great Thessalian victory. The fine situation of the town at the head of the Thermaic gulf, and on the great Egnatian road from Italy to Asia, gave it early importance, both commercial and political, which it has ever since retained; being still one of the most flourishing cities of the Turkish Empire, under the abbreviated name of Salonica or Saloniki. *A synagogue*, or more exactly, *the synagogue*, i. e. the well-known or famous synagogue; or still more probably, the only one to which they had yet come in Macedonia. The Jews appear to have been always numerous in this place, and at present constitute a large proportion of the population.

2. And Paul, as his manner was, went in unto them, and three sabbath days reasoned with them out of the Scriptures—

According to the custom (or *what was customary*) *to Paul, he went in*, &c. A similar practice of our Saviour is expressed in the same manner, Luke 4, 16. Paul was so far from having ceased his efforts to convert the Jews, that he still began with these wherever he went. (See above, on 13, 46.) This also afforded him the best means of access to serious and inquiring Gentiles. *Upon* (or *for*) *three sabbaths*, which implies a stay there of at least two weeks, but without forbidding the supposition of a much longer one, which some prefer, as more in keeping with the statements and allusions in the two epistles to the Thessalonians, presupposing a longer residence and a more intimate acquaintance with the people. Some, however, think a residence of two or three weeks quite sufficient to account for all that is there said; while others arbitrarily refer it to a later visit. *Reasoned*, or discoursed argumentatively, either in the way of dialogue, which is the primary meaning of the Greek verb (see above, on 1, 19. 2, 6. 8), or in that of formal and continuous discourse. *Out of* (or *from*) *the Scriptures*, as the source and starting-point of all his teachings. Some connect this with what follows, *out of the Scriptures opening*, &c. But although the division of the verses is without authority, it seems here to assume the true construction.

3. Opening and alleging, that Christ must needs have suffered, and risen again from the dead; and that this Jesus, whom I preach unto you, is Christ.

Opening, in Greek an emphatic compound, *opening out* or *through*, i. e. completely opening or explaining. The same word is elsewhere applied by Luke to the Scriptures themselves as the subject of instruction (Luke 24, 32), and also to the minds of those instructed (Luke 24, 45.) *Alleging*, or *propounding*, setting forth, as in Matt. 13, 24. 31. (For other senses of the same verb, see above, on 14, 23. 16, 34.) The distinction here is variously supposed to be that between particular and general instruction, or between synthetical and analytical ratiocination, but is more probably between elucidation or solution of difficulties, and the authoritative proposition of things to be believed. *It was necessary*, made so by the divine purpose as revealed in the Old Testament. *For the Christ* (the Messiah there predicted) *to suffer* (and especially to die, see above, on 1, 3) as a sacrifice for sin, a doctrine which the Jews had very commonly lost sight of. *And to rise from the dead*, as the appointed test of his divine legation, and a necessary proof that his great work was accomplished. *And that this* (suffering and rising Messiah foretold by the prophets) *is* (no other than) *the Jesus Christ whom I announce to you.* The usual construction (*this Jesus is the Christ*) is not so natural or easy; and the sense which it affords, though good, is less complete and less appropriate in this connection. We learn from this verse, that the two great doctrines preached by Paul at Thessalonica were those of a suffering Messiah and of his identity with Jesus of Nazareth.

4. And some of them believed, and consorted with Paul and Silas, and of the devout Greeks a great multitude, and of the chief women not a few.

The immediate success of his preaching appears to have been great. *Some of them*, i. e. of the Jews and Proselytes at Thessalonica. *Believed*, literally, *were persuaded* (or *convinced*) of the truth of Christianity. This inward conviction was followed by a corresponding outward profession or admission to the church. *Consorted with* (or more exactly, *were allotted to*) *Paul and Silas*, by divine grace, as their portion, or the fruit of their ministry. The effect thus produced upon the Jews extended also to the Proselytes, as the writer adds distinctly in the last clause. *And* (τε, as well as) *of the worshipping Greeks*, i. e. Gentiles (so called because Greek was now the general language) who worshipped in the synagogue, or worshipped the true God, whether professed converts to the Jewish faith or not. (See above, on 13, 43. 50. 16, 14.) *A great* (literally, *much*) *multitude*, an indefinite but strong expression, showing in a general but striking way the extent of the effect produced by the first preaching of the Gospel in the capital of Macedonia. *And* (τε, also, or as well as) *of the first women*, i. e. first in rank and social position. (See below, on v. 12, and above, on 13, 50.) The reference is still, as it would seem, to the Jewesses and female Proselytes, through whom, however, the Apostle, no doubt, obtained access to the Gentile population, out of which the church at Thessalonica seems to have been chiefly gathered. (See 1 Thess. 1, 9. 2, 14. 4, 5.) We have here indeed recorded only the beginning and the end of Paul's Thessalonian ministry. In his two epistles to the church there, we have a more particular account both of the method and the spirit of that ministry, as well as of Paul's self-denying labours to support himself and his companions. (See above, on 16, 40, and below, on 20, 34, and compare 1 Thess. 1, 5. 2, 1–11. 2 Thess. 3, 7–10.)

5. But the Jews which believed not, moved with envy, took unto them certain lewd fellows of the baser sort, and gathered a company, and set all the city on an uproar, and assaulted the house of Jason, and sought to bring them out to the people.

Unbelieving (and disobedient), see above, on 14, 2. *Moved with envy*, as in 7, 9, answers to a single word in Greek, and that an active participle, *envying* or *being jealous*, i. e. of the influence exerted by the strangers. (See above, on 5, 17. 13, 45.) *Taking to* (themselves), into their company and councils. *Certain fellows*, literally, *some men. Lewd*, or more generally, *wicked*, or as the word is sometimes used in such connections by the classical writers, *mean*, *low*, referring directly to their social standing, but by necessary implication to their moral character. This is perhaps the sense expressed by our version, *of the baser sort*, or this may correspond to another word in the original strictly meaning *of the market*, or belonging to the forum, but familiarly applied to idlers who frequented public places, without employment or respectability. Almost the same terms are combined by Aristophanes to describe a person of the same class in his own times. *Gathered a company*, or rather, *made a mob* (or *riot.*) *Set all the city on an uproar*, literally, *disturbed the city. Assaulted*, literally, standing over, coming suddenly upon, the actual attack being certainly implied, if not expressed. (See above, on 4, 1. 6, 12. 12, 7.) *Jason*, the Greek name borne by a Jewish resident, perhaps corresponding to the Hebrew *Joshua* (or *Jesus*, see above, on 7, 45.) It is here implied, and afterwards affirmed, that Paul was lodged or entertained by this man, possibly because he was of the same trade and could give him work, as Aquila did in Corinth. (See below, on 18, 3.) *To the people*, not the mob, but *into the assembly*, or the people in their corporate capacity, Thessalonica being a free city, like Tarsus, and not a Roman colony like Philippi. (See above, on 12, 22. 16, 1. 37.)

6. And when they found them not, they drew Ja-

son and certain brethren unto the rulers of the city, crying, These that have turned the world upside down are come hither also—

Not finding them, i. e. Paul and his companions, as in the preceding verse. *Drew*, violently dragged, the same verb that is used above in 8, 3. 14, 19. *Certain brethren*, some disciples or believers, converts to Christianity since Paul's arrival. *Rulers of the city*, in Greek one compound word, *Politarchs*, the proper designation of the elective magistrates of this free city, as distinguished from the Prætors or Duumviri (στράτηγοι) of a Roman colony. (See above, on 16, 20.) Luke's unstudied but exact precision in the use of these official titles has been justly urged as a strong incidental proof of authenticity. A further confirmation of his accuracy is afforded by an ancient arch still standing at Thessalonica, inscribed with the names of seven *Politarchs*, three of which, by a curious coincidence, are also the names of three Macedonians elsewhere mentioned as Paul's travelling companions, viz. Sopater, Gaius, and Secundus. (See below, on 20, 4.) *Crying*, shouting, or bellowing, a word suggestive of unusual excitement and confusion. *The world, the inhabited* (earth), the Roman empire. (See above, on 11, 28.) *Turned upside down*, elsewhere translated *made an uproar*, and *troubled*. (See below, on 21, 38, and compare Gal. 5, 12.) It is a verb belonging to the later Greek, and strictly meaning to produce a state of insurrection or rebellion, and therefore very nearly corresponding to *revolutionize* in modern English. The idea meant to be conveyed is evidently that of social disturbance and disorganization; but the figure of turning upside down is not in the original. (See below, on v. 30, where a similar but more objectionable liberty is taken by the common version.) *These also here are present*, implying that they had been often heard of elsewhere, which indeed is altogether natural, considering how long the Gospel had been preached, and the political tendencies with which it had been charged from the beginning. (See below, upon the next verse, and the passages there cited.) The Geneva version of this clause is, "these are they which have subverted the state of the world, and here they are!"

7. Whom Jason hath received; and these all do contrary to the decrees of Cesar, saying that there is another king, (one) Jesus.

Received under (his roof or his protection.) Compare the use of the same verb in Luke 10, 38. 19, 6. James 2, 25, in all which cases it is rendered by the simple verb *received*, although really expessing shelter and hospitable entertainment. *These all*, not merely Jason and his guests, but the whole sect or party which they represent. *Do*, act, practise, as distinguished from a single momentary action. *The decrees of Cæsar*, the laws or edicts (or in a wider sense, the sovereignty and government) of the Roman Emperors, who bore as an official title the name of their great predecessor, Julius Cæsar. It properly denoted one branch of the noble Julian race or family, but was adopted by Augustus and his successors, even after the race had ceased to reign, until Hadrian assigned it to the secondary emperor or heir-apparent, reserving that of Augustus for the actual sovereign. The particular violation of the imperial rights here charged was the proclamation of a rival sovereign. The word *king* (*rex*) was abjured by the Romans after the expulsion of the Tarquins, so that when monarchical institutions were restored with greater pomp and power than ever, the name assumed was really a military one (*imperator*, commander), although now considered higher than *king* itself. Had Luke been writing in Latin, the use of the word *king* would have been contrary to usage, and at least a pretext for some sceptical misgiving; but the Greek writers constantly applied the corresponding Greek word even to the Roman Emperors. The charge itself may be regarded either as a Jewish calumny, like that alleged against our Lord himself (Matt. 27, 11. 12. Mark 15, 2. 3. Luke 23, 2. John 18, 33–37. 19, 12), or as a misconception of Paul's Messianic doctrine, which appears to have been misapprehended even by the Thessalonian Christians. (See 1 Thess. 5, 1. 2 Thess. 2, 1.) *One*, supplied by the translators, makes the expression too contemptuous, implying that the name was never before heard there, which, however possible or even probable, is not suggested by the form of the original. (Wiclif's construction of the last clause is, *that Jesus is another king*.)

8. 9. And they troubled the people and the rulers of the city when they heard these things. And when they had taken security of Jason, and of the others, they let them go.

Troubled, disturbed in mind, as in 15, 24 above, a different verb from that in v. 6, which relates rather to external tumult and confusion. *The people*, populace, or mob, not the word so rendered in v. 5 above, and there explained. *Rulers of the city*, Politarchs, as in v. 6 above. *Hearing these things*, i. e. the charges first alleged against the Christians. *Having taken security*, literally *enough*, supposed to be a Latin law-phrase, the correlative of *satisdare*, to give bonds or security. *From Jason and the others* (or *the rest*), not Paul and his company, but the *certain brethren* mentioned in v. 6 above. *Let them go*, discharged them, a judicial term employed above in 16, 35. 36, and often elsewhere. The security was probably to keep the peace, or to abstain from every thing opposed to the imperial government, or possibly to send away the causes or occasions of this tumult, as they did.

10. And the brethren immediately sent away Paul and Silas by night unto Berea, who coming (thither) went into the synagogue of the Jews.

The brethren, disciples, Christians, acting in one body, as the same class had done long before, in a similar emergency, at Damascus and Jerusalem. (See above, on 9, 25. 30.) *Immediately*, no doubt upon the same day, or in the course of the ensuing night. *Sent away* (or out from Thessalonica) *both* (τε) *Paul and Silas*, i. e. not only Paul, whose safety was particularly cared for, but also Silas, who might perhaps have been expected to remain, as he did at the next place from which Paul was driven. (See below, on v. 14.) *Berea*, another town of Macedonia, southwest of Thessalônica. It is a curious coincidence that Cicero, in his oration against Piso, represents him as escaping from the same Thessalonica to the same Berea. *Coming thither*, being there, having got there or arrived. (See above, on 5, 21. 22. 25. 9, 26. 39. 10, 32. 33. 11, 23. 13, 14. 14, 27. 15, 4.) *Went*, or more exactly, *went away*, went out, perhaps because the synagogue was out of town, as at Philippi. (See above, on 16, 13.)

11. These were more noble than those in Thessalonica, in that they received the word with all readiness of mind, and searched the Scriptures daily, whether those things were so.

These, i. e. the Jews of Berea, whose synagogue had just been mentioned. Calvin, it is true, understands it of the higher ranks, or first families in Thessalonica (*the more noble of those in Thessalonica*), a construction which appears to be adopted also in the Vulgate, and by Luther; but with these exceptions, interpreters appear to be unanimous in understanding it as a comparison between the Thessalonian and Berean Jews, the latter being represented as *more noble* in a moral sense, i. e. more candid and impartial, just and devoted to the truth. *Received the word*, i. e. listened to the preaching of the Gospel. *Readiness of mind* (Wiclif, *desire;* Tyndale, *diligence of mind;* Geneva, *readiest affection;* Rhemish, *greediness.*) They were not only open to conviction, but predisposed in favour of the new religion. (*Day*) *by day*, a strengthened form of the expression used above, in 2, 46. 47. 3, 2. 5, 42, denoting not mere occasional but constant and assiduous investigation. *Searching*, the verb employed above in 4, 9. 12, 19, and properly denoting an official or judicial inquisition, thus suggesting the idea that they acted not as advocates or partisans, but judges, i. e. with unbiassed equanimity and conscientious love of truth. *These things*, i. e. the things taught by Paul and his companions, which had just been called *the word*. *Were so*, literally, *had* (themselves) *so* (see above, on 7, 1. 12, 15), i. e. as the Christian teachers represented.

12. Therefore many of them believed; also of honourable women which were Greeks, and of men, not a few.

Therefore, or rather, *so then* (see above, on 1, 18. 2, 41. 8, 4. 25. 9, 31. 11, 19. 12, 5. 13, 4. 14, 3. 15, 3. 30. 16, 5), as might have been expected from these predispositions. *Many of* (or *from among*) *them*, the Berean Jews who had been just described. *Believed* in Christ, were converted, became Christians. *And of the Grecian* (i. e. Gentile) *women*, *the respectable* (see above, on 13, 50.) The female converts were probably most numerous, and perhaps most distinguished, but *of men too* (there were also) *not a few*, i. e. there were many, as in v. 4, above.

13. But when the Jews of Thessalonica had know-

ledge that the word of God was preached of Paul at Berea, they came thither also, and stirred up the people.

Paul's labours at Berea were disturbed precisely as they had been at Lystra on his former mission. (See above, on 14, 19.) Both cases serve to show not only the inveterate hostility, but the intelligence and energy, of these dispersed Jews, who appear to have been well informed of what was passing even at a distance, and habitually ready for decided action. *Of* (literally, *from*) *Thessalonica*, i. e. belonging to that place (see above, on 10, 23. 38. 15, 5. 19), not simply coming from it upon this occasion, for their coming is recorded in the last clause. *The word of God*, the Gospel, as a special revelation. (See above, on 4, 31. 6, 2. 7. 8, 14. 11, 1. 12, 24. 13, 5. 7. 44.) *Preached*, declared, announced, proclaimed (see above, on v. 3, and on 4, 2. 13, 5. 38. 15, 36. 16, 7. 21) *of Paul*, i. e. by Paul. *Thither*, literally, *there*, which some construe with what follows, *there also stirring up the multitudes*, because it is to this act, and not to that of coming, that the *also* must apply. *Stirring up*, exciting, agitating, elsewhere spoken both of bodily and mental agitation. (See above, on 2, 25. 4, 31. 16, 26.)

14. And then immediately the brethren sent away Paul to go as it were to the sea; but Silas and Timotheus abode there still.

Immediately then, i. e. as soon as this commotion had begun. *The brethren*, as in v. 10, implying the formation of a Christian society or church here also, as the fruit of the Apostle's short and interrupted visit. *Sent away* is not the same verb that is used in v. 10, but a somewhat more expressive double compound, meaning they sent out and away (to a distance, as in 7, 12. 9, 30. 11, 22. 12, 11.) *To go*, go away, depart, travel, journey. (See above, on 16, 7. 16. 36.) *As it were* is in Greek a single word (ὡς) strictly meaning *as*, but often used by the best prose writers, with the preposition following it here (ὡς ἐπί), to signify the mere direction in which any thing or person moves, or at most the design to move in that direction. The full force of the phrase may be, to journey as (he must if he would get) to the sea. This idiom is so common in Thucydides, Polybius, and Xenophon, that it cannot be considered as implying an intention to elude pursuit, by seeming to go to the sea, but really journeying by land. That he actually went by sea, although not absolutely certain, is made highly probable, not only by its being easier and usually shorter than the land route, but also by Luke's silence as to any of the places through which he must have passed if he had gone by land. *Both* (τε) *Silas and Timothy*, not only Silas but Timothy, one of whom might have been expected to attend the Apostle. (See above, on v. 10.) *Abode*, not permanently, as the word in modern English usually means, but *remained*, continued, for a time, no doubt, according to Paul's constant practice, to watch and train the infant church there. It is very remarkable, considering the description above given (v. 11) of the class from which this church must have been chiefly formed, that it is never again mentioned, especially when such abundant evidence exists of Paul's solicitous regard for the Christians of Thessalonica and Philippi, in his three epistles to those churches still preserved in the New Testament canon. This silence has been variously explained, by supposing that although the word of God was preached in Berea (see above, on v. 13), no permanent society or church was formed there; or that it soon declined and died out; both of which hypotheses are far from having any antecedent probability.

15. And they that conducted Paul brought him unto Athens, and receiving a commandment unto Silas and Timotheus for to come to him with all speed, they departed.

Those conducting (or *escorting*) *Paul*, a different word from that in 15, 3, and descriptive of a different proceeding, not, as in that case, the affectionate and honorary act of accompanying one for a short distance and then taking leave of him, but the more substantial service of attending him throughout a journey, both for guidance and protection. The word here used means strictly, *putting* (or *setting*) *down*, as a deposit in a place of safety, and is stronger than the corresponding phrase in English, as specially applied to the conveying of a person in a carriage to his home, or any other point along the way, while the carriage proceeds further. In the sense of conveying to one's destination, or his journey's end, the Greek verb is employed by the best ancient writers, and by Homer with specific reference to a voyage by sea. *Brought* (led, or conducted) *him as far as* (or *even unto*) *Athens. For to come* (see above, on 5, 31.) The Greek construction is, *that they as soon as possible* (with all speed, or immediately) *should come to him.* This seems to favour the opinion that Silas and Timothy were merely left behind for safety, or to cover Paul's retreat, and that for want of time no church had been gathered at Berea, notwithstanding the favourable predispositions of the Jews there. (See above, on v. 14.) The urgent message sent to Silas and Timotheus may imply a wish for their assistance in the work which he believed to be awaiting him in Athens. But it may just as well imply a wish for such assistance in his work at Corinth, and an intention to remain at Athens only until they should join him. (See below, on v. 23.) The occurrences recorded in the rest of this chapter may have hastened his departure, so that his companions did not really rejoin him until after his arrival in Corinth (see below, on 18, 5.) It would seem, however, from his own words elsewhere (1 Thess. 3, 1), that Timothy did come to him at Athens, but was sent back to Thessalonica; unless we understand that passage, as some have done, of what happened at Berea, and of Paul's prospectively consenting to be left alone at Athens, as he was when his Macedonian escort had returned. *Departed,* literally, *went out* (or *away*) from Athens on their way home.

16. Now while Paul waited for them at Athens, his spirit was stirred in him, when he saw the city wholly given to idolatry.

Having thus disposed of Paul's arrangements for his further travels and his messages to Silas and Timothy, Luke turns to his short but memorable stay in Athens. *But in Athens itself,* literally, *in the Athens,* a more definite expression than the one in the preceding verse. This city had for ages been the source and centre of Hellenic culture, the metropolis of Gentile science, art, and wisdom. Although now deprived of all political importance by the Roman conquest, it was still revered throughout the civilized world for what it had accomplished in the cause of human freedom, as well as for its literature and its genius. The Athenian schools were still frequented by the flower of the Roman youth, and the great names of its history idolatrously cherished. There is something, therefore, very striking in the contrast here effected between Jewish, Christian, and Hellenic wisdom in the visit of St. Paul to the intellectual metropolis of Greece and of the Roman Empire. *Paul awaiting them* (or while he waited for them), i. e. for Silas and Timotheus, whom he had left in Berea, but had summoned to rejoin him. It is a natural though not a necessary implication, that he only stopped in Athens for this purpose, which may help to account for his impatience and excitement, though its main source was a deeper one, as here described. *Stirred*, or more exactly, *sharpened*, set on edge, the verb from which comes *paroxysm*, violent excitement, as a medical term signifying the access or fit of an acute disease, as an ethical term commonly applied to anger (see above, on 15, 37), but admitting of a wider application here, where we may readily suppose Paul to have felt, not only indignation in the proper sense, but grief, shame, wonder, and compassion likewise. *In* (or *within*) *him* may imply that for a time he was obliged or disposed to stifle his emotions, or at least to abstain from publicly expressing them. *When he saw* is more expressive in the Greek, where it agrees directly, as an active participle, with the pronoun which immediately precedes, *his spirit was stirred within him seeing*, or surveying as a spectacle (see above, on 3, 16. 4, 13. 7, 56. 8, 13. 10, 11.) *Wholly given to idolatry*, a paraphrase (copied from the Vulgate) of the Greek phrase, *being idol-full* (or *full of idols.*) The original epithet occurs here only, but is formed on the analogy of many adjectives, compounded with the same preposition, and expressing the abundance of the object which the noun denotes (Κατάδενδρος, full of trees; κατάμπελος, full of vines, &c.) It was peculiarly appropriate to Athens, which is repeatedly described by ancient writers as not only crowded with images and temples, but as containing more such objects than all other cities or the rest of Greece. Xenophon, poetically though in prose, refers to it as one great altar, one great sacrifice, etc. These general descriptions are abundantly sustained by the existing relics of these ancient structures, and still more completely by the enumeration and account of them in ancient writers. It was this peculiarity of Athens, visible and palpable to every one however ignorant or vicious, and not its mere moral aspect as devoted to idolatry, that Luke expresses here as the occasion of Paul's "paroxysm" while detained there.

17. Therefore disputed he in the synagogue with

the Jews, and with the devout persons, and in the market daily with them that met with him.

In order to give vent to his emotions, he resorted to his customary method of communicating with the public. *He disputed* (or discoursed, the word translated *reasoned* in v. 2 above, and there explained.) *With the Jews* (literally, *to* them) *and to the devout persons* (literally, *worshipping*, a term explained above, on v. 4.) We find therefore, here, as in Berea and Thessalonica, the same two classes of native or hereditary Jews, and Gentile proselytes or worshippers of Jehovah in the synagogue, with or without a formal profession of the Jewish faith. But finding this mode of access to the native mind of Athens still inadequate, Paul was obliged to employ the old Socratic method, handed down by a perpetual tradition, of conversing in the public squares or markets with the people whom he happened to encounter there. It has been disputed whether by the *Agora* (or *Forum*), here translated *market* (see above, on 16, 19), is intended the Ceramicus (the ancient Forum) or the Agora Eretria (the new one); but it seems rather to be used generically, just as we might say *the street*, without intending any one exclusively. *Daily* is a still stronger phrase than that in v. 11, and means *on* (or *throughout*) *every day*, which seems to imply a sojourn or detention of considerable though uncertain length. *Met with him*, in English, may suggest the idea of a formal meeting or a previous appointment, both which are expressly excluded in the Greek phrase, meaning those who chanced or happened to be by, so that Thucydides employs substantially the same form to denote the first comer (i. e. any body), and the neuter of the same to denote whatever may turn up (i. e. any thing). No form of speech could therefore have been chosen to express more clearly a fortuitous or random intercourse with people in the public places, a circumstance not wholly without interest, because of its exact agreement, which has been already mentioned, with the old Athenian and Socratic method of instruction. The facility with which the great Apostle of the Gentiles here adopts peculiar national and local habits, for the sake of reaching the Athenian mind, is one of the most striking illustrations and examples of the holy art, with which he ever stood prepared to become "all to all," that he might "by all means save some" (1 Cor. 9, 22.)

18. Then certain philosophers of the Epicureans, and of the Stoics, encountered him. And some said, What will this babbler say? other some, He seemeth to be a setter forth of strange gods; because he preached unto them Jesus and the resurrection.

Out of the promiscuous mass with which Paul thus came into contact, Luke now singles two well known schools or classes of philosophers. That he says nothing of the still more illustrious schools founded by Plato and Aristotle, has been variously explained, by supposing that these had lost their influence even in their native city; or that they were more employed in abstruse speculation, and took less interest in practical discussions; or that their principles were less immediately assailed by Christianity; or finally, that the only schools who happened to be represented in the Agora, when Paul appeared there, were the two here mentioned. The Epicureans, or Philosophers of the Garden, owed their name to Epicurus, who died at Athens in the year 270 before the birth of Christ, leaving his house and garden to be the constant seat of his philosophy, which was accordingly maintained there till the time of which we are now reading. He taught that the highest good and great end of existence was serene enjoyment, which his followers interpreted as meaning pleasure, and that often of the grossest kind. He ascribed the creation of the world to chance, and although he acknowledged the existence of the gods, described them as indifferent to human interests and human conduct. The Stoics, or Philosophers of the Porch, were so called from the Stoa Pœcile or Painted Porch, adjoining one of the Athenian squares or markets, where their founder, Zeno, taught at the same time with Epicurus. The Stoics acknowledged the supremacy of moral good, and even affected to deny the difference between pain and pleasure. They also acknowledged a supreme God and a Providence, but the former confounded with the world or universe, the latter governed by a fatal necessity. In later times, the Epicurean system was a favourite with the Greeks, and the Stoical with the Romans, as suiting their national characters respectively; but each had adherents in both races, one of the most eminent Stoics (Epictetus) being a Greek of Asia Minor, and one of the most eminent Epicureans (Lucretius) a Roman poet. *Encountered* is the verb translated *convened* in 4, 15 above, and *met with* in 20, 14 below, which last may be the meaning here, to wit, that in his public walks and conversations he fell in with some philosophers of these two schools. It may, however, have the more specific meaning of *conferring*, or comparing views, in conversation. *Babbler*, literally, *grain-picker*, or *seed-gatherer*, an epithet at first applied to birds, then to beggars who collect and live on scraps, and finally, as an expression of contempt, to any low or worthless character, or more specifically to a retailer of borrowed sayings, which is very nearly the idea suggested by the English version. Some derive the same sense from a different etymology, according to which the compound strictly means a *sower* (or *scatterer*) *of words*. *Setter forth*, announcer or proclaimer, a noun corresponding to the verb employed in vs. 3. 13 above, and often elsewhere. *Strange*, not wonderful or singular, but foreign, which in the mouth of an Athenian necessarily suggests the accessory idea of barbarous, or to use a homely English term, outlandish. *Gods*, or *demons*, a word which has only a bad sense in the New Testament, but which in classic Greek was used to designate the gods of secondary rank, who in Latin were called *Dii Minores*, or more indefinitely, deities, divinities, or superhuman beings in general. The last clause has been variously understood as meaning that they, really or in pretence, took *Jesus and Anastasis* (Resurrection) for a god and goddess; or that *gods* is a generic plural, meaning Jesus only; or that it has its proper meaning, and refers to Jesus and the God who raised him from the dead. Although not necessary, it is very natural to understand these two characteristic speeches as proceeding from the Epicureans and the Stoics, as they had just been mentioned, and as the words themselves agree so well with the levity and gravity for which they were respectively proverbial. *Preached*, or announced as good news (see above, on 15, 35. 16, 10.)

19. And they took him, and brought him unto Areopagus, saying, May we know what this new doctrine whereof thou speakest (is)?

Taking him, or *laying hold upon him*, not with force or violence, as in 16, 19, but in a friendly manner, as Barnabas is said to have laid hold on Saul in 9, 27, in both which cases the same verb is used. The most that can be meant here is a sort of mock arrest, in allusion to the place whither they were taking him. *Areopagus*, or *Hill of Mars*, a rocky ridge facing the Acropolis, where Mars was said to have been tried for murder, and from which the highest court of ancient Athens took its name. The seats of the judges, hewn in the solid rock, are said to be still visible. Some have supposed the name in this case to denote the court itself, before which Paul was now arraigned, as Socrates had been 450 years before, for the same offence of introducing strange or foreign gods. The objection to this supposition is, not that the court had been dissolved or deprived of its authority, which is uncertain, but that the ensuing context is without a vestige of judicial process, and that Paul, at the close of his address, went out, as it would seem, without the slightest molestation. (See below, on v. 33.) He was no doubt taken to the Areopagus as a convenient and customary place for public speaking, but with a sort of half jocose allusion to its being a seat of justice, and to the whole proceeding as a species of mock trial, which is perfectly in keeping with the national humour and traditions since the days of Aristophanes, and serves to explain his being taken up the steep hill, no doubt by the rocky steps which still remain, instead of being led into the more capacious Pnyx which was close at hand, or suffered to discourse in the Agora itself, or one of its adjacent porches. It seems to have been very much as if a stranger, preaching in the streets of any modern town, should be taken, not before a court, but to a court-house, as a convenient and appropriate locality in which to answer for himself before the public. In the self-same spirit, and in exquisite agreement with Athenian taste and manners, is the half-comic courtesy of the request recorded in the last clause. *May we know*, literally, *can we*, are we able, i. e. morally, is it lawful, will it be allowed; a mode of address wholly out of place in a judicial trial, but exactly suited to the temper and the motives of the people, as described above. Another slight but striking trait of genuineness and consistency in this whole passage is the use of *doctrine*, not in its usual sense in this book and the Gospels (see above, on 2, 42. 5, 28. 13, 12), but in that of the truth taught or the sentiment propounded. *Whereof thou speakest*, literally, *by thee spoken*, told, or talked of (see above, on 16, 13. 14), i. e. in his previous colloquial discourses in the Agora or market (see above, on v. 17.)

20. For thou bringest certain strange things to our ears: we would know therefore what these things mean.

Strange is not the word so rendered in v. 18, but the participle of a cognate verb, which might be Englished *strange-seeming*, i. e. startling or surprising. Elsewhere in Acts the Greek verb means to receive or entertain a stranger (see above, on 10, 6. 13. 23. 32, and below, on 21, 16. 28, 7, and compare Heb. 13, 2), but is twice employed by Peter in the kindred sense of thinking strange, or wondering (1 Pet. 4, 4. 12.) *To* (or rather *into*) *our ears* (or hearing), although not without classical analogies, seems to savour of the comic or half-serious tone of this entire proceeding. *We would know* (literally, *desire to know*) *what these things mean*, or rather, *what they may be*, or more closely still, *what they would wish* (or *choose*) *to be*. Of this peculiar idiom we have already had an instance (see above, on 2, 12.)

21. For all the Athenians, and strangers which were there, spent their time in nothing else, but either to tell or to hear some new thing.

This is Luke's explanation of the eagerness with which the multitude at Athens, unlike that of other cities, sought to hear this stranger, without any disposition to believe his doctrine, or any sense of spiritual want. *All the Athenians*, not as elsewhere the more leisurely or idle classes, but the people as a body. *Strangers*, temporary residents or sojourners. *Which were there*, the same word that is used above in 2, 10, and there explained. This class was very numerous at Athens,* as a famous seat of learning, still frequented from all quarters, both by students and by men already famous, of which we have an earlier example in the life of Cicero, who spent much time here and with great delight. These temporary residents would share of course in the peculiar habits of the natives with whom they had come there to hold intercourse. *Had time* (or *leisure*) *for nothing else*, a strong expression for their social and restless disposition. *Some new thing*, literally, *something newer*, i. e. newer than the last news heard before. The very same description, and with some of the same terms, is found in Theophrastus and in two orations of Demosthenes.†

* Πολλοὶ ἐπιδημοῦσι ξένοι. Theophr. Char. 8.

† "Tell me, do you still wish going round to ask throughout the market, is there any news? Can any thing be newer (τι καινότερον) than that a Macedonian, &c." Demosth. Philippic. 1. "We sit here doing nothing but trifling,

These ancient and authentic witnesses agree not only with Luke's own description, which he might be charged with having borrowed from them, but with the whole course of proceedings upon this occasion, which he could not have obtained in the same manner.

22. Then Paul stood in the midst of Mars' hill, and said, (Ye) men of Athens, I perceive that in all things ye are too superstitious.

Stood, literally, *standing*, or, as the form in Greek is passive, *being placed*, or *made to stand*. *Mars' Hill*, the translation of the name retained in v. 19. The margin here has, "or court of the Areopagites;" but see above, on v. 19. *Men of Athens*, literally, *Athenian men* (or *gentlemen*), the form of address common with the Attic orators and constantly occurring in the speeches of Demosthenes. (See above, on 1, 11. 16. 2, 14. 22. 5, 35. 13, 16.) *In all things*, or in all respects, entirely, altogether. *Ye are*, literally, *as*, i. e. as being. *Too superstitious* is in Greek one word, and that a comparative, like the one translated *new* in the preceding verse. *Superstitious*, literally, *god-fearing*, or more exactly, *demon-fearing* (see above, on v. 18), a word used by the classical Greek writers, both in the good sense of *religious* or *devout*, and in the bad sense of *superstitious*, i. e. slavishly afraid of the divine wrath. This equivocal expression seems to be deliberately chosen here, as justly descriptive of the Athenians, and yet not liable to shock their vanity or prepossessions in the very outset of this great discourse. A multitude of passages has been collected from the ancient writers, which agree with this in representing the Athenians as the most religious (in their way) of all the Greeks, and indeed of all the ancient heathen. Of this distinction they were naturally proud, and Paul avails himself of that well-known feeling to secure attention and conciliate his hearers. This end, however, would have been defeated by directly and explicitly denouncing them as superstitious in the very first sentence that he uttered. It is not, however, on the other hand, to be regarded as mere praise, much less as empty compliment or flattery, but simply as conceding to them what they might have justly claimed, the

and voting, and inquiring in the market whether any thing newer is reported (τι νεώτερον.)" Ep. Phil.

credit of superior devotion in the heathen sense, which, at the same time, to a Christian, was the grossest superstition. *I perceive*, behold, contemplate (see above, on v. 16), stands last in the original, *in all things as* (*being*) *more devout* (than others) *you I behold*, with some surprise and admiration, not of their idolatrous delusions, but of their assiduous devotion to what they regarded as the true religion.

23. For as I passed by, and beheld your devotions, I found an altar with this inscription, TO THE UNKNOWN GOD. Whom therefore ye ignorantly worship, him declare I unto you.

As I passed by, literally, *coming through*, which may mean simply passing through the streets, but it may also mean, passing through the city, on his way from Macedonia to Corinth (see above, on v. 16.) *Beholding*, an emphatic compound form of the verb used in the preceding verse, here suggesting the additional idea of attention, curiosity, or interest. *Devotions*, in the sense of religious services or worship, is an inexact translation. The one given in the margin of the English Bible (*gods that you worship*) is more accurate, but too restricted, as the Greek word denotes every thing connected with their worship, not its objects merely, but its rites and implements, including temples, images, and altars. *Found* seems to denote something more than *saw*, perhaps implying that the altar was not in public view, but in some corner or less frequented place, where Paul had unexpectedly discovered it or come upon it. *Also an altar*, the first of which words is omitted in the version, but essential to the sense, as meaning in addition to the well known and more obvious appurtenances of the heathen worship. *With this inscription*, literally, *in* (or *on*) *which had been written* (or *inscribed.*) The pluperfect form of the Greek verb may be intended to suggest the same idea of neglect, or at least of great antiquity. *To an unknown* (not THE unknown) *God*, a species of inscription not uncommon in antiquity, especially at Athens, where Pausanias and Philostratus bear witness to the existence of anonymous altars. Some light is thrown upon their origin by the statement of Diogenes Laertius, that when Epimenides was brought from Crete to stay a plague at Athens, he directed white and black sheep to be driven from the Areopagus, and where they first lay down, new altars to be built to the appropriate God (τῷ θεῷ προσήκοντι), i. e. to the divinity by whom the plague had been inflicted, and by appeasing whom it was to be removed. The practice, thus established or exemplified, of trying to propitiate an offended deity without even knowing who it was, agrees with the statements of the other writers above mentioned, that there were altars there to anonymous or unknown gods. Of this fact, plainly showing the uncertain and unsatisfying nature of the heathen superstition, which required so many gods to be appeased, and left it doubtful after all whether some had not been overlooked, the Apostle takes advantage, to show his cultivated but deluded hearers "a more excellent way." For *whom* and *him*, the oldest manuscripts and latest editors read *what* and *that*, which gives a better sense, because the object of their worship in such cases was not the true God, but a mere nonentity or vague abstraction. Jerome's arrogant and foolish statement—that the fact was not as Paul asserted, but that the altar was inscribed to the gods of Europe, Africa and Asia, and that Paul, having need of only one, so represented it—if worthy of regard at all, proves only that there was such an inscription as Jerome describes in his day, but not (as some seem to imagine) that there was none such as Paul describes four hundred years before. *Ignorantly* is in Greek a participle (*not knowing*), and *worship* a compound form of the verb commonly so rendered (see above, on vs. 4. 17, and on 13, 43. 50. 16, 14), expressing the idea of peculiarly devout or pious reverence. (Compare the use of the correlative adjective in 10, 2. 7 above.) *What ye worship without knowing* (what it is), *that I declare unto you.* The reference is not directly to Jehovah, as one of the foreign deities to whom they had erected altars; nor to the yearnings after the Supreme God, which are said to underlie the grossest forms of polytheism; but simply to the practical acknowledgment of insufficiency and worthlessness, included in the very fact that their religion allowed the worship of an unknown god. As if he had said, 'I perceive from one of your neglected altars, that you recognize another god (or other gods) besides the many which you worship formally by name, and I announce to you that under this indefinite description falls the very Being whom you ought to serve to the exclusion of all others. What yourselves acknowledge to exist and to be worthy of religious reverence, although you cannot even name it, I make known to you this day, in the person of the only true and living God.'

24. God that made the world and all things therein, seeing that he is Lord of heaven and earth, dwelleth not in temples made with hands—

The God, whom he thus proclaimed to them, is the maker, and by necessary consequence the sovereign, of the universe, described in one clause as *the world and all things in it*, and in the other as *heaven and earth*, which is plainly an equivalent expression (see above, on 4, 24. 7, 49. 14, 15.) *Seeing that he is*, in Greek a single word, *existing*, being (see above, on 16, 3. 20. 37.) The inference from these two facts, to wit, that God is the Creator and therefore the Lord (or Sovereign) of the universe, is that he does not dwell in artificial (literally, *hand-made*, manufactured) *shrines* (or *temples*, see above, on 7, 48, and below, on 19, 24.) The error here denied is that of Heathenism and corrupted Judaism, namely, that the Deity could be confined or unchangeably attached to any earthly residence, not the genuine Old Testament doctrine of Jehovah's real and continued dwelling in the tabernacle and temple. There seems to be an evident allusion here to Stephen's words, which had been heard by Paul himself. (See above, on 7, 48. 58.)

25. Neither is worshipped with men's hands, as though he needed any thing, seeing he giveth to all life, and breath, and all things—

Another necessary inference from the doctrine of creation and divine sovereignty is God's entire independence of all human care and service as essential to his blessedness or glory. *With* (literally, *by*) *the hands of men*, i. e. by men (as the agents) with their hands (as the instruments.) *Worshipped* is not exactly the idea conveyed by the original expression, which means *cared for*, taken care of, in the way of service, by supplying want and (in the case of human subjects) healing sickness (see above, on 4, 14. 5, 16. 8, 7, and the Gospels passim.) *As though he needed* (literally, *needing*) *any* (*thing*), or *any* (*one*), as the pronoun may be either masculine or neuter. It is somewhat singular that this same sentiment is uttered by Lucretius, the Epicurean poet, and by Seneca, the Stoic moralist. But in flagrant contradiction to these speculative doctrines was the whole religious practice, of philosophers as well as of the multitude, implying the necessity of human service to the divine blessedness. *Seeing he giveth* (literally, *himself giving*) *to all* (without exception or distinction) *life and breath* (the word translated *wind* in 2, 2), as a necessary incident and condition of life. The phrase is, therefore, not a mere hendiadys for *vital breath*, though this is the essential meaning. *And all the* (*things*) required for the support of life.

26. And hath made of one blood all nations of men for to dwell on all the face of the earth, and hath determined the times before appointed, and the bounds of their habitation—

This relation of the maker to the made is uniform and universal. With respect, not only to the local pride of the Athenians, as *autochthones* or *aborigines*, distinct from other races and the offspring of their own soil, but also to the general connection between the belief in many gods and that in many races, Paul here asserts the original unity of men, as the creatures of the same God and subjects of the same providential government. *Blood* is omitted in some manuscripts and versions and editions; but this omission is more easily explained than the insertion of an expression so unusual, although intelligible and appropriate, as evidently meaning a community of nature and of origin. *Made* may either mean *created* (as in 4, 24. 7, 50. 14, 15, and v. 24, above) for the purpose of dwelling, &c., or *caused* (as in 3, 12. 7, 19) *to dwell*, &c. The difference is one of mere construction, the creation of the race being as certainly implied in one case as it is expressed in the other. The great fact here alluded to, though frequently assailed and sometimes given up by the defenders of revealed truth, is confirmed by every new discovery in science, showing that the actual diversities among mankind are not more real or more marked than those which can be clearly traced in the same species of other animals. *All nations* (literally, *every nation*) *to dwell* (or more specifically *settle*), begin to dwell (see above, on 1, 19. 2, 5. 9. 14. 4, 16. 7, 2. 4) *on all the face* (or *surface*) *of the earth*, a studied generality of language, apparently intended to exclude all reservation and exception, even in favour of the Greeks or the Athenians. *Having determined* (or *defined*), not in the metaphorical or secondary sense of the verb elsewhere (see above, on 2, 23. 10, 42. 11,

29), but in its proper sense of marking boundaries or limits, either in reference to time (Heb. 4, 7) or space, or both, as in the case before us. *Times*, set times, junctures (see above, on 1, 7. 3, 19. 7, 20. 12, 1. 13, 11. 14, 17), meaning here the dates of history, the turning points in the experience of nations. *Before appointed*, or according to the latest critics, simply *appointed* or *commanded*. *Bounds*, literally *bound-settings*, limitations, definitions of extent and mutual relation. *Habitation*, settlement, the noun corresponding to the verb *dwell* (or *settle*) in the preceding clause. In this verse Paul claims for the Most High the right to govern, and indeed the actual control of the vicissitudes of nations, whether temporal or local, as a part of his great providential plan or purpose.

27. That they should seek the Lord, if haply they might feel after him and find him, though he be not far from every one of us—

A further statement of the end for which this one race was created and established in the earth. *To seek the Lord*, or according to the critics, *God*, which may, however, be an emendation founded on the supposition that *the Lord* does not express God's true relation to the Gentiles; but in this case it is perfectly appropriate, as meaning the divine authority or sovereignty, arising from the act of creation, and explicitly affirmed in v. 24 above. *If haply* (or *by chance*, implying contingency and doubt) *they might feel* or *grope after him* (as in the dark) *and find him* (even under all these disadvantages), a vivid and expressive exhibition of the state in which the Gentile world was placed, without a written revelation or direct communication with their Maker, yet with light enough to make their ignorance of God inexcusable. (See above, on 14, 15–17, and compare Rom. 1, 18–21.) *Though he be*, literally, *though being*, or existing, the same verb that is employed above, in v. 24, and here the last word in the clause or sentence. *Not far*, an instance of the figure called litotes or meiosis, the idea suggested being that of the closest and most intimate proximity. *Each* (or *every*) *one of us*, i. e. of men in general, mankind, the human race.

28. For in him we live, and move, and have our being; as certain also of your own poets have said, For we are also his offspring.

The relation thus existing between God and man is not a mere external nearness, but an intimate, essential oneness. *For in him*, not merely *by* or *through* him, which gratuitously weakens the Apostle's meaning, but in vital union with him, and included in him, as the source and sphere of our existence. *Have our being*, literally, *are*, the ordinary verb of existence, not the one employed in vs. 24. 27. Some suppose a climax in these words, the first denoting animal life, the last existence in the highest sense. Others suppose an anticlimax, *live* meaning spiritual life, *move* animal life, and *are* bare being or existence. Another view of the meaning is that without (or out of) God we could not live, nor even move, as some things without life can do, nor even (which is less than both) exist at all. But all these explanations are perhaps too artificial, and the words may be regarded as substantially equivalent, a cumulative or exhaustive expression of the one great thought, that our being and activity are wholly dependent on our intimate relation and proximity to God our Maker. That this was no peculiar tenet either of the Jews or Christians, Paul evinces by a sentence from a heathen poet, his own countryman, Aratus of Cilicia, who had lived in the third century before Christ, and who, in his astronomical poem, the Phenomena, translated into Latin by at least two illustrious Romans (Cicero and Germanicus), has these very words as part of a hexameter. The same idea, but conveyed in a direct address to Zeus or Jupiter, is found in an old hymn of Cleanthes the Stoic. Hence the plural form, *some of your own poets*, or *of the poets among you* (or belonging to you.) That Paul was familiar with the classics, although not deducible from this quotation, is much more probable, considering the reputation of his native city as a seat of learning (see above, on 9, 11. 30. 11, 25), than that his training was exclusively rabbinical. The use here made of heathen testimony is not an abuse, or even an accommodation, of the language quoted, which although applied by Aratus and addressed by Cleanthes to a mythological divinity, could only be regarded, even by themselves, as true of the Supreme God, as distinguished from all others. The *for* belongs to the quotation, and refers to nothing in this context. *We also*, as well as other orders of intelligences nearer to him. *Offspring*, family or race (see above, on 4, 6. 36. 7, 13. 19. 13, 26.)

29. Forasmuch then as we are the offspring of God,

we ought not to think that the Godhead is like unto gold, or silver, or stone, graven by art and man's device.

The relationship existing between God and man must be chiefly spiritual, not corporeal. To deify matter, therefore, is to make God inferior to man, the Creator to the creature. *Forasmuch then as we are*, literally, *therefore being*. *Ought not*, are bound not, as a matter both of interest and moral obligation. *Graven*, literally, *with carving*, *sculpture*. *Art and man's device* disturbs both the order and the syntax, the first and last noun being equally dependent on the second, *art and device of man*. The two ideas here combined are those of skill and genius, the power of execution and the power of invention or artistical creation, neither of which, nor both together, can change matter into spirit, much less clothe it with divine perfections. *The Godhead*, literally, *the divine*, i. e. the divine nature or essence. The corresponding abstract term in English is *the Deity*. The original order of this sentence, although scarcely reproducible in English, is peculiarly striking and expressive, the first word being *offspring*, and the last, *the Godhead to be like.*

30. And the times of this ignorance God winked at, but now commandeth all men every where to repent—

A thought to be supplied between the verses is, that this degradation and denial of the Godhead had been practised universally for ages, i. e. in the whole heathen worship and mythology. *The times of this* (literally, *the*) *ignorance* (of what God was and what was due to him from man) include the whole of the preceding ages or the past history of the Gentile world. *Times* is not the word employed in v. 26, but one denoting periods, as distinguished from mere points or junctures. (See above, on 1, 7. 3, 21. 7, 17. 23. 8, 11. 13, 18. 14, 3. 28. 15, 33.) *Winked at* is not only an inaccurate translation, but a very objectionable although unintended degradation of the subject, by applying to the Most High, even in a figure, a bodily gesture trivial in itself and its associations, and entirely wanting in the Greek, which simply means, *having overlooked*, or passed by, i. e. suffered or endured, without declaring his disapprobation. (See above, on 14, 16, and compare Rom. 3, 25.) This period of forbearance is now past. The revelation of God's will is confined no longer to a single nation. *Now*, in emphatic opposition to the past times of man's ignorance and God's forbearance (see above, on 4, 29. 5, 38.) *Commands*, peremptorily requires or orders (see above, on 1, 4. 4, 18. 5, 28. 40. 10, 42. 15, 5. 16, 18. 23.) *All* (*men*) *every where*, a double expression of the universality of the command, made still more striking in the Greek by the use of two cognate terms (πᾶσι πανταχοῦ), which might be Englished, *everybody everywhere*. *To repent*, to change their minds and reform their practice (see above, on 2, 38. 3, 19. 5, 31. 8, 22. 11, 18. 13, 24), with special reference to this sin of idolatry, but not excluding a more general and comprehensive revolution both of heart and life.

31. Because he hath appointed a day, in the which he will judge the world in righteousness by (that) man whom he hath ordained; (whereof) he hath given assurance unto all (men), in that he hath raised him from the dead.

Because refers directly not so much to what immediately precedes as to an intermediate thought, which is suppressed but may be readily supplied, to wit, this divine command is not without a sanction and a penalty. Its violation will be made the subject of judicial inquest, before one who has already been appointed and accredited by God himself. *Appointed*, set, or fixed (see above, on 1, 23. 4, 7. 5, 27. 6, 6. 13.) *A day*, i. e. a definite or set time, with particular but not exclusive reference to the final judgment. See above, on 10, 42, where Peter presents Christ in his judicial character and office to another company of Gentiles. *In the which*, an obsolete redundancy or pleonasm in English, meaning neither more nor less than *in which* without the article, there being nothing corresponding to it in Greek, either here or elsewhere. *Will judge*, is about (or just about) *to judge* (see above, on 3, 3. 5, 35. 11, 28. 12, 6. 13, 34. 16, 27.) *The world*, literally, *the inhabited* (earth), here put for the whole world or its inhabitants, the whole human race. (See above, on v. 6 and 11, 28.) *In righteousness*, not merely righteously or justly, as an epithet of quality or manner, but in the actual and active exercise of righteousness or justice as a moral attribute or trait of character. (See above, on 10, 35. 13, 10.) The judgment here predicted will not only be a just one, but a grand display of God's essential justice. (Compare Rom. 1, 17. 3, 25.) *By that man*, literally, *in a man*, not merely through the agency, but in the person, of a man as yet unknown to Paul's immediate hearers, but about to be more definitely set forth and identified. *Ordained*, the same verb with *determined* in v. 26, but here, as applied to a person, meaning *designated*, pointed out, as well as chosen and appointed. (See above, on 2, 23. 10, 42, and compare the use of the same verb in Rom. 1, 4.) *Wherefore he hath given assurance*, literally, *having offered faith* (as in the margin of the English Bible), i. e. having made it possible by furnishing the necessary evidence. *In that he hath* (literally, *having*) *raised him from* (among) *the dead*, the same expression that is used above in 13, 34, and there explained. The resurrection of Christ established his divine legation and the truth of all his doctrines and pretensions (see above, on 1, 22), among which was his claim to the judicial functions here ascribed to him by Paul. As this discourse was interrupted (see below, upon the next verse), we have no right to describe it as a mere lesson in natural theology, nor even to assume (with Calvin and some others) that it is less fully reported in the last than in the first part. The Apostle showed his wisdom, in addressing such an audience, by setting out from principles of natural religion, and gradually introducing the distinctive doctrines of the Gospel, as he begins to do in this verse. That he did not fully carry out his plan, was the fault of his hearers, not his own.

32. And when they heard of the resurrection of the dead, some mocked, and others said, We will hear thee again of this (matter).

When they heard, literally, *having heard* (or *hearing*.) *Mocked*, derided, ridiculed, the same verb that is used above, in 2, 13, although the latest critics give it there a compound and therefore more emphatic form. The possibility of resurrection after death was not only no part of the Greek creed, either philosophical or popular, but was positively repudiated as a gross absurdity. The universal faith may be summed up in the poetical but strong and clear phrase of Æschylus, "Once dead, there is no resurrection." This incredulity appears to have been felt, not only by the mockers of the first clause, but also by the graver and more courteous class mentioned in the second. *Others said* (or *some said*), *We will hear thee again about this*, not the resurrection merely, but the whole theme of his discourse. This is commonly explained as a polite refusal to hear further, even on the part of those who did not mock or ridicule the speaker, and has sometimes been compared to the procrastinating speech of Felix to the same Apostle (see below, on 24, 25.) Some, however, understand it as a serious proposal, which was never carried into execution, while some even think it was, and that one more conference at least was held, but as it led to no result, was not recorded. Here again, though not a necessary supposition, it is certainly more natural than any other, that the classes whom Luke so distinctly characterizes, by the few words which he puts into their mouths, were the gay Epicureans and the graver Stoics. (See above, on v. 18.)

33. So Paul departed from among them.

And (omitted in some copies) *so* (or *thus*), not a mere connective or continuative particle, but like the same word as employed by Stephen (see above, on 7, 8), summing up the substance of what goes immediately before. *And thus* rejected, thus derided by one portion of his hearers, thus put off to a more convenient season by another, and perhaps regarded with indifference by the rest, the Apostle of the Gentiles *went out from among* (or *from the midst of*) *them*, fortuitous but real representatives of Gentile wisdom and of Greek civilization. The way in which his going forth is here described shows clearly that he was not on his trial or under any personal restraint whatever (see above, on v. 19.) Whether he merely left the Areopagus, or now took his departure from the city, is a question which depends, in some degree, upon the explanation of the following verse.

34. Howbeit certain men clave unto him, and believed, among the which (was) Dionysius the Areopagite, and a woman named Damaris, and others with them.

Had the story of Paul's ministry at Athens ended with the foregoing verse, it would have seemed to be entirely fruitless. To correct this false but natural impression, an addition is here made to the whole narrative, the very form of which betrays its supplementary or qualifying purpose. *Howbeit*, yet, but, notwithstanding the apparent ill success of the Apostle's labours in this famous city, they were not without fruit after all. *Some men* (and one woman), *cleaving to him*, an expression which implies the sacrifice involved in doing so, adhering to him in the face of ridicule and opposition, *believed* his doctrine, and in Christ, as the Redeemer whom he preached to them. As if to make up for the fewness of the converts in this famous city, one of them was chosen from among the judges of the Areopagus itself, the most august tribunal of the ancient world. As usual in all such cases, the tradition of the church describes him as the first Christian bishop of Athens (so Eusebius), and a legend of much later date as having suffered martyrdom there (so Nicephorus.) A still less credible tradition has attached the name of *Dionysius the Areopagite* to certain mystical and hierarchical productions of a later age, which influenced both practice and opinion in the medieval church to a remarkable degree. The other name particularly mentioned here is *Damaris*, which differs only in a single letter from the favourite Greek female designation, *Damalis*, a heifer (compare Dorcas and Tabitha, 9, 36, and Rhoda or Rhode, 12, 13.) Some suppose her to have been the wife of Dionysius; but she would hardly have been simply called *a woman*. Some infer from her being so particularly mentioned, that she was a person of distinction; others, from her mixing with the crowd on this occasion, in direct violation of Greek usage, that she was a woman of bad character. More probable than either is the supposition that she was the only female convert, and is therefore named with Dionysius as the most distinguished male one, while the rest are indefinitely classed, at the beginning and the end of the sentence, as "certain men" and "other (men)," besides or with them.

CHAPTER XVIII.

We have here the conclusion of Paul's second mission, and the commencement of the third. The first of these divisions is entirely occupied with his ministry at Corinth. Becoming acquainted with Aquila and Priscilla, he takes up his abode with them, and works as a tent-maker, at the same time preaching in the synagogue (1–5.) The Jews opposing him, he leaves them for the Gentiles, and converts many of both classes (6–8.) Encouraged by a special revelation, he continues thus employed eighteen months (9–11.) The Jews accuse him before Gallio, but are ignominiously defeated (12–17.) Sailing from Cenchrea, he visits Ephesus, and with a promise to return, proceeds upon his journey to Jerusalem, and thence to Antioch (18–22.) While he is beginning his third mission by revisiting Galatia and Phrygia, Apollos makes his first appearance at Ephesus, but removes to Corinth before Paul's arrival (23–28.)

1. After these things Paul departed from Athens, and came to Corinth —

After these things, an indefinite expression, which cannot be rendered more determinate by any calculation or conjecture. *Departed* is in Greek a passive participle meaning *parted*, separated, as if by force or against one's will, (See above, on 1, 4, and compare Matt. 19, 6. Mark 10, 9. Rom. 8, 35. 39.) It may here imply that Paul left Athens with reluctance and regret. *Corinth*, a famous Grecian city, mentioned by Homer, situated on the Isthmus between Northern Greece and the Peloponnesus, with a port on each side, hence called by Horace *bimaris* (on two seas). The town was famous in remote antiquity for commerce, riches, luxury, and vice. It was destroyed by the Roman Consul Mummius, in the same year with Carthage (B. C. 146), but rebuilt by Julius Cæsar. It was now the capital of Achaia, one of the two great provinces into which Greece was divided by the Romans, the other being Macedonia. (See above, on 16, 9. 10. 12, and below, on v. 27. 19, 21.) It is now an inconsiderable town of two thousand inhabitants, with few remnants of the splendid buildings which gave name to the Corinthian order of architecture. Its identity is clearly ascertained, not only by its singular position, but by the Acrocorinthus, a hill eighteen hundred feet high, upon which stood the Corinthian Acropolis. Paul was no doubt directed to this place, as one peculiarly adapted to become a radiating centre of Christian influence.

2. And found a certain Jew named Aquila, born in Pontus, lately come from Italy, with his wife Priscilla, because that Claudius had commanded all Jews to depart from Rome, and came unto them.

Finding, meeting unexpectedly, falling in with; or perhaps it may mean, finding after search, upon inquiry (see above, on 11, 26.) *By name Aquila, by birth* (or *race*) *a Pontian*, or *native of Pontus*, one of the northern provinces of Asia Minor. By a curious coincidence, Suetonius speaks of a Roman senator named Aquila Pontius, a contemporary of Cæsar and Cicero, who also names him in his private letters. Hence some have hastily concluded that the Jew here mentioned was a freedman (or emancipated servant) of the senator, and according to the Roman custom, bore his name. But nothing can be more precarious than an inference from mere coincidence of names, a circumstance by no means rare either in history or real life. In this case the coincidence is double, as Aquila, the Greek translator of the Old Testament, is also said to have been born in Pontus. *Lately*, recently, a term originally applicable only to fresh or newly killed meat, then extended to fruits and flowers, and in the later Greek employed in a generic sense, without regard to its etymology and primary usage. *Priscilla*, a diminutive of *Prisca*, which form is itself used in 2 Tim. 4, 19. *On account of Claudius's having ordered all the Jews* (not indefinitely, *all Jews*, but specifically, *all the Jews* there resident) *to depart* (the verb used in the preceding verse and there explained). Suetonius relates that Claudius expelled the Jews because they were continually making a disturbance (*assidue tumultuantes*) under the influence, or at the instance, of one Chrestus (*Chresto impulsore*), which some regard as the proper name of a person now unknown, but others as a mistake for *Christus* (which Tertullian mentions as a frequent error.) The reference may then be either to the Jewish doctrine of a reigning and conquering Messiah, or to the Christian doctrine of our Lord's Messiahship, which was a constant subject of disturbance and dispute among the Jews, with whom the Christians were as yet confounded. There is less probability in the opinion that the edict here referred to is one of the same emperor, recorded by Tacitus, in which all astrologers (*mathematici*) were banished. *Came to them*, i. e. to their house or dwelling, for he had already found them or become acquainted with them. His coming to them seems to imply that they were Christians, although some take *Jew* and *Jews* in the distinctive sense, and suppose that Aquila and Priscilla were among Paul's converts.

3. And because he was of the same craft, he abode with them, and wrought; for by their occupation they were tent-makers.

Besides the national and spiritual tie, there was also a professional or business one. *On account of being a fellow-craft*, or of the same trade, literally *art*, a term originally signifying manual employment, i. e. such as requires skill and not mere strength. It was an ancient Jewish custom to teach all boys some trade, even those who received a liberal education, both as a means of subsistence and a moral safeguard. *He abode*, continued, or remained with them, how long is not expressed (but see below, on v. 11.) *Wrought*, the old and genuine past tense of *work*, now superseded by the so-called regular form, *worked*. It is here used in its proper sense of manual labour. The last clause is explanatory of the "fellow-craft" in that before it. (He was of the same trade) *for they were tent-makers*. There was a great demand for tents in ancient times, both for travellers and soldiers. They were sometimes made of leather, whence Chrysostom explains the compound term here used as meaning curriers or leather-dressers; but still more frequently of hair-cloth, and especially of the coarse hair furnished by a species of goat which abounded in Cilicia, whence the Latin name (*cilicium*) for hair-cloth. As Paul was a native of that country, this may help to account for his having acquired this particular trade. As the demand for tents, though great, was variable, it is not improbable that those who made them went from place to place, which would account for Aquila and Priscilla having lived at Rome, and for their being there again when Paul wrote his epistle (Rom. 16, 3–5.) These migrations may, however, have had other causes.

4. And he reasoned in the synagogue every sabbath, and persuaded the Jews and the Greeks.

Here again Paul addresses himself first to the Jews, who were very numerous in Corinth, on account of its extensive trade and advantageous situation near the confines, not only of Peninsular and Continental Greece, but of Europe and Asia, and its immediate intercourse both with East and West by sea. As in Salamis (13, 5), Antioch (13, 14), Iconium (14, 1), Thessalonica (17, 1), Berea (17, 10), and Athens (17, 17), so in Corinth, he avails himself of the facilities afforded by the synagogue for addressing both the Jews and the devouter Gentiles, whether formal proselytes or mere inquirers. *Reasoned*, or *disputed*, both which equivalents are used in the translation of the same Greek verb in the preceding chapter. (See above, on 17, 2. 17.) The second idea is rather suggested by the context than expressed by this word, which denotes argumentative discourse, even as uttered by a single person. *Persuaded*, endeavoured to convince, and in many cases did convince, *both Jews and Greeks*, i. e. Gentiles who frequented the synagogue. In such connections, all such Gentiles may be called Greeks, on account of the prevailing use of the Greek language; but in this case, as in 17, 4 above, the word may have its primary and strictest sense.

5. And when Silas and Timotheus were come from Macedonia, Paul was pressed in the spirit, and testified to the Jews (that) Jesus (was) Christ.

There is some doubt both as to the reading and the sense of this verse. Instead of *spirit*, the latest editors read *word*, as found in several of the oldest manuscripts. The original meaning of the verb is *held together*, or *compressed*, as in 7, 57 above, and in Luke 8, 45. Sometimes it seems to denote a painful pressure on the mind or heart, as in Luke 12, 50. Phil. 1, 23, and perhaps 2 Cor. 5, 14. This is the sense commonly adopted here, to wit, that Paul was painfully affected *in his spirit*, or constrained *by the Holy Spirit* to pursue a certain course. If the other reading be preferred, the sense may be, that he was painfully occupied in preaching (or constrained to preach) the gospel (compare 1 Cor. 9, 16.) There is also some doubt as to the connection between what is here affirmed of Paul and the fact recorded in the other clause, to wit, the arrival of Silas and Timothy from Macedonia. The usual assumption seems to be, that their arrival gave him a new impulse, or imposed a new sense of necessity and obligation. But this is neither so intelligible in itself, nor so consistent with the form of the original, the verb being in the imperfect tense, as the supposition that this second clause describes, not the effect of their arrival, but the state in which they found him. And when Silas and Timothy came down from Macedonia, *Paul was* (already) *pressed in spirit* (or 'had been already pressed by the Holy Ghost'); or, according to the other text, 'Paul was solicitous about (or wholly taken up with) the word,' i. e. the preaching of the gospel. The effect of this pressure or constraint is given in the last clause. *Testifying to the Jews*, and through them to the Gentiles who were present at their worship. *That Jesus was Christ* is in Greek but two words, *Christ Jesus*, the sense of which, however, is correctly given in the English version. Testifying to the Jews, and all who were acquainted with the Hebrew Scriptures, that the Messiah there predicted was identical with Jesus of Nazareth. (See above, on 2, 36. 5, 42.)

6. And when they opposed themselves and blasphemed, he shook (his) raiment, and said unto them, Your blood (be) upon your own heads; I (am) clean; from henceforth I will go unto the Gentiles.

The course of events here described is very similar to that at Antioch in Pisidia (see above, on 13, 45–47), but precisely such as might have been expected wherever there were unbelieving Jews. *They resisting* (or *opposing*) is in Greek a military term, and strictly means, *arraying themselves*, as an army to resist an enemy, implying not mere private or fortuitous but systematic and concerted opposition. *Blaspheming*, either in the lower but more classical sense of reviling, abusing (i. e. Paul and his companions), or in the stronger Hellenistic sense of impiously maligning (God or Christ.) See above, on 6, 11. 13. 13, 45. *Shaking*, or *shaking out*, the same verb which in 13, 51 means *shaking off* the dust, for the same purpose which is there explained. The accompanying words, however, are here different. *Your blood*, i. e. the blame of your destruction, *be* (or *is*, or *shall be*, as the verb is not expressed in Greek) *upon your* (*own*) *heads*, i. e. rest upon yourselves. (See Matt. 23, 30. 35. 27, 25, and compare Lev. 20, 9. Deut. 19, 10. Ezek. 18, 30. 33, 5.) *Clean* (*am*) *I*, or *pure*, i. e. guiltless of your ruin. (See below, on 20, 26.) *From the now* (i. e. the present moment), henceforth, *to the nations* (i. e. other nations, Gentiles) *I will go*, i. e, as an apostle and a preacher. This and the parallel passage in 13, 46 illustrate one another, by showing that Paul's language in such cases has immediate reference only to the place or the community in which he uttered it.

7. And he departed thence, and entered into a cer-

tain (man's) house, named Justus, (one) that worshipped God, whose house joined hard to the synagogue.

Removing, as the same verb is twice translated in Matt. 17, 20. *Thence*, not from the house of Aquila, as some suppose, for which no motive is assignable, but from the synagogue, where this conflict with the unbelieving Jews had taken place. *Entered*, came or went in, not at that time merely, or once for all, but as a permanent arrangement. He began to preach there, as he had done in the synagogue. *A certain man*, literally, *some* (*one*). *Named*, literally, *by name* (see above, on 5, 1.) *Justus*, a Latin name, which we have already met with, as the Roman surname of Joseph Barsabas (see above, on 1, 22.) There is a singular diversity of reading in the manuscripts and versions as to this name, *Justus*, *Titus Justus*, *Titius Justus*, *Titus son of Justus*, *Titus*. Some have hence inferred that the Justus mentioned here was really the Titus often named in Paul's epistles (Gal. 2, 1. 3. 2 Tim. 4, 10. Tit. 1, 4. 2 Cor. 2, 13, et passim), but never elsewhere in the Acts, an omission which these textual variations may have been intended to supply. (See above, on 15, 4.) If the supposed connection or identity has any historical foundation, the tradition of the Church has not preserved it. Both names are Roman, which agrees well with the description of Justus as *worshipping the* (*true*) *God*, a phrase commonly applied to Proselytes or Gentiles who acknowledged and adored Jehovah. (See above, on 13, 43. 50. 16, 14. 17, 4. 17.) He had now, no doubt, gone further, and recognized the Jesus whom Paul preached as the Messiah. *Joined hard*, an old English phrase for *next*, *adjoining*, or *contiguous*. It was no doubt for this reason that Paul chose it, as his removal and resort to it would be a kind of public declaration and memorial of his permanent secession from the unbelievers and blasphemers of the synagogue. A comparison of *synagogue* in this verse with the same word in 14, 43, will illustrate the transition from the primary and proper sense of *meeting* to the secondary one of *meeting-house*.

8. And Crispus, the chief ruler of the synagogue, believed on the Lord, with all his house; and many of the Corinthians, hearing believed and were baptized.

Crispus, another Roman name, but in this case certainly belonging to a Jew, perhaps a proselyte, as Gentile birth might not disqualify him for his office. *Chief ruler of the synagogue*, in Greek a single word, the plural form of which is rendered simply *rulers of the synagogue* in 13, 15. The *chief* may have been added on account of the article (*the ruler*), supposed by the translators to imply that there was only one. But the definite form of the expression may merely designate him as a person of some note, 'Crispus the (well known) ruler of the synagogue,' just as we say, "the Apostle Paul," "the Prophet Daniel," although there were many other Prophets and Apostles. There is also reason to believe, that these rulers of the synagogue were not elective officers, but the hereditary elders of the Jews, of whom there would of course be a plurality in every synagogue or congregation. (See above, on 4, 5. 8. 23. 5, 21. 6, 12, and below, on 23, 14. 24, 1. 25, 15.) If this be so, the position occupied by Crispus, although highly respectable among the Jews, was not so eminent, especially in Gentile eyes, as our translation may suggest to English readers. It could hardly be the reason, as some think, for Paul's baptizing this man with his own hand, as we know that he did from his own explicit statement in his first epistle to this very church. (See 1 Cor. 1, 14.) It is well observed by Paley, that the correspondence here between the letter and the narrative is just sufficient, in degree and kind, to prove the authenticity of both, without exciting the suspicion of collusion or assimilation. If the epistle had been framed to suit the history, the names of Stephanas and Gaius would not have been added; in the contrary case, they would not have been omitted. Paul's departure from his ordinary practice in these cases, far from implying that they were peculiarly important, or entitled to particular attention upon his part, seems to be treated by himself as something accidental or fortuitous. (See above, on 13, 9, and compare 1 Cor. 1, 13–17.) *Believed on* (or *in*) *the Lord* (Jesus), as the true Messiah and the only Saviour. (See above, on 9, 42. 11, 17. 14, 23. 16, 31.) *With all his house*, or more exactly, *with his whole house*, household, family. (See above, on 11, 14. 16, 15. 31.) That they were all baptized is not affirmed, but seems to be implied both here and in Corinthians. The same thing is recorded, in the last clause of the verse before us, as to *many of the Corinthians*, i. e. Greeks or Gentiles, who, *hearing* (not *of it*, i. e. that Crispus was converted, but the gospel as Paul preached it in the house of Justus), *believed*, or were converted, became Christians, in the same sense as before.

9. Then spake the Lord to Paul in the night by a vision, Be not afraid, but speak, and hold not thy peace—

And the Lord, i. e. the Lord Jesus, as in 9, 17. *Said by vision*, i. e. a divine communication, with or without a visible appearance. See above, on 16, 9, where the word *appeared* is expressly used. *Fear not*, perhaps implying that he was disposed to shrink from the dangers of his new position. *Speak and be not silent*, as he may have been tempted to remain. Or this may be merely the idiomatic combination of a positive and negative expression, as in other cases. The idea of some writers, that Paul was dejected, when he came to Corinth, by the failure of his ministry at Athens, and by a consciousness of having erred there in his mode of preaching, is at variance, not only with his apostolical authority, but also with recorded facts. The way in which he introduced the Gospel to his Athenian hearers is among the strongest proofs of his extraordinary wisdom. That he did not preach Christ fully to them, was because they would not hear, and not because he had begun with an appeal to the principles of natural religion. The divine approbation was attested by several conversions, perhaps many (see above, on 17, 34.) The reference in the verse before us can be only to such natural misgivings as may be felt by the best and most courageous men.

10. For I am with thee, and no man shall set on thee to hurt thee; for I have much people in this city.

This verse assigns the reason why he should not fear, by assuring him of the divine presence and protection. *I am with thee*, in a special and extraordinary sense, to aid and guard thee. (See above, on 10, 38.) The effect of this protection is then stated. *No man*, literally, *no one* (see above, on 5, 13. 23. 9, 7. 8. 10, 28.) *Set on thee*, an old English phrase, of which a kindred form still current is the noun *onset*. The Greek verb strictly means *to place* or *lay upon*, *impose*, a burden (as in 15, 28), a yoke (as in 15, 10), stripes (as in 16, 23), the hands (as in 8, 17. 19. 9, 12. 17. 13, 3), the latter always as a spiritual or religious act; whereas a kindred phrase (*to throw hands upon any one*) means to seize or arrest (as in 4, 3. 5, 18. 12, 1.) The other verb may here have a reflexive sense, to place or set one's self against, i. e. to assail, attack, in which sense it is also used by Xenophon and in the Septuagint (Gen. 43, 18.) *To hurt* (or *harm*) *thee*, i. e. for the purpose of so doing, or as the actual result. (For the usage of the Greek verb, see above, on 7, 6. 19. 12, 1. 14, 2.) The last clause gives another reason why he should not fear. The meaning is not that there were already many converts in the place who would protect him, but that there were many yet to be converted, for whose sake his life must be preserved. (Compare John 10, 16.)

11. And he continued (there) a year and six months, teaching the word of God among them.

Paul believes the promise and obeys the order. *He continued there*, literally, *he sat*, implying safety and tranquillity, perhaps with some allusion to the customary attitude of ancient teachers. (But compare Luke 24, 49, where the same Greek verb is rendered *tarry.*) *A year and six months*, a much longer stay than any one before recorded in Paul's missionary life, and affording time for the abundant and extensive labours presupposed in his epistles to the Church of Corinth. The period here mentioned may be either that of his whole residence at this time, or the part of it extending to the incident recorded in the next verse. In the latter case, the sense will be, that he continued quietly and safely at his work for eighteen months, when it was unexpectedly disturbed and interrupted. Some prefer this explanation on the ground that it vindicates the truth of the Lord's promise (see above, on v. 10), that he should not be attacked, whereas he was attacked before he left Corinth. But this, though plausible, is inconclusive, as the promise may be understood to mean that no one should assail him with success, or so as really to hurt him, either personally, or by interrupting his work as an Apostle. *Teaching among* (literally, *in*) *them* (the Corinthians) *the word of God* (the true religion, see above, on 4, 31. 6, 2. 7. 13, 5. 7. 44. 17, 13.)

12. And when Gallio was the deputy of Achaia, the Jews made insurrection with one accord against Paul, and brought him to the judgment-seat—

Gallio was the brother of Seneca, the famous Stoic, who describes him in his letters as a man universally beloved on account of his amiable disposition, and refers to his having caught a fever in Achaia (the province of which Corinth was the capital.) This relationship probably gave rise to the tradition and the fabrication of a correspondence between Seneca and Paul. According to one account, Gallio shared his brother's fate, being put to death by Nero; according to another, he destroyed himself. *Gallio being* (or *acting as*) *proconsul*, the Greek verb corresponding to the noun used in 13, 7. 8. 12, and there explained. Here again Luke's accuracy, even in minute points, is remarkable. One historian (Dio Cassius) says that Achaia was at first an imperial province, and therefore governed by Proconsuls (see above, on 13, 7); another (Tacitus) that it was afterwards transferred to the Senate, which would cause it to be governed by a Prætor; but a third (Suetonius) records its restoration to the Emperor before the time of these events; so that the nomenclature of the narrative is perfectly correct. Since Gallio's proconsulate is here assigned as the date of the new movement, it is probable that he arrived and entered on the office during Paul's abode there, and that his reputation as a man of easy temper led the Jews to make the attempt here recorded. *Made insurrection*, or *rose up against*, a strengthened form of the Greek verb used in 4, 1. 6, 12. 17, 5, and there explained. *With one accord*, unanimously, which implies not only joint action, but preconcert and a systematic plan. (For the etymology and usage of the Greek word, see above, on 1, 14. 2, 1. 46. 4, 24. 5, 12. 7, 57. 8, 6. 12, 20. 15, 25.) *Brought*, led, not necessarily implying force or violence, but only the presenting of his person as a prisoner before the magistrate. *The judgment-seat*, or the *tribunal* of the governor, to which the Romans attached great importance and a kind of sanctity, so that the Prætors and Proconsuls, sent into the provinces, sometimes carried their tribunals with them. (For the meaning of the Greek word here used, see above, on 12, 21, and compare Matt. 27, 19. John 19, 13.)

13. Saying, This (fellow) persuadeth men to worship God contrary to the law.

Saying that (ὅτι), the usual Greek formula of citation, even when the very words are given; whereas we use it only when we give the substance. It is omitted in translation here, as it was in 2, 13. 5, 23. 25. 6, 11. 14. 11, 3. 13, 34. 16, 36. 17, 6.

In the few places where it is expressed (7, 6. 15, 5), there is a slight change of construction to accommodate our idiom. *Fellow* is not expressed in Greek, but supplied by the translators, to convey the contemptuous meaning commonly attached to the demonstrative (*this*) when absolutely used. But besides the uncertainty of the alleged usage, the simple idea of *this man* (or *person*) would have been expressed precisely in the same way. *Persuadeth*, an emphatic compound of the verb so rendered in v. 4, and in 13, 43. 14, 19. above. *To worship God*, the Greek verb so repeatedly applied to the worship of Jehovah by the Gentiles. (See above, on v. 7, and compare 13, 43. 50. 16, 14. 17, 4. 17.) *Against the law* is understood by some to mean the Roman law, which, like those of Turkey and some Christian states, recognized certain kinds of worship or religion besides that established, and allowed no others. To the supposition that it means the law of Moses, these interpreters object, that with this the Roman magistrates had no concern, either as interpreters or executioners. But as this is just what Gallio says in the next verse, the objection rather favours that construction. It is possible, however, that the phrase was meant to be equivocal by those who used it, so that what was really a violation only of their own law might be taken by the inexperienced Proconsul as an offence against the Roman government, and as such punished.

14. And when Paul was now about to open (his) mouth, Gallio said unto the Jews, If it were a matter of wrong or wicked lewdness, O (ye) Jews, reason would that I should bear with you—

Paul being about (see above, on 3, 3. 5, 35. 11, 28. 12, 6. 13, 34. 16, 27. 17, 31) *to open his mouth* (see above, on 8, 35. 10, 34), i. e. to speak in his own defence and in answer to the charge just brought against him. Some suppose Gallio's interruption to be here recorded as a disrespectful or contemptuous act towards Paul himself. But it seems to have been rather like the practice in the English courts of hearing only one side when the case is too plain to require discussion, and stopping the party in whose favour the decision is to be. Thus viewed, the interruption was a virtual decision in Paul's favour, or at least an intimation that he needed no defence. The reason is given in the other clause by Gallio himself. *If indeed*, a particle suggesting that the case is only a supposed one. *A matter of wrong*, literally, *an injustice*, or a legal injury, a violation of your civil rights. *Lewdness* is too strong and too specific a version of a Greek word near akin to that translated *mischief* in 13, 10, and denoting undue facility of action, i. e. recklessness, unscrupulousness, here determined by the epithet (*wicked*) to denote an immorality, perhaps as distinguished from an illegal act, which had just been mentioned. The two together are intended to describe the whole class of offences, of which the civil magistrate was bound to take cognizance. *Reason would* is an obscure translation of a dubious Greek phrase, which may either mean, *according to reason*, or *throughout* (*your*) *speech.* 'I would hear you as in duty bound,' or 'I would hear you to the end.' The verb does not literally mean *to hear*, but *to bear* or *bear with.* 'I would think it rational or right to bear with your complaints,' or, 'I would bear with you, as long as you thought fit to speak,' if your complaints had reference either to legal or to moral wrong.

15. 16. But if it be a question of words and names, and (of) your law, look ye (to it); for I will be no judge of such (matters). And he drave them from the judgment-seat.

But if, as you know to be the case, which is equivalent to *since*, the conditional particle not always signifying doubt (see above, on 4, 9. 16, 15.) *A question*, literally, something sought, that is a subject of inquiry and dispute (see above, on 15, 2, and below, on 23, 29. 25, 19. 26, 3.) *Words*, literally, *a word*, or language, speech, as opposed to action. *Names* does not necessarily denote the names *Messiah*, *Christ*, and *Jesus*, although these may be included, as may those of *Christian*, *Jew*, &c. But the term has rather a generic sense, as when we say proverbially "names are things." The sentence is descriptive of mere verbal controversy or logomachy, as opposed to questions of principle or fact. *And of law*, *the* (*law*) *with you*, or that belonging to, prevailing among you, not us. The preposition and construction are the same as in 17, 28 (*your own poets*, i. e. yours, not ours.) *Look ye to it*, literally, *ye shall see* (i. e. must see to that) *yourselves*, a very similar expression to that used by the chief priests in reply to Judas, when he repented of his crime and returned the price of blood (Matt. 27, 3–5.) *For a judge of these things I do not wish* (or *choose*) *to be.* .Nothing could be more characteristic of a Roman, such as Gallio is reputed to have been, than this contemptuous indifference, unmixed with any thing like spite or anger, towards the Jews and their internal feuds and broils. The perfect truth of these unstudied portraits, without any thing like formal or avowed description, is among the strongest incidental proofs of authenticity. (See below, on 25, 18–20.) In perfect keeping with this speech is the act by which it was accompanied (v. 16), and which is not to be regarded as an act of brutal violence, but merely as a summary and practical expression of the resolution which he had expressed in words. *Drave* (or *drove*) *them from the judgment-seat* (tribunal, as in v. 12), i. e. peremptorily dismissed them and refused to hear them further. This attenuated meaning of the verb is found in the best Greek writers, who apply it to banishment, and even to the marching of an army.

17. Then all the Greeks took Sosthenes, the chief ruler of the synagogue, and (beat) him before the judgment-seat; and Gallio cared for none of those things.

Instead of *Greeks*, some manuscripts read *Jews*, according to which text the sense would seem to be, that they ascribed their failure to the way in which their case had been presented to the governor by Sosthenes. Another still less probable opinion is that Sosthenes, like Crispus (see above, on v. 8), was a Christian convert, and was beaten by the Jews on that account. But if Gallio would not even hear their charges against Paul, he surely would not have allowed such violence against his followers. According to the common text, the meaning seems to be, that when the governor so cavalierly sent them off, the Greeks who had been looking on expressed their indignation, or perhaps gave vent to their long cherished hatred of the Jews, by beating their official representative. The latest critics omit both words (*Greeks* and *Jews*), which leaves the clause indefinite, or refers it to all present; but as these must have been mostly Greeks or Gentiles, the essential meaning still remains the same. There is no need of assuming that Sosthenes was the successor of Crispus, or the ruler of another synagogue, as the office probably was not elective, and was held by a plurality of persons (see above, on v. 8.) That this is "Sosthenes the brother," named in the beginning of Paul's second epistle to the Corinthians, is not impossible, and rather favoured by the identity of name; but it rests on no other proof, and requires us to assume that he was afterwards converted. *And none of these things concerned Gallio* (or *was a care to him.*) The original construction is impersonal, like that in John 12, 6, where the same form of the verb is used, whereas in every other case it is the present tense (see Matt. 22, 16. Mark 4, 38. 12, 14. Luke 10, 10. John 10, 13. 1 Cor. 9, 9. 1 Pet. 5, 7), and in one the imperative mood (1 Cor. 7, 21.) The immediate reference in *these things* is to the disorderly proceedings of the multitude before the very judgment-seat of Gallio, whose silence and indifference is recorded as a token of his nonchalance or stoical apathy, and only indirectly of that callousness or coldness in religion, which is commonly regarded as the principal thing here intended; so that Gallio has become a standing type, and "Gallio-like" a stereotyped simile, in our religious phraseology. That he knew little and cared less about the true religion, is most probable; that he was equally indifferent to all religions, true or false, is possible; but neither of these facts is here disclosed, except by inference from what is really affirmed, to wit, that when the Jews accused Paul he refused to hear them, and when Sosthenes was beaten by the mob he suffered it, and none of these things troubled or concerned him.

18. And Paul (after this) tarried (there) yet a good while, and then took his leave of the brethren, and sailed thence into Syria, and with him Priscilla and Aquila, having shorn (his) head in Cenchrea, for he had a vow.

The original construction is, 'And Paul, having still remained (continued on, or staid over) many days (literally, days enough), having taken leave of the brethren, sailed, &c.' *After this*, supplied by the translators, may be said to represent the particle with which the Greek verb is compounded, and which properly denotes addition or continuance. It may here suggest that he remained there longer than he first intended, as another compound of the same verb does in 10, 48. 15, 34. *The brethren*, the converts who composed the infant church of Corinth. *Sailed thence*, literally, *sailed out*, a kindred form to that in 13, 4 (*sailed away.*) *Into Syria*, i. e. on his way to Antioch, though not by a direct course (see below, on vs. 19. 22.) *Having shorn* (or *shaved*) *the head in Cenchrea*, one of the two ports of Corinth, on the east side of the isthmus (see above, on v. 1.) It has been a subject of dispute for ages, and especially since Chrysostom and Jerome, whether this relates to Paul or Aquila. In favour of the latter construction, it is urged that Aquila not only is the nearest antecedent, but is postponed to Priscilla, as if to bring him into closer connection with the verb that follows. The force of this argument is much diminished by the fact that the names occur in the same order elsewhere (Rom. 16, 3. 2 Tim. 4, 19), perhaps because Priscilla was more active and intelligent or better known. The position of the name is also neutralized by the construction, in which there is a series of participles, all relating to Paul, unless this be an exception. If Aquila were meant, the natural expression would have been, *who shaved* (not *having shaved*) *his head in Cenchrea*. There is, moreover, no sufficient reason for the mention of a circumstance so unimportant in relation to a minor personage like Aquila. If meant to show Paul's tolerance of ceremonial observances among his followers and friends, which is by no means an obvious supposition, this design would doubtless have been more distinctly stated. But admitting that the words refer to Paul, there are still two questions to be answered. The first is, how this ceremonial act is to be reconciled with Paul's anti-judaic principles and practice. The answer is, that during the anomalous interval between the day of Pentecost and the downfall of Jerusalem, the observance of the ceremonial law, whether stated or occasional, was always lawful, sometimes necessary, often expedient, as a means of safety or conciliation. (See above, on 2, 46. 16, 3.) In the present case it may have had respect to persons with whom Paul expected soon to meet, either in Jerusalem or Antioch, where some suppose the conference referred to in Gal. 2, 11–14, to have taken place soon after this, although it has been commonly referred to a much earlier date. The other question has respect to the nature of the vow here mentioned. Its form resembles that of the Nazarites, who abstained from strong drink and allowed their hair to grow for a specific time, at the close of which they shaved their heads and offered certain sacrifices, as prescribed in Num. 6, 1–21. But as these rites could be performed only at the temple, or at least in Palestine, the most probable conclusion, on the whole, is that this was a personal or private vow, such as we read of elsewhere (e. g. Gen. 28, 20. Lev. 27, 2. Num. 30, 2. Deut. 23, 21. Judg. 11, 30. 1 Sam. 1, 11. 2 Sam. 15, 7. Ps. 65, 1. Ecc. 5, 4), the outward formalities of which would naturally be conformed to those of which the law took cognizance. Some suppose that the shaving of his head was the assumption of the vow, but this is contrary to all analogy and usage. (See below, on 21, 24, and compare Num. 6, 13. 18.)

19. And he came to Ephesus, and left them there: but he himself entered into the synagogue, and reasoned with the Jews.

Came down upon (or *into*) *Ephesus*, arrived there (see above, on 16, 1.) Ephesus being opposite to Corinth, on the eastern side of the Egean Sea, may have been a customary stopping-place in voyages from Greece to Syria. *Left them* (Aquila and Priscilla) *there* (in Ephesus.) The relation of the clauses is obscure and doubtful. Some suppose the synagogue at Ephesus, as at Berea (see above, on 17, 10), to have been outside of the city, and that Paul went out to it, leaving his companions in the town. But this, even if true, was too minute a circumstance to be recorded, which objection does not lie against the common opinion, that the leaving here meant was at Paul's departure to resume his journey eastward, and that after mentioning it, Luke reverts to his short stay there, for the purpose of noting that he did not neglect even this occasion of addressing the Jews in the synagogue. As if he had said, Aquila and Priscilla went no further, leaving Paul to complete his voyage alone, but not till he had gone into the synagogue and there addressed the Jews, showing how far he was from having abandoned the desire and hope of their salvation. (See above, on v. 6, and on 13, 46; and for the meaning of the verb translated *reasoned*, on v. 4. 17, 2. 17.)

20. 21. When they desired (him) to tarry longer time with them, he consented not; but bade them farewell, saying, I must by all means keep this feast that cometh in Jerusalem: but I will return again unto you, if God will. And he sailed from Ephesus.

When they desired him, literally, *they asking him* (see above, on 3, 3. 10, 48. 16, 39.) *To tarry longer time*, literally, *for more time to remain*. This request implies that they were favourably impressed with Paul's address, and, as some suppose, with his ceremonial act at Cenchrea. *Consented*, a Greek verb originally meaning *nodded*, as a natural and customary gesture of assent or affirmation. *Bade farewell*, the same verb that is rendered *took his leave* in v. 18. *I must*, or *it is necessary for me* (δεῖ με.) *By all means*, or *at all events*, whatever else may happen, in familiar English, *any how*. *The feast*, *the coming* (one), that now approaching or at hand. This is commonly supposed to have been Pentecost, as navigation was not commonly resumed before the passover, and no other annual solemnity was absolutely called "the feast." *Keep*, literally, *make*, which may either mean *observe*, celebrate, or *spend*, pass, as applied to time in 15, 33, above. The latter is commonly preferred, because it seems less probable that Paul considered himself bound to keep a Jewish festival, than that he wished to take advantage of it as an opportunity of meeting with great numbers from all quarters. (See above, on 2, 5.) Some of the latest critics expunge this clause, as an interpolation from 20, 16, on the ground of its omission in several of the oldest manuscripts and versions. But others, with much more probability, account for this omission by supposing, that these old transcribers and translators fell into the natural mistake, still made by many readers, of believing that no visit to Jerusalem is mentioned in the context, and therefore thought it necessary to omit a promise which was not fulfilled (but see below, upon the next verse.) There is no doubt that the last clause of v. 21 is genuine. *God willing*, Vulg. *Deo volente*. *Sailed*, not the verb used in v. 18, but that in 13, 13. 16, 11.

22. And when he had landed at Cesarea, and gone up, and saluted the church, he went down to Antioch.

When he had landed, literally, *having come down* (i. e. from the vessel) *into Cesarea, and gone up* (i. e. to Jerusalem), *and saluted the church* (i. e. the mother-church there, the only one that would be absolutely so called), *he went down* (from Jerusalem again) *to Antioch*, thus returning to his point of departure, as he did at the close of his first mission (see above, on 14, 26.) It may seem more obvious and natural at first sight to apply the middle clauses of this verse to Cesarea, which is actually mentioned, while Jerusalem is not. But why should he have gone out of his way to Cesarea, if not in execution of the purpose so explicitly avowed in the preceding verse? And why should his saluting the church there be mentioned as a circumstance of any moment? He is also said to have *gone up*, for which no reason can be given at Cesarea, whereas it is the constant usage with respect to Jerusalem. (See above, on 11, 2. 15, 2, and compare Matt. 20, 17. Mark 10, 32. Luke 2, 42. John 5, 1. 7, 8. 11, 55. 12, 20. Gal. 1, 17. 18. 2, 1. 2.) The same is true of *going down* from Jerusalem to Antioch (see above, on 8, 5. 9, 32. 11, 27. 12, 19. 15, 1); but in what sense could he *go down* from Cesarea to the same place? To all these reasons may be added a conclusive one derived from the preceding verse. If Paul was not really in haste to reach the Holy City, how can his declaration there be justified, or what could be his motive for making it? If, on the other hand, this was his purpose, when was it carried into execution? Or if it was prevented, why is not that recorded, to explain and justify the failure? The only method of avoiding all these difficulties is by adopting what is now the usual interpretation of the verse before us.

23. And after he had spent some time (there), he departed, and went over (all) the country of Galatia and Phrygia in order, strengthening all the disciples.

A chapter might conveniently have been begun here, at the opening of Paul's third foreign mission. *Having made* (i. e. spent, see above, on v. 21 and 15, 33) *some time* (at Antioch, see above, on 4, 28.) *Departed*, literally, came out, went forth (see above, on 7, 4. 10, 23. 11, 25. 12, 17. 14, 20. 15, 24. 40. 16, 3. 10. 40. 17, 33.) *Went over*, literally, *coming* (i. e. passing) *through* (see above, on 8, 4. 40. 9, 32. 10, 38. 11, 19. 22. 13, 6. 14. 14, 24. 15, 3. 41. 16, 6. 17, 23.) *Galatia and Phrygia*, interior provinces of Asia Minor, mentioned together with the same brevity as here, and with the same peculiar formula (*the Galatian region*) in the account of Paul's second mission (see above, on 16, 6), but in the opposite order (*Phrygia and Galatia*), to which some refer the phrase *in order* here used; but it rather has respect to the methodical successive visitation of the churches, the details of which were probably diversified by no extraordinary incidents, as both visitations are so briefly mentioned. *Strengthening*, the same word that is rendered *confirming* (or *confirmed*) in 14, 22. 15, 32. 41, in all which cases, as in this, it denotes not a ceremony but an intellectual and spiritual process of instruction and conviction.

24. And a certain Jew, named Apollos, born at Alexandria, an eloquent man, (and) mighty in the Scriptures, came to Ephesus.

Having thus despatched in a single sentence Paul's revisitation of Galatia and Phrygia, Luke proceeds to the more important part of his third mission, namely, his residence at Ephesus; but first, as a preliminary topic, introduces the appearance of Apollos there before Paul's arrival. *A Jew*, by birth and education, in which sense Paul himself was one. *Apollos by name*, most probably a contracted form of *Apollonius.* (For similar contracted forms in *as*, see above, on 15, 22.) *An Alexandrian by birth* (*race* or *nation*, see above, on v. 2. 4, 36.) *Alexandria* in Egypt, so called from its founder, Alexander the Great, was at this time, not only a great commercial mart, but an illustrious seat both of Greek and Hebrew learning. A multitude of Jews were settled here under the Ptolemies or Macedonian kings of Egypt, and were thus brought into contact with the Greek philosophy and civilization. It was here that the Septuagint version had its origin, and the school of Platonizing Jews represented by Philo. There was no place where greater advantages of education were enjoyed in the age of the Apostles, among which may be reckoned the greatest library of the ancient world. *Eloquent*, a Greek word also meaning *learned*, especially in history; but the first sense is more common with the later writers, and is probably the prominent one here, as Apollos's scriptural learning is separately mentioned in the last clause. The original order is, *arrived at Ephesus, being mighty in the Scriptures.* This collocation, which is not retained in English, seems to separate the qualities ascribed to Apollos, as if one were previous and the other subsequent to his arrival; or as if the first were of a general nature, and the second had a more specific reference to the object of his visit. He was eloquent and educated, but when he appeared at Ephesus, displayed another special qualification, that of intimate acquaintance with the word of God, and an extraordinary power in expounding and enforcing it, both which ideas are suggested by the pregnant phrase, *mighty in the Scriptures.*

25. This man was instructed in the way of the Lord; and being fervent in the spirit, he spake and taught diligently the things of the Lord, knowing only the baptism of John.

Was instructed might be understood to mean after he arrived at Ephesus; but the original expression is the usual form of the pluperfect passive, *he had been instructed*, i. e. already, or before he came there. The verb itself is one peculiar to the Hellenistic and Ecclesiastical Greek, and is used to denote oral elementary instruction, being the root of the words catechism, catechize, &c. (Compare Luke 1, 4. Rom. 2, 18. 1 Cor. 14, 19. Gal. 6, 6, and see below, on 21, 21. 24.) *The way of the Lord* is a phrase used elsewhere only in relation to the ministry of John the Baptist, as our Lord's forerunner (see Matt. 3, 3. Mark 1, 3. Luke 3, 4. John 1, 23), and as John's baptism is expressly mentioned in the last clause, it has been suggested, and is not impossible, that it here means the religion taught by John, i. e. the doctrine of a Messiah come or coming, and of his kingdom as at hand (see Matt. 3, 1. 2. 11. 12.) It is commonly, however, understood to mean the gospel, or the doctrine of Christ himself, elsewhere called *the* (*this* or *that*) *way.* (See above, on 9, 2, and below, on 19, 9. 23. 22, 4. 24, 14. 22.) *Fervent* (literally, *boiling*) *in spirit*, is a phrase used by Paul in Rom. 12, 11. *Spake* (or *talked*) *and taught* may signify private and public teaching (see above, on 16, 13. 32.) *Diligently* is not the meaning of the Greek word, but *exactly*, accurately, or correctly, i. e. as far as he knew or had as yet been taught, if by *the things of* (or *about*) *the Lord* we understand the gospel. But if that phrase means John's prospective preaching of the Saviour, the adverb may be taken in its strongest sense. *Knowing*, knowing well, a stronger word than that which is commonly so rendered (see above, on 10, 28. 15, 7, and below, on 19, 15. 25. 20, 18. 22, 19. 24, 10. 26, 26.) *The baptism of John* may be either the rite properly so called, or John's whole ministry and doctrine (see above, on 1, 22. 10, 37.) The meaning cannot be, that Apollos did not know that the Messiah had actually come, or who he was; for John had identified him and baptized him before the close of his own ministry. (See Matt. 3, 13. Mark 1, 9. Luke 3, 21. John 1, 29-36. 3, 26-36.)

26. And he began to speak boldly in the synagogue; whom when Aquila and Priscilla had heard, they took him unto (them), and expounded unto him the way of God more perfectly.

This same man (οὗτός τε), or *this man also*, besides talking and teaching as above related, now began to speak publicly and plainly (see above, on 9, 27. 29. 13, 46. 14, 3) in the synagogue of Ephesus, where, as a native Jew, he had liberty not only of worship but of speech (see above, on 13, 5. 14. 15.) *But Aquila and Priscilla* (whom Paul had left at Ephesus, v. 19), *having heard him*, in the synagogue which they still frequented, or to which they were attracted by the fame of this new preacher, *took him unto (them)*, into their society or company, the same verb that is used above in 17, 5. *Expounded*, set forth, stated, and explained, the same verb that is used above in 11, 4, and in a very different sense, in 7, 21. *The way of God*, i. e. his method of salvation, and the doctrine of his Son. The latest critics omit *God*, and simply read *the way*, which may then be an abbreviation of the phrase used in v. 25. That it means the same with that phrase, seems to follow from their teaching him this way *more accurately* or *exactly*, the comparative form of the adverb in v. 25. The English versions are peculiarly unfortunate in rendering this adverb by two entirely different English ones (*diligently* and *perfectly*), neither of which expresses its true meaning. The sense of this clause may be either that they gave him a more accurate idea of the gospel, the Christian system; or that they taught him more exactly what the way of the Lord was which John came to prepare.

27. And when he was disposed to pass into Achaia, the brethren wrote, exhorting the disciples to receive him; who, when he was come, helped them much which had believed through grace.

When he was disposed (literally, *he desiring*) *to pass*, or go through, i. e. through the intervening space (see above, on v. 23) *into Achaia*, and no doubt to Corinth, as the most important place in the province (see above, on v. 1.) This wish may have been prompted by the representations and advice of Aquila and Priscilla, who perhaps preferred that he should build at Corinth upon Paul's foundation, rather than anticipate Paul's work in Ephesus. *The brethren* may denote the same two persons, but perhaps includes some other Christians whom they had found or gathered there. It is not impossible indeed that the Ephesian church was organized already, as Paul in his epistle to it nowhere claims to be its founder, as he does in other cases. (Compare 1 Thess. 1, 5. 6. 9. Phil. 1, 5. 6. Gal. 1, 8. 9.) There is here an ambiguity in the original, which has not been retained in the translation. *Exhorting* stands before *the brethren wrote*, and is by some supposed to mean *exhorting* (*him*), i. e. encouraging him in his purpose. But most interpreters explain *exhorting* as a statement of what they wrote, the verb and participle indicating simultaneous acts, as in 1, 24. 19, 2. *When he was come*, or, *having arrived*, i. e. in Achaia, and no doubt at Corinth (see below, on 19, 1.) *Helped*, or contributed, the same verb that is used above in 4, 15. 17, 18, and below, in 20, 14. *Had believed*, or been converted, not through his preaching, but through Paul's, before Apollos came. These he assisted, as appears from the next verse, in their controversy with the unbelieving Jews. *Through grace* is by some connected with the remoter verb, contributed or helped through grace, i. e. by special divine influence. To the other and more obvious construction with *believed*, it is objected that the statement would be here superfluous and out of place, as Luke is not relating how they became Christians at a former time, but how Apollos now assisted them. It may be doubted whether this consideration is sufficient to outweigh the argument derived from the collocation of the words.

28. For he mightily convinced the Jews, (and that) publicly, shewing by the Scriptures that Jesus was Christ.

The way in which he helped them is particularly stated. *Mightily*, intensely, vehemently, which may refer either to the force of his arguments, or to the warmth of his delivery, most probably to both together. (Compare Luke 23, 10, where the Greek word is the same.) *Convinced*, refuted, or confuted utterly, in Greek an emphatic double compound verb, denoting not a change of mind in the opponents, as the English version would imply, but their logical discomfiture or failure in argument, and the complete triumph of Apollos over them. The adverse party were the unbelieving Jews, with whom he was particularly qualified to deal (see above, on v. 24.) *Publicly* (see above, on 16, 37, and below, on 20, 20), no doubt in the synagogue (see above, on v. 26.) *Showing*, evincing, or demonstrating. *By* (or *through*) *the Scriptures*, as the only means of proof (see above, on 17, 2. 11.) *The Christ*, the Messiah of the Prophecies (see above, on v. 5.)

CHAPTER XIX.

We have here the history of Paul's long residence and ministry at Ephesus. He first receives into the church twelve disciples who had only been baptized with the baptism of John (1–7.) He then preaches three months in the synagogue, and two years in another place, until the whole province had heard the gospel (8–10.) His preaching is attested by extraordinary miracles, which certain Jews attempt to imitate, but to their own discomfiture (11–17.) This is followed by a general confession and destruction of magical writings (18–20.) Paul prepares for his departure and sends two of his attendants into Macedonia before him (21–22.) Meantime the city is aroused against him by interested persons (23–34.) The tumult is allayed by the authority and reasonings of a public officer (35–41.)

1. And it came to pass, that, while Apollos was at Corinth, Paul having passed through the upper coasts came to Ephesus; and finding certain disciples —

It came to pass (or *happened*), a connective formula, resuming and continuing the narrative of Paul's third mission, which was interrupted (18, 24) to record the first appearance of Apollos. *While Apollos was*, literally, *in his being*. He was gone to Corinth, therefore, before Paul arrived in Ephesus. *Coasts*, in the old English sense of borders, districts (see above, on 13, 50.) The Greek word here used properly means *parts*, i. e. divisions of the country. *Upper*, i. e. inland, perhaps with some allusion to the mountains in the interior of Asia Minor. The parts here meant may be Phrygia and Galatia (see above, on 18, 23), or the country between them and Ephesus. This last was a very ancient city of Ionia, near the mouth of the Cayster, famous for its wealth and commerce, and for the temple of Diana just without its walls, built in the sixth century before Christ, burnt down in the fourth, on the night that Alexander the Great was born, and rebuilt in such a style as to be reckoned by the ancients one of the seven wonders of the world. (See below, on v. 24.) Ancient Ephesus was always flourishing, and under the Roman domination, the greatest city of Asia Minor, whereas now it exists only in ruins, near the Turkish village of Asayaluk; while Smyrna, by a singular but not uncommon contrast, is now more flourishing and populous than ever. In fulfilment of the promise made on his way from Corinth to Jerusalem (see above, on 18, 21), Paul now commences his long residence at Ephesus, of which the fruits were so abundant and so durable. *Finding*, unexpectedly, and on his first arrival (see above, on 18, 2.) *Certain* (i. e. some, a few) *disciples*, not of Apollos, or of John the Baptist, but of Christ, as the word always means when absolutely used (see above, on 18, 23. 27), and as appears from the way in which Paul treated them.

2. He said unto them, Have ye received the Holy Ghost since ye believed? And they said unto him, We have not so much as heard whether there be any Holy Ghost.

Did ye receive the Holy Ghost when ye believed (or *were converted*)? not, have you received it since? which would be otherwise expressed in Greek. The verb and participle denote simultaneous actions, as in 1, 24. 5, 30. 10, 39. 18, 27. *The Holy Ghost*, i. e. his extraordinary influences, with their miraculous effects, by which baptism was so frequently accompanied (see above, on 2, 38. 8, 17. 9, 17. 10, 44–48. 11, 15. 16. 15, 8.) It might seem indeed to have been an invariable conjunction from Paul's question; but this question may have been occasioned by something else not here recorded; or it may have been customary in such cases, to ask whether these extraordinary gifts had been received or not, without implying that they were essential or invariable in every case of genuine conversion. Paul's doubt as to their baptism did not arise from the absence of these gifts, but from their imperfect knowledge of the true religion. If they had simply answered No, he might have questioned them no further; but the singular form of their denial led him to pursue the subject. *We have not so much as heard*, may be more exactly rendered, *but* (or *why*, i. e. so far from receiving it) *we did not even hear if* (or *whether*) *there is a Holy Spirit.* That they had literally never heard of his existence is incredible, even if they were mere Jews (whose Scriptures contain references to him), or disciples of John, or of Apollos, much more if they had believed in Christ, which is the constant meaning of the verb *believe* when absolutely used. (See above, on 2, 44. 4, 32. 11, 21. 13, 12. 39. 48. 14, 1. 15, 5. 7. 17, 12. 34. 18, 8. 27.) *Heard* is in Greek an aorist relating, not to a long interval, but to a single point of time, to wit, the date of their conversion or profession. They did not then hear the Holy Spirit mentioned, any more than if there had been no such being. Far from receiving his extraordinary gifts, they were not even baptized in his name, or instructed in relation to his work and office. The expression of this fact is strong but natural, and not without analogies, even in the dialect of common life. As if an Englishman were asked whether he swore allegiance to the Queen on a particular occasion, he might simply say that no such oath was tendered to him; but if he wished to make his negative peculiarly emphatic, might express the same idea by declaring that he did not hear her named; or still more strongly, that he did not hear that there was such a person, without any risk of being understood to mean that he had never heard of her.

3. And he said unto them, Unto what then were ye baptized? And they said, Unto John's baptism.

This second question is not founded on the first, but on their strange and unexpected answer. He does not mean to ask them how they could have been baptized at all without receiving these extraordinary gifts, for the two things did not always go together (see above, on 8, 16); but how they could have been baptized without so much as hearing of the Holy Spirit. This implies, what is otherwise most probable, that

Christian baptism was administered from the beginning in the form prescribed by Christ himself (Matt. 28, 19), and that no one therefore could receive it without hearing of the Holy Ghost, in whose name, as well as in the Father's and the Son's, every convert was baptized. Since they could not be baptized into Christ (see above, on 8, 16) without so much as hearing of the Holy Spirit, Paul infers that they had not been so baptized at all, and asks them into what they were baptized, i. e. into what profession or communion, into what creed or system, into what faith or religion, they had been initiated by the rite to which they had submitted. *Unto*, in both clauses, should be *into*, as the usual and strict sense of the Greek word, and as more expressive of the main idea here suggested, namely, that of initiation, union, and incorporation. But how could they be *baptized into a baptism?* Not at all, if by *baptism* be understood the sacrament or rite itself. They might be baptized *with* it, or *according to* it; but neither of these senses is expressed in the original, which means simply *into* it, as just explained. The solution of the difficulty is afforded by the use of the word *baptism* elsewhere to denote John's ministry or mission (see above, on 1, 22), and the subject of his preaching (see above, on 10, 37.) Retaining this sense here, to be baptized into John's baptism is to be initiated, by that rite, into the doctrine, system, or religion which he taught. This was the doctrine of repentance (see above, on 13, 24), or reform of heart and life, not as sufficient of itself or practicable by itself, but as a preparation for something else, namely, faith in the Messiah, whose way John himself came to prepare. This Messiah he identified as Jesus of Nazareth (John 1, 29–36. 3, 26–30), who must therefore be acknowledged by all who were baptized with the baptism of John. There is no ground, therefore, for supposing that these men knew nothing of Jesus as the true Messiah; for this was an essential part of John's doctrine, and without this they would not have been called *disciples* (see above, on v. 1.) Their deficiency consisted in their stopping short at the Messiahship of Jesus, without any knowledge of his doctrine, miracles, atoning death, resurrection, ascension, and effusion of the Spirit, in a word, of any thing distinctively or characteristically Christian.

4. Then said Paul, John verily baptized with the baptism of repentance, saying unto the people, that

they should believe on him which should come after him, that is, on Christ Jesus.

Paul explains to them the prospective and preparatory character of John's ministry, who exhorted the people to believe, not on himself, but *on the coming* (*one*); and this *coming one* was Jesus. Though not expressed, it is implied that John had no church or religion of his own, into which men were initiated by his baptism, but merely introduced men to his principal, by whom alone they could be saved, or even fully instructed. Where this effect did not ensue, but men stopped short at the baptism of John, it was deprived of its whole meaning and effect.

5. And when they heard (this), they were baptized in the name of the Lord Jesus.

And hearing, they were baptized. There is here a remarkable ambiguity of syntax, which has led to two entirely different interpretations of the narrative. Some of the older writers understand this as a part of what Paul said, and therefore as referring to the people mentioned in v. 4. *And hearing* (what John said about believing in the coming one) *they were baptized* (as so believing) *into the name of the Lord Jesus* (i. e. into union with him as the only Saviour.) The objection usually made to this construction, that John did not, in point of fact, baptize into the name of Jesus, begs the question here at issue, as this passage, if a part of Paul's discourse, would be sufficient to establish what is thus denied, though not in the most obvious meaning of the words. Paul may, in that case, have intended to describe, not the formula which John used, but the end he had in view. As if he had said, 'Since John called the people to believe on a Messiah yet to come, and this Messiah was Jesus, those who received his baptism were really (though not ostensibly) baptized into the name of the Lord Jesus.' This view of the passage is preferred by some who are unwilling to admit the fact of a rebaptism. Most interpreters, however, are agreed that these are not the words of the Apostle, but of the historian, describing the effect of what Paul said upon his hearers. *Hearing* (his statement in relation to John's baptism, as deriving all its worth and meaning from its relation to the Saviour) *they were baptized in* (or *into*) *the name of the Lord Jesus.* The question why this was required or permitted has been variously answered. Some say, because John's baptism was essentially distinct from that of Christ and could not answer the same purpose. But we do not read that Apollos was rebaptized, or our Lord's own disciples, some or all of whom had been baptized by John. It is true, however, that Peter, on the day of Pentecost, requires all to be baptized, without inquiring whether any had been John's disciples. To reconcile these seeming contradictions, some suppose that there was no fixed rule, but that baptism was administered or not, at the discretion of the minister, or even at the option of the convert, who might wish to be assured of his legitimate admission to the church, by a repetition of the rite, even where it was unnecessary, as for instance in the case before us. Another explanation is, that they were not again baptized with water, but for the first time with the Holy Spirit; an idea nowhere else expressed by the phrase, baptized into the name of Jesus. Perhaps the most satisfactory solution is the one afforded by the intimate relation between John and Christ, and the entire dependence of John's baptism upon faith in Christ for its whole meaning and validity. Where this was understood, and those baptized by John went on, as he instructed them, without undue delay or interruption, to embrace Christ as their Saviour and his doctrine as their faith, rebaptism would have been a ceremonial mockery. This was probably the case with most of Christ's disciples who were resident in Palestine. But where, from their removal or return to foreign countries, or from other providential interruptions, they had gone no further than this first step, but continued at the threshold to which John had led them, long after the conclusion of his ministry and life, the work had as it were to be begun *de novo*, not because John's baptism was invalid or even insufficient, when correctly understood and followed up, but because by being insulated and divided from the work of Christ and of the Holy Ghost, to which it was a solemn introduction, it became useless and unmeaning, and must therefore be renewed from the beginning. This hypothesis not only serves to throw light on the case before us, but to harmonize it with the other facts which have been mentioned. That these men regarded John himself as the Messiah, as we know him to have been by later heretics, is inconsistent with Luke's calling them *disciples* (v. 1), and Paul's speaking of the time when they *believed* (v. 2.) A similar question of construction has occurred before in 15, 5; but a still more striking parallel is that in Luke 7, 29. 30, because the reference is there, as well as here, to John the Baptist's preaching, and to its effect upon his hearers.

6. 7. And when Paul had laid (his) hands upon them, the Holy Ghost came on them; and they spake with tongues, and prophesied. And all the men were about twelve.

Paul having laid (*his*) *hands upon them, they prophesied*, not foretold, but spoke by inspiration. (See above, on 2, 17. 18.) The effect is similar to that described in 8, 17. 10, 44, except that in the latter case baptism had not yet been administered, and there was no imposition of hands. Those who explain v. 5 as the words of Paul, regard this as a confirmation of their previous baptism; those who do not, as a confirmation of that just administered. Such confirmation cannot now be practised, as it had relation, not to the sanctifying influences, but to the miraculous endowments, of the Holy Spirit, which have long since ceased. *All the men were about twelve*, is an unusual expression, meaning something more than a simple designation of the number. It may have been intended to preclude the false impression, that all the brethren in Ephesus (see above, on 18, 27) were in this infantile state of ignorance and backwardness. *All* may then be understood to mean *all told*, or at the most. 'So far was this from being universal, that the men concerned in this transaction, on the highest computation, were not more than twelve.'

8. And he went into the synagogue, and spake boldly for the space of three months, disputing and persuading the things concerning the kingdom of God.

The occurrence just related took place at the time of Paul's arrival in Ephesus. Luke now begins the history of his residence and labours there. He gives his first attention to the Jews, not only in accordance with his general practice, but because they had invited him to come among them. (See above, on 18, 20.) *Disputing* (or *discoursing*) *and persuading* may describe his preaching as both doctrinal and practical, didactic and hortatory; or the first term may describe his preaching, and the second its effect. (See above, on 18, 4.) The subject of his preaching was all that related to the kingdom of God, the new dispensation, the doctrine and church of Christ. (See above, on 1, 3. 8, 12.)

9. But when divers were hardened, and believed not, but spake evil of that way before the multitude, he departed from them, and separated the disciples, disputing daily in the school of one Tyrannus.

When, literally, *as*, suggesting both the time and the occasion of Paul's conduct. *Were hardened*, became obstinate in unbelief. *Believed not*, in Greek a single word which may be rendered *disbelieved*, denoting not a mere negation, but a positive refusal. The Greek verb also suggests the idea of disobedience or resistance to authority. (See above, on 14, 2. 17, 5.) *Speaking evil*, vilifying, or reviling, here used as an equivalent to *blaspheming* (see above, on 13, 48. 18, 6), in its original or lower sense, and also in the secondary higher sense, so far as the evil speaking was directed against God or Christ. *That way*, literally, *the way*, i. e. the new religion, elsewhere more fully called the way of God, of the Lord, and of salvation. (See above, on 16, 17. 18. 25. 26.) The same abbreviated form occurs above, 9, 2. *Before the multitude*, i. e. the congregation in the synagogue, as appears from the preceding verse. The opposition was probably so violent and noisy as to make all further efforts in the same place useless or impossible. *Departing*, not merely going out from one place to another, but seceding, formally withdrawing. (See above, on 15, 38.) From the bad sense of the Greek verb here used comes the noun *apostasy*. (See below, on 21, 21, and compare 2 Thess. 2, 3.) *Separated the disciples*, drew a line between them and the unbelieving Jews, withdrew them from the synagogue, and formed a separate society or church. This was no new measure (see above, on 13, 46–49. 18, 6. 7), but is mentioned here as having been occasioned by the violent resistance to the truth at Ephesus, which is the more remarkable because this very class or body, and most probably some of the same individuals, had urged Paul to remain upon his former visit. (See above, on 18, 20.) *Disputing*, reasoning or discoursing, see above, on v. 8, and on 17, 2. 17. 18, 4. 19. The word has reference, no doubt, to the polemic, argumentative character imparted to Paul's preaching by the opposition of the unbelieving Jews. *School*, a Greek word originally meaning leisure or spare time, then study or instruction, then a place for teaching. *One Tyrannus*, or *a certain Tyrannus*, as the pronoun is translated elsewhere. (See above, on 5, 1. 10, 1. 12, 1. 13, 1. 15, 1. 16, 1. 18, 2. 24.) As *Tyrannus* originally means a king, Calvin thinks it not impossible that the place here mentioned was a school or college built by some former sovereign of the country, who reigned before the Roman Conquest. It is commonly agreed, however, that it is a proper name, of which use there are numerous examples both in classical and hellenistic Greek. Whether this Tyrannus was a Jewish rabbi, and his school a *beth-midrash* or private synagogue; or a Greek sophist, with his school of rhetoric; is as doubtful and as unimportant as the questions, whether he and Paul occupied the room together, and whether it was hired or only borrowed.

10. And this continued by the space of two years; so that all they which dwelt in Asia heard the word of the Lord Jesus, both Jews and Greeks.

This, i. e. this practice of discoursing daily in the school of Tyrannus. *Continued*, literally, *happened*, came to pass, was done, the same Greek word with which the chapter opens. *By the space of*, an obsolete and needless paraphrase of the preposition *for*, as in v. 8. *Two years*, from the time of his removal to the school of Tyrannus, and therefore exclusive of the three months mentioned in v. 8. (See below, on 20, 31.) *All those inhabiting Asia*, i. e. Asia Proper, or Proconsular Asia, of which Ephesus was the capital. (See above, on 2, 9. 6, 9. 16, 6.) *All*, a natural hyperbole, and not a strong one, as it may have been literally true, that the entire population of that province heard the new doctrine, not all by coming to Ephesus, nor all directly from the lips of Paul, but some from him or his assistants, in their journeys through the province. It was probably at this time that the seven churches of Asia, to which the epistles in the Book of Revelation are addressed, were originally founded. To this time, likewise, are now commonly referred the epistle to the Galatians and the first to the Corinthians, which last contains a reference to Paul's Ephesian labours, in perfect harmony with what is here recorded. (See 1 Cor. 16, 8.) *The word of the Lord* (*Jesus*), that of which he is both the author and the subject. (See above, on 8, 25. 13, 48. 49. 15, 33. 36. 16, 32.)

11. 12. And God wrought special miracles by the hands of Paul, so that from his body were brought unto the sick handkerchiefs or aprons, and the diseases departed from them, and the evil spirits went out of them.

Special miracles, literally, *powers*, *not the common* (*ones*), or still more closely, *not those happening* (readily or often.) The same phrase occurs again in this book, and is rendered, *no little.* (See below, on 28, 2.) *Powers* or *forces* is a term applied to miracles, as being proofs and actual exertions of omnipotence. (See above, on 2, 22. 8, 13.) What distinguished these from ordinary miracles was not their number or intrinsic magnitude, but the way in which they were performed, through articles of dress, which had been in contact with Paul's body. *Handkerchiefs* and *aprons* are both Latin words in the original, the former strictly meaning *sweat-cloths* (*sudaria*, elsewhere translated *napkin* (Luke 19, 20. John 11, 44. 20, 7), from *sudor*), and the latter *half-girdles* (*semicinctia*), i. e. going only half round the body, covering the front of the person. It here denotes most probably a workman's apron, perhaps those of Paul himself, if we suppose, as some do, that the articles here mentioned were his own, and were carried to and fro between him and the persons to be healed. It seems more natural, however, to suppose that the people brought their handkerchiefs or aprons and applied them to Paul's person, for the purpose of securing a miraculous effect. *Or* (not *and*) may be intended to suggest, that it mattered little what the garment was, or that it was not always the same; as if he had said, handkerchiefs, aprons, or other articles of dress, that could be easily removed and carried. *Brought unto* (or *upon*), i. e. applied, imposed; but according to some critics, the true text is *brought away. His body*, properly, *his skin* (or *surface*), not implying that these articles were worn there, which was not the case with either, but that a mere superficial touch or contact was sufficient to impart the healing virtue. The idea of a vulgar superstition, with which Paul had no concern, and which was mercifully countenanced by the event, is as gratuitous and groundless here as in the case of Peter's shadow. (See above, on 5, 15.) In either case, there was a special divine ordering, intended to communicate a healing influence to greater numbers and a greater distance, yet without allowing any doubt as to the source or channel of communication, such as might have arisen if the miracles had been performed by mere word of command, without actual proximity or contact, mediate or immediate, with the object. *Departed*, were got rid of, or escaped from, as the Greek word properly denotes. (Compare Luke 12, 58. Heb. 12, 15.) As in other cases of the same kind, demoniacal possessions are distinctly mentioned, as the worst form of disease, because entirely preternatural and arising from the real though mysterious agency of evil spirits, the expulsion of which furnished the most striking proof of a divine legation and authority. (See above, on 5, 16. 8, 7.) These were "the signs of an Apostle," by which Paul's commission was attested in Ephesus as well as Corinth (2 Cor. 12, 12.)

13. Then certain of the vagabond Jews, exorcists, took upon them to call over them which had evil spirits the name of the Lord Jesus, saying, We adjure you by Jesus whom Paul preacheth.

Then (δὲ) *undertook*, took in hand, or attempted. (See above, on 9, 29, and compare Luke 1, 1.) *Certain*, some, see above, on vs. 1, 9. *Of*, literally, *from*, i. e. from among (see above, on 12, 1. 13, 23. 15, 5. 17, 13); but the latest critics, following the oldest manuscripts, read *some also* (καί). *Vagabond Jews, exorcists*, is too strong a version, as the first Greek word (*going about, wandering*) is descriptive of their mode of life and not their character. (Compare its use in 1 Tim. 5, 13. Heb. 11, 37.) The whole phrase rather means, *itinerant Jewish exorcists*, as the second word may be either an adjective or substantive. (See above, on 13, 6.) These were men who undertook to expel demons by the use of spells or charms, some of which, according to Josephus, were said to have been handed down from Solomon. Such exorcists were very numerous in the days of Christ and his Apostles, partly because there was a general taste for mysteries and occult science in that age, partly because the number of demoniacs was unusually great. (See above, on 5, 16, and compare

Matt. 12, 27.) They used the name of Jesus, no doubt, because they had heard Paul so use it, and desired to try its efficacy for themselves. *Over* or *upon*, implying personal proximity, not merely *as to* them, in their behalf. *We* (or according to the oldest copies, *I*) *adjure you*, i. e. solemnly require you to come out of those whom you have thus possessed. These are here actively described as *having evil spirits*, as a sick man may be either said to have a disease, or to be seized, held, by it. As *Jesus* (or *Joshua*) was a common name among the Jews (see above, on 7, 45. 13, 6), the person meant is here distinguished as *the Jesus whom Paul preached*, or proclaimed as the Messiah.

14. And there were seven sons of (one) Sceva, a Jew, (and) chief of the priests, which did so.

This may either be a single case among those mentioned in v. 13, or a more specific statement of the only one there meant; as if he had said, 'the exorcists who did this were certain sons,' &c. *Some* or *certain* (omitted in our version) may be construed, as a qualifying term, with *seven*, in the sense of *some* (or *about*) *seven*. But it suits the collocation of the Greek words better to take them separately, one as an indefinite, the other as a definite description of the same persons, 'certain sons of Sceva, seven (in number.)' *A chief priest*, resident at Ephesus, is something strange, and has been variously explained according to the different senses of the Greek word. (See above, on 4, 4.) It is not impossible that a member of the sacerdotal race, entitled to be thus distinguished, may have been residing there. But it is also possible that *chief-priest* here has reference to the worship of Diana, and that this Sceva was a renegade or apostate Jew. This is the less improbable because the Greek word (ἀρχιερεὺς) was not only in general use among the heathen, but occurs repeatedly on coins and in other inscriptions relating to the worship of Diana at Ephesus. The word *Jew*, as in 18, 23, and often elsewhere, relates only to his origin. The name *Scæva* occurs both in Greek and Latin writers.

15. And the evil spirit answered and said, Jesus I know, and Paul I know; but who are ye?

And answering, responding to this impious invocation.

The evil spirit, i. e. wicked, fallen, as distinguished from good angels. The same idea is sometimes expressed by the phrase *unclean* (or *impure*) *spirits*. (See above, on 5, 16. 8, 7. Luke 4, 36. 6, 18. 8, 29. 9, 42, and compare Luke 7, 21. 8, 2. and vs. 12. 13, above.) *The evil spirit said*, through the vocal organs of the man whom he possessed, but probably in such a manner as to indicate the presence of two personal agents. (See above, on 8, 7.) *I know* is expressed by two entirely distinct Greek verbs, the last of which is commonly explained to mean a more familiar knowledge, though the first is applied even to our Lord's omniscience (e. g. in John 2, 24. 25. 5, 42. 10, 14. 15. 27.) The difference meant to be expressed, if any, is probably rather one of quality than quantity, the first verb being more reverential and the second more familiar. 'I know who Jesus is, and as for Paul, I am well acquainted with him.' One writer paraphrases, 'Jesus I know (to my cost);' but this can hardly be included in the meaning of the verb, nor is it even necessarily suggested by the context, though readily deducible from other passages. (See Mark 1, 24. Luke 4, 34.) The question (*Who are ye?*) is expressive both of indignation and contempt, in which sense it is familiar to the dialect of common life. It is here equivalent to saying, What right have you to use this venerable name, at which the very devils tremble? (See James 2, 19.)

16. And the man in whom the evil spirit was leaped on them, and overcame them, and prevailed against them, so that they fled out of that house naked and wounded.

The verbal expression of contempt is followed up by corresponding acts, which are here ascribed to the man himself, as the words in the preceding verse are to the evil spirit, a variation altogether natural, as both belonged to both. Under the resistless power of the demon, the demoniac attacked the presumptuous exorcists. *Overcame them*, mastered them, lorded it over them, the same verb that is used in Matt. 20, 25. Mark 10, 42. 1 Pet. 5, 3. *Prevailed* (literally, was strong or powerful) *against them*. *Naked*, i. e. with their clothes torn partially or wholly off. The Greek word sometimes means imperfectly or badly clothed (e. g. Matt. 25, 36. John 21, 7. James 2, 15.) This violence was permitted both as a proof of real demoniacal possession, and as a punishment of the exorcists. Some of the oldest manuscripts and latest critics read *against them both*, as if only two of the seven were actually thus maltreated. But this may be a mere correction by some copyist who thought the disproportion too great between one and seven.

17. And this was known to all the Jews and Greeks also dwelling at Ephesus; and fear fell on them all, and the name of the Lord Jesus was magnified.

This occurrence was recorded, not for its own sake merely, though sufficiently remarkable, but on account of its effect in discouraging all such attempts, and vindicating Paul's miraculous performances from the charge or the suspicion of magical imposture. *Was known*, or became known, by report, to many who were not eye-witnesses. (See above, on 1, 19. 9, 42.) *Jews and Greeks* (or *Gentiles*, see above, on v. 10, and compare 14, 1. 16, 1. 3. 17, 4. 18, 4. 17), the two great classes or divisions of the people as to religion. Both are particularly mentioned, either because the Jews were very numerous in Ephesus and formed a large proportion of the population, or because they were primarily interested in this incident, as having taken place among themselves (but see above, on v. 14.) *Jews and Greeks also*, or *both Jews and Greeks*. *Fear*, not mere terror, or dread of similar discomfiture to that experienced by the sons of Sceva, but religious awe, a sense of the divine presence, such as signal providences sometimes produce, even in irreligious men. (See above, on 2, 43. 5, 5. 11.) This feeling had particular respect to the Lord Jesus, as the Saviour whom Paul preached (see above, on v. 13), and whose name had been profaned by the exorcists, but was now *magnified*, extolled, and honoured, by their ignominious defeat and punishment.

18. And many that believed came, and confessed, and shewed their deeds.

A further effect of this remarkable occurrence was to touch the consciences of many converts and constrain them to acknowledge their malpractices. *Many too* (τε) *of those who had believed* (in Christ) or been converted to the true religion. This may mean those who were converted now, on this occasion, in consequence of this event. But the past form of the participle rather seems to indicate those who had before believed or been converted, but were now re-awakened by this singular occurrence, and the proof which it afforded, both of Paul's divine legation, and of God's displeasure at all magical and occult arts. *Came*, no doubt to Paul, but whether publicly or privately, is not recorded, though the former is more probable from what is mentioned in the next verse. *Came*, not once for all, or all at once, but, as the form of the verb indicates, *were coming*, or continued to come, came from time to time. *Confessing*, or acknowledging, a Greek verb sometimes used in a good sense (e. g. Matt. 11, 25. Luke 10, 21. Rom. 14, 11. 15, 9. Phil. 2, 11. Rev. 3, 5.) Hence some of the old writers understood this verse as meaning, that those who had already been converted, and had gone forth to convert others, now came back to the Apostle, as the twelve and seventy returned to Christ (Mark 6, 30. Luke 10, 17), *acknowledging and reporting*, thankfully acknowledging and joyfully announcing (or reporting) their proceedings and performances, i. e. what they had been enabled to accomplish for the good of others. This construction, though it yields a good sense, and removes the appearance of tautology or needless repetition in the next verse, is otherwise less favoured by the context and the usage of the terms employed. Such a report from the Ephesian converts would be out of place between the reference to exorcism in the previous context and to magic in what follows. The word translated *deeds*, though in itself generic or indifferent (see Matt. 16, 27. Rom. 12, 4), is commonly used in a bad sense (see Luke 23, 51. Rom. 8, 13. Col. 3, 9.) That the verb *confess* is also so used, see Matt. 3, 6. Mark 1, 5. Jas. 5, 16. It is therefore commonly agreed, that *deeds* means evil deeds or sins, and the verb the confession of them, either privately to Paul, or publicly before the people. Some understand this as a general confession of misdeeds, occasioned by a new conviction or alarm of conscience; others, more specifically, that of magical or occult practices continued since their baptism; others still, that of having dealt with sorcerers or wizards, whose own confession is recorded separately in the next verse.

19. Many of them also which used curious arts brought their books together, and burned them before all (men), and they counted the price of them, and found (it) fifty thousand (pieces) of silver.

And (or *but*) *many*, not the word so rendered in the verse preceding, but one which literally means *enough*, and is of frequent occurrence in this book (see above, on 5, 37. 8, 11. 9, 23. 43. 11, 24. 26. 12, 12. 14, 3. 21. 17, 9. 18, 18.) *Used*, literally, *practising*, the verb corresponding to the noun translated *deeds* in v. 18. *Curious arts*, in Greek an article and adjective, *the curious* (*things*). The adjective originally means officious, over-busy; then meddlesome, inquisitive, as to the concerns of others (see 1 Tim. 5, 13); then as to invisible realities with special reference to futurity, occasioning the use of magical or occult arts, as means of information and discovery. *Curious* means inquisitive in this sense, i. e. prying into the secret things of God (Deut. 29, 29.) (The sense of rare or singular belongs to later usage.) For such practices Ephesus was famous in the ancient world, so that "*Ephesian letters*" or "*inscriptions*" (ἐφέσια γράμματα) was almost proverbial as a designation of written charms, amulets and talismans. These were connected with the worship of Diana there, on whose image certain mystical and unintelligible words (such as *aski*, *lix*, &c.) are said to have been inscribed, and thence transferred to the *grammata* aforesaid. To this bad eminence the city seems to have attained very early. Crœsus, king of Lydia, is reported to have muttered some of these Ephesian charms upon his funeral pile, and Eustathius relates a famous story of an Ephesian wrestler at Olympia, who could not be thrown until he was deprived of an Ephesian amulet about his ankle. It is not strange, therefore, that one of the effects of Christianity in Ephesus was to reveal this class of evil deeds. Some identify the persons here referred to with those mentioned in v. 18; others, with more probability, distinguish them as sinners of a certain sort from sinners in general, or as practitioners of occult arts from their patients or employers. *Books*, in a wide sense, writings, papers, so as to include the charms already mentioned and the large rolls or volumes which contained the rules and formulas of incantation. The converted sorcerers attested their sincerity by burning these instead of selling them, as they might have done for the enormous price mentioned in the last clause. *Counted*, calculated, or computed. *Found*, as the product of this reckoning, an expression often used in Greek, to signify an arithmetical result. *Fifty thousand* (literally, *five myriads*) *of silver*, but of what denomination is not mentioned, although commonly supposed to be the Attic drachma, varying in value from fifteen to seventeen cents of our money, making a total of at least seven or eight thousand dollars. This sum would be tripled or quadrupled by supposing the coin meant to be the Jewish shekel, which, however, is less probable, as Luke was writing for Greek readers, and is here relating what occurred in a Greek city. It must be remembered that all ancient books were dear compared with ours, and that books of the class here described are always rated far beyond their real worth and even their commercial value.

20. So mightily grew the word of God and prevailed.

So mightily, in English, means with such force and rapidity, as that just mentioned. But in Greek, the first word does not necessarily qualify the second, but has an independent meaning, namely, *thus*, in this way, or by this means. *Mightily*, in Greek a compound phrase, *with power*, or *by force*. *The word of God* (the gospel, the Christian religion) *grew*, in extent of influence and number of adherents, and *prevailed*, became strong, as in v. 16 above. (See also, 6, 7. 12, 24.)

21. After these things were ended, Paul purposed in the spirit, when he had passed through Macedonia and Achaia, to go to Jerusalem, saying, After I have been there, I must also see Rome.

As (or *when*) *these* (things), not the growth and prevalence just mentioned, but the occurrences respecting the exorcists. *Were ended*, literally, *filled* or *fulfilled*, i. e. finished or completed. *Purposed*, literally, placed or set, i. e. settled or determined (see above, on 1, 8.) *In the spirit*, i. e. under the divine direction, or in his own mind as determined by the Holy Ghost. *Going* (or *having gone*) *through Macedonia and Achaia*, the two great provinces into which Greece was divided at the Roman conquest (see above, on 16, 1. 18, 1.) *To go*, depart, or journey (see above, on 1, 25. 8, 26. 9, 3. 12, 17. 17, 4.) *To Jerusalem*, to carry the collections which he had been making, or was now about to make, for the poor saints there, as appears from the first epistle to the Corinthians, written from this place and about this time. (See 1 Cor. 16, 1–9, and compare Rom. 15, 25. 26. 31.) *Saying*, either to himself in meditation, or to his friends in consultation. *After having been there*, or arrived there; having come so far, I must go further. *I must* (or *it is necessary for me to*) *see Rome also*, not to gratify a private wish and lawful curiosity, but as a part of the divine plan which he was engaged in executing, by the establishment of radiating centres at great points of influence throughout the empire, which of course would have been incomplete if Rome had been neglected. The same purpose or desire is expressed in his epistle to the Romans, written probably at Corinth, after leaving Ephesus (see Rom. 15, 28. 29), but with a further intimation of his purpose to go by them into Spain. (On the perfect but unstudied agreement of these passages with that before us, and the evidence of genuineness thence arising, see Paley's Horæ Paulinæ.)

22. So he sent into Macedonia two of them that ministered unto him, Timotheus and Erastus; but he himself stayed in Asia for a season.

And having sent away into Macedonia, i. e. probably to Thessalonica and Philippi, *two of those serving him* (or *ministering to him*), both as personal attendants and as fellow-labourers in the Gospel. (See above, on 13, 5, and compare 1 Thess. 3, 2. 2 Cor. 8, 23. Rom. 16, 21. Phil. 2, 25. Col. 4, 11. Philemon 13.) These were probably sent before to set on foot the collections above mentioned. (See 1 Cor. 16, 1. 10.) Most interpreters distinguish the Erastus here named from the one mentioned Rom. 16, 23 (compare 2 Tim. 4, 20), because the latter was the steward (or chamberlain) of Corinth; but he may not have become so until afterwards, and even while he held the place, it may not have required his constant presence, especially as it is quite uncertain what the office was, and whether it was shared by more than one incumbent. The general presumption is of course in favour of identifying persons who are called by the same name, without some positive reason for distinguishing them. (See above, on 18, 17, and below, on v. 29.) *But* is supplied by the translators, being rendered necessary by their change of the construction. *Stayed*, literally, *held on*, an expression similarly used in colloquial English. (For a very different application of the same verb, see above, on 3, 5, and compare Luke 14, 7. 1 Tim. 4, 16. Phil. 2, 16.) *For a season*, literally, *a time*, without a particle prefixed, an indefinite expression like our English *some time.*

In Asia, literally, *into Asia*, which some regard as a mere interchange of prepositions; but the more exact philologists explain it as a pregnant construction implying motion. The sense may then be that he stayed behind, and carried the Gospel further into Asia, i. e. Asia Proper or Proconsular (see above, on v. 10.)

23. And the same time there arose no small stir about that way.

This verse introduces an account of the extraordinary interruption to Paul's work in Asia after the departure of Erastus and Timotheus. About that time, the new religion, which had been triumphantly but quietly advancing since the defeat of the exorcists (see above, on vs. 17. 20), gave occasion to a violent and sudden outbreak of hostility, the causes and effects of which are circumstantially recorded in the remainder of the present chapter. (*At* or *about*) *the same time*, the preposition being here omitted, as it is supplied in the preceding verse. *There arose*, happened, came to pass, began to be, implying previous tranquillity or freedom from disturbance. *Stir*, commotion, tumult, the same word that is so rendered in 12, 18, and with the same qualifying adjunct. *No small* (literally, *few*, which can be used in English only with the plural), i. e. by a natural meiosis or litotes, *very great*. (See above, on 14, 28. 15, 2. 17, 4. 12.) *About that way* is ambiguous in English, and may seem to mean, *in those parts*, or *in that place*, namely, Ephesus or Asia. But neither noun nor preposition has a local sense here, and the meaning of the phrase is, *about*, (i. e. respecting or concerning) *the way*, i. e. Christianity considered as a way of thinking, living, and salvation. (See above, on v. 9, and compare 9, 2.)

24. For a certain (man) named Demetrius, a silversmith, which made silver shrines for Diana, brought no small gain unto the craftsmen—

For introduces or assigns the ground and the occasion of the uproar. *One Demetrius by name*, or *a certain man by name Demetrius*, a famous name in history, and also one in common use, derived from *Demeter*, the Greek name of the goddess *Ceres*. It occurs again in 3 John 12, where some suppose it to denote the same man, and infer that he had been converted in the mean time. (See above, on 18, 17.) *A silversmith*, silver-beater, one who works in silver, used by Plutarch to denote a coiner, but here a manufacturer of silver wares, described more particularly in the next clause. *Making*, manufacturing, habitually, as his constant business. *Shrines for Diana*, literally, *temples of Artemis*, the Greek goddess corresponding most nearly to the *Diana* of the Roman mythology. Whatever may have been the points of resemblance, there was also a great difference, at least between the Diana of the Latin poets and the Artemis of Ephesus, the former being usually represented in the succinct garb of a huntress armed with bow and arrow, while the latter was a less pleasing form distinguished by its many breasts, supposed to represent the prolific and nutritive attributes of nature. The temples here meant were not *shrines for Diana*, to be used in the great temple, but either medals stamped with its image, or more probably small models of the edifice itself, which were sold in great numbers, to be used in devotion, or as charms and amulets, a practice common in the heathen world, and not unknown in certain parts of Christendom, for instance at Loretto, where such models of the Virgin Mary's house, (transported by the hands of angels through the air from Nazareth to Italy) furnish the staple of a constant traffic. *Brought* (afforded, yielded) *no small* (i. e. very great, as in the verse preceding) *gain*, or work, employment, which is the primary meaning of the Greek word, and from which the other sense is readily deducible. (See above, on 16, 16.) *To the craftsmen*, artisans, or artists, those employed by Demetrius, or, in a wider sense, all who worked at the same trade. (See above, on 18, 3.)

25. Whom he called together with the workmen of like occupation, and said, Sirs, ye know that by this craft we have our wealth.

Whom having gathered, or *assembled*, the Greek verb, by its very etymology, suggesting the idea of masses or great numbers, which is not necessarily implied in *calling them together*. *With the workmen*, literally, *and the workmen*, or as it might be rendered, *even the workmen*, i. e. those already mentioned. But it seems more naturally to express another class besides these. Some suppose the distinction to be that between *artists* and *artisans*, those who devise and those who execute, or those who execute the finer and the coarser parts of the same work. But this distinction belongs rather to modern than to ancient usage, in which *art* (τέχνη) not only comprehends mechanical employments, but originally signifies no other, being applied by Homer to ship-building, the working of metals, &c. It is therefore more probable that the distinction here, if any be intended, is between the workmen whom Demetrius himself employed, and others *of like occupation*, or as the words literally mean, *the* (*other*) *workmen about such* (*things.*) *Sirs*, literally, *men* (or *gentlemen*); see above, on 1, 11. 16. 7, 26. 14, 15. 15, 7. 13. 17, 22.) *Ye know*, or know well, ye are well aware, without my telling you. (See above, on v. 15. 10, 28. 15, 7. 18, 25.) *Craft*, trade, business (see above, on 18, 3), a word used in modern English chiefly in a bad sense, that of cunning or deceit. The Greek word is the one translated *gain* in the preceding verse, but even there denoting not so much the gain itself as the employment which produced it. *Wealth*, affluence, abundance, comfort, a Greek noun corresponding to the verb employed above in 11, 29, and there explained. *We have our wealth*, literally, *our wealth is*, or according to the oldest manuscripts and latest critics, *wealth to us is.* He rouses their attention by appealing, first to their cupidity or selfish interest, and then to their religious feelings. (See below, on v. 27.)

26. Moreover ye see and hear, that not alone at Ephesus, but almost (throughout) all Asia, this Paul hath persuaded and turned away much people, saying that they be no gods which are made with hands —

Ye see, behold, contemplate as a spectacle, as something more than ordinary sights. (See above, on 3, 16. 4, 13. 7, 56. 8, 13. 10, 11. 17, 16. 22.) *And hear*, from others, what you do not see yourselves, referring probably to that part of Paul's work which is mentioned in the next clause as extending beyond Ephesus. The names *Ephesus* and *Asia* may be either genitives of place, as in the English version, or dependent in construction on the following noun, *a great crowd not of Ephesus only, but of almost all Asia.* The latter syntax is more regular, the first more natural and simple, both essentially the same in meaning. *Having persuaded*, or *persuading*, i. e. both convincing and alluring. (See above, on v. 8.

5, 40. 12, 20. 13, 43. 14, 19. 17, 4. 18, 4.) *Has turned away*, diverted, or perverted, from their former faith. The same verb, with the same essential meaning, is applied to Saul's removal, either from office or from life. (See above, on 13, 22.) *Much people*, literally, *a sufficient crowd.* (See above, on v. 19.) *They be*, an old English form of the verb, simply equivalent in such constructions to the modern one, *they are.* The exact translation of the clause is, *they are not gods*, *the* (*ones*) *by hands made* (literally, *being*, made to be.) The doctrine here ascribed to Paul is substantially identical with that which we have heard him preach at Athens. (See above, on 17, 29.)

27. So that not only this our craft is in danger to be set at nought; but also that the temple of the great goddess Diana should be despised, and her magnificence should be destroyed, whom all Asia and the world worshippeth.

So that, literally, *and* or *but.* *Craft* is not the word so rendered in v. 25, but one meaning simply *part* or *portion*, as in 2, 10. 5, 2, and in the first verse of this chapter, where it is translated *coasts.* Here it may either mean *this portion*, share, which we enjoy; or *this part*, department, of our business, as they were not merely manufacturers of shrines, but silversmiths or jewellers, though the former was much the most profitable part of their employment, and perhaps the only one in many cases. *Is in danger to us*, for us, with respect to us, and by necessary implication, to our loss and damage. (The English version treats the dative as a genitive and translates it *our.*) *To be set at nought*, literally, *to come to* (or *into*) *confutation*, a word occurring nowhere else, perhaps coined for the occasion, but admirably expressive of the speaker's meaning, as its obvious etymology determines it to signify not mere contempt in general, but logical or rational contempt, arising from a *reductio ad absurdum*, in allusion to Paul's arguments against the very being of a man-made god. We have here the transition from their own loss to that of their patroness or tutelary goddess. *The temple*, not the word translated *shrine* in v. 24, but a neuter adjective denoting *sacred*, i. e. set apart, appropriated to the deity, and constantly applied to the whole enclosure or consecrated ground, both at Jerusalem and among the heathen. (See above, on 2,

46. 3, 1. 4, 1. 5, 20.) *The great goddess* is not merely an expression of praise and admiration, on the part of the speaker or his hearers, but a sort of standing epithet or proper name, by which she was distinguished, not only from inferior deities, but also from all others bearing the same name of *Artemis* or *Diana.* Thus Xenophon describes an Asiatic Greek as swearing by his national ancestral god, "the great Ephesian Artemis." This eminence was partly owing to the peculiar oriental attributes ascribed to this divinity, and altogether different from those of the Hellenic Artemis and Roman Diana (see above, on v. 24), whose name was given to her, no doubt, on account of some minor and fortuitous resemblance, in accordance with the Greek and Roman custom of transferring the names of their own gods to those of other nations, though belonging to a system altogether different. (See above, on 14, 12.) This method being practised by both nations, not only with respect to the barbarians, but to one another, is a chief source of the endless contradiction and confusion of the classical mythology. Another cause of the peculiar greatness, universally ascribed to the Ephesian goddess, was the greatness of her temple, which has been already mentioned (see above, on v. 1) as extremely ancient, and rebuilt after its destruction by Herostratus, on a scale and in a style which caused it to be reckoned among the seven wonders of the world. Besides the admiration which it thus commanded, it was built at the joint expense of many cities, who had thus a common interest, not only in its sustentation, but in the honours of the resident and tutelary deity, *the great goddess Diana.* Both these, the temple and the goddess, Demetrius here tells his associates, are now *in danger to be reckoned for nothing*, a much stronger expression than *despised.* The next clause, on account of its peculiar idiomatic form, can scarcely be translated into English, though its meaning is entirely clear. By a slight irregularity or change of construction, Luke proceeds as if, instead of giving the exact words of Demetrius, he were merely telling what he said in substance. This is what the old grammarians call the change from direct to indirect narration. *And that her greatness was about to be destroyed*, a Greek verb originally meaning *to be taken down* or *pulled down*, and therefore peculiarly appropriate, both in its strict sense to the threatened ruin of the temple, and in its figurative sense to the dishonour of the goddess. *Whom the whole (of) Asia* (or *all Asia*) *and the world doth worship*, no unmeaning boast, nor even an ex-

travagant hyperbole, considering the facts already mentioned and the usage of the word here rendered *world*, the same that we have had repeatedly before (see above, on 11, 28. 17, 6. 31), and which originally means *inhabited*, but is indefinitely used to signify the whole world, or the Roman Empire, or some one of its divisions, as the writer chooses or the context may require.

28. And when they heard (these sayings), they were full of wrath, and cried out, saying, Great (is) Diana of the Ephesians.

But (or *then*) *hearing* (*these sayings* is supplied by the translators) *and being* (or *becoming*) *full of wrath* (anger, passion), *they cried* (in the imperfect tense, *were crying*, or continued to cry), *saying*, *Great* (is) *Diana of the Ephesians* (or *the Ephesians' Artemis!*) Here again, this is not a mere doxology or panegyric, but an assertion of their grand religious tenet, namely, that the goddess whom they worshipped was, in the strictest and the highest sense, entitled to be called The Great.

29. And the whole city was filled with confusion; and having caught Gaius and Aristarchus, men of Macedonia, Paul's companions in travel, they rushed with one accord into the theatre.

Having caught, or rather, seizing and carrying along with them, the same verb that is used above in 6, 12, and below in 27, 15. The original order of the sentence is, *they rushed with one accord into the theatre, seizing Gaius*, &c. The latter is therefore only a secondary or accompanying act, and not the main one, as the English may suggest. *The theatre*, among the Greeks, was used not only for dramatic exhibitions but for public meetings, particularly those in which the whole population was assembled. A modern analogy is that of the theatre at Oxford, which is never used for dramatic purposes at all, but only for academical solemnities. The Greek theatres were vast unroofed enclosures, semicircular in form, with tiers of stone seats rising one above another. The *amphitheatres*, in which were held the fights of gladiators and wild beasts, were double theatres, or rather mere elliptical enclosures, with spectators' seats surrounding the arena. The theatre at Ephesus was one of great size, as appears from the enclosure, which may still be traced, although the seats, &c. have long since disappeared, the materials having been employed in other buildings. *With one accord*, or by a common impulse, such as often actuates a mob, without implying any definite design or knowledge of each other's purpose (see below, on v. 32.) *Gaius*, the Greek form of the Latin *Caius*, was a very common name among the Romans and their subjects, which greatly weakens the presumption (see above, on v. 22), that wherever it is used in the New Testament, it designates one and the same person. This, however, is by no means impossible; for although the Gaius mentioned afterwards in this book (see below, on 20, 4) is described as a Derbean; and the Gaius of whom Paul writes (Rom. 16, 23. 1 Cor. 1, 14) would appear to have been resident in Corinth; and the Gaius to whom John writes (3 John 1) may have lived long after; none of these circumstances is sufficient to disprove the identity; the date of John's epistle being doubtful, and there being reason to believe that many of the early converts often changed their place of residence, both for prudential and religious reasons, like Priscilla and her husband. (See above, on 18, 2. 18. 26, and compare Rom. 16, 3. 1 Cor. 16, 19.) *Aristarchus* is more commonly agreed to be the same who afterwards attended Paul to Palestine, and shared in his imprisonment. (Compare Col. 4, 10. Philem. 24.) Both are here called *Macedonians* (or as the English version has it, *men of Macedonia*), which agrees with the description of Aristarchus elsewhere as a *Thessalonian* (20, 4), and a *Thessalonian Macedonian* (27, 2.) They are also here described as *Paul's companions in travel*, or more exactly, those who were away from home with him. (Compare the use of the same word in 2 Cor. 8, 19.)

30. And when Paul would have entered in unto the people, the disciples suffered him not.

And Paul wishing (or *intending*) *to go in*, though not carried in by the people, probably because he was not in their way, as his companions were, who do not seem to have been sought for and arrested, but swept along by the living stream in its resistless course. (See above, on v. 29.) *Unto the people*, or *into the assembly*, the Greek word being that used to denote the people as a sovereign, or as acting in a corporate capacity. What was merely a mob or rabble (ὄχλος) in the streets, became a popular assembly (δῆμος), although not a legal one, when seated in the theatre. (See above, on 1, 15, and below, on v. 39.) This attempt of Paul evinced that it was not from fear, or any other personal motive, that he was separated from the others. *The brethren*, his own converts, the Ephesian Christians, who appear to have been no less anxious for his safety than the same class at Damascus, Jerusalem, Lystra, and Thessalonica (see above, on 9, 25. 30. 14, 20. 17, 10.) *Suffered him not*, did not allow him or permit him.

31. And certain of the chief of Asia, which were his friends, sent unto him, desiring (him) that he would not adventure himself into the theatre.

Some of the Asiarchs, not civil magistrates, nor priests in the ordinary sense, although their office was connected with religion. They were annually chosen in the cities of the province, to conduct the sacrificial services and public games in honour of Diana. They derived their title from the name of the province, as the corresponding officers in Cyprus, Syria, and Lydia, were called Cypriarchs, Syriarchs, Lydiarchs, &c. Those of Asia are said to have been ten in number; but whether equal and co-ordinate, and whether always resident at Ephesus, is doubtful. As the ancient narrative of Polycarp's martyrdom at Smyrna says that "Philip the Asiarch" refused to loose the wild beasts when required by the people, it has been inferred that there was only one such officer on duty at the same time, and with more probability that they exercised their functions at the different cities of the province in rotation, or as occasion might require. As the games and sacrifices over which these Asiarchs presided, were provided at their own expense, they were always chosen from the richest class, and may be said to represent the highest rank of the community. It is therefore no slight indication of Paul's standing with the highest class of heathen, that these Asiarchs are said to have been *his friends*, or rather *friendly to him* (αὐτῷ φίλοι), i. e. personally well disposed, without implying any faith in his new doctrine, which indeed seems inconsistent with their social and official station, as conductors of ceremonies altogether heathenish. It is worthy of remark, however, that the church-councils of the third and fourth centuries were sometimes called upon to lay down rules for the direction of those Christians who were summoned by official or hereditary duty to perform this very service. It is possible, therefore, that these Asiarchs were converts, or at least inclined to become Christians, though the terms of the narrative are satisfied by simply assuming a respectful and benevolent feeling upon their part towards the great Apostle. Even this throws an interesting light upon his character and social position in the midst of that idolatrous community, by showing that his teachings and his miracles were not done in a corner, and that he was most respected by the most intelligent and wealthy classes. (See below, on v. 37.) *Sending to him*, messengers or letters, but more probably the former, from their residence, private or official, or perhaps from the place where they were actually engaged in their public duties, and which may have been forsaken by the people when the tumult about Paul arose. *Exhorted* or *besought him*, the same verb that is used above in 2, 40. 8, 31. 9, 38. 11, 23. 13, 42. 14, 22. 15, 32. 16, 9. 15. 39. 40. *Not to give* (risk, or venture) *himself into the theatre*, already filled with the infuriated populace, whose conduct and condition are described in the next verse.

32. Some therefore cried one thing, and some another; for the assembly was confused, and the more part knew not wherefore they were come together.

So then (μὲν οὖν), the resumptive particle so often used in this book after an interruption of the narrative or argument. (See above, on 8, 2. 25. 9, 31. 11, 19. 12, 5. 13, 4. 14, 3. 15, 3. 30. 16, 5. 17, 12. 17. 30.) Having told how the people rushed into the theatre, and then paused to relate what happened outside, Luke now resumes his account of what was done in the assembly. The description given in this verse is admirably true to nature, being perfectly appropriate in all its parts to many a convention and conventicle among ourselves. *The more* (*part*), the majority, the greater number. This clause shows that the *one consent*, with which they rushed into the theatre (v. 29), had reference only to that act, or at most to the general purpose of consulting what to do, but not to any definite proposal, which had been concerted, if at all, only between the leaders, i. e. those immediately connected with Demetrius. This agrees so exactly with the mode of managing such matters now, that it imparts to the whole narrative a striking character of authenticity and graphic truth.

33. And they drew Alexander out of the multitude, the Jews putting him forward. And Alexander beckoned with the hand, and would have made his defence unto the people.

And from (or *out of*) *the crowd* (assembled in the theatre) *they* (i. e. some, indefinitely) *brought forward Alexander.* Calvin and others have supposed this to be *Alexander the coppersmith*, of whom Paul says (2 Tim. 4, 14) that he did him much evil (literally, showed him many evils), but whether at this time or afterwards, they are not agreed. The identity of name proves still less here than in the case of Gaius (see above, on v. 29), on account of its frequency in Jewish usage ever since the time of Alexander the Great. (See above, on 4, 6, and compare Matt. 15, 21. 1 Tim. 1, 20.) The identity of business, too, is not sufficiently exact, although the Greek word used by Paul might possibly have some degree of latitude, or one who was properly a coppersmith (or brazier) might be led, by the prospect of extraordinary profit, to engage in the same business with Demetrius. But apart from this question of identity, and even granting that the person here named is one otherwise unknown, interpreters are much divided as to his relation to the parties and the matter now at issue. As the Jews put him forward, some suppose that he was to defend them from the charge of having any thing to do with Paul, and to explain the difference between Jews and Christians. Others think that he was himself a convert to the new religion (which is not inconsistent with the statement in the next verse), and that the unconverted Jews maliciously invited the attention of the Gentiles to him, in order to divert it from themselves. In either case, it was the Jews who put him forward, either to defend them or himself. *Would have made his defence* is too specific, as the Greek phrase simply means, *wished to apologize*, or *make defence*, but whether for himself or others, is not here expressed. *Beckoned with his hand*, or more exactly, shook it downwards, almost but not precisely the same phrase with that employed in 12, 17. 13, 16, and there explained. *To the people*, not as a mere mob, but as an organized assembly. (See above, on v. 30.)

34. But when they knew that he was a Jew, all with one voice about the space of two hours cried out, Great (is) Diana of the Ephesians.

But (they) knowing, recognizing, or discovering, the same verb that was used above in 3, 10. 4, 13. 9, 30. 12, 14, and there explained. How they perceived or ascertained this, we are not told, possibly by something Jewish in his looks or language; or the information may have been communicated orally from those who knew him to the others, and eventually to the whole assembly. *That he is*, in the present tense, as if the scene were actually passing, a graphic trait of which we have had several examples. (See above, on 7, 25. 9, 22. 26. 38. 12, 3. 9.) *A Jew*, i. e. by birth or nation, and therefore equally descriptive of an unconverted and a Christian Jew. (See above, on v. 33, and compare 10, 28. 16, 1. 20. 18, 2. 24.) *There was one voice* (or *one voice arose*) *from all*, a similar expression to the one in 4, 32, but there relating to one heart and soul. *Crying* (or *shouting*) *about the space of* (literally, *as for*) *two hours*. The cry is the same as in the last clause of v. 28, and is here repeated, not as a mere act of adoration or religious praise, but as a kind of watch-word, an expression of their zeal and resolution in the cause of their insulted and endangered goddess. Viewed in the former light, it may be reckoned as a sample of the *battology* or "vain repetitions," which our Lord describes as characteristic of the heathen worship. (See Matt. 6, 7, and compare 1 Kings 18, 26.)

35. And when the town-clerk had appeased the people, he said, (Ye) men of Ephesus, what man is there that knoweth not how that the city of the Ephesians is a worshipper of the great goddess Diana, and of the (image) which fell down from Jupiter?

The first words, as thus rendered, seem to refer to something previously mentioned ('when the town-clerk had thus stilled the crowd'); whereas in the original, a new character appears upon the stage ('the town-clerk, having stilled the crowd, says, &c.') *Appeased* implies that they were satisfied, or reconciled to something which before offended them; whereas the Greek word means to *put down*, quell, subdue, not by persuasion, which was yet to come, but by authority and influence of character or office. In describing this effect,

Luke, with great exactness of expression, substitutes the word denoting *crowd* or *mob* for that denoting an assembly of the people. (See above, on vs. 30. 33.) It was in the former, not the latter character, that they were shouting and extolling Artemis. This significant though slight variation may illustrate at the same time the resources of the language and Luke's power to employ them. *Town-clerk* is evidently much too modest a description of the person, whose appearance seems to have immediately restored the mob to order. The Greek word is *Grammateus*, the one so often rendered *scribe* (see above, on 4, 5. 6, 12), and like it means a writer, or one who has official charge of writings, whether sacred scriptures or official records. Like the English *clerk* and *secretary*, it admits of numberless gradations in the rank of those to whom it is applied, extending from a *town-clerk* (or still lower) to a *secretary of state*, which last is probably much nearer than the former to the meaning of the title here. Whether it be so rendered, or, as some prefer, *recorder*, *actuary*, *chancellor*, &c., it undoubtedly denotes a functionary whom the people were accustomed to respect, and whose very presence was sufficient to compose them; for until this was effected, he could neither reason with them nor exhort them. Besides abundant proof that *Grammateus* is used in classic Greek to signify not only humble but exalted office, there are extant inscriptions of Ephesian origin, in which this title is combined with that of *Asiarch*, before explained (on v. 31), in such a way as to suggest the question, whether the person here referred to was not a religious rather than a civil officer, and therefore the more likely to command a hearing, when the honour of the goddess was itself at stake. This is still more probable if, as Domninus says, the Grammateus at Antioch, on similar occasions, was the representative or spokesman of Apollo. But however this may be, it is unquestionable that the person here meant awed the multitude, as well by his official rank or personal character as by his arguments which follow, and the drift of which is to convince them that their riotous proceedings were superfluous and dangerous. *Ye men of Ephesus*, literally, *Ephesian men* (or *gentlemen*), the usual Greek formula of popular address (see above, on v. 25.) *What man*, in Greek, *for what man*, as if referring to something previously said but not recorded, possibly to something said before the noise was wholly stilled. (Q. d. 'Be silent, cease this uproar which is both unnecessary and alarming; for what man, &c.')

Who does not know is a form of rhetorical interrogation, also used by Demosthenes in speaking of a certain and notorious fact. *How that*, an old English pleonastic phrase, to which nothing corresponds in the original, the form of which is foreign from our idiom, consisting of a noun and participle, both in the accusative, *who does not know the city being*, &c. *City of* (*the*) *Ephesians*, like *Diana of* (*the*) *Ephesians* (see above, on vs. 28. 34) seems to have been a favourite formula in preference to *city* (and *Diana*) *of Ephesus*, like "Emperor of the French," and "King of the Belgians," instead of "Emperor of France," and "King of Belgium." *A worshipper*, or as the margin more exactly renders it, *a temple-keeper*. The Greek word is commonly explained to mean, at least in the first instance, *temple-sweeper;* but one of the old Greek lexicographers (Suidas) denies that there is any reference to sweeping, and declares the true sense to be that of decking or adorning. Hence some compare it with the English *sexton*, others with *church-warden*, the only difference being one of dignity and rank, as the essential idea is, in either case, that of one who has charge (or takes care) of a temple. This, even in its lower sense, was reckoned a great honour, when connected with the service of such a deity as Artemis, and such a temple as the one at Ephesus. (See above, on vs. 24. 27.) Even to sweep that sacred and magnificent abode was a distinction for which cities and crowned heads contended. The very epithet here used is found upon Ephesian coins still extant, and applied not merely to the city but the state or body politic (δῆμος νεωκόρος.) *And of the Jove-fallen* (*image*), a phrase used by Euripides in application to the same divinity as worshipped at Tauris. According to Pliny and other ancient writers, there was a wooden image of Diana at Ephesus, so old that it had outlived seven restorations of the temple, and was therefore fabled to have dropped from heaven, no unusual belief among the ancient heathen. Other examples are the famous Palladium at Troy and Rome, and an image of Cybele at Pessinus, as described by Livy. This notion has by some been traced to the real fall of meteoric stones; but in the case before us, we are told not only that the image was a wooden one, but also, by different authorities, of what wood it was made (vine, ebony, &c.)

36. Seeing then that these things cannot be spoken against, ye ought to be quiet, and to do nothing rashly.

The reference just made to their most highly prized distinction as a city was intended, partly as a solace to their national or local pride, and partly as the basis of an argument against tumultuous proceedings, which he now propounds distinctly. *Undeniable, therefore, being these* (*things*), namely, that their city was confessedly the constituted guardian of Diana's temple and its heaven-descended image. *It is necessary* (i. e. morally, in Greek a participial form, like *binding* and *becoming*) *for you to be* (or *that ye be*), continue, or begin to be (the same verb that is used above, in 5, 4. 8, 16. 14, 8. 16, 20. 17, 27, and there explained.) *Quiet* is in Greek the passive participle of the verb at the beginning of v. 35, and might be here translated *settled* or *subdued*, but is still more exactly rendered in the Vulgate by the Latin word *sedatos*, which is really a corresponding form, and from which comes *sedate* in English. The idea meant to be conveyed is not that of coercion by superior authority or power, but a dignified and reasonable self-control. *Rashly*, literally, *headlong* or *head-foremost*, then *precipitate*, which means the same in Latin, but is always tropically used in English, as a synonyme of hasty, inconsiderate, or rash, as applied to human character and conduct.

37. For ye have brought hither these men, which are neither robbers of churches, nor yet blasphemers of your goddess.

With a skill showing natural sagacity as well as great experience in argument and public speaking, he now insinuates without asserting that they had actually fallen into the great error against which he had just warned them. Instead of saying that they had already acted rashly, he describes the act itself, without express qualification or description, which their own minds, influenced by what he had before said, would immediately supply. The only application which he makes himself is by the use of the word *for*, referring to the thought which he had first suggested but without expressing it. This aposiopesis (as the Greek grammarians called it) may be thus completed or filled up. 'You have the strongest grounds for doing nothing rash, and yet you have been acting, and are acting now most rashly; for,' &c. *Ye have brought* (or *ye brought* just now, in Greek an aorist) *these men*, not an expression of contempt, but rather of respect, the Greek noun being that employed above in vs. 25. 35, and there explained. *Hither*, supplied by the translators, is correct, but hardly adequate to give the full force of the speaker's language, which suggests not only the idea of locality (brought them into this place or assembly), but also that of mode or manner (brought them violently and disgracefully.) The rashness tacitly imputed to their whole proceeding lay in the fact that there was no sufficient ground for it afforded by the conduct of the prisoners themselves. *These men* (being, or who are) *neither temple-spoilers* (and so chargeable with sacrilege) *nor revilers of* (literally, *reviling*) *your goddess* (and so chargeable with blasphemy.) *Robbers of Churches* is a Christian phrase put into the mouth of a heathen, less absurd but not more accurate than the change of *Passover* to *Easter* elsewhere. (See above, on 12, 4.) The latter statement of the Grammateus, in reference to Paul and his associates, has been very variously understood, by some as a mere falsehood, meant to calm the mob; by others as a true description of Paul's abstinence from all direct warfare against idol-worship; by a third class, as describing only his forbearance as to particular deities, or forms of heathen worship, which, according to Josephus, was practised also by the Jews; and lastly, as denying not even this kind of attack, but only an offensive and insulting method of conducting it. Shaftesbury's reflection upon Paul for allowing false witness to be borne in his behalf, when he was not present, and could not have spoken if he had been, is both false and foolish.

38. Wherefore if Demetrius, and the craftsmen which are with him, have a matter against any (man), the law is open, and there are deputies; let them implead one another.

So then, as in v. 32, where it resumes the narrative, as it here does the argument, after a momentary interruption in v. 37, which is a kind of parenthetical allusion to their conduct as at variance with the rule which he had laid down. 'You ought to do nothing rashly—as you have done by your treatment of these persons—so then, if Demetrius, &c.' *Craftsmen*, artisans or artists (see above, on v. 24.) *With him*, not merely in his company, or in the same place, but on his side, in his interest, associated with him, members of his party. (See above, on 5, 17. 14, 4.) *Matter*, literally, *word*, here used like the corresponding Hebrew term, in a judicial or forensic sense, for *cause*, complaint, or accusation. (See Ex. 18, 16. 22. 22, 8. 24, 14, and compare the full phrase, *word of judgment*, 2 Chron. 19, 6.) *Any* (*man*), or more generically, *any* (*person*), the same pronoun that is so often rendered *certain*. (See above, on vs. 1. 13. 14. 24. 31.) *The law is open*, a mere paraphrase, the version being given in the margin, *the court-days are kept.* From a Greek word (ἀγορά) meaning both a market and a court (see above, on 16, 19. 17, 17) comes an adjective (ἀγόραιος), applied in 17, 5 to idlers or frequenters of the public places, but here employed in the higher sense of *forensic* or *judicial*, and most probably agreeing with *days* understood. The verb (*are led*, *passed*, or *passing*) may be expressive either of a general fact (there are such times or terms of court), or of what was actually taking place at that time (there are such terms now held or holding.) *There are deputies*, a word before applied to Sergius Paulus (see above, on 13, 7. 8. 12, and compare the corresponding verb 18, 12), and there explained to be the Greek translation of *Proconsul*, the appropriate title of one who governed an imperial province (see above, on the passages just cited), such as Asia Proper was, and therefore often called *Proconsularis.* The only difficulty here arises from the facts, that the Proconsul was the highest judicial magistrate, and that there was never more than one in the same province. The plural form (*Proconsuls*) has been variously explained, as comprehending the legates or assessors of the governor; or as including the proconsuls of adjacent provinces, who may have been attending the Ephesian festival; or as denoting two procurators who about this time had murdered the Proconsul, and perhaps usurped his title; or finally, as a generic plural, representing the whole class, and not the individual, examples of which usage have been found by some in Matt. 2, 20, where the plural is supposed to denote Herod, and in 17, 18, above, where it is supposed to denote Jesus. Whether this be the true grammatical analysis or not, it is no doubt the essential meaning, which has reference not to the person but the office of the judges, whether one or many, whose existence and judicial functions are asserted as notorious facts. *Implead* (i. e. plead against) *each other* is a good translation of the Greek verb, which, although it strictly means *accuse* or *charge*, is here applied apparently to both the parties, although only one had been expressly mentioned.

39. But if ye inquire any thing concerning other matters, it shall be determined in a lawful assembly.

Having shown them how all private litigation should be settled, he now gives them similar advice in reference to questions of more public interest, municipal or legislative matters. *Ye*, i. e. Demetrius and his associates, of whom he had just spoken in the third person, but to whom he may now have turned or specially addressed himself. It is equally admissible, however, and perhaps more simple, to understand these words as still addressed to the assembly, all of whom were really concerned in what is here asserted. *Inquire*, not merely in the popular or vague sense of seeking or desiring (as in 12, 19. 13, 7, above), but in the more specific one of controverting or disputing, commonly expressed by another compound of the same Greek verb. (See above, on 6, 9. 9, 29. 15, 2. 7.) 'If you want a decision upon any other question not within the jurisdiction of the courts just mentioned.' *Assembly* is a general expression for all public meetings, but especially applied in classic Greek to legislative bodies, as in Scripture to the Congregation of Israel, and ultimately to the Christian Church. (See above, on 2, 47. 5, 11. 7, 38. 8, 1. 3. 11, 22. 26. 12, 1. 5. 13, 1. 14, 23. 27. 15, 3. 4. 22.) *A lawful assembly* seems to be contrasted with an unlawful or forbidden one. The Romans, however, did not deprive their Grecian subjects of their darling right to hold public meetings, the abuse of which, by needless gatherings and speeches "in the theatre," Cicero (in his defence of Flaccus) represents as a chief cause of their political misfortunes. This Ephesian meeting, therefore, could be called *unlawful*, only with respect to its disorderly, tumultuous proceedings, and the opposite expression would denote nothing more than one decorously conducted; which would not be an appropriate antithesis or supplement to what had been already said about the court-days or assizes. It is plain that the Grammateus is stating two ways of determining two kinds of controversy, private and public, or forensic and municipal. The former must be settled by the regular tribunals, the latter in a general assembly, but of what kind? Not merely *lawful* or permitted by the laws; for such was this one, in itself considered. Not merely orderly and well-behaved; for such was this, since he had been addressing it. The true sense of the words is, *the* (not *a*) *legal* (or constitutional) *assembly*, i. e. the one held at certain periods (as at

Athens thrice a month) for the transaction of public business. (Hence, in the margin of the English Bible, *lawful* is exchanged for *ordinary*.) The assembly now in session is described by implication, not as unlawful or forbidden, but as informal and without authority; just as a voluntary meeting or convention, although perfectly lawful, differs now from a judicial or legislative body. The word translated *lawful*, therefore, here means, not *permitted*, but *required* or *constituted by the laws*. *Shall be determined*, literally *solved*, implying doubt and difference of judgment, in relation to the principles or facts involved. (Compare the use of the same Greek verb in Mark 4, 34, and of the corresponding noun in 2 Pet. 1, 20.) This phrase, in the original, emphatically ends the sentence, *in the legal assembly it shall be determined*. The same argument is urged by Seneca against tumultuous and riotous proceedings.

40. For we are in danger to be called in question for this day's uproar, there being no cause whereby we may give an account of this concourse.

Having shown that their tumultuous proceedings were gratuitous, there being other more legitimate methods of accomplishing their lawful ends, he now suggests a still more serious consideration, namely, that the same proceedings were extremely dangerous, not only to the persons who took part in them, but also to their whole community. The danger arose from the extraordinary strictness of the Roman government in reference to every thing like riotous disturbances among their subjects and dependents. It was not the mere act of assembling, even in large numbers (see above, on the preceding verse), which was prohibited, but what is here called *uproar* and *concourse*, corresponding to the Latin terms *cœtus et concursus*, which appear to have been technical expressions of the Roman law, and descriptive of a capital offence. *We are in danger*, the same verb that was used by Demetrius (see above, on v. 27.) *To be called in question*, also a single word in Greek, the same that was explained above (on v. 38), as strictly meaning *to be charged* or *accused*. The original construction is, *to be accused of riot for to-day* (or *this day*, see a similar construction of *to-morrow*, 4, 3. 5), i. e. concerning, on account of, this day's conduct or proceedings. The danger was not merely that of being charged, but that of being left without excuse and unable to defend themselves. *There being no cause*, a judicial term, elsewhere translated *fault* (see Luke 23, 4. 14), and here denoting, not a cause in general, but a guilty cause upon the part of those accused. *There being* (or *existing*, see above on v. 36) *no crime* or *offence whereby* (literally, *as to* or *concerning which*) *we can*, or adhering to the future form of the original, *we shall be able*, in the case supposed, of their being charged or called in question. *Give* (render or deliver, an emphatic compound, used above, 4, 33. 5, 8. 7, 9, and there explained.) *Account*, literally, *word*, the one translated *matter* in v. 38, but sometimes signifying an account or reckoning, both in a financial and a moral sense. (Compare Matt. 12, 36. 18, 23. Phil. 4, 17. Heb. 13, 7. 1 Pet. 4, 5.) In all the passages referred to, there is more or less distinct allusion to judicial process and self-vindication, which is here the main idea, and as such expressly mentioned. *Concourse* is the literal translation of the Greek word, and denotes a violent tumultuary *running together*. The idea of *conspiracy*, or lawless combination, may be also implied, but is not prominent in this case, as it is in 23, 12 below.

41. And when he had thus spoken, he dismissed the assembly.

And these things having said (or *saying*), *he dismissed* (or *dissolved*, the verb explained above, on 3, 13. 4, 21. 23. 5, 40. 13, 3. 15, 30. 33. 16, 35. 36. 17, 9) *the assembly* (the *ecclesia*, as in vs. 32. 39.) This is evidently mentioned as an act of authority, implying that the tumult had entirely ceased, and that the people quietly dispersed; an important and remarkable effect, but not at all incredible, considering the proverbial mobility from which the mob derives its name, and also the extraordinary force and skill, with which the Grammateus appealed to their religious feelings, local pride, municipal usages, and selfish fears. The intrinsic merit of this speech, with reference to the end in view, its congruity and suitableness to the speaker and the hearers, and its total unlikeness to the other speeches here recorded, stamp it as palpably original and genuine. And this internal evidence instead of losing gains strength from the low views entertained by some of Luke's ability as a writer and the literary merit f the book before us.

CHAPTER XX.

THIS division of the text contains the account of Paul's return from his third mission, from his leaving Ephesus to his leaving Miletus. We have first his visit to the Grecian provinces (1–3.) Then comes a list of his seven companions who went before to Troas and were followed by Paul and Luke (4–6.) Paul there preaches and performs a miracle (7–12.) His course from Troas to Miletus is recorded with great minuteness (13–15.) Passing by Ephesus, he sends for the elders of the church there to Miletus, and delivers a farewell discourse to them (16–35.) He then prays with them and takes leave of them (31–38.)

1. And after the uproar was ceased, Paul called unto (him) the disciples, and embraced (them), and departed for to go into Macedonia.

The cessation of the tumult is not given as the cause of Paul's departure, but as a mere specification of time, or rather an indefinite description, since the length of the interval is not recorded (see above, on 19, 22.) *Embraced* is a secondary usage of the Greek verb, which originally signifies to greet or welcome, but is also used by Xenophon and later writers in the sense of taking leave or bidding farewell, which is the meaning here. *Departed*, literally, *went out* (see above, on 16, 36. 40.) *For to go*, depart, or journey (see above, on 5, 31.) *Into Macedonia*, as he had before designed, and whither he had already sent Timothy and Erastus (see above, on 19, 22.)

2. 3. And when he had gone over those parts, and had given them much exhortation, he came into Greece, and (there) abode three months. And when the Jews laid wait for him, as he was about to sail into Syria, he purposed to return through Macedonia.

Having gone (or *passed*) *through those parts*, i. e. Macedonia, and perhaps some adjacent regions (see Rom. 15, 19.) *Given them much exhortation*, literally, *having exhorted them* (i. e. the Christians in those parts) *with much speech* (or many words.) *Greece*, properly so called, or what the Romans named Achaia, to distinguish it from Macedonia (see above, on 16, 1. 18, 12. 27. 19, 21.) *Having made three months*, i. e. passed or spent them, but perhaps with an implication of active employment (see above, on 15, 33. 18, 23.) This is the more worthy of attention, as Luke gives us no details of this second missionary tour in Greece, the greater part of which was probably spent at Corinth, where he is commonly supposed to have written the epistle to the Romans. *Being about to sail into Syria*, i. e. to enter on the voyage which was to terminate at Antioch, as in the case of his two previous missions. (See above, on 18, 18, and below, on 21, 3.) The words express his purpose, not the actual event, which was altogether different, as he did not reach Antioch, but was arrested in Jerusalem, and after being long detained in Cesarea, sent to Rome. *A plot* (the same word that occurs above in 9, 24) *being made* (or *formed*) *against him by the Jews*. What was the nature or occasion of the Jewish plot here mentioned, we have no means of determining. We only know that Paul was led, no doubt by the detection or divine revelation of it, to relinquish his design of setting sail from Corinth or Cenchrea (see above, on 18, 18), and to revisit Macedonia for that purpose. *Purposed to return*, literally, *there was a purpose* (or it became his purpose) *to return*. The Greek noun properly means judgment or opinion, but is used by the purest Attic writers in the sense of will or purpose.

4. And there accompanied him into Asia Sopater of Berea; and of the Thessalonians, Aristarchus and Secundus; and Gaius of Derbe, and Timotheus; and of Asia, Tychicus and Trophimus.

There followed with him, an expression which implies both association and subordination. They were in his company, not as his equals, but as his adherents and attendants. *As far as Asia*, in the usual restricted sense (see above, on 19, 10. 22. 26. 27.) *As far as* may have reference to their waiting for him at Troas. It does not necessarily imply that they attended him no further, although only two of them are afterwards expressly named as being with him. (See below, on 21, 29. 27, 2.) *Sopater*, an abbreviation of *Sosipater*, and probably denoting the same person whom Paul mentions (Rom. 16, 21) as a kinsman who was with him in Corinth. Some of the oldest manuscripts and versions have *Sopater* (son) *of Pyrrhus*, which seems more likely to have been omitted than inserted without reason. *Of Berea*, literally, *a Berean*, an inhabitant or native of that place in Macedonia, where the Jews gave Paul so cordial a reception and so candid a hearing (see above, on 17, 11.) *Secundus*, a Latin name, occurring only here in the New Testament. *Gaius* (or *Caius*), commonly supposed to be a different person from the one so called in 11, 29, because he is there called a Macedonian and here a Derbean, or citizen of Derbe, which was in Lycaonia (see above, on 14, 6.) Some connect *Derbean* with *Timotheus*, and thus make Gaius a Thessalonian; but this construction is forbidden by the *and* between *Derbean* and *Timotheus*, unless, by another arbitrary supposition, we can change the form of the Greek particle (from καί to δέ.) Some add, that Timothy was certainly of Lystra, not of Derbe; but that fact is too doubtful to decide the question here at issue (see above, on 16, 1. 21), especially as Derbe and Lystra are so often named together, as if constituting one community. It is not certain, although commonly assumed, that these local adjectives denote the native place or constant residence of those to whom they are applied, as they may possibly denote the last place of abode, or some official position in the church or representative relation to it. The question is, however, less important, as Caius was one of the most common Roman names. In favour of the identity is the slight but noticeable circumstance, that the name is in both cases joined with that of Aristarchus. According to the usual construction, Timothy has no local epithet connected with his name, perhaps because his origin was generally well known. But besides the construction which has been already mentioned as forbidden by the syntax, we may read, *Gaius a Derbean and* (also, or from the same place) *Timotheus*, against which it may again be urged, but not more conclusively than in the other instance, that he was from Lystra. *Of Asia*, literally, *Asians*, Asiatics, i. e. representatives of Asia Minor, or rather of that part of it called *Asia Proconsularis*. *Tychicus* is several times named by Paul, as his messenger to the churches, and the bearer of two of his epistles. (See Eph. 6, 21. Col. 4, 7. 2 Tim. 4, 12. Tit. 3, 12.) *Trophimus* was with him at Jerusalem, and there became the innocent occasion of his arrest and long captivity (see below, on 21, 29.) He is also mentioned in the latest of Paul's epistles, as having been left sick at Miletus (2 Tim. 4, 20.) The presence of these seven men on this occasion has been variously explained and understood. That it was not fortuitous, i. e. that they did not merely happen to be travelling the same way at the same time, is evinced by the formality and fulness of the catalogue, if not by their being named at all. That they simply attended Paul to aid him in his missionary work, is peculiarly improbable at this point, where he is about to leave his field of labour and to have less need of such assistance than before. That they accompanied him as a body-guard, or to protect him from the violence or machinations of the Jews, seems inconsistent with the fact recorded in the next verse, that at the very outset of his journey, and before he left the country where his life had been in danger, they were sent before him, and thus separated from him, at least five days, and possibly much longer. Perhaps the most felicitous conjecture which has been proposed, is that these men went as representatives of the Gentile churches lately founded, in the presence of the mother-church and the Apostles; three representing Europe and four Asia, two of the latter the interior and two the western coast of Asia Minor. If they were also bearers of a general contribution from the Gentile churches for the poor saints at Jerusalem, as some infer from certain passages in Paul's epistles written about this time or not long before (e. g. 1 Cor. 16, 1–4. 2 Cor. 8, 1–5. Rom. 15, 25–28), the whole number (seven) may have had some reference to that of the almoners or deacons in the mother-church itself (see above, on 6, 3, and below, on 21, 8.)

5. These going before tarried for us at Troas.

These, i. e. the seven named in the preceding verse, and not merely the two last, as some explain it, which is perfectly gratuitous and arbitrary. *Awaited* (waited for) *us*, i. e. for Paul and the historian himself, a form of expression which has not occurred before since the sixteenth chapter, and the re-appearance of which here has justly been regarded as a proof that Luke rejoined Paul at Philippi, where he had been left by him so long before. (See above, on 16, 40.) It also shows that the writer was not Timothy, who is not only named in the preceding list, but explicitly said to have gone before and waited for the writer, as well as for Paul, at Troas.

6. And we sailed away from Philippi after the days of unleavened bread, and came unto them to Troas in five days, where we abode seven days.

After the days of unleavened bread, i. e. the week following the Passover. (See above, on 12, 3.) This not only fixes the season of the year, but, as some suppose, assigns the reason for Paul's staying at Philippi, while the seven went immediately to Troas, namely, that he wished to keep the feast. But although such observance was by no means incompatible with Paul's principles of Christian liberty, it can hardly be supposed that he would have deferred his voyage on that account, or have attached as much importance to the spending of a paschal week in Philippi, as he might have done in Jerusalem. It is equally probable, at least, as Luke alone remained with him, while all the rest went on to Troas, that this delay had some connection with the state of the Apostle's health; or that he waited until Luke had made his preparations to withdraw from the place where he had probably been resident for several years, without detaining the whole company on that account. On either of these latter suppositions, *the days of unleavened bread* may be regarded as a mere date or chronological specification (see above, on 18, 21), like Christmas and Easter in modern parlance, when employed to designate the season, without reference to religious observance. *In five days*, literally, *unto* (or *as far as*) *five days*, the same particle employed above (v. 4) in its proper local sense, but here applied to time, and suggesting two ideas, namely, that this number was the maximum or limit, that they were not more than five days on the way, and also that this number was unusually great, as appears moreover from the fact, that on his first voyage from Troas to Philippi, he was only two days going the same distance, a diversity no doubt arising from a difference of wind. *Abode seven days* is the sense but not the form of the original, in which the last word is directly governed by the verb meaning *passed* or *spent*. (See above, on 12, 19. 14, 3. 28. 15, 35. 16, 12.) These minute chronological specifications are in perfect keeping with the previous intimation that the writer had again rejoined Paul. (See above, on 16, 11.)

7. And upon the first (day) of the week, when the disciples came together to break bread, Paul preached

unto them, ready to depart on the morrow, and continued his speech until midnight.

Cranmer's version, *upon one of the sabbath-days*, seems at first sight more exact, but is not even grammatical, the Greek numeral and noun being of different genders. Equally incorrect is Tyndale's version, *the morrow after the sabbath-day*, except that it retains the reference to the first day of the week. We have seen already that the Hebrew word *sabbath*, in its Aramaic form, resembles a Greek plural, and is often so inflected, even when a single day is meant. (See above, on 13, 14. 16, 13.) Still more natural is the use of the plural to denote the interval between two sabbaths, or rather a whole week, a division of time connected, both in origin and usage, with the religious observance of one day in seven. Even in Hebrew, *weeks* and *sabbaths* are convertible terms (compare Lev. 23, 15 and Deut. 16, 9.) In the Greek of the New Testament, *a week* is once or twice expressed by *sabbath* in the singular (see Mark 16, 9. Luke 18, 12), but usually by the plural (see Matt. 28, 1. Mark 16, 2. Luke 24, 1. John 20, 1. 19. 1 Cor. 16, 2), which, however, as explained above, is only such in form, but in reality a singular. The substitution of the cardinal (*one*) for the ordinal (*first*) is not a Hebrew idiom, but a usage equally well known to other languages, as in our own familiar phrases, "number one," "chapter two," etc. Thus the phrase which, rendered word for word, would mean *one of the sabbaths*, is determined by analogy and use to mean (*the*) *first* (*day*) *of the week*, a striking illustration of the curious fact, that literal translation is not always the most faithful. In the case before us, it is not a simple date or chronological specification of the day on which this meeting happened to be held; for such a circumstance was too minute to be recorded for its own sake, and is never given elsewhere. The only satisfactory solution is, that the observance of the first day of the week, as that of our Lord's resurrection, had already become customary, so that the assembling of the church at that time for the purposes here mentioned, was a matter of course, with or without special notice and arrangement. This agrees well with the form of the expression here, *being assembled* (i. e. as usual) *to break bread, etc.*, and also with the words of Paul in 1 Cor. 16, 2, where the designation of the day would be gratuitous and inconvenient, unless founded on a previous and familiar custom. The observance itself, though not explicitly enjoined, nor even formally recorded, seems to date from the very day of Christ's resurrection. Compare John 20, 19. 26, where "eight days" is a common idiomatic expression for a week, and "again" implies a periodical reunion, not by chance, but by order or agreement, on the same day as before. The original or Jewish sabbath may have been observed, at least by Jewish Christians, either alone or in conjunction with the first day of the week, until the downfall of Jerusalem and final abrogation of the old economy, after which the former was entirely superseded by the latter, except among the Ebionites and Judaizing Gnostics, who were really, as well in form as spirit, rather Jews than Christians. In all the places which have now been cited, the expression used is simply, *the first day of the week.* *The Lord's Day* is a phrase derived from Rev. 1, 10, which is also commonly regarded as a proof of apostolical observance, although some interpreters identify it with *the day of the Lord* (or *of Jehovah*), so often mentioned and foretold in prophecy. *The disciples being assembled*, or, according to the oldest manuscripts and latest critics, *we being assembled*, which renders still more prominent the fact that the historian himself was an eye-witness of the facts recorded. (See above, on v. 5.) *Assembled*, literally, brought together, gathered, but not necessarily implying a special convocation, being elsewhere applied both to stated and occasional assemblies. (See above, on 4, 6. 26. 27. 31. 11, 26. 13, 44. 14, 27. 15, 6. 30.) It is in fact the verbal root of the noun *synagogue*, the most generic hellenistic term for any meeting, though especially applied to worshipping assemblies. (See above, on 6, 9. 13, 43. 15, 21. 18, 7.) *To break bread*, socially and sacramentally, according to the primitive and apostolic usage, which attached the eucharist to an ordinary meal, as in its original institution. (See above, on 2, 42. 46, and compare 1 Cor. 11, 20–22.) *Ready* is in Greek the participle of a verb denoting mere futurity, to which we have no exact equivalent in English, and which is therefore very variously rendered. (See above, on v. 3. 11, 28. 12, 6. 13, 34. 16, 27. 17, 31. 18, 14. 19, 27.) It might have been translated here, *intending* (as in 5, 35), or still better, *being about* (as in 3, 3, and v. 3, above.) *To depart*, or go out, go away, i. e. from Troas (see above, on v. 1.) *On the morrow*, or the next day (see above, on 4, 3. 5. 10, 9. 23, 24. 14, 20. *Preached*, the word translated *reasoned* and *disputed* elsewhere (see above, on 17, 2. 17. 18, 4. 19. 19, 8. 9.) As it primarily signifies colloquial discourse or conversation (being the root both of *dialogue* and *dialect*), some understand it to have that sense here, as agreeing better with the extraordinary length referred to in the next clause. It is probable, however, both from the usage of the word in this book (see the places above cited), and from the circumstances of the present case, that it was not a desultory talk, but an act of official or professional instruction, however informal and unshackled by rhetorical or other rules. The length of the discourse depends upon the time when it began, which is not specified; but that it was unusual, seems to be implied in the suggestion that it was his last opportunity of meeting with them, and also in the incident recorded in v. 9 below. It is still more explicitly affirmed in the ensuing clause of this verse, where *continued* is a stronger word in Greek, meaning stretched out or protracted, i. e. beyond the time to which they were accustomed in such cases. Some infer from this verse, that the meetings of the Christians were already held at night, as they were afterwards in times of persecution; others that this was an extraordinary meeting held in view of Paul's departure. It is possible, however, that he spent the whole day in the manner here described, as he seems to have done afterwards at least on one occasion (see below, on 28, 23), not in continuous discourse, but in animated conversation, with occasional intervals of rest or silence.

8. And there were many lights in the upper chamber where they were gathered together.

Lights, literally, *lamps*, but in a wider sense than that which we attach to it, including torches, candles, lanterns, etc., and therefore, both in etymology and usage, corresponding very nearly to the word used in the English version. *Upper chamber*, commonly the chief room in an ancient house, and best adapted to accommodate large numbers. (See above, on 1, 13. 9, 37. 39.) The mention of a circumstance, apparently so unimportant, has been variously and sometimes strangely accounted for. Some refer to the ancient (Jewish and heathen) use of lights, for ornament as well as use, in solemn ceremonies. Others suppose it to be intimated that the Christians of Troas took this method of avoiding the suspicious and malignant charges sometimes provoked by their nocturnal meetings. A third opinion is, that the multitude of lights is mentioned to account for the drowsiness of Eutychus; a fourth, to explain why his fall was instantly observed. More natura. than either is the simple supposition, that the lights are mentioned, not with any definite design, but as a part of the scene strongly impressed upon the writer's memory, and therefore serving, in conjunction with the intimations previously given, to remind the reader that he is again receiving the report of an eye-witness. (See above, on vs. 5. 6. 7.) As Luke, in orally rehearsing this same narrative long after the occurrence, might have said to those who heard him, 'My recollection of that night is still so vivid, that I seem almost to see the upper chamber brightly lighted up, the crowd, the young man in the window, etc.,' so in recording it, first for Theophilus, and then for us, he might naturally use some of the same expressions, without any pragmatical or utilitarian design at all. *Many*, the word so rendered in 9, 23. 43. 12, 12. 14, 21. 19, 19. *They were gathered*, or according to the oldest copies, *we were gathered*, as in the preceding verse. In both these cases later copyists seem to have entirely overlooked the graphic and authentic character imparted to the passage by the use of the first person, or rather to have looked upon it as an incongruity, and so expunged it. It is certainly remarkable that these slight emendations of the text, supported as they are by such external evidence, should not only render the whole narrative more lifelike, but assimilate it still more completely to the context, and enhance the proof that the Apostle of the Gentiles had recovered his "beloved physician" (Col. 4, 14.)

9. And there sat in a window a certain young man named Eutychus, being fallen into a deep sleep; and as Paul was long preaching, he sunk down with sleep, and fell down from the third loft, and was taken up dead.

There sat (literally, *sitting, seated*) *in a window* (literally, *on the window*), i. e. on the ledge or window-seat. The definite form (*the window*) does not necessarily imply that there was only one; or denote one looking towards Jerusalem, as some suppose; but is exactly like our own familiar phrase, to look out of the window, without any reference to number or position. His sitting in the window has been thought to imply, that he was a careless, inattentive hearer; but with more probability, that there was no room elsewhere. The occurrence of the same name (*Eutychus*) in old inscriptions, as the name of freedmen or emancipated slaves, is no sufficient ground for the conjecture that this person was a servant. *A young man* is in Greek one word, corresponding to our *youth*, but even more indefinite. That it does not mean a *child*, see below, on v. 12, and above, on 7, 58. The marked resemblance of this scene to one of our own public meetings, with its many lights and even crowded windows, serves to stamp the narrative as that of an eye-witness. *Fallen* and *sunk* are different participles of the same verb, strictly meaning *borne* (or *carried*) *down*, and specially applied in Greek to the effects of sleep, not only when the latter is expressed, as in our phrase *to fall* (or *drop*) *asleep*, but also when the verb is absolutely used. The medical Greek writers even use a cognate noun (καταφορά) to designate the lethargy. The present participle here denotes the natural relaxing influence of sleep, the aorist an additional corporeal movement as its result, by which he lost his balance. *Into* and *with*, although substantially correct, do not exactly reproduce the form of the original, in which the first is represented by the dative (ὕπνῳ), and the second by a preposition (ἀπό) meaning *from*. The final consequence was that he actually *fell down from the third loft*, i. e. floor or story, probably the highest in the house, as the *upper room* was usually next the roof (see above, on 1, 13.) *Taken up*, raised, lifted from the ground, an uncompounded form of the verb used above (in 1, 9) to denote the first stage or incipient movement of our Lord's ascension. *Dead* must of course be strictly understood, unless afterwards explained or qualified.

10. And Paul went down, and fell on him, and embracing (him) said, Trouble not yourselves, for his life is in him.

Going down, descending, to the street, or to the inner court, around which an oriental house is built, and into which "the window" may have opened. *Embracing*, not the word so rendered in the first verse, but a double compound, strictly meaning *to seize with and around*, often used by the classics in the figurative sense of comprehending or including, but here in its etymological import of folding or encircling in the arms. *Said*, to those who stood by, probably to such of the assembled Christians as had come down with Paul, or before him, and immediately after the occurrence of the accident. *Trouble not yourselves* (or *be not troubled*) seems in English to refer exclusively or chiefly to internal perturbation or disorder, and to mean, 'be not anxious or alarmed.' But the Greek verb properly, and almost constantly, expresses outward disturbance, and particularly noise or uproar, as the kindred noun is rendered in the first verse of this chapter, and the verb itself in 17, 5, above. Its specific application here derives some illustration from its use in Matt. 9, 23. Mark 5, 39, where it evidently signifies the noisy and tumultuous expression of grief, which was customary at an oriental funeral. Such a demonstration had perhaps begun in this case, and Paul may then be understood, not merely as forbidding them to grieve, but as exhorting them to keep silence or be quiet. The reason he assigns has been very variously understood. *His life* (or *soul*) *is in him*, is by some explained to mean, 'he is not dead, as you imagine.' (Compare the words of Christ himself in the passages last cited.) Paul's language, thus explained, is then used to qualify Luke's absolute expression, in v. 9, as meaning, 'he was taken up for dead,' or 'he was taken up dead, as they supposed.' This reasoning, however, may be just as easily reversed, and the terms of v. 9 made to qualify those here employed, instead of being qualified by them. As we are there expressly told that *he was taken up dead*, Paul may here be understood to mean, *his life is* (again) *in him*. The "again" in this construction is no more forced into the text than "still" is in the other; so that in this respect they stand at least on equal ground. In favour of a real death, besides the positive assertion in v. 9, is the act, here ascribed to Paul, of falling on the body and embracing it, in obvious allusion to the conduct of Elijah and Elisha in cases of miraculous resuscitation (see 1 Kings 17, 21. 2 Kings 4, 34.) That this act was in either case designed to ascertain the fact of life or death, is far less probable than that it was intended to connect a miraculous effect with the person by whom it was caused or brought about. (See above, on 5, 15. 19, 12.) The present case is altogether different from that of Paul himself in 14, 19, where the words, "supposing him to be dead," seem to give us a discretion, or an option, not afforded by the absolute expression, *he was taken up dead*. A further proof that this was a miraculous recovery from death may be founded on the fact that it is introduced at all, which cannot be explained by the startling impression or the vivid recollection of the accident; for although this may be sufficient to account for the minuteness and vividness of the details, it does not serve to show why Luke should thus have paused in his relation of this memorable journey, to record what happened to a person otherwise unknown and insignificant, unless it was accompanied by some display of Paul's miraculous endowments as the signs of his apostleship (2 Cor. 12, 12.) Thus his last recorded visit to this place was rendered memorable by a signal miracle, as the first was by a vision and a special revelation. (See above, on 16, 9. 10.)

11. When he therefore was come up again, and had broken bread and eaten, and talked a long while, even till break of day, so he departed.

Having then (δέ) *gone up*, to the room in the third story, where the Christians were assembled, and from which the youth had fallen. *Eaten*, literally, *tasted*, which may be strictly understood, as in Matt. 27, 34. John 2, 9. Col. 2, 21. But the wider sense of eating, taking food, partaking of a meal, is found, not only in the later classics, but in Xenophon. (See above, on 10, 10, and below, on 23, 14.) Most interpreters identify this breaking of bread with that mentioned in v. 7 above, and which had been deferred by Paul's protracted conversation or discourse. It is possible, however, that the love-feast and the eucharist had been observed as soon as they assembled, and that the eating here described was what we call an early breakfast, preceding the departure of these honoured guests. *Talked*, the nearest Greek equivalent to our *converse*, both in its narrower and wider sense. (See above, on 10, 27, and below, on 24, 26, and compare Luke 24, 14. 15.) It is somewhat curious that although this verb denotes familiar conversation, as distinguished from more formal or elaborate discourse, it was afterwards applied, in ecclesiastical usage, to the latter, and is the root or theme of the words *homily* and *homiletics*. (For a somewhat analogous change, see above, on 13, 2.) *A long while*, literally, *for sufficient* (*time*), or (*time*) *enough*, a favourite expression in this book, and one which has already been repeatedly explained. (See above, on v. 8.) The strict sense is retained here by the Vulgate (*satis*) and its English copyists (Wicl. *spake enough*. Rhemish Vers. *talked sufficiently*.) This second mention of Paul's long continued talk illustrates his vivacious and communicative habits, and implies the interest with which the brethren or disciples heard him. *Break of day*, or rather, broad day-light, the Greek word properly denoting *brightness* and particularly sunshine. *So*, not *so then*, as a mere connective or resumptive (see above, on 19, 32. 38), but *thus*, in this way, i. e. discoursing or conversing to the very last. (See above, on 7, 8. 14, 1. 17, 33. 19, 20.) *Departed*, literally, *went out*, not only from the room, or from the house, but from the city (see above, on v. 1.)

12. And they brought the young man alive, and were not a little comforted.

The sense is not, as some suppose, that in the mean time they had taken him home, but that now, about the time of Paul's departure, they brought him in, and showed him to the company, alive and well. Both verbs refer to the disciples, whose assembly had been so abruptly interrupted, and appeared to be completely broken up by this distressing casualty. *Comforted*, relieved from the shock which they had felt at first, and from their subsequent solicitude as to the issue. The word may indeed suggest still more, to wit, the natural reaction from distress of this kind to unusual excitement and exhilaration. *Not a little* is in Greek *not moderately*, an example of the figure called meiosis or litotes, which employs a negative expression to convey a very positive idea, such as *much* or *greatly*. (See above, on 12, 18. 14, 28. 15, 2. 17, 4. 12. 19, 23. 24.) *Young man* is not the word so rendered in v. 9, but one which answers to our *boy* (Geneva Bible) or *lad* (Rhemish version), and like it may be substituted both for *son* and *servant*. (See above, on 3, 13. 26. 4, 25. 27. 30.) Wiclif's version (*child*) is here at variance with the previous description of him as a youth or young man (see above, on v. 9.)

13. And we went before to ship, and sailed unto Assos, there intending to take in Paul; for so had he appointed, minding himself to go afoot.

We, i. e. the writer and his company, which here excludes Paul, as it did the others in v. 6 above. *Going* (or *having gone*) *before*, i. e. before Paul's own departure, although previously mentioned. (See above, on v. 11.) The idea seems to be, that they had left him in the house with the assembled

Christians. *To ship*, or more exactly, *to the ship*, i. e. the one in which they were to sail. It is not necessarily implied that this was the same ship in which they came to Troas; or if it was, that they had chartered it, and kept it waiting on their movements. For their own protracted stay of seven days in one place may have been the consequence, and not the cause, of the ship's delay there, for the purpose of refitting, loading, or awaiting a more favourable wind. (See above, on v. 6.) *Sailed*, the same nautical expression used above in v. 3, and in 13, 13. 16, 11. 18, 21, and there explained. *Unto Assos*, literally, *into Assos*, which appears to be the technical or customary form in such connections, being found in all the passages just cited. Some of the oldest manuscripts, however, have a different preposition in the case before us. *Assos* (or *Apollonia*), a Mysian seaport, opposite to Lesbos, and a few miles south of Troas, on a spot still marked by a wretched hamlet. *There*, literally, *thence*, from that place. *Intending* is too strong a term, especially as it was not their purpose, but his own, that was to be accomplished. The Greek verb is the one denoting mere futurity (see above, on vs. 3. 7), and here means simply that they *were to take him*, in pursuance of his own plan as expressed in the next clause. *To take in*, literally, *to take up*, i. e. from the land, which in nautical language is described as lower than the water. (See above, on 18, 22, and below, on 27, 3. 28, 12.) *He had appointed* is in Greek a passive form, and may be therefore more exactly represented by *determined* or *resolved*. (For the meaning of the verb itself, see above, on 7, 44. 18, 2.) *Minding*, the same participle just translated *intending*, but here too, although purpose is implied, expressing only futurition (that he was to go, or being about to go.) *Afoot* (in modern parlance, *on foot*) may be strictly understood, as the distance was so short; but the verb is used by the best Greek writers (such as Xenophon and Aristotle) to denote a journey or march by land, as distinguished from a voyage by sea. The cognate adverb is employed in the same way by Herodotus and Thucydides, and may be so explained in Matt. 14, 13. Mark 6, 33. The cause of this arrangement has not been recorded and can scarcely be conjectured. Whether designed for health, or safety, or retirement, or intercourse with others, the unstudied mention of this fact without explanation, so far from discrediting the narrative, imparts to it a fresh air of reality and simple truth. In every such case there are acts and incidents, which naturally dwell upon the memory of those who witnessed them, although they neither can nor need be fully understood by others, not because they are mysterious or important, but perhaps for a reason diametrically opposite.

14. And when he met with us at Assos, we took him in, and came to Mitylene.

When, literally, *as*, an idiom common to both languages. (See above, on 1, 10. 18, 5. 19, 9. 21.) *Met*, a Greek verb which primarily means to *throw* (or *put*) *together*, but has several secondary senses, three of which occur in this book. (See above, on 4, 15. 17, 18. 18, 27, and compare Luke 2, 19. 14, 31.) It here means something more than *met*, which might have been fortuitous, whereas Paul *joined* (or *rejoined*) *them* by express preconcert. *Us*, including the historian (as in vs. 5. 6. 7. 8. 13), whose continued presence is evinced, moreover, by the minute specifications both of time and place which follow. *At Assos* is the same phrase that is rendered *unto Assos* in v. 13. *Took him in*, took him up, as in the same verse. *Mitylene*, the capital of Lesbos, on the east side of the island, famous as the birthplace of Sappho and Alcæus, described by Cicero as noble, by Horace as beautiful, by Vitruvius as magnificent. It is now called Castro. The preposition is the same with that prefixed to *Assos*.

15. And we sailed thence, and came the next (day) over against Chios; and the next (day) we arrived at Samos, and tarried at Trogyllium; and the next (day) we came to Miletus.

We have here Paul's itinerary given with all the precision of a journal, or the vivid recollection of one personally present. *Sailing away*, a different verb from that in v. 13, and a different compound of the one in v. 6. *Came*, came down upon, the verb employed above in 16, 1. 18, 19. 24. *Over against*, opposite to, implying that they did not land or touch there, but simply passed in sight of it. *Chios*, a beautiful and fertile island, near the coast of Asia Minor, between Lesbos and Samos. It is now called Scio, and is famous for the Turkish massacre in 1822. *Arrived*, a Greek verb, literally meaning to place one thing by or near another, for comparison or any other purpose. Hence in Mark 4, 30, it means to compare, and is the root of the word *parable*. As a nautical expression, it means to come to, touch, or land, at any place. *Samos*, an island of the Archipelago, south-west of Ephesus, the birth-place of Pythagoras. *Having remained*, probably all night. *Trogyllium*, the name both of a promontory and a town, upon the coast of Asia Minor, opposite to Samos. *Miletus*, a famous seaport, about thirty miles from Ephesus, in Ionia, but near the Carian border, famous as the birth-place of Thales, and at one time the chief commercial town of Asia Minor. It is a curious circumstance, that *the next day*, thrice repeated in this verse, answers to three different Greek phrases, meaning *the coming* or *ensuing* (day); *the other* (day); and *the adjoining* or *adjacent* (day), the same expression that occurs in the latest text of 13, 44, and is there explained.

16. For Paul had determined to sail by Ephesus, because he would not spend the time in Asia: for he hasted, if it were possible for him, to be at Jesusalem the day of Pentecost.

This verse assigns the reason of Paul's visiting Miletus when he did not visit Ephesus, although much more important and attractive. *Determined*, literally, *judged*, implying not mere arbitrary resolution, but a deliberate opinion and conclusion (see above, on 3, 13. 15, 19.) *To sail by*, i. e. without stopping, though it really lay in his way (see above, on 18, 18. 19.) *Because he would not spend the time*, though correct as a paraphrase, is not an exact version. *That it might not happen to him* (against his own will and judgment) *to spend the time in Asia*, which he felt bound to spend elsewhere. One fine trait, not apparent in the common version, is the Apostle's wise distrust of his own constancy suggested in the beginning of this clause. As if he had said, 'Who knows what may happen, when I find myself again among my old friends and old enemies? In spite of present views and resolutions, I may be induced to waste time there, which I ought to be redeeming elsewhere.' *Asia*, i. e. Asia Proper or Proconsular, the province to which Ephesus belonged (see above, on v. 4.) *For he hasted*, was impatient, or solicitous (see 2 Pet. 3, 12.) *If it were possible*, implying some doubt, and at the same time some anxiety. The last clause may be construed, *that the day of Pentecost should be* (*observed* or *spent*) *in Jerusalem*, without material change of meaning. (As to *Pentecost*, see above, on 2, 1, and compare 1 Cor. 16, 8.) It has been disputed whether this desire had reference to the observance of the feast, or to the multitudes assembled at it; but there seems to be no reason for excluding either motive, though the latter may have been the main one (see above, on 18, 21.)

17. And from Miletus he sent to Ephesus, and called the elders of the church.

Sending to Ephesus, he called for, called to him, summoned (see above, on 7, 14. 10, 32.) *The elders of the church*, and as such its official representatives, as well as its divinely constituted rulers. (See below, on v. 28, and above, on 11, 30. 14, 23. 15, 2. 4. 6. 22. 23. 16, 4.) *The church*, i. e. the church of Ephesus, considered as one organic whole, whatever may have been its subdivisions or affiliated congregations. Whether this description is to be extended beyond the bounds of Ephesus itself, is a disputed question. Irenæus, followed by some later writers, understands *the church* to mean the church of the whole province or surrounding country. But this construction is intended merely to account for the use of the word *bishops* in v. 28 below, without relinquishing its later sense of prelates or diocesans. As Ephesus alone is mentioned; as a general citation would have taken time, of which Paul certainly had none to spare; and as the principle of such interpretations is precarious, and admits of an indefinite extension; it is safest to abide by the letter of the narrative, and understand *the church* to mean the Christian body then existing in the place which is expressly named. That he should cite these presbyters alone, is altogether natural, considering their central and conspicuous position, and the influence which they must have exerted on the other churches of the province. It is possible, indeed, and perfectly consistent with the apostolic mode of church extension (see above, on 19, 21), that these other churches were supplied and governed by the elders of Ephesus, or that their own elders went and came to Ephesus, as the Apostles still did to Jerusalem, both as the mother-church, and as a central source of radiation (see above, on 15, 2.) But however this may be, there can be no doubt that what Paul said to the elders of Ephesus on this occasion, he said through them to the other presbyters, not only of that province, but of the whole church, not only then, but ever since, and through all ages, for which end it has been left on record. It is therefore a comparatively trivial question who were personally present, as they virtually represented those who were not. The objection to supposing a citation of all the Asiatic churches does not lie with equal force against the notion entertained by some, that the elders of Miletus were among the persons here addressed, and not expressly named because, being on the spot, they were not sent for. There is no proof, however, that a church existed there at this time, or even at the date of 2 Tim. 4, 20, which was some years later. Perhaps, indeed, the natural impression made on every reader by the narrative itself, is rather that Paul, wishing, for the reason before given, not to stop at Ephesus itself, sent for the elders of the church to meet him in a place where there was none, but where they could conveniently confer together.

18. And when they were come to him, he said unto them, Ye know, from the first day that I came into Asia, after what manner I have been with you at all seasons —

When, lit. *as*, see above, on v. 14. This discourse of Paul to the Ephesian elders has been justly regarded, not only as a masterpiece of apostolical and pastoral fidelity, but also as extremely characteristic of its author, and therefore affording a strong proof of its own genuineness, and of Luke's fidelity as a reporter. (See above, on 3, 26.) Besides a multitude of verbal similarities between this speech and the epistles, too minute and indirect to be regarded as the product of a studied imitation, the discourse is full of those impassioned vindications of himself from various malignant charges, which occasionally burst forth in his writings, and especially pervade his second letter to the Church at Corinth. Some of these coincidences will be indicated in the exposition, but the greater part of the minuter ones, although by no means the least interesting, must be left to the reader's own comparison and observation. He first appeals to their own recollection of his faithful and unwearied ministry among them (17–21.) He then adverts to the dubious prospect now before him, but only to assert again his own fidelity and freedom from responsibility for their perdition (22–27.) He exhorts them to a like fidelity, and warns them of the perils that await them, still returning to the subject of his own unwearied labours, as a model for their imitation (28–31.) He finally commends them to the divine favour, with a parting protestation of his own disinterested toil among them, winding up with a memorable saying of the Saviour, nowhere else recorded (32–35.) The charge of egotism and boasting, brought by infidels against this valedictory discourse, never occurs spontaneously to any devout reader, a sufficient proof that it is not only false but artificial and factitious. Every such reader feels that these are not ebullitions of personal vanity or pride, but as it were official claims to apostolical fidelity, by one who had been placed there by the Holy Ghost, not only as an oracle to be believed, but as a leader to be followed, and an exemplar to be sedulously copied. Lest the whole effect of this divine arrangement should be lost on his departure, he concentrates in this last discourse expressions which might otherwise have been expanded over many, and details in words what otherwise might rather have been said in action. It is this necessity of uttering as much as possible, and in as strong a form as possible, on one occasion, that imparts to this incomparable speech the air which has been mentioned, but which none can fail to understand correctly, who have any sympathy with Paul's affections or his situation when the words were uttered. It may be added, that throughout the whole discourse, the idea is spontaneously suggested of malignant calumnies against Paul, possibly invented since he "fought with beasts at Ephesus" (1 Cor. 15, 32), and designed not only to affect him personally, but to stop the progress of the new religion. That the Jews of Asia were among his most inveterate enemies, appears from their connection with his subsequent arrest (see below, on 21, 27. 24, 18.) The heathen feeling towards him we have seen displayed already (see above, on 19, 23–34.) By supposing, as we naturally may, that this address was designed in part to be a general and final answer to such charges, we obtain another explanation of the prominence here given to himself and his Ephesian ministry. These general remarks upon a common misconception or perversion will preclude the necessity of dwelling on it, in connection with the several expressions which have given rise to it, as they present themselves. *Ye know*, or more emphatically, ye yourselves are well aware (see above, on 10, 28. 15, 7. 19, 25.) He thus appeals to their own memory, in proof of what he is about to utter. As if he had said, 'whatever others may allege, as to my ministry among you, I abide by your testimony; you at least have been acquainted with my whole course since I first appeared among you.' *That I came*, literally, *from which I entered*, with reference not merely to arrival but to public appearance on this stage or field of action. *Asia*, in the same sense as before (see above, on v. 16.) *At all seasons*, literally, *the whole time*, which is understood by some to mean that he was never absent; but the emphasis is evidently on the adverb *how*, or as the English version justly but diffusely phrases it, *after what manner*, i. e. in what way. *I was with you*, not merely in the local sense of being personally present, but in that of intercourse, association. They were well aware of his relations to them, or connections with them, during the whole period of his residence in Asia.

19. Serving the Lord with all humility of mind, and with many tears, and temptations, which befell me by the lying in wait of the Jews—

The sentence is continued and the *how* of the preceding verse explained and amplified. Ye know how I was with you, namely, *serving the Lord*, not as a private Christian, but as a preacher and apostle, in which sense Peter, James, and Jude, as well as Paul, use the cognate noun (*servant*) to describe themselves in their epistles. (See James 1, 1. 2 Pet. 1, 1. Jude 1. Rom. 1, 1. Gal. 1, 10. Phil. 1, 1. Tit. 1, 1, and compare Rev. 1, 1.) *Humility of mind*, in Greek a single word, but compounded of the two expressed in English. It is sometimes rendered *lowliness* (Eph. 4, 2) or *lowliness of mind* (Phil. 2, 3.) The adjective answering to *humble* has commonly a bad sense in the classics, namely, that of mean, base, abject, although sometimes used by Xenophon and Plato to express a virtue. Christian or evangelical humility was something unknown to the heathen, both in theory and practice. *All humility*, i. e. all kinds and degrees that were appropriate to his condition. This may be taken, in accordance with a previous suggestion, as a tacit answer to the charge of pride, which may have been alleged against him. *Many tears*, or according to the latest critics, simply *tears*, the *many* being reckoned an interpolation or unauthorized assimilation to Paul's language in 2 Cor. 2, 4. Even the weaker phrase conveys a strong idea of Paul's sufferings in his ministry at Ephesus. One specific cause or occasion of these sufferings is here presented. *Tears and temptations*, i. e. tears arising from temptations, not in the restricted sense of allurements or inducements to commit sin, but in the primary and wider sense of *trials*, including troubles or afflictions, when regarded as a test of character. (Compare the use of the same Greek word in James 1, 9. 12. 1 Pet. 1, 6. 4, 12. Rev. 3, 10.) The trials thus referred to are then specified as *those occurring to me* (or *befalling me*) *in the plots* (or *machinations*) *of the Jews. In* does not merely mean *by means* (or *on account*) *of*, but suggests the additional idea of his being in the midst of them, surrounded by them. The Greek noun is the same with that in v. 3, and in 9, 24 above, 23, 30 below, in all which cases it is rendered by the English phrase, *laid wait* or *lying in wait*, a metaphor not found in the original, which simply means a *plan*, plot, or design against one. What these plots were we have now no means of determining; but the fact of their existence agrees fully with the glimpse which we obtained of Jewish policy and feeling in the riot of Demetrius (see above, on 19, 33.) The same machinations still beset his path in Greece (see above, on v. 3.) The Jews of the Diaspora appear to have maintained an active intercourse among themselves, as well as with Jerusalem, and this enabled them to operate with more effect against the Christians (see above, on 14, 19. 17, 13, and below, on 28, 21.) This verse, then, describes Paul's ministry at Ephesus as any thing but ostentatious and self-pleasing.

20. (And) how I kept back nothing that was profitable (unto you), but have shewed you and have taught you, publicly and from house to house —

Having thus described the spirit and external circumstances of his mission, he proceeds to state its more substantial qualities of faithfulness and diligence, instructiveness and soundness. He first alleges negatively, and as if in answer to some charge of negligence or partiality, that he had withheld nothing and neglected no means to promote their improvement and salvation. *How* (or *that*) connects this sentence with his previous appeal to their own recollection. As they knew how humbly and amidst what trials he had toiled among them, so they knew that he had *kept back nothing of the things expedient*, i. e. to be known in order to salvation. In the other places where the verb occurs, it means to shrink, recoil, or draw one's self back. (See below, on v. 27, and compare Gal. 2, 12. Heb. 10, 38.) Here, being construed with an expressed object, it denotes the act of holding back what ought to be presented or exhibited. *Expedient* is in Greek a participial form, the etymology and usage of which both give it the sense of *conducing* or *contributing*, i. e. to the benefit of those concerned. (Compare 1 Cor. 7, 35. 10, 33. 12, 7. Heb. 12, 20.) The verb itself is used impersonally (like the Latin *expedit*, from which *expedient* is derived) except in 19, 19, above, where it has its physical and proper sense of *bringing together*. *But have showed you* is the sense but not the form of the original, which literally means, *so as not to show you*, and describes not what he did but what he would have done, if he had kept back any thing to which they were entitled. What kind of withholding he is here disclaiming, is apparent from the last clause, where the same negative construction is continued, *so as not to tell you and to teach you.* The first of these verbs is the one variously rendered *showed* (19, 18), *told* (16, 38), *declared* (15, 4), *rehearsed* (14, 27), but strictly meaning to *announce*, to bring news, and in this connection, therefore, nearly equivalent to *preach*, in which sense it is joined with *teach*. (See above, on 4, 2. 18. 5, 21. 25. 28. 42. 4, 26. 15, 35. 18, 11. 25.) It appears, then, that what he here denies having held back from them is the word of God, instruction in the truth, and the negative assertion that he did not so withhold the truth as not to preach and teach, is equivalent to the strongest affirmation that he did thus preach and teach it. *Publicly*, or (*in*) *a public* (*place*), before the people, in assemblies. *From house to house*, or *in houses*, as distinguished from the public meetings previously mentioned. (See above, on 2, 46. 5, 42. 8, 3, where the singular number of the Greek noun is employed in the same manner.) Thus the two modes of instruction, which have ever since been found most efficacious, are here combined in Paul's description of his own Ephesian ministry. The church has yet invented nothing to supply the place or rival the effect of church and household preaching.

21. Testifying, both to the Jews and also to the Greeks, repentance toward God, and faith toward our Lord Jesus Christ.

Having claimed for his ministry in Ephesus the praise of being humble, affectionate, diligent, and faithful, he now describes its specific character or substance, what it was and wherein it consisted. In the first place, it was testimony to the truth, a common description of Christian and particularly Apostolic preaching. (For the usage of the Greek verb, see above, on 2, 40. 8, 25. 10, 42. 18, 5.) The subject of this testimony he reduces to two great heads of doctrine and of duty, repentance and faith. There is no distinctive reference to Jews and Gentiles, both being equally in need of both. Nor is it intimated that repentance can be exercised without regard to Christ, or faith without regard to God the Father. *Repentance toward God* (or with respect to God) is that change of heart and life which every sinner owes to God as his rightful sovereign, irrespectively of any offered mercy, although never really experienced till this has been revealed and apprehended. *Faith toward our Lord Jesus Christ* is that belief or trust, of which he is the specific object, and which cannot therefore be reposed in God as God, without regard to mediation or atonement. The two together constitute the whole of practical religion, and comprise all the lawful and obligatory themes of evangelical instruction. He who preaches the repentance and the faith here spoken of, in all their fulness and variety, will need to seek no other topics, and may humbly boast of having kept back nothing that was profitable to his hearers.

22. And now, behold, I go bound in the spirit unto Jerusalem, not knowing the things that shall befall me there —

He now turns from the past to the future, from the recollection of his former labours to the anticipation of approaching trials. *And now* often marks the transition from one topic to another as a sort of logical connective (see above, on 3, 17. 7, 34. 10, 5. 13, 11); but here it may be taken in its proper sense, *and now*, at present, at this time, as distinguished from the former times of which he had reminded them. *I go*, or rather, *I am going*, journeying (see above, on v. 1, and on 19, 21.) *Bound in spirit* has been variously understood as meaning, *bound to the Spirit*, i. e. under his controlling power; or encircled, guarded, and protected by him; or prospectively, though not yet really, a prisoner; or constrained in my own mind (see above, on 18, 5, and compare 7, 59. 15, 16. 18, 25.) Perhaps the meaning of the phrase is given in the next clause, *not knowing the (things) about to meet* (encounter or befall) *me*. *Bound in Spirit* may then mean, kept in ignorance, restrained from knowing, either in his own mind, or more probably by the Holy Ghost, who did not vouchsafe to reveal this to him. It thus appears that Paul's inspiration, though infallible, was not unlimited as to its objects, and did not extend to some things in which he was personally most concerned. *There*, literally, *in it*, or *in her*, i. e. in the Holy City, which he had just mentioned.

23. Save that the Holy Ghost witnesseth in every city, saying that bonds and afflictions abide me.

The negative statement just made is now qualified. The ignorance in which he had been left was not a total one. *The Holy Ghost* is here expressly mentioned as the source of what he knew upon the subject, and therefore probably as the concealer or withholder of that which he did not know, or in other words, as *the Spirit* by whom, according to the figurative language of the verse preceding, he was *bound* or kept in ignorance. *In every city* is too strong a version, the Greek phrase being not universal but distributive, *city by city*, or *from town to town*, which necessarily denotes no more than an occasional communication, here and there, as he proceeded. *Witnesseth*, the verb translated *testifying* in v. 21. *Saying*, either by direct revelation to himself, or by means of such communications as are afterwards recorded (see below, on 21, 10–12.) That no such intimations have been previously mentioned, does not prove that they were not received, as they may frequently have been of such a nature as to be observed and understood by no one but himself. It is possible, however, that the reference is after all to internal revelations, which might just as well be made progressively as outward warnings. *Bonds*, imprisonment, captivity, a form of suffering which he had frequently inflicted upon others. (See above, on 8, 3. 9, 14, and below, on 22, 4. 5. 26, 10.) *Bonds and (other) afflictions*, a specific and generic term combined. *Abide*, await, re ready for me.

24. But none of these things move me, neither count I my life dear unto myself, so that I might finish

my course with joy, and the ministry, which I have received of the Lord Jesus, to testify the Gospel of the grace of God.

None of these things move me is a very free paraphrase of the original, which strictly means. *I make account of* (i. e. value, care for) *nothing*. (For this use of the Greek noun, see above, on 19, 40.) The verb is in the middle voice, and therefore means to value for one's self, or on one's own account. This profession of indifference is then made still stronger. *I do not even hold my life dear* (i. e. valuable, precious) *to myself* (here expressed by a reflexive pronoun.) The Greek adjective is that used in 5, 34, and there explained. The necessary qualification of these strong expressions is contained in the last clause. *So as to finish* (perfect, or complete) *my course* (or race) *with joy*, in allusion to the joy of victory in the athletic games or contests, from which Paul so often draws his illustrations. (See above, on 13, 25, and compare Rom. 9, 16. 1 Cor. 9, 24. 26. Gal. 2, 2. 5. 7. Phil. 2, 16. 3, 14. Heb. 12, 1. 2 Tim. 4, 7.) *So as to finish* is equivalent to saying, *so that* (or *provided*) *I may finish*. This is the condition on which, or the good compared with which, he cared for nothing, no, not for life itself. That this *course* or *race* was not his personal experience merely, is apparent from the last clause. *And the ministry*, i. e. (in fact, though not in form) even the ministry, to wit the ministry. This ministry was that of the Apostleship (see above, on 1, 17. 25, and compare Rom. 11, 13.) He valued it even more than life, not only for its fruits, but for its author. *Which I received from the Lord Jesus*, i. e. at the time of my conversion (see above, on 9, 15. 17, and below, on 22, 15. 21, and compare Rom. 1, 1. Gal. 1, 1.) This definite allusion to a critical juncture in his history is weakened by translating the verb, *have received*. (See above, on 19, 2.) Wherein this ministry consisted, he again tells, as if never weary of the repetition. *To testify* (the same verb as in vs 21. 23, meaning not only to proclaim but to attest as true) *the gospel* (good news or glad tidings) *of the grace of God*, i. e. the good news that he can and will be gracious even to the chief of sinners who believes in Christ. (Compare Rom. 3, 26. 1 Tim. 1, 15.)

25. And now, behold, I know that ye all, among

whom I have gone preaching the kingdom of God, shall see my face no more.

The formula in v. 22 is repeated, perhaps because he had recurred for a moment to his previous ministry, and now comes back to his anticipations of the future. In both cases, *lo* (*behold*) as usual suggests something unexpected. As if he had said, 'See to what our friendship comes at last; after all our intimate relations, we are now to part, and part for ever.' The original order is, *no more shall see my face ye all among whom I have gone*, literally, *I went through* (see above, on 9, 32), i. e. when I was resident among you. This does not necessarily imply, as some suppose, the presence of elders from other parts of Asia besides Ephesus (see above, on v. 17); nor is it an impassioned apostrophe to all among whom Paul had laboured, whether present or absent. It is simply an address to the Ephesian elders, not as individuals merely, but as representatives. We have here still another description of his ministry, but one with which we are already well acquainted, *preaching* (heralding, proclaiming) *the kingdom of God.* (See above, on 1, 3. 8, 12. 14, 22. 19, 8.) Some suppose that this was merely an opinion or surmise of Paul without divine communication or direction; but this idea was expressed in v. 22 by the phrase *not knowing*, and it surely cannot be assumed that knowing and not knowing mean precisely the same thing. If *not knowing* there denotes that it was hidden from him and remained uncertain, then *I know* must mean that it had been revealed in some way and was certain. To attach the same sense to directly opposite expressions, in the same context, and in reference to the same subject, is to nullify the use of language. The only natural interpretation of Paul's statement is, that he *did not know* in detail what should befall him, but he *did know* that imprisonment and other sufferings awaited him, and he *did know* that all those among whom he went about in Ephesus should see his face no more. The only motive for preferring a different construction is that Paul, according to some writers, was released from his captivity at Rome and did revisit Asia Minor. But this historical uncertainty, instead of altering the sense of plain words, must itself be qualified or settled by them. There is no need even of avoiding the supposed contradiction by insisting on the strict sense of the word *all*, as if Paul meant to say that he would never more be seen by every one then present, though he might be seen by some, perhaps by most of them. This, which is always true of every large assembly, with respect to one who is about to leave them, would not have been entitled to such solemn utterance. The obvious meaning of the words is that he was about to take a final leave of them and of their country.

26. Wherefore I take you to record this day, that I (am) pure from the blood of all (men.)

I take you to record seems to mean, I cite (or summon) you as witnesses, as he had actually done in vs. 18–21. But the Greek verb here used means, *I testify*, I myself bear witness, or at most, with reference to the customary form of oath, I call God to witness. (Compare the use of the same verb in Gal. 5, 3, and especially in Eph. 4, 17, where the divine name is expressed, *I testify in the Lord.*) *This day* is very strong in the original, the noun *day* and the adverb *to-day* being both expressed, a combination which can only be imperfectly retained in English by such phrases as *this very day*. The very strength of the original expression shows that it was meant to be emphatic and significant, implying even more than *now* in vs. 22. 25. As if he had said, on this the last day we shall spend together, or the last day of our meeting upon earth, I testify, etc. The fact thus solemnly attested is, that if they perished it would not be his fault, or for want of faithful warning and instruction upon his part. This idea is expressed in scriptural and oriental form by saying, *I am clean* (pure, without stain, innocent) *from the blood* (i. e. the murder, or the guilt of the destruction) *of all* (i. e. of all among whom he had laboured.) *Clean from*, which has by some been represented as a Hebraism, occurs in classical Greek writers. There is obvious allusion in this passage to Ezek. 3, 17–21. 33, 1–9.

27. For I have not shunned to declare unto you all the counsel of God.

Shunned, the same verb that occurs above in v. 20, but without an expressed object as in that place. The essential meaning is, however, still the same, namely, held or drew back so as not *to tell*, announce, report, another verb occurring in that passage, and with the same infinitive construction. *The whole counsel* (plan or will) *of God*, respecting your salvation, comprehending the two cardinal requisites of repentance and faith. (See above, on v. 21.)

28. Take heed therefore unto yourselves, and to all the flock, over the which the Holy Ghost hath made you overseers, to feed the church of God, which he hath purchased with his own blood.

Having thus affirmed his own fidelity, he urges them to follow his example. *Take heed*, the same verb that is used above, in 5, 35. 8, 6. 10. 11. 16, 14, and there explained. It denotes not mere attention but attendance, sedulous and anxious care. *To yourselves*, to your own safety and salvation, as a prerequisite of usefulness to others. *The flock*, a term applied by Christ himself to his disciples (Luke 12, 32), and by Peter to the church already organized (1 Pet. 5, 2. 3). It is a favourite figure with the prophets for the chosen people or the church of the Old Testament. (See Isai. 40, 11. 63, 11. Jer. 13, 17. 23, 2. 31, 10. 51, 23. Ezek. 34, 3. Mic. 7, 14. Zech. 10, 3. 11, 4. 7. 17.) Our Lord describes himself as the good shepherd, and believers as his sheep (John 10, 1–16.) Peter describes him as the shepherd and bishop (or overseer) of souls (1 Pet. 2, 25), and as the chief shepherd (5, 4), to whom ministers are under-shepherds. *Over the which* is not a correct version, as it makes the overseers entirely distinct from and superior to the flock, whereas the original makes them a part of it, although superior in office. *In which*, in the midst and as a part of which. *The Holy Ghost made*, literally, placed or set, not only by creating the office, but by choosing the incumbents, either by express designation (as in 13, 2), or by directing the choice of others (as in 6, 5.) *Bishops* is the Anglicised form of the Greek word, which means *overseers*, *inspectors*. It is here applied to the same persons who were before described as *elders* (see above, on v. 17), proving clearly that the titles are convertible in this case, as they are in Tit. 1, 5–7; a conclusion strengthened by the otherwise inexplicable fact, that both are never named together as distinct classes of church officers. (See above, on 11, 30. 14, 23. 15, 2. 4. 6. 22. 23. 16, 4, and compare 1 Tim. 3, 2. 5, 1. 17. 19. 1 Pet. 5, 1.) That these bishops were diocesans with presbyters under them, is inconsistent with their being themselves called presbyters or elders. That they were subject to diocesans not mentioned, is precluded by the improbability that these, though superior in rank, should have passed unnoticed. That the office of diocesan was vacant at this time, is not only a gratuitous assumption, but at variance with the fact that

Paul, when he warns the elders of approaching dangers, makes no allusion to their future prelate, but addresses them as if they were about to be left in sole charge of the flock. There is no tenable ground, therefore, but the obvious and simple one, now commonly adopted even by Episcopalians, that bishops and presbyters, when Paul spoke and when Luke wrote, were the same thing, a fact affirmed also by Theodoret and Jerome. When it is added that the name bishop was afterwards assumed by a higher order who succeeded the apostles, it is only true in reference to a subsequent though early deviation from the apostolic theory and practice. Throughout the New Testament the same class of officers are called both presbyters and bishops. *To feed* is a very inadequate translation of the Greek word, which means *to act as* (or *do the duty of*) *a shepherd*, and includes, not only feeding, but protection, regulation, and the whole care of a shepherd for his flock. (Compare the use of the same verb in Rev. 2, 27. 12, 5. 19, 15, where the sense of feeding is entirely merged in that of ruling.) *The church of God*, or according to the latest critics, *of the Lord.* Both readings are very ancient, the latter being found in several of the oldest manuscripts, the former in the oldest one of all. The phrase *church of God* is of frequent occurrence (see 1 Cor. 1, 2. 10, 32. 11, 16. 22. 15, 9. 2 Cor. 1, 1. Gal. 1, 13. 1 Thess. 2, 14. 2 Thess. 1, 4. 1 Tim. 3, 5), whereas *church of the Lord* is without example elsewhere. But this fact is urged as an argument on both sides, some contending for the usage as decisive of the question, others accounting for the change of reading as an unauthorized assimilation of this one place to the others which have just been cited. The interest of the question arises from its bearing on the divinity of Christ, whose blood, according to the common text, is here described as the blood of God, a phrase found in several of the earliest Christian writers (such as Ignatius and Tertullian) as if in allusion to some text of Scripture. In favour of this reading it may also be alleged that the apparent incongruity of the expression would naturally tempt men to amend it, while the very same cause would prevent its introduction if it were not genuine. The blood of God is of course the blood of Christ who, though a man, was a divine person. *Purchased*, a Greek verb meaning properly to cause to remain over, then to save or lay by, then to acquire or gain. The middle voice denotes specifically to acquire for one's self, both here and in the only other place where it is used in the New Testament

(1 Tim. 3, 13.) The corresponding noun occurs more frequently and always in reference to redemption or salvation. (See Eph. 1, 14. 1 Thess. 5, 9. 2 Thess. 2, 14. Heb. 10, 39. 1 Pet. 2, 9.) The motive here urged for fidelity is not, as in v. 27, that their office was created by the Holy Ghost, but that the church itself was purchased by the blood of Christ.

29. For I know this, that after my departing, shall grievous wolves enter in among you, not sparing the flock.

I know this can have no other meaning here than that belonging to the same words in v. 25. How he knew it, we are not informed in either case; but that he knew it, is explicitly affirmed in both. *This*, this too, besides what he professed to know before. *Departing*, in the original a noun, used by the old Greek writers (as Herodotus) to signify *arrival*, but by Plato and Demosthenes, a going home again, and then in the Apocrypha and here, departure in general, which may either refer to his death or to his leaving them at this time, the two things coinciding as to practical effect. (See above, on v. 25.) *Wolves*, the natural enemies of sheep, and therefore used as a figure for those who ravage or lay waste the Church. (See Matt. 7, 15. 10, 16. Luke 10, 3. John 10, 12.) *Grievous* (from the Vulgate *graves*), literally, *heavy*, but explained by the context to mean cruel and destructive. (See below, on 25, 7.) *Enter in among you* (or *come in to you*), i. e. from without, as distinguished from those mentioned in the next verse. *Not sparing*, a litotes or meiosis (see above, on v. 12) for devouring or destroying.

30. Also of your own selves shall men arise, speaking perverse things, to draw away disciples after them.

Another class of enemies or wasters shall arise from a very different quarter, namely, *of* (i. e. out of, from among) your own selves. *Men*, not as opposed to wolves, which were also representatives of human beings, but a like class described without a figure. Wolves were to come in from without, i. e. wicked and destructive men, and such men were also to arise within. Some suppose the wolves, or enemies from without, to denote persecutors, as distinguished from errorists; but the only distinction here intended seems to be that between wasters from within and from without. *Shall arise*, appear, come forward. (See above, on 5, 36. 37. 7, 18.) *Perverse*, perverted, or distorted, i. e. from the standard of truth and rectitude. (See above, on 13, 8. 10, and compare Matt. 17, 17. Luke 9, 41. 23, 2. Phil. 2, 15.) *So as to draw away*, the same infinitive construction that occurs above in vs. 20. 27. It may here denote either the design, or the effect, or both. They should not only teach error in the church, but rend it by schismatical divisions, forming schools or parties. *Disciples* seems to mean disciples of their own; but in the original it is *the disciples*, i. e. of Christ, by drawing whom away from the belief of the truth and the communion of the Church, these schools or sects were to be formed. *After* (or *behind*) *them*, implying not only influence and imitation, but dependence and subjection. With this prediction of the evils which were to invade the church at Ephesus after Paul's departure, may be compared the description of its actual condition many years later in the epistle of the Saviour to it, as recorded by John (Rev. 2. 2–7.) We there learn that the church had been visited by false apostles, and infested by the Nicolaitans; but that although she had left her first love and fallen from her high estate, and was in danger of losing what she still possessed, she had endured and laboured in her master's cause, and had especially unmasked the false apostles, and abhorred the practice of the Nicolaitans; all which may be regarded as the fruit and the fulfilment of this very prophecy and exhortation.

31. Therefore watch and remember that by the space of three years I ceased not to warn every one night and day with tears.

Therefore, because these dangers threaten you, and you have been forewarned of them. *Watch*, in the primary and strict sense of the verb, both in Greek and English, *be awake*, be wakeful (1 Thess. 5, 6. 10), and also in the secondary and more common sense, *be on your guard* (1 Pet. 5, 8.) *Remembering*, as a motive and example of such vigilance, that Paul himself had exercised it night and day for three years, when the danger was less imminent. *By the space of* is supplied by the translators, as in 7, 42. 19, 10 (compare 13, 20, 21. 19, 8. 34), unless it be regarded here as a part of the translation of the Greek noun, which denotes a period or interval of three years, like the corresponding Latin form (*triennium*.) This is here a round number, including the two years and a half expressly mentioned (see above, on 19, 8. 10), together with the undefined period that Paul may have remained there after the two years expired. *Night and day*, a natural hyperbole, familiar in all languages, for *constantly*, unceasingly, at all times when he could be so employed, without regard to his own ease and comfort. *Ceased not*, paused not, another hyperbolical expression, to be understood in the same way. *With tears*, still another, meaning not that he was literally always weeping, but that his whole ministry was something more than a cold and heartless exhibition of the truth, being warmed and animated by the tenderest affection towards them, and a heartfelt desire for their salvation. *Warning*, literally, putting in mind, or into the mind, so as to include the ideas of instructing and reminding. This verb and the corresponding noun are used in the New Testament by Paul alone, with whom they are favourite expressions. *Each one* (or *every one*) who came within the reach of his instructions. This expression seems descriptive not of public but of personal or private warning.

32. And now, brethren, I commend you to God and to the word of his grace, which is able to build you up, and to give you an inheritance among all them which are sanctified.

And now, a third effort to conclude (see above, on vs. 22. 25), the others having failed, as it were, from strong emotion and unwillingness to leave them. *Commend*, commit, deposit for safe keeping (see above, on 14, 23, and compare the very different use of the same verb in 16, 34. 17, 3.) The same idea is expressed, but by another verb, in 14, 26. 15, 40. *The word of his grace* may either mean the doctrine of salvation through God's mercy (see above, on v. 24. 14, 3, and compare 11, 23. 13, 43), or his gracious word of promise. In the latter case, what follows must refer to God himself; whereas in the other case, it may be construed with *the word* or doctrine, which is able, as an instrument or means, to accomplish what is thus ascribed to it. *To build up* (or *edify*), another favourite of Paul's, who often uses it to signify spiritual progress or increase upon a firm foundation and a certain plan. (See 1 Cor. 3, 10. 12, 14. Eph. 2, 20. Col. 2, 7. Jude 20, and compare the uncompounded form of the same verb explained above, on

9, 31. *Inheritance*, possession by a filial right, the portion of sons. *Sanctified*, made holy, as the very end of their salvation (1 Thess. 4, 3. Heb. 12, 14.)

33. I have coveted no man's silver, or gold, or apparel.

His labours had been not only faithful and affectionate but disinterested. *Silver or gold or raiment of no one did I covet*, i. e. when I was among you. *Raiment* or *clothing* is often alluded to in Scripture, as a principal kind of riches in the east, where the fashion of dress seldom changes, and the son not unfrequently inherits the apparel of his father. Hence the reference to moth as well as rust in Matt. 6, 19. 20. A similar profession of disinterestedness is made by Samuel in relinquishing his office (1 Sam. 12, 3.)

34. Yea, ye yourselves know, that these hands have ministered unto my necessities, and to them that were with me.

Here, as at the beginning of the whole discourse (v. 18), he appeals to their own knowledge of the facts which he asserts. The original order of the following words is, *that to my wants, and to those being with me, ministered these hands*, a much more pointed and emphatic collocation. Whether he showed his hands, as some suppose, exhibiting the marks of labour, is a doubtful question. There can be no doubt, however, that the form of expression is peculiarly appropriate to a person speaking, and would scarcely have occurred to a mere writer. *To those with me*, that is, to their wants, or to them considered as among his own wants. The word translated *wants* (or *necessities*) is one of very frequent occurrence in Paul's writings. *Ministered*, served, provided for. (See above, on 13, 26, and below, on 24, 23.) Although Paul teaches clearly that the preachers of the Gospel are entitled to support, he refused to avail himself of this right in the Gentile churches, lest his motives should be liable to misconstruction. (See 1 Cor. 9, 11-15. 2 Cor. 11, 7-12. 12, 13-16. 2 Thess. 3, 7-12.)

35. I have shewed you all things, how that so la-

bouring ye ought to support the weak, and to remember the words of the Lord Jesus, how he said, It is more blessed to give than to receive.

Showed, the same verb that is used above, in 9, 16, and there explained. *All things* may be either the object of the verb, as in the English version, or an adverbial expression meaning *always*, or by all means, or in all things. This last construction is not only favoured by the collocation of the words in Greek, but by Paul's usage elsewhere (see 1 Cor. 10, 33. Eph. 4, 15.) *So labouring*, i. e. as I did, with my own hands, and without compulsion. *Ye ought* is in Greek a more indefinite expression, *it is right* (or *necessary*), as a general fact or principle of duty. The same word (δεῖ) is translated *we ought* elsewhere (see above on 5, 29.) *To support*, a most expressive Greek verb which, according to its etymology, originally signifies to lay hold of any one (or some thing) opposite, as if to hold it up. (Compare the use of the same verb in Luke 1, 54. 1 Tim. 6, 2.) *The weak*, in Greek a participle commonly denoting weak in body, i. e. from disease (see above, on 9, 37. 19, 12), but sometimes weak in faith or conscience, i. e. scrupulous (compare Rom. 4, 19. 14, 1. 2. 21. 2 Cor. 8, 9. 11. 12.) Some prefer the latter meaning here, viz., that Christians ought to waive their privilege in this respect, in condescension to the doubts or prejudices of others. This agrees well with Paul's principle and practice, but scarcely with the strong expression *to sustain*, support, or hold up. It is better, therefore, to explain *the weak* as meaning all who stand in need of such support from any cause. This also agrees better with the words which follow, and which speak of giving, not of refusing to receive or to depend on others. *To remember too* (τε), i. e. we ought (or it is right and necessary) so to do. *The words of the Lord Jesus*, nowhere else preserved, but breathing the spirit of his life and doctrine. As neither all his words nor deeds have been recorded (see John 21, 25), there is no need of supposing that Paul here sums up several expressions of the Saviour scattered through the Gospels, as Matthew does the prophecies of his humiliation in the words, "He shall be called a Nazarene." (See above, on 2, 22, and compare Matt. 2, 23.) It is much more natural in this case to regard the words as literally spoken by our Lord, and incidentally recorded here. The words themselves are exquisitely simple, but embody an important truth and principle of action.

Blessed, happy, or conducive to happiness, the very word used in our Lord's *beatitudes* (see Matt. 5, 3–11. Luke 6, 20–22), and often elsewhere, so that it may be described as one of his favourite expressions, which confirms the authenticity of Paul's quotation. The same sentiment is found in Aristotle, but with far less clearness and directness of expression; and the spirit of heathenism is no doubt much better embodied in the opposite maxim of an old poet, "silly the giver, lucky the receiver."

36. And when he had thus spoken, he kneeled down, and prayed with them all.

These things having said (or *saying*), *placing his knees* (upon the ground), *with them all he prayed.* The mention of his kneeling seems to imply that it was not his customary posture in public prayer, but one occasioned by the strength of his emotions. Long after, as we learn from Justin Martyr and others, it was the practice of the church to stand in public prayer upon the Lord's Day, although kneeling was no doubt used in smaller circles, as it is still by those who stand in public, or on special occasions, like the one before us. *Prayed with them*, no doubt in the sense attached to the words now, to wit, that of leading the devotions or praying in the name of all.

37. And they all wept sore, and fell on Paul's neck, and kissed him,

There was (or *arose*) *a great* (or *sufficient*) *weeping of all, and falling on his neck* (i. e. embracing him) *they kissed him* (an emphatic compound form denoting frequency or tenderness.) This childlike expression both of love and sorrow is to be explained, not merely from ancient or oriental usage, but as a proof of the intense regard, which Paul appears to have commanded on the part of all who were in bonds of spiritual friendship with him. As in many other cases, this attachment seems to have borne due proportion to the malice of his enemies.

38. Sorrowing most of all for the words which he spake, that they should see his face no more. And they accompanied him unto the ship.

Sorrowing, or in the passive form, *distressed, grieved.* The strength of the expression may be learned from its application elsewhere to maternal anguish and the torments of the damned. (See Luke 2, 48. 16, 24. 25.) *Most* (*of all* is supplied by the translators), chiefly, or especially, the usual superlative adverb. *The word*, not the whole speech as the Greek noun sometimes means (see above, on 2, 41. 6, 5. 18, 14), but a particular expression in it (compare John 6, 60. 7, 36. 18, 9. 19, 8. 21, 23.) *Spake*, or retaining the pluperfect form, *had spoken*, which suggests that it was not the close of his discourse that thus affected them, but something which he had said before, viz. in v. 25 above. *That they no more are* (*about*) *his face to see*, behold, contemplate (see above, on 7, 56. 8, 13. 10, 11. 17, 16. 22. 19, 26.) *Accompanied*, escorted, literally, sent him forward. (For the verbal and the social usage, see above, on 15, 3.)

CHAPTER XXI.

THIS division of the text contains the conclusion of Paul's voyage from Greece to Syria, his last recorded visit to Jerusalem, and the close of his active ministry or labours as a freeman. The chapter opens with a very particular itinerary of his route from Miletus to Tyre (1–3.) He spends a week there, and one day at Ptolemais (4–7.) He next visits Cesarea, where Agabus foretells his imprisonment, and his friends endeavour to dissuade him from continuing his journey (8–14.) The next stage is Jerusalem, where he is welcomed by the brethren and the elders with James at their head (15–18.) They rejoice in the conversion of the Gentiles, but describe the converted Jews as numerous and zealous for the law, and prepossessed against Paul as one who taught men to neglect it (19–21.) They advise him to conciliate these zealots by an act of ceremonial conformity, while at the same time they reiterate the previous decision as to Gentile converts (22–25.) Paul accepts their counsel, but while acting on it, is attacked tumultuously by the Jews with a design to kill him (26–30.) He is rescued by the Roman soldiers, but pursued by the infuriated mob (31–36.) The Roman commander takes him for another person, but on being undeceived, allows him to address the people (37–40.)

1. And it came to pass, that after we were gotten from them, and had launched, we came with a straight course unto Coos, and the (day) following unto Rhodes, and from thence unto Patara—

And when (or *as*) *it happened that we sailed*, i. e. from Miletus, where the previous discourse was uttered. (See above, on 20, 17.) *After we were gotten*, literally, *having been torn from them*, which means more than mere departure, namely, painful and reluctant separation. (See above, on 1, 4. 18, 1. 2.) *Ran straight*, the same Greek compound as in 16, 11. *Coos* (or *Cos*), a small but fertile island near the coast of Caria, famous of old for wine, silk, cotton, the worship of Esculapius, and the residence of Hippocrates. It is now called *Stanco*, said to be a mere corruption of a Greek phrase meaning *to* (or *into*) *Cos*. *Following*, literally, *in order*, next. *Rhodes*, another Carian island, one of the Sporades, with a city of the same name, famed for its Colossus, or gigantic statue of Apollo, which however was now prostrate or in ruins. *Patara*, a town on the coast of Lycia, near the mouth of the Xanthus, where Apollo was believed to utter oracles at certain seasons, and hence derived one of his epithets or titles (*Patareus*.) The minuteness and exactness of this narrative evince that it proceeds from an eye-witness, while the nautical phraseology shows him to have been familiar with the sea, though not a seaman by profession.

2. And finding a ship sailing over unto Phenicia, we went aboard and set forth.

Sailing over, crossing, passing through the intervening sea, which may either mean, about to do so now, the present being then used for the future, or accustomed to do so periodically, in which case the present participle has its proper sense. *Phenicia*, see above, on 11, 19. 12, 20. 15, 3. There was an open sea, and no doubt constant trade, between the Lycian and Phenician ports. *Went aboard*, literally, *ascending*, mounting, but applied (as here) to going on board ship by

Mark (6, 51) and John (21, 3.) *Set forth*, the word translated *launched* in v. 1, and explained above, on 13, 13. 16, 11. 18, 21. 20, 3. 13.

3. Now when we had discovered Cyprus, we left it on the left hand, and sailed into Syria, and landed at Tyre; for there the ship was to unlade her burden.

When we had discovered is another technical expression, being in form a passive participle, not easily translated into English. The nearest approach perhaps is *being* (or *having been*) *shown Cyprus*, i. e. made to see it at a distance, passing in sight of it. As to the island itself, see above, on 4, 36. 11, 19. 20. 13, 4. 15, 39. The apparent play upon words here (*left it on the left*) is confined to the translation, the original containing two entirely different terms, the last literally meaning *well named* (or *of good name*) and then *lucky*, in which secondary sense it was applied, by a superstitious euphemism, to the left hand or side, which was regarded by the ancients as unlucky, though they did not dare to call it so. *On the left hand* is in Greek a single word, and that an adjective agreeing with the noun or pronoun (*leaving it sinister* or *left.*) They sailed therefore to the south of Cyprus, as Paul, on his first missionary voyage, had traversed its whole length from east to west (see above, on 13, 5. 6.) *Sailed into Syria*, i. e. completed our voyage to it. (See above, on 20, 3, and compare 18, 18.) *Landed*, literally, *were brought down*, the converse or correlative expression to the one employed above in v. 1. (See below, on 27, 3. 28, 12.) *Tyre*, the famous sea-port and commercial city of Phenicia, which with Palestine formed part of the Roman province of Syria. (See above, on 12, 20.) *There*, literally, *thither*, which may here have the former sense, as it seems to have elsewhere (see below, on 22, 5), or be strictly understood as implying previous motion (going thither to unload), or motion from the harbour to the town itself. *Was to unlade*, literally, *was unlading*, which admits of the same two constructions as the participle *crossing* (see above, on v. 1.) *Her burden*, literally, *the load* (or *cargo*), elsewhere put for merchandise or wares in general (see Rev. 18, 11. 12.)

4. And finding disciples, we tarried there seven days; who said to Paul through the Spirit, that he should not go up to Jerusalem.

Finding, after search or previous inquiry. (See above, on 11, 26, where the less emphatic uncompounded form is used.) The gospel had been early introduced into Phenicia (see above, on 11, 19. 15, 3); but the Tyrian Christians were probably few in proportion to the whole population, though enough to verify, at least prospectively, the prophecy in Isai. 23, 18 (compare Ps. 87, 4.) *Tarried*, staid over, remained longer than they had expected (see above, on 10, 48. 12, 16. 15, 34.) This was probably because the ship was long discharging its cargo. The abrupt construction of the relative in English is exactly copied from the Greek. *Through the Spirit*, under his influence, by inspiration. (See above, on 1, 2. 11, 28.) *Not to ascend* (or *go up*), the expression commonly employed in speaking of motion to the Holy City. (See above, on 11, 2. 15, 2. 18, 22.) This was not a divine command to Paul, but an inference of the disciples from the fact, which was revealed to them, that Paul would there be in great danger. It was not revealed to them, as it was to him, that he must go up at all hazards. *Should not go up*, besides being an unnecessary deviation from the form of the original, suggests the idea of a moral obligation more distinctly than the simple infinitive, *not to go up*, i. e. if he valued his own ease and safety.

5. And when we had accomplished those days, we departed and went our way; and they all brought us on our way, with wives and children, till (we were) out of the city; and we kneeled down on the shore, and prayed.

And when it happened (or *befell*) *us to complete the days*, i. e. the days of this involuntary stay at Tyre. Some understand the verb, however, in the sense of thoroughly equipping or supplying (compare 2 Tim. 3, 17), and refer it to the ship, *when we had got* (it) *ready* (during) *the days;* but this construction is less natural. *Going out we journeyed* (or departed), *all escorting us* (see above, on 15, 23. 20, 38) *until* (or *as far as*) *outside of the city; we were* is supplied by the translators. *Placing the knees*, precisely as in 20, 36, but with the local specification here, *upon the shore* or *beach* (see below, on 27, 39. 40.) *We prayed*, i. e. the whole company, though led no doubt by the Apostle, as in 20, 36.

6. And when we had taken our leave one of another, we took ship, and they returned home again.

Taken our leave, the verb translated *saluted* in the next verse and in v. 19 below, and in 18, 22 above (in 20, 1 it is *embraced.*) *Took ship*, the same verb that is rendered *went aboard* in v. 2, but without the noun, which is here expressed. *Home again*, literally, *to their own* (things or places, as in John 19, 27), not *to their own friends* (as in 24, 23 below), the *own* being masculine there and neuter here. (Both forms are combined in John 1, 11.) The mention of these unimportant but impressive circumstances would not have occurred to any but a witness of the scene which he describes.

7. And when we had finished (our) course from Tyre, we came to Ptolemais, and saluted the brethren, and abode with them one day.

But we, as the other party, here opposed to those whom we have just seen going home. *Having finished the voyage*, not merely from Tyre, but the whole of their journey by water. *From Tyre came down to Ptolemais* (see above, on 16, 1. 18, 19. 24. 20, 15.) The Greek collocation makes the construction less ambiguous, *the voyage having finished, from Tyre we came.* The aorist participle may denote a simultaneous act, as in 1, 24. 19, 2. *Finishing the voyage* (or the maritime part of our journey), *we came down*, i. e. in the act of coming down we finished it. *Ptolemais*, one of the oldest and most celebrated places in the world, the *Acco* of the Old Testament, which name it still retains among the Arabs, while its modern European name is *Acre*, or in French more fully, *St. Jean d'Acre*, from the Hospitallers, or Knights of St. John, by whom it was once occupied. It is situated north of Mount Carmel, and is still the best harbour on the coast. It was assigned to the tribe of Asher, but never actually occupied by them (Judges 1, 31.) It was so near the frontier, that the ancient geographers assigned it to Phenicia, and a dictum of the Talmud says that it is and is not in the land of Israel. It was called Ptolemais no doubt as a compliment to some of the Ptolemies or Macedonian kings of Egypt. It is famous in history for its sieges, not only during the Crusades, and in the wars occasioned by the French Revolution, but also in the latest times, having been bombarded by Ibrahim Pacha in 1832, and by the Austrians and English in 1840.

8. And the next (day) we that were of Paul's company departed and came unto Cesarea; and we entered into the house of Philip the Evangelist, which was (one) of the seven, and abode with him.

The next day, literally *on the morrow*, as in 10, 9. 23. 24. 14, 20. 20, 7. *We that were of Paul's company*, literally, *those about Paul*, the idiomatic phrase employed above in 13, 13, and there explained, but here rejected by the latest critics, as not found in the oldest manuscripts, and probably added to begin a pericope or lesson. The reading then is simply, *we departed*, literally, *going out*, i. e. from Ptolemais. *Cesarea*, the new sea-port on the Mediterranean, built by Herod the Great upon the site of Straton's Tower, and when Paul was there the residence of the Roman Procurator of Judea. (See above, on 8, 40. 9, 30. 10, 1. 12, 19. 18, 22, and below, on 23, 23. 24. 33.) *Entered* (literally, *entering*) *into the house of Philip the Evangelist* (not the Apostle, but) *one of the seven* (whose appointment is recorded in 6, 5. 6.) It has been disputed how he could be absent from Jerusalem, unless he had resigned his office there. Some say the office was itself a temporary one (but see Phil. 1, 1. 1 Tim. 3, 8. 12.) A more satisfactory reply is furnished by the history itself, from which we learn that in the persecution on the death of Stephen, all the church at Jerusalem were scattered abroad throughout Judea and Samaria except the Apostles (see above, on 8, 1.) Among those thus dispersed was Philip, who seems never to have gone back after the re-organization of the church in which he was ordained a deacon. In the mean time he had "purchased (or acquired) to himself a good degree" (1 Tim. 3, 13), and had long been doing "the work of an *evangelist*" (2 Tim. 4, 5.) This word strictly means a preacher of the Gospel, but is specially applied to a particular office in the primitive church. It does not express, as in modern times, the negative idea of a minister without charge, or a mere itinerant preacher; nor the more positive idea of a missionary, or a commissioner invested with extraordinary powers for a special or temporary purpose; but a stated office in the apostolical church of great importance. While the local government and ordinary teaching of the church were committed to its elders, the work of preaching was performed by the Apostles, and by others whom they sent forth for the purpose, and who are called Prophets when inspired, but Evangelists in reference to their essential functions, just as the same persons were called Presbyters and Bishops (see above, on 20, 28.) This was a temporary system, suited to the period of organization and formation, and to be gradually superseded by the pastors and teachers of particular congregations, who began to take the place of these itinerant instructors before the end of the Apostolic age, as appears from Paul's enumeration of church-offices in Eph. 4, 11, "he gave some apostles, and some prophets, and some evangelists, and some pastors and teachers," with an obvious reference in the following verses to the temporary nature and design of the arrangement. This important office Philip had been executing since he left Jerusalem, if not before, although his ordination to it is not expressly recorded, as his being made a deacon is, not for its own sake, but as a preliminary to the martyrdom of Stephen and the great events occasioned by it. (See above, on 6, 5.) It is not improbable that Paul and Philip had been formerly acquainted, being both Hellenists and in Jerusalem together (see above, on 6, 5. 7, 58.) But however this may be, the Apostle would naturally take up his abode with Philip, not only as a labourer in the same field with himself, but as being now, perhaps, the stated pastor and teacher of the Gentile church at Cesarea, formed at the conversion of Cornelius. (See above, on 10, 48. 11, 18.)

9. And the same man had four daughters, virgins, which did prophesy.

With respect to Philip's family, an interesting fact is stated, namely, that his four unmarried daughters, no doubt still residing with him, were inspired, literally, *prophesying*, not as public teachers, which would be wholly inconsistent with Paul's principle, as laid down both before and after these occurrences (1 Cor. 14, 34. 35. 1 Tim. 2, 12), but in private, perhaps actually prophesying in the strict sense at the time of Paul's arrival, i. e. predicting what was to befall him, like the Tyrian disciples (see above, on v. 4.) This would account for the mention of the circumstance, without assuming, as some Romish writers do, that Philip's daughters were the first nuns of the Christian church. Their virginity is probably referred to, only as a reason for their being still at home, and not as having any necessary connection with their inspiration. We read of prophetesses under the old economy, not only wives of prophets (Isai. 8, 3), but themselves inspired, from Miriam (Ex. 15, 20) and Huldah (2 Kings 22, 14), to Noadiah (Neh. 6, 14) and Anna (Luke 2, 36.) Joel's promise of extraordi nary spiritual gifts was to servants of both sexes, and to daughters as well as sons. (See above, on 2, 17. 18.) It is possible, however, that the present participle (*prophesying*) was not intended to describe a constant but a special momentary inspiration *pro hac vice*, which would make what they predicted still more striking and impressive.

10. And as we tarried (there) many days, there came down from Judea a certain prophet, named Agabus.

We remaining (longer), staying over, the same verb as in v. 4. *Many*, literally, *more*, i. e. more than one, equivalent to our modern use of *several.* (See above, on 13, 31.) That the prophesying of Philip's daughters had respect to Paul's captivity, is rendered still more probable by this verse, which immediately connects with it another intimation of the same sort from a very different quarter. As if he had said, 'these prophetic warnings of the four inspired virgins were confirmed, before we left the place, by a prophet from Judea.' This last expression may denote Jerusalem (see above, on 11, 1. 29), or that part of Judea nearest to Cesarea, where Agabus may have been when he heard of Paul's arrival. The former is more probable, as he is said to have *come down*, although this might have reference merely to the site of Cesarea on the seacoast. There seems to be no reason for disputing the identity of this man with the prophet who foretold the famine, and gave occasion to Paul's first official mission to Jerusalem. (See above, on 11, 27–30.) That two contemporary prophets of Judea should have borne the not very common name of Agabus, though not incredible if well attested, is in itself much more improbable than that Luke might mention him a second time without referring to his previous appearance. (Compare the reference to Barnabas in 4, 36. 9, 27.) It does not follow from these two cases of prediction, that Agabus was a prophet only in the strict sense, and not in the wider and more usual New Testament sense of an inspired teacher. If these had been the only instances of his foretelling things to come, they would still have been entitled, from their very nature, to a more explicit record than his ordinary teachings, although equally inspired.

11. And when he was come unto us, he took Paul's girdle, and bound his own hands and feet, and said, Thus saith the Holy Ghost, So shall the Jews at Jerusalem bind the man that owneth this girdle, and shall deliver (him) into the hands of the Gentiles.

Coming to us, i. e. to the house of Philip, either as the place of usual resort for Christians, or because Paul and his company were lodged there. It is probably though not necessarily implied that Agabus came to Cesarea expressly for the purpose of uttering this prediction. *Taking*, or more exactly, *taking up* (as in 20, 9 above), or *taking away* (as in 8, 33 above.) If the former, the idea is that Agabus picked up Paul's girdle, which he had laid aside while in the house (see above, on 12, 8.) If the latter, that he took it from his person, which may then have been a part of the symbolical action, or prophecy by deed as well as word, of which we have repeated instances in the old Testament, and one relating also to a girdle. (See Jer. 13, 1. 10, and compare Isai. 20, 2. Ezek. 4, 1. 8. 5, 1. 1 Kings 22, 11, &c.) The girdle was made use of, in the case before us, not because it happened to be lying near, or simply as an article of dress, but because it was essential to all active movement, and therefore a familiar metaphor or emblem of vigorous and energetic action. (See Job 12, 18. 21 Ps. 18, 32. Prov. 31, 17. Isai. 5, 27. 11, 5. Luke 12, 35. Eph. 6, 14.) To bind him with his own girdle, therefore, expressed far more than to bind him with the strongest cord or heaviest chain. *His own hands and feet* is the unequivocal reading of the five oldest manuscripts (ἑαυτοῦ) and latest critics. The received text is ambiguous (αὐτοῦ or αὑτοῦ) and may be referred either to Paul or Agabus. But although the former reference may seem to agree better with the fact that it was Paul's girdle, not his own, the other is not only required by the true text, but is in itself more probable, as the acting or binding Paul himself for such a purpose would have been indelicate and inconvenient. *Thus* (literally, *these* things) *saith the Holy Ghost*, a formula equivalent to *Thus saith the Lord* in ancient prophecy, and claiming for the words of Agabus direct divine authority. The original order of his words is, *The man whose is this girdle, so shall bind in Jerusalem the Jews, &c. Thus* (or *so*), i. e. in such a manner as to paralyze or cripple his extraordinary energy. *Deliver* is the true sense of the Greek verb, which does not necessarily imply a treacherous proceeding, although frequently applied to the betrayal of our Lord by Judas. (See above, on 3, 13, and compare the use of the same verb in 6, 14. 7, 42. 8, 3. 12, 4. 14, 26. 15, 26. 40. 16, 4.) *The Gentiles*, literally, *nations*, i. e. other nations, not Jews (see above, on 4, 27. 7, 45. 9, 15. 10, 45. 11, 1. 18. 13, 42. 14, 2. 15, 3. 18, 6.) This whole prediction, with its symbolical accompaniment, though derived remotely from an ancient usage, takes its form directly from our Saviour's prophecy of Peter's martyrdom, recorded in John 21, 18. 19.

12. And when we heard these things, both we and they of that place besought him not to go up to Jerusalem.

Both we (i. e. the writer and the others who came with him) *and they of that place*, literally, *the local* (Christians), i. e. those of Cesarea. *Besought*, an expressive and significant Greek word, which means in different connections, to invite, entreat, exhort, console, which last sense would here be inappropriate. (See above, on 8, 31. 9, 38. 11, 23. 13, 42. 14, 22. 15, 32. 16, 9. 15. 39. 40. 19, 31. 20, 2. 12.) This unanimous importunate request was prompted by the concurrent and accumulating tokens of impending danger. It implies, of course, that they were only acquainted with this fact, and not with the express communication of the divine will, which had been made to Paul alone. (See above, on v. 4, and below, on v. 13.) These Christians, therefore, were not guilty of dissuading Paul from obeying a divine command, but simply exercised the right, which all possess, of judging for themselves or others in a doubtful case.

13. Then Paul answered, What mean ye to weep and to break mine heart? for I am ready not to be bound only, but also to die at Jerusalem for the name of the Lord Jesus.

Then, but, or and (δέ.) *What mean ye to weep*, literally, *what do ye weeping?* i. e. what is this that you are doing? or, without interrogation, see what you are doing, or consider the effect of your own conduct, which is simply to aggravate my present sufferings, without diminishing my danger, or affecting my unalterable resolution. *To break* (literally, *crushing*, shivering) *my heart*, i. e. weakening, as far as in you lies, my courage, and endeavouring to shake my resolution, by working on my own fears and my sympathy with your distress. The same verb (in its uncompounded form) is used by Aristophanes and Xenophon to signify the moral weakness caused by vicious indulgence. *For* has reference to something not expressed, e. g. 'it is in vain,' or 'cease these fruitless efforts to unman me.' The original order is, *for I, not only to be bound, but also to die, at Jerusalem, am ready, &c.* This last phrase is in Greek still more expressive, and might be rendered, *hold* (myself) *in readiness.* It is elsewhere used only by Paul (2 Cor. 12, 14) and Peter (1 Pet. 4, 5.) *For the name of the Lord Jesus*, not merely for his sake, or for the honour of being called by his name, but for all that his name or names import, viz. his sovereignty, Messiahship, and saving grace. (See above, on 5, 41, 9, 16. 15, 26.)

14. And when he would not be persuaded, we ceased, saying, The will of the Lord be done.

He not being persuaded, or *not obeying*, both which ideas are suggested by the Greek verb, in accordance with its usage and its form, which may be either passive or middle. The word may have been employed here to express the pregnant sense of an obedience prompted by conviction, as distinguished from concession to mere force or even to authority. Of this sense we have had already three examples in a single chapter (see above, on 5, 36. 37. 40), and in the present case it is peculiarly appropriate, as conveying the distinct but perfectly compatible ideas, that Paul was not convinced by their representations, and therefore did not yield to their mistaken wishes, being fortified not merely by his natural decision, but also by his certain knowledge of the divine will that he should go up to Jerusalem, whatever might befall him there. Though he does not seem to have avowed this knowledge even now, his friends appear to have inferred it from his fixed determination. *We ceased*, or more exactly *acquiesced*, not merely held their peace, but submitted to his positive decision, as appears from their own words here recorded. (For the meaning of the Greek verb, see above, on 11, 18.) *The will of the Lord be done* (or happen, come to pass) is understood by some as a quotation or allusion to the third petition of the Lord's Prayer (Matt. 6, 10. Luke 11, 2), the substance and indeed the very terms of which were no doubt daily in the minds and on the lips of the first Christians. These words might also be explained as an expression of submission to the Lord's will in allowing Paul to rush, as it were, blindfold to his own destruction; but the natural impression, made perhaps on every reader, is the one already given, to wit, that of acquiescence in Paul's own decision, as itself indicative of what the Lord would have him to do. (See above, on 9, 6, and below, on 22, 10.)

15. And after those days we took up our carriages, and went up to Jerusalem.

After these days, i. e. at the end of the *several* (or *many*) *days* mentioned in v. 10. *Carriages* is here used in its old English sense of things carried, bearing the same relation to the verb *carry*, that *luggage* does to the verb *lug*, and *baggage* to the verb *bag*. This use of the noun occurs in Spenser and in several other places of the English Bible. (See Judg. 18, 1. 1 Sam. 17, 20. 22. Isai. 10, 28.) It was here gratuitously introduced by the last translators, being found in neither of the older versions. (Wiclif: *were made ready*. Tyndale: *made ourselves ready*. Cranmer: *took up our burthens*. Geneva: *trussed up our fardels*. Rheims: *being prepared*.) The whole phrase answers to one Greek word, a participle, which might be more exactly rendered, *having packed away* (our baggage); either in the sense of *stowing away* what they did not need upon their journey to Jerusalem, or in that of *packing off* (or *forwarding*) all their effects. The latter explanation presupposes that the particle (ἀπό), with which the verb is here compounded, gives it the sense of packing up and sending off, the nearest approach to which in classical usage is the sense of clearing dishes from a table, which is found in Suidas. To the first sense above given it has been objected that if they wished to stow away superfluous incumbrances, they would have done so at Ptolemais, where their sea-voyage ended (see above. on v. 7.) But the plan may have been formed after leaving that place; or, which is still more probable, Paul may have expected to return very soon to Cesarea on his way to Rome (see above, on 19, 21.) He would sail in that case, not from Ptolemais but from Cesarea, as he actually did, but not till after a delay and imprisonment of more than two years. (See below, on 24, 27. 27, 1.) All these constructions have respect to the received text (ἀποσκευασάμενοι), for which the latest editors, on the authority of several of the oldest manuscripts, have substituted another compound form of the same verb (ἐπισκευασάμενοι), more common in the classics, where it means to fit, prepare, or furnish (as a meal, a horse, a ship, etc.), in which sense Tyndale, and the Rhemish version understand it here, while the modern writers take it in the more specific sense of packing up, and so preparing for a journey. *Went up*, literally, *go up*, in the present tense, a graphic form of narrative, much used not only by ancient, but by modern, and especially by French historians.

16. There went with us also (certain) of the disciples of Cesarea, and brought with them one Mnason of Cyprus, an old disciple, with whom we should lodge.

And (δέ) at the beginning of the sentence is omitted in the English version, or perhaps merged in the *also*, which however corresponds to a distinct Greek particle (καί.) *Disciples*, i. e. Christians, members of the church there. *Of* (or *from*) *Cesarea*, which may either mean belonging to it (as in 10, 23. 12, 1. 15, 5. 19, 13), or denote more strictly motion from it (as in vs. 1. 7. 10 above.) *Went* (or *came*) *with us*, means of course to Jerusalem, there being nothing to restrict or qualify the language, as in v. 5, and in 15, 3. 20, 38. The construction in the last clause is unusual and ambiguous, so as to leave the meaning doubtful upon one point. This is the question, whether the disciples brought Paul to Mnason in Jerusalem, or Mnason to Paul in Cesarea. In the one case the construction is, 'bringing (us to one) with whom we might be lodged'—in the other, 'bringing (one) with whom we might be lodged,' &c. The English version changes the order of the sentence, and inserts "with them," which is not in the original. The first construction is now commonly preferred, and is certainly favoured by the fact that the disciples went with Paul to Jerusalem, whereas they might have brought Mnason to him without leaving Cesarea. There is less force in the argument that the other construction supposes Mnason to have been in Cesarea, though his home was in Jerusalem, a circumstance by no means strange on any supposition, but especially as Mnason was a Cyprian, and may have been returning now from Cyprus. It is not even necessary to assume that he was living in Jerusalem, since multitudes, like Paul himself, were on their way to Pentecost (see above, on 20, 16), and Mnason may have simply invited them to share his lodgings. Whether he was an old acquaintance or even a convert of Paul's during his visit to Cyprus (see above, on 13, 4-12), we have no means of determining. *Old* does not here mean personally aged, though he must have been so, but ancient, old as a disciple or a Christian. The Greek adjective, and the noun from which it is derived, are both applied in this book to the beginning of the Gospel or the Christian dispensation (see above, on 11, 15. 15, 7.) There is therefore no absurdity in the conjecture that this man was a disciple of our Lord himself, or at least a convert on the day of Pentecost, and possibly one of the "Cyprians," by whom the Gospel was first preached in Antioch (see above, on 11, 19. 20.) It is worthy of remark how many points of contact are presented in this book between the apostolical history and the isle of Cyprus.

17. And when we were come to Jerusalem, the brethren received us gladly.

We being come, or having got there (see above, on 9, 3. 13, 5. 19, 21. 20, 16, and compare the compound form in 5, 21. 22. 25. 9, 26. 39. 10, 32. 33. 13, 14. 14, 27. 15, 4. 17, 10. 18, 27. 20, 18.) *The brethren*, not their personal friends merely; nor the whole church as an organized body; nor its elders, whom they seem to have met for the first time on the next day; but such individual believers as they met with on the day of their arrival. *Received us gladly*, the same adverb that is used above in 2, 41. *Us*, as well as Paul himself, and that not only upon his account, but as the representatives of Gentile Christendom or Christianity. (See above, on 20, 4.)

18. And the (day) following Paul went in with us unto James; and all the elders were present.

The day following, or coming on, ensuing (see above, o 7, 26. 16, 11. 20, 15), supposed by some to be the day of Pentecost. *Went in with us*, i. e. introduced us, showing plainly, that his travelling companions had a part to play in this transaction, as the circumstance that they were with him (or rather he with them) would be otherwise unworthy of repeated mention. There is not the slightest ground for doubting the identity of this James with the one already named in 12, 17. 15, 13, as president at Jerusalem. It is far less certain, although on the whole most probable, that this was James the Less (Mark 15, 40), so called to distinguish James the Son of Alpheus from James the Son of Zebedee, whose death is recorded in this book (see above, on 12, 2.) The anomalous condition of the church until the downfall of Jerusalem, sufficiently apparent from this very chapter, required the constant presence of an Apostle, while the others were engaged perhaps on distant missions. This responsible and arduous commission, which was far more than the pastoral care of any single church, however eminent or important, would not have been assigned to one of less than Apostolic rank, and is therefore a sufficient proof that James was an Apostle.

19. And when he had saluted them, he declared particularly what things God had wrought among the Gentiles by his ministry.

Saluted (greeted) *them*, in words of kindness and respect, which is far more probable, in this connection, than the idea, entertained by some, that he embraced or even kissed them. (See above, on vs. 6. 7, and compare 18, 22. 20, 1.) *Declared*, expounded, set forth in detail, the same verb that is used above, in 10, 8. 15, 12. 14, and there explained. *Particularly* is in Greek *by each* (or *every*) *one*, or giving to the particle its usual distributive force, *every* (*thing*) *one by one*. This strong expression shows that Paul's report of his missionary labours was by no means a mere vague or general account, but an exact and circumstantial statement. (See above, on 14, 27. 15, 12.) The original construction is, *each one of the things which God did in the nations*, or among the Gentiles (see above, on v. 11.) Here, as elsewhere, the efficient agency is ascribed to God, that of Paul being only instrumental. *By* (or *through*, by means of) *his ministry*, i. e. his labours as an Apostle, both in the strict sense of a witness and an organizer, and in the wide one of a missionary and itinerant preacher. (See above, on 1, 7. 25. 6, 4. 14, 4. 14. 20, 24.)

20. And when they heard (it), they glorified the Lord, and said unto him, Thou seest, brother, how many thousands of Jews there are which believe; and they are all zealous of the law—

They, i. e. James and the Elders, all of whom were present, as we learn from the preceding verse. *Hearing* (or *having heard*) Paul's report, confirmed by the presence of Gentile converts from the principal churches founded by him. *Glorified the Lord*, or *God*, which is the reading of the oldest manuscripts and latest critics. The effect is the same with that ascribed to previous disclosures of God's favour towards the Gentiles, made in one case to the Gentile converts themselves. (See above, on 11, 18. 13, 48.) The Greek verb is appropriate only to some signal exhibition and exercise of the divine perfections, as for instance to a miracle (see above, on 3, 13. 4, 21, and here to an extension of God's mercy, which the Jews no doubt considered equally miraculous.) *Glorified*, not only in their hearts, but with their lips, confessing it to be in truth the work of God. *And said*, or *said too* (τε), i. e. besides glorifying God, they also said to Paul what follows. The indefinite and plural form here used is worthy of attention, as James is often incorrectly mentioned as the sole author of the statement and advice here given; whereas it is not even said that he concurred in it, although most probably he did, and even acted as the spokesman of the Presbytery. It can hardly be unmeaning or fortuitous, however, that the narrative so carefully ascribes what is here said, not to an individual, not even to a sole Apostle, but to the whole assembly, in which he presided, and with which he acted jointly. (See above, on 15, 2. 4. 6. 22. 23. 16, 4.) *Thou seest*, beholdest as a spectacle, the verb employed in 3, 16. 4, 13. 7, 56. 8, 13. 9, 7. 10, 11. 17, 16. 22. 19, 26. 20, 38, in all or nearly all which cases it expresses more than simple vision, and implies something strange and striking in the object. It cannot here refer to what he saw before him, which was only an assembly of the elders (see above, on v. 18, and below, on v. 22), but must rather denote what he had already seen and learned from his experience, the present tense imparting force and point to the expression, as in v. 15 and elsewhere. *Brother*, an expression both of personal affection and official recognition, the highest title given in the primitive church, even to Apostles. It is here important, as evincing the unhesitating recognition of

Paul's claims as the Apostle of the Gentiles, even by the mother-church and Jewish Christians of Jerusalem. *How many myriads* (or *tens of thousands*) is not a mathematical but an indefinite and popular expression, meaning what great numbers, or (at most) vast multitudes, without defining their extent or sum. This is the primary sense of the original expression in the classics, where the definite idea of ten thousand is entirely posterior to Homer. It is also a favourite hyperbole of Paul himself, who writes to the Corinthians of their having had ten thousand teachers, and of his uttering ten thousand words in an unknown tongue (1 Cor. 4, 15. 14, 19), in both which cases he can only mean what we mean when we say "innumerable," "numberless," or "endless," not to define or specify a number, but to convey the vague idea of a multitude, which is itself a relative expression, meaning more or less according to the context or the circumstances in which we employ it. These considerations are sufficient to remove the necessity of carefully inquiring where these myriads of Christian Jews were to be found, or what became of them afterwards, or how this statement can be reconciled with Origen's, that all the Jewish converts in the world would not amount to the apocalyptic number of a hundred and forty-four thousand (Rev. 7, 4. 14, 1.) It is not the statistics of the Jewish Church that we have now before us, but a strong yet natural expression of the fact that they were very numerous, a fact which is altogether credible, especially if we remember, that many of these Jewish converts afterwards apostatized or separated from the church as Ebionites or Judaizing heretics. This may also throw light on the character here given of them, although strictly applicable and explicitly applied to those Jews who had really believed or been converted. But that this conversion was not always real, we may learn from the use of the same word in reference to Simon Magus (see above, on 8, 13.) *And all*, as a body or a class, no doubt with individual exceptions. *Zealous*, literally, *zealots*, the name given by Josephus to the ultra or fanatical anti-Roman party, whose excesses finally occasioned the destruction of the Jewish state and of the temple at Jerusalem. It is here, no doubt, applied to Christian or converted Jews; but such, in every age, have often brought into the Church the spirit of their old profession, and the Christian zealots, here described, may have partaken largely of the violent fanaticism, which was already teeming and fermenting in the bosoms of their unconverted brethren. The verb stands in Greek at the end of the sen tence, and is not the ordinary verb of existence (*are*), but that more emphatic form, with which we have already met repeatedly, and which in this connection, as in others, seems intended to suggest the idea of continuance, and might almost be ren dered *still are* (or *continue*) *zealots of the law*, as they were perhaps before conversion. (See above, on 5, 4. 8, 16. 16, 3, and compare 2, 3. 3, 2. 6. 4, 34. 37. 7, 55. 10, 12. 14, 8. 16, 20. 37. 17, 24. 27. 29. 19, 36. 40.)

21. And they are informed of thee, that thou teachest all the Jews which are among the Gentiles to forsake Moses, saying that they ought not to circumcise (their) children, neither to walk after the customs.

Are (or *have been*) *informed* is a correct though not an adequate translation of the Greek verb, which properly denotes oral elementary instruction (see above, on 18, 25, and compare Luke 1, 4. Rom. 2, 18. 1 Cor. 14, 19. Gal. 6, 6), and is here descriptive, not of mere report or rumour, but of careful inculcation on the part of Paul's opponents. The Christian zealots of Jerusalem, or of the Holy Land, had been not simply *told* but *taught* by his calumniators what here follows. *Of thee*, not by thee (as in 2, 24. 4, 11. 10, 33. 38. 41. 42. 12, 5. 15, 4. 16, 4. 14. 17, 13), but about, concerning thee (as in 1, 1. 31. 5, 24. 7, 52. 8, 34. 9, 13. 11, 22. 13, 29. 15, 6. 17, 32. 18, 15. 25.) *Among*, not the particle so rendered in v. 19, but a stronger one which might be rendered *through*, *throughout* (as in 8, 1. 9, 31. 42. 10, 37), implying an extensive dispersion among various nations. These were the Jews of the *Diaspora*, so called in the original (though not in the translation) of John 7, 35. James 1, 1. 1 Pet. 1, 1. *To forsake Moses*, or more emphatically and at the same time more exactly, *apostasy from Moses*. (Compare the verbal root or theme, as used above, in 5, 37. 38. 12, 10. 15, 38. 19, 9.) *Saying that they ought not* (or more simply and exactly, *telling them not*) *to circumcise their children*, *nor to walk after* (i. e. live according to) *the customs* (institutes, or institutions) of the ceremonial law or old economy. (See above, on 6, 14. 15, 1. 16, 21.) This account of Paul's teaching with respect to the Mosaic rites was true only in the sense of his denying their necessity to personal salvation, but not in that of representing them as worthless or unlawful while the temple was still standing. (See above, on 2, 46. 16, 3. 18, 18.)

22. What is it therefore? the multitude must needs come together: for they will hear that thou art come.

What is (it) therefore might be understood to mean, what is the truth as to the subject of these accusations? What is really your theory and practice in relation to the law? But as they do not wait for or require an answer, it is better to explain the words, with most interpreters, as meaning, *what then is (to be done)?* how shall this false impression be removed? The very question, thus explained, implies that the Presbytery, as a body, did not credit the malicious accusation. They speak throughout of Paul's accusers, and of those whom they had prejudiced against him, as a class entirely distinct from themselves. *The multitude* should rather be *a multitude*, the article not being used, and cannot therefore mean the church or body of believers as a corporate or organized society, but rather a promiscuous assemblage, or an accidental concourse, of such zealots as had first been described (in the preceding verse), of whom great numbers were assembled in Jerusalem to keep the feast (see above, on 2, 1.) *Must needs* (or *by all means*, i. e. unavoidably) *come together*, not in orderly assemblies to discuss the question, but in crowds or mobs to gratify their curiosity. The latest critics have expunged the words, *the multitude must come together*, but retain the adverb (πάντως) and connect it with the last clause, *by all means* (or inevitably) *they will hear that thou art come.* As the oldest manuscripts and versions are divided between these two readings, it is safer to retain the words in question, the omission of which it is at least as easy to explain as their insertion. Even the shorter reading, but still more the longer, gives us a clear glimpse of the interest with which Paul and his movements were regarded, both by friends and foes.

23. Do therefore this that we say to thee. We have four men which have a vow on them —

The original order is, *this therefore do. Therefore*, because there are so many zealots prepossessed against thee and because they will unquestionably come together, when they hear of thy arrival. *We say to thee*, not *I James*, but we the assembled elders of the representative or mother-church (see above, on 15, 2. 6.) *We have*, literally, *there are to us*, i. e. among us and belonging to our body, but also under our control, at our disposal. They must therefore have been Christians, and not unconverted Jews. The number (*four*) may have been fortuitous, there happening to be so many just at that time in the ceremonial condition here described. Or the elders may have chosen four out of a greater number, as sufficient for the purpose, and yet not so many as to give unnecessary trouble. A single subject would not have attracted public notice, while a dozen might have proved unmanageable or produced confusion. *Having a vow upon them*, no doubt that of Nazarites, provided for in Numbers 6, 1–21, and explained above, on 18, 18. This was not, however, as in that case, an informal private vow, externally conformed to legal usage, but a regular and normal case of ceremonial observance, as no other would have answered the proposed end of evincing Paul's respect for the Mosaic institutions.

24. Them take, and purify thyself with them, and be at charges with them, that they may shave (their) heads, and all may know that those things, whereof they were informed concerning thee, are nothing, but (that) thou thyself also walkest orderly, and keepest the law.

Them take, literally, *these* (*men*) *taking*, i. e. to thyself, into thy company. The Greek verb is the same with that employed above, in 15, 39. 16, 33, in both which cases, as in this, it denotes not momentary contact but prolonged association. *Purify thyself*, or rather, as the Greek verb is a passive form, *be purified* (by others, i. e. by the priests), submitting to the necessary ceremonial rites. This is usually understood to mean, become a Nazarite like them, assuming the same obligation, and undergoing or performing all that they do. This agrees well with the general usage of the Greek word, and with its special application in the Septuagint version of Numbers 6, 3, to the Nazarite abstinence or separation. But as this hypothesis creates some difficulty in explaining the details that follow, some understand the verb as signifying, not the Nazaritic vow itself, but those preliminary rites of purification which preceded every solemn act of ceremonial worship, as required by the law (see Ex. 19, 10. 14) and still practised in the time of Christ (see John 11, 55.) The exhortation, thus explained, is not that he should make himself a Nazarite, but merely that he should perform such preparatory rites as would enable him to take part with these Nazarites in the conclusion of their solemn service. *Be at charges with them*, literally, *spend* (*money*) *on them*, i. e. pay the expenses of their offerings and other ceremonial forms attending the conclusion of their vow. (Compare the use of the same Greek verb in Mark 5, 26. Luke 15, 14. 2 Cor. 12, 15, and especially in James 4, 3, where the construction is the same, though not the preposition.) *That they may shave their heads* (literally, *the head*), one of the chief external badges of the Nazaritic vow being long hair (Num. 6, 5), and its public cutting off or shaving the appointed sign of its completion (Num. 6, 18.) Nothing is said of Paul's own hair, which no doubt was short already (see 1 Cor. 11, 14), but only of his paying what was necessary to enable the four Nazarites to cut theirs likewise. That such participation in the vows of others by advancing money, was a practice not unknown in that age, we may learn from the statement of Josephus, that Agrippa (the Herod mentioned in the twelfth chapter of the book before us) on coming to Jerusalem from Rome, in this very way enabled many Nazarites to shave their heads. His motive was probably the same here suggested by the Presbyters to Paul, namely, to vindicate his doubtful claim to be esteemed a Jew, by publicly conforming to the rites and ceremonies of the law. *All may know* (or according to the latest critics, *will know*) *that of the* (*things*) *which they have been informed* (or *taught*) *about thee, there is nothing* (i. e. there is no truth in them or foundation for them), *but that thou thyself also walkest* (or *that thou walkest even thyself*) *keeping the law.* The verb translated *walkest* is a military term, and means to keep the ranks or march in order, then to walk by any rule, i. e. to act or live according to it. It is a favourite word of Paul's, occurring elsewhere only in his writings (see Rom. 4, 12. Gal. 5, 25. 6, 16. Phil. 3, 16.) *Keeping*, in the proper sense of watching, then observing or obeying (see above, on 7, 53. 12, 4. 16, 4.)

25. As touching the Gentiles which believe, we have written (and) concluded that they observe no such

thing, save only that they keep themselves from (things) offered to idols, and from blood, and from strangled, and from fornication.

All that the Elders had said thus far went upon the supposition that the charges against Paul were false, and that he looked on the continued observance of the ceremonial services as lawful in the case of Jewish Christians. But it might have seemed to be their purpose to lay down the same rule for converted Gentiles, which would have been directly contrary to all Paul's principles and practice. (See above, on 16, 3. 18, 18.) To preclude this false impression of their purpose, they expressly add, that as to the *believing Gentiles* (literally, the nations who had believed or been converted), they had nothing new to ask or offer, but adhered to their own previous decision (that recorded in the fifteenth chapter), that they should be only required to abstain from what was unavoidably offensive to their Jewish brethren. *Written and concluded*, literally, *sent* (by letter or in writing) *judging* (or *deciding*.) *Observe*, a different verb from that at the end of the preceding verse, but like it originally meaning to watch or keep (as in 12, 5. 6. 16, 23), and then to observe or obey (as in 15, 5. 24.) *No such thing*, i. e. nothing ceremonial as a permanent observance or as necessary to salvation. These words (*that they observe no such thing save only* or *except*), though found in several uncial manuscripts, are wanting in the oldest, and therefore excluded by the latest critics, but on insufficient grounds. *That they keep* (or *guard*) *themselves*, the middle or reflexive form of the verb used in the last clause of v. 24. The specific prohibitions are the same as in 15, 29, except that the genitive is here exchanged for the accusative throughout, and the plural for the singular in the first noun, and also in the third according to the latest critics.

26. Then Paul took the men, and the next day purifying himself with them entered into the temple, to signify the accomplishment of the days of purification, until that an offering should be offered for every one of them.

Then is not the continuative particle (δέ) often so translated, but the adverb of time (τότε) strictly meaning *then* or afterwards, i. e. when he had thus been counselled by the elders. *Took*, literally, *taking* (see above, on v. 24.) *The men*, the four who had been previously mentioned (see above, on v. 23.) *Next*, the word employed in 20, 15 above, and there explained. *The temple*, in the wide sense of the sacred enclosure (see above, on 2, 46. 3, 1. 4, 1. 5, 20. 19, 27.) *To signify*, literally *announcing*, giving notice, i. e. to the priests on duty. *The accomplishment*, fulfilment, or completion, of the days of purification, which may either mean the term of the Nazaritic vow, or the time of the concluding service. *Should be offered*, literally *was offered*, the form of the Greek verb being indicative and not subjunctive. This has led some to understand the verse as meaning that Paul notified the priests that the term of the vow was already finished, and then waited at the temple till the necessary offerings were actually made. The more usual interpretation is that the notice was prospective, or that Paul announced how soon the vow would be expired, in order that the priests might make arrangements for the sacrifices when the time for offering them should arrive.

27. And when the seven days were almost ended, the Jews which were of Asia, when they saw him in the temple, stirred up all the people, and laid hands on him—

And when (*nearly*, or *as*) *the seven days were almost* (literally, *about to be*) *ended.* It has been much disputed what *the seven days* were. Some suppose that the duration of the Nazaritic vow was optional, and that in this case it continued only for a week. But although the law prescribes no term ("the seventh day" in Num. 6, 9, having reference to an unexpected interruption and renewal of the vow), a week would be too short a time to make the growth of the hair perceptible, and a month is mentioned as the customary period, both by Josephus and the Talmud. Another supposition is, that those who undertook to pay for others were allowed to keep a shorter term, and that when Paul joined these Nazarites, there were only seven days of separation left. But as this solution rests upon a mere conjecture, some understand *the seven days* to mean the first week after Paul's arrival, which is thought to be at variance with other chronological specifications (see below, on 24, 11.) Others suppose a whole week to have been observed at Pentecost as at the Passover; for which however there is no ground either in the law or in historical tradition. Others still explain *the seven days* as seven sabbaths, or the interval of seven weeks between the two great festivals (Lev. 23, 15. 16.) The question, although difficult, is unimportant, and its very difficulty, far from discrediting the narrative, confirms it by this natural reference to facts, with which Luke's Jewish readers must have been familiar, although some of them to us are necessarily obscure. The essential point, in this case, is that the time of Paul's ceremonial conformity was almost ended, when the following occurrences took place. *The Jews from Asia*, i. e. from the western part of Asia Minor (see above, on 20, 4. 16. 18), and especially no doubt from the Ephesian district. The idea expressed in the common version (*which were of Asia*) is really suggested by the preposition here used (see above, on v. 16.) *Having seen* (or *beheld*) *him*, with an implication of something strange and unexpected in the sight. (See above, on 1, 11. 8, 18, and compare the like use of another verb in v. 20, and the places there referred to.) The Jews of Ephesus, among Paul's most malignant enemies (see above, on 20, 19), may not have been prepared to meet him in the Holy City. Regarding him as an apostate, and as such no longer entitled to the privileges of a Jew, they were naturally moved with indignation, when they saw him in the temple, and perhaps engaged in ceremonial duties. These excited feelings they of course endeavoured to impart to others. *Stirred up*, literally, *poured together*, threw into confusion (see above, on 2, 6. 9, 22. 19, 29. 32.) *All the people*, more exactly, *all the crowd*, the promiscuous assemblage or mixed multitude which filled Jerusalem at such a season. With his usual exactness in the use of such terms, Luke does not describe them as *the people*, either in the Greek sense (τὸν δῆμον) or the Jewish (τὸν λαόν), but as the mob or rabble (τὸν ὄχλον), all which terms are carefully distinguished in the usage of this book. (Compare 12, 22. 17, 5. 19, 30. 33 with 3, 43. 4, 1. 2. 10. 10, 2. 41. 12, 4. 11. 13, 31. 15, 14. 18, 10. 19, 4, and with 1, 5. 8, 6. 14, 1. 16, 22. 17, 8. 19, 33. 35.) Emboldened by the presence, and perhaps by the applause, of the assembled masses, *they laid hands on Paul*, i. e. arrested, seized him. (See above, on 4, 3. 5, 18. 12, 1.) This, though not perceived to be so at the moment, either by himself or others, eventually proved to be the end of his ministry at large, and the commencement of his long apostleship in bonds.

(See Phil. 1, 7 13. 14. 16. Col. 4, 18. Philem. 10. 13. Heb. 10, 34. 2 Tim. 2, 9.)

28. Crying out, Men of Israel, help! this is the man that teacheth all (men) every where against the people, and the law, and this place; and further brought Greeks also into the temple, and hath polluted this holy place.

We have here the way in which they acted on the multitude, to wit, by appealing to their national and theocratic prepossessions. *Men of Israel* (literally, *Israelites*), not merely sons of Israel or Jacob (compare Gen. 32, 28), but as such members of the ancient church or chosen people, in which capacity the people are here summoned to the rescue. *Help*, succour, a verb, which from its very etymology, was specially appropriate in outcries like the one before us, being compounded of the two verbs *cry* and *run*, and often used by the Greek poets in like manner. The whole phrase corresponds to a well-known one in Latin (*cives adeste!*) It was not therefore as a mob, though truly such, but as the house of Israel, that the people were now summoned to protect the temple. The last clause clearly implies Paul's celebrity or notoriety among his unconverted countrymen. *This is the man*, of whom you have all heard, and whom some of us have often seen in other places. *That teacheth*, literally, *the* (*one*) *teaching*, i. e. habitually, constantly. *All men every where*, a double hyperbole or exaggeration, showing clearly what importance was attached by such men to the acts and influence of the apostle. *Against the people*, not the populace as such, but the chosen or peculiar people, against whose privileges Paul is represented as contending. *The law*, the whole Mosaic system under which they lived, and by which they were segregated from the other nations. *This place*, Jerusalem, the seat of the theocracy, and more especially the temple, as the heart and centre of the ceremonial law. This hostile cry must have painfully reminded Paul of that in which he had himself joined against Stephen, and in consequence of which he was arraigned before the council. (See above, on 6, 12. 14.) But the charge against himself was more specific and exciting still. *And further also* (or moreover, in addition to all this), nearly the same expression that is used above in 2, 26, and there explained. *Greeks*, not in the national or local sense, but in the wider one of Gentiles, so called from the general and almost universal use of the Greek language among all known nations. Hence the perpetual antithesis of *Jews and Greeks* in the New Testament. (See above, on 11, 20. 14, 1. 16, 1. 3. 17, 4. 18, 4. 17. 19. 10. 17. 20, 21, and compare Paul's epistles passim.) *Into the temple*, or sacred enclosure (see above, on v. 26), and especially the inner courts, from which all foreigners (or Gentiles) were excluded upon pain of death, by a stone wall and pillars with inscriptions warning against all profane intrusion. According to a speech which Josephus puts into the mouth of Titus, the Jews were suffered by the Romans themselves to kill a Roman who was guilty of such violation. *Polluted*, desecrated, rendered common, the verb employed above in 10, 15. 11, 9, and there explained. *Holy*, consecrated, set apart, devoted to divine use (see above, on 6, 13.) Considering the character and spirit of the men by whom this cry was uttered, we might well regard it as a spiteful fiction, framed expressly to excite the Jewish zealots against Paul, but for the candid and impartial explanation which is given in the next verse.

29. For they had seen before with him in the city Trophimus an Ephesian, whom they supposed that Paul had brought into the temple.

The charge contained in the preceding verse was founded on a natural though inexcusable mistake of those who made it. *Seen before*, i. e. before they saw Paul in the temple, on the occasion just referred to. *Trophimus*, one of those who sailed from Greece before Paul and awaited him in Troas (see above, on 20, 4.) He and Tychicus were there described as Asians (or of Asia), which is here made more specific, *Trophimus the* (not *an*) *Ephesian*, i. e. the one previously mentioned in more general terms, and also the one well known, both by name and person, to these Jewish countrymen. *In the city*, no doubt in the streets, beyond the temple-area. *They supposed*, were of opinion, or believed, a false impression which might easily have been corrected, which they consequently had no right to propagate, but which exonerates them from the charge of sheer invention or malignant falsehood. This is not to be explained away by saying that they used equivocal expressions, so that a mere inference or guess of theirs was taken by the people as a positive assertion of a fact. This would be a forced construction of the words before us, which are wholly unambiguous, and furnish a remarkable example of the fairness with which every thing is stated in the sacred history, whoever may be honoured or dishonoured by it, and however slow interpreters may be to own it.

30. And all the city was moved, and the people ran together; and they took Paul, and drew him out of the temple, and forthwith the doors were shut.

All the city, the whole city, i. e. its entire population, a hyperbole so natural as scarcely to appear one. (See above, on 13, 44, and compare Matt. 8, 34. 21, 10. Mark 1, 33. 6, 33. Luke 8, 1. 4.) *The people ran together*, literally, *there was* (or *arose*) *a concourse of the people* (see above, on 19, 40.) This rush was no doubt to the temple, whence the cry proceeded. *They took*, or rather, *laying hold on Paul*, the same verb that is used above in 16, 19. 18, 17, but sometimes not implying violence (see above, on 9, 27. 17, 19), which is here suggested by the context. *Drew*, on the contrary, does imply it, and might be translated *dragged*, both here and in the other place where it occurs (James 2, 6.) *Out of the temple*, in the same sense as before, i. e. the court or enclosure of the temple (see above, on vs. 26. 27. 28.) *Forthwith*, immediately, without delay. *The doors*, or gates, of the enclosure before mentioned, either those communicating with the city, or more probably those separating one court from the other, i. e. the inner court or court of the Israelites from the outer court usually called (at least in later books) the court of the Gentiles. The shutting of the doors has been variously understood. According to some, it was intended to prevent Paul's taking refuge at the altar, as Adonijah and Joab did (1 Kings 1, 50. 53. 2, 28. 29), although the law of Moses recognizes no right of asylum, except in the case of unpremeditated homicide (Ex. 21, 12–14.) Others suppose that it was meant to save the sacred precincts from the defilement of Paul's blood, whom they were now about to put to death. A third opinion is, that the shutting of the doors, during the time of ceremonial service, was a formal suspension of that service. Equally satisfactory with any of these explanations, and perhaps more natural than either, is the simple supposition, that the Priests or Levites upon duty in the temple, when they saw Paul violently dragged out, shut the doors, in order to exclude both him and his assailants, with a view not only to their own security, but also to preserve the sanctuary from being made the scene of a tumultuous brawl.

31. And as they went about to kill him, tidings came unto the chief captain of the band, that all Jerusalem was in an uproar—

Went about, in the old English sense of sought, endeavoured. (Compare John 7, 19. 20. Rom. 10, 3, where the Greek verb is translated in the same way.) The literal translation is, *they seeking to kill him*. The subject of the verb here is not necessarily the same as in vs. 27. 28, but more indefinite, referring not specifically to the Jews of Asia, but to the nearer antecedents in v. 30, i. e. *the city* and *the people*. *Tidings*, or rather, *a report*, either in the sense of rumour, or in that of official information, probably conveyed by the Roman sentries, on or near the spot, to their superiors. *Came*, went up, ascended, both in a figurative sense, from the lower to the higher military ranks, and in a literal or local sense, from the area of the temple to the tower of Antonia which overlooked it. This fortress was an ancient one, but had been several times rebuilt, and named by Herod the Great in honour of his friend and protector, Anthony. Josephus represents it as a lofty structure, at the north-west corner of the temple-area, with which it communicated both by stairs and by interior passages. It was constantly occupied by a Roman garrison, to watch and overawe the Jews, especially in times of more than ordinary concourse, as for instance during the great festivals. This is the force here called *the band*, corresponding to a Greek word which originally means a roll or coil (being the root of our word *spiral*), but in military dialect a maniple, the third part of a cohort, or two centuries. It is here supposed by most interpreters to signify the cohort itself, or a thousand men. Hence the commander of the force is called a *chiliarch*, or leader of a thousand, corresponding to the Latin *tribune*. Both these military terms are elsewhere used in the New Testament to denote the levitical guard of the temple and its Jewish leader. (See above, on 4, 1. 5, 24. 26, and compare John 18, 3. 12.) As the Jews at this time were peculiarly impatient of the Roman yoke, and insurrections had been frequent (see below, on v. 38, and above, on 5, 36. 37, and compare Mark 15, 7. Luke 23, 19. 25), the garrison was no doubt more than usually vigilant, particularly when the population was increased by multitudes of strangers in attendance on the yearly feasts (see above, on 2, 5.) *Was in an uproar*, literally, *has been confounded*, i. e. thrown into confusion (see above, on v. 27.)

32. Who immediately took soldiers and centurions, and ran down unto them; and when they saw the chief captain and the soldiers, they left beating of Paul.

Taking with him, or along with him, the same verb as in vs. 24. 26. *Centurions*, commanders of a hundred men, whom Mark calls by their Latin name (Mark 15, 39. 44. 45), but Luke and Matthew by the corresponding Greek one (*hecatontarchs*, Matt. 8, 5. 8. 13. 27, 54. Luke 7, 2. 6. 23, 47.) His taking more than one centurion implies that he was followed by at least two hundred men. *Ran down*, literally, from the fort or castle to the street or the exterior enclosure of the temple, and also in the figurative sense of rushing on, assailing, or attacking. *Unto them*, or more exactly, *on them*, i. e. on the mob who were attempting to kill Paul. *And when they saw*, or more exactly, *but they seeing*. *Left*, literally, paused or ceased. *Beating of Paul*, i. e. beating Paul, there being nothing in the Greek corresponding to the pleonastic preposition. This instantaneous effect illustrates the immense disproportion between mobs and armies, and at the same time the habitual submission even of the zealots to their heathen masters, till the national antipathy, exasperated by religious bigotry, finally burst through all restraints and brought about the great catastrophe.

33. Then the chief captain came near, and took him, and commanded (him) to be bound with two chains, and demanded who he was, and what he had done.

Then (τότε), at that time, afterwards, or in the next place (see above, on v. 26.) *Came near*, coming near, approaching. *Took him*, laid hold upon, arrested, seized him, the same verb that is used above in v. 30. Paul was thus treated as the evident occasion of the uproar, whether innocent or guilty, which could only be decided by a subsequent investigation. In the mean time the tribune was bound to keep the peace and tc secure the person who had caused the breach of it. *With two chains*, or two ligatures, applied to the hands and feet respectively, as some suppose, but more probably to both arms, fastening the prisoner to a soldier on each side, a Roman method of safe-keeping, which we have already seen exemplified in Herod's imprisonment of Peter. (See above, on 12, 6, where the same Greek terms are used as in the case before us.) *Demanded*, asked, inquired, not of Paul himself, but of the people round him. *Who he was*, or rather, *who he might be*, the contingent particle prefixed to the Greek optative expressing a high degree of doubt and curiosity, whereas the other question, although similar in English, is in Greek more direct and categorical. *What he had done*, literally, *what he is having done*, a combination foreign from our idiom, consisting of the perfect participle of the verb *to do* with the present tense of the verb *to be*. The use of this peculiar form has been accounted for, upon the ground of the chief captain's knowing that he must have done something. But then the same form should have been used in the other case, for the chief captain was no less certain that he must be somebody.

34. And some cried one thing, some another, among the multitude; and when he could not know the certainty for the tumult, he commanded him to be carried into the castle.

Nothing can be more lifelike or more true to nature than this picture, which could scarcely have been drawn from hearsay or imagination. The highly idiomatic form of the first clause (*others cried some other thing*) does not admit of an exact translation; but the meaning is correctly given in our version. (For another instance of the same idiom, see above, on 19, 32.) *When he could not* (literally, *not being able to*) *know the certainty* (*the certain*, sure, infallible), i. e. the true state of the case. *For the tumult*, on account of the confusion, noise, and uproar (see above, on 20, 1.) *Carried*, in the wide sense of conveyed, conducted. not in the specific sense of borne or lifted, which is mentioned in the next verse. *The castle* is supposed by some to mean the fortress of Antonia described above (on v. 31), by others a fortified camp within it, or the barracks (quarters) which the soldiers occupied. The later classics sometimes use it to denote an army drawn up in a certain manner (compare Heb. 11, 34), but commonly to signify a camp (compare Heb. 13, 11. 13), both which senses have been put upon the word in one place (Rev. 20, 9.)

35. And when he came upon the stairs, so it was, that he was borne of the soldiers for the violence of the people.

Came, became, was, or began to be, the same verb that is used above, in vs. 1. 5. 14. 17. 30. *The stairs*, leading up from the area of the temple into the castle of Antonia, and particularly mentioned by Josephus in describing it. *So it was*, or rather, it occurred, chanced, happened, implying that what follows was entirely unintentional and unexpected. (For the use of the verb, see above, on 3, 10. 20, 19.) *Borne*, lifted, carried, not as an act either of hostility or kindness, but *for the violence* (or from the pressure) *of the crowd* (which followed.) This little circumstance is mentioned, not to show how carefully the Roman soldiers guarded and protected Paul, but simply as a vivid reminiscence of the scene by Luke, who well remembered seeing his beloved teacher, as the soldiers led him up the stairs, completely lifted from his feet by the resistless pressure of the crowd behind, so that without intending it, the soldiers carried him instead of leading him. (See above, on 20. 8, 13, and for the usage of the verb, on 3, 2. 9, 15. 15, 10.)

36. For the multitude of the people followed after, crying, Away with him.

Three of the collective terms, or nouns of multitude, which Luke elsewhere so carefully distinguishes, are used successively in this connection, each in its proper and distinctive sense, although the English version has confounded two of them. Having stated in the foregoing verse that Paul was lifted from his feet by the pressure of *the crowd* (τοῦ ὄχλου), Luke now adds, by way of explanation, that *the mass* (τὸ πλῆθος) of *the people* (τοῦ λαοῦ), i. e. of the Jews, *was following*, the imperfect tense of the Greek verb denoting both continuous and simultaneous action. While the soldiers were removing Paul, the mob was following. (For the usage of the two first nouns of multitude, see above, on vs. 27, 30; for the third, on 2, 6. 4, 32. 6, 2. 14, 4. 15, 12. 30.) *Crying*, calling with a loud voice, shouting (see above, on 7, 57. 60. 14, 14. 16, 17. 19, 28. 32. 34.) *Away with him*, literally, *take him* (*away*), the same verb that was used above in v. 11, and the same cry that was uttered near the same spot, many years before, by a deluded and infuriated rabble, thirsting for the blood of the same person whom, within a week, they had welcomed with hosannas, as the true Messiah. (Compare Luke 19, 38. 23, 18. John 12, 12. 13. 19, 15.) The verse before us furnishes an explanation of what otherwise might seem strange, that although Paul was now in the possession of the soldiers, he was nevertheless closely pressed by his pursuers, who were following him even up the castle stairs.

37. And as Paul was to be led into the castle, he said unto the chief captain, May I speak unto thee? Who said, Canst thou speak Greek?

Being about to be led into the camp (or *castle*) *Paul says to the chiliarch* (or *tribune*), the present tense, in this as in many other cases, representing the whole scene as actually passing (see above, on v. 15.) *May I*, literally, *if it is permitted* (or *allowable*) *for me, to say something to thee.* For the use of the conditional in asking questions (*if it is*, meaning, tell me if it is), see above, on 1, 6. 5, 8. 7, 1. 19, 2. The latest critics omit *something* (τι) although found in several of the oldest manuscripts, and read, *speak to thee.* *Who said* (or rather, *and he said*), *Canst thou speak Greek* (literally, *dost thou know Greek?*) The original for *Greek* is an adverb, corresponding to the Latin *Graece*, which is used by Cicero in a connection very similar to that before us, when he says of those who do not understand the language, *qui Graece nesciunt.* (See above, on 14, 11, and compare John 19, 20, where three such adverbs stand together.)

38. Art not thou that Egyptian, which before these days madest an uproar, and leddest out into the wilderness four thousand men that were murderers?

Art not thou seems to foresee an affirmative answer, and imply that the commander still regarded Paul and the Egyptian as identical; whereas he must have been convinced of his mistake as soon as Paul began to speak. This agrees exactly with the Greek phrase, which is hardly interrogative at all, and might be rendered, *thou art not then* (or *so then thou art not*) *the Egyptian.* He is evidently speaking of events still recent, and in which he may have been concerned himself. *Before these days* is an indefinite expression, which determines nothing as to the precise date, since it may mean just before, or long before, according to the context. *Madest an uproar* is the verb translated *turned upside down* in 17, 5, and *trouble* in Gal. 5, 12, in both which cases, as in this, it means to revolutionize, or violently alter the existing state of things, and might be rendered here, *who made* (i. e. tried to make) *a revolution;* or if this is too strong, *uproar* is as much too weak, and *insurrection* may be taken as a mean between them. *Leading out into the wilderness the four thousand men of the assassins.* The omission of the article before the last two nouns materially affects the sense, by making the chief captain seem to speak of something known to him but unknown to his hearers; whereas *the four thousand men* of course means those four thousand men, of whom you have so often heard, or rather whom you well remember, not as *murderers* merely, but as *the assassins*, a defined and well remembered body, once perhaps the terror of the country. *Assassins* is in the original a Greek inflection of the Latin word (*Sicarii*), so called from *sica*, a short sword or dagger, and described by Josephus as a kind of robbers who concealed short swords beneath their garments, and infested Judea in the period preceding the destruction of Jerusalem. Such a band had been led by the Egyptian here referred to, who is also mentioned by Josephus, but in terms at once extravagant and inconsistent. In one place he describes him as the leader of thirty thousand men, of whom the most part were destroyed, while in another place he states the number of the latter at four hundred. It is not impossible to reconcile these statements with each other and with that before us by assuming what is altogether probable and common in such cases, that the number of his followers, small at first, was vastly multiplied by popular delusion and fanatical excitement, and eventually thinned again as this subsided, or the government began to use its strength against them. The four thousand may in that case be regarded as the military force of the Egyptian, and the thirty thousand as the aggregate number of his followers, in the height of his success, while the four hundred may have been the remnant finally destroyed when that success was at an end. That he should ever have enjoyed it is the less incredible because Josephus calls him a false prophet, which implies that he gained influence not only by appealing to political dissatisfaction, but to popular delusions. That the cases are the same is clear from the Egyptian origin of both, and from the date, to wit, the government of Felix (see below, on 23, 24.) It seems that this Egyptian knew no Greek, which accounts for the chief captain's wonder when he heard Paul speak it, not because Egyptians did not usually do so, but because he knew that this one did not.

39. But Paul said, I am a man (which am) a Jew of Tarsus, (a city) in Cilicia, a citizen of no mean city: and, I beseech thee, suffer me to speak unto the people.

A Jew of Tarsus, literally, *a Tarsean Jew*, the same form of expression as in 9, 11. The translators having introduced the name of Tarsus, place the following words in apposition with it, thereby changing the entire construction. The syntax, although not the collocation, of the second clause in Greek is, *a citizen of no mean city of Cilicia*, Tarsus being meant of course, but not expressly named, though really suggested by the adjective connected with the word *Jew* in the first clause. *Mean*, in the original, is negative, and might be rendered *undistinguished*. The Greek word is said to have been once applied to unmarked cattle and uncoined money. The very phrase here used, with its litotes or meiosis, meaning really illustrious or famous, is found, with very little difference of form, in the Greek poets, one of whom (Euripides) employs it, just as Paul does, to describe a city. Having thus asserted his respectability, he makes it the ground of a request, not for his own advantage, but for that of his kinsmen according to the flesh (Rom. 9, 3), his love for whom could not have been more clearly proved than by his asking to address them at such a juncture, when his life had just been rescued from their fury by the interposition of a Roman soldier. *To the people* (λαόν), not the multitude (πλῆθος), or the rabble (ὄχλον), but he chosen people as there represented.

40. And when he had given (him) license, Paul stood on the stairs, and beckoned with the hand unto

the people; and when there was made a great silence, he spake unto (them) in the Hebrew tongue, saying—

Given license is the same verb that is rendered *suffer* in the verse preceding. *Standing on the stairs*, where he had stopped when just about to go into the camp or fort to which they led (see above, on vs. 35. 37), and where the crowd was no doubt still in contact with him (see above, on v. 36.) There is something grand in the position here assigned to the Apostle of the Gentiles, in the custody of Gentiles, yet by their permission speaking to the Jews, not only in the Holy City, but in sight of the temple, and on the very verge of its sacred enclosure, which he had just been accused of wantonly profaning. So far, he could not have begun his passive ministry, or rather his apostleship in bonds, in a more imposing or auspicious manner. *Beckoned* (in modern English, motioned, gestured, made a sign) *with the hand*, an action previously ascribed in this book both to Paul and others (see above, on 12, 17. 13, 16. 19, 33.) *Much silence being*, or arising, beginning, the same verb that means *came* in v. 35. The silence was probably occasioned by the presence of the Roman officers and soldiers; by the sight, if not the hearing, of what passed between the Tribune and his prisoner; by Paul's unexpected presentation of himself upon the stairs and offer to address them; but above all by the circumstance recorded in the last clause, that he spake in Hebrew, not because they would not have understood Greek, but because he wished to rouse their better feelings, and to prove himself an Israelite indeed by using their own sacred language, or at least the kindred dialect in use among them. Some suppose an allusion to the Tribune's question, Canst thou speak Greek? 'Yes, but I would now speak Hebrew.'

CHAPTER XXII.

The passive ministry of Paul, or his Apostleship in bonds, may be divided into trials or defences before various tribunals, the first of which is recorded in this chapter, with the subsequent occurrences until the second. He gains attention by respectfully accosting them in their own language (1. 2.) He avows himself a Jew by birth and education (3.) He describes his persecuting zeal against the Christians (4. 5.) He relates his miraculous conversion (6–11.) He shows that even his reception into the new body was by Jewish agency (12–16.) He comes at last to his Apostleship among the Gentiles, which he represents as unsought by himself and forced upon him by divine authority (17–21.) He is interrupted by an outburst of fanatical excitement (22. 23.) He is rescued from their fury by the Romans, and from the severity of the Romans themselves by avowing his citizenship (24–29.) He appears before the Sanhedrim, to make his second apology or self-defence (30.)

1. Men, brethren, and fathers, hear ye my defence (which I make) now unto you.

To the customary form of address, *Men (and) brethren*, or *Men (who are) brethren* (see above, on 1, 16. 2, 29. 37. 13, 26. 15, 7. 13), Paul, like Stephen, and perhaps in imitation of him (see above, on 7, 2), adds *Fathers*, either as a general expression of respect, or, as most interpreters suppose, with reference to such priests or elders as he may have seen or known to be among the multitude (but see below, on 23, 1.) *Hear*, as in other cases of the same kind, seems to bespeak their patience in the hearing of what might offend their prejudices (see above, on 2, 22. 7, 2. 13, 16. 15, 13.) *Defence*, in Greek *apology*, but without any implication of confession or acknowledgment. Thus the ancient Apologies, or defences of Christianity, presented to the heathen emperors, involved no admission of fault or error in the system thus defended, but on the contrary were often bold attacks upon the heathen superstitions. *My now* (i. e. my present, actual) *defence unto you.*

2. And when they heard that he spake in the Hebrew tongue to them, they kept the more silence; and he saith—

It seems to be implied that Greek would have been equally intelligible, even to the native Jews. His not employing it appears to have surprised as well as pleased them. *The Hebrew dialect* may either be the ancient Hebrew, which was still the sacred and the learned language of the Jews, or that

Aramaic modification of it which had now become their vernacular dialect (see above, on 1, 19); more probably the latter, as he was not addressing the Sanhedrim but the populace, composed both of native and foreign Jews (see above, on 6, 1.) His wisdom in adopting this mode of suggesting his own Jewish origin and education was approved by the effect as here recorded. *Spake*, was calling to, addressing them, the same verb as in 21, 40, often used by Luke elsewhere (see Luke 6, 13. 7, 32. 13, 12. 23, 20, and compare Matt. 11, 16.) *The more*, i. e. even more than at first, as mentioned at the close of the preceding chapter. *Kept silence*, literally, *afforded quietness*, not the same word that was used before (21, 40), but a stronger and more positive expression, denoting not mere silence but a studied stillness and attention. (Compare the still more expressive use of a cognate verb in 11, 18. 21, 14.) This breathless stillness of the multitude so lately raging adds to the sublimity of Paul's position, standing between the Jewish temple and the Roman fortress, and about to address, for the first and last time, his assembled brethren.

3. I am verily a man (which am) a Jew, born in Tarsus (a city) in Cilicia, yet brought up in this city at the feet of Gamaliel, (and) taught according to the perfect manner of the law of the fathers, and was zealous toward God, as ye all are this day.

With admirable art and skill, he renders prominent whatever marked him as a Jew, in order to refute the charge on which he was arrested, namely, that of traitorous hostility to the religion of his fathers. *Verily* should rather be *indeed* (or *it is true*), a concessory particle which qualifies this whole clause, or its second member. 'I am a Jew, born *it is true* in Tarsus, but nevertheless a Hebrew of the Hebrews (2 Cor. 11, 22. Phil. 3, 5), and brought up among you.' The Jews of the Diaspora (see above, on 21, 21), who did not intermarry with the Gentiles, claimed an absolute equality with those of Palestine (see above, on 2, 39.) His being a Hellenist was therefore nothing to his disadvantage, especially as his early life was chiefly spent, not only in the Holy Land, but in the Holy City. *Tarsus of Cilicia*, i. e. belonging to it, situated in it. (See above, on 6, 9. 9, 11. 30. 11, 25. 15, 23. 41. 21, 39.) *A man which am a Jew* a needless and enfeebling circumlocution for *a Jewish man*, the Greek word (ἰουδαῖος) being properly an adjective which means belonging to the tribe of Judah or the country of Judea. (See above, on 2, 14. 19, 13.) *Brought up*, reared, or nourished, strictly denoting the nurture of children (as in 7, 20. 21), but commonly explained here as denoting mental culture, on account of what immediately follows, *at the feet of Gamaliel.* Some, however, understand it strictly, as meaning that Paul was not only a pupil of Gamaliel, but an inmate of his family, perhaps a relative. There is no ground for disputing the identity of this Gamaliel with the eminent Pharisee and member of the Sanhedrim, who appears before in this same history, and often in the Jewish traditions (see above, on 5, 34–40.) *At the feet* is commonly explained as an allusion to the customary posture of the ancient teachers and their pupils, but is much more probably a natural figure for their mutual relation. (See above, on 4, 35. 37. 5, 2. 10, and compare Luke 10, 39.) *At the feet* will then convey the two distinct ideas of intimate nearness and subjection to authority. The meaning of this verse depends somewhat upon its punctuation. For a reason already suggested, some divide it thus, *brought up in this city, at the feet of Gamaliel trained* (or *educated.*) But as both the other participles (*born* and *brought up*) precede the words which qualify them, this would be a harsh inversion. Most interpreters avoid the supposed incongruity of making Gamaliel Paul's nurse as well as his instructor, by treating both verbs as substantially synonymous, and here intended to express the same idea of education in the widest sense. The second verb means more than *taught* in English, namely *trained*, implying systematic discipline. (See above, on 7, 22, and compare 2 Tim. 2, 25. Tit. 2, 12.) Its most frequent use in the New Testament, however, is in the secondary sense of correcting or chastising, as a necessary part of all such discipline. (See Luke 23, 16. 22. 1 Cor. 11, 32. 2 Cor. 6, 9. Heb. 12, 6. 7. 10. Rev. 3, 19.) *Perfect manner*, literally, *strictness* or *exactness* (compare the corresponding adverb, as explained above, on 18, 25. 26.) The reference is here to the Pharisaic rigor, both of theory and practice, as contrasted with the Sadducean laxity and latitudinarianism. (See above, on 4, 1.) *Zealous towards God*, literally, *a zealot of God*, i. e. in his service, for his honour, as he then understood it (see above, on 21, 20.) The last clause intimates that he had passed through what they now experienced and gone beyond it.

4. And I persecuted this way unto the death, binding and delivering into prisons both men and women.

He proved the sincerity of his convictions by persecuting all that contradicted them. *This way*, this new sect or religion (see above, on 9, 2. 19, 9. 23.) *Unto death*, not only in desire and intention, but in fact, as we know him to have done in Stephen's case (see above, on 6, 1, and below, on v. 20), and probably in others (see below, on 26, 10.) With the rest of this verse compare 9, 1.

5. As also the high priest doth bear me witness, and all the estate of the elders, from whom also I received letters unto the brethren, and went to Damascus, to bring them which were there bound unto Jerusalem, for to be punished.

This was no secret, resting only on his own assertion, but matter of record, or at least of recollection on the part of others. *The* (then) *high priest*, from whom he had received his commission, and who was still living, perhaps present. This is commonly supposed to have been either Theophilus or Jonathan, who had been displaced in the mean time by the Romans (see above, on 4, 6.) *Doth bear me witness*, literally, *testifies to me*, which may simply mean, he is my witness, or the witness whom I cite in proof of these things; though the words seem rather to imply a personal appeal to him as actually present. 'Do you ask for proof? There is the very high priest who commissioned me.' *The estate of the elders*, a needless paraphrase of one Greek word, *Presbytery*, which is retained in the translation of 1 Tim. 4, 14, while in Luke 22, 66, it is simply rendered *Elders*. *Estate* is here used in the old sense of a national assembly, as in the phrases *third estate*, *states general*, *etc.* The body described is the Sanhedrim, as chiefly composed of elders or hereditary representatives, even the priests being elders of their own tribe (see above, on 4, 5.) It was therefore under national authority that Paul went to Damascus (see above, on 9, 1. 2.) *To the brethren*, i. e. to the Jews in Syria, not against the Christians there, a form of speech which, if not unintelligible, would have been offensive to Paul's Jewish hearers, and out of keeping with the rest of his discourse, in which, if ever, he became to the Jews as a

Jew (1 Cor. 9, 20.) *There*, literally, *thither*, which some understand as implying previous removal, perhaps flight from the persecution in Jerusalem (see above, on 21, 3.) *About to bring also those there being*, i. e. in addition to those previously seized at home. *For to be*, literally, *that they might be* (see above, on 5, 32.)

6. And it came to pass, that, as I made my journey and was come nigh unto Damascus, about noon suddenly there shone from heaven a great light round about me.

Here begins Paul's own account of his conversion, which should be compared throughout with that of Luke in 9, 3–19, and need not be explained, except as to the points of difference. These are merely formal, and precisely such as might be naturally looked for in two free unstudied statements of the same occurrence. Some modern critics have affected to contrast the two accounts, as independent and discordant narratives, forgetting that the one before us was as much at Luke's disposal as his own, and that his not attempting to assimilate them is a clear proof that he looked upon them as harmonious, or he would not have inserted them in one and the same history. This verse is parallel with 9, 3, and differs from it chiefly in grammatical forms, the infinitive being twice exchanged for a participle, and once for an aorist, of the same verbs, the preposition *from* for *out of*, *etc.* The only additions here are that of the epithet *great* (literally, *sufficient*) to the noun *light*, and that of the precise time when the scene occurred, to wit, *about noon* (or *midday*), the same Greek word that is elsewhere used in the secondary sense of *south* (see above, on 8, 26.) These variations and additions are not only perfectly consistent with the truth of both accounts, but far more natural than perfect uniformity.

7. And I fell unto the ground, and heard a voice saying unto me, Saul, Saul, why persecutest thou me?

This verse is parallel to 9, 4, from which it differs, in addition to the use of the first person for the third throughout, by substituting for the word *earth* (or *ground*) one which originally means a bottom or foundation, then a floor or pavement, and may here have reference to a paved road leading to or into Damascus. Still less important is the change of prepositions (*on* to *into*), and of the case of the noun *voice* (from the accusative to the genitive), though the latter is connected with the explanation of a seeming discrepancy to be noticed afterwards (see below, on v. 9.)

8. 9. And I answered, Who art thou, Lord? And he said unto me, I am Jesus of Nazareth, whom thou persecutest. And they that were with me saw indeed the light, and were afraid, but they heard not the voice of him that spake to me.

V. 8 is parallel to 9, 5, and differs from it chiefly in the change of *said* to *answered*, the addition of the pronoun (*to me*), and of the epithet (*Nazarene*) after *Jesus*. V. 9 answers to 9, 7, from which it varies more than either of the two preceding verses from their parallels. *The* (*men*) *who were* (or *being*) *with me* is less full and explicit than the phrase there used, *the* (*men*) *journeying with him*, although perfectly consistent. *Speechless* is here *afraid*, the cause being put for the effect or outward indication. There is, however, a much greater variation, and one which has been sometimes represented as a contradiction. Paul's companions are described in 9, 7, as *hearing the voice but seeing no one*, whereas here it is affirmed, that *they saw the light indeed, and were afraid, but the voice they heard not of the* (*person*) *talking to me.* Besides the gross improbability of Luke's inserting what directly contradicted his own statement, there are several possible solutions of this seeming inconsistency, each one of which is more entitled to belief than the hypothesis of contradiction. One consists in referring the two statements to successive points of time, so that they are said to have heard the voice at last, but not at first, or *vice versa.* Another makes a difference between the accusative and genitive construction of the verb to *hear*, the one denoting mere sensation, the other intellectual perception. Substantially identical with this, but simpler and more natural, is the distinction between hearing a voice speak and hearing what it says, as nothing is more common in our public bodies than the complaint that a speaker is not heard, i. e. his words are not distinguished, though his voice may be audible and even loud. In these two obvious and familiar senses, it might be said, with equal truth, that Paul's companions heard the voice, i. e. knew that it was speaking, and that they did not hear it, i. e. did not know what it said. Whether this distinction was designed to be suggested by the difference of construction or the change of case already mentioned, is a doubtful point, but one which does not affect the validity or truth of the solution. It is positively favoured, on the other hand, by the only remaining variation, namely, that instead of *the voice* (9, 7), we have here the more explicit phrase, *the voice of the* (*one*) *speaking to me*, which, though it does not necessarily suggest, admits and justifies the supposition, that the voice which they did not hear was a speaking (i. e. an articulate, distinguishable) voice, and not mere vocal sound or utterance, without regard to words or language. A remarkable analogy is furnished by the case recorded in John 12, 28–30, where some said that it thundered, and others that an angel spoke, implying that it was a voice (and not a mere sound) that they heard, while the Evangelist records the very words that it pronounced. In this case, as in that before us, it might well be said of the first class mentioned, that they did and that they did not hear the "voice from heaven." Their mistaking it for thunder proves, at the same time, that they heard it in the one sense, and that they did not hear it in the other.

10. And I said, What shall I do, Lord? And the Lord said unto me, Arise, and go into Damascus, and there it shall be told thee of all things which are appointed for thee to do.

This verse corresponds to 9, 6, by a slight transposition or inversion, wholly unimportant and in strict accordance with the usages of common life, in which the same occurrences are seldom related, even by the same speaker, in precisely the same order. The first clause of 9, 6, as we have already seen, is rejected by the latest critics, as an unauthorized assimilation to the one before us. Even admitting the correctness of this criticism, we are still in possession of the dialogue there given, although not precisely in the same form (see above, vol. i. p. 359.) The mental and bodily effects there mentioned (*trembling and astonished*) are omitted here, and the question (*what wilt thou have me to do?*) is abridged (*what shall I do?*) In the other clause, admitted to be genuine, there are only formal variations, some of which are not perceptible in the translation. *Arise* is an imperative in that place, and a participle in this. *Go* is there *enter*, here *proceed* (or *journey.*) For *the city* we have here the proper name, *Damascus.* Before the verb, the adverb *there* is here inserted. *What thou must do* is amplified, without a change of meaning, into *about* (i. e. concerning) *the* (things) *which have been appointed* (or *ordained*) *for thee to do.* (For the usage of the leading verb in this clause, see above, on 13, 48. 15, 2.)

11. And when I could not see for the glory of that light, being led by the hand of them that were with me, I came into Damascus.

This verse corresponds to 9, 8, a comparison with which will show that the narrative is here abridged, though otherwise unvaried. *I could not see* is the sense but not the form of the original, which strictly means, *I did not see*, or was not seeing. The only addition here made to the narrative is the statement that his blindness arose *from the glory* (i. e. the celestial or divine effulgence) *of that light*, already mentioned in v. 6 above. That he was not merely dazzled but miraculously blinded, is suggested by the use of the word *glory*, which denotes something supernatural (see above, on 7, 2. 55), and still more necessarily implied in v. 13 and the parallel passage.

12. And one Ananias, a devout man according to the law, having a good report of all the Jews which dwelt (there) —

Here again the narrative is abridged on one hand, and supplemented on the other. Paul omits what passed between the Lord and Ananias (see above, on 9, 10–16), and proceeds at once to the interview between the latter and himself (9, 17.) But in describing Ananias, he is more particular than Luke, in order to conciliate the Jews by showing that his introduction to the Christian Church was through a well-known Jew, of high repute among his brethren at Damascus. *The certain disciple* of 9, 10, now becomes *a pious* (or *devout*) *man*, not merely in the Christian sense, but *according to the law*, i. e. the law of Moses, the religion of the Jews. But not content with this description of his spiritual character, he adds that he was *certified*, attested, recommended (see above, on 6, 3. 10, 22. 16, 2) *by all the Jews residing* (for the time, or permanently settled) at Damascus. (See above, on 1, 19. 2, 5.) The emphasis and fulness with which Paul insists upon these circumstances, altogether wanting in Luke's narrative, although it does not in the least impair the harmony between them, calls for explanation; and this is furnished by the circum stances and occasion of his speaking at this time at all, and more particularly by his obvious desire to render prominent whatever was most Jewish in his own biography, and even in the mode of his professing Christianity, especially his being introduced into the Church, not by a Gentile minister, but by the hands of one whom all the Damascene Jews might be said to have endorsed, as a devout and exemplary member of their body. This shows a definite design in this address of Paul, but one involving no duplicity or evil purpose.

13. Came unto me, and stood, and said unto me, Brother Saul, receive thy sight. And the same hour I looked up upon him.

Coming to me (in the house of Judas), *and standing over me* (as he sat or lay there.) *Brother Saul*, or retaining the original order, both of this verse and the parallel passage, *Saul* (*my*) *brother* (see above, on 9, 17.) *Receive thy sight* and *looked up* are imperative and indicative forms of the same Greek verb, and ought to have been so translated, the recovery of sight being not expressed but implied, whereas the relative position of the two men is expressly mentioned, and the natural relation of the order and its execution ought not to be hidden by a needless change in the translation. Ananias, standing over him, says, Look up, which he could not do unless his sight had been restored, and therefore when it is added that he did immediately look up as he was told, it is the strongest way of saying, though by implication, that his eyes were opened. *Looked up upon him*, i. e. Ananias, still standing by or hanging over him, was the first object of his restored vision. *The same hour*, i. e. time or moment (see above, on 16, 18. 33.)

14. And he said, The God of our fathers hath chosen thee, that thou shouldest know his will, and

see that Just One, and shouldest hear the voice of his mouth.

The words ascribed to Ananias in the parallel accounts differ not only in order but in substance, some things which in one place are described as having been addressed by Christ to Ananias being spoken in the other by Ananias to Paul. But this only shows that neither statement is complete, Ananias having naturally repeated much that he had heard, a repetition which was needless in the record. What is contained in this verse, therefore, was no doubt said to Paul by Ananias, although not recorded in the parallel passage. *The God of our fathers*, another intimation that both he and Ananias were native Jews, like those whom he was now addressing (see above, on 3, 13. 25. 5, 30. 7, 2. 11. 14. 15. 19. 38. 40. 45. 13, 17.) *Chosen*, appointed, or prepared beforehand. (For a distinct but similar expression, see above, on 10, 41.) *To know his will*, by special revelation, and *to see the Righteous* (or *that Just One*), the Messiah, who is expressly so called elsewhere (see above, on 3, 14. 7, 52.) *To see* is no doubt to be strictly taken (see above, on 9, 17.) *The voice of his mouth*, literally, *a voice from* (or *out of*) *his mouth*, i. e. his immediate instructions, without any human intervention. This was necessary to put Paul upon a level with the twelve Apostles. (See above, on 13, 3, and compare Gal. 1, 1.)

15. For thou shalt be his witness unto all men of what thou hast seen and heard.

What was just before implied is here expressed, that is, the reason why it was necessary that Paul should see and hear the Lord himself, to wit, because he was to be an Apostle, although not one of the twelve, and the essential function of that office was to testify of Christ, not from hearsay, but from personal acquaintance and direct communication with him. (See above, on 1, 8. 22. 2, 32. 3, 15. 5, 32. 10, 39. 13, 3.) *His witness*, i. e. sent forth and commissioned by him, or *a witness to him*, i. e. testifying of him. (Compare the two readings in 1, 8 above.) The extent of this official witness-bearing is determined or defined in a twofold manner. *To all men*, without social, personal, or national distinctions, Greeks and Barbarians, Jews and Gentiles, wise and unwise, bond and free. (Compare Rom. 1, 14. Col. 3, 11.) *Of what* (or *of the things which*) *thou hast seen and heard*, i. e. especially, though not perhaps exclusively, in vision and by revelation, or direct communication, from the Lord himself. (See below, on vs. 17, 18, and above, on 16, 9. 18, 9, and compare Gal. 1, 12. 2, 2. 2 Cor. 12, 1. Eph. 3, 3.) The nearest parallel to this verse, although very different in form, is that contained in 9, 15.

16. And now why tarriest thou? arise, and be baptized, and wash away thy sins, calling on the name of the Lord.

The other narrative records the execution of this proposition, but not the proposition itself. As Ananias here calls upon Saul to be baptized, so in 9, 18, we read that *he received sight forthwith and arose and was baptized. Why tarriest thou*, literally, *what art thou about* (to do?) or rather, *why art thou about* (i. e. still just about to act) instead of acting really? *Arise and*, literally, *arising*, which may either mean, address thyself to action, or be taken in the strict sense of arising from a sedentary, prostrate, or recumbent posture. (See above, on 9, 18.) *Be baptized* is not a passive, as in 2, 38, but the middle voice of the same verb, strictly meaning, *baptize thyself*, or rather, cause thyself to be baptized, or suffer (some one) to baptize thee. The form of the next verb is the same, but cannot be so easily expressed in English, as it has a noun dependent on it. This peculiarity of form is only so far of importance as it shows that Paul was to wash away his own sins in the same sense that he was to baptize himself, i. e. by consenting to receive both from another. As his body was to be baptized by man, so his sins were to be washed away by God. The identity, or even the inseparable union, of the two effects, is so far from being here affirmed, that they are rather held apart, as things connected by the natural relation of a type and antitype, yet perfectly distinguishable in themselves and easily separable in experience. *Calling on the name of the Lord* (or according to the latest critics, *his name*), i. e. invoking it in worship, recognizing Christ's divinity and sovereignty, as an indispensable prerequisite of baptism. (See above, on 2, 21. 7, 59. 9, 14. 21.)

17. And it came to pass, that, when I was come again to Jerusalem, even while I prayed in the temple, I was in a trance—

The historical formula (*it came to pass*) betokens a transition, or the introduction of another topic. The Apostle now approaches the most delicate and doubtful part of his assumed task, that of explaining and defending his peculiar mission to the Gentiles. Having traced the history of his profession as a Jew and his conversion as a Christian, without being interrupted or denounced as an apostate, he was probably encouraged to believe that even this most trying part of his defence would be received in the same spirit. He is not on that account, however, the less careful to connect this difficult portion of his task, as well as that which he had now accomplished, with the sacred places which he was accused of wantonly profaning. It was true that he had preached among the Gentiles, not of his own choice, but by express divine command, communicated to him not abroad, but in the Holy Land, but in the Holy City, but in the Holy House, i. e. within the precincts of the temple at Jerusalem. He therefore speaks of his return thither after his conversion, passing over many intermediate events, and leaving the chronology indefinite, though most interpreters identify this visit with the one described above, in 9, 26–29. Nor is it merely his return to Palestine and to Jerusalem that he insists upon, but also his return to the temple, as a place of stated and habitual resort. *It happened to me, having returned to Jerusalem, and I praying in the temple*, i. e. in the inner court or customary place of prayer. (See above, on 2, 46. 3, 1. 5, 20. 21, 26–30.) The abrupt change of construction, from the dative to the genitive, might almost seem intended to give prominence to Paul's own person as the actor in these strange proceedings. As if he had said, 'You seem to think that after I became a Christian, I forsook the temple and the Holy City and my old associations as a Jew; but you are very much mistaken. I, even I Paul (1 Thess. 2, 18. Philem. 9), came back to Jerusalem, and to the sanctuary; and it was while I Paul was actually praying there, that what I am about to tell occurred; so far is my conversion or apostleship from having severed my connection with the fathers and the covenants, the law, the service, and the promises to Israel (see Rom. 9, 4.)' *It came to pass* (while I was there and thus employed) *that I was in a trance* (or *ecstasy*), i. e. under special divine influence, and in direct communication with my Master. (See above, on 10, 10. 11, 5, and compare the use of the same word in 3, 10.)

18. And saw him saying unto me, Make haste, and

get thee quickly out of Jerusalem; for they will not receive thy testimony concerning me.

The construction is continued from the verse preceding, (*it came to pass that I was in a trance*) *and that I saw him*, i. e. saw him again, with obvious allusion to the sight recorded in v. 14, where precisely the same verbal form is used in Greek. The person here meant therefore is the same as there, to wit, the Just One, i. e. the Messiah. His name may be suppressed because Paul was unwilling to offend his hearers by an unnecessary repetition or obtrusion of what he believed but they did not, and because he was still more unwilling to expose that name to their irreverence and even blasphemy, if they should be so offended. He may possibly have wished moreover to convey the idea, that in going to the Gentiles he had acted by divine authority, without expressly stating that this authority was that of Christ, whom he regarded as divine, but they as an impostor. By saying *I saw him* he might be understood to mean a theophany or vision of Jehovah, without specifying in or under what form he appeared to him. (For a somewhat similar ambiguous allusion to our Lord by Peter, but addressed to Gentiles, see above, on 10, 38.) It appears, however, from what follows, that his hearers must have understood him as referring to a vision or appearance of our Lord himself (see below, on v. 19.) The unusual combination, *saw him saying*, is not to be explained away by taking the last verb in the diluted or extenuated sense of perceiving either by the eye or ear, which is equivalent to making *see* and *hear* synonymous. The true explanation is that *saw him* is a substantive or independent proposition, and that *saying* is an afterthought or subsequent description of the way in which he was employed when seen. The expression may be amplified or paraphrased as follows. *I saw him* (and when I saw him, he was) *saying, etc.*, or, *I saw him* (and at the same time heard him) *saying, etc.* This implies, however, that the seeing was not a mere incidental circumstance but something of intrinsic moment. So it is, when considered as a proof of Paul's Apostleship and of his being qualified to testify of Christ from personal acquaintance and communication (see above, on v. 14.) 'Once more, as his Apostle and his witness, I was suffered to behold him, and on this occasion heard him saying,' etc. *Hasten and go out quickly* (literally, *in quickness*, or *with speed*), a repetition which, together with the sudden and abrupt address, seems to imply that Paul had been already too long in Jerusalem, or even that he ought not to be there at all. This agrees well with the evidence which follows of his having entertained a false view of his own vocation. *They* (i. e. the Jews, or the people of Jerusalem) *will not receive* (as true or credible) *thy testimony about me*, to bear which was the very task imposed upon him, and the vital function of his apostolic office (see above, on v. 14.) This was therefore a distinct annunciation, that he was not an Apostle to Jerusalem or to the Jews, as Peter and the twelve were (see above, on 1, 22. 26.)

19. And I said, Lord, they know that I imprisoned and beat in every synagogue them that believed on thee —

We have here another instance of that singular reluctance on the part of God's most honoured instruments, and of that freedom in expressing such reluctance, which have been already noticed in the case of Ananias (see above, on 9, 13.) To the observations there made, it may here be added, that the opposition is in all such cases momentary, and succeeded by implicit acquiescence, whether produced by rational conviction, or by simple iteration of the order as in this case (see below, on v. 21.) The words of Paul, as here reported by himself, are in fact, though not in form, an argument against the Saviour's requisition, and in favour of his own preconceived idea of the way in which he might expect most effectively to aid the cause which he had once sought to destroy (see above, on 9, 21.) It is not a formal argument, because he only states the premises or data, without venturing to draw the bold conclusion, which, however, is too obvious to be mistaken. *Lord*, both in Greek and Aramaic, an ambiguous expression, which might either be addressed to man or God, though really applying here to Christ, in whom both natures were united. *They know* is very strong in the original, the pronoun and the verb being both emphatic, *they* (*themselves*) *know* (*well*), as if he had said, none know better. (For the usage of the Greek verb, see above, on 10, 28. 15, 7. 18, 25. 19, 15. 25. 20, 18.) *Imprisoned and beat*, or more exactly, *was imprisoning and scourging*, i. e. was continually doing it. The last word properly means flaying, skinning, but is used to denote the most severe and cruel kind of flogging. (See above, on 5, 40. 16

37.) *In every synagogue* is too strong, like *in every house* (5, 42. 8, 3), *in every city* (15, 21. 36. 20, 23), in all which cases the Greek preposition might be rendered *through* or *throughout* (as in 8, 1. 9, 31. 42. 10, 37), *throughout the synagogues*, or (as in 2, 46. 20, 20), *from synagogue to synagogue. Those believing on thee*, a periphrasis for Christians, which of course implies that Christ is the person here addressed, and therefore shows that Paul, though reserved in the use of our Lord's name where it was liable to be dishonoured, had no thought of dissembling his religion, which indeed was so notorious as to have occasioned his misfortunes upon this occasion.

20. And when the blood of thy martyr Stephen was shed, I also was standing by, and consenting unto his death, and kept the raiment of them that slew him.

To this general description of his own participation in the persecutions of the church, he adds one particular example, as the earliest in date, and most indelibly impressed upon his memory, as having given the first impulse to his youthful zeal in this fanatical and murderous direction. Bloodshed is probably here put by a familiar figure for loss of life by violence, without necessarily implying a specific mode of killing, although stoning may have been accompanied by literal effusion of blood. *Martyr* is itself a Greek word meaning *witness*, and repeatedly occurring in the book before us (see above, on v. 15, and on 1, 8. 22. 2, 32. 3, 15. 5, 32. 6, 13. 7, 58. 10, 10. 41. 13, 31), but in English having the specific sense of one who dies for his religion, or seals his testimony to the truth with his blood. The transition from the general sense of *witness* to the specific sense of *martyr* is traced by some in this verse and in Rev. 2, 13. 11, 3. 17, 6. Our translators would, however, have done better to retain the usual term, *witness*, which is found in all the older English versions. *I also* is in Greek still stronger, as the pronoun means *myself*, or *I myself*. 'Not only other men, but even I, or I myself too,' possibly with reference to his youth, 'not only older men, but even I' (but see above, on 7, 58.) *Was standing* is precisely the construction which occurs in the preceding verse, and here as there denotes continued action, but confined to one occasion. As if he had said, 'all the time that they were shedding Stephen's blood, I was *standing by*,' or more emphatically, *standing over* (see above, on v. 13), that is, on some spot which overlooked the scene of murder, or literally over Stephen's body as he knelt or lay upon the ground (see above, on 7, 60.) *Kept the raiment* (literally, guarding, watching, the upper garments) *of those killing* (or despatching) *him*, which they had thrown off for convenience in the act of stoning. This circumstance, recorded by Luke likewise (see above, on 7, 58), would of course be deeply impressed upon the memory of Saul, even after his conversion. As mere reminiscences, these facts would have been out of place, both as originally uttered in the temple, and as here repeated on the castle stairs. The only way in which they can be made significant or relevant, is by supplying the conclusion evidently meant to be deduced from them, to wit, that as the first scene of Paul's persecutions, and of Stephen's martyrdom from which they took their rise, was in Jerusalem, that was the place for the convert and Apostle to retrieve his character, and there the most inviting field of labour in the cause which he had once sought to destroy, but which he now lived only to promote, because the last place where his motives or the truth of his conversion could be questioned, in the face of all the suffering and reproach which it had brought upon him. That the argument suggested (not expressed) in these words is a strong one, every reader feels, and has often been attested by its application to a multitude of later cases, as for instance when converted Jews or popish priests are sent to labour among those whom they have lately left, upon the very ground, at least substantially, which Paul here urges for remaining in Jerusalem. The frequent failure of such missions may be owing partly to neglect or misconception of the way in which Paul's argument was answered, as recorded in the next verse.

21. And he said unto me, Depart, for I will send thee far hence unto the Gentiles.

Though Paul may have expected a more formal answer to his tacit argument, derived from the facts mentioned in the two preceding verses, he could not have received one more cogent and conclusive than this stern and peremptory iteration of his Master's orders. The words derive a high degree of dignity and grandeur from the very absence of all ratiocination, and their purely imperative or jussive character. There is something also very striking in the childlike simplicity with which Paul here recites this crushing answer, i. e. crushing to his self-complacent and ambitious prepossessions, although no doubt long since fully justified and hallowed, even to himself, as proofs of the divine benevolence as well as wisdom. It is possible, however, that he might not have been willing to recite so publicly his own humiliating disappointment, which would otherwise never have been known, if he had not wished to use it as a proof that his devotion to the Gentiles sprang from no indifference to the interests of Israel, but from an absolute divine decree. *And he said unto me* (without any direct answer to my plea for license to remain), *Depart* (set out upon thy journey), *because I to nations far off am about to send thee out away*, the first and last verb both implying distance. (See above, on 1, 10. 8, 26. 9, 3. 18, 6. 21, 5, and on 7, 12. 9, 30. 11, 22. 12, 11. 17, 14.) Although uncertain, it is not impossible, nor inconsistent with this passage, to suppose that the departure here required is the one already mentioned in 9, 30, and there referred to outward dangers and the anxious care of the brethren at Jerusalem. That the operation of such secondary causes is entirely compatible with an express divine command, is not only matter of experience, but exemplified in other cases upon record (see above, on 15, 1. 4.) We have only to suppose, what is altogether probable and suited to Paul's character, that notwithstanding the impending dangers and the counsel of the brethren, he refused to leave the post of danger, till convinced that it was not the post of duty, and could not therefore be the post of honour. This conviction may have been effected by the argument in this verse, which may be resolved into the simple statement, that whatever God or Christ commands, it must be right, and safe, and wise to do, whatever man may have to say against it.

22. And they gave him audience unto this word, and (then) lifted up their voices, and said, Away with such a (fellow) from the earth, for it is not fit that he should live.

Notwithstanding the consummate skill with which Paul seemed to have conducted his defence, it was not to prove successful. What the Lord had said to him in vision long before was now to be verified anew, "they will not receive thy testimony concerning me" (see above, on v. 18.) If any thing had been required to confirm his acquiescence in the former disappointment of his hopes and wishes, it must have been afforded by this fresh proof, that his time and toil would have been thrown away upon his "kinsmen according to the flesh." *Gave him audience* (as in 13, 16. 15, 12), literally, *heard*, were hearing, or continued still to listen. (See above, on 14, 9, and compare 16, 25.) *Unto*, until, as far as, but no further, an expression applied sometimes to space (11, 5. 13, 6. 20, 4), but commonly to time (1, 2. 2, 29. 3, 21. 7, 18. 13, 11. 20, 6. 11), and once or twice exclusively to neither (as here and in v. 4 above.) *This word*, not the word *Gentiles*, as the English reader may suppose, for it is not the last word in the Greek sentence, and *word* will bear a wider meaning, such as that of saying, proposition, or expression. The *word* meant is no doubt the last part of Paul's discourse, in which he undertook to justify his mission to the Gentiles on the ground of an express divine command, and more especially the last verse, in which that command is given *totidem verbis*. *Voices*, literally *voice*, as that of one man (see above, on 19, 34, and compare the like use of the singular in 2, 6. 4, 24. 7, 57. 8, 7. 14, 11.) *Away with*, literally *take away*, remove, i. e. by death, the same cry that was raised against our Lord himself almost upon the same spot. (See Luke 23, 28. John 19, 15.) The contemptuous term, *fellow*, is supplied by the translators, but in perfect keeping with the tone of this ferocious acclamation. *Fit*, becoming, the original word being also a participle in the common text, with which a verb must be supplied, (*it is*) *not becoming*. But all the oldest copies have the past tense meaning, *it was not fit*, or was not right, probably in reference to their previous attempt to kill him, and his rescue by the Romans. The sense will then be, 'We were right at first, it was not fit that he should live, as we declared before.' This allusion to their first attack upon him is of some importance, as explaining why they now refused to hear him further, and broke out with these intemperate expressions. It could not be the simple mention of the Gentiles that provoked them; for among these many of the Jews now present had their homes and business. It was not the intimation that the Gentiles might be saved, for this had always been conceded, and the Pharisees were famous for their proselyting zeal (see Matt. 23, 15.) But Paul's claim to a divine commission as Apostle of the Gentiles (see above, on vs. 17–21) was immediately connected by his hearers with the previous charge against him (see above, on 21, 28) of apostasy and blasphemy and sacrilege, which seemed to be confirmed by what he now said, so that they broke out afresh against him, not simply because he said he had been sent forth to the Gentiles, but because his saying this convinced them that he did reject the law, and had profaned the temple.

23. And as they cried out, and cast off (their) clothes, and threw dust into the air —

This verse describes the outward signs of rage, with which the words just given were accompanied. The construction is that of the genitive absolute, *they crying*, an unusual intensive form in Greek, which might be rendered by some stronger term in English, such as yelling, shrieking, screeching. *Cast off their clothes* conveys the false idea that they stripped themselves, which would be wholly unnatural and out of place, as well as foreign from the true sense of the words, which do not even mean that they *cast off their upper garments*, as a preliminary to the act of stoning (see above, on v. 20, and on 7, 58.) This, though an appropriate Jewish punishment (see above, on 5, 26. 7, 59. 14, 5. 19), was here out of the question, as the Romans had Paul in possession, and the Jews would scarcely have expressed the mere desire to stone him, when they knew they could not, by so violent and troublesome a gesture. Besides, we know that when they had him in their power and sought to kill him, it was not by stoning but by beating (see above, on 21, 31. 32.) The verb, moreover, is not the compounded one which elsewhere means to *cast off* (see below, on 27, 43), but a frequentative form of the primitive verb, meaning to throw about, to toss. The act described here may be either that of tossing up their loose cloaks or outer garments, or that of violently shaking them without removal; not as a gesture of concurrence or applause, in which sense agitation of the dress is sometimes mentioned in the classics, but as a spontaneous expression of intense and irrepressible excitement. *Throwing dust into the air*, not, as it has sometimes been explained, that it might descend upon their own heads as a sign of mourning, an idea probably connected with the false assumption that they rent their garments, whereas they only shook or tossed them. The act described is to be understood precisely like the one before it, as an outward symptom of internal rage, resembling its expression in the lower animals, and said to be still common in the East, upon the part of whole crowds, when impatient or exasperated.

24. The chief captain commanded him to be brought into the castle, and bade that he should be examined by scourging, that he might know wherefore they cried so against him.

They thus acting, i. e. while and because they did so, the Roman Tribune, or commander of the garrison, saw that the time was come for a second interposition and rescue. But while he thus provided for the safety of the prisoner, he felt constrained to use some other means for the discovery of his crime, or of the charge alleged against him. This he had not learned from the speech of Paul, either because he did not understand the language, or because it would convey no definite idea to a Roman, even if complete, much less when violently broken off. The method of discovery to which he now resorted was no proof of peculiar cruelty or ill-will to his prisoner, but only of the rigour of the Roman discipline. *To be examined by scourging* (literally, *scourges*) was a species of judicial torture, intended like the similar but worse devices of the Inquisition and some other civilized but barbarous tribunals, to supply the want of proof or information, by extorting a confession or compelling a prisoner to accuse himself. From this use torture has acquired a euphemistic name, the application of the rack, the iron boot, the thumb-screws, and a hundred other hellish cruelties, being known in history as putting men (or women) to the *question*. In comparison with these refinements, there was something merciful in the Roman practice of examining by scourges. *That he might know*, discover, ascertain, a compound of the verb *to know*, employed above in 3, 10. 4, 13. 9, 30. 12, 14. 19, 34, and there explained. *For what cause*, in the general sense of motive, ground, or reason (see above, on 10, 21), or in the more specific one of a judicial cause, a crime or accusation (see above, on 13, 28.) *So*, as usual, is not an expletive or idiomatic pleonasm (see above, on 1, 11. 3, 18. 7, 8. 13, 47. 14, 1. 17, 33. 19, 20. 20, 11. 35. 21, 11), but means, *in such a manner*, i. e. here with such extraordinary fury, without any visible occasion or intelligible explanation. *Cried*, an entirely different word from that in the beginning of v. 23, derived from *voice*, and elsewhere used by Luke, once to denote the acclamation or idolatrous applause of Herod by his flatterers just before the Angel smote him (see above, on 12, 22), and once the awful cry of "crucify him" by the rabble of Jerusalem (see Luke 23, 21.)

25. And as they bound him with thongs, Paul said unto the centurion that stood by, Is it lawful for you to scourge a man that is a Roman, and uncondemned?

Bound with thongs (or *straps*), a word used elsewhere only to denote the straps of shoes or sandals. (See Mark 1, 7. Luke 3, 16. John 1, 27.) Our translation here supposes it to mean the straps by which the person to be scourged was fastened to a post or other fixture, or according to some writers, was suspended in the air. To suit this explanation, the preceding verb is rendered *bound*, but without authority from usage. It really means *stretched forth* or extended, and may here be literally understood of bodily position, or taken in a figurative sense, such as presented, subjected, or exposed, for which however there is less authority. This latter explanation of the verb requires the *thongs* (or *straps*) to be explained as meaning the lashes of the scourges to which they were about subjecting or exposing him. The same explanation of the noun may be combined with the literal or strict sense of the verb, to wit, that *they stretched him out for the whips*, i. e. in a suitable position for receiving them. All these interpretations coincide in one point, and the only one of much importance, namely, that the clause describes the preparation made for Paul's immediate scourging. This was prevented by a similar avowal of his civil rights to that made at Philippi and before recorded (see above, on 16, 37.) *That stood by*, literally *the (one) standing*, i. e. standing there to see the Tribune's order carried into execution. The Roman historians sometimes speak of centurions as presiding over punishment, and an officer of that rank seems to have had charge of our Saviour's crucifixion (see Matt. 27, 54. Luke 23, 47. Mark 15, 39. 44. 45.) *And uncondemned*, i. e. not even tried, an aggravating circumstance which Paul had long before urged at Philippi (see above, on 16, 37.) *Is it lawful*, the impersonal verb so rendered 16, 21, but elsewhere by the auxiliary *let* (2, 29) or *may* (8, 37. 21, 37.) (*Tell me*) *if it is lawful*, see above, on 1, 6. 5, 8. 7, 1. 19, 2. 21, 37. *For you*, the Roman soldiery, who ought to be the guardians and protectors of your fellow-citizens.

26. When the centurion heard (that), he went and told the chief captain, saying, Take heed what thou doest; for this man is a Roman.

Having heard (the question just recorded) *the centurion coming to* (him) *reported* (what he had thus heard) *to the chiliarch* (or tribune.) The last verb is the one employed in 4, 23. 5, 22. 25. 11, 13. 12, 14. 17. 15, 27. 16, 36, and there explained. For the meaning of the military title here used, see above, on 21, 31. *Take heed*, literally, *see* (*to it*), a phrase synonymous though not identical with that in 13, 40, but omitted here by all the oldest manuscripts and latest critics, who make the sentence interrogative, *what doest thou?* or more exactly, *what art thou about to do?* the first verb being that employed above in v. 16, and often elsewhere (see above, on 3, 3. 5, 35. 11, 28. 12, 6. 13, 34. 16, 27. 17, 31. 18, 14. 19, 27. 20, 3. 7. 13. 38. 21, 27. 37.) *For* assigns the reason of his ask ing, or according to the other text, his warning, which indeed is equally implied in the interrogative construction. *A Roman*, not by birth or residence, but in right and privilege, a Roman citizen. As to the nature and the value of this *civitas* or citizenship, see above, on 16, 37. 38.

27. Then the chief captain came, and said unto him, Tell me, art thou a Roman? He said, Yea.

Neither the centurion nor the chiliarch appears to have suspected Paul of claiming what was not his due, perhaps because of the severity with which false claims were punished (see above, on 16, 38.) The centurion without hesitation goes to his commander, saying, This man is a Roman. The commander, it is true, interrogates the prisoner, but rather from surprise and curiosity than doubt or incredulity, which would have led him to stay where he was, instead of hurrying back to question him. *Tell me if thou art*, the full form of the abbreviated question in v. 25. The oldest manuscripts, however, omit *if*, so that the form of the interrogation is precisely that presented in the English version, except as to the order of the words, which in Greek is, *Tell me, thou a Roman art?* This might be construed as an exclamation, which would make the expression of surprise still stronger. *Yea*, in modern English, *yes*, a form scarcely used in the English Bible. The Greek particle occurs above in 5, 8.

28. And the chief captain answered, With a great sum obtained I this freedom. And Paul said, But I was (free) born.

With (or *for*) *a great sum* (literally, *much capital*) *this freedom* (literally, *polity*, citizenship) *I obtained* (acquired or purchased, as in 1, 18 above.) The chiliarch was probably surprised that one of Paul's appearance should possess the right at all, and still more that he should have the means to purchase it, the customary mode of acquisition, and the only one familiar to his own experience. The sale of such rights was undoubtedly a common practice in the reign of Claudius, and was especially promoted by his infamous wife, Messalina, who at first exacted the highest prices, but afterwards expressed her contempt for the distinction by allowing men to purchase it for almost nothing. *But I was free born*, literally, *but I also have been born*, an unusual expression, which most probably means, 'I not only have this freedom in possession, as it seems that you have, but was *also born* to it, as you were not.' It was not merely as a citizen of Tarsus that Paul claimed this birthright; for although that city received important grants from Julius Cæsar and Augustus, this was not among them. If it had been, Paul would have escaped imprisonment and stripes before, by simply stating his nativity (see above, on 22, 39.) It was not a local but a family distinction, how or when acquired is now unknown, most probably by service which his father or some other ancestor had rendered to the state, or the successful party, during the long civil wars. As to his motive in avowing it precisely at this juncture, it was no doubt essentially the same as at Philippi (see above, on 16, 37), but regulated by the same discretion which he exercised in that case. Here, besides exemption from a painful and disgraceful process, it seems to have procured for him the opportunity and honour of appearing in the presence of the Sanhedrim, as he had already in the presence of the people (see below, on v. 30.)

29. Then straightway they departed from him which should have examined him: and the chief captain also was afraid, after he knew that he was a Roman, and because he had bound him.

Then, not a particle of time, but a logical connective meaning *therefore*, i. e. because Paul had thus avowed his birthright as a Roman citizen. *Straightway*, immediately, without even waiting, it would seem, for an order from the Tribune, although some assume that it was given, but omitted in the record, as a matter of course or of routine. *Departed*, drew off, left him to himself (see above, on 5. 38. 12, 10. 15, 38. 19, 9.) *Those about to examine him*, i. e. by scourging (see above, on v. 24.) That they were influenced by fear in thus abandoning their task, appears from what immediately follows, *and the chiliarch also was afraid* (or *frightened*), not the subalterns or soldiers merely, but their chief commander. *Knowing*, or having ascertained, the same verb that is used above in v. 24. *That he wàs a Roman*, literally, that he *is* one, thus recalling the whole scene to mind as actually passing. *And becauśe he had bound him*, not at first, as mentioned in 21, 33, for this restraint still continued (see the next verse), and was lawful till the charge against him could be tried. The reference is rather to the binding mentioned in v. 25, in order to his being scourged, a measure inconsistent with Paul's civil rights, as well as with the statute of Augustus, still preserved in the Digest of the Civil Law, that process never must begin with torture (*non esse a tormentis incipiendum.*) It is not impossible, however, that the Tribune's fears had reference to Paul's imprisonment, but were not strong enough to put an end to it, especially as he was yet in doubt as to the charge against him.

30. On the morrow, because he would have known the certainty wherefore he was accused of the Jews, he loosed him from (his) bands, and commanded the chief priests and all their council to appear, and brought Paul down, and set him before them.

Because he would have known, in Greek simply, *wishing to know* (see above, on 14, 18. 19.) *The certainty*, in Greek, *the certain* (or *infallible*), i. e. the true state of the case, the real facts. (Compare the use of the same phrase above, in 21, 34.) The article is here used in a way peculiar to the Greek idiom, and therefore not expressed in the translation, which would literally be, *the why* (i. e. the question or the reason why) *he is accused*, the present tense as in the verse preceding. *By* (or according to another reading, *from*, on the part of) *the Jews.* *Loosed him*, freed him from personal restraint. *From his bands* is omitted in the oldest manuscripts and latest critical editions. *Commanded*, or required, no doubt by virtue of official powers in cases of emergency belonging to the governor when present, but devolving in his absence on the commander of the forces in Jerusalem, most probably the second Roman officer or magistrate in all Judea. (See below, on 23, 24.) *The chief priests* are mentioned as the most important class of counsellors, and then *all the Sanhedrim*, the pronoun *their* being omitted by the latest critics. *To appear*, literally, *to come*, which would naturally mean, to him, into the castle; but the oldest reading is *to come together*, to assemble, i. e. in their customary place of meeting. This had once been in the temple, but according to an old tradition, was at this time in a hall upon Mount Zion. The former situation seems to be implied, however, in the phrase, *brought Paul down*, i. e. from the camp or castle of Antonia, by the stairs already mentioned (see above, on 21, 35. 40), into the area or enclosure of the temple. *Set him*, set him up, caused him to stand (see above, on 1, 23. 4, 7. 5, 27. 6, 6. 13.) *Before them*, literally, *into them*, i. e. into the midst of the assembled council. This last attempt of the commander to find out what Paul had done or been accused of, by making a national affair of it and bringing him before the senate, was most probably suggested by his previous discovery that the prisoner, at first so harshly and contemptuously treated, was a Roman citizen of equal privileges with himself (see above, on v. 28.) The whole narrative illustrates the perplexity in which the Roman rulers of the Jews were constantly involved, and to which Paul owed this unexpected opportunity of making his second Apology before the highest court of Israel.

CHAPTER XXIII.

It is highly important here to bear in mind, that Paul was not a mere chance visitor to Jerusalem, accidentally involved in a disturbance there, but the Apostle of the Gentiles, specially commissioned to make, as it were, a last appeal to Israel, before he finally transferred his centre of operations to the great metropolis and mistress of the heathen world. All that is recorded of his acts and sufferings, in his farewell visit to the Holy City, must be viewed as having an official character on his part, and a representative or national significancy on the part of those with whom he came in contact, both as friends and foes. Having borne his testimony to the people from the castle stairs and been rejected by them, he now appears, for the same momentous purpose, in the presence of the Sanhedrim, of which he had once been a member, or at least an emissary. But the rejection of his testimony here is still more prompt and violent than in the other case (1–5.) Under the influence of party spirit, the Pharisees espouse his cause, but only for the moment, and so as to increase his personal danger, from which he is a third time rescued by the Romans (6–10.) The disappointed zealots form a plot against his life, from which he is a fourth time rescued by the Romans (11–22.) Having been thus repeatedly rejected by the Jews and protected by the Gentiles, he is finally delivered from the power of the former, and entrusted to the keeping of the latter, being transferred by the Tribune at Jerusalem to the Procurator at Cesarea (23–35.)

1. And Paul, earnestly beholding the council, said, Men (and) brethren, I have lived in all good conscience before God until this day.

Gazing steadily (or *intently*), a favourite word of Luke's, especially in this book (see above, on 1, 10. 3, 4. 12. 6, 15. 7, 55. 10, 4. 11, 6. 13, 9. 14, 9), and therefore not to be explained here in any special sense, as denoting or implying weakness of sight, but in accordance with its general usage as expressive of earnestness and boldness, and especially of that *good conscience* which is afterwards expressed in words. *Men (and) brethren*, without the still more deferential title, *fathers*, which he used in the beginning of his speech to the people (see above, on 22, 1), although here, as it would seem, peculiarly appropriate when he was addressing the Senate or Eldership of Israel (see above, on 22, 5.) If the difference was not accidental and unmeaning, or belonging rather to the ummary report than to the actual discourse, it may be understood as an indirect assertion of his equality with those whom he addressed, and as having forfeited no rights which he had once possessed, as a member of the body, or at least of the theocracy, a claim which is also then expressed in words. The notion that it was mere rudeness, or at best forgetfulness in Paul, is an absurd device of that neology which loves to pick flaws even in the manners of Apostles. Anticipating, probably, the interruption which ensued, Paul puts into a single sentence the sum total of what he wished to say, to wit, that so far from being an apostate or a renegade, he claimed to be still a faithful member of the chosen people, and to have uniformly acted in accordance with his theocratical obligations. This involved the doctrine which he always taught, that Christianity was the genuine developement of ancient Judaism, so that he, and not his adversaries, held fast to the true design and spirit of the Mosaic institutions. The word *conscience* and the phrase *good conscience* are confined (with the exception of John 8, 9) to the dialect of Paul and Peter. (The full phrase occurs only in 1 Tim. 1, 5. 19. Heb. 13, 18. 1 Pet. 3, 16. 21.) It here means consciousness of rectitude and faithfulness, not merely in the general, but with specific reference to those peculiar rights and obligations which are suggested by the accompanying verb in the original, though not at all by the translation. *Lived* is a gratuitous attenuation of a Greek verb derived from the noun *citizen*, and meaning therefore to act the part, enjoy the rights, perform the duties, of a citizen, or one belonging to some state or body politic. The only such organization that can be referred to here is the Theocracy, or ancient church, in its twofold form, ecclesiastical and national, of which the Sanhedrim was still the ostensible representative, but which was really continued in the Christian Church, without its national restrictions, and of which Paul therefore was more really a citizen than those whom he addressed. In this same proper sense, and not as a mere figure or accommodation, he applies the Greek word to the Christian life, in the only other place where it occurs (Phil. 1, 27), and where it is no less diluted by the English version, although not precisely in the same form. The specific sense of *theocratic citizenship* is given to the verb here by the phrase, *to God*, which does not mean *before God*, i. e. in his presence, nor is it a superlative expression (see above, on 7, 20) meaning *truly* or *completely*, but is to be strictly understood as qualifying what precedes, *I have lived as a citizen to God*, or of that body in which God is the immediate sovereign. That this sense of the terms is agreeable to Hellenistic usage, may be seen from the occurrence of the same verb in the apocryphal but ancient books of Maccabees, in reference to the practice of the Jews' religion, and accompanied by qualifying phrases corresponding to the one here used, e. g. *to the law*, *to the laws of God*, *according to the customs* (ἔθη) *of their forefathers* (2 Macc. 6, 1. 11, 25. 3 Macc. 3, 4.) Thus understood, the clause before us is not a vague profession to have acted conscientiously, either before or after his conversion, but a definite and bold claim to have acted theocratically, i. e. as a faithful member of the Jewish church, from which they represented him as an apostate. *Until this day*, or to this very day, not only while he persecuted Christianity, but still more since he was converted to it.

2. And the high priest Ananias commanded them that stood by to smite him on the mouth.

This was not an unmeaning act of brutal violence, nor a mere expression of resentment at Paul's not addressing them as Fathers, as it might have seemed to be if the preceding verse only contained the first words of his address without disclosing what he meant to say. But as it really contains the sum and substance of his whole defence, which he could only have explained and amplified if suffered to proceed, the action here recorded was an arbitrary but significant reply to it, clothed in the form of a symbolical gesture, like stoning and the rending or shaking of the garments. Striking on the mouth implies a previous unlawful use of it, as well as an injunction to cease speaking. This mode of silencing improper self-defence upon the part of accused persons is said to be still practised at the court of Persia. Translated into language it was here equivalent to saying, that Paul's claim, not only to integrity and innocence as some suppose, but to the highest theocratical fidelity, was false in itself, and grossly insulting to his judges, whom it charged, by necessary implication, with being themselves unfaithful to their great national and religious trust. (See above, on 7, 51–53, where Stephen urges the same accusation in express and most offensive terms.) Whether this practical repudiation of Paul's theocratic claims can be regarded as the act of the whole body, depends upon the doubtful and disputed question, as to the position occupied by Ananias. It is commonly assumed, as a matter of course, or as the only sense that can be put upon this verse and v. 4 below, that he was the actual High Priest at this time, and as such presiding in the Sanhedrim (see above, on 4, 6. 7, 1.) That there was a High Priest of this name about the time in question, is expressly stated by Josephus, who describes him as an avaricious, overbearing man, and represents him as having been involved in a dispute with the Samaritans, in consequence of which the Roman governor, Quadratus, sent him to answer for himself before the Emperor. But whether he was there detained or sent back to Judea, and if so, whether he continued or was re-appointed High Priest, are disputed points, in reference to which Josephus has been variously understood, although the latest writers are inclined to the opinion that he did return, which vindicates Luke's accuracy in referring to him here. But even upon this hypothesis, it still continues doubtful whether he retained his office, or usurped it during a vacancy, or merely held a place among the many High Priests who had been successively put up and down by Roman intervention. (See above, on 4, 6.) It should be remembered that the intricacy and confusion of the history on these points is not necessarily the fault of the historian, but arises from the actual irregularities existing at this crisis of the Jewish history, when every thing was tending to the outbreak of that war in which the Hebrew commonwealth was finally destroyed. As the same Greek word is rendered *High* and *Chief Priests*, and as there certainly were many titular High Priests at once, it is highly arbitrary to insist upon the strict interpretation of the title here, as meaning the one recognized and acting at the time here mentioned, although this is certainly the natural presumption, unless something in the context should require or suggest the wider meaning which is equally agreeable to usage. *Those standing by him* might denote those members of the council who were nearest to the prisoner; but the verb *commanded* seems to favour the opinion that the phrase denotes the ministerial officers or attendants of the council. There is no need, however, of taking *bystanders* in the specific sense of servants or attendants, which it is thought to have in Luke 1, 19. John 18, 22 (but compare John 19, 26), as this would require us to read, *standing by* (or *near*) *himself*, i. e. the High Priest, whereas the natural construction is, *those standing by* (or *near to*) *Paul.* If Ananias is here introduced, not as the actual High Priest presiding in the council, but as previous incumbent and the leader of a faction, this command may be addressed to his own adherents or those standing near to him, as the leaders in the English Parliament describe those acting with them as the gentlemen around or nigh them. The question as to Ananias cannot be conclusively determined without some regard to the ensuing verses.

3. Then said Paul unto him, God shall smite thee, (thou) whited wall; for sittest thou to judge me after the law, and commandest me to be smitten contrary to the law?

Shall smite, literally, *is* (or *is about*) *to smite*, the first verb denoting simple futurity (see above, on 22, 16. 26. 29), without expressing (although it of course implies) intention or determination on the part of God, much less a desire on the part of Paul himself; so that the old idea of a (human) curse or imprecation is at variance with the very form of the original. The only sense consistent with this form is that of a prediction or prophetical denunciation, not of the general fact that condign punishment awaits such sinners (compare Gen. 9, 6. Matt. 26, 52), but of the specific fact that this man was himself to be smitten of God. This is not only the natural meaning of the words, but is confirmed by the event, as we learn from Josephus that this Ananias, in the beginning of the Jewish War, was taken from an aqueduct where he lay concealed, and put to death by sicarii or assassins, perhaps some of the same zealots, whose fanaticism he encouraged and inflamed on this occasion. *Whited*, i. e. either washed or plastered with lime, as the original word signifies. *A whited wall* is a familiar figure for a fair outside, behind which or within which all is foul and filthy. Our Saviour uses the still stronger image of a *whited sepulchre* (Matt. 23, 27.) In this case, as in that, there is reference, no doubt, to personal hypocrisy; but as the essential idea is a wider one, to wit, that of false appearances in general, it is natural to give the phrase a wider meaning, as applied not only to the private character of Ananias, but to the hollow and unreal nature of the very office which he held or had held, and indeed of the whole system which it represented. Nothing could well be more descriptive of the Ceremonial Law, as it was suffered to subsist till the destruction of Jerusalem, a mere shell or framework, venerable and beloved for the fathers' sake, but from which the vitality or essence had now passed into another form, than this homely figure of a whited wall, behind which there was nothing, at least nothing good or even sightly. Thus explained, Paul's language may be paraphrased as follows. 'You command me to be smitten, but a far worse stroke from God himself awaits you, the unworthy claimant of an office once ordained of God, but now itself a mere mask and disguise of human corruption under the name and garb of institutions, which have done their office and are soon to vanish even from the sight of men.' That this severe denunciation was a burst of sinful passion, is entirely at variance with Paul's whole position in this narrative, and not supported in the least by his complaint of the injustice done him, which he had a right to utter, even if only personally interested, much more when thus treated in his official representative capacity. *For sittest thou*, literally, *and thou sittest*, the conjunction having a peculiar force in such connections, nearly equivalent to *then* or *so then* (as in Luke 10, 29, and elsewhere.) *Sitting* is probably in all languages and nations the appropriate judicial posture. (See Judg. 5, 10. Ps. 9, 7. 122, 5. Prov. 20, 8. Isai. 28, 6.) *Sittest judging* (or *to judge*) *me*, does not necessarily imply that Ananias was presiding, because every member of the Sanhedrim was acting as a judge on this occasion, and because by his command to smite Paul he had volunteered a premature decision of the case before he heard it, whether acting as the president or as an individual. (For a similar abuse of the same verb, but in another application, see above, on 15, 19.) *Contrary to the law* is in Greek a participle, and means *breaking the law*, or *acting lawlessly*. (Compare the corresponding noun in 2 Pet. 2, 16.) The lawlessness was twofold and consisted, first, in the unworthy and unjust treatment of Paul's person; then, in arbitrarily condemning him before he heard him. Here let it be again observed, that Paul was not on trial simply for himself, but for his Master, whose pretensions as the true Messiah were involved in Paul's defence before the Sanhedrim. The truth of his assertion in the first verse, that he had been faithful to the church of the Old Testament, depends entirely on the fact that Christ had not destroyed its institutions but fulfilled them. Here then, as well as in v. 6 below, he identifies his own cause with the cause of Christianity, and therefore when he speaks of having been unjustly dealt with, the complaint has reference to something more than personal maltreatment, and cannot possibly be reckoned as an ebullition of mere private feeling.

4. And they that stood by said, Revilest thou God's high priest?

This has often been regarded as conclusive evidence that Ananias was the actual High Priest, because no other would be called *the High Priest of God.* But the force of this argument depends entirely on the persons so describing him. As we have seen before (on 4, 6), the actual possession of the office was determined, not by the Mosaic law, but by the Roman government, who looked upon the priesthood chiefly as a national or civil function, representing the whole body, and the most convenient medium of communication with its foreign masters. This seems to be the only explanation of the fact that, while in other points the Jews were left in undisturbed possession of their own religion, the High Priesthood was subjected to continual change, at the caprice or discretion of the Romans. In the eyes of all strict Jews, however, there could be but one legitimate High Priest living at the same time, and his rights were founded on descent from Aaron, not on the decisions of a heathen power. There might indeed be adverse claims among the Jews themselves, and more than one competitor might be supported, each by his own adherents, as the legitimate incumbent. That there were such rivalries and conflicts, is not only in itself a probable result of causes which we know to have been in operation, but the natural impression made by the contemporary history. If *they that stood by* are the same in this verse as in that before it, where, as we have seen, the words may have respect to the immediate friends and partisans of Ananias, then the phrase *God's High Priest* only proves that his adherents so regarded him, while others may have been preferred by other Jewish factions, and still another recognized and upheld by the Romans in the actual possession of the title and prerogatives belonging to the office. If, on the other hand, Ananias was the actual High Priest, *they that stood by* will have the same sense as in v. 2, either the general one of persons present, or the more specific one of officers, attendants. On any of the suppositions which have been suggested, the adherents of the High Priest would of course regard Paul's prophetic denunciation as impious and insolent.

5. Then said Paul, I wist not, brethren, that he was the high priest: for it is written, Thou shalt not speak evil of the ruler of thy people.

The fashionable sentimental view of this verse is, that Paul acknowledges his having spoken in a fit of passion, and apologizes for it. But besides the sheer impossibility of making *I wist not* (i. e. *did not know*) mean *I did not consider* (or remember at the moment), the acknowledgment itself would be at variance with all the facts and circumstances of the case. The objection is not, as some seem to imagine, that the great Apostle was entirely free from human weakness, but that its exhibition is precluded by the special commission under which he acted as a witness for his Master at Jerusalem, both to the masses and the rulers of the Jews. In what imaginable juncture of his history, if not in this, could he expect Christ's promise to be verified, "but when they deliver you up, take no thought how or what ye shall speak; for it shall be given you in that same hour what ye shall speak; for it is not ye that speak, but the Spirit of your Father which speaketh in you" (Matt. 10, 19. 20. Mark 13, 11.) After having been directed to postpone his long-desired voyage to Rome, for the very purpose of this farewell visit and appeal to his own people, and then so providentially brought into contact, first with the representative assemblage from all nations in the area of the temple at the feast of Pentecost, and now with the official representatives of Israel in their aggregate and organized capacity, there is something monstrous in the supposition that a single act of violent injustice, added to the thousands which he had before experienced, betrayed him into an intemperate expression of unsanctified resentment, and that Luke has solemnly recorded this unhappy and unseasonable burst of feeling, for the sake of showing how inferior Paul was to his Master, and yet how gracefully and frankly he could make amends for such offences. Jerome's famous contrast between Paul's behaviour and that of Christ's upon a similar occasion (John 18, 22. 23), though often quoted with applause, contains a double fallacy; first, in assuming that our Saviour literally acted on his own rule, that when smitten upon one cheek we must turn the other also (Matt. 5, 39), whereas he expostulated and resisted no less really, though certainly in milder terms, than Paul himself; and then in taking it for granted that the conduct of his followers was to be governed by his own example in a situation to which theirs was never perfectly analogous, rather than by his immediate and express instructions with respect to the particular emergency in which they were to act. That Paul was thus directed and restrained, is not explicitly affirmed, but is really included in the promise above cited, which of course extends to Paul as an Apostle, and in perfect keeping with the whole series of events by which he had been brought into his present trying situation. Another fallacy, which runs through some interpretations of this verse, is that of confounding Paul's supposed infirmity of temper with the sins of Patriarchs and other holy men, so frequently and candidly recorded in the Scriptures. But in all such instances, the act is sinful in itself, and incapable of any other explanation, which is very far from being the case here; or the divine displeasure is distinctly indicated, either in express words, or by retributive judgments, or by both, as in the case of David (2 Sam. 12, 10. 11); whereas no case can be found in which a Prophet or inspired man, acting by express divine direction, in a most momentous crisis, was allowed to fall into such errors in the very act of executing his commission, or another man inspired to record his weakness. (See below, on v. 11.) To the view now taken of the passage no objection can be drawn from the quotation in the last clause, which is simply tantamount to saying, 'I know the law that you refer to (Ex. 22, 28), but I am not guilty of its violation.' This is at least as natural and easy a construction as the one which supposes the sudden recollection of the law in question to have brought Paul to his senses and convinced him of his indiscretion. But the question still remains, in what sense Paul could say, *I wist not that he was the High Priest*, or as the words ought to be translated, *I knew not that he is the High Priest.* Some say that Paul was not acquainted with his person, on account of his long absence and the frequent changes in the office. The reply often made to this, that the official dress and seat of the High Priest must have revealed him even to a stranger, much more to one so familiar with the Jewish forms and usages as Paul was, is only true upon the doubtful supposition, that this Ananias was the acting High Priest, in the strict sense of the terms, and as such presiding upon this occasion. Another answer is that Paul, from weakness of sight, or looking in a different direction, or the general confusion, did not know from whom the order had proceeded. But besides the statement in v. 3, that Paul addressed the words *to him*, i. e. to Ananias, this would not have been an answer to the general charge of speaking evil of the rulers of his people. Another objection to both these solutions is that they suppose Paul to mean, 'I did not know him but I know him now,' whereas the present tense (εστι) necessarily implies, that his ignorance, whatever it might be, still continued. The combination of the past and present forms can only be explained by understanding him to mean, 'I did not know (and I do not now know) that he is the High Priest.' This is referred by some to his irregular appointment, or to his having been deposed, or, by a sort of irony, to his personal unworthiness. 'I did not know that such a man could be the High Priest.' But the most satisfactory solution is, that Paul means to deny that Ananias was in any such sense High Priest, as to make him a violator of the law in Exodus. And this he might affirm, on either of the previous suppositions as to this man's actual relation to the office, i. e. whether he was acting now as High Priest, or was only one of many who had filled the office and still bore the title (see above, on v. 2.) This distinction is of less exegetical importance, because Paul's denunciation was not meant to terminate upon the individual, but through him aimed at the entire system, of which he claimed to be the representative. That this is not more clearly stated is a part of that reserve and toleration which distinguish the whole apostolic mode of treating the Mosaic institutions, during this anomalous and doubtful interval. As Paul could at the same time teach the independence of salvation upon all ceremonial observances, and yet conform to them himself for safety or conciliation, so he might virtually represent the priesthood, and the law of which it was the centre, as an abrogated system, without saying so explicitly, as long as God permitted the external framework to continue; a reserve which may have had respect to the prepossessions of the Christian Jews, of which they were not wholly disabused until the great catastrophe, a few years after these events. (See above, on 21, 20.) If the views here taken of this difficult and interesting passage are correct, Paul's reply to the reproach of the bystanders may be paraphrased as follows. 'You upbraid me with insulting the High Priest of God; but whom? or which of those who bear the name? The very presence of so many claiming this distinction shows how utterly your practice has departed from the ancient one, and makes it scarcely possible to know who is, or who is not the legitimate successor of Aaron. When I reproved this man, and threatened him with condign judgments for his malice against me and against him whose I am and whom I serve, I did not know, and do not now know that he is the High Priest of God. I know, though you do not, that the office exists only in appearance and in name, and that even that will soon be done away, so as to leave not a vestige of that ancient and divinely constituted priesthood, which I could not have reviled without a flagrant violation of the law, Thou shalt not speak evil of the ruler of thy people.'

6. But when Paul perceived that the one part were Sadducees, and the other Pharisees, he cried out in the council, Men (and) brethren, I am a Pharisee, the son of a Pharisee: of the hope and resurrection of the dead I am called in question.

When Paul perceived might seem to mean that among those present he now recognized persons belonging to both parties; but the meaning of the Greek is simply, *Paul knowing*, i. e. knowing it beforehand as a standing fact, and not that he discovered it as something new, by looking round him upon this occasion. *Were Sadducees*, or more exactly, *is* (composed) *of Sadducees, and the other of Pharisees.* These were the two great parties, commonly called sects, between which the nation was divided, and the representatives of which were no doubt as continually present in the Sanhedrim as Whigs and Tories in the British Parliament. (See above, on 4, 1. 5, 17.) *Men* (*and*) *brethren*, the same friendly but not flattering address which he had used before (in v. 1.) *Son of a Pharisee*, or as the oldest copies, versions, and Fathers have it, *son of Pharisees*, which some refer to both his parents, others to the whole line of his ancestry, as far back as these party lines existed, which are commonly hereditary, though the plural form does not exclude particular exceptions. The essential fact asserted is, that his connections had been always with that party, which contended for the national peculiarities of Judaism, in opposition to the liberal or latitudinarian concessions of the Sadducees. In their later and degenerated state, the former had been led to overload the law with mere traditions, and the latter to repudiate even some essential doctrines. Of one such difference between them Paul avails himself by crying, *Of* (i. e. about, concerning) *hope and resurrection of* (*the*) *dead I am called in question*, literally, *judged* or *tried.* By *hope and resurrection* many understand the hope of such a resurrection, by the figure called hendiadys (see above, on 2, 42.) More probably, however, one is a generic and the other a specific term, *the hope* (of Israel) *and* (as a necessary part of it, or necessarily connected with it, that of the) *resurrection of* (*the*) *dead.* Now the hope of Israel, when absolutely used, must mean the hope of the Messiah (see below, on 26, 6. 7), and this, in Paul's view, was inseparable from the great fact of his resurrection, which again, as he demonstrates in one of his epistles, is the pledge and foretaste of a general resurrection (1 Cor. 15, 12–20.) Thus explained, the brief phrase, *hope and resurrection of the dead*, embraces all that was believed, as to the future, by the Jews in general, and by the Pharisees in particular. There was, therefore, something which the Christians held in common with the Pharisees, but not with the Sadducees, to wit, the doctrine of the resurrection; so that Paul, in making this last effort to conciliate his kinsmen according to the flesh, appeals of course to this remaining link between himself and the school to which he once belonged, abandoning the Sadducees as destitute of any thing on which to found the hope of reconciliation. *I am a Pharisee* means, therefore, as to this great point of difference between you; nor is this qualification merely left to be inferred, but distinctly intimated in the last clause. As if he had said, 'I am and always have been on the Pharisaic side, and opposed to the Sadducean doctrine with respect to resurrection, which indeed, as I connect it with the hope of a Messiah, is the real although not the obvious occasion of my standing here this day before you.' So a converted Papist might exclaim in an assembly of his former brethren, where the most contradictory opinions were asserted in relation to the doctrines of grace, 'I am a Jansenist and always was a Jansenist,' without intending or being understood to express any further acquiescence in their views than as they stood opposed to those of Jesuits and Semipelagians. This view of his meaning, as suggested by the whole connection and the circumstances under which the words were uttered, will prepare us to appreciate the twofold charge which has been urged against him, in addition to the one already mentioned (see above, on v. 5), namely, that he used an unworthy artifice in order to divide his enemies, and that he misrepresented the true nature of the charge against him. The first objection is connected with the arbitrary notion, that this policy was suddenly suggested to him, when forbidden to proceed with his defence; whereas it probably formed part of the defence itself. The other rests upon the false assumption that he gives this as the formal charge alleged against him; whereas he means to say the very opposite, to wit, that this was not the formal charge at all, but that it might be easily reduced to this, as the great principle at issue.

7. And when he had so said, there arose a dissension between the Pharisees and the Sadducees, and the multitude was divided.

He having said this (literally, *this he having said*) *there arose* (happened, came to pass, began to be) *a dissension*, not a mere difference of opinion, but an actual dispute (as in 15, 2), or a violent commotion (as in 19, 40), not in reference to doctrinal divisions, but to Paul and to the charges which had been alleged against him, as a teacher of apostasy and a profaner of the temple (see above, on 21, 28.) *The multitude* does not mean the people as distinguished from the Sanhedrim or council, but the whole mass or body of the Sanhedrim itself, as distinguished from the parties into which it was divided. (For a like relative use of the same Greek word, see above, on 2, 6. 4, 32. 6, 2. 5. 15, 12. 30. 19, 9. 21, 22.) *Divided*, rent, split, the Greek verb from which *schism* is derived (see above, on 14, 4, where the whole phrase occurs, both in Greek and English.) The division here described was not a permanent or new one, but a sudden paroxysm of their usual antipathy and party-zeal, immediately produced by Paul's avowal of his Pharisaic sentiments on one important subject, which would irritate one party in the same proportion that it pleased the other.

8. For the Sadducees say that there is no resurrection, neither angel, nor spirit; but the Pharisees confess both.

This is Luke's explanation of the effect produced by Paul's appeal to the Pharisees, consisting in a statement of the points of difference between the parties, so far as they affected this division. *For*, literally, *for indeed*, or on the one hand, corresponding to the *but* in the other clause, the two correlative particles employed to balance a Greek sentence or make it antithetical in form (see above, on 1, 5.) *For Sadducees* (without the article) *indeed say* (i. e. are accustomed so to say or teach) *that there is no resurrection* (literally, *not to be a resurrection) neither angel nor spirit*, i. e. any other *spirit*, the genus of which *angel* is a species. Or *spirit* may be used in the specific sense of a disembodied human soul (as in Heb. 12, 23.) This additional difference is mentioned, either on account of its connection with the other, since the resurrection of the body necessarily implies a previous separate existence of the disembodied spirit, or because of the allusion to it, made by the Pharisees themselves, in v. 9. It has been disputed how the Sadducees could reconcile their unbelief on this point with their reception of the Pentateuch, if not of the entire Old Testament, in which the reference to angels is so frequent. Some explain this by supposing, that the Sadducees regarded such appearances as transient, or believed that angels were created *pro hac vice*, and as soon as they had done their work, annihilated or absorbed into the Deity. But without resorting to such methods of solution, we may be content to know from all experience, that no limits can be set to the capacities of sceptical interpretation, which can easily eliminate from Scripture even its most palpable contents. *But Pharisees acknowledge both*, i. e. both the doctrines which the Sadducees had just been said to disbelieve, that of a future resurrection, and that of the existence of pure spirits. *Angel* and *spirit* are so evidently used to express one great idea, that it seems absurd to count them separately, so as with *resurrection* to make three, and then to ask how *both* can be applied to more than two. Chrysostom, who ought to be acquainted with Greek usage, says that it was so used; but this, though available in case of exegetical necessity, is not so satisfactory as the explanation which has just been given.

9. And there arose a great cry, and the scribes (that were) of the Pharisees' part arose, and strove, saying, We find no evil in this man; but if a spirit or an angel hath spoken to him, let us not fight against God.

That the whole affair was one of passionate excitement, not of rational conviction, is sufficiently apparent from this mention of the cry or clamour. *Arose* is here employed, not only to express two different ideas, but to render two distinct Greek verbs. The first is that used in v. 7, meaning *happened* or *began to be*. The other is a participle and means *standing up*, arising from their seats, in tumultuous confusion. *The*

Scribes of the part (i. e. *party*) *of the Pharisees* (considered as a portion or division of the council), their learned men and professional leaders, the official guardians and expounders of the law (see above, on 4, 5.) These would naturally take the lead in doctrinal discussion, or in any other controversy growing out of it. Some suppose that all the Scribes were Pharisees, since none are mentioned, here or elsewhere, as belonging to the other party; while the opposite conclusion has been drawn by others from the form of expression here, which is really ambiguous and may be construed either to mean, 'such Scribes as were of the party of the Pharisees,' or 'the Scribes who were all of the party of the Pharisees.' The truth lies probably between the two extremes, to wit, that the majority of Scribes, as of the Jews in general, was on the Pharisaic side. Such was the magical effect of Paul's avowed agreement with them, that these Scribes, for the time, became his friends and champions, at least as much in opposition to the Sadducees, as from sincere conviction of his innocence. *No evil*, i. e. crime or ground of condemnation. *If a spirit did speak to him or an angel* is supposed by some to be a reference to Paul's visions, mentioned in his speech the day before (see above, on 21, 14. 17.) There is also an obvious allusion to the Sadducean disbelief, and an indirect profession of their own faith in angels and spirits. In the previous disputes, the Sadducees may possibly have urged these visions as objections to the truth of the Apostle's story. *Let us not fight against God* is in Greek a compound verb, corresponding to the adjective in 5, 39, from which the latest critics suppose it to have been interpolated here, as it is wanting in the oldest manuscripts and versions, and was probably inserted to complete the sentence, which without it is an instance of the figure of speech called *aposiopesis*. *If a spirit did speak to him or an angel* (what of that? or what is there incredible in that?) Some modern writers make it interrogative throughout, (what) *if a spirit did speak to him or an angel?* which amounts to the same thing. In favour of the common text it has been urged, that an interpolation would have probably retained the very form used by Gamaliel (see above, on 5, 39.)

10. And when there arose a great dissension, the chief captain, fearing lest Paul should have been pulled

in pieces of them, commanded the soldiers to go down, and to take him by force from among them, and to bring (him) into the castle.

Much dissension arising, the same noun and verb as in v. 7 above. *Fearing*, in Greek a passive, meaning *frightened* or *alarmed*, and corresponding to *afraid* in its original participial form (*affrayed*), though now used only as an adjective. *Pulled in pieces*, literally, *drawn asunder* (or *apart*), which is no doubt to be figuratively understood, as implying that both parties seized him and endeavored to secure his person. Here again the ever watchful care and solicitude of the Roman commander is exemplified. *The soldiers* is in Greek a collective singular, translated *army* in v. 27 below, but really meaning in both cases a detachment, or a body of troops, whether large or small. *Going down* (from the tower or castle of Antonia into the enclosure of the temple, where the Sanhedrim must therefore have been meeting) *to seize* (or *snatch*) *him from the midst of them, to bring him too* (τε) *into the camp* (or fortified enclosure, see above, on 21, 34. 37. 22, 24.)

11. And the night following the Lord stood by him, and said, Be of good cheer, Paul; for as thou hast testified of me in Jerusalem, so must thou bear witness also at Rome.

It is not surprising that Paul, after this extraordinary series of apologies, rejections, and rescues, should have needed some express encouragement and indication of divine approval. *The coming* (or *ensuing*) *night*, the corresponding phrase to that in 7, 26. 16, 11. 20, 15. 21, 18. The night here meant is that which followed the exciting scenes described in vs. 1–10. *The Lord*, i. e. the Lord Jesus Christ, as in 22, 8. 10. 16. 19. *Standing by* (or *over*) *him*, perhaps as he lay upon his bed, though not necessarily in a dream, but rather in a waking vision. *Be of good cheer* (or *courage*), be courageous, cheerful. Such exhortations do not necessarily imply excessive or unusual dejection, but are simply assurances of the divine favour and approval. As if he had said, 'Be not troubled or discouraged by this opposition and rejection of thy testimony; it is enough that I approve and will reward thee.' The last clause intimates that he had now performed his mission in Jerusalem, and must turn his face towards Rome for the same purpose. The length of time and various events which were to intervene of course formed no part of this soothing and encouraging disclosure. But what was the testimony thus approvingly referred to as already borne, if not that very utterance to which a sentimental age would now attach the sense of an apology for hasty language and unbridled temper, and that last appeal to Pharisaic orthodoxy, which the scrupulous morality of modern sceptics brands as Jesuitical. If Paul's address to the people was a part of his apostolic testimony, so of course was his defence before the Sanhedrim, and nothing can be more unreasonable than the supposition of his having interrupted this official witness-bearing with a burst of sinful anger, except the supposition that in case he did so, his testimony would have been approved, as it appears to be in this verse, without qualification or reserve. This clause is not a simple warning that he was to suffer in Rome as he had done in Jerusalem, but a promise that having now discharged his functions in the Holy City, he should complete his work as the Apostle of the Gentiles, by appearing in that character at Rome itself.

12. And when it was day, certain of the Jews banded together, and bound themselves under a curse, saying that they would neither eat nor drink till they had killed Paul.

It being (or *having become*) *day*, *certain of the Jews*, or according to the oldest text, simply *the Jews*, these zealots representing really the spirit and temper of the whole contemporary generation. *Banded together*, literally, *made a combination*, the same Greek word that is used above, in 19, 40, and there rendered *concourse*, but here more nearly corresponding to the kindred term *concurrence*, i. e. concert and collusion. *Bound themselves under a curse*, in Greek *anathematized themselves*, i. e. pronounced themselves anathema or cursed of God, unless they executed this engagement. *Anathema* originally means a deposit, then more particularly something set up or suspended in a temple as a votive offering. Among the Jews it seems to have been used to represent a Hebrew word denoting an irrevocable vow, or something consecrated either to God's special service or to irremissible destruction. (Compare the usage of the Hebrew noun, Lev. 27, 21. 28. 29. Num. 18, 14. Deut. 7, 26. 13, 18. 1 Kings 20, 42. Isai. 34, 5. Zech. 14, 11. Mal. 3, 24.) Later ecclesiastical usage gave it the sense of excommunication, as in the ancient formula by which the councils of the church condemned essential errors, or denounced the man by whom they were believed or taught, (ἀνάθεμα ἔστω) "let him be anathema," a custom founded on the words of Paul in Gal. 1, 8. 9 (compare Rom. 9, 3. 1 Cor. 12, 3. 16, 22.) By such a curse these Jews had bound themselves, i. e. they had invoked the curse upon themselves if they should prove false to the pledge which they had given. *Saying* (promising, engaging) *neither to eat nor drink*, an ancient form of oath or vow, of which we have examples in 1 Sam. 14, 24. 2 Sam. 3, 35. By engaging to abstain from the most essential act or means of life until their promise was redeemed, they gave the strongest proof of their sincerity, and at the same time the most potent stimulus to prompt and energetic action on their own part.

13. 14. And they were more than forty which had made this conspiracy; and they came to the chief priests and elders, and said, We have bound ourselves under a great curse, that we will eat nothing until we have slain Paul.

That this was not a scheme for the commission of an ordinary murder, is evinced by two things, first, that it was not the act of one or two desperadoes, but the joint resolution of no less than forty, probably well known in the community. The other reason is that it was not kept secret, but submitted to the Sanhedrim, whose tacit approbation gives it both a national and religious character. We have here a specimen of that fanatical yet conscientious zealotry, which ultimately brought about the downfall of Jerusalem (see above, on v. 5, and compare 1, 13. 21, 20.) We learn from Josephus, that this bigoted and sanguinary zeal was gradually ripening for years before the great catastrophe. The repetition in the last clause seems designed to show the grave deliberation and formality with which they set about their task, not as a crime, but as a pious act by which they thought to do God service, as predicted by our Lord himself (John 16, 2.) *To taste nothing* may be simply equivalent to *neither eat nor drink* in v.

12 (see above, on 10, 10. 20, 11), but the idea naturally suggested is that of still more total and exclusive abstinence.

15. Now therefore ye with the council signify to the chief captain that he bring him down unto you tomorrow, as though ye would inquire something more perfectly concerning him; and we, or ever he come near, are ready to kill him.

The Chief Priests and Elders were not only made acquainted with this plot, but summoned to take part in it, not as individuals but as a body, by bringing Paul into the power of his murderers through false representations to his Roman protector. It was evidently by a vote or act of the whole council that this plausible request was to be made, as it was founded on Paul's previous appearance in that body, and perhaps upon the fact that he had not obtained a hearing, which these zealots now propose to grant him, but with the avowed determination not to let him even reach the council hall alive. The same thing is suggested by the word translated *signify*, which properly denotes a formal or official notice. Some suppose that this flagitious proposition was made only to the Chief Priests and elders of the Sadducean party, as the Pharisees had openly espoused Paul's cause. But as this effect was owing to a momentary impulse, and as both parties afterwards accused him before Felix (see below, on 24, 15), it is better to make no limitation not suggested by the text or context. *Bring him down*, from the tower of Antonia to the council-chamber, probably within the enclosure of the temple (see above, on v. 10.) *As* (*if*) *about* (or *intending*) *to know thoroughly* (or *ascertain*) *more accurately* (or *exactly*) *the* (*things*) *concerning* (or *about*) *him.* For the use of the Greek adverb, which is never accurately rendered in our version, see above, on 18, 25. 26, and compare the corresponding noun in 22, 3. *Or ever*, an old English phrase, precisely equivalent to *before. Ready to kill*, or ready for the killing, an unusual construction and peculiarly expressive. The proposal was not to despatch him in the council, but to relieve that body of the whole responsibility, by killing him while still afar off. If the Sanhedrim assented to this proposition, they were guilty of the grossest hypocrisy, as well as of complicity in the proposed murder.

16. And when Paul's sister's son heard of their lying in wait, he went and entered into the castle, and told Paul.

The execution of the plot is prevented by its premature disclosure to the Romans. The providential instrument of this disclosure was a relative of Paul himself, not elsewhere mentioned, and the blank attached to whose name it is vain to fill with fanciful conjectures, as for instance, that his mother, the companion of Paul's childhood, was residing in Jerusalem, or that he was sent there, as his uncle had been, to receive his education; or that he accompanied him on this journey. Not only is there nothing gained by such conjectures, but they really detract from the air of authenticity imparted to all narratives by unexplained and incidental reference to facts intrinsically not improbable though often wholly unimportant. (See above, on 20, 13.) What is more natural and likely than that Paul should have a nephew, otherwise unknown to history, but providentially employed to baffle the designs of his bloodthirsty enemies? *Their lying in wait*, literally, the *ambuscade* or *ambush*, not in the figurative sense of plot, but with a literal allusion to their plan of watching for him and despatching him while on the way. *Heard of* seems to imply that it had come to him by rumour, or that he had overheard their secret plottings. But the Greek text simply represents him as *hearing the* (plan of) *ambuscade* itself, i. e. hearing it proposed in some assembly, probably the Sanhedrim, as stated in v. 14. The whole affair appears to have been publicly concerted, at least so far as related to the Jews, the only concealment necessary being from the prisoner himself and from his Roman guardians. The providential fact that a near relative of Paul was in the midst of them, and in attendance on their meetings, was of course unknown to them and unsuspected; yet to this was owing the defeat of the whole project. *Entered into the castle*, which was probably accessible to any person, but especially to Paul's friends, as we know to have been the case at Cesarea (see below, on 24, 23.) *Told him*, reported to him, brought him word, the same word that is used above in 4, 23. 5, 22. 25. 11, 13. 12, 14. 17. 15, 27. 16, 36.

17. Then Paul called one of the centurions unto (him), and said, Bring this young man unto the chief captain, for he hath a certain thing to tell him.

The graphic minuteness with which all the details of this transaction are recorded may be due to Paul's own vivid recollection of the scene, but still more naturally seem to imply that the historian witnessed it himself, although we have no certain information whether Luke was with Paul till the time of his setting sail from Palestine to Italy (see below, on 27, 1), when the use of the first person is again resumed (see above, on 16, 10. 20, 5.) *One of the centurions* on duty near him, or perhaps in charge of him (see above, on 22, 25.) *Bring*, literally, *take* (or *lead*) *away*, implying that the Tribune was not close at hand. *This youth*, the word applied to Paul himself upon his first appearance in the history (see above, on 7, 58.) *To tell him*, or report to him, as in the close of the preceding verse.

18. So he took him, and brought (him) to the chief captain, and said, Paul the prisoner called me unto (him), and prayed me to bring this young man unto thee, who hath something to say unto thee.

The deference paid to Paul's request may have been partly owing to humanity and partly to an interest in his mysterious character and mission, but perhaps more than either to his recognition as a Roman citizen (see above, on 22, 25. 26.) *The prisoner Paul* may mean no more than that he was confined to the precincts of the camp or castle; but it may be, that the bonds, which are described as loosed in 22, 30, had been now replaced and that he was again chained to a soldier (see above, on 12, 6. 21, 33.) *Calling me to (him) asked*, may have been intended to suggest that the centurion had not volunteered his services or begun the conversation, which might have seemed to show too great an interest in the prisoner and too familiar an acquaintance with him. *Bring* is the strict translation of the verb here used, which is the simple uncompounded form of that employed in the preceding verse. *Who hath*, literally, *having*, an active participle which agrees grammatically with *young man* or *youth*.

19. Then the chief captain took him by the hand, and went (with him) aside privately, and asked (him), What is that thou hast to tell me?

Taking his hand, or *taking him by the hand*, a mark of

affability and kindness, which are not so strange and misplaced in a Roman officer of rank, as to imply a special divine influence compelling him to act in opposition to his real dispositions, although this, as well as every other part of the transaction, was undoubtedly controlled and ordered by an all-wise Providence, as means to an important end. *Aside privately*, are not in Greek two adverbs in immediate juxtaposition; but the former is included in the compound verb, which means to withdraw or retire (compare Matt. 4, 12. 12, 15. Mark 3, 7. John 6, 15), and from which, in its later application, is derived the English *anchorite*. *Privately*, apart, alone. The seeming eagerness of this interrogation is explained not only by Paul's sending him, but also by the commander's anxious wish to know the cause of Paul's arrest, and also perhaps the state of public feeling. No military service, probably, was ever more solicitous or harassing than that of Roman officers in Palestine, at this eventful epoch, when the whole nation was in such a state of feverish mobility, that a popular outbreak might be daily looked for. This anxiety was naturally heightened, in the case before us, by imperfect information and a want of personal acquaintance with the language and the institutions of the country. It would be amusing to observe the symptoms of this ignorant solicitude, combined with great professional sagacity and promptness, and with traits of natural nobility, if it were not all connected with the painful trials of the great Apostle, and the fearful doom impending over Israel.

20. And he said, The Jews have agreed to desire thee that thou wouldest bring down Paul to-morrow into the council, as though they would inquire somewhat of him more perfectly.

Although the facts had all been previously stated, they are here repeated, no doubt in the very words employed by Paul's nephew, who most probably addressed both his uncle and the officer in Greek. *The Jews* again implies that this was only a fortuitous display of the spirit which now governed the whole nation (see above, on v. 12.) *Agreed*, literally, *put together* or *combined*, i. e. concerted or devised a plan. (Compare the use of the same verb in Luke 22, 5. John 9, 22.) *To ask*, desire, or request (see above, on v. 18. 3, 3. 10, 48. 16, 39. 18, 20), implying that they could not claim it as a right, or at least chose to ask it as a favour. *As though*, &c., precisely as in v. 15, except that *know* is here exchanged for *inquire*, both verbs in Greek usage meaning secondarily *to ascertain*.

21. But do not thou yield unto them; for there lie in wait for him of them more than forty men, which have bound themselves with an oath, that they will neither eat nor drink till they have killed him; and now are they ready, looking for a promise from thee.

But should be *then* or *therefore*, i. e. because the real motive of their plausible request is what he then proceeds to state. *Yield to them*, literally, *be persuaded by them*, as in 5, 40, where it is translated by the verb *agreed*. *Lie in wait*, the verb corresponding to the noun in v. 16 above. *Of them*, literally, *out of*, from among them, which again implies that there was nothing peculiar in the spirit or the conduct of these forty zealots, but that they were merely representatives and agents of all Israel. *Bound with an oath*, the same verb that is rendered, *bound under a curse* in v. 12, but in the margin, *with an oath of execration*. *That they will*, &c., literally, *neither to eat nor drink*. *Killed*, not the verb used in vs. 12. 14, but that in v. 15, and often elsewhere, corresponding very nearly to *despatch* or *make away with* (see above, on 2, 23. 22, 20.) *Looking for* (i. e. expecting or awaiting) *a promise* (i. e. an assent to their proposal, an agreement to produce Paul as they wished.) Some prefer the sense of *order*, others that of *notice* or *announcement*, both which are agreeable to Classical but not to Hellenistic usage, or at least not to that of the New Testament, in which it always means a promise. For the usage of the book before us, see above, on 1, 4. 2, 33. 39. 7, 17. 13, 23.)

22. So the chief captain (then) let the young man depart, and charged (him, See thou) tell no man that thou hast shewed these things to me.

So then the chiliarch dismissed the youth, charging (or *having charged*, i. e. strictly ordered) *him*. (For the meaning of the first verb, see above, on 3, 13. 4, 21. 23. 5, 40. 13, 3. 15, 30. 33. 16, 35. 36. 17, 9. 19, 41; for that of the second, on 1, 4. 4, 18. 5, 28. 40. 10, 42. 15, 5. 16, 18. 23. 17, 30.) The

English version changes the construction for the sake of uniformity, the Greek abruptly passing from the third to the first and second persons. *Charging him to tell no one, that thou hast disclosed these (things) to me.* The same end might have been secured by inserting *saith he*, as in 1, 4. *To tell*, or more exactly, *to speak out*, or as we say in English, *let out*. *Disclosed*, the verb translated *signify* in v. 15 above. This prohibition was of course intended to gain time for sending Paul away, before the zealots knew that their design had been betrayed.

23. And he called unto (him) two centurions, saying, Make ready two hundred soldiers to go to Cesarea, and horsemen threescore and ten, and spearmen two hundred, at the third hour of the night—

Calling to (him) some (or *certain*) *two* (an idiomatic phrase not easily expressed in English) *of the centurions* (under his command, of whom there were usually ten in a legion, as denoted by the titles, *chiliarch*, commander of a thousand, and *centurion*, commander of a hundred men. (See above, on 10, 1. 21, 31.) *Make ready* is in Greek a single word, *prepare*, provide. *Soldiers*, when absolutely used, denotes the heavy-armed infantry of ancient warfare. *To* (as far as) *Cesarea*, on the Mediterranean coast, the Roman capital of Judea. (See above, on 8, 40. 9, 30. 10, 1. 24. 11, 11. 12, 19. 18, 22. 21, 8. 16.) Since the death of Herod Agrippa, recorded in this book (see above, on 12, 23), Judea had again become a part of the great Roman province of Syria, and was governed by deputies (or procurators) of the Syrian proconsul. *Spearmen* is in Greek a word occurring nowhere else in ancient Greek, supposed by some to be a term in popular but not in written use, apparently compounded of *right hand* and *take*, and variously explained as meaning those who take the right hand of the king, or of the general, or of the army; or those who take a weapon in the right hand, as a spear or dart; while one of the oldest manuscripts presents a different form compounded of *right hand* and *cast* or *throw*, a reading also found in the Peshito or old Syriac version. It is now commonly agreed that it denotes some kind of light troops, as distinguished from the heavy infantry and cavalry which are separately mentioned. Surprise has sometimes been expressed that so large a force should have been needed to protect Paul against forty zealots. But besides that these were only representatives of the popular feeling in Jerusalem, the country was at this time in a most unsettled state, and travelling particularly dangerous to strangers. *At* (literally, *from*, i. e. beginning, setting out from) *the third hour of the night*, according to the Roman computation, about nine o'clock of our time (see above, on 2, 15. 3, 1. 10, 3. 9. 30.) This was late enough to escape observation, and early enough to give them a long night-journey.

24. And provide (them) beasts, that they may set Paul on, and bring (him) safe unto Felix the governor.

Beasts too (τε) *to provide* (or *furnish*), i. e. riding animals, horses, mules, or asses. *That mounting Paul, they might bring* (*him*) *safe* (literally, *save him through*) *to Felix the governor.* The last word is generic (meaning leader or a leading man) and applied in Greek to any class of Roman governors. *Claudius Felix*, or *Antonius Felix*, as the different historians call him, perhaps because he was a freedman or emancipated slave of the emperor Claudius and also of his mother Antonia. His brother Pallas was a favourite of Nero, and through his influence Felix was made Procurator of Judea, at first either jointly with Cumanus or alone. He is described by his contemporaries as a cruel, avaricious and licentious man. Tacitus, in one of his most famous sentences, exhibits him as one who exercised the power of a king in the spirit of a slave. He showed great energy, however, in suppressing the commotions of the country, and especially in quelling the insurgent zealots, commonly called thieves or robbers, but not in the ordinary sense of the expression. (Compare Matt. 21, 13. 26, 55. 27, 38. Luke 10, 30. John 10, 1. 8. 18, 40. 2 Cor. 11, 26.) On the other hand, he hired assassins to kill Jonathan the High Priest, to whose influence he partly owed his own appointment.

25. 26. And he wrote a letter after this manner: Claudius Lysias unto the most excellent governor Felix (sendeth) greeting.

Writing (or *having written*) *an epistle containing this type*, i. e form of words, though some prefer the opposite sense of sketch or draught, as distinguished from the very words, in which sense the term is said to be employed by Plato. V. 26 discloses, for the first time, and in a very natural and simple way, the name of the Tribune or Chief Captain, with whom the narrative has made us so familiar. Both names are common, one in Latin, one in Greek, which last is supposed by some to have been his native language, as he was only a Roman citizen by purchase (see above, on 22, 28.) As Greek was in such extensive use, there is no need of supposing that this letter is translated from the Latin. It is not impossible that Paul obtained it at the time from Felix or the officer in charge of him, though some suppose that it was sent to Rome and Luke there found it in the public archives. *Most excellent*, the word so rendered in Luke 1, 3, and *most noble* in 24, 3. 26, 25 below. It was a title of respect to public officers, like *honourable*, *right honourable*, *excellency*, *etc.* *Sendeth greeting*, literally, *to rejoice*, the usual salutatory formula in Greek epistles, used above in that from the council at Jerusalem to the Syrian and Cilician churches, and also in that of the Apostle James (see above, on 15, 23, and compare James 1, 1.)

27. This man was taken of the Jews, and should have been killed of them; then came I with an army, and rescued him, having understood that he was a Roman.

The original construction is, *this man, having been seized by the Jews, &c., I rescued him*, the last pronoun being pleonastic. *Should have been killed* is now an equivocal expression, which might seem to mean, he ought to have been killed, whereas the Greek means simply, *and about to be dispatched* (for the usage of the two verbs, see above, on vs. 15. 21.) *Then came I*, literally, *standing over*, the same verb that occurs above in v. 11, but here applied to sudden attack, as in 4, 1. 6, 12. 7, 5. *With an army*, with the garrison, the forces under his command (see above, on v. 10, where it is translated *soldiers.*) *Rescued*, literally, *took out* (or *away*) *from them* (see above, on 7, 10. 34. 12, 11, where *deliver* or *delivered* is the English version.) *Having learned* (or *learning*) *that he is a Roman.* This inaccurate expression has been often represented as a wilful falsehood on the part of Claudius Lysias, intended to conceal his own precipitate treatment of a Roman citizen and at the same time to display his zeal for the honour of the Roman name. But this elaborate invention, which a word from Paul or the accompanying soldiers would have instantly refuted, is far less natural and likely than the supposition of mere negligence, precisely such as a commanding officer might readily fall into, when reporting his own actions. As he did eventually save a Roman citizen from Jewish fury, he could scarcely be expected to report his first mistake and subsequent correction. This very negligence, in point of fact as well as of expression, is a much stronger proof of authenticity than that afforded by the supposed falsehood.

28. 29. And when I would have known the cause wherefore they accused him, I brought him forth into their council: whom I perceived to be accused of questions of their law, but to have nothing laid to his charge worthy of death or of bonds.

Wishing to know the cause for which (or *on account of which*) *they were accusing him, I brought him forth* (literally, *down*, as in vs. 15. 20, and in 22, 30) *into their council*, consistory, *synedrion*, of which *sanhedrim* is a corruption (see above, on 4, 15.) *Perceived*, literally, *found*, discovered, with an implication of surprise and novelty. *Accused of questions* seems to represent the questions as themselves the crimes of which he was accused; whereas the meaning is, *accused concerning questions*, i. e. charged with crimes involving or relating to such questions (or discussions) of their law, the law of Moses, the whole Jewish system. *But having no charge* (i. e. being charged with nothing) *worthy of death or bonds* (i. e. confinement or imprisonment.) Compare this Roman estimate of Jewish strifes with that of Gallio (in 18, 14. 15), and that of Festus (in 25, 18. 19.)

30. And when it was told me how that the Jews laid wait for the man, I sent straightway to thee, and gave commandment to his accusers also to say before thee what (they had) against him. Farewell.

But a plot against the man having been reported to me, (*as*) *about* (or *that it was about*) *to be* (attempted) *by the*

Jews. For the word *plot*, see above, on 9, 24. 20, 3. 19; *reported*, compare John 11, 57. 1 Cor. 10, 28.) *To be* (or come into existence) *by* (or on the part of) *the Jews*, is an unusual construction, both in Greek and English; but the sense is plain. *At once* (forthwith, the word employed in 10, 33. 11, 11. 21, 32), without further hesitation or delay. *Having charged* (or *ordered*, the verb used above in v. 22) *the accusers also, to say the* (*things*) *concerning* (or *against*) *him before thee*, a peculiar phrase appropriated to judicial hearing, as in Matt. 28, 14, where the meaning is, *if this come to be heard before the governor*, or tried at his tribunal. The order mentioned in this verse was no doubt given after Paul's departure, but before the letter could reach Felix, and is therefore mentioned in the past tense, not with an intention to deceive, but in accordance with ancient epistolary usage, which has reference in such forms to the time of reading, not of composition. *Farewell*, be strong or healthy, the usual concluding formula of Greek epistles (see above, on 15, 29, where the plural of the same Greek word occurs.)

31. Then the soldiers, as it was commanded them, took Paul, and brought (him) by night to Antipatris.

The danger being greatest near Jerusalem, a large part of the military escort only went about two-thirds of the distance, leaving Paul to be conducted to his journey's end by the smallest of the three divisions, which was mounted. *Soldiers*, in the first clause, may be used generically for the whole detachment, or specifically, as in v. 23, for the heavy-armed infantry, who constituted the main force of every Roman army, whether large or small. In favour of the latter explanation is the form of expression in the first clause of v. 32. *So then*, as in v. 22, i. e. accordingly, in execution of these plans and orders. *As it was* (literally, *according to the thing*) *commanded them*, referring to the orders before given (see above, on vs. 23. 24.) *Took*, or more exactly, *taking up*, which is not only the original and proper sense of the Greek verb, but its invariable usage in this book (see above, on 1, 2. 11, 22. 7, 43. 10, 16. 20, 13. 14.) It may here have reference to Paul's being mounted (see above, on v. 24.) *Commanded*, not the verb employed in vs. 22. 30, but the one used in 7, 44. 18, 2. 20, 13, and originally meaning to arrange, with special application to military disposition or array, in which sense it may here be taken, as the orders had specific reference to the arrangements of the march and escort. *Brought*, led, conducted, as in vs. 10. 18 (compare 21, 34. 22. 24.) *By night*, literally, *through* (or *in the course of*) *the night* (see above, on 1, 3. 16, 9), which naturally seems to mean the first night, or the same night upon which they set out. *To* (or *into*) *Antipatris*, according to Josephus anciently called Capher Saba, but rebuilt by Herod the Great and named in honour of his father, Antipater the Idumean. The Crusaders identified it with a town upon the sea-coast; but the description in Josephus shows that it must have been some miles in the interior. He also speaks of it as situated on a stream; but this may have been nothing more than an occasional or temporary torrent flowing through the adjacent valley from the mountains. If so, there can be no doubt that the place is that described by Smith and Robinson, and still called by the ancient name, though partially concealed by needless variations of orthography. This is one of the most striking and instructive instances of old names surviving, in the local or popular tradition, those which had displaced them by authority or in the dialect of books, eighteen hundred years ago. According to the old itineraries, Antipatris was twenty-six Roman miles from Cesarea, and forty-two from Jerusalem. On the ground that this distance was too great to be accomplished, even by a forced march, in a single night, some suppose that the night meant is the second after their departure from Jerusalem, which seems to make the time as much too long; others, that the chief part of the journey was performed at night, but that they arrived at Cesarea in the course of the next day.

32. 33. On the morrow they left the horsemen to go with him, and returned to the castle; who, when they came to Cesarea, and delivered the epistle to the governor, presented Paul also before him.

The meaning of the first phrase, *on the morrow* (or *the next day*), will depend of course upon that of the one just explained in the preceding verse. According to the sense there preferred, the day here meant will be either the first or second after their departure from Jerusalem. *Left*, or more exactly, *let*, i. e. suffered or permitted (as in 5, 38. 14, 16. 16, 7. 19, 30) *the horsemen to go* (go on, proceed, or journey, as in v. 23, and in 8, 26. 9, 3. 16, 7. 17, 14. 19, 21. 20, 1. 21, 5. 22, 5. 21.) The grammatical subject is the same as in v. 31, to wit, *the soldiers*, who are here distinguished from the *horsemen*, and must therefore have the more restricted meaning in both cases. The spearmen or light infantry are not here mentioned, but as being an auxiliary force they probably accompanied the main force on its return to its camp or quarters in the castle of Antonia (see above, on 21, 34. 37. 22, 24. 23, 10. 16.) There is something in the promptness and precision of these movements, both as to the order and its execution, that is perfectly in keeping with all that we know otherwise of the Roman discipline, and therefore the less likely to have been invented by a Greek physician, or any other foreign and unmilitary writer. *Who*, at the beginning of v. 33, refers back to *horsemen* in v. 32, a syntax less abrupt in the original, because the pronoun here employed, though often used precisely like the simple relative (as in vs. 14. 21 above), sometimes refers to the remoter antecedent (as in 17, 11), or resumes an interrupted construction (as in 21, 4.)

34. 35. And when the governor had read (the letter), he asked of what province he was. And when he understood that (he was) of Cilicia, I will hear thee, said he, when thine accusers are also come. And he commanded him to be kept in Herod's judgment hall.

The governor is not found in the oldest manuscripts and latest critical editions, but is readily supplied from the preceding verse. *Reading* (or *having read*), perhaps aloud, as an official form, which is the stricter and more ancient application of the verb in Greek, though afterwards employed (like the corresponding verb in Hebrew, which originally means to *call*) even in reference to silent reading. (See above, on 8, 28. 30. 32. 13, 27. 15, 21. 31.) The object of the verb is not expressed but easily supplied, to wit, *the letter*, mentioned in v. 33, or the pronoun *it*, referring to the same. *Having asked*, not merely out of private curiosity, but in a judicial or official way, as seems to be suggested by the Greek verb, which is that employed in 5, 27, and there explained (but see above, on 1, 6.) *Province, eparchy*, the domain, jurisdiction of an *eparch*, a term used by the later Greek historians to denote the Roman ruler of a conquered country. *He was*, or more exactly, *is*, the direct form of narration being gradually substituted for the indirect, as in v. 22 above, but less abruptly; or the present tense may be intended to call up the scene as actually passing (see above, on vs. 5. 6, and compare 7, 25. 9, 26. 38. 12, 9. 19, 34. 22, 29.) *Having learned* (or ascertained) by inquiry, which the verb itself denotes (see above, on vs. 19. 20, and compare 4, 7. 10, 18. 29. 21, 33), and which is here expressly mentioned in the clause immediately preceding. *That* (*he is* or *was*) *of* (or more exactly *from*, i. e. belonging to, as in 6, 9. 10, 23. 14, 19. 15, 5. 19. 17, 13. 21, 16. 27) *Cilicia* (see above, on 6, 9. 15, 23. 41. 21, 39. 22, 3.) *Hear thee*, or more emphatically, *hear thee through*, i. e. examine thy whole case from the beginning, as the Roman magistrates were required to do, by a law still extant in the Pandects of Justinian, when a prisoner was sent from an inferior tribunal or authority, with a statement of the charge against him, technically called *elogium*. (*Qui cum elogio mittuntur ex integro audiendi sunt.*) The hearing meant is therefore a judicial audience and investigation. (See above, on v. 30, and compare the place in Matthew there referred to, where the simple verb *to hear* has the same judicial meaning.) *Thy accusers*, the Jews mentioned in the letter of Claudius Lysias, as having been directed to appear before the Procurator (see above, on v. 30.) *Are come*, are present, on the ground, arrived, the same verb that is used in v. 16, and often elsewhere (see above, on 5, 21. 9, 26. 10, 32. 11, 23. 13, 14. 14, 27. 15, 4. 17, 10. 18, 27. 20, 18. 21, 18.) The connection of these clauses is historical not logical, as some suppose, who understand Luke as saying that Felix would not undertake to hear the case, until he knew that Paul was of Cilicia; just as Pilate, when he heard that Christ was of Galilee, sent him to be tried by Herod (Luke 23, 7.) But the cases are not parallel, as Felix only ruled Judea as a deputy (or procurator, see above, on vs. 23. 24), and had no authority whatever in Cilicia. His question in relation to Paul's province is to be connected, not with what follows but with what precedes, that is to say, with the statement which he had just read in the *elogium* of Claudius Lysias, that Paul was a Roman citizen, and as such probably enrolled or registered in some division of the empire, to determine which the question was proposed, and not as a condition of the promise in the next clause, which was not dependent upon Paul's nativity or residence, but absolutely binding as a part of the governor's official duty. *He com-*

manded him too (τε) *to be kept* (or guarded as a prisoner, see above, on 12, 4) *in the Praetorium of Herod.* The *Praetorium* was originally the commander's tent in an encampment (from the ancient military sense of *Praetor*), but the term was afterwards applied to the official residence of governors, and finally to any large palatial building. Here, no doubt it has the second of these senses, and denotes the palace of the Roman governor at Cesarea, at this time actually occupied by Felix. It is probably called *Herod's*, because built by Herod the Great, or perhaps by his grandson Herod Agrippa, for his own use when the sovereign of the country, and the scene of his melancholy death; for although smitten in the theatre, he lingered five or six days, both which circumstances are recorded by Josephus and entirely consistent with Luke's narrative (see above, on 12, 23.) When Judea was again annexed to Syria and consigned to Procurators (see above, on v. 23), this palace of the former kings at Cesarea would of course become the official residence of their successors, and from them most probably derived the Latin name by which it is described in this verse. From these local statements, and from what is said in 24, 23 below, it is plain that Paul, although under confinement or arrest, was not committed to a common prison.

CHAPTER XXIV.

This chapter contains Paul's third Apology or self-defence, delivered before Felix (1–21), and his subsequent transactions with that governor (22–27.) He is formally accused by the High Priest and Elders through an advocate (1–4.) The charges are the old ones of sedition, schism, and sacrilege (5. 6.) There is also a complaint of the Chief Captain's interference, and a reference to him for further information, with a full assent to all these statements, on the part of the Jews present (7–9.) Paul congratulates himself on the Procurator's knowledge of the country and the people, states the time and purpose of his visit to Jerusalem, denies the charge of having disturbed the public peace, and all the other charges brought against him (10–13.) He then more positively defines his relation to the Jewish Church and the Theocracy (14–16.) He then recurs to the time and purpose of his coming, tells how and where he was arrested, complains of the absence of his first accusers, and challenges those present to bring any other charge against him (17–21.) Felix, perceiving how the matter stands, postpones it, and commands Paul to be mildly treated (22–23.) To gratify his wife, he summons Paul again before him, not to defend himself, but to explain the new religion, in hearing which his conscience is alarmed and he remands the prisoner (24–25.) During the next two years he often talks with him, but only for the purpose of extorting money, failing in which attempt, and anxious to conciliate the Jews at the close of his administration, he leaves Paul still a prisoner at his departure (26–27.)

1. And after five days Ananias the high priest descended with the elders, and (with) a certain orator (named) Tertullus, who informed the governor against Paul.

The *five days* have been variously reckoned from Paul's arrival in Cesarea, and from the order given to the Sanhedrim (see above, on 23, 30); but nothing of historical or exegetical importance is dependent on this question, though the mention of the fact is an incidental proof of authenticity. *Descended*, went down, from Jerusalem to Cesarea, implying both a physical and moral difference of elevation (see above, on 9, 32. 18, 22, and often elsewhere.) *The High Priest Ananias*, who was previously mentioned in the same terms (see above, on 23, 2.) Even here, though natural, it is not necessary, to explain the title in its strictest sense, as a well known chief priest (or former high priest) might be sent to represent the actual incumbent, more conveniently perhaps than he could leave Jerusalem himself. The necessity for this interpretation, however, is removed if, according to the latest investigations, Josephus does represent Ananias as acquitted and sent back from Rome, and still retaining his High Priesthood. He is then to be regarded here as representing, not an official superior, but the whole Sanhedrim and nation. *With the elders*, or as several of the oldest manuscripts and versions have it, *some* (or *certain*) *elders*, which is no doubt implied (though not expressed) in the received text, as the whole Presbytery, or estate of elders (see above, on 4, 5. 22, 5), could appear at Cesarea only by their delegates. *A certain orator*, a Greek word originally meaning *speaker*, but specially applied to public speakers in the national assemblies, then to advocates, and finally to teachers of eloquence or *rhetoricians*, a word derived from that here used. It is here used, no doubt, in the last but one of these senses, to denote what the Romans called an *orator forensis* or *causidicus*. From the name *Tertullus* (a diminutive of *Tertius*, like Catullus from Catius, and Lucullus from Lucius), and the well-known custom, to which Cicero refers, of young Romans practising at first in the provinces before they ventured to appear at home, some have inferred that the advocate here mentioned was of this description, and that he must have spoken in Latin. But the Jews of that age, and of every other till the present time, have been so accustomed to bear Gentile names, that nothing can be gathered from this circumstance with certainty (see above, on 1, 13. 23. 6, 5. 13, 9. 17, 7. 18, 2. 7.) And even if Tertullus was a Roman, there was nothing strange in their employing him to plead their cause before a Roman magistrate, especially if (as Valerius Maximus affirms) the Latin language was employed in all the tribunals of the empire, even Greeks and orientals being forced to use it or to plead through an interpreter. On the other hand, a later Greek historian (Dio Cassius) represents his own tongue as continually heard in the Senate and the courts of Rome itself. Both statements may be reconciled, not only by referring them to different dates, but even at the same time by supposing such a joint use of the languages as now exists in Canada and Louisiana, where speeches are delivered, in the same assemblies, on the same occasions, both in French and English. *Who*, the relative employed above in 23, 14. 21. 33, and here intended to include the remoter antecedent (*Ananias*) as well as the nearer (*the elders* and *Tertullus*), as taking part in the act described. *Informed*, in the forensic or judicial sense, of which we have examples in the English terms, *informer*, *criminal information*, *etc.* The Greek verb literally means to *show* or make appear, and is the same with that employed in 23, 15. 22. The Geneva version (*appeared before the governor*) is inconsistent both with the form and usage of the Greek word. Whether this information was in writing or by word of mouth, is not determined by the narrative, and happily of no importance. The original expression may include both modes of accusation, i. e. written charges amplified in oral argument, an English parallel to which is furnished by the technical and popular sense of the word *pleading*.

2. And when he was called forth, Tertullus began to accuse (him), saying, Seeing that by thee we enjoy great quietness, and that very worthy deeds are done unto this nation by thy providence—

He (Paul) *having been called* (cited or summoned to appear), according to the Roman law, which suffered no man to be judged without a hearing and an opportunity of self-defence (see below, on 25, 16.) *Began to accuse* is not a pleonasm (see above, on 1, 1. 2, 4. 11, 4. 18, 26), but may be intended to suggest that only the beginning of Tertullus's oration is recorded, at least with any fulness, the rest being given in a summary or abstract. As if he had said, 'Tertullus then accused him in a speech, of which the exordium was as follows.' This exordium is an apt example of the conciliatory introduction (*captatio benevolentiae*) prescribed by Cicero and other rhetoricians, and from its very nature complimentary, so that the charges of gross flattery and lying, brought by almost all interpreters against Tertullus, although not without foundation, are a little overcharged, as will appear from the particulars recorded in the next verse.

3. We accept (it) always, and in all places, most noble Felix, with all thankfulness.

The change of collocation in the version partially conceals the rhetorical and classical form of the original, which opens with the leading or emphatic words, *Much peace enjoying through thee, etc.* *Peace*, not in the vague sense of prosperity, nor even in the more precise one of tranquillity or quiet, but in the proper and specific one of freedom or deliverance from war and the commotions which attend it. To such disturbances the Holy Land had long been subject (see above, on 23, 12. 23), partly from religious causes, and in quelling them Felix had been active and successful, having seized and sent to Rome a famous robber (i. e. zealot or guerilla partisan) named Eleazar, besides suppressing the rebellion spoken of in 21, 38 above, and other prompt and energetic measures mentioned by Josephus. For these administrative acts the terms here used by Tertullus can scarcely be regarded as extravagant, or certainly not more so than was warranted by Greek and Roman usage. That the crimes of Felix are not also set forth, is a negative objection, which applies with equal force to the Apology of Paul himself. Nothing is gained by these exaggerated charges of deception, even against wicked men, which are often copied by one writer from another, till they finally almost become as disingenuous as that by which they were at first provoked. Apart from these traditional invectives, the oration of Tertullus is an average sample of forensic adulation in all ages. *Enjoying*, or obtaining, lighting upon, happening to acquire or be possessed of. (See above, on 19, 11, where the participle of the same verb is employed to denote what usually happens and is therefore common.) *By* (or *through*) *thee*, by thy means or agency. *Very worthy deeds*, in Greek a single word denoting what is rightly done (*recte facta*, as Cicero defines it), but specially applied to martial achievements or exploits, and therefore here appropriate to the military or coercive measures which had just been mentioned. The Vulgate version (*multa corrigantur*), which makes it mean reformatory measures, rests upon another reading (διορθωμάτων for κατορθωμάτων) found in several of the oldest manuscripts, but not regarded by the critics as the true text. *Done*, happened, come to pass, or brought about, the same verb as in 23, 7. 9. 10. 12. *This nation* is supposed by some to imply necessarily that the speaker was a Gentile; but although the conclusion is probably correct, the proof is insufficient, as Paul uses an analogous expression (*this people*) in speaking to the Jews themselves (see above, on 13, 17.) *By* (or rather *through*) *thy providence* (or *foresight*) as an attribute of administrative wisdom. This was a favourite mode of flattery in that age, as appears from its occurrence on imperial coins (*Providentia Cæsaris*), a part of the idolatrous process, by which the Roman Emperors arrogated to themselves divine honours. *Always and everywhere*, or, preserving the original alliteration, *at all times and in all places*. Some connect this with what goes before, as a part of the description of the Procurator's merit, 'done to this nation through thy constant and universal providence;' but most interpreters connect it with what follows, *always and everywhere* (not merely now and in thy presence) *we accept*, and by implication thankfully acknowledge. (For the strong sense of the Greek verb, see above, on 2, 41. 15, 4. 18, 27.) *Most noble*, excellent, or honourable, the same honorary epithet employed by Claudius Lysias in his letter (see above, on 23, 26), and afterwards applied by Paul himself to Festus (see below, on 26, 25), as it is by Luke to the person for whom both his books were originally written (see above, on 1, 1, and compare Luke 1, 3.) But for these examples, the use of the term here would probably have been among the sins imputed to Tertullus. As the epithet relates to the office, not the person, it was just as appropriate to Felix as to Festus, although very different in moral character (see below, on v. 27.) *With all thankfulness*, or all the gratitude to which such favours are entitled, whether great or small, and therefore not to be denounced as hypocritical exaggeration. The Greek noun is used elsewhere only by Paul (e. g. 1 Cor. 14, 16. 1 Tim. 2, 1), and John (Rev. 4, 9. 7, 12), but in later ecclesiastical usage was applied specifically to the Lord's Supper or Communion, on account of the thanksgiving (*eucharist*) by which it was accompanied. In both these cases, it denotes not merely the internal feeling but its audible expression. (For the sense of *all*, as here used, see above, on 4, 29. 5, 23. 12, 11. 13, 10. 17, 11. 20, 19. 23, 1.)

4. Notwithstanding, that I be not further tedious unto thee, I pray thee that thou wouldest hear us of thy clemency a few words.

Notwithstanding indicates an opposition or antithesis which does not really exist, the Greek word being nothing but the usual continuative particle (δέ), so often rendered *but* or *and*. *That I may not more detain* (or *hinder*) *thee*, a verb originally meaning to *cut in* or *into*, then to stop one's way (as by a ditch), or cross one's path, to intercept, impede a person's progress. *I pray* (invite, exhort, beseech) *thee*, the verb so used in 8, 31. 9, 38. 13, 42. 16, 9. 15. 39. 19, 31. 21, 12. *To hear us*, the Jews, with whom he identifies himself, as actually being one of them, or as an advocate, who makes his client's cause his own. *Of thy clemency*, or in thy moderation and impartiality (compare the cognate adjective in Phil. 4, 5.) The essential idea is not so much that of kindness or gentleness, as that of fairness, reasonableness, freedom from extremes of every kind. This is a peculiarly judicial virtue, and is therefore pertinently here appealed to. *A few words* is in Greek an adverb, corresponding, both in etymology and sense, to our *concisely*, an abbreviated but intelligible phrase for *hear us speak concisely.* This promise to be brief might almost seem to have been caused by some appearance of impatience in the Procurator, at the prospect of a formal and elaborate harangue. There would then be no need of supposing that the rest of the oration has been less fully given than the introduction (see above, on v. 2), the difference, on that supposition, being not in the report but in the speech itself.

5. For we have found this man a pestilent (fellow), and a mover of sedition among all the Jews, throughout the world, and a ringleader of the sect of the Nazarenes—

The exordium being ended, he proceeds to the statement of the case itself. *For* may have reference to the request and implied promise in the verse preceding. 'We only ask your impartial attention to a few words; for all we have to say is, that having found, &c.' *A pest* (or *plague*), a natural and common figure in all languages for one who is at the same time troublesome and mischievous. It is so used by the two great orators, Demosthenes and Cicero, who speaks of different persons as the pest of the republic, of the state, and of the empire (*pestis reipublicae, civitatis, imperii.*) *Pestilent fellow,* though essentially correct, is a needless departure from the form of the original. *Finding* may either have its strict sense, and refer to their detection or discovery of Paul in the temple; or be taken in the secondary sense of ascertaining, finding out. Upon the meaning of this verb depends the construction of the clause, which may be either 'having found this man (who is) a pest,' or, 'having found this man (to be) a pest.' In either case, the syntax is irregular, the sentence having no finite verb, except in its relative dependent clause (see v. 6.) The sense is clear, however, and such freedom of expression may be found in the best writers of all languages, in whom it is frequently applauded as a beauty, while in Scripture it is censured as an imperfection. Here, however, it is perfectly in keeping as a natural effect of the orator's precipitate attempt to cut short what he saw would rather give offence than please. *Moving,* stirring up, exciting, see above, on 21, 30. *Sedition* (literally, *rising,* standing up) may either have its proper sense of insurrection, or its secondary sense of strife, dissension (see above, on 15, 2. 19, 40. 23, 7. 10.) Paul was really accused of both crimes, that of sowing strife among the Jews themselves, and that of rousing them against their Roman masters (see above, on 16, 20. 21. 17, 6. 7. 18, 13. 21, 28.) The ambiguous term may have been selected to suggest both these ideas; but the former is the one especially presented in the context. *To all the Jews*, not only among them, but to their injury or disadvantage. *Throughout the inhabited* (or civilized world), i. e. the Roman Empire, or indefinitely everywhere, in all directions. (See above, on 11, 28. 17, 6. 31. 19, 27.) *A ringleader too* (τε, introducing an afterthought or supplementary idea, see above, on 1, 13), not only a public pest in his own person, but the leader of a dangerous organization. The Greek noun is a military term, used by Thucydides to signify the front man on the right of an army in array, but afterwards more generally to denote a front rank man, and metaphorically, any leader. *The sect* (or *party*, see above, on 5, 17. 15, 5) *of the Nazarenes*, the followers of *the Nazarene*, contemptuously so called (see above, on 2, 22.) Although this designation in the plural form occurs only here, it was probably in common use among the Jews, as *Christians* was among the Gentiles (see above, on 11, 26), until after the destruction of Jerusalem, when Nazarene became the name of a Christian sect, which still adhered to the Mosaic law, but with less exclusive rigour, and with worthier notions of the Saviour, than the kindred party of the Ebionites (see above, on 21, 20.)

6. Who also hath gone about to profane the temple; whom we took, and would have judged according to our law.

An additional specification of the general charge. He was not only a pest, and a ringleader of the Nazarenes, but had attempted a particular offence against the law and the religion of the Jews, that of profaning the temple, literally, rendering accessible, depriving of its consecration, making common (see above, on 10, 14. 15, where the verb, however, is not the same, as it is in Matt. 12, 5.) *Hath gone about*, an old English phrase for *sought* or *tried*. (See above, on 21, 31, where it represents a synonymous Greek verb.) The charge of actual desecration (see above, on 21, 28) is here softened down to that of merely attempting it, perhaps because they had discovered their mistake (see above, on 21, 29), or because they were unable to prove what they at first alleged. *Whom als*, (καί, not expressed in the version), corresponding to *who also* in the first clause, both belonging to the summary or recapitulatory style, like the Latin *item* in an enumeration of particulars, and showing either that we have only a brief abstract of the speech, or that Tertullus found it necessary simply to recite the heads or salient points of the charge which he would otherwise have stated at full length. As if he had said, 'Another point is his connection with the Nazarenes; another his attempted profanation of the temple; another, the way in which we were prevented from trying him ourselves.' *Whom also we took*, laid hold on, seized, arrested (see above, on 2, 24. 3, 11.) *And would have judged*, in modern English, *wished*, desired to do so (see above, on 7, 39. 10, 10. 14, 13. 16, 3. 19, 33.) *Judged*, i. e. tried, according to due form of law (see above, on 17, 31. 23, 3. 6.)

7. But the chief captain Lysias came (upon us), and with great violence took (him) away out of our hands —

Coming by (or *along*), as if by accident, the idea of attack being not expressed but suggested by what follows. *With great violence* (or *much force*) *out of our hands took* (literally, *led*) *him away*. There are several points here, in which the facts are, no doubt wilfully, misrepresented, so as to exhibit the conduct of the Jews in a more favourable light than that of Paul and Claudius Lysias, whose interference was at once injurious to their interests and humbling to their pride. That they wished to try Paul according to their law, is wholly at variance with the fact that they were beating him to death when the chief captain rescued him (see above, on 21, 31. 32.) That rescue, therefore, was not from the peaceful protection of the law by brute force, as they here insidiously intimate, but from their own brute force by a lawful exercise of military power. The misrepresentation is the worse for being rather hinted than expressed; and although this may be ascribed in part to the professional adroitness of Tertullus, it no doubt entered into the concerted policy of those for whom he pleaded, and from whom he had of course received his instructions.

8. Commanding his accusers to come unto thee,

by examining of whom thyself mayest take knowledge of all these things, whereof we accuse him.

The first clause adds a supplementary complaint against the Tribune, who had not only thus deprived them of the privilege of trying Paul according to the law which he was charged with breaking, but had put them to great inconvenience by requiring them to come to Cesarea and accuse him before Felix. Here again the fact is truly stated, very much as Claudius Lysias had stated it himself (see above, on 23, 30); and yet the whole connection irresistibly conveys the impression that they had not been well treated, and evinces a strong feeling of resentment against Lysias, who had acted so decidedly and conscientiously in opposition to their murderous designs. This clause, however, with the whole of the preceding verse, is rejected by the latest critics because not found in the oldest extant manuscripts; but this omission makes the speech, already brief, so strangely meagre, and the introduction of the passage is so hard to be accounted for, that its genuineness is, on the whole, more probable than its interpolation, as it may have existed in still older copies now no longer extant. Upon this question of criticism depends the meaning of the other clause, which is admitted to be genuine. *Of whom* (i. e. *from whom*), if the disputed words are genuine, refers most naturally to Claudius Lysias, whom the Jews then desire Felix to examine, as the most important witness on their side. But if the disputed words are spurious, Claudius Lysias is not named at all, and *from whom* must refer to Paul himself. But such a proposition, to examine the prisoner on the truth of their assertions, would be either monstrous or superfluous; a further argument in favour of the genuineness of the words in question, to which may be added the extreme improbability that nothing would be said of Claudius Lysias in this complaint to Felix. The future form (*thou wilt be able*, in the English version, *mayest*) seems to refer to something which could not be done upon the spot, but would require time, whereas the examination of the prisoner might take place at once. Lastly, the reference to Claudius Lysias, rather than to Paul, though not made certain, is made highly probable by the ground on which Felix postpones the case (see below, on v. 22), and which would seem gratuitous unless proposed by one of the parties. But if, for these or other reasons, the words *from whom, &c.*, be referred to Claudius Lysias, the genuineness of the clause in which his name appears becomes a necessary consequence. *Examining*, i. e. judicially (see above, on 4, 9. 12, 19), without any reference to torture, which is not suggested by the context, as in 22, 24. The reference of *from whom* to the plural noun *accusers*, although natural in English, is impossible in Greek, where the relative itself is in the singular number. *Take knowledge*, i. e. gain it, ascertain, discover (see above, on 3, 10. 4, 13. 9, 30. 12, 14. 19, 34. 22, 24, 29.) The spirit of this verse, as just explained, is, 'Such are our charges, and the witness by whom we sustain them, is the very man who sent us here to make them, after interrupting our proceedings at Jerusalem, to whom we now refer you for all further information.'

9. And the Jews also assented, saying that these things were so.

The Jews, as represented by the High Priest and the Elders (see above, on v. 1.) *Also*, i. e. in addition to the charge made by Tertullus in their name and as their advocate. *Assented* is the meaning of the common text (συνέθεντο); but all the oldest manuscripts and late editions have a double compound form of the same verb (συνεπέθεντο), which yields the stronger sense of *jointly set upon* (compare the use of the single compound in 18, 10), unitedly attacked him, or concurred in the attack made by Tertullus. *Saying*, not the ordinary verb so rendered, but a more emphatic form, elsewhere translated *professing* (Rom. 1, 22) and *affirming* (see below, on 25, 19.) Not content with simply *saying*, they formally and solemnly *declared, asserted these things* (those just stated by Tertullus) *so to have* (themselves), i. e. to be. (For this idiomatic usage of the verb *have*, see above, on 7, 1. 12, 15. 17, 11.)

10. Then Paul, after that the governor had beckoned unto him to speak, answered, Forasmuch as I know that thou hast been of many years a judge unto this nation, I do the more cheerfully answer for myself—

Then answered Paul, having signed to him the governor to speak. Signed, literally, *nodded* (compare John 13, 24, and the compound form in 18, 20 above.) There is a striking contrast here between the order and fairness of this Roman process, though conducted by a wicked man, and the passionate confusion of the Sanhedrim, although composed of Priests, Scribes, and Elders of the People (see above, on 23, 2–10.) It seems as if the Jews and Gentiles were beginning to change places as the guardians of the church, a transposition afterward brought out in terrible relief at the destruction of Jerusalem, where Titus was as temperate and humane as the Zealots were ferocious to themselves and others. This circumstance imparts new interest to the crisis which we have now reached, and in which Paul begins his third Apology, or Apostolical defence of Christianity and of himself, not uttered, like the first, to a vast crowd of Jews from all parts of the world assembled to observe the feast of Pentecost; nor like the second, in the presence of the Sanhedrim or Eldership of Israel; but before a Roman magistrate, and under the protection and restraint of Roman arms, yet in the presence of the High Priest and a deputation of the Elders, so that he was still appealing to the chosen people, and before these Gentile witnesses attempting, for the last time, to convince them of the true relation between Law and Gospel, Christ and Moses. He begins, like Tertullus (see above, on vs. 2. 3), with a regular *captatio benevolentiae*, by ascribing to Felix at least one most important qualification for his present duty, that of long experience and thorough knowledge of the men with whom he had to deal. Here again the leading words stand first in the original, though needlessly displaced in the translation. As Tertullus had begun with *much peace enjoying through thee*, Paul begins, *since many years a judge unto this nation*. *Since*, literally, *from*, i. e. dating or beginning to compute from. *Many*, here as elsewhere, is a relative expression, and as Felix had been governor at least six years—still longer, if as Tacitus relates, he shared the power of Cumanus, his immediate predecessor—this was a long time, in the view of the Apostle, when compared with the ignorance and inexperience of a Roman just arrived among the Jews, even though he might be such an one as Porcius Festus (see below, on 25, 1.) *More cheerfully*, or readily, with less apprehension of the issue, than if I were arraigned before a novice or an ignoramus. The latest critics, with the oldest manuscripts, read *cheerfully* without the *more*, which really implies the same as the comparative, though in a less emphatic form. (As to) *the* (*things*) *about myself*, (i. e. in my own case or behalf) *I make defence* (the same verb as in 19, 33. Luke 12, 11. 21, 14.) The similarity of form between this exordium and that of Tertullus is too strong to be fortuitous. Even in substance, there is less diversity than those are willing to admit, who exaggerate the advocate's professional laudation into servile flattery and shameless lying. Each gives the Procurator credit for possessing what he really possessed, indomitable energy and long experience; while both are silent, as they should have been on this occasion, with respect to his bad qualities. That Paul's forbearance was not cowardly, we know from his deportment at another and more private audience (see below, on v. 25.) The unfairness of Tertullus, as we have already seen, lies rather in the substance of his speech than in the oratorical exordium.

11. Because that thou mayest understand, that there are yet but twelve days since I went up to Jerusalem for to worship.

This is not a deduction from the fact just stated, that Felix had been many years a magistrate in Palestine, but an additional reason for Paul's cheerfully defending himself, namely, because Felix had the best means of knowing how lately he had come into the country, and how groundless was the charge of his being a disturber of the public peace. *Because that thou mayest understand*, an awkward circumlocution likely to mislead the English reader, as it has misled a noble and devout interpreter of recent date (Lord Lyttelton), who explains it thus, "I speak so that thou mayest understand." The original construction is the genitive absolute, *thou being able to know*, i. e. since thou hast it in thy power, both from thy office and thy place of residence, to ascertain how long it is since I went up from Cesarea to Jerusalem (see above, on 21, 15–17.) With this appeal to the Procurator's means of information, Paul confidently states the time himself. *There are to me* (i. e. I have lived or spent) *not more than twelve days since* (or from the day that) *I went up, etc.* A vast amount of calculation and discussion has been lavished on the question, how these twelve days are to be reckoned, all agreeing in the only point of any moment, namely, that Paul's statement may be justified in several ways, the variation having reference chiefly to the *seven days* spoken of in 21, 27, and to the admission or exclusion of the days which had elapsed since his return to

Cesarea (see above, on v. 1.) *To* (or *about to*) *worship* is in Greek a future participle, the same with that in 8, 27, and like it denoting, not an incidental or fortuitous occurrence, but the very end and purpose of the journey. There is no need of explaining this away, as inconsistent with the statement in v. 17, for neither statement is exclusive of the other; or as at variance with his principles, for these not only suffered but constrained him to perform acts of worship in the temple upon fit occasions (see above, on 21, 26.) While the temple was still standing, and the framework of the ceremonial law unbroken, even Paul the Apostle of the Gentiles could not go up to Jerusalem without some devotional as well as business purpose. By an almost insensible transition from his exordium to his argument, he here alleges two facts, bearing on his own defence; first, his recent arrival in the country, leaving him no time for such proceedings as were charged against him; and then, the avowed religious end for which he went up, to perform the duties of that very faith, which they accused him of renouncing.

12. And they neither found me in the temple disputing with any man, neither raising up the people, neither in the synagogues, nor in the city —

The third point of his defence consists in a direct denial of the charge of having moved sedition (see above on v. 5.) He had been but twelve days in the country, and in those twelve days they had detected him in no disturbance of the peace or violation of decorum. They had found him neither publicly *discoursing* (the same verb as in 17, 2. 17, 18, 4. 19. 19, 8. 9. 20, 7. 9), nor in any other way *raising up the people*, literally, *making a gathering of a mob*. This he boldly affirms, not only in the general, but with specific mention of the only places where he could have done it, *in the temple*, *in the synagogues*, *and through the city*, i. e. in the streets, perhaps including private houses, so as to exhaust the list of possible localities. This bold assertion that he not only had not had the opportunity of doing that which they alleged against him, but still more categorically, had not done it, could never have been made in the presence of accusers who were capable of proving what they charged. Its very utterance is tantamount to a denial that the charges were susceptible of proof at all.

13. Neither can they prove the things whereof they now accuse me.

Not content with the implied denial in v. 12, he now repeats it in a definite and formal manner. Or the logical relation may be that of a deduction from admitted data. As if he had said, 'Since I have been only twelve days in Jerusalem, and during that time they have found me nowhere publicly or privately exhibiting the character which they would fasten on me, as a mover of sedition and a sower of dissension among the Jews throughout the world, I am entitled to conclude that they have no proof to adduce of that calumnious description, or of any charge which they have brought against me.' The confident and sweeping terms which Paul employs in these two verses seem to imply that he had carefully abstained during this visit to the Holy City, even from those customary modes of usefulness to which he was addicted in his proper sphere as the Apostle of the Gentiles, and as a necessary consequence, that his present mission was a temporary, special, and restricted one.

14. But this I confess unto thee, that after the way which they call heresy, so worship I the God of my fathers, believing all things which are written in the law and in the prophets—

Having thus answered one of the two charges in v. 5, to wit, that which described him as "a pestilent fellow and a mover of sedition," he now takes up the other, which described him as "a front-rank-man (or leader) of the sect (or party) of the Nazarenes." The exquisite transition here is worthy of Demosthenes. Thus far he had denied and contradicted; now he comes to acknowledge and confess. *But I own this to thee*, perhaps with emphasis upon the pronoun, 'I have nothing to confess to them, and yet to thee I own that there is one charge which is true, though not in the sense put upon it by its authors.' The flattering charge of being a ringleader he modestly and wisely passes by in silence, but admits the more important fact that he was really a "Nazarene." *According to the way which they call sect* (or *schism*), *I do thus worship the paternal God.* The translation *heresy*, though found in all the English versions, is doubly objectionable; first, because it puts a meaning on the Greek word which it never has in the New Testament (see above, on 5, 17, 15, 5); and then, because it hides from view the striking correspondence between this defence and the accusation in v. 5, by using different English words to render the same Greek one. Tertullus calls him a ringleader of the sect (or party) of the Nazarenes. Paul admits that he belongs to it, but not that he is guilty of apostasy from Moses. *The way* (of thinking, living, worshipping, etc.) seems to have been a common Jewish name for doctrinal and practical diversities among themselves; a supposition which accounts for its repeated application to the Christian faith in this book (see above, on 9, 2. 19, 9. 23. 22, 4), not as a specific but as a generic designation, i. e. representing it as one out of many such diversities existing in the bosom of the Jewish church itself. *Heresy*, as here used in its ancient sense of school or party, is a more specific term, and as such is distinguished here by Paul himself. 'That peculiar way of thinking, living, etc., which my accusers call a sect or schism, but which I deny to be so.' But how could Paul deny that in becoming a Christian he had ceased to be a Jew? This question is answered in the next clause by himself. *So* (i. e. in this peculiar way described by my accusers as schismatical) *I worship the paternal God*, i. e. the God of my forefathers and of theirs. There is great propriety and beauty in the use of the adjective *paternal*, constantly applied in the classics to the tutelary and ancestral gods of nations, families, and places. In addressing Jews, he employs the Scriptural phrase, *God of our fathers* (see above, on 3, 13. 5, 30. 22, 14), which, in addressing Felix, he exchanges for a classical expression, more familiar yet to all intents and purposes synonymous. The idea commonly attached to this clause ('I worship as a Christian') is but half its meaning, and the least important half in this connection. Assuming that as undisputed and notorious, he asserts that when he worships as a Christian, he adores no new God, but the same who had been worshipped by his fathers, or in other words that Christianity was really the genuine continuation of Old Testament Judaism. This, although presented in a new form, is precisely the same claim that Paul asserted in the single sentence which comprised his defence before the Sanhedrim (see above, on 23, 1.) As addressed to Felix, and adapted to his heathenish associations, it may thus be paraphrased. 'They charge me with abandoning our old religion, and with worshipping some strange god;

but the very God, whom I thus worship, is our own ancestral God, whom I would no more leave than you would abandon your hereditary deities; and this I prove by my adherence to the sacred books of our religion, to that Law and to those Prophets, of which even you have often heard, as the very basis of our faith, and in which I now believe as firmly as I ever did, and more sincerely than the men who charge me with rejecting them.'

15. And have hope toward God, which they themselves also allow, that there shall be a resurrection of the dead, both of the just and unjust.

The relation of the clauses here is often misconceived, as if Paul meant to say that he indulged a certain hope, and then as a subordinate or incidental circumstance that other Jews indulged the same; whereas this sameness is the main idea here expressed, and that on which his argumentative defence entirely turns. *Having a hope towards God which these (men) also themselves entertain* (or *look for*, i. e. for its realization, as in Tit. 2, 13.) This, it must still be borne in mind, is addressed to Felix, and intended to explain to him the true relation between Judaism and Christianity, so far as it could thus be made intelligible to a heathen, and thereby to meet the charge of having apostatized from his religion. The amount of this explanatory statement, as contained in this and the preceding verse, is that he still worships the same God; and still believes in the same sacred books; and still cherishes the same hope for the future. With these points of agreement, how could he be cast out as a schismatic or an apostate? But what was the hope which he still held in common with the unconverted Jews? It seems to be explained, in the last clause, as the hope of a general resurrection. But this was not held by the Sadducees, nor is it elsewhere represented as the great distinctive hope of Israel. Considering the brevity of this defence, or the abbreviated statement of it here presented, it is allowable to fill up its omissions and elucidate its darker places, by comparing it with the fuller (or more fully reported) Apology before Agrippa as contained in ch. xxvi. This will be done more particularly in the exposition of that chapter; it will here be sufficient to anticipate the inference, hereafter to be drawn (from 26, 6–8. 22. 23), that the national hope referred to, even here, was the hope of the Messiah, and the resurrection, here connected with it, that of Christ himself, but represented as the pledge and foretaste of a general rising, here expressed by saying, *both of the just and unjust*, i. e. of all kinds and characters without exception (compare Matt. 5, 45.) The three points of adherence, then, to ancient doctrines, here alleged by Paul, are one God, one Scripture, one Messiah.

16. And herein do I exercise myself, to have always a conscience void of offence, toward God and (toward) men.

Herein (or *in this*), i. e. in this adherence to the God, the revelation, and the hope of Israel. *I exercise* (*myself*), a verb originally denoting any kind of hard work; then specially applied to athletic strife or training; and then to moral discipline, especially to that of the severest kind, in which sense it is the etymon or theme of *ascetic* and its cognate forms. It here denotes, not only constant or habitual practice, but methodical and systematic effort. *Void of offence*, in Greek a single word, suggestive of the two ideas, *unoffended* and *unoffending*, i. e. a conscience neither wounded by transgression nor allowing me to be the means of tempting others. The same word occurs once in the Apocrypha, but in the New Testament is confined to Paul and to the conscience (see 1 Cor. 10, 32. Phil. 1, 10), a strong though incidental mark of genuineness in the passage now before us. *Toward* (i. e. in relation or regard to) *God* (as the head of the theocracy) *and to men* (as my fellow-citizens or fellow-members.) *Always*, not perhaps in the restricted modern sense (*at all times*), but in the wider sense suggested by its etymology (*in all ways*), which agrees well with the form and original meaning of the Greek word (*through all*, or *by means of all*.) This word, though dislocated in the version, emphatically closes the whole verse in tne original. If this verse merely meant, as many readers may imagine, that Paul was conscientious in his whole deportment, it would be a very needless and unmeaning close of the preceding argument in proof of his fidelity to the theocracy or ancient church. It is in fact the winding up of that whole argument, with obvious allusion to his words before the Sanhedrim, for which Ananias had required him to be smitten on the mouth (see above, on 23, 2), and which he here takes occasion to explain and justify. As if he had said, 'In this sense and on those grounds, I affirmed before and now affirm again, that far from being an apostate or a renegade, I am and always have been, both before and since my confession of Christ, a conscientious and consistent Jew.'

17. Now after many years I came to bring alms to my nation and offerings.

Now, the usual continuative particle, translated *and* in v. 16, *but* in v. 14. *After*, literally, *through*, or in the course of (see above, on 23, 31), but often used to signify the close as well as the duration of a period (see Matt. 26, 61. Mark 2, 1. 14, 58.) *Many*, not the word so rendered in v. 10 above, but its comparative, strictly meaning *more*, and like the corresponding words in Latin and German, used in the modern English sense of *several*, i. e. more than one, in this case meaning about four years (see above, on 18, 22. 23.) Having now defined his relative position to the Jews and their religion, Paul reverts to the purpose of his visit to Jerusalem, and to the charge of having come as a mover of sedition. In contradiction to this groundless calumny, he had already said (in v. 11) that he came *to worship*, to which he now adds that he came *to bring alms* (literally, *to do* or *make*, i. e. dispense them). This is perfectly consistent with the other motive, and is added to it as a proof that his whole object was pacific and religious, not divisive or disorderly. But what were these alms? Not the private charities of Paul himself, which must have been comparatively small, and could not have occasioned his long voyage and journey. He must refer to more extensive and important contributions, of which he was the channel or dispenser. But none such are mentioned in this book, a seeming difficulty which, when properly explained, becomes a striking incidental proof of authenticity. While Luke says nothing in his narrative of these "alms," Paul himself, in his epistles written just before this journey, is abundant in allusior to them (see above, on 19, 21. 22. 20, 1–4, and compare Rom. 15, 25–31. 1 Cor. 16, 1–4. 10. 11. 17. 2 Cor. 8, 1–24. 9, 1–15.) From these allusions it appears that at his own suggestion a general contribution had been made throughout the churches in the two great provinces of Greece for the relief of the poor saints at Jerusalem, and that one important object of Paul's visi' was to deliver or distribute these benevolent donations. As hey were not designed for Gentiles he expressly adds, *unto my nation*, thus suggesting that such conduct towards his kinsmen according to the flesh was incompatible with hating or despising them. *And offerings*, not the alms just mentioned; first, because the repetition would be needless; secondly, because the collocation of the words, both in Greek and English, shows that something additional or supplementary was meant to be expressed; and lastly, because the word here used is never applied elsewhere to mere charities, but always, either in the literal or figurative sense, to the oblations of the Mosaic ritual. (See Heb. 10, 5. 8. 10. 14. 18. Rom. 15, 16. Eph. 5, 2.) It was to sacrifice, as well as pray, that Paul had gone up to Jerusalem. This might be understood as nothing more than a specification of the phrase *to worship* in v. 11. But a more precise sense is suggested by the fact that the very same term (*offering*) occurs above in 21, 26, with reference to the sacrifices of the Nazarites, the cost of whose ceremonial purification Paul had undertaken. Here then are offerings, in the strict sense, which we know him to have actually made, or to have been upon the point of making, at the time of his arrest; a clear proof that he was not a despiser and blasphemer, even of the legal ceremonies, as his enemies alleged. It is certain, therefore, that the *alms* and *offerings* of this verse are distinct from one another, though adduced for the same purpose, that is, to establish his fidelity and loyalty to that which he was represented as rejecting and attempting to destroy. But the alms and offerings, though not the same thing, may have been connected if, as some suppose, the money spent by Paul upon the Nazarites was taken from the fund which he had brought from Greece, as a real compliance with the wishes of the donors, perhaps authorized if not proposed by the Elders at Jerusalem, though not recorded in the narrative of their conference with Paul (see above, on 21, 23. 24.) But this, though in itself entirely credible, and serving to account for the peculiar way in which the *alms* and *offerings* are here put together, is a mere conjecture, and must not be forced upon the passage as a part of its essential meaning. To the question how Paul could be said to have gone up for a purpose, which was first suggested after his arrival, it may be answered, that perhaps this suggestion was but the occasion of performing what had been before projected, or communicated by the Holy Ghost; and also, that without this supposition, the peculiar way in which the *offerings* are added, by a kind of afterthought, may be intended to exclude them from his original design and to describe them as a subsequent expedient. 'How could I come up to defile the temple and divide the people, when I brought relief to many poor among them; yes, and while there actually offered sacrifices at the very sanctuary which I am accused of trying to profane.'

18. Whereupon certain Jews from Asia found me purified in the temple, neither with multitude, nor with tumult.

Whereupon should be *in which*, i. e. in which deeds or employments, aiding the poor saints and performing sacrifice. 'In the very act of proving my devotion to the race and my respect for the Mosaic law, they seized me, and have since arraigned me, as an enemy of both!' Some of the oldest manuscripts have *which* in the feminine form, and therefore necessarily referring to the feminine nouns *alms* and *offerings*, which only makes the reference more definite, without a real change of meaning. The defensive argument, implied in this clause, is still further carried out by adding, *purified* (i. e. undergoing ceremonial purification, see above, on 21, 24. 26) *in the temple* (i. e. in its courts or area, see above, on vs. 6. 12, and compare 2, 46), thereby proving his respect for the Mosaic law in reference to two of its great parts or features, sacred rites and sacred places. The fact that Paul was thus engaged when seized and charged with sacrilege, was a genuine *reductio ad absurdum* for his false accusers. They could not even say that, although present at the temple, and apparently engaged in ceremonial duties, he performed them in an unbecoming or disorderly manner. *Not with crowd* (or concourse), so as to attract undue attention and disturb the devotions of his neighbours, *nor with tumult* (uproar, as in 20, 1. 21, 34), a stronger term denoting the natural result of mobs or lawless gatherings. There is here a question of grammatical construction, closely connected with one of textual criticism. This cannot be intelligibly stated to the English reader without restoring the original order of the sentence, which is this, *whereupon* (or *wherein*) *found me purified in the temple*, *not with crowd nor with tumult*, *certain Jews from Asia.* As the last words evidently constitute the subject of the verb *found* (which is plural), the translators have transposed them in accommodation to English usage. But the latest critics have inserted the continuative particle (δέ) after *some* (or *certain*) from a few of the old manuscripts, thus separating *certain Jews* from the preceding verb, and leaving the latter to be construed indefinitely, *they* (i. e. my enemies and false accusers) *found me purified, &c., but* (or *and*) *certain Jews from Asia.* The authorities for this emendation, although strong, are not decisive, as the oldest copy extant (Codex Vaticanus) either has the common text or has not yet been collated as to this point. Even admitting the proposed change, the construction may be made at least intelligible, although still singular, by repeating or supplying something from the first clause. *They found me purified in the temple, not with crowd or tumult, but certain Jews from Asia* (were the cause of these.) *Jews from Asia*, the same Greek phrase that is rendered *Jews which were of Asia* in Luke's account of the transaction here referred to. The preposition indicates that they not only came from but belonged to Asia Proper or Proconsular (see above, on 21, 27.)

19. Who ought to have been here before thee, and object, if they had aught against me.

The mention of the Jews from Asia, as the real authors of the tumult at the temple, leads Paul to urge another circumstance, showing the unfairness and irregularity of this whole process. Who had accused him of profaning or attempting to profane the temple? *Certain Jews from Asia.* Why were they not present to sustain their accusation, either as witnesses or parties? Why was their place supplied by Ananias and Tertullus, who knew nothing of the facts except as they had heard them from those Asiatic Jews, whose absence could not be supplied by a contemptuous reference to Claudius Lysias as the only witness (see above, on v. 8.) *To have been here* (literally, *to be present*) *before thee* (i. e. as a judge, or at thy bar, the preposition used above in 21, 30, and there explained.) This was no forensic quibble or finesse, but a legitimate objection to the whole procedure as evincing bad faith and a conscious inability to prove their charges. *Object* should be *accuse*, the same verb as in vs. 2. 8. 13, and in 22, 30. The variation in the version here obscures the meaning by suggesting as Paul's meaning, that they ought to have been there to make objections to the method of proceeding or to his defence; whereas he means that they ought to have appeared as his prosecutors or accusers. *If they had aught* (or *any thing) against me*, is in Greek peculiarly expressive from the use of the optative mood, implying that the case was purely hypothetical, or in other words, that they had really no charge against him.

20. Or (else) let these same (here) say, if they have found any evil doing in me, while I stood before the council.

Or else seems to imply that Paul is here presenting an alternative, proposing two things, one of which ought to be done. 'Either let the Jews from Asia be brought forward, *or else* let these, &c.' But what he really says is, not that they ought now to be produced, but that they ought to have appeared from the beginning as his prosecutors. He proposes nothing as to this point, but merely censures what had been already done. With this relation of the verses agrees the connective particle which simply denotes *or*, the *else* being introduced by the translators. *Or* (as it is now too late to remedy this error, and the Jews from Asia have perhaps gone home) *let these* (Ananias and the Elders) *themselves* (not merely through an advocate, but in their proper persons) *say, if they found any wrong* (or according to the oldest copies, *what wrong they found*) *in me, while* (or *when*) *I stood* (lit. *I standing*) *before the council* (the *Synedrium* or *Sanhedrim*, see above, on 4, 15.) The allusion is of course to the scene described in 23, 1-10. *Wrong*, the word translated *matter of wrong* in 18, 14, and there explained. *Before*, the same word as in v. 19, at their bar, at their tribunal. Having shown, from the absence of the original accusers and of all other witnesses, that the charge of sedition was abandoned, he now challenges the High Priest and the Elders to bring forward any other accusation which they could establish, even by their own testimony. They had not witnessed the alleged desecration of the temple; they had only seen him as he stood before the council (see above, on 22, 30); if they knew any thing against him from their own observation, it must have happened then, and he accordingly gives this specific form and limitation to his challenge.

21. Except it be for this one voice, that I cried standing among them, Touching the resurrection of the dead I am called in question by you this day.

Except it be, in Greek a single letter, meaning *than*, i. e. other than, besides, except. *For* (or *about*) *this one voice* seems dependent in construction on a verb suppressed; or it may be connected with the phrase *found wrong* in the preceding verse, *unless* (they found fault or condemned me) *for this one voice*, i. e. utterance, not only the words said, but the act of saying them. *Among them*, literally, *in them*, i. e. in their circle, in the midst of them. (For the idiomatic use of ὅτι, *that*, omitted in the version, see above, on 2, 13. 3, 22. 5, 23. 25. 6, 11. 7, 6. 11, 3. 13, 34. 15, 1. 16, 36. 19, 21. 23, 20.) His quotation of his own words agrees as nearly with Luke's narrative in 23, 6 as would be natural in any case of repetition. The only variations are that he omits *hope* before *resurrection*, and adds, *this day by you*. *Called in question*, here as in the other case, means *judged*, tried, put upon my trial, summoned to defend myself. As this was the expression which created the division in the council (see above on 23, 7), it has been disputed whether those to whom Paul here appeals (though not directly) were Pharisees or Sadducees. But this is a question of no moment, as he is not here appealing to their diverse principles or prepossessions, but is simply recalling what had happened on a recent occasion, for the purpose of strengthening his previous statement, that they could have nothing to allege against him. 'They have only seen me in their council at Jerusalem, and surely I did nothing there for which I must be tried, unless it was my uttering those words which threw them into such confusion.' The reference is not so much to what he said as to his having said so little, and that little so inadequate to justify their conduct. At the same time the Apostle, with consummate skill, by thus repeating his own words before the Sanhedrim, renews his enigmatical but solemn declaration, that so far from having given up his Messianic hope, it was because he held it fast in its original intent, it was because he had embraced the true Messiah when he came, while Israel at large denied him, this was the very reason of his being now a prisoner and called on to defend himself. That he still described his hope of the Messiah as a hope of resurrection, may have been intended to disguise a doctrine which the Jews would instantly regard as nullifying all that he had said in proof of his own loyalty to Israel and Moses. The key to this enigma of his being both a Christian and a Jew was furnished by his holding that Messiah had already come. But as this, distinctly stated, might have prevented their attending to his further statement, he excites their curiosity and gains their ear by speaking only of the resurrection, as the crowning attestation of our Lord's Messiahship, reserving a fuller explanation of his meaning for his last Apology and last appeal to Israel, before he left the Holy Land for ever (see below, on 26, 6.) It is not to be forgotten that although this third apology was formally addressed to Felix, and was really intended to apprise him of the true state of the case which had been so misrepresented by the Jews, it was virtually an additional appeal to the Jews themselves, as there officially and representatively present, a further effort to convince them of the false position which they occupied in reference to Christ and Moses.

22. And when Felix heard these things, having more perfect knowledge of (that) way, he deferred them, and said, When Lysias the chief captain shall come down, I will know the uttermost of your matter.

Having heard these things is omitted by the oldest manuscripts and latest critics, according to whom the verse begins, *And Felix put them off*, which comes next in the original. *More exactly* (see above, on 18, 26. 23, 15. 20) *knowing the* (*things*) *about the way* have been explained by some as the words of Felix himself. 'More exactly knowing (i. e. when I do know more exactly) the things concerning this way, said he, when Claudius Lysias,' &c. But this construction is condemned by the harsh transposition it involves and by the sense it puts upon the participle (εἰπών.) *The way* has here been variously understood to mean the present case; or the character and practice of the Jews; or the Christian religion, as in v. 14, and other places there referred to. This usage seems decisive in favour of the last interpretation; but the question still arises in what sense Felix is said to have understood the new religion more exactly. Some suppose the comparative to be here used, as it often is in Latin, to express a moderate degree of something (knowing pretty accurately), which, however, is by no means very natural or obvious. Others give the comparative its proper sense, but differ as to the things compared (knowing more exactly than was usual with Romans, or than could have been expected, or than the Jews imagined, &c.) all which supply something not expressed or necessarily suggested by the context. The simplest syntax and the best sense are obtained by supposing these words to describe the effect of Paul's discourse on Felix, whom, as we have seen, it was intended to enlighten with respect to the relation between Judaism and Christianity, a subject always puzzling to the Romans, though important to the exercise of their authority (see above, on 18, 15. 23, 29.) What Gallio and Lysias could not comprehend had now been made in some degree perspicuous to Felix by the masterly discourse of the Apostle. *More exactly knowing* (than he did before, the true state of the case) *about the way* (of living and believing) to which Paul adhered and which the Jews had represented as an absolute rejection of their whole religion. Seeing this charge to be a false one, and the whole proceeding frivolous and spiteful, he determined to get rid of it, but not by openly acquitting Paul, and thereby putting an affront upon the Jews, as represented in his presence by the High Priest and the Elders. This, as we shall see below (on v. 27), he had personal and selfish reasons for avoiding, while he must have seen that there was not the slightest ground for the proceeding against Paul. In this dilemma he resorts to the cowardly expedient of delay, embracing for that purpose the suggestion offered by Tertullus (see above, on v. 8), that the Tribune should himself be made to testify. *When Lysias the chiliarch comes down* (from Jerusalem, as in v. 1 above), *I will know the things concerning you* (or in which you are interested.) Some regard this as a threat that when he did obtain the necessary information, they might expect to be put upon their trial in their turn. But this agrees neither with the character of Felix, nor with his actual position, as Josephus describes both; nor with the natural import of the terms employed. The compound Greek verb (διαγνώσομαι) might be explained to mean, I will discriminate, and so decide (Geneva Bible); but usage is in favour of the sense, I will know (your matters) thoroughly (or through and through), perhaps with some allusion to the forensic use of knowledge to denote judicial cognizance or jurisdiction. The first of these ideas (that of knowing thoroughly) was no doubt meant to be conveyed by Tyndale's paraphrastic version, retained in King James's Bible, *I will know the uttermost of your matter.* That this adjournment was a mere device to end the whole proceeding, may have been apparent, even at the time, from the extreme improbability that Lysias could leave his post at such a turbulent and anxious juncture, and is now confirmed by the silence of the history in reference to any such appearance of the Tribune as a witness in this matter.

23. And he commanded a centurion to keep Paul, and to let (him) have liberty, and that he should forbid none of his acquaintance to minister or come unto him.

The impression made upon the governor by Paul's defence is further shown by the directions which he gave for his safe-keeping. He was still to be detained, because not yet acquitted, and for other reasons afterwards disclosed, but *to have remission* (relaxation, mitigation of his bondage.) The translation *liberty*, if strictly understood, makes the sentence contradict itself. *To be kept* (watched, guarded), and at the same time *to have liberty*, are incompatible conditions. (For the true sense of the Greek word, compare 2 Cor. 8, 13. 2 Thess. 1, 7.) Some suppose an allusion to the technical distinction between different kinds of custody practised by the Romans, such as the *custodia publica*, or confinement in the common prison; the *custodia militaris*, or perpetual surveillance by a soldier, and in its severer forms attachment to his person by a chain; and the *custodia libera*, in which the prisoner was entrusted to a magistrate or other well known person, who received him into his own household and was answerable for his safety. This last might seem to be the liberty which Felix ordered Paul to have; but it was practised only in the case of prisoners of great distinction, and it seems to be implied in the words before us that the centurion still had charge of him. That this was the centurion who escorted him to Cesarea (the other having gone back from Antipatris, see above, on 23, 23. 32), although possible, cannot be inferred from the definite expression (*the centurion*), because this may only mean the one on duty, or the one who was entrusted with such matters. *To forbid none of his own* (friends or acquaintances, see above, on 4, 23. 21, 6), *to wait upon him*, minister to him, take care of him, supply his wants (compare the use of the same verb in 13, 36. 20, 34.) *Or come to him*, have access to him, visit him, even without performing services so intimate and confidential. To the latter class we may perhaps refer Philip and his household (see above, on 21, 8. 9); to the former Trophimus (see above, on 21, 29), Aristarchus (see below, on 27, 2), but above all, Luke, "the beloved physician," and the author of this history, which may owe much of its contents to this renewal of the intercourse between them (see below, on v. 27.)

24. And after certain days, when Felix came with his wife Drusilla, which was a Jewess, he sent for Paul, and heard him concerning the faith in Christ.

After certain (i. e. *some*) *days*, an indefinite expression, but suggestive rather of a short than of a long time (see above, on 10, 48. 15, 36. 16, 12.) *Came*, coming, being there, the same as in v. 17. 23, 16. 35, and often elsewhere (see above, on 5, 21.) According to Tacitus, the wife of Felix was Drusilla, daughter of Juba the Numidian king, and grand-daughter of Anthony and Cleopatra. According to Josephus, she was Drusilla, daughter of Herod Agrippa, whose death is recorded in 12, 23, and great-grand-daughter of Herod the Great. This might seem to be total contradiction, but for the statement of a third historian (Suetonius), that Felix was the husband of three queens, by which he no doubt means three wives of royal lineage. This would comprehend and reconcile the statements of Josephus and Tacitus, although there may have been some confusion of names, the double Drusilla being certainly remarkable. The Jewish Drusilla was betrothed in childhood to Antiochus Epiphanes of Comagene, but he refusing to comply with the conditions of the contract by receiving circumcision, she was actually married to Azizus king of Emesa, who did become a Jew. Felix, according to Josephus, was smitten with her beauty, and through the agency of Simon, a magician from Cyprus, but supposed by some to be the same with Simon Magus (see above, on 8, 24), persuaded her to leave her husband. As the ordinary word for *wife*, in Greek as well as French, is *woman*, and as some manuscripts omit the pronoun, it might be understood as a contemptuous expression, *with the woman Drusilla*, like *the woman Jezebel* in Rev. 2, 20. But the pronoun is expressed in many manuscripts, and two of the most ancient have the strong expression, *with his own wife;* so that most interpreters agree that she is so described, but in a popular sense, without implying that the marriage was a lawful one. If it took place about this time, of which we have no other evidence, the words of Luke might naturally mean, *Felix arriving with his wife Drusilla*, i. e. bringing her home for the first time, a circumstance more likely to be mentioned so distinctly than their merely going from one house to another, or, as some suppose, from one apartment to another in the same. *Being a Jewess*, by birth and probably by actual profession, and as such naturally curious to hear the famous Christian preacher and learn something of the strange sect which was everywhere spoken against (see below, on 28, 22.) That it was for her gratification that the Procurator sent for Paul, is clear from the difficulty of explaining otherwise the formal mention of her name and her religion. *Heard him* (not preach an ordinary sermon, but explain what was peculiar) *about the faith in Christ*, i. e. the new religion, of which Christ is the centre, the foundation, and the topstone, and a personal faith in him its only method of salvation (see above, on 4, 11. 12.)

25. And as he reasoned of righteousness, temperance, and judgment to come, Felix trembled, and answered, Go thy way for this time; when I have a convenient season, I will call for thee.

As he reasoned, literally, *he discoursing* (see above, on 17, 2. 17. 18, 4. 19. 19, 8. 9. 20, 7. 9, and v. 12 of this chapter.) *Righteousness*, not justification, as the other terms denote human virtues, but justice, in the wide sense, or the rendering to every one his due (see above, on 10, 22. 35.) *Temperance*, not in the restricted modern sense of abstinence from strong drink, but in that of self-control and moderation as to all the appetites, with special reference, in ancient usage, to chastity or continence, which last is derived directly from the Latin word answering to the one here used. The Christian doctrine upon these points must have been peculiarly awakening to the Roman's conscience, as his whole life seems to have been one of unjust tyranny and sensual indulgence, so that Tacitus uses, to describe his moral character, two of the strongest words afforded by the language (*saevitiam et libidinem.*) For another portrait, by the hand of the same master, see above, on 23, 24. There is no need of supposing, as some have done, that Paul purposely went out of his way to gall the conscience of his hearers, or, as others imagine, that he preached the Law exclusively without the Gospel. This is not the apostolical method, which presents the two together, and convicts the individual, not by personal invective, but by manifestation of the truth, commending itself to every man's conscience in the sight of God (2 Cor. 4, 2.) Paul no doubt complied with the request that he would state to them "the faith in Christ," in doing which he could not fail to treat of Christian virtues and their corresponding vices, as the fruits of faith and unbelief respectively; and this plain statement, without digression or exaggeration, would suffice to reach the conscience and to rouse the apprehension of that *coming judgment*, literally, *the judgment, that about to be*, the same verb that occurs above, in v. 15, and five times in the preceding chapter (23, 3. 15. 20. 27. 30.) *Becoming fearful* (or *alarmed*), *Felix answered*, or responded to this terrible discourse, so unlike what he had looked for, as a gratification of Drusilla's curiosity or his own. *For this time* is in Greek an idiomatic phrase which can hardly be translated into English, consisting of an article and participle in the neuter gender, *the having*, i. e. the time having itself (being) now. (See above, on v. 9, and the places there referred to.) This is equivalent to our phrases, as the matter now is, for the present, and some others, different in form, but of the same essential import. *Go thy way*, in Greek a single word, *depart*, (*begone!*) *Having got time*, or *obtained an opportunity, I will send for thee* (*again*). It is a curious instance of the way in which a text may be severed from its context by the tradition of the pulpit, that the three points commonly made prominent in this verse are entirely adventitious and have no trace in the text itself. *Trembled* is merely Tyndale's loose translation of a phrase denoting inward feeling, not its outward indications; *convenient* is an epithet added by the same hand to the bare noun *time* or opportunity; and lastly, the traditional assertion, that the season never came, is directly contradicted by the following verses.

26. He hoped also that money should have been given him of Paul, that he might loose him; wherefore he sent for him the oftener, and communed with him.

At the same time also, a phrase only partially translated in our Bible, which throughout this passage follows Tyndale closely. At the same time that he thus dismissed him, *hoping that money will be given him by Paul.* The remaining words, *that he might loose* (or *free*) *him*, although no doubt a true statement of the motive, are omitted by the latest critics, because not found in the oldest copies extant. *Wherefore*, because he entertained this mercenary hope, *the oftener* (or *even oftener*, than he would otherwise have done so) *sending for Paul* (from the Prætorium to his own house, or from the prisoner's apartments to his own, if they were under the same roof) *he conversed with him*, the verb employed in 20, 11, above, and there explained. That Paul abstained from all religious conversation in these frequent interviews, is utterly at variance with his character and practice (see above, on 20, 20. 21. 26. 27. 31, and compare Col. 1, 28.) It cannot, therefore, be alleged that although Felix often talked with Paul, it was exclusively on business, and he never found an opportunity of hearing him again "concerning the faith in Christ." The very fact that Felix, while his conscience trembled, could conceive the plan of getting money out of him, shows that he would not shrink from hearing him reason of righteousness, temperance, and future judgment, every day, if thereby he might gain his darling end. This hope of bribe or ransom must have rested on the zeal of Paul's friends and his influence upon them, not without some reference to the foreign alms of which he was the bearer (see above, on v. 17.) The same spirit that collected these would surely do still more for the Apostle's liberation. But however plausible the expectation, it was disappointed.

27. But after two years Porcius Festus came into Felix' room; and Felix, willing to shew the Jews a pleasure, left Paul bound.

A biennium (or period of two years) *having been completed* (or elapsed since Paul's imprisonment), *Felix received a successor*, *Porcius Festus*. The date of this change has been commonly assigned to the summer of the year 61; but the latest chronological investigations make it probable, at least, that it occurred a twelvemonth sooner, in the summer of A. D. 60, ten years before the destruction of Jerusalem. *Wishing too* (τε) *to deposit favours with the Jews*, i. e. to place them under obligations, thereby laying up in store a future claim upon their gratitude or kindness. The same figure is employed by Demosthenes and other classical Greek writers. It may seem strange that a ruler so unscrupulous as Felix, who practised every method of extortion and oppression on this very people, should be so desirous of securing their good will when he was taking leave of them for ever. But like Pontius Pilate, and some others of his predecessors, he was recalled to answer the complaints of the oppressed Jews, and was therefore anxious to propitiate them and perhaps induce them to withdraw their charge, before he made his appearance at the emperor's tribunal. From contemporary history we learn that he escaped through the intercession of his brother Pallas, then a favourite of Nero, but a few years later put to death by him, perhaps involving Felix in his own destruction.

CHAPTER XXV.

We have here the narrative of Paul's fourth Apology, or public appearance, as a prisoner, in defence of himself and his religion, together with the circumstances which prepared the way for the fifth, recorded in the following chapter. The one related here, like that before it, was at the tribunal of the Roman governor, but in the presence of Jewish representatives, and like it also exhibits only a brief summary of the defence itself, with a fuller statement of the interlocutory proceedings. The chief points of difference are those of character and situation between Felix and Festus, and the step in advance which the Apostle here takes by appealing to the Emperor. The chapter naturally falls into two parts, the first of which contains the direct transactions between Paul and Festus (1–12). Under this head are included the arrival of Festus, his first visit to Jerusalem, the renewal of the charge and plot against Paul, the refusal of the Procurator to remove him, and the appointment of a new trial at Cesarea (1–5). Then comes the trial itself, with a summary statement of the charges and defence (6–8). Paul refuses to be tried once more at Jerusalem, and appeals to the Emperor in person, which appeal the governor allows (9–12). The remainder of the chapter describes the occasion and preliminaries of his fifth appearance (13–27). Among these is a visit from Agrippa to Festus, and a statement of Paul's case by the latter to the former, with an expression of Agrippa's wish to see and hear him (13–22). Then follows an account of the meeting for this purpose, a second statement of the case by Festus, with his own reason for desiring Agrippa to hear the prisoner himself (23–27).

1. Now when Festus was come into the province, after three days he ascended from Cesarea to Jerusalem.

Festus is also mentioned by Josephus, in both his histories, as the successor of Felix in the government of Judea, and as having been occupied, during his short administration, in suppressing the Sicarii (or Assassins) and other disturbers of the public peace, including an impostor who had tried to raise the people in rebellion by fanatical delusions (see above, on 5, 36. 37. 21, 38.) In these respects his government was very similar to that of Felix (see above, on 23, 24. 24, 2. 3), but his personal character much better, as appears, not so much from any positive description, as from the way in which Josephus contrasts him with his successor Albinus, a man who governed in a manner altogether different, and had a hand in every kind of wickedness. According to the latest chronological authorities, Festus administered the government a little less than two years, from the autumn of A. D. 60 to the summer of A. D. 62. From an incidental statement of Josephus (that the Emperor, hearing of the death of Festus, sent Albinus to Judea as his Procurator), we learn that, unlike most of his predecessors and successors, he died in office. In justice to the memory of this short-lived and comparatively upright magistrate, he ought to be carefully distinguished from his predecessor (Felix), with whom, no doubt from the resemblance of the names, he has sometimes been confounded, not only by superficial readers, but by learned writers. *Festus then* (or *therefore*), a resumption of the statement in the first clause of 24, 27. *Having come*, literally, come up, mounted, or ascended, sometimes applied to embarkation on board a vessel (see above, on 21, 2. 6, and below on 27, 2), but also to entrance or arrival in a country (see above, on 20, 18); and as this is perfectly appropriate here, there is no need of resorting to the figurative sense of *entering on his government* (or *office*), which however, although not expressed, is necessarily implied in his arrival and the acts that follow. *After three days* may be strictly understood as meaning three whole days, or, according to a common ancient idiom, as implying that he took one entire day of rest between his arrival at Cesarea and his journey to Jerusalem. This prompt departure to the Holy City may evince both official promptness and a natural curiosity to see a place so famous even in the history of empires.

2. Then the high priest and the chief of the Jews informed him against Paul, and besought him—

Then (δὲ) *the High Priest*, or according to the oldest copies and the latest critics, *the High* (or *Chief*) *Priests*, in the plural number. The actual High Priest, at this time, as we learn from Josephus, was not Ananias (see above, on 23, 2. 24, 1), but Ishmael the son of Phabi, nominated to that office by Agrippa (see below, on v. 13.) *The chief* or *first* (*men*) *of the Jews*, a general description of the class commonly described as *elders* (see above, on 4, 5. 8, 23. 6, 12. 23, 14. 24, 1), with whom they are identified by Festus, in relating this very occurrence (see below, on v. 15.) *Informed*, the same verb, with precisely the same meaning, as in 24, 1, where it is explained. This revival of the criminal information against Paul, after an interval of two years, shows the national importance which the Sanhedrim attached to the proceeding, if not the personal malignity and rancor of its leading members, which, at all events, is evident enough from the petition here recorded. (For the usage of the last verb, see above, on 2, 40. 8, 31. 16, 40. 20, 12. 21, 12. 24, 4.)

3. And desired favour against him, that he would send for him to Jerusalem, laying wait in the way to kill him.

Not content with renewing their old accusation, they present a petition of the most extraordinary kind. *Asking* (for themselves) *favour* (or *a favour*) *against him*, the idea of gratuity or special favour being doubly suggested, by the added noun and by the form of the verb, which is in the middle voice and has the same reflexive sense as in many other places (see above, on 3, 14. 7, 46. 9, 2. 12, 20. 13, 21. 28.) This direct demand for partial judgment, or respect of persons, a sin so frequently forbidden in their own law (see above, on 10, 34), would seem to imply an unfavourable estimate of the new Procurator's character and judgment, were it not more easily referred to that insane delusion, under which the Jews, at this eventful crisis of their history, appeared to act, and which has been already mentioned as transforming them, in temper and spirit, from devout Jews to ferocious heathen (see above, on 24, 10.) One of the clearest premonitions that the days of Israel, as a church and as a state, were numbered, is this very loss of the true theocratical spirit, and this callousness of conscience both as to means and ends; a change made known to us, not only or most vividly in Scripture, but in the writings of the contemporary Jewish historian. It is possible, however, that the words, *asking favour*, in the verse before us, relate not to the form of the request, but merely to its secret motive. The sense will then be, not that they entreated Festus to confer this favour on them, but that they simply asked him to transfer the trial to Jerusalem, as a matter of right or of convenience, while the real purpose of this proposition would have made the granting of it by the governor a gross act of judicial partiality or favour to one party at the cost and hazard of the other. This may seem more natural and credible, in itself considered; but the other is more readily suggested by the language of the narrative. *Laying wait*, literally, *making an ambuscade* (or *ambush*), either in the strict sense, or in that of plotting. (See above, on 23, 21, and compare the use of the cognate verb in 23, 16 and Luke 11, 54.) If literally understood, the present participle (*making*) may be used for the future, or imply that they were actually making preparation to way-lay Paul. *To kill* (despatch, or make away with) *him in* (by or along) *the road.* (For the usage of the verb, see above, on 2, 23. 9, 23. 16, 27. 22, 20. 23, 15; and for that of the preposition, on 5, 15. 8, 36. 16, 7.)

4. But Festus answered, that Paul should be kept at Cesarea, and that he himself would depart shortly (thither).

But, or *so then*, the resumptive particle, following the parenthetical statement in the last clause of the third verse (see above, on 1, 6. 2, 41. 8, 4. 9, 31. 11, 19. 12, 5. 13, 4, 16, 5. 19, 32. 23, 18, 22. 31.) *Should be kept* is not the meaning of the Greek verb, which is in the infinitive mood and present tense, and according to Greek usage means that he was actually then kept (i. e. watched or guarded, see above, on 12, 5. 6. 16, 23. 24, 23.) The governor's reply to their exorbitant or treacherous petition was, that Paul was already in safe-keeping at the seat of government, and as the governor expected to be there himself before long, his removal was unnecessary and indeed would be inconvenient. *Would depart*, or was about to set forth (see above, on 9, 28, and on 24, 15. 25.)

25.) *Thither* (i. e. to Cesarea) is unnecessarily, but not erro neously, supplied by the translators.

5. Let them therefore, said he, which among you are able, go down with (me), and accuse this man, if there be any wickedness in him.

Therefore, i. e. because it would not be convenient to remove him. *Able*, i. e. able to do so, as in 11, 17 above (compare Luke 14, 31. Rom. 4, 21. 11, 23. 14, 4. 2 Cor. 9, 8. 2 Tim. 1, 12. Tit. 1, 9. Heb. 11, 19. James 3, 2.) The meaning then is, 'Such of you as have it in your power to attend there.' But although this usage of the Greek word is established by the passages just cited, and by its frequent construction with the infinitive in the classics, most interpreters prefer the stronger sense of *powerful*, which occurs above, in 7, 22. 18, 24 (compare 1 Cor. 1, 26. 2 Cor. 10, 4. 12, 10. 13, 9. Rev. 6, 15.) This may then be taken either as a vague description of the leading men (like *first* or *chief* in v. 2), or as a more specific designation of the persons authorized, by office or by special delegation, to perform the duty here prescribed, and represent the Sanhedrim at Cesarea. The first interpretation, although favoured by a similar but rare use of the Greek word by Josephus and Thucydides, is less appropriate and natural, as being a mere complimentary description, than the other, which denotes official rank and obligation. The word *wickedness*, although not printed in italics, is supplied by the translators, being found neither in the common text nor in the critical editions ; but several of the oldest copies have a Greek word (ἄτοπον) elsewhere rendered *harm* (28, 6), *amiss* (Luke 23, 41,) *unreasonable* (2 Thess. 3, 2.) The idea of fault or crime is of course suggested even by the shorter reading, 'if there be any thing in this (or the) man.'

6. And when he had tarried among them more than ten days, he went down unto Cesarea, and the next day, sitting on the judgment seat, commanded Paul to be brought.

Having spent (or *passed*), the same verb as in 12, 19. 14, 3. 28. 15, 35. 16, 12. 20, 6. The marginal reading, *not more than eight or ten days*, is now regarded by the critics as the true text. The difference between this and the common reading is, that the latter seems to represent the sojourn as a long one ('he said he would set out soon, but he really remained there more than ten days'); while the other refers to it as very short ('he said he would set out soon, and accordingly he staid there only eight or ten days.') *Going down to Cesarea, on the morrow sitting* (or taking his seat) *upon the bench* (or *tribunal*, see above, on 12, 21. 18, 12. 16. 17.) Here again Festus is presented to us as a prompt and active man of business (see above, on v. 1), punctual to his engagements and exacting punctuality of others.

7. And when he was come, the Jews which came down from Jerusalem stood round about, and laid many and grievous complaints against Paul, which they could not prove.

Come, arrived, i. e. either from the prison to the palace, or from one apartment of the latter to another (see above, on 24, 17. 24.) *Having* (or *who had*) *come down*, in obedience to the procurator's order, and as representatives of the national council (see above, on v. 5.) *Stood around him*, according to some ancient copies, which is commonly regarded as the true sense, although not perhaps the true text. Some interpreters, however, understand it to mean, *round about* (the judgment-seat); but this is really included in the other, which suggests the additional idea of the eagerness with which they crowded round their long-lost victim. The charges are described in general terms as *many and grievous*, literally, *heavy*, which might here have been retained, as it could not be in the translation of the same word in a former case (see above, on 20, 29.) *Complaints*, charges, accusations, grounds of punishment, a kindred form to that in 13, 28. 22, 24. 23, 28, and primarily meaning *causes*. The nature of these charges may be gathered from the former accusation (see above, on 24, 5. 6), and from the abstract of Paul's answer in the next verse. *Laid*, literally, *bearing, bringing*, which is equally agreeable to Greek and English usage. *Which* (complaints or charges) *they were not strong* (enough, or *able*) *to prove* (literally, *show forth*, as in 1 Cor. 4, 9. 2 Thess. 2, 4), i. e. show to be true. (See above, on 2, 22, and for the usage of the preceding verb, on 6, 10. 15, 10. 19, 16. 20.)

8. While he answered for himself, Neither against the law of the Jews, neither against the temple, nor yet against Cesar, have I offended any thing at all.

Paul's defence is stated in the same compendious and summary form. *He apologizing*, saying in his own defence (see above, on 19, 33. 24, 10), not once for all, perhaps, or in a continuous discourse, but, as the absolute construction seems to intimate, from time to time, replying to each charge as it was opened or alleged against him. (*That*, omitted in the version, as at variance with English usage, see above, on 24, 21.) *Against*, or more exactly, *as to*, with respect to, the idea of hostility or opposition being really suggested by the context. (See above, on 2, 25. 6, 11. 9, 1. 17, 21. 20, 21. 24, 15. 24.) From what Paul here denies we learn what his enemies affirmed, to wit, the same old charges of schism or apostasy (from the law), sacrilegious desecration (of the temple), and treacherous revolt (against the emperor.) These are substantially the charges urged, two years before, at the bar of Felix, by Tertullus (see above, on 24, 5. 6.) *Cesar*, properly the name of a patrician Roman family, from the most illustrious of whom (Julius Cesar) it was derived by his adopted son (Augustus), and from him by his adopted son (Tiberius), and from him by his successors (Caligula, Claudius, and Nero), under whom it had become a royal title, equivalent to Emperor (see above, on 11, 28. 17, 7.)

9. But Festus, willing to do the Jews a pleasure, answered Paul, and said, Wilt thou go up to Jerusalem, and there be judged of these things before me?

To do the Jews a pleasure, almost the same phrase with the one applied above (in 24, 27) to Felix. The variation between *do* and *show* belongs exclusively to the translation, which, however, is in neither case exact, the Greek verb meaning to deposit or lay up in store. A real difference of form, not observed in the translation, is that between the plural (*favours*) in the other place and the singular (*favour*) in the one before us. This may have reference to the fact that Felix had used many such means of conciliation, whereas this was the first and perhaps the last attempt upon the part of Festus. It cannot be denied, however, that the sameness of expression in these cases shows that Festus, though apparently less selfish and unscrupulous than Felix, was in some measure actuated by the same desire to secure the good will and the good word of his subjects, when he should come to give account at Rome of his administration. The means by which they undertook to gain this common end, however, were extremely different. While Felix, after keeping Paul in prison two years, left him still in bondage at his own departure, Festus merely asked him if he would consent to undergo another trial at Jerusalem. This might indeed be regarded as a wholly unobjectionable proposition, made by a new-comer, unacquainted with the murderous designs of the accusers, and regarding their request as one of little moment. But this favourable view of the Procurator's conduct must be very materially qualified by the tone and substance of Paul's answer, as recorded in the next two verses. It should also be remembered that Paul had just been tried already, as we read of charges and defences summarily but distinctly spoken of in vs. 7. 8 above. This was therefore a proposal to be tried once more, and that before the Sanhedrim, though in the presence of the governor, and subject to his ultimate decision. (See above, on 23, 30. 24, 19. 20.)

10. Then said Paul, I stand at Cesar's judgment seat, where I ought to be judged; to the Jews have I done no wrong, as thou very well knowest.

To the unreasonable proposition in the ninth verse, which could only be intended to conciliate the Jews by a gratuitous reiteration of a process which had been already several times repeated with the same result, Paul replies by re-asserting, for the third time, his immunities and rights as a Roman citizen. (See above, on 16, 37–39. 22, 25–29.) At Philippi he had done this to reprove the magistrates for scourging and confining him; at Jerusalem, to prevent the repetition of that outrage; but now at Cesarea, to secure himself from being sacrificed by Festus, even through mere ignorance or weakness, to the malice of his enemies. *I stand at* (or *before*) *Cesar's judgment-seat* (i. e. the tribunal of the Emperor.) This is not to be confounded with the appeal at the close of the next verse, but explained as a preliminary to it. *I am standing* (*now*) *at Cesar's bar*, i. e. before his representative, as the very title *Procurator* signified, and not at that of the

Jewish Sanhedrim. He here claims the protection of that Roman power, to which the Jews had virtually betrayed him, and by which he had been long robbed of his liberty. *Where* (i. e. in the Roman not the Jewish courts) *I ought to be* (or still more strongly, *must be*) *tried* (if tried at all.) This naturally followed from the fact that he was actually in Roman hands and under Roman jurisdiction, and that no reason could be given for removing his case elsewhere. It followed, still more clearly and conclusively, from his being a hereditary Roman citizen, and as such entitled to the full advantage of the Roman laws. These claims would have been valid, even if a case had been made out against him by the Jews; how much more when they had utterly failed so to do. This third ground is stated in the last clause, with a confident appeal to Festus's own judgment, as to the nature of the charge against him. *The Jews I have* (*in*) *nothing wronged*, in the judicial sense, i. e. they have no ground of charge against me. If this was merely a profession of his innocence, it would be no argument at all, as it would really be tantamount to saying, 'I am not guilty, and therefore ought not to be tried,' a mode of reasoning which would put an end to all judicial process, except in the case of persons pleading guilty. This absurd sense has been sometimes put on Paul's expressions by interpreters who overlook the fact that this was not a mere preparatory meeting, a discussion about trying him, but that he had just been tried on many grievous charges, and defended himself against them (see above, on vs. 7. 8), and that he here asserts his innocence, not as a witness in his own behalf, but with explicit reference to the result of the preceding trial. 'With respect to the Jews, I am not guilty, having just been proved so by their total failure to substantiate their charges.' This view of the matter also serves to explain the last clause of the verse, which has very much perplexed interpreters. *As thou also* (not expressed in the translation, i. e. thou thyself, as well as I and others) *knowest right well* (literally, *better.*) This comparative expression, like the one applied to Felix (see above, on 24, 22), has been variously explained as a superlative, or as meaning better than could be expected, better than thou choosest to acknowledge, &c. But in this, as in the other case, the simplest and most satisfactory hypothesis is that which compares his present with his previous knowledge, *as thou also knowest better* (now than thou didst a little while ago.) Besides the simplicity of this construction, the strict sense which it puts on the comparative expression, and the analogy afforded by the other case just cited, it is furthermore confirmed by the usage of the verb translated *knowest*, which elsewhere means to recognize, discover, ascertain, or come to know what was previously unknown or misunderstood. (See above, on 3, 10. 4, 13. 9, 30. 12, 14. 19, 34. 22, 24. 29. 24, 8.) As thus explained, the whole verse may be paraphrased as follows. 'Why do you ask me such a needless question? Can you really expect a Roman citizen, already standing at the Roman bar, to consent to undergo another trial at the tribunal of these Jews, who have just failed again to prove their charges against me, and have therefore not the slightest claim upon me, as you must yourself be now convinced, if you knew it not before?'

11. For if I be an offender, or have committed any thing worthy of death, I refuse not to die; but if there be none of these things whereof these accuse me, no man may deliver me unto them. I appeal unto Cesar.

This verse shows still more clearly that the ground assumed by Paul in that before it, is the ground of his own innocence, not merely as asserted by himself but as judicially established. He indignantly disclaims a base desire to shun investigation or to escape any punishment of which he may be proved worthy. *For* relates to this disclaimer—'I am not merely seeking to shun danger, for if,' &c. *If I am guilty*, the same technical expression used in v. 10, although here translated by a different phrase (*if I be an offender*), which obscures the connection to the English reader. *If I have done, etc.*, i. e. if I am proved on trial to have done so; if such is the result of the investigation just concluded, then *I do not refuse*, literally, *beg off*, ask to be exempted as a favour from the punishment which I deserve. (Compare the less emphatic use of the same verb in Luke 14, 18. 19. 1 Tim. 4, 7. 5, 11. 2 Tim. 2, 23. Tit. 3, 10. Heb. 12, 19. 25.) *If there be none of these things*, i. e. if their charges have been proved already to be frivolous and groundless. This is really equivalent to saying, since they have been proved to be so, the conditional expression being often so employed in Greek (see above, on 4, 9. 11, 17. 23, 9.) *No (one) can* (i. e. lawfully) *deliver me*, a very inadequate translation of the Greek verb, which means to do a favour, or bestow a gift (see above, on 3, 14, and below, on 27, 24), and should be taken in its strict sense here. 'If I have been found guilty, let me suffer, without further trial. If I have not, to remand me to their bar would be to make a present of me to my enemies, which no man, no, not even you, can rightfully or justly do.' From this reply of Paul, we learn that Festus, although not unfriendly, and no doubt convinced of his innocence, had made a gratuitous and dangerous proposal, simply to gratify the Jews, by conceding what appeared to him a matter of indifference, or at most a matter of mere form. By this proposal he betrayed such a deficiency, either of judgment or of knowledge, that no uprightness of intention or amenity of temper could have made the cause of the Apostle safe so long as it was under his control. By a prompt and unexpected movement, therefore, he removes it instantly beyond the reach, not only of the Jews, but of the governor himself. *I appeal unto Cesar*, or, as the words primarily signify, *Cesar I invoke*, the same verb that is elsewhere used to denote the religious invocation of our Lord by his disciples (see above, on 2, 21. 7, 59. 9, 14. 21. 22, 16.) The essential meaning may be that of calling to one's aid, invoking help, either in prayer to a superior being, or by appeal to a superior tribunal. The right of appeal to the people, in a body or as represented by the tribunes, was one of the most valued rights of Roman citizens, and still continued to be so regarded, even after the supreme judicial power of the people had been transferred to the emperors. Particular importance was attached to the right of appeal from the judgments of provincial magistrates. According to ancient writers, no delay or written form was requisite, the only act necessary to arrest the judgment being the utterance of the word *Appello!* The magic power of this one word is described as similar to that of the talismanic phrase, *Civis Romanus sum!* (See above, on 16, 37. 21, 25.) Indeed the two things coincided, as it was the Roman citizen, and not the mere provincial subject of the empire, who could thus transfer his cause from any inferior tribunal to that of the Emperor himself. The possession of this citizenship, therefore, was the providential means of saving Paul, at this critical juncture, not only from the power of his Jewish foes, but also from the weakness of his Roman friends. For it will now be seen, that while in v. 10 he contrasts the Jewish courts with that of Festus, as the representative of Roman justice, in the close of that before us, he ascends even from the bar of Festus to the tribunal of his lord and master. (See below, on v. 26.)

12. Then Festus, when he had conferred with the council, answered, Hast thou appealed unto Cesar? unto Cesar shalt thou go.

Having conferred (literally, *talked* or *spoken*) *with the council*, not that of the Jews, which was not present as a body, and is never so described, the Greek word elsewhere always meaning consultation, Matt. 12, 14 not excepted; but his own assessors or advisers, a kind of local court or jury, who assisted the provincial magistrates in their judicial functions. The conference, in this case, was occasioned not so much by any doubt or difficulty as by the surprise which Paul's abrupt appeal occasioned. According to the ancient legal books, there were some excepted cases, in which the right of appeal was suspended or entirely withheld; but it seems to have been only where the public peace or safety was endangered by delay, as when a pirate or insurgent was detected in the very act. However this may be, the Procurator's council could see no ground for refusing Paul's appeal, and Festus therefore entertains it. *Hast thou invoked* (or *appealed to*) *Cesar?* may be also read affirmatively, as in the oldest English versions and the best modern commentaries, *thou hast appealed unto Cesar*. It is objected, that the interrogative construction makes the clause more spirited and pointed; but the very argument against it is, that it imparts to this reply of Festus a flippant and sarcastic tone, which does not properly belong to it. Without the question, the words simply mean, '(As) thou hast appealed to Cesar, unto Cesar thou shalt go,' which may have been the customary formula in granting or sustaining such appeals. By this decided and sagacious step, Paul, acting under the divine direction, although not perhaps entirely aware of what was to ensue, not only placed himself beyond the reach of his vindictive enemies, but secured his long designed and promised visit to Rome. (See above, on 19, 21. 23, 11, and compare Rom. 1, 15.)

13. And after certain days king Agrippa and Bernice came unto Cesarea to salute Festus.

The appeal recorded in the verse preceding put an end to all judicial process against Paul, both in the Jewish and the Roman courts of Palestine. It might have seemed, therefore, that he could have no further opportunity of self-defence or argumentative appeal to his own nation. And yet he did appear once more, before its highest representative, and there delivered what, in some respects, is the most characteristic and complete of his Apologies. This singular and unexpected close of Paul's extraordinary mission to Judea seemed to call for explanation, to afford which is Luke's purpose in the remainder of this chapter, where he states distinctly the apparently fortuitous occasion of this last appearance. *After certain days*, literally, *some days having intervened*, or happened, come to pass, between (see below, on 27, 9, and compare Mark 16, 1.) *Agrippa the king*, sometimes called Agrippa the Second or Younger, to distinguish him from his father, Agrippa the First, always called Herod in this book, whose miserable death is recorded in 12, 23 above. When that event took place, the Emperor Claudius, the friend and patron of the younger Agrippa, who had been brought up at Rome, was dissuaded by his counsellors from giving to a youth of seventeen the whole dominion of his father (see above, on 12, 1), but bestowed upon him the kingdom of Chalcis which had belonged to his uncle Herod, and afterwards gave him the tetrarchate of his uncle Philip, and certain parts of Galilee and Perea, with the royal title. To this was eventually added the guardianship of the temple, the keeping of the sacred vestments, and the right of nominating the High Priest. Here again the writer's truthfulness and knowledge of his subject are evinced by the precision and the confidence with which he steers through all these complicated changes without once committing even an anachronism or misnomer. Three times, in the course of the New Testament history, we find a Herod on the throne, yet always with some variation in the circumstances, which would have proved a snare to a fictitious writer. Thus the two Agrippas were both kings, but not of the same kingdom, the father reigning over Judea, while the son was present only as a visitor, and the province was again annexed to Syria and governed by a Procurator (see above, on 23, 23.) He is represented by Josephus as a zealous Jew, at least externally, and even in the Talmud there is a story of his weeping at the public reading of the law forbidding any Gentile to bear rule in Israel, whereupon the people cried out to console and reassure him. According to Josephus, he was not regarded by the Jews with much affection or respect, on account of his heathen education and equivocal position between Jews and Gentiles, which was afterwards defined by his adhering to the Romans, in the final struggle which destroyed the Jewish church and commonwealth. During the short administration of Festus, he and Agrippa were involved in a controversy with the Jews, occasioned by the king's erecting an apartment in his palace on Mount Zion, from which he could see all that passed in the enclosure of the temple, even when reclining at his meals, to obstruct which view the people built a wall before his windows. This dispute was carried up to Rome, and finally decided in favour of the people through the influence of Nero's wife, Poppæa, whom Josephus speaks of as devout, that is, a secret or avowed adherent of the Jewish faith. All this was subsequent to what is here recorded; for we find Agrippa paying a visit of congratulation to the newly arrived governor, with whom he may have been acquainted formerly at Rome. The incestuous marriages, for which the Herods were proverbial, are said to have had one example in the case of this Agrippa and his eldest sister Bernice, who now attended him to Cesarea. Her first husband was her uncle, Herod king of Chalcis, after whose death she resided with Agrippa, till, in order to avoid reproach and scandal, she persuaded Polemon, king of Cilicia, to become a Jew and marry her, which he did for the sake of her supposed wealth, but afterwards forsook both his wife and his religion, whereupon she returned to her brother, and at length crowned her infamous career by becoming the mistress of two successive Roman Emperors, father and son, Vespasian (so says Tacitus) and Titus (so says Suetonius.) With such representatives of Judaism long resident at Rome, it is no wonder that the poet Juvenal, in one of his most bitter and severe allusions, should combine the sabbath and abstinence from swine's flesh with the incest of Bernice and Agrippa, as characteristics of the race and the religion. This odious relation, as a key to Agrippa's moral character, is thought by some to be suggested by the prominence here given to Bernice, without any designation of her rank or lineage. That these corruptions were not merely personal, but tainted the whole family, may be inferred from the description previously given of Drusilla, a younger sister of the two here mentioned. (See above, on 24, 24.) Some suppose Agrippa's visit upon this occasion, though ostensibly designed to welcome Felix, to have had some reference to the case of Paul, which he may have regarded as belonging to his own jurisdiction as the guardian of the temple and protector of the Jews, though not the civil ruler of Judea. But as no such motive is suggested in the context, and as both Agrippa and Bernice paid a similar visit to the Procurator Gessius Florus, it is better to explain it as a complimentary attention, or perhaps as an official recognition of the Roman sovereignty by the successors of the native kings.

14. And when they had been there many days, Festus declared Paul's cause unto the king, saying, There is a certain man left in bonds by Felix—

When (literally, *as*, or while) *they had been* (literally, *were spending time*) *there*, the same Greek verb that is used above in v. 6. *Many*, literally, *more*, i. e. more than one, several, a few (see above, on 13, 31. 21, 10. 24, 17.) *Declared Paul's cause*, or more exactly, *stated* (or *referred*) *the* (*things*) *concerning Paul.* (Compare the use of the same verb by Paul himself, Gal. 2, 2.) The idea is not that of official reference or report, but rather of a casual colloquial statement, although Festus, if the motive afterwards expressed was real, may have meditated such a course from the beginning. This narrative of Festus is as near to that of Luke as would be natural in such a case, although there may be some exaggerations or embellishments, as we shall see below. *In bonds*, literally, *a prisoner*, or *imprisoned*, the Greek word being used in the classics as an adjective, but in the New Testament always elsewhere as a noun (see above, on 16, 25. 27. 23, 18, and compare Matt. 27, 15. 16. Mark 15, 6.) In Paul's epistles, written during his captivity, he uses this word as a favourite description of himself (see Eph. 3, 1. 4, 1. 2 Tim. 1, 8. Philem. 1, 9.)

15. About whom, when I was at Jerusalem, the chief priests and the elders of the Jews informed (me), desiring (to have) judgment against him.

About (concerning, with respect to) *whom*, *I being at* (or *to*, i. e. having previously come to) *Jerusalem*. *Informed*, as in v. 2 and in 24, 1 above. *Desiring to have*, literally, *asking* (for themselves), the same verb in the middle voice employed above in v. 3. The expression here is not so strong, however, since instead of *favour*, they are said to have asked *judgment*, not *condemnation*, as the Greek word elsewhere means from its connection (see below, on 28, 4, and compare 2 Thess. 1, 9. Jude 7, in all which places it is rendered *vengeance*), but *justice*, i. e. a fair trial, which was the pretext of the application, as appears from Luke's account of it (see above, on vs. 3. 9.) They desired Paul's condemnation, no doubt, as the issue of his trial at their bar; but all they dared to ask was justice.

16. To whom I answered, It is not the manner of the Romans to deliver any man to die, before that he which is accused have the accusers face to face, and have license to answer for himself concerning the crime laid against him.

This reply is altogether different from that in v. 4, where the application is refused from mere considerations of convenience. It is altogether possible, however, that both answers were returned, and that Luke has chosen to record each only once. Another explanation of the difference, less pleasing in itself and less creditable to Festus, is that he embellished his statement to Agrippa, by relating not only what he said but what he might have said on that occasion. The reply itself has always been regarded as a true and honourable testimony to the Roman love of justice, the most real and conspicuous of the national virtues. *Manner* (or *custom*) is a feeble reproduction of the Greek word (ἔθος), which, in reference not only to the Jews (see above, on 6, 14. 15, 1. 21, 21), but to the Gentiles (see above, on 16, 21), would necessarily suggest the additional ideas of established law and religious usage. The practice here repudiated was to the Romans both illegal and irreligious. *To deliver*, as a gift, or as a means of gratifying others, the same expression that occurs above in v. 11, and which Festus may have borrowed from Paul's speech on that occasion, a remark admitting of a wider application to the whole of this fine Roman sentiment, for which the judge was very possibly indebted to the prisoner at his bar. *To die*, literally, *to* (or *for*) *destruction* (or *perdition*, see above, on 8, 20); but these words are not found in the oldest copies, and are therefore omitted by the latest critics, the idea being certainly implied, if not expressed. *He which is accused*, or more simply and exactly, *the accused*, corresponding, both in form and sense, to *the accusers*. The combination of the singular and plural form was probably suggested by the case in hand, where one man was accused by many. *Face to face*, literally, *to (his) face*, i. e. before him, in his presence (see above, on 3, 13), which may be regarded as an abbreviation of the other phrase (see 1 Cor. 13, 12, and compare the marginal translation of 2 John 12. 3 John 14.) *License to answer for himself*, or more exactly, *place of apology* (or *self-defence*), which some take literally in the sense of a place where he may defend himself, but most interpreters in that of opportunity, including a sufficient space of time. (Compare *place of repentance*, Heb. 12, 17, and the corresponding Latin phrase, *poenitentiae locus*, used by Livy, Tacitus, and Pliny.) *The crime laid against him* is in Greek a single word meaning *charge* or *accusation*, as explained above (on 23, 29.)

17. Therefore, when they were come hither, without any delay, on the morrow, I sat on the judgment seat, and commanded the man to be brought forth.

When they were come hither, literally, *they having come together here*, i. e. at Cesarea, in obedience to the order here omitted but before recorded (see above, on v. 5.) *Without any delay*, literally, *making no delay* (or *postponement*), a noun corresponding to the verb used above (in 24, 22) of Felix, to whose gratuitous procrastination there may here be a complacent reference, though true in fact, as the testimony of Festus is confirmed by that of Luke himself (see above, on v. 6.) *Sitting* (or *having sat down*) *on the bench* (or judgment-seat, tribunal, see above, on vs. 6. 10), *I commanded the man to be brought* (*in* or *forth*, i. e. from the prison, as supplied by the translators.)

18. Against whom when the accusers stood up, they brought none accusation of such things as I supposed—

Against whom, literally, *about whom*, which may either mean, *concerning whom*, as in the last clause of v. 16, or have its primary and local sense, *around him standing*, an idea before expressed by a verb compounded with this same preposition (see above, on v. 7.) This construction is now commonly preferred, as it connects the first words of the verse together and at the same time makes the scene more lively by describing the accusers not as standing merely, but as standing or gathering around the accused. *None*, as an adjective directly coupled with a noun, belongs to old English usage, the modern dialect, in all such cases, substituting *no*. (Other examples of the old form may be seen in Deut. 28, 66. Mic. 3, 11. 1 Cor. 10, 32. 1 Tim. 5, 14.) *Of such things as* (or *those things which*) *I supposed* (surmised, suspected, or conjectured), implying a want of clear and definite knowledge (see above, on 13, 25, and below, on 27, 27.) Festus here refers, no doubt, to that which Gallio expressly named upon a like occasion (see above, on 18, 14), namely, legal or moral wrong, as distinguished from mere error of opinion. The resemblance between these two speeches, although not so great as to impair their individuality, is just what might have been expected from the similarity of circumstances, both the governors in question being strangers or new comers, and entirely unacquainted with the Jews' religion.

19. But had certain questions against him of their own superstition, and of one Jesus, which was dead, whom Paul affirmed to be alive.

Questions, the plural of the word employed by Gallio, in 18, 15, and there explained. *Against him*, literally, *to* or *at him*, as the person whom they charged with heresy, the preposition signifying not hostility directly, but the object of address or controversy (see above, on 11, 2.) *Of* (about, concerning, as in v. 16) *their own religion*, an equivocal expression, upon which the speaker and the hearers were at liberty to put their own construction, as denoting either piety or superstition. It is a kindred word to that employed in the exordium of Paul's discourse at Athens (see above, on 17, 22) and there explained. From the use of this word (in the sense of *superstition*) it has been inferred that Agrippa could not be a Jew, or Festus would not have insulted him so grossly. But the argument is all the other way, to wit, that as we know Agrippa to have been a Jew (see above, on v. 13, and below, on 26, 3 27), the word must at least admit of a good sense. That this speech is not copied from the speech of Gallio, is apparent from the circumstance that while the latter uses terms of general description (*words* and *names* and *law*), Festus fastens on a single question, that of Christ's resurrection, and describes it just as might have been expected from a Roman of good sense, but not acquainted with the Jewish Scriptures or the Christian doctrines. The transition from the general to the special statement of the points at issue is indicated by the *and* —'about their own religion and (especially) *about one* (or *a certain*) *Jesus* (now) *dead* (or *a certain deceased Jesus*), *whom Paul affirmed* (or solemnly declared, the same verb as in 24, 9) *to live* (i. e. to be alive), which may either mean to *live still* (i. e. not to have died), or to *live again* (i. e. to have revived or risen from the dead.) The very ambiguity of this expression corresponds no doubt to the precise state of the speaker's mind on this perplexing and confounding subject, as he probably was not aware precisely what Paul meant beyond the general assertion that the man in question was alive. The charge of scornful and incredulous misrepresentation, brought by some of the old writers against this description of the controverted question, is at variance with what we know besides of Festus, and far less natural in this connection than the view just taken of the passage, as exhibiting precisely the impression likely to be made upon the mind of even an intelligent and candid heathen, by the complicated issues of the controversy between Jews and Christians. This character of truthfulness is made more striking by the fact that the specific point, which Festus singles out in his description of the charges against Paul, is precisely that which Paul makes even strangely prominent in his own discourses (see above, on 23, 6. 24, 15. 16, and below, on 26, 6–8.) The more inexplicable this proceeding upon Paul's part may as yet appear, the more surprising is the strict fidelity with which it is reproduced by Festus, to whom it must have been still more enigmatical, and whose account of it is therefore a strong proof of authenticity and genuineness in the record. Besides the points of similarity and difference between the words of Gallio and Festus, they may also be compared with those of Claudius Lysias in his letter to Felix (see above, on 23, 29), where the same natural perplexity appears, but with more reference to practical than speculative difficulties, and with a more negative description of the "questions," as involving no offence deserving death, or even imprisonment.

20. And because I doubted of such manner of questions, I asked (him) whether he would go to Jerusalem, and there be judged of these matters.

Because I doubted, literally, *being at a loss*, perplexed, confounded (see above, on 2, 12, where the etymology and usage of the Greek verb are explained.) The marginal version of the next words (*how to inquire hereof*) is probably nearer to the sense of the original than that given in the text, though both are paraphrases rather than translations. *Being perplexed* (or *at a loss*) *as to the inquiry about these* (*things*), i. e. how such matters could be judicially investigated. The word here rendered *inquiry* is a cognate form to that so often rendered *question* (see above, on 15, 2. 18, 15. 23, 29, and below, on 26, 3), but with a difference of termination (ζήτησις and ζήτημα), regarded by the best Greek philologists as expressing two distinguishable shades of meaning, namely, the subject and the act of disputation. The *questions* mentioned in v. 19 were themselves perplexing to the mind of Festus; but the particular perplexity, of which he here complains, was in relation to the method of inquiry or investigation. 'Being doubtful how such questions could be made the subject of inquiry in a court of justice.' This seems a natural and reasonable ground for wishing to transfer the case to Jewish hands; but it is not found in Luke's account of what was said on this occasion, which ascribes the Procurator's proposition to a very different motive (see above, on v. 9.) Nor is any such reason presupposed or recognized in Paul's reply, which treats the proposition as unreasonable and unfair, and makes it the occasion of his own appeal. From all this it is probable that Festus, like too many men in similar circumstances, instead of simply stating what he said before, avails himself of what has since occurred to him upon reflection, and improves the logic of his speech at the expense of its historical exactness. He originally made the proposition, as Luke tells us, to conciliate the Jews, but afterwards excogitated reasons of a higher kind, by which it might be plausibly supported. Such variations may be made almost unconsciously, and cannot therefore be adduced as proofs of *mala fides* or *malus animus*, although they may evince, as in the case before us, a greater care for one's own credit than for truth or for the interests of others. *These* (*things*) is the reading of the oldest manuscripts and latest critics; the received text is *this*, in the singular number, which in Greek may be either masculine or neuter, *this* (*man*), i. e. Jesus, whose life or death was in dispute, or *this* (thing), i. e. this whole matter or affair, which is substantially the same thing with the plural reading. *I asked him* (literally, *said*) *if* (or *whether*) *he would go*, not an auxiliary tense but two distinct verbs, *whether he desired* (or *was willing*) *to go*. (See above, on 17, 20. 18, 15. 19, 30. 22, 30. 23, 28; and for the like use of a different verb, on 7, 28. 39. 10, 10. 14, 13. 16, 3. 17, 18. 19, 33. 24, 6.) *Go*, depart, or journey, a verb implying distance and removal (see above, on v. 12.) *Judged*, tried, put on trial (see above, on vs. 9. 10.) *Of* (about, concerning) *these* (*things*), or about these questions, which to Festus were so puzzling and inscrutable. The impression naturally made by this whole statement must have been, that Paul had not been tried at all since Festus came into the province, but had stubbornly refused to be so, and in order to avoid it had appealed to Cesar. But this impression is to us corrected by the narrative of Luke himself, from which we learn that it was after Paul had been accused and heard in his defence by Festus, with an utter failure, on the part of his accusers, to substantiate their charges, that the governor had asked him to be tried again at Jerusalem, from which gratuitous and dangerous proposal, whether made ignorantly or insidiously, Paul was obliged to escape by suddenly appealing to the Emperor. Whatever impression this misstatement may have made upon Agrippa, it has not been without effect on some interpreters, who seem to take their views of Paul's case rather from what Festus asserts here than from what Luke relates in vs. 7–12 above.

21. But when Paul had appealed to be reserved unto the hearing of Augustus, I commanded him to be kept till I might send him to Cesar.

Paul appealing (or *having appealed*) *to be reserved* (or *kept*) seems at first an incongruous construction; but the first verb really includes the sense of *claiming*, which would here be perfectly appropriate. He appealed (and thereby virtually claimed) to be reserved, etc. *Hearing* (margin, *judgment*) is in Greek *diagnosis*, a term still employed in medicine to signify the critical discrimination of diseases, but applied more widely in the classics to any discriminating judgment or decision. (For the usage of the primitive or cognate verb, see above, on 23, 15. 24, 22.) *Augustus*, like the Greek word which it here translates, is properly an adjective denoting venerable, reverend, august. It is strictly a religious title, and describes its subject as entitled to divine honours, in which sense it was idolatrously given by the Roman Senate and people to Octavian Caesar, the first Emperor, from whom it was inherited by his successors, as an official title or description. It is here applied to Nero, not by Paul, who uses only the family name *Cesar* (see above, on vs. 8. 10. 11, and compare Phil. 4, 22), but by Festus, not as a mere honorary title, but no doubt in its highest and most heathenish acceptation, though he also uses the less flattering name in this same sentence. *To be kept*, another tense of the verb rendered in the preceding clause, *to be reserved*, both suggesting the additional idea of being watched or guarded (see above, on v. 4, and on 12, 5. 6. 16, 23. 24, 23.) *Until* (the time when or at which) *I might* (should or could) *send him to Cesar*. The delay referred to might have reference to legal forms required in such cases, or to military orders for the escort of the prisoner, or to an opportunity of safe and speedy passage from Judea into Italy. The interval, however, was not probably a long one (see below, on 27, 1.)

22. Then Agrippa said unto Festus, I would also hear the man myself. To-morrow, said he, thou shalt hear him.

Would hear, like *would go* in v. 20, is not a compound tense of one verb, as in English, but a phrase consisting of two distinct and independent verbs, the first of which means to *desire* (or *wish*), and is here in the indicative imperfect form. The simplest and most obvious version, therefore, would be, *I desired* (or *I was wishing*), with respect to past time, more or less remote. Some accordingly explain it as referring to a wish excited in Agrippa's mind while listening to Festus ('I was wishing just now that I could myself hear him'); others to a wish of earlier date and longer standing ('I desired to hear him long ago,' or 'before I came upon this visit'), which might then be understood as implying that he came at least in part for this purpose. This construction is especially preferred by those who think it not unlikely that Agrippa came to Cesarea, with a view to claim at least concurrent jurisdiction with the Procurator over Paul's case, as that of a native Jew, and as such under his protection and control (but see above, on v. 13.) Most interpreters, however, and especially the most exact philologists of modern times, explain the Greek verb, like the similar imperfect used by Paul in Rom. 9, 2, as the indirect expression of a present wish, correctly rendered in the English version. The nice distinction in Greek usage, as explained by these authorities, is that the present tense would have represented the result as dependent on the speaker's will (as in Rom. 1, 13. 16, 19. 1 Cor. 16, 7. 1 Tim. 2, 8); the imperfect with the qualifying particle (ἄν) would have meant, *I could wish* (but I do not); whereas this precise form is expressive of an actual and present wish, but subject to the will of others, 'I could wish, if it were proper, or if you have no objection.' This courteous suggestion or request is promptly responded to by Festus, who was no doubt glad of such important aid in settling this vexatious question. The dramatic movement of the sentence is still more marked in two of the oldest extant manuscripts, which omit the verb *said* in the first clause, and its subject or nominative (ὁ δέ) in the last clause.

23. And on the morrow, when Agrippa was come, and Bernice, with great pomp, and was entered into the place of hearing, with the chief captains, and principal men of the city, at Festus' commandment Paul was brought forth.

On the morrow, a favourite expression in this book, though not always uniform in English, being sometimes rendered *the next day*. (Compare 10, 9. 23. 24. 20, 7. 22, 30. 23, 32, with 14, 20. 21, 8, and v. 6 above, in all which places the original expression is the same.) *Agrippa having come* (or *coming*) *and Bernice*, again named as his companion, and again without describing her relation to him, perhaps for the reason before hinted (see above, on v. 13.) *With great pomp*, literally, *much fantasy*, a Greek word current in old English, in the restricted sense of *fancy*, which is really contracted from it, but in ancient usage meaning show, display, parade, pomp, as it is here correctly rendered. This might be nothing more than the usual and necessary state maintained by royal personages, as the only means of distinguishing their rank; but most interpreters suppose it to be here recorded in the way of censure, as a needless and excessive ostentation, throwing light upon the character of these two persons, and made doubly odious by their mutual relation and by the local circumstance, that this display was made almost upon the very spot where their father, a few years before, was smitten by an angel and devoured by worms, for the indulgence of a pride very similar to that supposed to be here charged upon his children. (See above, on 12, 21–23.) *Entered*, literally, *coming in*, a compound form of the verb *coming* in the first clause. *Place of hearing* is in Greek a single word, not used by the ancient classics, and supposed to have been formed upon the model of the Latin *auditorium*, which properly means any place of hearing, such as a lecture-room or court-room; but as this last usage, even of the Latin word, did not become fixed till the second century, its Greek equivalent most probably denotes, not a place constantly appropriated to this use, but one appointed for the present occasion, no doubt an apartment of the Praetorium in Cesarea (see above, on 23, 35.) The other persons mentioned were probably invited to give eclat to the audience, which in this respect was therefore the most brilliant and imposing of all Paul's appearances. *Chief captains*, chiliarchs, commanders of a thousand men, i. e. of cohorts (see above, on 10. 1. 21, 31), five of which, as Josephus mentions twice, were stationed at Cesarea, as the political capital of the province. *Principal men*, literally, *men by (way of) eminence* (or *prominence*), the prominent or leading men of Cesarea, whether *ex officio* or as private citizens.

24. And Festus said, King Agrippa, and all men which are here present with us, ye see this man, about whom all the multitude of the Jews have dealt with me, both at Jerusalem and (also) here, crying that he ought not to live any longer.

For the information of the strangers present, and perhaps to justify the singular occurrence of what seemed to be another trial after an appeal to the supreme tribunal, Festus opens the assembly with an explanatory statement of the previous proceedings and of his own design in this. *King Agrippa* (in the original, *Agrippa King*) is first addressed by name, as the highest in rank of the spectators, and the one for whose gratification this assembly had been really, though not perhaps ostensibly, convened. *And all the men* (or gentlemen) *present with us* (*here* is supplied by the translators.) *Bernice*, although present, is not named, because a woman could not be considered as taking part in judicial business, without a violation both of Oriental and Roman usage. *Ye see*, behold, survey, contemplate as a strange sight (see above, on 7, 56. 8, 13. 10, 11. 17, 16), or imperatively, *see, behold* (the man of whom you have so often heard.) *All the multitude* (or *mass*, see above, on 2, 6. 6, 2. 15, 30. 23, 7) may be either a hyperbole, relating to the priests and elders, or a reference to some popular movement not recorded elsewhere, although perfectly consistent with the known facts of the case, and with the habits of the people at Jerusalem (see above, on 21, 36.) *Dealt with me*, applied to me, petitioned me, a Greek verb originally meaning to fall in with or encounter, then to meet, confer, converse, negotiate, intercede, either for, as in every other place where it occurs (Rom. 8, 27. 34. 11, 2. Heb. 7, 25), or against a person, as in this place. *Crying*, shouting, and thereby showing the passionate excitement under which they acted. *Here*, at Cesarea, in allusion, no doubt, to the deputation from Jerusalem, of which we read in vs. 5. 17 above. As no popular commotion is recorded to have taken place there, it is not improbable that even what is said in the preceding clause has reference to the Sanhedrim and not to the rabble at Jerusalem.

25. But when I found that he had committed nothing worthy of death, and that he himself hath appealed to Augustus, I have determined to send him.

When I found, literally, *apprehending*, ascertaining, or perceiving (see above, on 4, 13. 10, 34) *him to have done nothing worthy of death*, another proof that Paul had actually been tried before Festus, when the latter made the proposition which occasioned his appeal (see above, on vs. 7. 8. 20); for on what other ground could Festus here assert his innocence? Had Festus promptly acted on the strong conviction here expressed, by setting Paul at liberty, the latter could have no pretext for appealing. It was because Festus, though convinced of his innocence, instead of giving judgment in his favour, weakly and unreasonably asked him to submit to a new trial, at another and most prejudiced tribunal; it was therefore that Paul found himself compelled to gain deliverance from both by an assertion of his civil rights. *This* (*man*) *himself having appealed to Cesar*, from what decision, or for what cause, Festus carefully abstains from saying, either here or in his previous and private statement of the case to Agrippa. *I determined to send him*, not by an arbitrary act of will, or even by a peremptory act of judgment, which is not the meaning of the Greek verb (see above, on 3, 13. 4, 19. 15, 19. 20, 16. 21, 25), but I came to this conclusion, I was satisfied hat this was the true course, as it was in fact the only one .eft to his discretion (see above, on v. 12.) Before proceeding to the next verse, it is indispensable to get a just view of the painful and embarrassing position, to which Festus had reduced himself by a vacillating and time-serving policy. Here was a man who had been tried before him (see above, on vs. 7. 8), with an utter failure, on the part of his accusers, to substantiate their charges, as the governor himself admits in this verse. He was therefore virtually though not formally acquitted, and his appeal was not from a decision in his favour, which would be absurd, but from the Procurator's failing or refusing to pronounce such a decision, unless Paul would submit to a new trial at Jerusalem.

26. Of whom I have no certain thing to write unto my lord. Wherefore I have brought him forth before you, and specially before thee, O king Agrippa, that, after examination had, I might have somewhat to write.

Having seen the false position in which Festus had been placed by his attempt to please the Jews instead of acting on his own sense of justice and conviction of Paul's innocence, we come now to his own disguised confession of the error into which he had thus fallen. *Of* (about, concerning) *whom* (as in v. 24) *any* (thing) *safe* (infallible or certain, see above, on 2, 36. 5, 23. 16, 23. 24. 21, 34. 22, 30) *to write unto the Lord I have not; wherefore* (for the reason just assigned, that he had nothing definite or certain to report) *I brought him forth* (or *forward*) *before you, and especially before thee* (as a judge, which idea is suggested by the Greek preposition, as in v. 9, and in 23, 30. 24, 8. 19. 20.) Not that Agrippa was to be a real judge in this case, or could possibly decide it after the prisoner's appeal to Nero; but by acting just as if he could do this, he might relieve the governor from some perplexity.

That the inquest (or *examination*) *having taken place, I might have somewhat to write* (or according to the latest critics, *have what I may write.*) This plausible address, without directly violating truth, is suited, and was probably intended, to convey the false impression, that the governor's embarrassment arose entirely from his ignorance of Jewish usages and doctrines, and could therefore be removed by the assistance of a person so well skilled in all such matters, and at the same time so exalted in position, as the king Agrippa. But this embarrassment, though real when the cause first came before him, must have been removed in a great measure by the trial spoken of in vs. 8. 9, or he could not have pronounced Paul guiltless, as he does in v. 25. The real difficulty of his present situation lay in the necessity of sending Paul to Rome, because he had himself neglected to perform his duty, and was therefore utterly unable to report the case to Nero without self-crimination, unless something should occur in this mock-trial or rehearsal of the one before the Emperor, to put a new face on the whole affair, of which he seems to have indulged some vague and groundless expectation. *The Lord* (or *Master*) in this verse is not a synonyme for *sovereign*, in the ordinary secular or civil sense, but like *Augustus* (see above, on v. 21), a religious or idolatrous description of the Emperor as a divine person (see above, on 24, 2.) There is here a strong proof of the writer's intimate acquaintance with the facts to which he even incidentally alludes, or rather of the absolute fidelity with which he has reported what was said by others, in the circumstance that this very title (*Dominus*) had been indignantly rejected by Augustus, and in imitation of him by Tiberius, but afterwards accepted by Caligula and Claudius, and exacted by Nero, to whom Festus here applies it. (For kindred arguments derived from the right use of the titles corresponding to *proconsul*, *king*, *etc.*, see above, on 13, 7. 17, 7. 19, 38.)

27. For it seemeth to me unreasonable to send a prisoner, and not withal to signify the crimes (laid) against him.

Unreasonable might perhaps be still more exactly rendered *irrational*, *absurd*, something not only unbecoming or improper, but a suitable subject of contempt and ridicule. This strong expression, which would hardly be appropriate to such an error if arising from mere ignorance of Jewish laws, betrays a secret consciousness that he had played the fool, as well as failed in duty, by allowing Paul to take advantage of his weakness and escape from his control before he had passed judgment in the case, and while he was gratuitously urging a new trial, with the risk of an unrighteous condemnation, merely because the Jews desired it, though convinced by what had passed already in his presence, that the prisoner was guiltless of the capital offence with which he had been charged (see above, on v. 25.) It is very probable that Festus would have forced Paul to submit to a new trial at Jerusalem, not for the purpose of destroying him, but simply to gain favour with the Jews, if such coercion had been in his power. But from this the Apostle was delivered by his *civitas* or citizenship, which enabled him, by one decisive act, to overleap the heads both of the High Priest and the Procurator into the presence of the Emperor himself. To this, no doubt, he was divinely guided, as the providential means, not only of prolonged life and of safe escape from Palestine after he had done his errand, but also of a final apostolical appearance at the bar of Nero (see below, on 28, 30. 31.) *To send* (literally, *sending*) *a prisoner, and not withal* (literally, *not also*) *to report* (or *signify*, but not in the same sense as in 11, 28 above) *the charges* (literally, *causes*, grounds of punishment or prosecution, as in v. 18) *against him* (*laid* is introduced by the translators.)

CHAPTER XXVI.

This division of the text contains Paul's fifth Apology, the one before Agrippa, representing both the Jewish and the Roman power, at whose joint tribunal the Apostle recapitulates or sums up his defence, thereby closing his extraordinary mission to the Holy Land with another attempt to gain his kinsmen according to the flesh. The chapter requires and admits of no division beyond that afforded by the progress of the argument or drift of the discourse. Being called on by Agrippa to defend himself, he expresses satisfaction at the opportunity of doing so before one so familiar with all Jewish matters (1–3).

Then referring to his early Pharisaic life, as well known to the Jews, he points out the remarkable circumstance, that his old associates now accused him of believing their own doctrines (4–8). Then resuming his narrative, he paints in the strongest colours his own persecuting agency, with aggravating circumstances not recorded elsewhere (9–11). This is followed by a third account of his conversion, with a fuller statement of his great commission then received from Christ himself (12–18). This commission he had faithfully fulfilled, and by so doing had been brought into his present situation (19–21). He continues to maintain, however, that his teaching is in strict accordance with the ancient Scriptures, as to the Messiah's being both a sufferer and a saviour (22, 23). At this point Festus interrupts him with a charge of madness, to which Paul replies by courteously denying his assertion and reminding him that this defence was not addressed to him, but to a person well acquainted with the subject, and indeed a believer in the Scriptures (24–27.) Agrippa acknowledges the power of Paul's argument, and agrees with Festus that the charges were without foundation, but reminds him that he ought to have discharged the prisoner before, instead of letting him appeal to Nero (28–32).

1. Then Agrippa said unto Paul, Thou art permitted to speak for thyself. Then Paul stretched forth the hand, and answered for himself:

Agrippa here begins to act his part as judge in this mock-trial, which was a sort of rehearsal or anticipation, on a small scale, of what might be expected to take place before the Emperor. *It is permitted to thee for thyself to speak.* The first verb, in the classics, usually means to commit or to entrust, but sometimes to permit, which is its only sense in the New Testament. (See above, on 21, 39. 40.) *Then*, in the first clause, is the usual connective (δέ) ; in the last clause, the adverb (τότε) meaning at that time, or after that, as soon as he received permission. (See above, on 21, 26. 33. 23, 3. 25, 12.) *For himself* is not expressed, as *for thyself* is, by a pronoun and a preposition, but by the middle voice of a verb which originally means to *talk off*, or save from punishment by speaking. (See above, on 19, 33. 24, 10. 28, 8.) *Extending* (or *stretching out*) *the hand*, not motioning for silence, as in 12, 17. 13, 16. 19, 33. 21, 40, where the Greek verb means to shake or shake down; but either as a customary gesture at the opening of a speech; or a specific recognition of Agrippa, as the one whom he consented to address; at the same time intended to remind him and the others of Paul's unjust confinement, by exhibiting the chain, with which he was fastened to his guard in prison. (See above, on 24, 23, and below, on v. 29.)

2. I think myself happy, king Agrippa, because I shall answer for myself this day before thee touching all the things whereof I am accused of the Jews —

Paul begins, as he did before Felix (see above, on 24, 10) with a conciliatory exordium (*captatio benevolentiae*), but more strongly expressed, as might have been expected from the difference in the judges. Here again the original order of the words is more sonorous and rhetorical than in the version "As to all the things of which I am accused by Jews, king Agrippa, I have thought myself happy, before thee being about this day to defend myself." *By Jews* (not by *the Jews*), i. e. by persons of the same religion which the king professed, and with which Paul describes him as being so familiar. *Happy*, a much stronger term than *cheerfully* in 24, 10. *Have thought*, in the perfect tense, i. e. since I heard of this appointment or arrangement, which was probably announced to him as soon as it was made. *Being about*, the verb expressive of futurity, so often used in this book (see above, on 24, 15. 25. 25, 4.) *To defend myself*, the same verb as in v. 1. *Before thee*, not merely in thy presence, but at thy tribunal, as appointed *pro hac vice* to sit in preliminary judgment on the case before it is submitted to the Emperor.

3. Especially (because I know) thee to be expert in all customs and questions which are among the Jews; wherefore I beseech thee to hear me patiently.

Especially may either indicate his principal reason for rejoicing, namely, because Agrippa was expert, etc., or may qualify what follows, *expert* (in other things no doubt but) *especially*, etc. The words, *I know thee*, are supplied by the translators, the original construction being the comparatively rare one of the accusative absolute. *Expert*, literally, *a knower*, corresponding to the French *connoisseur*, but without its restricted application. *Customs*, legal and religious institutions (see above, on 6, 14. 15, 1. 16, 21. 21, 21. 25, 16.) *Questions*, controversies, subjects of dispute (see above, on 15, 2. 18, 15. 23, 29. 25, 19.) *Among* is in Greek a stronger word, meaning *through*, throughout, and thus suggesting the idea that the things in question were of universal not of local interest. (See above, on 8, 1. 9, 31. 42. 10, 37. 11, 1. 13, 1. 18, 15. 21, 21. 24, 5. 12.) This was not an idle compliment, but a fact of great importance in relation to Paul's testimony or defence both of himself and his religion. Of the four apologies already past, two were delivered to the Jews, but in the presence of the Gentiles, and two to the Gentiles in the presence of the Jews. (See above, on 21, 39. 40. 22, 30. 24, 1. 25, 6. 7.) As a winding up of this extraordinary mission to Judea, he was now to recapitulate and close his whole defence, before a man who might be said to represent, in his own person, both religions and both governments; a Jew by education and profession, the official guardian of the temple and defender of the faith, but at the same time a crowned vassal of the Roman Empire, bound to it not only by political necessity, but by personal interest and predilection. There was certainly no man living who united in himself so many diverse qualifications for the singular position in which Providence now placed him; a knowledge of Roman affairs rare among the Jews; a knowledge of Jewish affairs still more rare among the Romans; official authority, both civil and religious, with the ad ventitious dignity belonging even to a tributary and dependent sovereign. No wonder that the "prisoner of the Lord" (Eph. 4, 1), after pleading his cause before the people and the Sanhedrim, and at the bar of Felix and of Festus, should have thought himself happy, i. e. highly favoured by the providence of God, in being suffered to sum up his cause before an auditor so singularly qualified and chosen. *Wherefore*, the rather as thou art thus qualified to understand my case and to appreciate the grounds of my defence, *I pray thee*, I make bold to ask thee, not as a mere favour but a right, arising from our mutual relations at this singular conjuncture, *to hear me patiently*, or with long-suffering, a Greek word modelled on a Hebrew phrase of frequent occurrence, especially in application to the divine forbearance with the sins of men. (Compare the Septuagint version of Ex. 34, 6. Num. 14, 18. Neh. 9, 17. Ecc. 7, 9. Prov. 29, 11.)

4. 5. My manner of life from my youth, which was at the first among mine own nation at Jerusalem, know all the Jews; which knew me from the beginning, if they would testify, that after the most straitest sect of our religion, I lived a Pharisee.

After this exordium he begins, as in his first Apology (see above, on 22, 3), with his early history, but instead of repeating the details, refers to them as well known to the Jewish population, and requiring no other proof than that which it could furnish. *My manner of life* is a correct paraphrase of one Greek word, meaning *life* or *living*, and occurring only here. *Which was at the first*, literally, *the* (*life*) *from the beginning past* (elapsed or happened.) *In my* (*own*) *nation*, not abroad, among the Gentiles. *In Jerusalem*, the capital and Holy City, not in any obscure province or provincial town. *Know all the Jews*, implying that he not only came very early to Jerusalem, but was there conspicuous and well known, either from his family connections, his relations to Gamaliel (see above, on 22, 3), or his personal ability, activity, and zeal. The fact that he was thus so well and generally known is repeated with great emphasis, as one of some importance to his own defence. *Knowing me before*, i. e. before these present troubles, as if he had said, 'I am no stranger or new acquaintance of these people, but an old familiar friend and neighbour.' *From the beginning* is the literal translation of the phrase rendered *at the first* in v. 4, and employed in v. 5 to express an adverb strictly meaning *from above* (as in Matt. 27, 51. John 3, 31. 19, 11. 23. James 1, 17. 3, 15. 17), but applied less frequently to time (see Luke 1, 3, and compare John 3, 3. 7. Gal. 4, 9.) *If they would testify*, i. e. are willing so to do (see above, on 7, 39. 10, 10. 14, 13. 16, 3. 24, 6. 25, 9.) This seems to imply that his accusers had affected to know nothing of his antecedents. *Most straitest*, an anomalous pleonasm, not found in the original, but handed down from Tyndale through the later English versions. *Straitest*, i. e. strictest, most exact, in reference both to doctrinal and practical rigour. (See above, on 18, 25. 26. 22, 3. 23, 15. 20. 24, 22.) *Religion* is in Greek a word denoting more especially the external form or mode of worship, and therefore peculiarly appropriate to the Jewish ritual, as rendered still more ceremonial by the Pharisees (see above, on 4, 1.) *I lived a Pharisee*, an excellent translation of a beautiful and pointed phrase, which would be greatly weakened by inserting *as*. He not only professed this form of Judaism, but lived it, exemplified, embodied it, in his life and practice.

6. And now I stand and am judged for the hope of the promise made of God unto our fathers —

And now, the usual transition from the past to the present (see above, on 3, 17. 10, 5. 13, 11. 20, 22. 25. 22, 17), but here suggesting an antithesis or contrast. 'Such was I of old, and now see what and where I am.' He here repeats, but more distinctly, the assertion made upon his trial before Felix (see above, on 24, 14. 15), that the real ground of his arrest and prosecution was not his having left the old religion, but his having too faithfully adhered to it. *For the hope of the promise*, i. e. founded on, excited by the promise; or the sense may be, the hope of its fulfilment. (See above, on 1, 4. 2, 33. 7, 17.) *Made*, happened, brought into existence (see above, on v. 4, and on 25, 15. 26.) *To the fathers*, i. e. to the Patriarchs and to the intervening generations. *Our*, which identifies the speaker with the Jewish race and church (see above, on 3, 13. 25. 5, 30. 7, 2. 11. 12. 15. 19. 38. 39. 44. 45. 13, 17. 15, 10. 22, 14), is omitted by the latest critics. *I stand and am judged*, literally, *stand* (or *have stood*, see above, on 1, 11. 9, 7. 21, 40. 24, 20. 25, 10) *being tried* (or on my trial.) The hope here meant is more explicitly described in the next verse.

7. Unto which (promise) our twelve tribes, instantly serving (God) day and night, hope to come. For which hope's sake, king Agrippa, I am accused of the Jews.

Promise is correctly supplied by the translators from the verse preceding, the antecedent being indicated by the gender of the relative in Greek. *Twelve tribes*, in the original a single word, not occurring elsewhere, but of obvious etymology and meaning, being properly a neutre noun denoting a collective body composed of twelve tribes. (Compare the words translated *two years*, *three years*, in 20, 31. 24, 27.) It is here put for the whole Jewish race or nation, either because it was at first composed of twelve tribes, although now reduced to a much smaller number; or because it virtually still consisted of twelve tribes, the ten being represented by the descendants of such as adhered to Judah after the Assyrian Conquest, and of such as returned with Judah from the Babylonish exile. The expression here used is equivalent to saying, the Theocracy or Jewish Church. *Instantly*, literally, *in tension*, i. e. with intensity, the Greek noun corresponding to the adjective in 12, 5. This may refer either to the traditional hereditary zeal with which the Jews adhered to the Mosaic law, or to the expectation, which is known to have been specially alive at this time, of Messiah's advent (see above, on 2, 5.) *Serving*, worshipping, a Greek word primarily signifying work for wages, and even in its higher use suggesting the idea of hard labour undergone with a view to some valuable recompense, an excellent description of the old economy with its burdensome impositions and restrictions (see above, on 15, 10), borne by some as meritorious, by others simply in obedience to the will of God, by others still as a provisional or temporary system until Christ should come. *Hope* (agreeing with the singular collective in the first clause) *to come*, come down, arrive at, or attain to. (For the local usage of the Greek verb, see above, on 16, 1. 18, 19. 24. 20, 15. 21, 7. 25, 13; for its higher application to spiritual attainments, compare Eph. 4, 13. Phil. 3, 11.) *Of* (about, concerning) *which hope, I am accused* (and that) *by Jews* (not *the Jews*, see above, on v. 2), i. e. by men whose whole religion rests upon the very hope which they accuse me of maintaining. The hope described in this verse cannot be that of a general resurrection, which is only partially revealed in the Old Testament, and was not held by all the Jews at this time (see above, on 24, 15.) The only hope answering to the description, as an ancient, national, and still intense one, is the hope of the Messiah, as promised to the Patriarchs, prefigured in the Law, predicted in the Prophets, and still ardently expected by the People. This was in fact the end at which the complicated legal system aimed, and towards which it continually pointed. The words, *king Agrippa*, are omitted by the latest critics, as an unauthorized repetition from v. 2, though several of the oldest manuscripts have one or both. The sense, in which Paul represents himself as charged with holding fast the hope of the nation, although not distinctly stated, must have been perceived by every Jewish hearer. Common to him and his accusers was the hope of a Messiah; the breaking point between them was the question whether he had come, which they denied and Paul affirmed. He could therefore say with perfect truth, that he was tried (or on his trial) about, concerning, in relation to this hope, i. e. to its fulfilment.

8. Why should it be thought a thing incredible with you, that God should raise the dead?

The first word may be also construed as an exclamation, *What! is it judged incredible, etc.?* This is now commonly preferred, as giving more vivacity and point to the apostrophe. *Is it* (not *should it be*) *judged incredible with you*, i. e. among the Jews, including Agrippa, whom Paul here addresses as their representative. *That God should raise*, or rather, *if God raises dead* (*men*), not as a mere possible contingency, but as an actual fact, equivalent to saying, since he has done so. (For this use of *if* in Greek, see above, on 4, 9. 11, 17. 16, 15. 23, 9.) The reference is plainly to the resurrection of Christ, as the crowning proof of his Messiahship, and thus the nexus between this verse and the one before it, which appeared to be abruptly broken, is completely re-established. As if he had said, 'they believe in a Messiah, so do I; but they expect him yet to come, while I believe that he is come already, not without grounds or on hearsay, but because God has identified him by raising him from the dead; and surely this, if properly attested, cannot be thought by any devout Jew to be beyond his power.' *Dead* (not *the dead*) is in Greek a plural, and by some explained as a generic form relating to a single person (see above, on 17, 18); but it is rather an allusion to the general resurrection, of which Christ's was the pledge and the example. (See above, on 24, 15, where this part of Paul's doctrine is more prominently brought to view.)

9. I verily thought with myself, that I ought to do many things contrary to the name of Jesus of Nazareth.

Verily, or rather, *so then*, the continuative particle resuming what had been previously dropped or interrupted (see above, on 8, 4. 25. 9, 31. 11, 19. 12, 5. 13, 4. 15, 3. 30. 16, 5. 17, 12. 17. 30. 18, 14. 19, 32. 38. 23, 18. 31.) It here connects this verse with the last words of the fifth (*I lived a Pharisee*), from which he had digressed to point out the remarkable fact that he was now accused by Pharisees for holding their own doctrines, and to which he now returns, by showing how his Pharisaic spirit was displayed in action. 'Well then, as I was saying, being such a Pharisee, I thought, etc.' *With* (*to* or *in*) *myself*, a pleonastic phrase, found also in the classics, and suggesting the idea both of independent judgment and of intimate conviction. *Ought* (or *must*), in Greek the infinitive of a verb used to denote both physical and moral necessity (see above, on 25, 10. 24.) *Contrary* (hostile, or in opposition) *to the name of Jesus the Nazarene* (see above, on 2, 22. 3, 6. 4, 10. 6, 14. 22, 8. 24, 5), i. e. opposed to the person so called in contempt, even by Saul the Pharisee himself; or, according to the usage of this book, against all that is denoted by his names and titles, which describe him as a Saviour, the Messiah, Prophet, Priest, King, etc. (See above, on 2, 38. 3, 6. 16. 4, 10. 12. 17. 30. 5, 41. 9, 15. 15, 14. 26. 19, 5. 13. 17. 21, 13.) It never simply means the person of Christ, nor those who bear his name. *Many* (*things*) may either signify a frequent repetition of the same acts, or various forms and modes of opposition.

10. Which thing I also did in Jerusalem; and many of the saints did I shut up in prison, having received authority from the chief priests; and when they were put to death, I gave my voice against (them).

Which also I did, i. e. I acted on this strong conviction of necessity and duty, beginning at Jerusalem. *The saints*, or *holy ones*, a designation of believers used three times in one chapter of the book before us (see above, on 9, 13. 32. 41), and still more frequently in Paul's epistles (see Rom. 1, 7. 8, 27. 12, 13. 15, 25. 26. 31. 16, 2. 15. 1 Cor. 1, 2. 4, 12. 14, 13. 16, 1. 15. 2 Cor. 1, 1. Eph. 1, 1. Col. 1, 2. 4. 12. 26. 1 Th. 3, 13. 2 Th. 1, 10. 1 Tim. 5, 10. Philem. 5, 7. Heb. 6, 10. 3, 24.) The use of the term here implies an acknowledgment of his former error in relation to these Christians, whom he now admits to have been saints of God. But while he thus confesses his own sin, he denounces that of the Jewish rulers, by declaring under what authority he acted, namely, that of the chief priests, here put for the whole Sanhedrim or national council (see above, on 4, 5. 23. 5, 24. 9, 14. 21. 22, 30. 23, 14. 25, 15.) *In prison*, literally, *in prisons*. *They also* (τε) *being executed* (or despatched, see above, on 25, 3), *I gave my voice* (literally, *brought a vote*) *against them*. This is literally understood by some, as proving that Saul was a member of the Sanhedrim, which others think improbable for various reasons, and explain the phrase as a figure for personal concurrence and assent, which is elsewhere spoken of in literal terms (see above, on 8, 1. 22, 20.)

11. And I punished them oft in every synagogue, and compelled (them) to blaspheme; and being exceedingly mad against them, I persecuted (them) even unto strange cities.

The second *and* is supplied by the translators. The original construction is, *and often punishing them, forced them to blaspheme. In every synagogue*, or more exactly, *throughout all synagogues*, a natural hyperbole, implying that this persecuting agency was not confined to one community or congregation, nor indeed to one country, as appears from the statement in the last clause. *Punishing*, no doubt by scourging, which was a customary form of punishment, and practised in the synagogues or public meetings for religious worship (see Matt. 10, 17. 23, 34. Mark 13, 9.) *Forced them to blaspheme* (or curse the name of Christ), not only tried to do so, but succeeded in the case of those whose faith was weak or spurious. In the reign of Trajan, forty years later, as we learn from one of Pliny's letters, the same thing was required of the persecuted Christians in Bithynia; but he says that none who really believed in Christ could be induced or forced to do it. The last clause is descriptive of the highest point to which his persecuting zeal attained, and which he here looks back upon as a paroxysm of insane excitement. *Exceedingly too* (τε) *raving* (being mad or furious) *against them, I pursued* (or *persecuted*) *them even also* (or *as far as even*) *to the foreign* (literally, *outside*) *cities.* As Damascus is the only one of these expressly mentioned, some suppose the plural here again to be generic (see above, on v. 8); others think that this one instance was selected out of many, because connected with such great events. Most probably, however, Paul's commission extended to other cities, but his progress was arrested at the first.

12. Whereupon as I went to Damascus with authority and commission from the chief priests —

In which (*things*), i. e. while thus employed (compare a

similar expression in 24, 18 above.) *As I went*, literally, journeying, proceeding (see above, on 24, 25. 25, 12. 20.) *Commission*, a noun corresponding to the verb employed above in v. 1. Paul insists upon his regular commission and authority, not so much as an extenuating circumstance in his own case, as because it proved the personal and national complicity of those who now accused him. As if he had said, Let it be observed that this fanatical mission, mad and wicked at it was, must not be reckoned a mere personal or private act, but one performed by national authority and under the most sacred auspices, to wit, those of the Priesthood and the Sanhedrim. In the account of Paul's conversion which now follows, it will only be necessary to advert to what is new, or to remove apparent inconsistencies between this and the two previous narratives of the same event. (See above, on 9, 1–9. 22, 6–11.)

13. At mid-day, O king, I saw in the way a light from heaven, above the brightness of the sun, shining round about me and them which journeyed with me.

Here, as in 22, 6, the time of day when this occurrence took place is particularly mentioned, namely, *mid-day* (or *the middle of the day*), which may be intended either to remind the hearers that this was no nocturnal vision, but an incident occurring in the blaze of noon, or as a vivid recollection, which would naturally dwell upon the mind of the chief actor, although just as naturally passed by in the narratives of others. An addition to the previous accounts is the description of the light from heaven as *above* (or *beyond*) *the brightness of the sun*, and as shining not only about Paul himself, but also about those journeying with him.

14. 15. And when we were all fallen to the earth, I heard a voice speaking unto me, and saying in the Hebrew tongue, Saul, Saul, why persecutest thou me? (it is) hard for thee to kick against the pricks. And I said, Who art thou, Lord? And he said, I am Jesus whom thou persecutest.

We all having fallen to the earth, i. e. Paul and his companions mentioned in the verse preceding. This is not at variance with the statement in 9, 4. 7, where Paul alone is spoken of as falling to the earth, and those who journeyed with him as standing speechless. But the verb *stood*, there used, may be rendered *had stood still*, or *stopped*, at the first appearance of the light, and is opposed not so much to lying prostrate as to going on. They may therefore have fallen after Paul did, whose prostration Luke records exclusively, as that of the chief actor and great subject of the history. *In the Hebrew dialect*, i. e. perhaps the ancient Hebrew, although commonly explained to mean its Aramaic corruption, then vernacular in Palestine (see above, on 21, 40. 22, 2.) The last clause is admitted to be genuine in this place, even by those who reject it in 9, 5, where it has already been explained as a proverbial expression, not for difficulty merely, but for danger as attending blind resistance to superior power. The question and answer in v. 15 are substantially the same in all accounts (but see above, on 22, 8), the chief variation being in the collocation of the words, which here follow, as in 9, 5 they precede, the proverbial expression just referred to. This is no contradiction, inasmuch as neither of the narratives professes to record the exact order of the incidents, which indeed is altogether unimportant.

16. But rise, and stand upon thy feet; for I have appeared unto thee for this purpose, to make thee a minister and a witness both of these things which thou hast seen, and of those things in the which I will appear unto thee —

ministers by witnessing; or each term may have its distinct meaning, one who administers and one who testifies, which is not only a simpler construction, but appropriate in this connection, where the things referred to in the last clause are the divine communications and commands, which Paul was both to execute and make known to others *Which thou sawest* (just now) or *hast seen* (on this occasion), referring to the whole interview or vision in which Christ appeared to him at his conversion. *And of the things which* (i. e. as to which or in which) *I will appear to thee*, communicate with thee, or make revelations to thee, hereafter. The causative construction (*I will make thee see*) is consistent neither with the form nor the usage of the Greek verb.

17. Delivering thee from the people, and (from) the Gentiles, unto whom now I send thee—

Delivering, rescuing from danger or the power of another, is the constant meaning of this verb in the New Testament (see above, on 7, 10. 34. 12, 11. 23, 27, and compare Gal. 1, 4), except where it is used in its primary and physical sense of *taking out* (as in Matt. 5, 29. 18, 9), from which, in classical usage, it derives that of *choosing* (picking out), and this is preferred by some modern writers in the case before us. But besides the settled Hellenistic usage, to which this would be almost the sole exception, there is something not entirely natural in representing Paul as *chosen* from among the Gentiles as well as the Jews. The words indeed admit of an intelligible sense (to wit, that he was chosen out of the whole field in which he was to labour), but by no means so appropriate and obvious as that which is obtained by adhering to the usage elsewhere, namely, that although he was to be in danger both from Jews and Gentiles, to whom Christ was now about to send him, he should be finally delivered from their enmity and power.

18. To open their eyes, (and) to turn (them) from darkness to light, and (from) the power of Satan unto God, that they may receive forgiveness of sins, and inheritance among them which are sanctified, by faith that is in me.

Having assured him of his own safety, the Lord now describes the work to which he was appointed, by a full specification of the moral changes to be wrought, through his agency, upon the Gentiles, as the words are usually understood, but, as some of the best modern writers understand them, both on Jews ("the people") and Gentiles ("the nations"), as the double antecedent of the relative (*to whom*) in the last clause of v. 17. This agrees not only with the form of the expression here, but with the fact which runs through Paul's whole history and writings, that wherever he had the opportunity he preached to Jews as well as Gentiles. (See above, on 9, 20. 29. 13, 5. 14. 14, 1. 16, 1. 3. 13. 17, 1. 18, 4. 19, 8, and compare Rom. 1, 16. 9, 3. 10, 1.) The effects themselves are stated both in a literal and figurative form. *To open their eyes*, i. e. remove their spiritual blindness and enable them to distinguish spiritual objects (1 Cor. 12, 14) by communicating both the object and the power of perceiving it, the truth itself and a believing apprehension of it. *To turn* (*them*), or *convert* them, which is only a corresponding Latin form, both denoting change of condition and especially of relative position, with respect to God, his service and his favour. *Darkness* and *light* are common figures in the New Testament, not only for ignorance and knowledge, especially of spiritual things, but for the several states or characters, of which these are necessary incidents, a state of sin and one of holiness. (See Matt. 6, 23. Luke 1, 79. John 3, 19. Rom. 13, 12. 1 Cor. 4, 5. 2 Cor. 4, 6. 6, 14. Eph. 5, 8. Col. 1, 13. 1 Thess. 5, 4. 5. 1 Pet. 2, 9. 1 John 1, 5. 2, 8–11.) The two worlds thus distinguished are then described by naming their respective sovereigns, *from the power* (or dominion) *of Satan* (the great adversary, see above, on 5, 3) *to God*, not only to his power or dominion, but to himself, implying a more intimate union and communion. This change of relation comprehends or carries with it exemption from punishment and guilt, or the *remission of sins* (see above, on 2, 38. 5, 31. 10, 43. 13, 38), and as its positive result, participation by a filial right in the holiness and happiness of those who are heirs of God and joint-heirs with Christ (Rom. 8, 17.) *By faith in me* does not qualify the last preceding clause alone, but is presented as the only means or principle by which any of the changes here described can be effected.

19. Whereupon, O king Agrippa, I was not disobedient unto the heavenly vision—

Whereupon, literally, *whence*, from which place (as in 14, 26 above and 28, 13 below), but sometimes logically used, from which cause, or for which reason (as in Matt. 14, 7. 1 John 2, 18), an idiom particularly frequent in the epistle to the Hebrews (2, 17. 3, 1. 7, 25. 8, 3. 9, 18.) This is the only sense appropriate in this place, where the reference is clearly to the previous description of the work to which he had been called. *For which cause*, i. e. because thus instructed in the nature of the work before me, *I was not* (or rather, *did not become*, in consequence of this disclosure) *disobedient to the heavenly vision*, or divine communication from the visible Redeemer, the extraordinary sight being put for the whole revelation which it accompanied and attested. (Compare the like use of a kindred verb in v. 16 above.) Thus understood, the verse seems to imply that if controlled by selfish motives, or a merely human wisdom, Saul would have recoiled from the responsibilities and hardships of the ministry, to which he was thus set apart by Christ himself.

20. But shewed first unto them of Damascus, and at Jerusalem, and throughout all the coasts of Judea, and (then) to the Gentiles, that they should repent and turn to God, and do works meet for repentance.

Far from refusing his commission, he accepted it and instantly began its execution, although not avowedly as an Apostle until long after his conversion (see above, on 13, 9.) The particular localities here named are probably designed to show how promptly and how fully he had executed his important mission. *But to the* (*Jews*) *in Damascus first*, the very place where he became a Christian (see above, on 9, 20–22), *and* (to those) *in Jerusalem* (as soon as he returned there, see above, on 9, 29), *I showed*, the verb so rendered in 11, 13. 12, 17, but elsewhere more exactly *told* (5, 22–25. 12, 14. 15, 27. 16, 36. 22, 26. 23, 16. 17. 19), and once *reported* (4, 23.) The act here described is that of preaching, considered as a publication or announcement of the Gospel. This was not confined to the metropolis, but penetrated *also* (τε) *into the whole region of Judea.* (For the English usage of the word *coasts*, see above, on 13, 50.) If this related to the beginning of his ministry, it would be inconsistent with his statement in Gal. 1, 22; but he here puts together his whole ministry among the Jews, before proceeding to the other and chief part of his commission, *to the nations*, i. e. other nations, Gentiles (see above, on v. 16.) Having shown his prompt obedience as to time and place, he now asserts his fidelity in reference to the subject of his preaching, as prescribed in his divine commission (see above, on v. 18), the substance of which is here repeated in another form. (Announcing both to Jews and Gentiles by authority, in other words commanding them) *to repent* (see above, on 2, 38. 17, 30), *and turn* (convert, or be converted) *unto God* (see above, on. v. 18, and on 3, 19. 9, 35. 11, 21. 14, 15. 15, 19. 20, 21), *doing* (habitually, practising, a word derived from that here used) *works* (acts, habits,) *worthy of repentance*, not merely consistent with it, but suited and proportioned to it, both as its necessary fruits, and as proofs of its existence and sincerity. This varied yet harmonious statement of Paul's great commission may throw light also on the ministerial work in general, and on that of the missionary in particular.

21. For these causes the Jews caught me in the temple, and went about to kill (me.)

Having stated his commission and its execution, he proceeds to connect it with his present situation as a prisoner. *For* (on account or for the sake of) *these* (*things*), i. e. because I had received and executed this commission, as a teacher and apostle (2 Tim. 1, 11) both to Jews and Gentiles. This was the true ground, even of the first charge against him, which occasioned his arrest (see above, on 21, 28. 29.) The alleged profanation of the temple would not have been thought of by the Jews from Asia, but for their previous knowledge of Paul's intercourse, as a religious teacher, not with Jews only, but with Gentiles, in their native country (see above, on 19, 8–10.) That he should venture to preach Jesus as the true Messiah, expected by the Jews and predicted in their Scriptures, and invite the Gentiles to partake of the advantages belonging to his kingdom, without even passing through the vestibule of Judaism; this was the real crime of Paul in Jewish eyes, for which they *seized* (*me*) *in the temple, and endeavoured to despatch* (or *make away with*) *me* by summary violence, without legal process, though the verb here used is elsewhere applied to the judicial murder of our Lord himself. (See above, on 5, 30, and compare the account of the attempt on Paul's life, 21, 31.)

22. Having therefore obtained help of God, I continue unto this day, witnessing both to small and great, saying none other things than those which the prophets and Moses did say should come —

The order in Greek is somewhat different. *Succour*, help and protection against enemies, which is the specific usage of the Greek word. *Then* (or *therefore*) is not to be pressed as a logical connective, though it really refers as such to an intermediate fact or thought, not here expressed, to wit, the failure of the murderous attempt just mentioned. 'They would gladly have despatched me, and repeatedly attempted it, but God confounded all their plots, and so (or therefore) etc.' *Having obtained*, experienced, met with, the same verb that is used above in 24, 2 (3), and there explained. *From God*, as the ultimate and sovereign author of this help, in whose hands the Romans were but instrumental agents, as declared by Christ himself to Pilate (John 19, 11.) *Unto this day*, from its position in the sentence, may be construed either with the words preceding it in Greek (*having obtained help from God*), or with those following it (*I continue*) both of which it qualifies in fact, although the last grammatical construction is entitled to the preference, because the other leaves the following verb too insulated. *I continue*, literally *stand*, or *have stood* (see above, v. 6, and on 1, 11. 9, 7), which means not merely, I am still alive in spite of these attempts to kill me, but more pointedly, I still maintain my ground, I hold fast my position, the idea expressed in Hebrew by the phrase, to stand in judgment (compare Ps. 1, 5.) But even this is not the whole of what Paul here claims. It was not only negatively true that he had been sustained as an innocent though accused party, but also positively true that he had stood fast as a witness to the truth. *Witnessing* (or *testifying*), not as a self-commissioned volunteer, but in execution of the charge which he received at his conversion (see above, on v. 16.) *Both to small and great*, an idiomatic phrase for all classes and varieties of condition, without exclusive reference to rank (high and low) or to age (old and young.) A similar expression (*from small to great*) is employed above in 8, 10 (and in Heb. 8, 11), though needlessly disguised by a superlative translation (*from the least to the greatest.*) Still nearer to the formula here used is one repeatedly employed by John in the Apocalypse (see Rev. 11, 18. 13, 16. 19, 5. 18. 20, 12.) If the common text (μαρτυρούμενος) be here retained, the clause will have a wholly different sense, this participle being always passive elsewhere (see above, on 6, 3. 10, 22. 22, 12, and compare Rom. 3, 21. 1 Thess. 2, 12, 1 Tim. 5, 10. Heb. 7, 8.) Some accordingly translate it here, *attested* (testified, accredited) *both by small and great* (as) *saying nothing, etc.* But besides that the expression, *small and great,* is not so natural on this construction, it contradicts the known facts of the history, as all did not bear witness to Paul's faithfulness in this respect, or he would not have been a prisoner or had occasion to defend himself at all. By a happy coincidence which does not often happen, the best sense here agrees with what the latest critics reckon the true text, four uncial manuscripts and several Greek Fathers having another reading (μαρτυρόμενος), the participle of a different though kindred verb, occurring elsewhere only in an active or deponent sense (see above, on 20, 26, and compare Gal. 5, 3. Eph. 4, 17.) The last clause then describes this testimony, not as something new or anti-jewish, but in strict accordance with the Hebrew Scriptures. *Saying none other things* (literally, *nothing saying*) *than* (literally, *outside of*, besides, except) *those which the prophets spoke of* (*as*) *about to come* (to pass, take place or happen.) For the usage of the two last verbs (μελλόντων γίνεσθαι) see above, on vs. 2. 4. 6. 19. Lest his profession of agreement with *the prophets* should be understood in too confined a sense, he adds, by a kind of afterthought, *and Moses*, not the other prophets merely, but the great prophetic legislator, from whom I am particularly charged not only with apostatizing, but with teaching apostasy to others also. (See above, on 21, 21.) The emphatic position of these words in the original is lost in the version by connecting them directly with *the prophets.*

23. That Christ should suffer, (and) that he should be the first that should rise from the dead, and should shew light unto the people, and to the Gentiles.

Having thus far spoken of his preaching as a testimony borne to small and great, perhaps with some allusion to the rank of those whom he addressed on this occasion, he now remembers, as it were, that it had also a polemic character, in reference to certain Messianic doctrines, upon which its truth depended, and which he had been under the necessity, not only of expounding but defending from the open opposition or corrupt interpretation of the Scribes and their disciples. What the version positively states as Paul's own doctrine, he himself states as a subject of discussion or debate between him and his Jewish adversaries. *That Christ should suffer*, literally, *if* (or *whether*) *the Messiah* (*is* or *was to be*) *passible* (susceptible or capable of suffering.) As we know, however, that the same parties who denied that the Messiah was to suffer, also denied that he was to be a divine person, the last word in this clause is probably to be taken, not in a philosophical or technical but rather in a popular and loose sense, as referring less to his capacity of suffering than to his suffering in fact, and the prediction of that fact by the ancient Prophets. Thus understood, it might be rendered, *whether the Messiah* (was to be) *a sufferer*. As the suffering meant is that of death (see above, on 1, 3. 3, 18. 17, 3), it would of course imply his resurrection, which is stated as another controverted question. *Whether* (*he, as the*) *first from* (*the*) *resurrection of* (*the*) *dead*) i. e. the first so to arise, *is* (or *is about*) *to proclaim light* (i. e. truth, holiness, and happiness, see above, on v. 18) *to the people* (of the Jews) *and to the* (other) *nations* (i. e. to the Gentiles.) As thus explained, the whole verse may be paraphrased as follows. 'Through the help of God, I have maintained my ground to this day, bearing witness of the truth to men of all conditions, and discussing the great question, whether the Messiah of the prophecies was to die and rise again, before he could be set forth as a Saviour, both to Jews and Gentiles.' Here at last we have the key to that mysterious connection between the doctrine of Messiah and the doctrine of a resurrection, which seems to be implied though not expressed in Paul's defence before Felix (see above, on 24, 14–16.) It is now clear that in speaking, upon that occasion, of the general resurrection as the hope of Israel, he tacitly connected it, perhaps expressly in his self-defence as actually uttered, with the resurrection of our Lord himself as the Messiah foretold in the Hebrew Scriptures; and on this ground claimed to be a strict adherent of the old religion, holding all that was taught in the law and the prophets, and therefore able conscientiously to claim his birthright as a faithful member of the Theocracy or Jewish Church, and as such guilty of no treason or disloyalty to God or man.

24. And as he thus spake for himself, Festus said with a loud voice, Paul, thou art beside thyself; much learning doth make thee mad.

As Paul had addressed himself directly to Agrippa (see above, on vs. 2. 7. 13. 19), and had therefore presupposed an acquaintance with the Jewish Scriptures and religion, much that he said must have been wholly unintelligible to the Romans present (see above, on 25, 23), while the warmth with which he uttered these mysterious doctrines would of course appear irrational to such a hearer. It is therefore altogether natural that Festus, without any feeling of malignity, or even of contempt, but simply as a Roman, ignorant of both religions now in conflict, as the same in principle but opposite in fact, should have uttered just such an apostrophe as that recorded in the verse before us. *He apologizing these* (*things*), i. e. saying these things in his own defence, seems to imply that Festus interrupted him, but probably not long before the meditated close of his discourse. The *loud* (or *great*) *voice* only implies eagerness and boldness, not contempt or insolence, which Paul could not consistently have answered as he does in the next verse below. *Thou art beside thyself*, in Greek a single word, *thou ravest*, thou art mad. *Much learning*, literally, *many letters*, which, according to its Greek etymology and usage, may denote either books and writings (as in John 5, 47), or the knowledge obtained from them (as in John 7, 15), i. e. literature, learning, as in our phrases, men of letters, polite letters, etc. The latter sense is given in the English version and preferred by most interpreters, although the other is no less appropriate and much more pointed. There is no need of supposing a specific reference to the books and parchments over which the governor had seen Paul poring while in prison (compare 2 Tim. 4, 13); but there does seem to be an obvious allusion to the Jewish Scriptures, from which his arguments were drawn, on the sense of which the truth or falsehood of his claims depended, which moreover were habitually designated by a kindred Greek word (γραφαί), and at least in one place (John 5, 47) by the very word here used (γράμματα.) The sense will then be not that learning in general had disturbed his reason, which a cultivated Gentile would be slow to think, but that Scripture learning in particular had this effect, which any Greek or Roman would have thought most natural. *Doth make thee mad*, literally, *turns thee round to mania*, which may either mean, inclines thee to insanity, or more emphatically, *overturns thee*, i. e. subverts thy reason, *to* (or so as to produce) *insanity*.

25. But he said, I am not mad, most noble Festus, but speak forth the words of truth and soberness.

I am not mad, the first person of the same verb, mood, and tense employed in the preceding verse, though rendered by a different one in English, thus destroying the antithesis which gives force and beauty to the answer. *I am not mad* may correspond in substance to the phrase, *thou art beside thyself*; but how much more exactly to the literal translation, 'Thou art mad . . . . . I am not mad.' *Most noble*, excellent, or honourable, an official title, not a personal description (see above, on 24, 3. 7.) As the use of it was optional, Paul's application of the term to Festus must be understood as a respectful recognition of his office, if not of his character, which would not have been uttered if the speech that called it forth had been an insolent or scornful one. As it is, the Apostle turns to Festus, whose proximity he seemed to have forgotten, saying, 'I am not surprised that your Excellency thinks me mad, but you are much mistaken.' *But words of truth and soberness*, or sanity, the opposite of madness, which is the precise sense of the Greek word here employed. *I speak out*, utter forth, as with authority, the Greek verb used above in 2, 7, and there explained.

26. For the king knoweth of these things, before whom also I speak freely; for I am persuaded that none of these things are hidden from him; for this thing was not done in a corner.

The tact and courtesy have always been admired, with which the Apostle here reminds the governor, that this Apology was not addressed to him, but to Agrippa. Festus had already sat in judgment on him, and by trying to conciliate the Jews at Paul's expense had forced him to appeal to Nero, thereby involving both the prisoner and himself in great embarrassment, from which he was now trying to escape by letting king Agrippa hear the case again, while Festus himself sat by as a spectator. He had no right, therefore, to disturb or interrupt a proceeding which he had himself requested, and in which he was incompetent to take an active part, as he had more than once acknowledged (see above, on 25, 20. 26.) To this Paul delicately here refers, as if he had said, 'It is not surprising that you cannot understand me, as I am not speaking now to you but to the king.' *For the king knows* (or is well informed, see above, on 19, 15. 25. 20, 18. 22, 19. 24, 10) *about these things* (the usages and questions mentioned in v. 3 above), *to whom* (not *before whom*, but directly *to whom*) *I speak freely* (or speak using freedom, see above, on 9, 27. 29. 13, 46. 14, 3. 18, 26. 19, 8.) The reference is not so much to boldness as to plainness or freedom from reserve, because he knew that what he said would be intelligible to his hearer, not only from his general acquaintance with the matters in debate, but from his previous knowledge of the facts in this particular case. *For any of these* (*things*) *to be concealed from* (or *escape*) *him, I do not believe* (literally, *am not persuaded*) *; for not in a corner* (i. e. in obscurity or secret) *has this* (*thing*) *been done*, i. e. this whole affair or series of events, in which Paul had been actively or passively concerned. In thus acknowledging the king's acquaintance with the subject and capacity to understand his statements, Paul's design is not to flatter or exalt him, but to humble Festus, without giving him offence, by reminding him that what appeared to him mere visionary raving might be perfectly coherent and intelligible to another, who was qualified by early education and experience to comprehend the subject of discussion.

27. King Agrippa, believest thou the prophets? I know that thou believest.

All that precedes might have been said, had Agrippa been a heathen, but familiar with the Jews' religion, which would certainly have given him a great advantage over any one as ignorant as Festus was of these things, however intelligent in other matters. But besides this mere difference of knowledge, there was one of more importance in the fact, that Agrippa was a Jew by education and profession, and as we here learn by sincere conviction that the Scriptures were inspired of God. This interesting circumstance Paul here turns to his own advantage, not by boldly stating it, but by a natural rhetorical expedient, carrying it home with tenfold force to all who heard him. *Believest thou,* (*oh*) *king Agrippa, in the prophets?* i. e. dost thou trust them and rely upon them as the spokesmen and messengers of God himself? With another stroke of skill and power worthy of Demosthenes, instead of waiting for an answer to his question, he replies to it himself, *I know that thou believest* (i. e. in the inspiration of the ancient prophets.) *I know* cannot mean *I think* or I conjecture, any more in this place than in 20, 25. 29. Even if the absolute expression did admit of this attenuated meaning elsewhere, it is here forbidden by the solemnity of the occasion, and especially of this appeal to the convictions of Agrippa, which would be greatly weakened if the last words only meant, 'I think you do.'

28. Then Agrippa said unto Paul, Almost thou persuadest me to be a Christian.

Without explicitly assenting to what Paul had said, Agrippa really responds to it by stating the impression which he had received from Paul's discourse, the argumentative effect of which depended wholly on the divine authority of those very writers, in whom he had just been represented as believing. This remarkable expression of Agrippa has been variously represented as a trivial jest, a bitter sarcasm, a grave irony, a burst of anger, and an expression of sincere conviction. Corresponding to these different conceptions of the temper in which the words were uttered are the senses put upon the words themselves, or rather on the first two words in Greek (ἐν ὀλίγῳ), which might be literally rendered, *in a few*, but that this word is exclusively employed with plural nouns, whereas the Greek word is a singular in form and meaning, and may therefore be translated, *in a little.* (See above, on 12, 18. 14, 28. 15, 2. 19, 23. 24.) *Almost*, the common English version, although very ancient, is immediately derived from the Geneva Bible, being found in none of older date. It supposes the Greek phrase to mean within a little, wanting a little, or the like, in which sense several kindred phrases are employed, but not the very one here used. Another objection to it is, that it requires the corresponding phrase in Paul's reply to mean *altogether*, which it never does elsewhere. Adhering to the strict sense, *in a little*, some supply *time*, in a little while, or soon; but this requires the present tense (*thou persuadest*) to be taken as a future, and the corresponding phrase (in v. 29) to mean, in a long time. Still more unnatural is the explanation of some recent writers, with little trouble, easily, which not only takes the words in an unusual sense, but assumes an irony, of which there is no other intimation. By far the simplest and most satisfactory interpretation, although not even mentioned by some modern writers, is the one found in the oldest English versions, in a little, i. e. in a small degree, (Tyndale and Cranmer, *somewhat.*) The idea then is, 'thou persuadest me a little (or in some degree) to become a Christian,' i. e. I begin to feel the force of your persuasive arguments, and if I hear you longer, do not know what the effect may be. This is neither sportively nor bitterly ironical, but rather complimentary and courtly, no doubt expressing a sincere admiration of Paul's eloquence and logic, and a strong persuasion of his innocence, but not a genuine conviction of the truth of Christianity, as may be gathered from the later history of this man, as recorded by Josephus, and from his use of the term *Christian*, which had not yet been adopted by the church itself, but was still a foreign if not a disrespectful designation. (See above, on 11, 26.)

29. And Paul said, I would to God, that not only thou, but also all that hear me this day, were both almost, and altogether such as I am, except these bonds.

The Apostle's answer to this courteous but evasive compliment, no doubt intended to ward off all appeals to the king's conscience, has been always praised as a model of Christian dignity and kindness, and a rhetorically admirable peroration. *I would to God*, or more exactly, *I could pray to God*, i. e. if it were proper and would not offend, I could now burst forth into an audible petition, which with graceful art he does indirectly, even while he seems to be deferring it. Another fine trait in this closing sentence is the ease with which he passes from Agrippa, hitherto the only auditor whose presence he had recognized, except when Festus for a moment interrupted him, to all those present, not by a direct address, which could not have been made becoming at the very end of his discourse, but by including all in his benevolent petition. *Were* (or rather, *might become*) *both in little and in much* (or in a small and great degree) *such as even I am, save these bonds* (which he again perhaps held up to view.) The exquisite mixture of severity and tenderness in this allusion to his own unjust confinement, and the accompanying wish for their exemption both from this and from a far worse bondage, forms a noble peroration of this great discourse, and an appropriate winding up of the whole series of Apologies, which occupies the history of Paul's last visit to the Holy Land.

30. And when he had thus spoken, the king rose up, and the governor, and Bernice, and they that sat with them —

When he had thus spoken (or *he having spoken these things*) is omitted in the oldest copies and excluded by the latest critics. Some suppose their rising to be here described as an abrupt one, prompted by the king's unwillingness to hear more; but the regular and beautiful conclusion, to which Paul's address was brought in the preceding verse, seems rather to imply that he had said what he intended, and that the purpose of the audience was accomplished. The persons who composed the assembly are enumerated in the order of their personal rank, and not of their official authority; first the King, as such, and on account of his relation to the Jews, although without political power in Judea; then the Governor, whose relative position was the converse of Agrippa's; then Bernice, as a person of royal lineage, and the sister of the highest dignitary present; after which the military officers and citizens (see above, on 25, 23) are grouped together as assessors, or those sitting with the chiefs just severally men tioned. These are little things, of no importance in themselves, but tending to confirm the supposition that the writer was a witness of Paul's last Apology in Palestine. (See above, on 24, 23.)

31. And when they were gone aside, they talked between themselves, saying, This man doeth nothing worthy of death or of bonds.

Some explain the first words, *and withdrawing*, or as they withdrew from the "place of hearing" (see above, on 24, 23), they conversed among themselves as follows. But the constant meaning of the Greek verb is to go aside for safety, privacy, or consultation (see above, on 23, 19, and compare Matt. 2, 12. Mark 3, 7. John 6, 15.) This is especially appropriate in this place, where the whole proceeding had a definite design (see above, on 25, 26), which would not have been accomplished without something more than a colloquial expression of opinion. The only question is, to whom this verse refers as thus withdrawing and consulting. Not to all those mentioned in v. 30, who would then be represented as withdrawing from themselves. The most probable solution is afforded by the next verse, where the two leading personages are expressly named, and may therefore be regarded as the subjects of the verb in this verse. The sense will then be, that Agrippa and Festus, withdrawing from the company, perhaps going aside but in the same apartment, there exchanged views in relation to the hearing which had just been held, and coincided in the judgment previously formed by Festus (see above, on 25, 25), that the prisoner was guilty of no crime deserving either the highest or the lowest form of punishment, imprisonment or death. Thus again the innocence of Paul had been triumphantly established, not only to the further satisfaction of the governor, by whom he had been virtually cleared before, but also in the judgment of the best informed and most disinterested arbiter before whom he had yet appeared.

32. Then said Agrippa unto Festus, This man might have been set at liberty, if he had not appealed unto Cesar.

If this meant only that the charges against Paul were groundless, it would be a needless and unmeaning repetition by Agrippa of what he and Festus had agreed upon already in the verse preceding. But Paul's was not the only case on which Agrippa was to sit in judgment. The very man who had requested his assistance as an arbiter in Paul's case, had by that act made him judge of his own conduct. We have seen already (on 25, 9 above), that Festus by neglecting to discharge Paul when his innocence was proved, had forced him to appeal, and at the same time placed himself in the embarrassing position of a magistrate sending home a prisoner, who might have been disposed of on the spot, but for his own neglect of duty. During this last hearing by Agrippa, Festus seems to have indulged a hope that something would occur to relieve him from his false position; but of this hope he was now deprived by the expression of Agrippa's jugdment here recorded. *This man could have been discharged* (or set at liberty), the technical expression for judicial liberation, used above in 3, 13. 4, 21. 23. 5, 40. 16, 35. 36. 17, 9. He does not say that he could now be set free, but that he might have been so at some former period, both verbs being in the past tense. This can refer only to the time of Paul's appearance before Festus (see above, on 25, 6. 25), and is therefore a civil way of saying that he ought to have been set free then. *If he had not appealed unto Cesar* is not added to exonerate Festus, but in reality to make him answerable for the whole result, as having forced Paul to appeal by his denial or delay of justice. It is worthy of remark that this appeal, though apparently precipitate on Paul's part, and embarrassing to him as well as to the Procurator, was the providential means by which he was removed from Palestine and brought to Rome, an end which might never have been reached, if he had not, as many of his friends no doubt lamented now, appealed to Cesar.

CHAPTER XXVII.

THIS chapter is entirely occupied with Paul's last recorded voyage, from his leaving Cesarea to his shipwreck on the island of Malta. It is chiefly remarkable for the fulness and exactness of its nautical details, which the latest and most critical investigations have only served to render more surprising in themselves, and more conclusive as internal proofs of authenticity and genuineness. This view of the chapter has been recently presented in a masterly monograph,* the valuable substance and results of which, omitting technical minutiae, are embodied in the following exposition. The original narrative begins with the delivery of Paul and other prisoners into the custody of a Roman officer, their embarkation in a ship of Asia Minor and short stay at Sidon, with their subsequent slow progress till they reach Myra in Lycia (1–5). Here they are transferred to an Alexandrian vessel bound to Italy,

* The Voyage and Shipwreck of St. Paul: with Dissertations on the Life and Writings of St. Luke, and the Ships and Navigation of the Ancients. By James Smith, Esq., of Jordanhill, F. R. S. etc. Second edition, with additional proofs and illustrations. London, 1856.

but are forced by contrary winds to the east and south of Crete, where they find a harbour, but, in opposition to Paul's warnings, leave it for another more commodious on the same coast (6–12). While prosperously nearing it, as they suppose, a violent and sudden change of wind drives them to the south-west and involves them in the greatest danger (13–19). When the storm has continued many days, Paul assures them, on divine authority, of their ultimate escape, but predicts an intervening shipwreck (20–26). In the fourteenth night they make land, and are now exposed to danger of another kind, which tempts the crew to leave the others to their fate; but their proposed desertion is prevented, at Paul's instance, by the soldiers (27–32). He then induces the whole company (the number of which is precisely stated), both by exhortation and example, to partake of food before the ship is lightened for the last time (33–38). As soon as daylight renders the land visible, they run the ship aground, but are still in a position of great peril, from which Paul is the occasion of their all escaping (39–44).

1. And when it was determined that we should sail into Italy, they delivered Paul and certain other prisoners unto (one) named Julius, a centurion of Augustus' band.

When (literally, *as*) *it was determined that we should sail*, or rather (*about*) *our sailing*, i. e. as to the precise time and mode of their departure, the general determination having been previously formed and recorded (see above, on 25, 12. 21. 25, and compare 26, 32.) *We*, including the historian, the first occurrence of this form of speech since the appearance of Paul and his companions before the presbytery at Jerusalem (see above, on 21, 18.) Paul's arrest no doubt separated these companions from him, at least until Felix ordered that his friends should have access to him (see above, on 24, 23.) *Sail*, literally, *sail away*, i. e. from Palestine, one of several compound forms of the same verb, belonging to the nautical dialect of Greece, and used by Luke in this book with great freedom and precision. (See above, on 13, 4. 14, 26. 15, 39. 18, 18. 20, 6. 21, 3, and below on vs. 2. 4. 6. 7. 24.) The one here employed suggests, more distinctly than the simple verb, the idea of separation and departure from the Holy Land, where his mission was now ended. The place of departure, though supposed by some to have been Ptolemais (see above, on 21, 7. 15), is commonly, and no doubt justly, understood to have been Cesarea, as being both the seat of government and the most frequented seaport on the coast, as well as the scene of the last previous transactions, without the slightest intimation of their setting out from any other point. *Into Italy*, i. e. as their final destination (compare *into Syria*, 18, 18. 20, 3. 21, 3), but not directly, as appears from the next verse. *They delivered* has been variously explained, as a generic plural meaning Festus only (see above, on 17, 18. 19, 38); or as a proper plural including his assessors and perhaps Agrippa (see above, on 25, 12. 23, 26); or, more probably than either, as a plural indefinite (like that in Luke 12, 20. John 15, 6) which, though comparatively rare in Greek, is one of our most familiar English idioms, the plural being used instead of the indefinite pronouns in French (*on*) and German (*man.*) For the most part it may be resolved into the passive, as in this case, *Paul was delivered, etc.* *Certain other prisoners*, who may have been accumulating for some time at Cesarea. *To a centurion*, strictly the commander of a hundred men, but used perhaps with some degree of latitude (see above, on 10, 1. 21, 32.) *Of a band* (called) *the August* (or *Augustan*), the feminine form of the word used above in 25, 21. (For the meaning of the word translated *band*, see above, on 10, 1. 21, 31.) As the epithet *August* appears too strong for a subdivision of the army, it is commonly explained to mean *Augustan*, i. e. belonging or related to the Emperor in some peculiar sense or manner. That this honorary title was bestowed on certain Roman legions, is a certain fact of history; but not that any such were stationed in the East. Hence some suppose the word to mean *Samaritan*, from *Sebaste*, the name given to the ancient Samaria when rebuilt by Herod (see above, on 8, 5); but although Josephus does speak of Samaritan battalions in the Roman service, he uses a different derivative, as Luke would no doubt have done also, to express the same idea. Some maintain that the Augustan rank (equivalent to that of imperial guard) was given not only to legions, but to cohorts and even to still smaller corps; others, that the title here describes the Procurator's body-guard, as that of the Emperor's official representative. All these explanations presuppose that Julius was detached, for this important service, from the army in Palestine; whereas it is at least as probable that he came from Italy, perhaps with a special commission, and was now returning thither, which removes the necessity of explaining the epithet *Augustan*, whether Julius be identified with any other person named in history or not.

2. And entering into a ship of Adramyttium, we launched, meaning to sail by the coasts of Asia; (one) Aristarchus, a Macedonian of Thessalonica, being with us.

There seems to have been no direct communication, just at this time, between Palestine and Italy, or at least no vessel of the requisite capacity about to sail immediately in that direction. Besides the *other prisoners*, who may have been numerous, as we read in contemporary history of many being sent from Judea to Rome together, the centurion commanded a military escort, as we learn from the mention of *the soldiers* in vs. 31. 42 below, and this detachment may have been a large one (see above, on 23, 23.) *Entering*, embarking, see above, on 21, 2. 6, and compare 20, 18. 25, 1. *Adramyttium*, a seaport of Mysia, on the western coast of Asia Minor, opposite to Lesbos (altogether different in form from *Adrumetum* on the coast of Africa.) This vessel, having sold its cargo, was now upon its homeward voyage, and Julius availed himself of its accommodations to reach Asia, where he knew that he should meet with vessels on their way to Italy; just as Americans who visit India often go by way of England, the circuitous route being more than made good by the greater certainty, frequency, and ease of the communication. Even this ship, however, was not going directly to its final destination, but *about to sail* (or *navigate*) *the places along Asia*, i. e. probably to carry on a coasting trade along the western and southwestern shore of the peninsula which we call Asia Minor (see above, on 21, 27. 24, 18.) *Meaning*, in Greek a verb denoting mere futurity (see above, on 26, 2. 22. 23), and according to the common text (μέλλοντες) agreeing with the subject of the verb (*we launched* or *sailed*), but in the oldest copies with the ship itself (μέλλοντι), as explained above. It is possible, however, that this clause has reference not to trade but to the necessary route from Cesarea to Adramyttium, which was also the course usually taken from Palestine and Syria to Italy. They were really, therefore, on their way until they reached the south-west corner of the peninsula, although obliged to seek another vessel to complete their voyage. *Launched*, set sail, departed, went out to sea, another nautical expression, of which we have already met with several examples (see above, on 13, 13. 16, 11. 18, 21. 20, 3. 13. 21, 12.) *One Aristarchus* seems to imply that he had not been previously mentioned; but see above, on 19, 29. 20, 4. He is here described by his country (*a Macedonian*) and his city (*a Thessalonian*, see above, on 17, 1. 11. 13.) How long he was separated from Paul, and when he rejoined him, can only be conjectured. The praise of constancy bestowed by some upon this man, though doubtless just, has no foundation in the text here (*being with us*) but only in the Vulgate version (*perseverante nobiscum.*) In two of Paul's epistles, commonly supposed to have been written during his captivity at Rome, Aristarchus is mentioned, once as his fellow-labourer (Philem. 24), and once as his fellow-prisoner (Col. 4, 10), which may have reference to his voluntary share in Paul's confinement during and after the voyage here described.

3. And the next (day) we touched at Sidon. And Julius courteously entreated Paul, and gave (him) liberty to go unto his friends to refresh himself.

Their first day's course, instead of being north-west towards the coast of Asia (Proper), was considerably east of north, along the coast of Palestine and Phenicia, so as to reach Sidon (see above, on 12, 20) on the next day (literally, *the other*, as in 20, 15) after leaving Cesarea. This movement may have been for purposes of trade, or simply occasioned by the westerly wind, which is almost as constant as a trade wind, in that part of the Mediterranean, during the summer and autumn. Such a wind would be a fair one between Cesarea and Sidon, and a day would thus be gained in their course towards the coast of Asia Minor, even if there were no business to be there transacted, either by the ship or the centurion. In favour of the latter supposition, however, is the fact, that the vessel remained long enough at Sidon to admit of Paul's visiting his friends there. *Courteously*, benevolently, philanthropically (a word of kindred origin with that here used.) *Touched*, came to, or landed, is in Greek a passive, literally meaning, *we were brought down*, i. e. from the high sea to the shore (see above, on 21, 3, and compare the converse or correlative expression in the first clause of the next verse. *Entreated*, in its old sense of *treated* (now superseded by that of *prayed*, besought) or *used*, which is the literal meaning of the Greek verb. This clause (*benevolently using Paul*) though relating strictly to the instance here recorded, may be also taken as a general description of the Roman officer's deportment towards his prisoner throughout the voyage. It is not to be regarded as implying any faith in Paul's religious doctrines, which would no doubt have been more distinctly mentioned, nor even as arising wholly from a personal regard for him. Whatever part of the result may have been owing to the free-will or discretion of the officer, there can be no doubt that he acted in obedience to specific orders, similar to those which Felix issued after Paul's defence before him (see above, on 24, 23), and prompted in both cases, not by mere humanity or good-will to the individual prisoner, but also by respect for his rights and privileges as a Roman citizen. (See above, on 16, 38. 22, 29.) *Gave him liberty*, literally, *permitted* (see above, on 21, 39. 40. 36, 1.) *Going to the friends* (whom he had there), either old acquaintances, or simply Christians, who as such were necessarily his friends, at Sidon no less than at Tyre (see above, on 21, 2–4), the other great city of Phenicia, into which country the Gospel had been early introduced (see above, on 11, 19.) These two cities are always named in the New Testament together, except here and in Luke 4, 26, where Sidon stands alone. It was much more ancient than Tyre, which is mentioned neither in the Pentateuch nor by Homer, whereas Sidon is named not only by Moses but by Jacob, as a well-known boundary or landmark even in the patriarchal age. (See Gen. 10, 19. 49, 13.) In the book of Joshua (19, 28) it is called *Great Zidon* (*Zidon Rabbah*) and apparently assigned to Judah, but remained unconquered (Judg. 1, 31. 10, 10, 12), and was afterwards eclipsed by Tyre (2 Sam. 5, 11. 1 Kings 5, 6. Isai. 23, 8. Ezek. 26, 15. 27, 8. 28, 21), subdued by the Assyrians, destroyed by the Persians but rebuilt, reconquered by Alexander the Great, alternately possessed by his successors, the Greek kings of Syria and Egypt, until finally wrested from them by the Romans. It is still a town of more than five thousand inhabitants, under the slightly altered name of *Saida*, and for some years past the seat of an American mission. The ancient geographers describe its harbour (or rather harbours, for it seems to have been double) as the finest on the mainland, from the shelter afforded by a natural breakwater or ridge of rocks; but it was filled up during the middle ages. *To refresh himself*, literally, *to obtain* (experience, meet with, as in 24, 2. 26, 22) *care*, attention, which may either denote hospitality in general, or more specifically nursing, care required by delicate or ill health, to which a Greek medical writer applies almost the same expression (ἐπιμέλεια σώματος.) As to Paul's bodily infirmities, see above, on 16, 10. 20, 6.

4. And when we had launched from thence, we sailed under Cyprus, because the winds were contrary.

And thence (from Sidon) *loosing* (setting sail, departing), in form as well as sense the converse of the verb translated *touched* in the preceding verse. *Launched* is applicable strictly only to boats or vessels which were drawn up on the land (as in Luke 8, 22.) *Undersailed* (or *sailed under*) *Cyprus* (see above, on 11, 19. 13, 4. 15, 39. 21, 3), another nautical expression, falsely understood by some as meaning *south of Cyprus*, and by others close beneath its shore; whereas the best authorities explain it to mean *under the lee of Cyprus*, i. e. between the island and the wind (or the point towards which the wind was blowing.) They did not therefore leave it on their right hand, which would have been the direct course to the coast of "Asia" with a favourable wind (compare Paul's last voyage in the opposite direction as described above, on 21, 3), but upon their left hand, i. e. to the west, sailing along the eastern coast and northward, as the only course permitted by the wind, and also for a reason brought to light by modern nautical investigation, that from Syria to the Archipelago, along the coast of Asia Minor, there is a constant current to the westward, so strong at certain times and places as to break into the cabin windows, even in calm weather. By getting into this strong current they would be able to make some way westward, even in the face of an unfavourable wind. This fact, derived from the familiar practice of those seas and attested by professional experience, not only stamps Luke's brief account as nautically accurate, but shows the ship to have been managed just as it would have been at this day by the most experienced and skilful mariners. It also confirms the previous statement, that they sailed not to the south but to the east of Cyprus, which is further shown by the repeated mention of the reason, *for* (or *on account of*) *the winds being contrary*,

i. e. from the west. Had they left the island on the right hand, this wind must have been directly in their face or nearly so, whereas by sailing to the north they were enabled to avail themselves of it as a side wind, and at the same time to secure the advantage of the current on the coast of Asia Minor. That they sailed close to the shore, though not expressed, may be implied, or is at least most probable.

5. And when we had sailed over the sea of Cilicia and Pamphylia, we came to Myra (a city) of Lycia.

That their course was northward, and to the east of Cyprus, now becomes still more apparent from their being next found in *the sea of* (or *along*) *Cilicia and Pamphylia*, i. e. that part of the Mediterranean which washes the two south-easternmost provinces of Asia Minor in the modern sense of that term, although not included in the ancient Asia, the neglect of which distinction by some writers on this passage has involved it in complete confusion. These are just the waters into which they would be brought by sailing towards the north along the eastern coast of Cyprus, and which Luke accordingly describes them as now *sailing through* (not *over*), another compound of the verb to *sail*, belonging to the technical vocabulary of ancient navigation (see above, on v. 1.) By the aid of the current which has been already mentioned, and the indentations of the coast of these two provinces, *they came down* (we are not told how soon), an active verb equivalent in meaning to the passive one in v. 3, both denoting arrival at a port or harbour. *Lycia*, a south-western province of Asia Minor, also included in the strict and ancient sense of *Asia*. It was only now, therefore, that the ship began to reach its destination, and *to navigate the places along* (*the coast of*) *Asia* (see above, on v. 2.) The first of these was *Myra*, now in ruins, but at that time an important city with its port Andriace, at the mouth of a small river with the same name (now Andriaki.) The size of the city in its palmy days is supposed to be indicated by that of its theatre, which may still be traced and is of vast extent. (See above, on 19, 29.) Lycia often changed its political relations, having been dependent upon Rhodes in the period of the Roman Republic; then a free state under the first Emperors; then deprived by Claudius of this honour on account of its perpetual commotions, and united with Pamphylia as one province, ruled by a Proconsul, as appears from inscriptions still extant; and at last separately organized with Myra for its capital. But these political vicissitudes do not affect its geographical position as a part of Asia Proper. Myra was still a place of note and resort during a great part of the middle ages.

6. And there the centurion found a ship of Alexandria sailing into Italy; and he put us therein.

The centurion's expectation of finding an immediate opportunity to Italy was fulfilled as soon as he arrived upon the coast of Asia. *And there* (at Myra) *finding an Alexandrian ship sailing* (then or periodically, see above, on 21, 2) *into Italy.* That a vessel bound from Alexandria to Italy should be found at Myra on the coast of Asia Minor, may seem at first sight purely accidental, as the direct route between those two countries was much further to the south, between the island of Crete and the coast of Africa. Yet Julius seems to have counted upon it as a matter of frequent if not usual occurrence. The solution of this difficulty is afforded by the fact that the same wind, which forced the ship from Cesarea to sail northward on the eastern side of Cyprus, might force the ship from Alexandria to the coast of Asia Minor, with the same advantage, on arriving there, of a powerful current setting westward and a local land wind in the same direction. Julius was justified, moreover, in expecting to find a ship from Alexandria, not only by the general trade of which that city was the centre, but by the special and extensive trade in wheat, with which at this time Rome was supplied chiefly from that quarter. The vessels built for this trade were of great size, fully equal, it is said, to the largest class of modern merchantmen, and therefore able to accommodate a much larger company than that which now embarked at Myra, and afterwards at Malta (see below, on 28, 11.) About this same time, as we learn from Josephus, he was shipwrecked in a vessel of this class with six hundred others. A few years later, Titus, after conquering Jerusalem, returned to Rome in one of these store-ships. In the second century, one was driven by stress of weather into Athens, where it was visited as a great curiosity, and is described in one of Lucian's dialogues. From all this it is plain that what Luke here records, far from being incredible or even strange, is in strict accordance with contemporary usage and familiar facts of history. *Put us therein*, embarked us, made us go aboard (compare the verb in v. 2.) That such changes and transfers were by no means rare upon that coast we have already had a proof in Paul's adopting the same measure, on his eastward voyage, at Patara, another port of Lycia (see above, on 21, 1. 2.)

7. And when we had sailed slowly many days, and scarce were come over against Cnidus, the wind not suffering us, we sailed under Crete, over against Salmone—

On leaving Myra and attempting to go further westward, they were met by the still prevailing wind from that direction, without the counteracting influence before exerted by the local wind and current of the southern shore. Hence their progress was not only slow but difficult. *In many* (literally, *sufficient*) *days slow-sailing*, a Greek word not found in the classics, but obviously belonging to the nautical dialect, only a small part of which would find its way into contemporary literature, as in modern cases of the same kind. *Scarce*, or *scarcely*, should rather have been rendered *hardly*, as in the next verse, and taken in its proper sense, *with difficulty*, namely, that of "working to windward," or advancing in the face of adverse winds. *Over against* (opposite or parallel to) *Cnidus*, a peninsula projecting between Cos and Rhodes (see above, on 21, 1) into the Ægean Sea (or Archipelago) of which it may be said to mark the entrance. The distance between Myra and Cnidus (about 130 geographical miles) being only one day's sail with a fair wind, the delay must have arisen from its being still adverse, as intimated in the next clause. This renders needless and gratuitous the supposition that they were becalmed, which also agrees less with the expression *hardly*, as explained above. *Not suffering*, another word unknown to classical Greek usage, and possibly belonging to the dialect of sailors. It is in form a compound of the verb to *let* (or *suffer*, see above, on 5, 38. 14, 16. 16, 7. 19, 30. 23, 32) and the preposition *to* or *into*, expressive either of addition or approach, advancement. Some understand it here accordingly to mean, *not admitting* (or *permitting*) *us to* (enter Cnidus), as a reason why they did not land there as at Myra. Others, including the best nautical authorities, explain it to mean, *not allowing us to proceed* (or *go further*) *in the same direction*,

i. e. west by south, from the point of the peninsula to Italy. The wind forbidding this, according to the same authorities, must have been what is popularly called north-west, the very wind which even now, as we have seen, prevails in those seas towards the end of summer. Repeated instances are quoted from the history of modern navigation, in which the same cause has produced the same effect, to wit, that of driving the vessel to the east and south of Crete, along the northern coast of which her direct course would have lain in this case. *Undersailed* (or *sailed under*) *Crete* has precisely the same sense as in v. 4, where it is applied to Cyprus. The only difference in the cases is, that in the one they would otherwise have sailed along the south and in the other on the north side of the island, but in both they actually sailed on the east side, so as to be under its lee, or protected by it from the wind. *Over against Salmone*, is no doubt the true translation of the Greek phrase which corresponds in form and sense with *over against Cnidus* in the first clause. *Towards* (or in the direction of) *Salmone*, the construction preferred by some, would be equally grammatical and equally agreeable to usage, but a needless variation from the sense which must be put upon the same phrase in the clause preceding, and yielding scarcely so appropriate a meaning, as they rather passed in sight of than sailed towards Salmone. This is still, slightly modified, the name of the extreme point of the island eastward.

8. And, hardly passing it, came unto a place which is called the Fair Havens, nigh whereunto was the city (of) Lasea.

Having *hardly* (or with difficulty, as in v. 7) passed or rounded this point, they were soon upon the southern coast of Crete, and therefore in the same relative position as before they left the coast of Asia, i. e. with a high indented shore upon their right, and perhaps with something of the same advantage from a land-wind and a westward current, which would account for their apparently soon reaching a comparatively safe port called Fair Havens, a name not unknown to modern and American geography. That they chose to get upon the southern coast because the northern had no harbours, is a common error founded on a statement of Eustathius, refuted by the now familiar fact that there are at least two excellent ones (Souda and Spina Longa) upon that side of the island. It is clear from the narrative of Luke that they were driven to the east and south of Crete against then will and by the north-west wind, which would also allow them to proceed as far as Cape Matala, where the coast begins to trend towards the north-west, thus exposing them without obstruction or defence to the wind from that direction. The harbour which they reached must, therefore, have been situated to the east of Cape Matala, and there accordingly it was discovered by Pococke in the seventeenth century, two leagues east of that point, and has since been repeatedly identified, both by the Greek name which it still retains almost unaltered, and by its position furnishing a shelter from the very wind to which Paul's vessel was now exposed, but not from all the winds by which it might be threatened during a whole winter (see below, on v. 12.) This place is described simply as a harbour (or harbours) but not far from the city of *Lasea* (or *Lasaia*), which was long supposed to have entirely disappeared, both from books and from the surface of the earth, but the remains of which, with the old name still preserved in the local tradition, were identified by two Scotch travellers (Brown and Tennent) in the year 1856.

9. Now when much time was spent, and when sailing was now dangerous, because the fast was now already past, Paul admonished (them) —

Now (δέ, and, or but), *much time* (literally, *time enough*, as in v. 7. 8, 11. 18, 18) *having passed* (elapsed, or happened, as in 25, 13), *and the sailing* (or *navigation*, rendered *course* in 21, 7 above, and *voyage* in v. 10, below) *being already unsafe* (a correlative expression to the one translated *safe* in Phil. 3, 1, *sure* in Heb. 6, 19, and *certain* in 25, 26 above) *because* (or *on account of*, the same construction as in v. 4) *the fast being already past* (or *gone by*), i. e. the annual fast of the Mosaic calendar, the great day of atonement, being the tenth day of the seventh month, corresponding partly to September and October. (See Lev. 16, 29–34. 23, 26–32.) It is here used simply to define the season of the year, like Pentecost in 20, 16, or like Michaelmas in English, which occurs about the same time. There is of course no reference to any physical connection of the close of navigation with the Jewish fast as a religious service, or, as some have strangely thought, with the abstinence of the crew from food during the previous toils and perils of the voyage (see below, on vs. 21. 33.) Others, though regarding it correctly as a simple designation of the season, would derive it from some fast connected with the Greek mythology and heathen worship, on the ground that the ship's company were not Jews; as if that would prevent Luke from using Jewish marks of time, with which his readers were familiar, any more than an English writer would abstain from saying Michaelmas to designate the season, although writing about Turks or Chinamen. The Roman period of the *mare clausum* (or suspended navigation) began later, reaching from about the middle of November to the corresponding part of March. It is probable, however, that the two preceding months were reckoned unsafe or precarious, although navigation was not absolutely interrupted. *Paul admonished* (or *exhorted*), a Greek verb used only in this chapter (see below, on v. 22), but originally meaning to commend, and then to recommend, advise, especially in public, as a speaker in the Greek assemblies. It is probable, therefore, that this exhortation was addressed to the whole company, not merely to the chiefs and officers (compare *the more part* in v. 12 below.)

10. And said unto them, Sirs, I perceive that this voyage will be with hurt and much damage, not only of the lading and ship, but also of our lives.

Saying to them, i. e. either to the whole ship's company, including sailors, soldiers, and the officers of both sorts, or, as some infer from the next verse, only to the latter (see above, on v. 9.) *Sirs*, an excellent translation of the Greek word literally meaning *men*, which in English would be rather disrespectful than the contrary. (See above, on 1, 11. 16. 2, 14. 22. 29. 37. 3, 12. 5, 35. 7, 2. 26. 13, 7. 16. 26. 14, 15. 15, 7. 13. 17, 22. 19, 25. 35. 21, 28. 22, 1. 23, 1. 6.) These may either be the words he uttered once for all, or the sum of what he said on more than one occasion, during their long stay at Fair Havens. *I perceive*, behold, contemplate (see above, on 25, 24), denoting something more than simply seeing. Whether it here means supernatural perception, inspiration, revelation, or mere human forecast and conviction, is disputed. In favour of the latter may be urged the very different assurance afterwards imparted on express divine authority (see below, on v

23.) The first is then to be regarded as an error; but the two may be reconciled without this supposition, by explaining *loss* and *damage* as concise expressions for the risk or danger of them, as in 15, 26 above. *Hurt*, a Greek word properly denoting *insolence* and *insult*, as the attributes or acts of human agents, but applied by Pindar and some other poets to the fury of the elements and its effects, which seems more natural in this connection than to understand it of the mariners themselves, 'with arrogant presumption on our own part and much loss, &c.' *Loss* and *damage*, both which negative and positive ideas are suggested by this one Greek word. *Lading*, load, freight, cargo, from the verb to *carry*, like the noun translated *burden*, 21, 3, from the verb to *fill*. *Lives*, the word so rendered in 15, 26, but *souls* in 15, 24 (compare 2, 27. 3, 23. 4, 32 with 20, 10. 24), the primary idea being that of the soul as living or a vital principle. *This voyage will* (or is about to) *be* stands last in the original, with some irregularity of syntax, not affecting the sense and occurring in the best Greek writers.

11. Nevertheless the centurion believed the master and the owner of the ship, more than those things which were spoken by Paul.

The centurion, as commander of the troops and guardian of the prisoners, appears to have possessed the chief authority, either because he had chartered or engaged the ship on that condition (see above, on v. 6), or as a necessary consequence of his official rank and special mission in the public service (see above, on v. 1.) *Believed*, literally, *was persuaded* (or *convinced*), the same passive verb employed above in 5, 36. 37. 40. 17, 4. 21, 14. 23, 21. 26, 26, and implying previous doubt and reasoning, as distinguished from the exercise of mere authority. *The master*, governor (a word of kindred origin with that here used), or pilot, who steered the vessel with his own hands, or at least, in modern parlance, sailed it. *Owner of the ship*, in Greek a single word, *ship-owner*, who in ancient times most commonly accompanied his vessel in person, although sometimes represented, as at present, by a supercargo. That Julius should defer to the opinion of these mariners, in preference to that of his own prisoner, was natural enough, and is here recorded, not as a reproach or censure, but as the unintentional occasion of the subsequent disasters (see below, on v. 21.)

12. And because the haven was not commodious to winter in, the more part advised to depart thence also, if by any means they might attain to Phenice, (and there) to winter; (which is) a haven of Crete, and lieth toward the southwest and northwest.

The haven (port or harbour) *being*, from the beginning, i. e. naturally, always (for the usage of the Greek verb, see above, on 3, 2. 14, 8. 16, 3. 17, 24. 21, 20. 22, 3.) *Incommodious*, unsuitable, badly situated, probably another technical expression, as it is not used by classical Greek writers. It is here to be comparatively understood, as meaning that the harbour did not afford shelter from all the winds to which the ship would be exposed if it should winter there (see above, on v. 8.) *To winter in* is not a verb in Greek (as *to winter* in the next clause is), but a cognate noun preceded by a preposition, *for wintering* (or *for a winter-station.*) Both words are used in classic Greek, and the verb by Paul in his epistles (1 Cor. 16, 6. 3, 12.) *The more* (*part* supplied by the translators) is in Greek a plural adjective, meaning *the more* (men or persons), i. e. the majority of those consulted, or of all on board the vessel, to whom the decision of this question seems to have been left. *Advised*, or as some explain the phrase, *gave counsel*, might be more exactly rendered, *laid a plan*, or adopted a resolution. The verb (meaning literally *placed* or *put*) is one used elsewhere in the strong sense of determined (see above, on 1, 7. 5, 4. 19, 21); the noun in that of *will*, design, or purpose (see above, on 2, 23. 4, 28. 5, 38. 13, 36. 20, 27.) According to this usage, the whole phrase denotes not mere advice but positive determination, whether that of the whole company or of the officers, decided by majority of voices, although not, most probably, by formal voting. *To depart*, the word translated *loosed* in 13, 13, *sailed* in 18, 21, and *launched* in v. 2 above, where its usage is explained more fully. *Thence*, i. e. from Fair Havens, where they still continued. The reading *and thence* (or *thence also*) is not found in the oldest manuscripts, and seems to be preferred by certain critics only on account of its embarrassing the syntax. *If by any means* (or *if perchance*), implying the uncertainty and hazard of the course proposed (compare Rom. 1, 10. 11, 14. Phil. 3, 11, the only other cases of its use in the New Testament.) *They might be able, coming down to* (or arriving at) *Phenice* (or more exactly, *Phœnix*, the masculine form of that occurring in 11, 19. 15, 3. 21, 2.) Although Ptolemy mentions such a place, its situation remained undiscovered till within a few years, when it was identified with what is now called Lutro, and in 1856 the ancient name was found, as in so many other cases, to have been preserved by popular or local tradition (see above, on v. 8.) The proof of the identity, however, is afforded by the fact that no other place upon the southern coast of Crete affords a shelter even from the winds to which it opens, and which never "blow home," but expend their force before they reach the roadstead. The only difficulty is that Lutro opens to the eastward, whereas Phœnix is here described as *lying* (literally, *looking*, an expression used by Cicero and modern writers to express the same idea) *toward the south-west and north-west*, here denoted by the Latin names of winds from those points of the compass. The obvious sense of this translation is that the harbour could be entered only from the south-west or the north-west; and this is insisted on by some as the only meaning which the Greek itself will bear. But as the preposition here used (κατά) is among the most variable in its application (see above, on vs. 2. 5. 7), and sometimes (with the genitive) denotes a downward motion (as in Mark 14, 3. 2 Cor. 8, 2), it may here mean *down the winds* in question, i. e. in the direction towards (not from) which they blow. The harbour then will be described as opening to the north-east and the south-east, which accords exactly with the site of Lutro, whether the double aspect be referred to an island in or near the mouth of the harbour, having two entrances at its extremities, or understood more generally as descriptive of a spacious entrance stretching far round in different directions. This construction, although certainly not the most obvious, is rendered less harsh by the doubtful meaning of the preposition, and more positively recommended by its reconciling the description with the features of the only port upon the southern coast of Crete where the ship can be supposed to have sought refuge. That Lutro is not now frequented or accessible to large ships, if a fact, which seems uncertain, may be readily accounted for by long neglect and by the gradual encroachment of the sand, which has destroyed so many fine ports in the Mediterranean.

(see above, on v. 3.) That the ancient ships sometimes wintered here, is clear from an inscription, found by recent visitors, in honour of the Emperor Nerva (himself of Cretan lineage), erected by a pilot (*gubernatore*) and the superintendent of some public work upon the island. It appears from this verse that the judgment of the captain and the owner, which the centurion preferred to Paul's, was not merely arbitrary or capricious, but founded on their knowledge of a harbour better suited to their purpose. It appears, moreover, that the hope of reaching Italy before the spring was now abandoned, and the only question where they might securely winter. Some indeed explain the cognate verb and noun in this verse, from one of the senses of the root (χειμών or χεῖμα), to mean shelter from the *storm* or *tempest* then upon them; but no example of this usage has been cited, while the other has the sanction of Demosthenes, Polybius, and Diodorus Siculus.

13. And when the south wind blew softly, supposing that they had obtained (their) purpose, loosing (thence), they sailed close by Crete.

The plan of removing to Phenice (or Phœnix) was not only reasonable in itself, because founded upon maritime experience, but apparently most feasible and on the eve of being carried into execution. *A south wind blowing gently*, literally, *underbreathing*, a beautiful Greek compound which, according to the usage of the particle (*under*) in composition, denotes a small degree or a subdued force (as *rideo* in Latin means to laugh and *subrideo* to smile.) *A south wind*, the Greek word used by Aristotle as the opposite of *Boreas* (compare Luke 13, 29. Rev. 21, 13), but applied by Hesiod to the south-west, and by Herodotus to both. A gentle south wind would, according to the nautical authorities, be altogether favourable to their course from Fair Havens to Cape Matala, lying four or five miles distant; and as Phenice was only thirty-four miles further to the west-north-west, it is not surprising that they looked upon their purpose as already accomplished. *Supposing* (thinking or believing, as in 12, 9. 26, 9) *to have gained* (or more emphatically, *mastered*, seized upon, obtained possession of, as in 2, 24. 3, 11. 24, 6) *the purpose* (see above, on 11, 23), i. e. the purpose of removing to Phenice (as stated in the verse preceding.) *Loosing*, not the word so rendered in 16, 11 (see above, on vs. 2. 4. 12), but one which primarily means *taking up* or *raising* (as in 4, 24. 20, 9), and in nautical language may be applied either to a boat (as in v. 17), a sail, or an anchor, with both which it is coupled by the ancient writers. As absolutely or elliptically used here it may be translated either *setting* (*sail*) or *weighing* (*anchor*), without effect on the essential meaning, which is that of leaving or departing from a port, to go to sea or to proceed upon a voyage. (See above, on vs. 2. 4.) *Sailed close by Crete* is the exact sense, but not the form, of a peculiar nautical Greek phrase, consisting of an adverb meaning *nearer*, i. e. nearer than usual or nearer than before, when coming to Fair Havens, as related in v. 8, and of the same verb that is there used, strictly meaning *they laid themselves* (or *laid their course*) *by* (or *along*) a certain place. (Compare the corresponding Latin phrase, *legere oram.*) This close adherence to the land between Fair Havens and Cape Matala, was at once their shortest and their safest course with such a wind.

14. But not long after there arose against it a tempestuous wind called Euroclydon.

Not long after, literally, *after not much*, i. e. probably as soon as they passed Cape Matala, beyond which the coast of Crete turns abruptly to the north and afterwards to the west, so that their direct course lay no longer close along the shore, but across a bight or bay of some extent. *Arose*, literally *threw* or *cast* (*itself*), of which reflexive sense examples may be found in Homer, who describes a river as throwing (i. e. throwing itself) into the sea, or as we should say in English, emptying (i. e. emptying itself and its contents.) *Against it* has by some been understood to mean against the purpose mentioned in the first clause of v. 13, and defeated by the change of wind here spoken of. Others refer it to the ship, although the pronoun is a feminine in form, and the noun in vs. 2. 6. 10 is neuter; to remove which grammatical objection, Luke is supposed to have had in his mind another noun of the feminine gender, which he actually employs below in v. 41, or still less probably, some part of the vessel (as the prow, the stern, etc.) A third interpretation refers the pronoun to the island; either in the sense *against it*, which is inconsistent with the facts, as they were driven from the island, not upon it; or in that of *down from it*, as the preposition (κατά) sometimes means (see above, on v. 12, and compare Matt. 8, 32. Mark 5, 13. Luke 8, 33.) This last construction is the one adopted by the latest philological and nautical interpreters, as being in accordance both with the usage of the language and the circumstances of the case. *Tempestuous*, in Greek *typhonic*, i. e. like a typhoon, a word still used to denote the hurricanes or whirlwinds of the eastern seas. In Greek it seems to have a mythological origin, such tempests being superstitiously ascribed to Typhon, Typhos, or Typhœus, a giant buried under Etna. *The (one) called*, suggesting the idea of a local name, such as Pliny says are particularly frequent with respect to winds. *Euroclydon*, accordingly, is not found elsewhere, and is here variously written in the manuscripts and ancient versions, though the weight of critical authority is strong in favour of the common text, which seems to be compounded of *Euros*, the south (or south-east) wind, and a noun denoting waves or billows, a combination somewhat incongruous and less descriptive of a wind than of a sea. Another reading is *Euruclydon*, which seems to mean *wide-wavy* (from the same noun with the adjective εὐρύς, *broad*), or wide-washing, wide-dashing (from a cognate verb.) As none of these poetical compounds seem appropriate to a wind, some of the best authorities, both nautical and philological, prefer still another reading, found in two of the oldest copies and the Vulgate (*Euroaquilo*), and denoting the *north-east wind*, which is just the one that would produce the effects afterwards described. Some prefer the supposition that the wind did not blow from any fixed point, but from various quarters at the same time or in quick succession. Such winds, however, are but momentary, whereas this one drove the vessel long and far in one direction. The sense of *north-east wind* is put by some even on the common text (εὐροκλύδων), which they regard as a corruption, very easy among sailors, of the original name (εὐρακύλων.) It is more than a fortuitous coincidence, that modern navigators speak of sudden changes from a gentle south to a tempestuous north wind as not only frequent but almost invariable in that part of the Mediterranean.

15. And when the ship was caught, and could not bear up into the wind, we let (her) drive.

And the ship having been (or *being*) *caught*, the same verb that is used above in 6, 12. 19, 29, and strictly meaning *seized together*, or carried along by some impetuous movement, swept away in its resistless course. *And not being able to face the wind*, or look it in the eye, an expressive compound very common in Polybius, who applies it to the facing of an enemy in war or battle. The transfer of this figure to a ship is much more natural and striking than the reference, assumed by most interpreters, to a practice still prevailing in the coasting craft of the Mediterranean, that of painting an eye on each side of the bows. *We let her drive*, literally, *giving up* (the ship or ourselves) *we were borne* (or carried along) without resistance (see above, on 2, 2), i. e. in nautical phraseology, they were forced to scud before the wind, and therefore towards the south-west.

16. And running under a certain island which is called Clauda, we had much work to come by the boat —

Running under, a technical expression similar to *sailing under* in v. 7, but distinguished from it by the nautical interpreters, both denoting that they sailed to leeward of the nearest land, but in that case with a side wind, and in this before the wind; a nice distinction, resting on professional authority, and showing Luke's precision in the use and application of sea phrases. *A certain island* or *islet*, the Greek noun being a diminutive in form. *Clauda* or *Claude*, written in the Vulgate *Cauda*, and in several other forms by ancient writers, now called *Gozzo*, a small island off the southern coast of Crete and south-west of Cape Matala. *Had much work* (literally, *were hardly able*) *to come by* (i. e. to obtain, or more exactly, to become possessed or masters of) *the boat.* Some of the older writers, disregarding the article, strangely understood this to mean that they had difficulty in procuring a boat from the people of the island; whereas the sense is, that the raging of the storm made it hard to secure the boat belonging to the ship and probably towed after it. This circumstance is mentioned as a proof of the elemental strife in which the vessel was involved.

17. Which when they had taken up, they used helps, undergirding the ship; and, fearing lest they should fall into the quicksands, strake sail, and so were driven.

Which (referring to the boat already mentioned) *having taken up* (see above, on v. 13), i. e. on deck from the surface of the sea where it was floating. *Helps*, not the assistance of the passengers, as some of the old writers thought, but either such extraordinary methods as are mentioned in the next clause, or perhaps the appliances and means provided for that purpose. *Undergirding*, not fastening the boat under the ship, as one interpreter absurdly thinks, a process equally useless and impossible, but strengthening the hull by compression, either by means of wooden stays within the vessel, or more probably by cables passed repeatedly around the outside and made fast on deck. This operation is still known to modern seamen by the technical name of *frapping*, and although not often practised now, has been resorted to in several well-known instances of recent date, among the rest especially by Captain Back on his return from his arctic voyage in 1837. In ancient navigation it was so habitually practised that the undergirding apparatus formed a part of every complete ship's provision, as appears from the inventory of the Athenian navy discovered a few years ago. The learned editor of that work, and some writers on the passage now before us, have supposed that the cables passed from end to end (or stem to stern) around the sides; but this would not be undergirding, or effect the purpose; and it has now been shown conclusively that both the ancient and the modern practice was to pass the cables vertically round the hull so as to tighten it by outward pressure. *Fearing*, in Greek a passive form like *being afraid* (see above on 22, 29.) *Fall*, or more exactly, *fall out*, an expression also used in classic Greek to signify the driving of a vessel from its course or from the high sea upon shoals and rocks. *Quicksands* is in Greek a proper name, *the Syrtis*, one of two sandy gulfs particularly dreaded by the ancient seamen on the northern coast of Africa, the Syrtis Minor near Cathale, and the Syrtis Major near Cyrene, which last is the one here meant, as being that to which a north-east wind would naturally drive them from the coast of Clauda. *Strake sail* is regarded by the latest nautical interpreters as not only incorrect but contradictory, denoting not a wise precaution against danger but a reckless rushing into it. The first word properly means loosing, slackening, then lowering (as in 9, 25 above.) The other is a very comprehensive term, which has no exact equivalent in English, corresponding more or less exactly to our *vessel*, *utensil*, *etc.* As a nautical term it is translated *gear* or *tackle*, and supposed in this place to denote, not the mast which was immovable in large ships then as now, but the yard with all that was attached to it, or more specifically what is called the "head-gear" or "top-hamper," i. e. the top-sails and other tackle used only in fair weather.

18. And we being exceedingly tossed with a tempest, the next (day) they lightened the ship—

We being exceedingly (or *vehemently*) *tempest-tossed*, a single word in Greek, used in the same sense by Thucydides and Plato. *The next* (*day*), see above, on 21, 1. 25, 17, where the same form occurs and is explained. This phrase is not to be connected, as in some editions both of the Greek and English text, with what precedes, as if the tempest were particularly violent the next day, but with what follows as the date of the proceeding there recorded. *The next day*, not after the beginning of the tempest, but the next day after they *used helps, &c.* *Lightened the ship*, literally, *made an out-cast* (or *ejection*) for that purpose, the translators having put the effect for the cause. The original expression is entirely different from the one so rendered in v. 38 below. What was thrown out in the first instance is not stated; but no doubt it was the least valued portion of the ship's contents.

19. And the third (day) we cast out with our own hands the tackling of the ship.

The third day, in reference to *the next* (or *second*) mentioned in the verse preceding. *With* (*our*) *own hands* is in Greek a single word (own-handed, self-handed), and implies that others besides the crew took part in this second operation. *The tackling*, a cognate form to that in v. 17, and meaning generally apparatus, equipage, &c., but in reference to a vessel, understood by some to mean its furniture, by others the passengers' baggage, but by the nautical interpreters some heavy portion of the rigging, such as the mainyard with its appurtenances, by throwing which overboard the ship would be materially lightened. All these methods of relief have been repeatedly exemplified in later voyages, from the narratives of which some writers have collected parallels, corresponding to the narrative before us, almost verse for verse.

20. And when neither sun nor stars in many days appeared, and no small tempest lay on (us), all hope that we should be saved was then taken away.

Neither sun nor stars appearing to (or *shining on*) *us for many days*, literally, *more days*, i. e. several (as in 25, 14.) *And no small tempest*, i. e. by a figure of speech common in this book, a very great one (see above, on 12, 18. 14, 28. 15, 2. 17, 4. 12. 19, 23. 24.) *Lying on* (us), i. e. pressing, weighing, as in Luke 5, 1 (compare John 11, 38. 21, 9), elsewhere metaphorically used to signify the pressure of necessity, duty, importunity, &c. (see Luke 23, 23. 1 Cor. 9, 16. Heb. 9. 10.) *Then*, or rather *thenceforth*, after that, literally, (*for*) *the rest.* (Compare Matt. 26, 15. 14, 41. 1 Cor. 7, 29. Heb. 10, 13.) *All hope of our being saved* (from death or shipwreck) *was taken away*, or, as the compound Greek verb strictly means, taken away all round, in which sense it is literally applied to the removal of the anchors in v. 40. As their state could not be rendered hopeless by the darkness mentioned in the first clause, nor even by the tempest mentioned in the second, which might possibly have driven them into some safe harbour, the nautical interpreters suppose it to be tacitly implied, though not expressly mentioned, that the vessel was already leaking, and their situation therefore looked upon as desperate.

21. But after long abstinence, Paul stood forth in the midst of them, and said, Sirs, ye should have hearkened unto me, and not have loosed from Crete, and to have gained this harm and loss.

Much abstinence (literally, *foodlessness*) *existing* (or *continuing*, see above, on v. 12, and on 5, 41), not a religious fast, nor a scarcity of food, as the vessel must have been provided for a much longer voyage, and indeed appears to have been loaded with wheat (see below, on v. 38), but that neglect of regular repasts, which is so frequent a concomitant of storms at sea, and so familiar to the readers of the history of shipwreck and marine disaster. *Then* (not expressed in the translation), i. e. after this long period of fasting or indifference to food. At this juncture Paul the prisoner comes forward, not as a mere adviser, but a cheerer and encourager of his companions in distress and danger. *Stood forth*, literally, *stand-*

ing, or still more exactly, *stationed*, i. e. having taken his stand in some conspicuous position, where he could address the whole ship's company. *In the midst of them*, among them, and surrounded by them (see above, on 1, 15. 17, 22.) *Sirs*, literally, *men* (or gentlemen, see above, on v. 10, and compare 7, 26. 14, 15. 9, 25.) *Ye should*, literally, *it was right* (or *necessary*, see above, on 1, 16. 17, 3. 24, 19.) *Have hearkened*, literally, obeying, yielding to authority, the same verb that is used above in 5, 29. 32 (compare Tit. 3, 1), and there explained. It has here a peculiar propriety and force (not preserved in the translation) because Paul had spoken with authority, not as a mariner, but as a person under divine influence, although they knew it not, until they learned their error by experience. As if he had said, 'You may now see that when I counselled you to stay where you were, I did not speak at random, but with an authority entitled to obedience.' He then reminds them what it was he had advised, namely, *not to loose* (sail or depart, see above, on vs. 2. 4. 12) *from Crete*, i. e. from the port in Crete where they were already safely housed, to wit, Fair Havens (see above, on vs. 10–12.) *And to gain* (or *to gain too*) *this harm and loss*, the same two nouns that are translated *hurt and damage* in v. 10 above, and which have certainly the same sense in both places; so that the first cannot mean presumption there, as this idea would be wholly inappropriate here. *To gain this outrage* (of the elements) *and injury*, may either be ironical, or mean to shun, escape, an idiom of which several examples have been quoted from the classics.

22. And now I exhort you to be of good cheer, for there shall be no loss of (any man's) life among you, but of the ship.

Lest they should regard this reference to his previous counsel as a taunt or a reproach, he immediately resumes the tone of consolation and encouragement. *And now*, the same peculiar formula of transition that occurred above in 20, 32 (compare 4, 29. 5, 38. 17, 30.) It is here equivalent to saying, 'but whatever may have been your error in rejecting my advice before, there is no need of desponding now.' *I exhort you* (see above, on v. 9) *to cheer up* (or be of good cheer), a verb corresponding to the adverb used in 24, 10. *Loss*, literally, rejection, casting away, as in Rom. 11, 15 (compare the cognate verb, Mark 10, 50. Heb. 10, 35.) *Of any man's life,* literally, *of life from (among) you. But* (only) *of the ship,* literally, excepting of the ship, an expression foreign to our idiom, but not unusual in Greek.

23. For there stood by me this night the angel of God, whose I am, and whom I serve—

He claims attention to this cheering assurance on the ground of its divine authority and origin. 'Do not regard this as an unauthorized assertion of my own, for, &c.' *Stood by me* (as in 1, 10. 4, 10. 9, 39. 23, 2. 4.) Not at a distance, but at hand, within reach of my senses. *The angel of God* (or rather, *an angel of the God,*) *whose I am,* i. e. whose property, to whom I belong) *and whom I serve* (or *worship,* see above, on 7, 7. 42. 24, 14. 26, 7.) This form of expression was particularly natural in addressing Gentiles, who knew little or nothing of the true religion, but to whom the word *angel* was familiar, not only in its general sense of messenger, but as more specifically meaning a messenger from heaven (see above, on 14, 12.)

24. Saying, Fear not, Paul; thou must be brought before Cesar; and, lo, God hath given thee all them that sail with thee.

Fear not (or be not terrified), the same expression as in 18, 9, where Paul, in the beginning of his ministry at Corinth, was encouraged by a similar divine communication. *Brought before,* the same tense (but a different mood) of the same verb that is rendered *stood by* in the verse preceding, and which here means *to stand before* (or *in the presence of*) *Cesar,* the Emperor Nero (see above, on 11, 28. 17, 7. 25, 8–12. 21. 26, 32.) This is an obvious allusion to his own appeal, as one link in a chain of causes and effects which could not be curtailed or broken. As if he had said, 'You have appealed to Cesar, and before Cesar you must stand, or the purpose of God will be defeated.' *And behold,* as usual, introduces something unexpected and surprising. Paul knew that he must go to Rome, but not that for the sake of securing this result, the lives of a multitude should be preserved. *God hath given thee,* presented to thee, or bestowed upon thee, as a free gift and a token of his favour (see above, on 3, 14. 25, 11. 16.) *All those sailing with thee*, i. e. their lives, here expressed as if their persons had been given to him.

25. 26. Wherefore, sirs, be of good cheer; for I believe God, that it shall be even as it was told me. Howbeit we must be cast upon a certain island.

Wherefore, because of this divine assurance, *cheer up*, be cheerful, or of good cheer. *Sirs*, as in vs. 10, 21. *For* assigns the reason of this exhortation, *I believe* (or *trust in*) *God*, not only in the general, but *that it will be* (come to pass or happen) *even as*, literally, *after what manner* (see above, on 1, 11. 7, 28. 15, 11) *it has been told* (or *spoken to*) *me*. *Howbeit* (δέ, *but*) *we must* (or *it is necessary for us*) *upon* (literally, *in* or *into*) *a certain island be cast* (literally, *fall out*, see above, on v. 17.) The name of the island, it would seem, was not revealed to Paul.

27. But when the fourteenth night was come, as we were driven up and down in Adria, about midnight the shipmen deemed that they drew near to some country—

When (literally, *as*) *the fourteenth night* (since leaving Crete) *was come* (occurred or took place, see above, on 23, 12.) *We being carried about*, literally *through*, a verb used in the classics, as the corresponding Latin verb (*differo*) is by Horace, to denote the driving of a vessel up and down or hither and thither by the wind. *Adria*, or the *Adriatic* (*sea*), not in the modern sense, which confines it to the gulf of Venice, but in the ancient sense, which makes it co-extensive with the central basin of the Mediterranean, between Sicily and Greece. This difference of usage is a point of some importance in identifying the place of Paul's shipwreck (see below, on 28, 1.) *About midnight*, literally, *towards* (or *near*) *the middle of the night*. *Shipmen*, sailors, mariners, the officers and crew belonging to the vessel, as distinguished from the soldiers, prisoners, and other passengers. *Deemed*, conjectured, or suspected (see above, on 13, 25. 25, 18) *that they drew near to some country*, literally, that *some country drew near to them*, or retaining the original construction, *they supposed some country to approach them*, in accordance with the optical illusion, mentioned by Cicero and other ancients, and familiar to all navigators now, according to which the vessel seems to stand still and the land to move. The word translated *country* does not mean *land* indefinitely as opposed to *water*, which is forbidden by the pronoun, but *a certain land* or country, not yet recognized (see below, on v. 39. 28, 1.) They discovered the proximity of land, not by the sense of smell, as some interpreters imagine, which supposes that the wind blew from the land, whereas their danger was occasioned by its blowing in the opposite direction; but by the sight or sound of breakers on the rocky coast.

28. And sounded, and found (it) twenty fathoms; and when they had gone a little further, they sounded again, and found (it) fifteen fathoms.

Having sounded (heaved the lead, to ascertain the depth), *they found (it) twenty fathoms.* The Greek word is derived from a verb meaning to stretch out, and properly denotes the space between the extremities of the outstretched arms, most measures of length, in all languages and ages, being taken from the human body (such as foot, handbreadth, span, ell, &c.) The ancient fathom and the modern coincide so nearly, that the nautical interpreters, in their calculations, treat them as identical. *Having stood apart a short (distance)*, or advanced a little further, *and again sounded, they found* (a depth of) *fifteen fathoms.* Such a diminution would of course be looked for, in approaching any land; but as the greater depth here mentioned must have been close to the spot where they perceived the nearness of the land, and in a certain direction from the second sounding, and at such a distance as to give time for the operation mentioned in the next verse; these data, when combined, may aid us in determining the place where the ship was run aground (see below, on 28, 1.)

29. Then fearing lest we should have fallen upon rocks, they cast four anchors out of the stern, and wished for the day.

Then, or more exactly, *also*, likewise, too, which may here be taken as equivalent to *and. Lest we should fall out* (from our course or from deep water, see above, on vs. 17. 26) *upon* (or *into*) *rocks*, literally, *rough* (or *rugged*) *places*, a technical term of Greek hydrography. *Casting* (or *having cast*) *four anchors from the stern*, which was not the customary mode in ancient vessels, although more frequently resorted to than now, from their different construction, and from their having both extremities alike. In a picture found at Herculaneum, and belonging to the period of which we are now reading, there is a figure of a vessel with the hawser and anchor at the stern. The same mode of anchoring has been occasionally used in modern times, for instance by Lord Nelson at the battle of the Nile, although the other is in ordinary circumstances more effectual in promptly stopping the ship's way or progress. *Wished for the day*, or more exactly, *prayed that day might be* (begin or come, the same verb as in v. 27.) The first verb properly denotes prayer as an expression of desire, and then desire in general, which most interpreters suppose to be the meaning here, although there seems to be no reason for excluding the idea that the crew, or the whole company on board, did literally pray to the objects of their worship for deliverance in their extremity.

30. And as the shipmen were about to flee out of the ship, when they had let down the boat into the sea, under colour as though they would have cast anchors out of the foreship —

The ship had been anchored to retain her in her actual position until morning, when she might perhaps be safely run aground. This precarious chance of safety did not satisfy the crew, who now, with natural but odious selfishness, determined to abandon both the ship and their companions in misfortune and escape at once to the shore, under the cover of a nautical manœuvre which they reasonably thought the others would not understand. *The shipmen* (sailors, see above, on v. 27) *seeking* (attempting, using means, see above, on 13, 8. 16, 10. 17, 5. 21, 31) *to escape out of the ship, and lowering* (the same verb as in v. 17) *the boat*, belonging to the ship, which had been taken up on deck soon after the beginning of the storm (see above, on v. 16.) (*Under*) *a pretext* (or *pretence*) *as being about to extend* (or *carry out*) *anchors from the prow* (or forepart of the ship), in addition to those previously cast from the stern (see above, on v. 29.) This was a measure the necessity of which could hardly be appreciated by a landsman, and which therefore furnished a convenient means to gain possession of the boat without endangering its being sunk by others crowding into it. This treacherous contrivance, founded on the ignorance of those who were to be abandoned, is not without its parallels in modern shipwrecks, and would no doubt have proved successful, but for a sudden interposition from an unexpected quarter, as related in the next verse.

31. Paul said to the centurion and to the soldiers, Except these abide in the ship, ye cannot be saved.

For the third time in this memorable voyage and tempest (see above, on vs. 10. 21), Paul the prisoner comes forward as the counsellor of those who seemed to have his life and liberty at their disposal. Perceiving, either by a natural sagacity, by nautical experience, or by special revelation, the ungenerous purpose of the crew, perhaps including both the captain and the owner (see above, on v. 11), he addressed himself to the military portion of the company, to wit, the centurion and the soldiers under his command, all of whom, with the prisoners committed to their charge, would have fallen victims to this murderous desertion of the vessel by the only men on board who knew how to control her, or could be expected to avail themselves of the precarious and dubious opportunity of safety which might be presented when the morning dawned. *Except* (or *unless*, literally, *if not*) *these* (mariners or sailors, who were in the act of lowering the boat, or had already done so) *abide* (remain, continue) *in the ship*, *ye* (the soldiers whom he was addressing). *cannot be saved* (from shipwreck or from instant death.) The condition thus prescribed, though often used to prove that the divine decrees are not absolute, is perfectly consistent with the previous assurance (in v. 22) that they should all escape, because the means are just as certainly determined as the end, which in this case was to be secured by the prevention of the seamen's flight, and that by the very exhortation here recorded, and its effect upon the soldiers, as related in the next verse.

32. Then the soldiers cut off the ropes of the boat, and let her fall off.

Then, not the mere connective (δέ) often so translated, but the adverb of time (τότε), meaning at that time, or afterwards, when Paul had thus addressed them, and by necessary implication, as a consequence of that address. *The soldiers*, indefinitely, meaning some of them, acting perhaps under the centurion's orders, but more probably prompted by the sense of their own danger and the instinct of self-preservation. *Cut off* (or cut away) *the ropes* (originally meaning rushes twisted into cords, but afterwards applied to ropes in general) *of the boat* (either those by which it had been lowered, or those by which it was still fastened to the ship, the sense preferred by nautical interpreters) *and let* (permitted, suffered, as in 14, 15. 16, 7. 19, 30. 23, 32, compare v. 7, above) *her* (the *boat*) *fall off* (or *out*), the same verb that is used above, in vs. 17. 26. 29, but here to be literally understood as meaning to fall from the ship into the sea, implying that she had not yet been entirely let down, unless the verb be taken in the less specific sense of separation or removal from the vessel.

33. And while the day was coming on, Paul besought (them) all to take meat, saying, This day is the fourteenth day that ye have tarried and continued fasting, having taken nothing.

For the fourth time Paul the prisoner assumes, as it were, the command of the vessel, or at least the direction of the company, wisely and carefully providing for the crisis which was now approaching, and in which they would have need of all their strength and spirits, unabated by neglect or insufficiency of food. *While the day was coming on*, or more exactly, *until it was about to become day*, implying that throughout the interval from midnight (or a little later) to the dawn of day, *Paul was exhorting them*, which is the proper force of the imperfect tense here used. (For the usage of the verb itself, see above, on 2, 40. 25, 2.) *The fourteenth day to-day expecting* (as in 3, 5. 10, 24), looking for, deliverance or shipwreck, *without food* (foodless, an adjective corresponding to the noun in v. 21) *ye complete* (or spend the time), i. e. continue or remain. *Having taken nothing* is not to be strictly understood, but as a natural and popular hyperbole, denoting the omission of all stated meals, with the deficient and irregular supply of food, which may be said to be invariable incidents of storms at sea, and as such recorded in most narratives of shipwreck and marine disaster (see above, on v. 21.) The irregularity arises partly from forgetfulness and want of appetite occasioned by anxiety or sense of danger, and partly from the difficulty of preparing, serving, and partaking of the usual repasts, amidst the disorder and confusion of a storm, by which the provisions are often damaged or swept away before they can be used. Some, with less probability, suppose an allusion to religious fasting; others to scarcity or failure of provisions, which is inconsistent with the facts recorded in the following verses.

34. Wherefore I pray you to take (some) meat; for this is for your health: for there shall not a hair fall from the head of any of you.

Wherefore, because you have already fasted so long, and because the consequent debilitation must unfit you for exertion, at the very time when you are most in need of all your energy and vigour. *I pray* (exhort, invite, entreat) *you* (the same verb that is used in the preceding verse) *to partake of nourishment* (or *meat*, in its wide old English sense of *food*, the only one belonging to the word in our translation.) *For this* (the act of eating, or the use of food) *is* (the same verb that is used above in vs. 12. 21) *for* (connected with, belonging or conducive to) *your safety*, the word usually rendered *salvation* (see above, on 4, 12. 13, 26. 47. 16, 17), but here used in the lower sense of rescue, or deliverance from danger. The common version (*health*) is too restricted, unless taken in the wider sense of welfare, safety. The second *for* has reference to an intermediate thought, implied though not expressed. 'What I advise is an appointed means to the appointed end of your deliverance, for, &c.' The collocation of the last clause is peculiar, *for of none of you a hair from the head* (i. e. a hair from the head of none of you) *shall fall* (to the ground), a proverbial expression for the slightest injury or loss. (Compare Matt. 10, 30. Luke 12, 7.) Instead of *fall*, which is the Hebrew or Old Testament formula (see 2 Sam. 14, 11. 1 Kings 1, 52), the oldest manuscripts and versions here have *perish*, which may however be a mere assimilation to the form of the same proverb used by Christ himself (see Luke 21, 18.)

35. And when he had thus spoken, he took bread, and gave thanks to God in presence of them all; and when he had broken (it), he began to eat.

Saying (or *having said*) *these* (*things*), *and taking* (or *having taken*) *bread, he thanked God before* (*them*) *all, and breaking* (or *having broken* it) *began to eat.* In this Paul is supposed by some to have acted as a Christian minister keeping a love-feast if not administering the communion; by others, as the father of a family, asking a blessing on his children's food; by others, as a pious Jew, acknowledging the Lord in all enjoyments. The most natural construction of his conduct is, that his primary design was to induce the rest to eat by his example, but that in so doing he did not forget the Christian practice of returning thanks for providential bounties. (See Matt. 15, 36. 26, 27. John 6, 11. 23. Rom. 14, 6. 1 Cor. 10, 30. 11, 24. 14, 17. Eph. 5, 20. 1 Thess. 5, 18.) This religious act was commonly connected, both by Jews and early Christians, with the breaking of bread as the formal commencement of the meal. It is not, therefore, necessarily implied that bread alone was eaten upon this occasion, though it may have been so; but in that case it is necessary to suppose a regular and orderly participation of this frugal fare, as distinguished from the scanty and occasional refections of the previous fortnight (see above, on v. 33.) *Began* is no more pleonastic here than elsewhere (see above, on 1, 1. 2, 4. 11, 4. 15. 18, 26. 24, 2), but denotes that he made a beginning which the rest continued, or that he began what others finished, as related in the next verse.

36. 37. Then were they all of good cheer, and they also took (some) meat. And we were in all in the ship two hundred threescore and sixteen souls.

Then (δέ, not τότε, as in v. 32) *being encouraged*, or *becoming cheerful* (see the corresponding verb in vs. 22. 25), *they also* (or *themselves too*) i. e. the whole ship's company as well as Paul himself. *Took*, the verb used in the last clause (and akin to that used in the first clause) of v. 33, and strictly meaning *took to* (*themselves*), as in 17, 5. 18, 26, where it is applied to persons. The same verb is found also in the received text of v. 34; but the oldest manuscripts and latest critics have the same form there as in the first clause of v. 33 (μεταλαβεῖν, *to partake.*) That this participation embraced all on board the vessel, is apparent from the statement in v. 37, which does not mean *we were in all* so many, for this would here be out of place between vs. 36 and 38, but we (who thus partook of this last meal) *were all the souls on board the ship* (amounting to) *two hundred and seventy-six.* This number, far from being incredible, as some have thought, is not unusually large, considering the size of these Egyptian storeships (see above, on v. 2), and compared with the statement of Josephus, that about this same time he was wrecked in the Adriatic with a shipload of six hundred.

38. And when they had eaten enough, they lightened the ship, and cast out the wheat into the sea.

And being satisfied (or sated), having eaten heartily, their first full meal since the commencement of the storm. *Lightened the ship*, the very phrase employed in v. 18 above to represent a Greek one altogether different from that here used, which is a technical term in ancient navigation. In this case we are told more particularly what it was that they threw overboard. *Casting out the wheat into the sea*, i. e. as some explain it, the remainder of the ship's provisions, as no longer needed, since they expected either to be rescued or to perish without long delay. To this it is objected that the provisions would have made but little difference in the burden of the ship; whereas the cargo, which had not been previously mentioned, would be naturally spared until the last, and would most probably consist of wheat, as this was the great staple of the trade between Italy and Egypt (see above, on v. 6.)

39. And when it was day, they knew not the land: but they discovered a certain creek with a shore, into the which they were minded, if it were possible, to thrust in the ship.

When it was (or *became*) *day* (see above, on v. 29), *they did not recognize the land*, as one already known to them (compare the use of the same verb in 3, 10. 4, 13. 12, 14. 19, 34.) *Discovered*, or as the verb strictly means, observed, examined closely, then discerned, distinguished (see above, on 7, 31. 32. 11, 6.) *A creek*, in its proper English sense of a small inlet, cove, or bay, metaphorically called in Greek and Latin a *bosom*. *With a shore*, literally, *having a beach*, and therefore suitable for landing. This specific usage of the Greek word is found in the best writers, and removes the ground of the objection that all creeks have shores, as well as the absurd construction founded on it, *a creek with a shore*, i. e. a shore with a creek. *They were minded*, i. e. they intended, purposed, such was their design (see above, on 5, 33. 13, 37.) *If it were possible*, lit., if they were able, if they could, the optative form suggesting the idea of contingency and doubt. *To thrust in*, or rather, *to thrust out*, the particle referring not to the creek but to the sea from which they there found refuge. (See the same verb as employed above, in 7, 45, and compare the kindred verb in vs. 27. 39 of the same chapter.)

40. And when they had taken up the anchors, they committed (themselves) unto the sea, and loosed the rudder bands, and hoisted up the mainsail to the wind, and made toward shore.

Having taken up (or away all round), the same verb that occurs above in v. 20, and which is here more correctly rendered in the margin of the English Bible (*cut the anchors*.) The same remark applies to the words following (*committed themselves unto the sea*) which the margin properly explains as still referring to the anchors, *and left them in the sea*, or as it may be still more exactly rendered, *let* (*them fall*) *into the sea*, the verb being the same with that applied in v. 32 to their letting the boat fall off or away. *At the same time* (ἅμα, in the version simply *and*) *loosing* (relaxing or unfastening, as in 16, 26) *the junctures* (ligatures or fastenings) *of the rudders*, which in ancient ships were two large oars on each side of the stern, and which in this case had no doubt been raised out of the water and lashed together while the ship was anchored by the stern (see above, on v. 29) but must now be loosed again in order to direct her movement towards the shore. *And raising* (hoisting) *the artemon*, an ancient nautical expression still retained in several modern languages, and variously applied to all the principal sails (the main-sail, mizen-sail, &c.) but believed by the latest and best nautical interpreters to mean the fore-sail, both on historical grounds and as the most appropriate in the circumstances here described, to which interesting parallels are cited from the history of modern navigation. *To the wind*, literally, *to the breathing* (*air*), or *blowing* (*breeze*), an ellipsis also found in Xenophon and other Attic writers. *Made toward*, literally, *held down*, i. e. by steering, kept her head in that direction. Herodotus combines the very same verb, particle, and noun (meaning *beach* or sandy shore, as in the verse preceding.)

41. And falling into a place where two seas met, they ran the ship aground; and the forepart stuck fast, and remained unmoveable, but the hinder part was broken with the violence of the waves.

Falling into, literally, *falling round*, embracing, but with the secondary sense of *falling among*, so as to be surrounded by (robbers, as in Luke 10, 30, or temptations, as in James 1, 2), or *falling within* (getting inside of) a place, as here. *Where two seas met*, in Greek a single word and that a compound adjective, analogous to *bimaris*, the epithet applied by Horace to Corinth on account of its position on an isthmus (see above, on 18, 1.) The same sense was adopted by the older writers here and referred to a projecting point or tongue of land, on which the vessel struck or ran aground. Later interpreters suppose it to denote the meeting of two opposite currents forming a shoal or sand-bank. But the modern nautical interpretation understands it of a narrow channel between two seas or two portions of the sea, as Strabo uses the same term in application to the Bosphorus. *Ran aground*, another technical term belonging to the nautical dialect of Greece and still preserved by other writers, such as Xenophon, Polybius, and Herodotus. *The forepart* (prow or bows), the word translated *foreship* in v. 30. *Indeed* (μέν), corresponding to the *but* (δέ) in the next clause, is omitted in the version (see above, on 1, 5. 5, 23. 11, 16. 19, 4. 22, 3. 9.) *Stuck fast*, literally, *leaning* (resting upon something), and then settling, fixing itself, in a certain situation, here most probably a bed of sand or clay. *Unmoveable* (in modern phrase, *immoveable* or *motionless*), a term used elsewhere only in a figurative sense (Heb. 12, 28.) *But* (δέ, in opposition to the μέν preceding) *the hinder part* (or *stern*, as it is rendered in v. 29) *was broken* (literally, loosened or dissolved, see above, on 2, 24. 7, 33. 13, 25. 43. 22, 30. 24, 26) *with* (or rather *by*) *the violence* (see above, on 5, 26. 21, 35. 24, 7, where it is applied to human subjects) *of the waves.* This is supposed by nautical writers to imply that the stern of the vessel was imbedded in mud and thus exposed to the action of the sea.

42. And the soldiers' counsel was to kill the prisoners, lest any of them should swim out, and escape.

As the sailors had their plot (see above, on v. 30), so the soldiers had their plan, but of a very different nature, not to save their own lives, but their honour and the charge entrusted to them, a proposal in the highest degree characteristic of the Roman discipline and spirit. *The soldiers' counsel was,* seems to imply a consultation and the asking of advice by the centurion from different classes, of which this was one. But this is not the sense of the original, which might be more exactly rendered, *of the soldiers there arose a plan* (or *proposition*), without reference to any other which had been proposed. *That they should kill the prisoners* (Paul and the others mentioned in v. 1), *lest some* (or *any one*), *swimming out* (or from the vessel) *should escape*, and thereby bring dishonour on the Roman arms, by which they had been guarded and protected. Far from seeking to preserve their own lives by the sacrifice of others, they proceeded rather on the supposition that they were to perish in the shipwreck, while some of those entrusted to them might escape, a thought intolerable to their stern fidelity and rude sense of military honour.

43. But the centurion, willing to save Paul, kept them from (their) purpose; and commanded that they which could swim should cast (themselves) first (into the sea), and get to land —

The centurion, as the first in rank and in responsibility, *willing* (or rather *wishing*, although never so translated in our Bible; see above, on 5, 28. 12, 4. 17, 20. 18, 15. 27. 19, 30. 22, 30. 23, 28. 25, 20. 22) *to save Paul*, literally, to save him through, or bring him safe through (see above, on 23, 24), which implies more hope of their escape from shipwreck than the soldiers seem to have indulged. Here again, as in v. 3 above, the language does not necessarily imply a personal regard for Paul, as the governing motive in the mind of the centurion, but rather a desire to execute his own trust and discharge his obligations, by bringing this important prisoner at least, through the perils which beset him, safe to Rome and into the imperial presence. Preferring the precarious chance of doing this to the desperate remedy proposed by the men under his command, *he kept them* (literally, *hindered* or *withheld them;* see the various versions of the same Greek verb in 8, 36. 10, 47. 11, 17. 16, 6. 24, 23) *from their purpose* (a kindred form to that translated *counsel* in v. 42), i. e. from its execution, as distinguished from the proposition or conception. *And commanded,* or commanded too (τε) *those able to swim, throwing* (themselves) *out first, upon the land to go forth* (from the ship or from the sea.) By issuing this unrestricted order, the centurion, boldly but prudently, incurred the risk of some among his prisoners escaping, for the even chance of saving all their lives and yet securing all their persons.

44. And the rest, some on boards, and some on (broken pieces) of the ship. And so it came to pass, that they escaped all safe to land.

The construction is continued from the verse preceding; we have here the second part of the centurion's order. (He commanded those who could to swim ashore) *and the rest* (who could not swim, to get to land) *some indeed* (μέν, as in v. 21) *on boards* (or spars, perhaps thrown over for the purpose), *but* (δέ) *others on some of the* (*things*) *from the ship*, i. e. articles of furniture or others which had been swept overboard, or broken pieces of the ship itself, as the English version rather paraphrases than translates it. *And so* (or *thus*) i. e. by these means, namely, swimming and floating with the aid of such appliances as those which had been just described, *it came to pass*, or happened after all, as something more than could have been expected, *that all* (without exception, sailors, soldiers, and prisoners, the whole ship's company of 276 souls) *escaped safe*, the passive of the verb translated *save* in the preceding verse, and strictly meaning in both places *to be brought safe through*, impending or surrounding perils. Although not expressed, there is an obvious allusion to the promise in vs. 22. 23. Not only was Paul's prophecy fulfilled, but the divine assurance upon which it rested shown to be no mere invention or imagination, but an authenticated, proved reality. Besides the singular position of authority, already occupied by Paul the prisoner (see above, on vs. 10. 21. 31. 33), he now stands forth in the extraordinary character of one to whom his God had made a present of 276 human lives, although he might have rescued him alone or with a few companions, thus displaying the benevolence as well as the omnipotence of Him whose worshipper and servant Paul professed to be, and whose immediate agency in this miraculous deliverance was placed beyond the reach of doubt by the distinct prediction of the danger (v. 10), of the ultimate escape (vs. 24. 34), and of their intervening shipwreck on an island (v. 26), a minute specification no impostor would have ventured, and which could not have been verified by accident.

CHAPTER XXVIII.

THIS chapter winds up the whole history by recording Paul's arrival at the great metropolis and centre of influence, and the beginning of his labours there. It may be divided into three parts, one of which describes his three months' residence in Malta (1–10); the second, his continued voyage to Rome (11–16); the third, his proceedings when he first arrived and through the following two years (17–31). They find themselves in Malta and are kindly treated by the natives, who regard Paul, first as a murderer, and then as a god (1–6). He is hospitably entertained by the chief man of the island, and performs a miracle of healing in his household, followed by many others, with a marked effect upon the population (7–10). Leaving the island in the spring, they touch at Syracuse and Rhegium, and land at Puteoli (11–13). Thence they proceed by land to Rome, on the way meeting two deputations from the church there; and on Paul's arrival he is treated with indulgence, although still a prisoner (14–16). He convokes the chief men of the Jews and vindicates himself before them, being his last Apology on record (17–22). At their own request, he expounds and proves his Messianic doctrine, with the usual diversity of effect upon the hearers (23–25). This last appeal to his brethren according to the flesh, he winds up by applying to them a well-known prophetic picture of judicial blindness, as exactly descriptive of their own condition (26–29). Having thus brought the Apostle to the end of his exertions for the Jews, and to the beginning of his work at Rome, Luke concludes with a brief statement of his unobstructed labours there for two whole years (30. 31).

1. And when they were escaped, then they knew that the island was called Melita.

Having been saved, or brought safe through, the same verb that is twice employed in the two preceding verses (27, 43. 44.) *They knew*, or according to the oldest manuscripts and latest critics, *we knew*, or rather came to know, discovered, ascertained (see above, on 27, 39), either by further observation, or from the natives, who are mentioned in the next verse. *Was called*, literally, *is called*, being still so called when Luke wrote. *Melita*, or *Melite*, now *Malta*, an island south of Sicily, described by Diodorus as a Punic or Phenician colony, and once a famous seat of Carthaginian manufactures, especially of cloth. There was another island of the same name, on the Illyrian coast and in the gulf of Venice, now called *Meleda*, which one of the Greek emperors of Constantinople, followed by some later writers, supposed to be the scene of the Apostle's shipwreck. The arguments in favour of this notion are, that Malta is not in the Adriatic; that its people were not barbarous but civilized; and that venomous animals are there unknown, though numerous in Meleda. But in ancient geography, the Adriatic was the whole central basin of the Mediterranean (see above, on 27, 27.) *Barbarous* (in vs. 2. 4) simply means not Greek or Roman, and was therefore applicable to the Punic population of Malta, but not to that of Meleda, which was probably of Greek or Roman origin. The presence of venomous reptiles in the latter is ascribed by the writers who assert it to the island's being damp and woody, which was once the case with Malta, but is so no longer. Precisely the same change, and arising from the same cause, has been noted in the Isle of Arran and in other countries. Against Meleda, as the place of shipwreck, it may be objected, that it lies entirely out of the course which the ship had been pursuing; that the presence of the other Alexandrian vessel there cannot be accounted for; that it does not agree with the subsequent course of the shipwrecked vessel, as it is described below in vs. 11–13; whereas Malta agrees perfectly with both, being in the way from Crete to Puteoli and south of Sicily. The bay of Saint Paul, on the north-east coast of Malta, which tradition assigns as the place of shipwreck, presents all the features mentioned in the narrative; a rocky shore with creeks or inlets; a place of two seas. both in the sense of a narrow channel and in that of a project ing point; a tenacious anchorage, with beds of mud contiguous to banks of sand and clay; soundings exactly answering to those recorded, and in the same relative position; and precisely such a coast, as to shape, height, breakers, currents, etc., as would account for a shipwreck taking place just here, in this case and in others of more recent date. If any thing is wanting to complete the resemblance, it is easily accounted for by changes which geologists regard as quite demonstrable. That the seamen did not recognize the island at first, is easily explained from the fact that it was not the most frequented part, and presented no marked features by which it could be readily identified. To all the coincidences which have been recited, it may now be added, that independent calculations, made by several experienced naval officers, as to the rate at which a ship would drive before the wind in such a storm as that described above, agree almost exactly in the singular conclusion, that the vessel, on the fifteenth morning after leaving Crete, must have been precisely where tradition has assigned the place of the Apostle's shipwreck.

2. And the barbarous people shewed us no little kindness; for they kindled a fire, and received us every one, because of the present rain, and because of the cold.

The barbarous (*people*), the same word that is rendered *barbarians* in v. 4, and applied by the Greeks, and afterwards by the Romans, to all nations but themselves, with reference rather to a difference of language than of civilization. In this connection, it is nearly equivalent to the common use of *natives* for the inhabitants of unknown countries. *Showed*, literally, afforded, or extended to us. *No little*, literally, *not common* (see above, on 19, 11.) *Kindness*, literally, *philanthropy* (see above, on 27, 3.) *Kindled*, literally, *touched* (or *lighted*) *up* (compare Luke 12, 49. James 3, 5.) *Received us to* (*it*), i. e. to the fire, or to their company (as in 17, 5. 18,

26.) *Every one*, literally, *all*, agreeing with the plural pronoun (*us.*) *Because* (or *on account*) *of the rain*, *the present*, literally, *having come upon* (*us*), which some refer to the preceding storm, but most interpreters, no doubt correctly, to a rain which followed it. The ideas of suddenness and violence (compare *lying on*, 27, 20) are not expressed by this word, but suggested by the context. *The cold* shows that the wind, which no doubt still continued, could not be the south-east or sirocco with its stifling heat, but must have been the north-east (see above, on 27, 14.)

3. And when Paul had gathered a bundle of sticks, and laid (them) on the fire, there came a viper out of the heat, and fastened on his hand.

Paul assists in keeping up the fire, which affords occasion for a new proof of the special divine care extended over him. *Having gathered*, literally, *turned* (or *twisted*) *together*, a verb corresponding to the noun applied, in 19, 40. 23, 12, to human gatherings and combinations. *Fire*, not the element so called, but a cognate form, meaning a heap or pile of burning fuel. *Came out*, or according to the latest text, *coming out through* the wood or sticks, in which it had been lying, no doubt in a torpid state, until aroused by the heat. *Out of*, or as some explain it, *away from*, or *because of*, as in Rev. 8, 11, which is a rare use of the preposition. *Fastened on*, literally, fitted (itself) down upon, i. e. with its mouth or teeth, though some infer from v. 5, that it merely coiled itself about his hand without biting it (but see below, on that verse.)

4. And when the barbarians saw the (venomous) beast hang on his hand, they said among themselves, No doubt this man is a murderer, whom, though he hath escaped the sea, yet vengeance suffereth not to live.

And when (literally, *as*) *the barbarians* (or natives, as in v. 2) *saw the beast* (a Greek word specially applied to venomous serpents) *hanging from* (or *out of*) *his hand*, which seems naturally to imply that he was bitten, although some suppose the viper to have merely clung to him without inflicting any wound (see above, on v. 3.) *No doubt*, or by all means, certainly (see above, on 18, 21. 21, 22.) *Saved* (*saved through*, or *rescued*, the same verb that occurs at the beginning of the first verse.) *Vengeance*, literally, *justice*, either as an act or an attribute of God (compare 2 Thess. 1, 9. Jude 7.) There is no need of supposing a personification, or a reference to the Nemesis, or goddess of retributive justice, represented by the Greek mythology as the daughter and avenger of the supreme Deity. *Suffereth*, literally, *suffered*, in the past tense, as denoting a result already fixed and certain. The inference drawn by the barbarians is supposed by some to imply that murder was punished in Malta by the bite of serpents, which appears gratuitous and far-fetched. Others suppose it to imply a popular belief that the guilty member would be providentially punished, but murder is not the only crime committed with the hand. The only natural supposition is, that seeing Paul to be a prisoner, perhaps still fastened to a soldier, they inferred that he was guilty of some crime, and seeing him assailed by a venomous animal, whose bite they well knew to be mortal, they concluded that his crime was that of murder, as the highest known to human laws, and one appropriately punished by the loss of life.

5. And he shook off the beast into the fire, and felt no harm.

And, or *so then*, the resumptive particle so common in this book, by which the writer, after telling what the natives said, returns to his main subject, and relates what Paul did. (See above, on 26, 4. 9.) *Shook* (or more exactly, *shaking*, having shaken) *off*, (the verb employed in Luke 9, 5, and a kindred form to that in 13, 51. 18, 6 above.) *The beast*, or reptile, as in v. 4. *The fire*, not the word so rendered in vs. 2. 3, but the primitive form, meaning fire in the proper sense, or fire itself. *Felt no harm*, literally, *suffered* (or *experienced*) *no evil*. This does not mean that the viper did not bite, or that it was not venomous, though so regarded by the natives, who must have been acquainted with its nature and habits, and who could not have expected such effects without a reason (see below, upon the next verse.)

6. Howbeit they looked when he should have swollen, or fallen down dead suddenly; but after they had

looked a great while, and saw no harm come to him, they changed their minds, and said that he was a god.

But they waited (or *were waiting*), the imperfect tense of the verb used above in 3, 5. 10, 24. 27, 33. Or, retaining the original construction and Greek idiom, *they expected him to be about* (see above, on 27, 2. 10. 30. 33) *to be inflamed*, the only sense supported by the usage of the Greek verb, that of *swelling* being either implied as an effect and sign of inflammation, or derived from a confusion of this verb with one which differs from it only in a single letter, and means strictly to be filled or filled up. Sudden and violent inflammation is described, both by Lucan and Lucian, as an effect of the bite of serpents. *Or to fall down suddenly dead*, an alternative suggested also by experience. ("Tremblingly she stood and on the sudden dropped," Shakspeare, Anthony and Cleopatra, 5, 2.) *But for much* (time, i. e. long, compare 16, 18. 27, 14), *they waiting* (or *expecting*), *and beholding* (see above, on 25, 24. 27, 10) *no harm*, literally, *nothing out of place*, i. e. amiss, injurious, elsewhere used only in a moral sense (see Luke 23, 41. 2 Thess. 3, 2.) *Come to him*, literally, *happening* (occurring, taking place) *to* (or towards, in relation to) *him* (see above, on 2, 25. 6, 11. 20, 21. 24, 15. 25, 8. 20. 26, 7.) *Changing* (themselves or their mind), a verb used in the classics, both without and with a noun, to signify a change of judgment or opinion. The change in this case was the opposite of that undergone by the idolaters at Lystra, who first tried to worship Paul, and then to kill him, or at least consented to his being stoned (see above, on 14, 11. 13. 20.) *A god*, not necessarily any particular deity of their own or of the classical mythology (Æsculapius, Hercules, etc.), but a divine person; not because the serpent was itself regarded as divine, but because he had escaped what they knew to be the usual, perhaps the invariable, effects of its virus.

7. In the same quarters were possessions of the chief man of the island, whose name was Publius; who received us, and lodged us three days courteously.

In the (parts) *about that place*, i. e. the place of shipwreck, on the north-eastern coast of Malta (see above, on v. 1.) *Were*, a verb implying permanent occupation (see above, on 4, 34. 37. 5, 4.) *Possessions*, literally, *places*, lands, the same word that is used above, 4, 34. 5, 3. 8, and the plural of that in 1, 18. 19. *Chief men*, literally, *first* (i. e. in rank or office. Compare the plural of the same Greek word in 13, 50. 17, 4. 25, 2.) That it does not denote mere superiority of wealth or social station, some infer from the fact that his father was still living, who, in that sense, would have had precedence. That it rather signifies official rank, may be inferred from the Roman name (*Publius*), and from the fact that two inscriptions have been found upon the island, one in Greek and one in Latin, in which the same title is preserved (MEL. PRIMUS ... ΠΡΩΤΟΣ ΜΕΛΙΤΑΙΩΝ) and in one of them applied to a Roman knight, most probably the Governor. Cicero, in one of his orations against Verres, speaks of Malta as dependent on the Prætor of Sicily, whose legate or lieutenant Publius may have been. *Receiving us*, in Greek a more emphatic term, implying cordiality and kindness, although not so strongly as the cognate form of the same verb in 2, 41. 15, 4. 18, 27. 24, 3. *Lodged*, in its modern sense, is too restricted to convey the force of the original, which means to entertain as guests, and comprehends all the rites of hospitality, as well as the mere furnishing of shelter for the night or even comfortable quarters (see above, on 10, 6. 18. 23. 32. 21, 16.) *Courteously*, not the word so rendered in 27, 3, but an analogous compound of the same verb or adjective with another noun, and meaning *benevolently*, amicably, kindly. *Three days*, i. e. probably until they could be otherwise accommodated for their residence of three months in the island (see below, on v. 11.) *Us*, not the whole ship's company, as some suppose, for this was too large to be so received, and probably dispersed at once; but, as in v. 10, Paul and his companions, Luke and Aristarchus (see above, on 27, 2), with probably the Roman officer, and possibly the whole detachment under his command.

8. And it came to pass, that the father of Publius lay sick of a fever and of a bloody flux, to whom Paul entered in, and prayed, and laid his hands on him, and healed him.

The Apostle was enabled to repay this kindness to himself and his companions in a very gratifying manner. *It came to pass*, or *happened*, either afterwards or at the time of this hospitable entertainment, *that the father of Publius lay*, or was lying down, the same verb that is rendered *kept his bed* in 9, 33, and repeatedly applied in the Gospels to a recumbent posture, both at meals (Mark 2, 15. 14, 3. Luke 5, 29) and on a sick bed (Mark 1, 30. 2, 4. Luke 5, 25. John 5, 3. 6.) *Seized*, confined, or held fast, elsewhere applied to pressure outward (7, 57) and inward (18, 5), and in the Gospels to the pressure or constraint of fear (Luke 8, 37) and illness (Matt. 4, 24. Luke 4, 38), which is the meaning here. *Dysentery and fever*, by which, in its worst form, it is commonly attended. *A fever*, literally, *fevers*, in the plural, a form of expression also found in the Greek medical writers, and supposed to refer to the intermittent paroxysms of the disease. This is one of the passages in which it is thought by some that Luke's professional habits may be traced. (See above, on 3, 7. 9, 18. 33. 12, 23. 13, 11. 20, 9.) It has been alleged that this disease is unknown on the island of Malta; but besides the changes wrought in this respect by lapse of time and the advance of cultivation, the assertion is disproved by the experience both of travellers and resident physicians. *Going in and praying* (or *having prayed*, but see above, on 1, 24), thereby avowing that he healed him, not in his own strength, but as an instrument of the divine mercy (see above, on 9, 40.) It has been well observed, that Paul experienced, almost at the same time, two fulfilments of his Master's promise, "they shall take up serpents; and if they drink any deadly thing, it shall not hurt them; they shall lay hands on the sick, and they shall recover (Mark 16, 18.)"

9. So when this was done, others also, which had diseases in the island, came, and were healed—

The healing of the father of their host was only the beginning of a series of such miracles, including, if the words are to be strictly understood, all the sick upon the island, or at least all who could be brought to the Apostle. Nor is this incredible, the population being probably a small one, and his stay protracted through the winter. *This therefore having taken place* (i. e. the miracle of healing mentioned in the verse preceding) *others* (or more exactly, *the rest*, those remaining, as in 2, 37. 5, 13. 17, 9. 27, 44) *having infirmities* (diseases, the noun corresponding to the adjective in 4, 9. 5, 15. 16, and the verb in 9, 37. 19, 12) *came* (or more exactly, *came to*, i. e. to him), as he could not go to them, being still a prisoner (see above, on v. 4) *and were healed*, or more exactly *cured*, the Greek verb meaning strictly *cared for*, but with special reference to the sick (see above, on 17, 25, and compare 4, 14. 5, 16. 8, 7.)

10. Who also honoured us with many honours; and when we departed, they laded (us) with such things as were necessary.

The effect of these extraordinary favours on the barbarians or rustic population is expressed by two of its external signs. *Who also* (i. e. not content with praising God, or simply thanking Paul) *honoured us* (the whole party) *with many honours* (or attentions), i. e. marks of affection and respect during our stay among them. As the word translated *honours* sometimes means *price* or *value*, and is always so used elsewhere in the book before us (see above, on 4, 34. 5, 2. 3. 7, 16. 9, 19), some retain that meaning here and understand the clause of fees or pecuniary gifts, to which the word *honorarium* is applied in Latin, and even the word *honos*, it would seem, in one of Cicero's epistles (*ut medico honos haberetur*), and the Greek word itself in 1 Tim. 5, 17 (compare v. 3 of the same chapter) as explained by some interpreters. But all these parallels, together with one found in the Apocrypha (Ecclus. 38, 1), are either doubtful or determined by the context; whereas here the wider sense is equally appropriate and much more natural, especially as these honours seem to have continued during their abode upon the island, and to be distinguished from the presents made to them at their departure. *Laded us*, literally, *laid upon us*, which denotes not merely that they put the things into the ship, but that the gifts were very numerous and abundant. *When we departed*, literally, *on us setting sail*, or setting out, the nautical expression for departure from a seaport, used above in 13, 13. 16, 11. 18, 21. 20, 3. 13. 21, 1. 2. 27, 2. 4. 12. 21. *Such things as were necessary*, literally, *the things* (pertaining) *to the use or need* (or according to the latest critics *needs or wants*) of Paul and his companions. For the usage of the Greek noun, see above, on 2, 45. 4, 35. 6, 3. 20, 34 (comparing Phil. 2, 25. 4, 16.) These gifts, consisting no doubt chiefly or entirely in provisions and other necessaries for the voyage, were particularly seasonable after the hardships and losses of the shipwreck.

11. And after three months we departed in a ship of Alexandria, which had wintered in the isle, whose sign was Castor and Pollux.

After three months, probably as soon as navigation was considered safe (see above, on 27, 9.) *We departed*, set sail, put to sea, the same verb that occurs in the preceding verse. *Which had wintered* (literally, *having wintered*) *in the island* (Malta), perhaps driven there as the other was, but more successful in avoiding shipwreck. *An Alexandrian* (vessel) like the other; this particular is added in the Greek text by a kind of afterthought to the statement of its having wintered in the island, as if he had said, 'which, by the way, was also a ship of Alexandria.' *Whose sign was*, in Greek a single word, and that an adjective, meaning signed, signalized, distinguished, designated by a badge. The ancient ships, besides the image of some tutelary god upon the stern, bore a carved or painted figure-head upon the prow, which gave name to the vessel; but in some cases, and perhaps in this, the *insigne* and *tutela* were the same. *Castor and Pollux*, in Greek *Dioscuri*, i. e. the boys or sons of Jupiter (and Leda), regarded by the ancients as the gods of navigation and the guardians of seamen. This particular is mentioned, not to show the piety or superstition of the mariners, nor to show how Paul was brought into compulsory contact with heathenish corruptions, but as a lively reminiscence on the part of an eye-witness. As to the number, size, and quality of these ships, see above, on 27, 6.

12. 13. And landing at Syracuse, we tarried (there) three days. And from thence we fetched a compass, and came to Rhegium; and after one day the south wind blew, and we came the next day to Puteoli—

Landing, literally, being brought down (see above on 21, 3. 27, 3.) *Syracuse*, the famous capital of Sicily, on the eastern coast, still in existence under the same name, but with not more than a twentieth of its ancient population. *Tarried*, remained over (see above, on 10, 48. 15, 34. 21, 4. 10), either for purposes of trade, or waiting for a favourable wind. *Fetched a compass*, literally, *coming* (or *going*) *round*, i. e. as some suppose, round the island or the southern point of Italy, or out to sea in order to avoid the coast, or along the windings of the coast itself; but most interpreters now understand it either of the zigzag movement technically known as tacking, or of the more irregular course caused by an unfavourable wind. *Came,* or came down, the verb used to denote arrival at a place in 16, 1. 18, 19. 24. 20, 15. 21, 7. 25, 13. 26, 7. 27, 12. *Rhegium*, now Reggio, a seaport near the south-west point of Italy opposite Messina. It was ruined by an earthquake in 1783, but is still the chief town of the province of Calabria in the kingdom of Naples, and has nearly twenty thousand inhabitants. *The south wind* (see above, on 27, 10) *springing up*, arising, a Greek verb used in the same sense by Polybius and Thucydides. *The next day* is in Greek a plural adjective analogous to *secondary*, but used in the specific sense of belonging to (or happening on) the second day (compare the similar derivation from *four* in John 11, 39.) Its application to persons (we of or on the second day) is wholly foreign from our idiom; but the sense is clear. One day would be sufficient with a fair wind to proceed from Rhegium to Puteoli, now Pozzuoli or Puzzuoli, seven miles south-west of Naples, once a place of great resort, both on account of its mineral springs from which or from their odour it derived its name, and as the landing place of the Egyptian corn-ships, the arrival of which was an occasion of great interest, as described by Seneca and Suetonius.

14. Where we found brethren, and were desired to tarry with them seven days; and so we went toward Rome.

Even here they found Christians, showing how extensively the gospel had already been diffused, though some suppose the "brethren" at Puteoli to have been Alexandrians residing there for purposes of trade. *We were desired*, invited or entreated (see above, on 27, 33. 34.) The very same verb followed by the same preposition has in 2 Cor. 7, 7 the sense of *being comforted in*, which some suppose to be the meaning here; but this requires a change of text, so as to read tarrying (not to tarry), an emendation without manuscript authority. It seems to be implied that this request was granted, which could not have been without the leave of the centurion, another proof of his indulgent treatment of his prisoner, whatever may have been the motive (see above, on 27, 3. 43.) *And so*, i. e. after these delays and interruptions, *we went toward Rome*, a phrase analogous to that in 27, 1 (*sail into Italy*) and others there referred to. But the best philological interpreters regard it as denoting their arrival, as it does in the beginning of v. 16, and explain what intervenes as a parenthesis or supplementary addition. 'So we came to Rome, but on the way, certain brethren came to meet us, &c.'

15. And from thence, when the brethren heard of us, they came to meet us as far as Appii Forum, and the Three Taverns; whom when Paul saw, he thanked God and took courage.

And thence (from Rome) *the brethren* (Christians there residing) *hearing* (or *having heard*) *the* (things) *about us* (or *concerning us*), i. e. of their arrival at Puteoli, their stay at which place would afford time for the news to be received at Rome. *Came out to meet us*, an attention similar to that so often paid at parting with distinguished and beloved guests (see above, on 15, 3. 20, 37. 21, 5.) There is no need of supposing a formal division into two companies, but only that some set out earlier than others, so that Paul found them waiting at two well-known stopping places on the Via Appia, the oldest and most famous of the Roman roads, leading from the capital to Capua and thence to Brundisium. Appii Forum was a market-place, and Tres Tabernae a group of shops or inns, the former above forty miles from Rome, the latter about ten miles nearer. Appii Forum is described by Horace in a well-known passage of great humour; and both are named together in one of Cicero's epistles, dated from Appii Forum and referring to another letter written a few hours before from Tres Tabernae. *Whom Paul seeing*, and beholding in them living representatives of that important church which he had so long purposed and desired to visit (see above, on 19, 21. 23, 11, and compare Rom. 1, 9–15), *having thanked God*, for his safe arrival and the fulfilment of his hopes so long cherished and deferred, *he took courage*, either in the passive sense of receiving encouragement from God, or in the active sense of rallying his jaded spirits, and rousing himself to new or more implicit trust in the divine protection.

16. And when we came to Rome, the centurion

delivered the prisoners to the captain of the guard; but Paul was suffered to dwell by himself with a soldier that kept him.

Having mentioned Paul's reception by the Christians (or the Church) at Rome, Luke now describes his treatment by the public authorities. *We came*, implying that the writer was still with him. *We came to* (or *into*) *Rome*, the same phrase with which v. 14 closes, the narrative there interrupted being here resumed after the statement (in v. 15) of what happened by the way. As if he had said, 'so then, when we got to Rome at last, the centurion, etc.' The special commission of Julius now expired on his delivering Paul to *the captain of the guard*, or as the Greek word literally means, *the commander of the camp*, i. e. of the Prætorian camp, occupied by the Prætorian or Imperial Guard, created by Augustus, and permanently organized under Tiberius by Sejanus. This formidable force, like the Janissaries of Turkish history, became the most powerful body in the state, and finally controlled the choice of the Emperor himself. There were usually two Prætorian Prefects, or commanders of this guard; but under Nero, the place was filled for a time by his preceptor Burrus without any colleague. Hence some have inferred that as only one is mentioned here, it must have been this person, and attempt to fix the time of Paul's arrival by the fact that Burrus was put to death in March, A.D. 62. It is evident, however, that no such conclusion can be drawn from the use of the singular number, which may just as well denote the one on duty, or be taken as equivalent to *one of the prefects* or commanders. The delivery of Paul to this high officer agrees exactly with an order of the Emperor Trajan, forty years later, to the younger Pliny, that a prisoner from his province should be sent to the Prætorian Prefects. (*Vinctus mitti ad praefectos praetorii mei.*) The first clause relates to the delivery of all the prisoners (see above, on 27, 1. 43), but the last to the disposal made of Paul in particular. *But to Paul it was permitted* (or allowed, as in 21, 39. 40. 26, 1. 27, 3), not by the centurion, whose power over him had ceased, but no doubt by the Prefect, who had now assumed the charge of him. *To dwell* (literally, *to stay*, remain, abide, continue) *by himself*, i. e. apart from other prisoners, but not entirely alone, as appears from what is added in the last clause, *with the soldier* (not *a soldier*, but the one already mentioned as) *keeping* (i. e. guarding, watching) *him.* (See above, on 12, 6. 21, 33. 22, 30. 23, 35. 24, 23. 26, 29.) The definite form of the expression has respect to the general method of confinement, not to the person of the guard, which was no doubt continually changed, thereby affording Paul the opportunity of talking with a multitude of the imperial guards in turn, to which some suppose him to allude in Phil. 1, 13. Even the confinement here described was indulgence in comparison with that to which most prisoners were subjected, and was probably owing to the favourable statements made by Festus in writing and by Julius orally. (See above, on 25, 25. 26, 31.)

17. And it came to pass, that after three days Paul called the chief of the Jews together; and when they were come together, he said unto them, Men (and) brethren, though I have committed nothing against the people, or customs of our fathers, yet was I delivered prisoner from Jerusalem into the hands of the Romans —

It came to pass is not a pleonastic or superfluous expression, but equivalent to saying, the next remarkable occurrence after Paul's arrival was that after three days, etc., thus marking, as it were, the stages or divisions of the narrative. *After three days*, during which interval Paul may have removed from the Prætorian camp to the private lodging mentioned in v. 23, and where the interview about to be recorded would more probably take place than in a camp or prison. *Paul*, or according to the oldest manuscripts and versions, *he*, without expressly naming him. *Called together*, to or for himself, which is the full force of the middle voice in Greek. *The chief*, or more exactly, *those being chief*, to wit, at that time, the actual existing chiefs, perhaps with some allusion to their banishment by Claudius (see above, on 18, 2) and restoration under the mild government of Nero during the first five years of his reign. The sense will then be, 'those who now again were recognized as chiefs and representatives of the Jews at Rome.' (Compare the similar expression used in 13, 1, and there explained.) It has been disputed whether these were elders and rulers of the synagogue, or merely heads of families and men of weight in the community; but the two classes are in fact coincident, the elders both of the Jewish and the early Christian church comprising most of those to whom the description above given would apply. Some have thought it strange that the Apostle's first communication should have been with unbelieving Jews, and not with that community of Christians, in whom he had long felt so deep an interest, and to whom he had addressed the greatest of his doctrinal epistles. But having related the readiness and eagerness with which the Roman Christians came forth to receive Paul, Luke might leave his readers to infer from that fact, as a matter of course, the cordial, confidential intercourse which afterwards took place between them, and instead of dwelling upon facts that any one could take for granted, might proceed to mention others not so easily conjectured, and for that very reason needing to be placed on record. The surprise felt at Paul's negotiation with these Jews is of itself enough to justify its being given at full length, while other matters are omitted, which if stated would have generated no surprise at all. As to the motive of this singular proceeding, it was not mere anxiety to stand well with the Jews at Rome, or to avoid their machinations, neither of which could give the great Apostle, after all that he had passed through, much uneasiness; but rather an intention to wind up his dealings with his unbelieving brethren by a solemn declaration of the truth as to himself and the religion which he now professed, and thus, through them as representatives, to bid farewell to Israel according to the flesh for ever. In this last appeal and apology, he uses his old formula, *Men and brethren*, thereby acknowledging them still, not only as his countrymen, but also as his coreligionists, or fellow-Jews. (See above, on 2, 29. 7, 2. 13, 26. 22, 1. 23, 1. 6.) *I having done nothing contrary* (or *hostile*, see above, on 26, 9) *to the people* (i. e. to the rights and privileges of the Jewish church or chosen race) *nor to the paternal* (or *ancestral*, see above, on 22, 3. 24, 14) *institutions* (see above, on 6, 14. 15, 1. 16, 21. 21, 21. 26, 3), (nevertheless as) *a prisoner from Jerusalem was delivered into the hands of the Romans.* Two questions have been raised as to the truth and ingenuousness of this statement. The first is, how Paul could deny that he had opposed the Jewish church and institutions, when his whole life as a Christian had been spent in maintaining that they were not necessary to salvation. The answer is the same that Paul himself gave before Felix (24, 14–16) and Agrippa (26, 6–8. 21–23), namely, that he did not embrace Christianity as a succedaneum for the old religion, but as its legitimate successor and predicted consummation, so that the Christian was in fact the best Jew, or rather the only Israelite indeed in whom there was no guile (compare John 1, 48.) The Mosaic ceremonies, having been intended for a temporary purpose now accomplished, could no longer be essential or even conducive to salvation. The other question is, how Paul could justly represent the Jews as having betrayed him to the Romans, when in fact he had himself declined the jurisdiction of the Sanhedrim and appealed to the imperial tribunal (see above, on 25, 9–12.) The answer is, that Paul is here referring not to the outward form of the proceedings, but to their secret springs and actual effects. His original transfer from the power of the Jews to that of the Romans, though immediately occasioned by the armed interference of the latter, was ultimately referable to the violence and malice of the former (see above, on 21, 31. 32.) So too, his final appeal to Cesar, though a voluntary act, was rendered necessary by the continued machinations of the Jews against his life and the apparent connivance of the Procurator Festus (see above, on 23, 12. 25, 3. 9–12.) It was therefore true, in fact if not in form, that Paul was forced into the power of the Romans and the presence of the emperor by the treacherous and murderous designs of his own countrymen. The immediate reference is here to his original transfer from the Jewish to the Roman power, as appears from what is added in the next verse.

18. Who, when they had examined me, would have let (me) go, because there was no cause of death in me.

As an aggravation of their guilt in thus betraying him, he adds, that they prevented his acquittal by the Romans when convinced that he was innocent, after a judicial investigation (for the usage of the Greek verb, see above, on 4, 9. 12, 19. 24, 8.) This is not a mere inference or conjecture, but a supplementary completion of Luke's narrative in 25, 8. 9, where we read that after Paul's refutation of the charges, Festus asked him if he would be tried again before the council at Jerusalem. The seeming abruptness of this proposition, and its destitution of all ground or reason, are in some degree removed by Paul's own statement to the Jews at Rome, which although perfectly consistent with the other narrative, completes it by informing us, that in the interval between Paul's defence and Festus's proposal, the latter had expressed a wish to set him free, but by the opposition of the Jews had been induced to offer a new trial as a sort of compromise. This, while it explains the Procurator's conduct, does not in the least extenuate his error in sacrificing Paul's rights to the wishes of his enemies, and proposing a new trial when he ought to have acquitted and discharged him. (See above, on 25, 12. 25. 26, 31. 32.)

19. But when the Jews spake against (it), I was constrained to appeal unto Cesar; not that I had aught to accuse my nation of.

The Jews contradicting or opposing (the proposal to acquit or set him free), *I was constrained* (compelled or forced) *to appeal to Cesar* (or invoke the emperor, see above, on 25, 11.) The compulsion here alleged is not a physical compulsion, forcing him against his will to take this step, but a moral force, depriving him of any other means by which he could ensure his safety. As the Jews were determined to destroy him, and Festus seemed unable or unwilling to protect him, he was forced, as his only means of safety, to assert his civic rights and to invoke the imperial protection. It was therefore simply a defensive measure, and involved no charge against the Jews as a nation, of which he here still claims to be a member. The idea is not that his persecution in Judea was a local one, for which the Jews at large were not responsible; for the sacred history uniformly treats the proceedings against Christ and his apostles as a national offence. The distinction drawn is not between the whole race and its subdivisions, but between offensive and defensive action on the part of Paul himself; and even this has reference only to his formal appeal. He does not say, and could not say with truth, that he had no complaint to make against his nation; nay, he had already made one in this very speech, to wit, that they had betrayed him to the Romans and prevented his acquittal and discharge. *Not that I had*, might have been translated more exactly, *not as having*, and immediately connected with the verb preceding, *I was forced to appeal to Cesar* (for my own protection) *not as having any thing to charge my nation with* (at this tribunal.) This view of the grammatical construction does away with an additional charge of disingenuousness, by evincing that the last clause of the verse before us has exclusive reference to the form and ground of Paul's appeal to Nero, which was purely a defensive act, involving no attack whatever upon others, whether innocent or guilty with respect to the appellant.

20. For this cause therefore have I called for you, to see (you) and to speak with (you), because that for the hope of Israel I am bound with this chain.

For this cause, not the one suggested in the last clause, as the English version seems to mean, but that involved in the preceding statement; because he had been passive in this whole affair, not active; because he was "more sinned against than sinning;" because his present errand to the court was not to bring a charge against his nation, but to save himself from their injustice; *for this cause he had called for* (or *invited*) them, *to see* (them) *and speak with* (or *talk to*) them, that they might not of themselves suspect, or be induced by others to believe, that he was an apostate and a traitor to the theocracy in which they gloried. *For* (not *because*, which changes the relation of the clauses), so far is this from being true, that I am actually suffering because of my fidelity to that religion which they charge me with abandoning. *On account* (or *for the sake*) *of the hope of Israel, I wear* (or *am surrounded by*) *this chain*, the one by which he was attached to the accompanying soldier. (See above, on v. 16, and compare the use of the same compound verb in Heb. 5, 2. 12, 1.) By this skilful but most natural conclusion, Paul connects the simple statement of his own case, and the purpose of his present visit, with the great Messianic doctrine which was at once the centre of the Jewish and the Christian systems. Here, as in 23, 6. 24, 15. 26, 6. 7, the hope of Israel is faith in the Messiah as predicted in the Hebrew Scriptures. Here too, as in his previous apologies just cited, he describes this hope as the occasion of his sufferings, because it was his Messianic doctrine that had caused the breach between him and his countrymen, and thus led to his loss of liberty and accusation as a renegade and heretic. But this doctrine, far from involving a rejection of the ancient Jewish faith, was in his view an inflexible adherence to it, and he thus comes back to the point from which he set out, namely, that the best Christian is the best Jew in the true sense of the term; "for," as he had said long before in writing to the Church at Rome, "he is not a Jew, which is one outwardly; neither (is that) circumcision, which is outward in the flesh; but he (is) a Jew, which is one inwardly; and circumcision (is that) of the heart, in the spirit, (and) not in the letter, whose praise (is) not of men, but of God." (Rom. 2, 28. 29.)

21. And they said unto him, We neither received letters out of Judea concerning thee, neither any of the brethren that came shewed or spake any harm of thee.

Paul's address presented two points to his Jewish hearers; his motive in appealing to the Emperor (vs. 17–19), and his firm adherence to the ancient doctrine (v. 20.) To both these they reply in the same order, to the first in this verse, to the second in v. 22. *Letters*, the same word that is rendered *learning* in 26, 24, the strict sense in both cases being *writings*. *Nor did any* (*one*) *of the brethren coming* (or *arriving* here) *report or tell any* (*thing*) *about thee* (that was) *evil*. *Report* and *tell* may possibly have reference to official and colloquial communication. *Any of the brethren coming* (or *that came*) may seem in English to imply that some had come, but that none of them had brought any bad account of Paul. In the Greek, however, there is no such implication, as the participle (*coming*) agrees with the singular pronoun (*any one*.) It is rather implied, though not explicitly affirmed, that no one had arrived who could have brought the news of Paul's appeal before him. This is not improbable, as he had left Judea near the close of navigation (see above, on 27, 9), and no doubt soon after his appeal (see above, on 26, 32. 27, 1), and any vessel sailing near the same time must have been arrested in the same way and could scarcely have reached Italy before him. This may serve to account for the fact here alleged by the Jews, without supposing that their banishment by Claudius had interrupted all communication with Judea, or that this denial was untrue and meant to avoid participation in a feud with which they had not been immediately concerned, and in which they may have seen the powers at Rome to lean in favour of the prisoner. This last hypothesis, though not at variance with the Jewish character in that or any later age, is less probable in reference to a number of the leading men than it would be in the case of a private individual.

22. But we desire to hear of thee what thou thinkest; for as concerning this sect, we know that every where it is spoken against.

This is their answer to his second point or closing intimation, that the cause of his imprisonment was not his abjuration of the old Jewish doctrine, but his close adherence to it. *We think it right* (perhaps with the suggestion of a wish, see above, on 15, 38) *to hear from thee what thou thinkest*, and how thou feelest, for the Greek verb denotes not mere opinion but affection (compare its use in Matt. 16, 23. Rom. 8, 5. 1 Cor. 13, 11. Phil. 2, 5. 3, 19. Col. 3, 2.) This is therefore a respectful proposition to do justice to Paul's doctrinal as well as his legal or forensic position, by allowing him to state his own views with respect to the great doctrine which divided between him and other Jews, and on which his pretensions to be still an orthodox and faithful Israelite of course depended. *For* (the reason why they wish or think it right to hear him) *as to* (or *concerning*) *this sect* (or schismatical party, see above, on 5, 17. 15, 5. 24, 5. 14. 26 5), meaning of course the Nazarenes or Christians, to whom Paul notoriously belonged, as he was no doubt understood by them to hint in the conclusion of his first speech (see above, on v. 20.) *We know*, literally, *it is known to us*, perhaps implying that they knew no more, as if they had said, 'all we know about it is, *that it is every where opposed* (or *contradicted*),' i. e. by the Jews, with whom they were in correspondence or communication. This, if not a prudent or contemptuous pretence, implies a singular want of information with respect to a religion represented by a large and famous church in Rome itself, whose faith had long been spoken of throughout the whole world (Rom. 1, 8.) This description of the Roman church by Paul himself, some years before the date of these events, precludes the explanation which might otherwise be drawn from the extent, confusion, and diversified interests of the imperial city, where two religious bodies might well co-exist in ignorance of one another. Some would account for the phenomenon in question by supposing that the temporary exile of the Jews from Rome, already mentioned, had prevented their knowing many things that had occurred there in their absence, and among the rest the rise and progress of the Christian Church. But the edict of Claudius is supposed by some judicious writers not to have been fully executed, or at least to have been soon repealed by

Claudius himself, and it certainly would seem from Rom. 16, 3, that Aquila and Priscilla had returned before the date of that epistle (see above, on 18, 2.) On the whole, the natural impression, made perhaps on most unbiassed readers, is that the Jewish leaders here dissemble or disguise their knowledge of the Christian sect, either from a supercilious disposition to disparage its importance in addressing one of its ringleaders (see above, on 24, 5), or from prudential motives and a natural unwillingness to be involved afresh in quarrels which perhaps had caused their previous misfortunes, but which certainly seemed likely now to bring them into conflict not only with the church itself but with the government which at this moment seemed disposed to favour it. This obvious and natural hypothesis accounts for all the facts, without being open to the same objection with the similar assumption in relation to the statement in the verse preceding.

23. And when they had appointed him a day, there came many to him into (his) lodging; to whom he expounded and testified the kingdom of God, persuading them concerning Jesus, both out of the law of Moses, and (out of) the prophets, from morning till evening.

Having appointed (or, as the Greek verb originally signi fies, arranged, agreed upon) *a day with* (or *to*) *him*, after how long an interval is not said, but the natural implication is a short one. *Many*, literally, *more*, which may be understood indefinitely, either of a great or small number (see above, on 2, 40. 13, 31. 21, 10. 24, 17. 25, 14. 27, 20), but is commonly explained here strictly as a comparative, meaning more than had attended the first interview. Besides the leading men then present, there were others now assembled, to hear Paul's account of the new religion. *Lodging*, a Greek word used by the older classics in the wide sense of hospitable entertainment (compare the cognate verb in v. 7), but by the later writers in the more restricted local sense expressed in the translation. Here (and in Philem. 22) it may denote a private house where Paul was entertained as a guest, perhaps that of Aquila and Priscilla (see above, on 18, 2, and compare Rom. 16, 3); but most interpreters identify it with the *hired house* mentioned in v. 30. One modern writer paradoxically holds that Paul was now at liberty, his trial and acquittal having taken place between the two meetings with the Jews here recorded. But the principal ground of this opinion, a provision of the Roman law requiring such appeals to be determined within five days, has been shown to be an error, that provision having reference, not to the trial of the merits, but to the preliminary forms, receiving the appeal, &c. (That Paul was still a prisoner at the close of this book, see below, on v. 30.) The terms used in describing Paul's address are very similar to those employed before on like occasions. *Expounded and testified*, literally, *expounded testifying*, not as two distinct acts, but as one, partaking of both qualities, and answering the twofold purpose of explaining and attesting the true doctrine. (For the usage of the Greek verbs, see above, on 2, 40. 8, 25. 11, 4. 18, 5. 26. 20, 21. 24.) *The kingdom of God*, the reign of the Messiah, the new dispensation, as predicted by the Prophets and fulfilled in Christ. (See above, on 1, 3. 8, 12. 14, 22. 19, 8. 20, 25.) *Persuading them too* (τε) *concerning Jesus*, i. e. not merely proving him to be the Christ, but striving to enlist them in his active service. (See above, on 13, 43. 18, 4. 19, 8. 26. 26, 28.) The verb denotes, not the actual result, nor yet the mere endeavour, but the whole subjective process as performed by Paul, without respect to the diversity of its effect. *Both out of the law*, as the source of his argument, or more exactly, *from the law*, as his starting-point, *and the prophets*, or remaining scriptures, as expounding and confirming Moses. (See above, on 3, 18. 21. 24. 10, 43. 13, 27. 24, 14. 26, 22. 27.) *From morning*, more exactly, *from early* (in the morning) *until evening*, i. e. all day long. The whole day was thus occupied, of course not in formal or continuous discourse, but partly in familiar and colloquial discussion (see above, on 20, 7.)

24. And some believed the things which were spoken, and some believed not.

As in most other cases where the auditors were Jews, the effect was a divided or diverse one. (See above, on 13, 43–45. 14, 1. 2. 18, 4–6. 8. 12. 19, 8. 9.) *Some believed* (or more exactly, *were persuaded* or *convinced by*) *the things spoken*, that Paul's doctrine as to the Messiahship of Jesus was correct, and as a necessary consequence that he and not his enemies had held fast to the old religion. (For the usage of the passive, see above, on 5, 36. 37. 40. 17, 4. 21, 14. 23, 21. 26, 26. 27, 11.) This effect was probably foreseen by Paul, who had not been led by accident to give this exposition of his Messianic doctrine, but had deliberately seized the opportunity, afforded by the Jews themselves (v. 22), of bearing witness to the truth before his kinsmen according to the flesh, however his testimony might be treated.

25. And when they agreed not among themselves, they departed, after that Paul had spoken one word, Well spake the Holy Ghost by Esaias the prophet unto our fathers —

Being discordant, a musical expression (literally, *unsymphonious*), but applied by Plato, as it is here, to diversity of feeling and opinion. *They departed*, not abruptly, or before Paul had accomplished his design, as may appear to be the meaning of the English version, but *they were dismissed* (or *sent away*) by Paul himself. (Compare the use of the same verb in 19, 41.) *Paul saying* (as they went), or *having said* (before they went), not as the reason or occasion of their going, which they would have done if he had added nothing, but as a solemn close of the whole interview, a last farewell to them and to the doomed race whom they represented. Here, as well as in the preceding verse, it is implied that the greater number persevered in unbelief and the rejection of the true Messiah (but see below, on v. 29.) *One word*, saying, dictum (see above, on 10, 37. 11, 16), full of fearful import, selected, not at random, but as an appropriate conclusion to Paul's dealings with his unbelieving brethren. *Well*, not properly or truly, which would be superfluous, if not irreverent, in allusion to words uttered by the Holy Ghost, but exactly or appropriately, as a description of the sons, no less than of the fathers, to whom and of whom it was primarily spoken. The form of expression is derived from Christ himself (see Matt. 15, 7. Mark 7, 6.) *Our fathers* still identifies the speaker with the hearers, as descendants of the same progenitors (see above, on 3, 13. 25. 5, 30. 13, 17. 15, 10. 22, 14. 26, 6.) But the oldest manuscripts and latest critics read *your fathers*, which appears more natural in this connection, just as Stephen, after using the first person ten times, suddenly adopts the second in his closing invective or anathema (7, 2. 11. 12. 15. 19. 38. 39. 44

45. 51. 52. For the idiomatic use of ὅτι, *that*, in a direct quotation, see above, on 2, 13. 3, 22. 5, 23. 25. 6, 11. 11, 3. 13, 34. 15, 1. 16, 36. 17, 6. 18, 13. 19, 21. 23, 20. 24, 21. 25, 8. 16. 26, 31.) The passage quoted is here recognized, not only as the genuine composition of Isaiah, but as a prophecy inspired by the Holy Ghost. (See above, on 1, 16. 4, 25.)

26. Saying, Go unto this people, and say, Hearing ye shall hear, and shall not understand; and seeing ye shall see, and not perceive —

The passage chosen for Paul's final utterance to the Jews is still found in the writings of Isaiah (6, 9. 10), where it constitutes a part of the renewed (or, as some think, the original) commission of the Prophet, after a solemn vision of Jehovah in the temple, and a symbolical assurance of his own forgiveness, as a preparation for the painful duty now to be imposed upon him. This consisted in preaching to the people, but with an assurance that it would have no effect, as to the mass, except to blind and harden them. *Hearing* (or *with hearing*) *ye shall hear and not* (at all) *understand* (the Greek negation being very strong), *and seeing ye shall see and not* (at all) *perceive* (or *looking ye shall look, and not see.*) *Hearing* and *seeing*, though alike in English, are entirely different in their Greek form, the last being the active participle of the verb *to see*, agreeing with the plural pronoun (*ye seeing*), and the first a noun derived from the verb *to hear*, and construed as the dative of means or manner. The distinction in both phrases is between sensation and perception, or between a mere impression on the organ and a corresponding intellectual effect (see above, on 22, 9.) The combination of the noun and participle with the cognate verb is designed to represent a common but peculiar Hebrew idiom, which joins an infinitive and finite verbal form, for the sake of emphasis in general, or of some particular intensive meaning. Thus in this case, it may either simply strengthen the expression (ye shall hear indeed, ye shall certainly hear), or suggest the accessory ideas of clearness (hear distinctly), or abundance (hear sufficiently), or continuance (hear on), or repetition (hear again), &c. The idea of hearing and seeing in one sense without hearing or seeing in another may have been proverbial among the Hebrews, as we know it to have been among the Greeks, from a similar expression of Æschylus, and still more clearly from another of Demosthenes, who expressly cites it as a proverb, "seeing not to see, and hearing not to hear."

27. For the heart of this people is waxed gross, and their ears are dull of hearing, and their eyes have they closed; lest they should see with (their) eyes, and hear with (their) ears, and understand with (their) heart, and should be converted, and I should heal them.

This part of the original prediction has the form of an ironical commission or command, in which the Prophet is required to stupefy and blind the people, which is only a strong and paradoxical mode of commanding him to do his duty or perform his office, with an accompanying intimation of its actual effect upon the people through their own perversity and unbelief. (Compare the similar command of Christ in Matt. 23, 32.) In this fearful process there are three distinguishable agencies expressly or implicitly described, the ministerial agency of the Prophet, the judicial agency of God, and the suicidal agency of the people themselves. The original passage makes the first of these most prominent (Fatten the heart of this people, dull their ears, shut their eyes, &c.) The quotation in John 12, 40, draws attention to the second (He hath blinded their eyes and hardened their heart.) That in Matt. 13, 15, like the one before us, dwells upon the third and represents the people as destroyed by their own insensibility and unbelief. We have thus a striking and instructive instance of the way in which the same essential truth may be exhibited in different parts of Scripture under several distinct aspects or successive phases. *Heart* is neither the affections nor the intellect exclusively, but the whole mind or soul as comprehending both. (See above, on 2, 37. 4, 32. 7, 23. 8, 21. 11, 23. 14, 17. 15, 9. 16, 14. 21, 13.) *Waxed gross*, literally, *fattened*, made fat, i. e. gross and stupid. *Their ears are dull of hearing*, literally, *with (their) ears they have heard heavily*, i. e. obtusely, dully, indistinctly. *Closed*, in Greek a strong expression, strictly meaning *shut down*, i. e. shut fast, and applied especially to sleep and death. The corresponding word in Hebrew is still stronger, meaning *smeared*, or glued fast, so that they cannot be opened. The moral effect of this insensibility is stated in the last clause. *Be converted*, literally, *turn*, i. e. to God by true repentance (see above, on 3, 19. 9, 35. 11, 21. 14, 15. 15, 19. 26, 18. 20.) As in the previous description, their own agency is prominently presented, so in this, without excluding that of God in either case. *Heal them*, forgive and save them, sin being often represented in the Scriptures as a spiritual malady. (Compare Ps. 41, 4. Jer. 3, 22. Hos. 14, 4. 1 Pet. 2. 24.) The terms of this quotation, not excepting the change of construction in the verse before us, are derived, with little variation, from the Septuagint version of Isaiah.

28. Be it known therefore unto you, that the salvation of God is sent unto the Gentiles, and (that) they will hear it.

Therefore, because you are thus hardened, and exhibit just the character and state described in this appalling passage as the fruits and symptoms of judicial blindness and abandonment by God. *Be it known unto you*, the same emphatic formula employed by Peter at Jerusalem (2, 14. 4, 10), and by Paul himself at Antioch in Pisidia (13, 38), to introduce a solemn and authoritative declaration. *Salvation*, not the Greek word commonly so rendered (as in 4, 12. 13, 26. 47. 16, 17), but one used only by Luke (Luke 2, 30. 3, 6) and Paul (Eph. 6, 17.) It is properly an adjective meaning *salutary*, *saving* (as in Tit. 2, 11), but here, and in the passages just cited, absolutely used without a substantive to signify God's method of salvation, the remedial system made known in the gospel. *Is sent*, literally, *was sent*, i. e. has already been sent. The past tense seems to be employed, and not the future, because what he here refers to was not something yet to be begun in consequence of what had just occurred, but something begun long before and still in operation, of which this was only the farewell annunciation, repeating to the Jews of Rome what Paul had previously said to those of Antioch (13, 46) and Corinth (18, 6), and no doubt in other cases not recorded. In the present case, however, it is made particularly impressive by its being the conclusion of Paul's efforts to convert the Jews, and the commencement of those undivided labours for the Gentiles, of which Rome was now to be the seat and centre. *To the Gentiles*, literally, *the nations*, i. e. other nations (see above, on 4, 25. 27. 9, 15. 10, 45. 11, 18. 26, 17. 20. 23.) *They shall hear it*, in the lower sense, i. e.

shall have the opportunity of doing so, *and* (many) *will hear it*, in the higher sense, i. e. give heed to it, accept it, and obtain salvation by it.

29. And when he had said these words, the Jews departed, and had great reasoning among themselves.

This verse is rejected by some critics, because not found in several of the oldest manuscripts and versions, but retained by others on account of the agreement as to form among the copies which do give it, and because its insertion is as hard to be accounted for as its omission. It contains a natural though not a necessary close of this transaction with the Jews at Rome, again recording that they were not all of one mind, but divided on the subject of Paul's Messianic teaching. *He having said* (or *saying*, i. e. as or while he said) *these words* (to wit, the *one word* mentioned in v. 25, but more especially his last words in v. 28), *the Jews departed*, not the passive verb so rendered in v. 25, but one which properly means *went away* (employed above, 4, 15. 5, 26. 9, 17. 10, 7.) *And had*, (literally, *having*, i. e. at the time, or as they went) *great reasoning*, literally, *much dispute*, the same word that is used above, 15, 2. 7 (compare the cognate verb in 6, 9. 9, 29) *among themselves*, literally, *in themselves*, which might be strictly understood of an internal conflict, as a like phrase is employed above in 10, 17. 12, 11, but for the preceding noun, which originally means joint inquiry or investigation, and therefore necessarily implies a plurality of persons. (For the use of *in* to mean *with* or *among*, see above, on 2, 29. 4, 12. 34. 5, 12. 6, 8. 7, 44. 12, 18. 13, 26. 15, 7. 22. 17, 34. 18, 11. 20, 25. 32. 21, 19. 34. 24, 21. 25, 5. 6. 26, 4. 18.) This is in one sense the conclusion of Paul's ministry, i. e. so far as it extended both to Jews and Gentiles. From the former it was now to be withdrawn, and during the remainder of his life exclusively directed to the latter, not so much, if at all, by travelling among them, as by setting a ministry in motion at the heart of the empire which should reach to its extremities, and giving an impulse to the energies of others that should still be felt when he had left the field of labour.

30. And Paul dwelt two whole years in his own hired house, and received all that came in unto him —

Having brought the Apostle of the Gentiles to the heart and centre of the Gentile world, and recorded his last dealings with the Jews, the history closes with the interesting fact, that he continued to exert his apostolical influence, from this great radiating point, without interruption or obstruction, during an interval of many months after his arrival. *Dwelt*, remained, continued (as in v. 16 above.) *Two whole years*, literally, *a whole biennium*, or period of two years, the same word that occurs above in 24, 27. The word *whole* shows, not only that the two years were elapsed when Luke wrote, but that the condition here described continued without any interruption for that length of time. *His own*, or as the word may mean, a *separate* or *private* dwelling, which amounts, however, to the same thing. (See above, on 1, 7. 19. 25. 2, 6. 8. 3, 12. 4, 23. 32. 13, 36. 20, 28. 21, 6. 23, 19. 24, 23. 25, 19.) *Hired house*, a single word in Greek, used in the Classics and the Septuagint to denote the act of hiring or the hire itself, but here the thing hired or rented, which the context determines to have been a place of residence, and therefore an apartment, if not an entire house. Whether this hired lodging was the same that is referred to in v. 23, or one to which he afterwards removed, is a question happily of little moment, as the narrative does not afford data for its satisfactory solution. *And received* (as visitors or guests) *all the* (persons) *coming in to him* (as such), a statement which implies that his intercourse with others was confined to his own dwelling, and as a necessary consequence that during these two years he was still a prisoner, an inference corroborated by the allusions to his bonds in the epistles written at this time. (Compare Philem. 1. 9. 10. 23. Col. 4, 18. Phil. 1, 13. 14. 16.)

31. Preaching the kingdom of God, and teaching those things which concern the Lord Jesus Christ, with all confidence, no man forbidding him.

These were not visits of mere courtesy or friendship, but connected with the great work even of his prison-life. (Compare Phil. 1, 12–21.) *Preaching*, proclaiming as a herald (see above, on 8, 5. 9, 20. 10, 42. 19, 13. 20, 25, and compare the cognate noun in 1 Tim. 2, 7. 2 Tim. 1, 11.) *The kingdom of God*, see above, on v. 23. *Teaching*, explaining, as well as heralding, announcing (see above, on 15, 35. 18, 25. 20, 20) *the* (*things*) *about* (*of* or *concerning*) *the Lord Jesus Christ*,

i. e. Jesus as a sovereign, and as the Messiah of the Scriptures, the predicted Prophet, Priest, and King, not of the carnal but the spiritual Israel. (See above, on 2, 30. 36. 8, 12. 9, 22. 15, 26. 17, 3. 18, 5. 19, 4. 20, 21.) *With all confidence*, the word translated *boldness* in 4, 13. 29. 31 (compare the kindred verb in 9, 27. 29. 13, 46. 14, 3. 18, 26. 19, 8), but always meaning strictly freedom and plainness of speech, as opposed, not only to a timid reserve, but to a partial and obscure exhibition of the truth (see above, on 2, 29. 26, 16.) This is the gift for which the twelve apostles prayed in persecution (see above, on 4, 29. 31), and of which Paul speaks repeatedly in his epistles, as essential to the full proof of his ministry. (Compare Eph. 6, 19. 20. Phil. 1, 20. 1 Thess. 2, 2.) *All*, i. e. all that was required for this purpose (see above on 4, 29, and compare the use of the same epithet in 5, 23. 13, 10. 17, 11. 20, 19. 23, 1. 24, 3.) The mention of this circumstance as something singular, or contrary to what might naturally have been looked for, serves to confirm the previous conclusion that throughout these two years he was still a prisoner (see above, on v. 30); and the same thing may be said of the emphatic adverb which concludes the whole book, and to which our language affords no nearer equivalent than *unforbidden* (or retaining the adverbial form, *unforbiddenly*), the essential meaning being that of the English phrase, *without let or hindrance.* This emphatic and sonorous close shows that the book is not unfinished, as so many have imagined, and then tried to account for its abrupt conclusion on the ground that Luke was interrupted, or intended to compose a third book (see above, on 1, 1), or that the original conclusion has been lost, &c. These are not only arbitrary and gratuitous assumptions in themselves, but are invented to explain a fact without existence. Because no account is given of what afterwards befell Paul, of his condemnation or acquittal, his release and re-arrest, and final martyrdom, it does not follow that the history is incomplete, but only that these interesting facts were not included in the writer's plan. The book is not a personal biography of Paul, who is not even named until the close of the first subdivision (see above, on 7, 57), but a history of the planting and extension of the church among the Jews and Gentiles, by the institution of great radiating centres at important points throughout the empire, beginning at Jerusalem and ending at Rome. The ministry of Paul, as the Apostle of the Gentiles fills a large part of the book, and as soon as he arrives at the last point in the series just referred to and commences operations there, the subject is exhausted and the history complete. All subsequent occurrences, however interesting in themselves, or useful for another purpose, belong rather to biography than history, or rather to the later apostolical history and the interpretation of the Pastoral Epistles, than to this succinct and well-defined account of the great process, by which Christianity was carried from its cradle at Jerusalem, not only to its secondary homes in Antioch, Philippi, Corinth, Ephesus, and other cities of inferior rank, but also to its throne in the Eternal City, the locality selected for its highest exaltation and its most profound abasement. To have added any thing beyond this point, except so much as might suffice to show that Rome did really become a radiating centre before Paul died, would have been to open a new history and not to close an old one. However tantalizing, therefore, the reserve of the historian may be to modern curiosity, it gives his work a unity and relative completeness, which could only have been marred by supplementary additions. He does not even stand in need of the apology, which some have made for him, that all the rest was well known to Theophilus, and therefore needed not to be recorded; as if the book, although inscribed to one man, was not meant from the beginning for the use of all men. It ends where it does, for no such personal or trivial reason, but because the writer's purpose is accomplished and his task performed. As soon as he has traced the course of Christ and Christianity from the Holy City to the Mistress of the World, he has already shown the virtual fulfilment of the promise and the plan with which the history begins, "Ye shall be my witnesses, both in Jerusalem and in all Judea and Samaria, and unto the uttermost part of the earth."

THE END.

www.ingramcontent.com/pod-product-compliance
Lightning Source LLC
LaVergne TN
LVHW020913110826
845150LV00004B/662